Also by Barbara Bush

C. FRED'S STORY

MILLIE'S BOOK

REFLECTIONS: LIFE AFTER THE WHITE HOUSE

Barbara Bush

A Memoir

Barbara Bush

A LISA DREW BOOK

Scribner

New York   London   Toronto   Sydney   New Delhi

A LISA DREW BOOK/SCRIBNER
An Imprint of Simon & Schuster, Inc.
1230 Avenue of the Americas
New York, NY 10020

This Scribner trade paperback edition May 2015

SCRIBNER and design are trademarks of The Gale Group, Inc.,
used under license by Simon & Schuster, Inc., the publisher of this work.

A LISA DREW BOOK is a trademark of Simon & Schuster, Inc.

For information about special discounts for bulk purchases,
please contact Simon & Schuster Special Sales at 1-866-506-1949
or business@simonandschuster.com.

The Simon & Schuster Speakers Bureau can bring authors
to your live event. For more information or to book an event
contact the Simon & Schuster Speakers Bureau at 1-866-248-3049
or visit our website at www.simonspeakers.com.

Designed by Laura Hough

Manufactured in the United States of America

10 9 8 7 6 5 4 3

Library of Congress Control Number: 94013829

ISBN 978-1-5011-2223-1
ISBN 978-1-5011-1778-7 (pbk)
ISBN 978-1-4516-0395-8 (ebook)

*To faith, family, and friends; and to George Bush, who taught me
that these are the most important things in life*

Contents

Forewords from
the Bush Children

Barbara Bush taught us how to live, love, and laugh. When asked whether she would be willing to uproot her young family and leave the comforts of Greenwich, Connecticut, to move to West Texas, she did not hesitate. She, of course, would say that she would go anywhere with the love of her life, our dad. I think it was more than that. I think she, too, has an adventuresome spirit; the idea of heading to the foreign culture of Texas intrigued her. She was not fearful of change. This was a pattern of her life. She, of course, was not the one who was offered the new challenges, but she was the one who charged ahead with no complaints and an eagerness to learn. Like her mate, she felt life was to be lived to the max. I smile when I think of Mom and her little yelpers (those would be her dogs) walking the beach in Kennebunkport. Her message is, Walk life's beaches for as long as you can.

Mom taught us how to love. No doubt her number one love was Dad. But she had plenty of love to spare for her children. She was always encouraging and never deflating (except the time she told me that I couldn't beat Ann Richards for governor of Texas). She was the disciplinarian in our family. She was quick to scold when I stepped over the imaginary good behavior line. She spoke her mind. There was not much subtlety. But once the tempest passed she was quick to move on. She did so because of the love in her heart.

Mom has a sharp and quick wit. She is not afraid to speak her mind. She is self-deprecating. She can spot a phony before most. She deflated the pompous and the arrogant. She is a pro at putting people at ease because she herself is at ease. On her dog walks she befriends all kinds of people. The local tomato salesman is one of her favorites. Of course she remembers the name of every dog. During my time in office, the number of people who said "I just love your mother" or "I wish I could just meet your mother" was astounding.

Mom taught me how to laugh, how to see irony, how to verbally joust. She had a doormat in our home in Houston that said "Birds fly high because they take themselves lightly." She always took her duties seriously, like that of First Lady. But never herself.

I could go on and on, but she might think that I was the pompous one by trying to dominate the introduction in her book. So I end knowing that I'm a lucky man to have had Barbara Bush as a mother.

—George W. Bush

I salute the publisher for reissuing my mother's memoir for the simple fact that we could all use a good dose of Barbara Bush's humor, her caring, and her plainspoken wisdom. I say that as a totally biased son, but am willing to wager that there are millions who would agree with that sentiment.

Barbara Pierce Bush is an American treasure.

As to what she has taught me, I would start with how to be a good parent. Mom has always had the firm belief that a successful life is defined first and foremost by loving your children with all of your heart and soul. How lucky we were to learn the habits that lead to a successful life from the best!

Mom did that. One of my earliest childhood memories is reading books chronicling the adventures of Babar the Elephant with her. Later it was Zelda the Zebra. I loved the pictures, and together we read those books hundreds of times—by which time I am sure Mom could recite each book from memory. Still, it was one of her first, and most important, gifts to me: the gift of reading.

The time she invested in us and the power of her example inspired me when my wife, Columba, and I were blessed with three wonderful children of our own.

Mom taught me plenty of other things as well. She taught me the importance of civility. She taught me not to take myself seriously. God help you if she ever caught you acting arrogant. You would get that Barbara Bush look and then you would be hit with her very quick and sharp wit that would put you in your place. Even today, when I am speaking to an audience, I feel her looming presence behind me whispering: "Don't brag. Don't toot your own horn too loud. Don't talk like a big shot."

Dad calls Mom "the Enforcer," because she tended to be the one who has meted out discipline through the years. Like many parents, my mother's style of discipline could often be fairly described as a "benevolent dictatorship." But if you had really messed up, she could just as readily discard the "benevolent" part. Looking back, I have to confess the punishment usually fit the crime.

Long before I ever considered entering politics, Mom also taught us the importance of "staying on message." If she ever gave you advice or corrected you, she was apt to repeat herself. On this front, my siblings and I challenged her patience on a regular basis. Still, hearing her impart the same piece of wisdom repeatedly became the first known instance of a phenomenon today called "Bush fatigue."

I suppose it would have helped things had we been faster learners, or better behaved.

Aside from family, Barbara Bush is the best friend to hundreds if not thousands of people. I imagine her time living in Washington taught her the true meaning of genuine friendship. Friends are with you through the good times and the bad ones too. As she details in the book, she also learned a lot about friendship after watching my sister Robin slip from their grasp at an innocent, early age. They will never forget the way their friends and neighbors in Midland rallied to their side.

Mom also taught us the importance of faith in God, but never in a preachy, showy kind of way. Again, it is in the consistent manner in which she has lived her life, reaching out to others, trying to leave this a better world than she found it. Working with her and her family literacy foundation, I can attest to the tens of thousands of lives she has touched, and lifted, and infused with new hope.

Now, having said all of this, let me confide that Barbara Bush would be the first to tell you she is not perfect. As president, my brother George got us both in trouble at a Florida event during which he teased Mom about her lack of total expertise in the kitchen. (Mom didn't buy my explanation that I was laughing just to be polite to the President of the United States.) More recently, I have learned that she can be somewhat deficient in explaining *certain* political endorsements!

But where Mom is totally wrong is in describing herself as the luckiest person in the world. That simply cannot be because it is us "kids," my siblings and I, who have been blessed beyond belief to have Barbara Pierce Bush raise us, and guide us, and instill in us a sense of values. Together with our father, she has given us the love and lessons we need to make our way in this complex and wonderful world.

—Jeb Bush

Mom's seventy-year devoted marriage, her public affection and support for her children and grandchildren, her sharp humor, her naturally elegant pearl-accented style and silver head of hair have endeared her to millions. Mom's commitment to literacy and support of so many worthy nonprofit agencies have inspired Americans to get involved in causes that make a difference in the lives of others. The truth is, Mom is a great role model, and millions have learned something from Barbara Bush, the First Lady.

On a very personal basis, as a son, Mom has taught me to be a better parent, a better person, and a better citizen. She has taught me to be a better parent by demonstrating the importance of unconditional love. I struggled with reading in elementary and middle school. Mom felt my pain and worked hard to find a diagnosis and solution. She stood by me, lifted my spirits, helped me find joy in things I did well, and made sure my life wasn't mired in self-doubt.

Mom taught me to be a better person by demonstrating core values that ground good behavior, lead to wise choices, and make life a whole lot better. Under her early leadership I learned to make my bed, to hang up used towels, and to use a bank account. She prepared me for living independently. Mom has also taught me to persevere through hardship. Mom has endured indescribable back pain, rarely complaining. She doesn't burden other people with tales of her woes. After double knee replacement or heart valve surgery, she recovered quickly, demonstrating amazing willpower. I've learned from her to muscle through pain, to endure jet lag, to bounce up after a fall and get back in the game. She taught us to be kind and respectful of others, to say thank you, and to be polite. She praises hard work and good deeds. And Mom is the gatekeeper for grounding her large flock of children and grandchildren. There are no inflated egos or feelings of entitlement in the Bush family. She advocates transparency and owning up to things. Often times it has to do with spending money. As a young couple with a bunch of kids, Mom and Dad didn't spend money on exotic family trips. They always preferred to save. Mom fiercely advocates frugality and living a debt-free lifestyle. Also, I've learned that there is no point in hiding stuff . . . she will find out about the ski vacation in Colorado or the beach trip to the Bahamas. I married a woman who shares Mom's aversion to debt, so at the age of sixty, I'm on the right track.

Truthfully, I'm still working to incorporate into my life some of the things that Mom has emphasized.

And finally I am a better citizen because I've seen Mom's active commitment to helping others throughout her life. Before she had the platform as First Lady, where her charitable works received lots of attention, Mom would selflessly volunteer in hospitals, in schools, and in the communities where she lived. It's no wonder that service has become a part of the Bush family culture, and I now serve as chairman of Points of Light, the largest organization in the world focused on volunteerism. What ignites my passion more than anything is work we are doing in Houston through the Barbara Bush Houston Literacy Foundation. I've drunk Mom's literacy lemonade and believe that there is no way a human can realize their God-given potential if they don't achieve an age-appropriate level of literacy. The hours I devote to Points of Light and the Barbara Bush Houston Literacy Foundation are inspired by Mom's remarkable commitment to serving others.

It is a blessing to have a strong, stable, loving, witty mother in my life. She fills my heart with joy and blankets me with unconditional love and support. If every family were led by a Barbara Bush, the world would be a much better place.

—Neil Bush

A few valuable lessons learned from my mom, Barbara Pierce Bush:

Be on time.

I felt like a lottery winner in October 1956 when I finally stuck my head out of Mom's womb and first laid eyes on that incredible woman. I've learned many lessons from her over the years, but the first one was impressed upon me on that day in October. The lesson? *Be on time!* Apparently she was raised to think that it was rude—and selfish—to keep people waiting, including herself, so she asked the doctor for a healthy dose of castor oil to expedite my birth at Midland Hospital. Lesson learned, Mom. Thanks to you I now get to social gatherings, airports, and business meetings with time to spare.

Be yourself.

When I was little I remember my mom changing her hair color so that she could appear younger than her prematurely gray hair suggested. Most of the shades were in the light brown to dark brown kaleidoscope, but one hairdresser left her with a color that could kindly be called "copper" or "rust." I think she looked in the mirror and didn't see a reflection that made her happy. I don't remember her saying a word about it, but a few weeks later, her hair was gray and there was once again an authenticity to her beauty.

My mom named me after her dad, Marvin Pierce. As a kid I would repeatedly tell her that I was the only guy I knew named Marvin and that no one has used the name since she and Dad unleashed it on me in the mid-1950s. Her response over the years varied from "Your dad and I didn't want to waste that beautiful name on one of your other brothers" to "Count your blessings; we were going to name you Maude if you were a girl." Of course, now I see it her way. I'm honored to be named after her wonderful dad and have become very comfortable with the uniqueness of the name.

⁓ A sense of humor can be your friend.

Mom will unanimously be inducted into the Self-Deprecation Humor Hall of Fame on the first ballot. I remember her response to a reporter who asked about the adjustments made after she and dad left Washington and the White House: "It's been different. I started driving again. I started cooking again. My driving's better than my cooking. George has discovered Sam's Club."

She taught us all early on that humor is a friend that can guide you out of the tightest jams or through the toughest times. When the "perfect storm" devastated Walker's Point in 1991, she and dad went to Kennebunkport to survey the damage. Worried, I called Mom to see how they were holding up. Her enthusiastic response: "Great, Marv, the only valuable we found on the rocks was your high school picture!" That picture of me with unruly hair, an ugly blue jean jacket, and a snarl that would make any parent cringe became a running joke between us. Every time we visited Maine my mom would prominently display the picture, much to my protestation. She knew how much I hated the picture but it brought her great joy that our running joke could continue.

⁓ We learned the definition of love.

There wasn't a moment that I've been on this planet that I didn't feel really loved by Mom. Her loyalty to her kids is legendary. I wouldn't call it "blind love," but it is close. Let's call it "blurry-to-blind love." She gave us a hug when one was needed, supported us through thick and thin, believed in us when we had our own doubts, and teased us when we needed what my dad calls "the needle." On the other hand, she was quick to discipline us when it was merited. We tested her like it was our day job and she responded like a mom who really loves her kids—with swift, consistent punishment.

Growing up, we had a front row seat at one of the greatest love stories that ever existed. My parents can't get enough of each other. Their love has grown stronger with each passing year. They laugh at each other's goofy jokes, hold hands when no one is around, and generally look at each other like teenagers in love. Being one of my mom's offspring, I sometimes feel like saying, "Enough, you two, get a room." Knowing my mom, she would respond with something like "I have a room and the best roommate in the world."

—Marvin Bush

As the only daughter among my parents' five children, I have the unique designation of being the only woman in history to see both her father and her brother become president. While I feel honored to have this credential, I feel even more honored to be able to say that I am Barbara Bush's daughter.

When I consider everything I've learned from my remarkable and very colorful mother, the list is long. So I might as well begin with the first thought that came to mind: Miss Rumphius.

Miss Rumphius by Barbara Cooney is one of my mother's favorite children's books; it is no surprise that this was my first thought given my mom's love of reading and passion for literacy. In the book, Miss Rumphius is instructed by her grandfather to leave the world a better place. She decides to do so by spreading flower seeds wherever she goes in the hope that she will help make the world more colorful, and thus more beautiful. While my mother may not have spread actual flower seeds throughout the world, she certainly makes it a more colorful and beautiful place.

My mother is known for speaking her mind in the most unique and entertaining way possible. When I was growing up and I did something right, she might say something like, "That's using your head for something other than a hat rack!" On the other hand, if I did something she did not think was very bright, she would say, "Don't be a stupenagel" (whatever that means!).

Mom is also known for saying things that she (at times) later regrets. Once there was a rather plumpish guest visiting our family in Maine, and when my mom spotted him, she simply stated, "There's the whale up by the pool!" She always keeps us guessing about what she might say next! But the truth is my mother's unpredictable and colorful language has led to a life filled with laughter and joy.

My mother takes this colorful attitude and reflects it in her style as well. When she was given a collection of Keds sneakers in a rainbow of colors for her birthday, she wore them all with gusto. She even went one step further and mismatched them, strutting out in one green sneaker paired with another blue sneaker or a red one matched with a yellow one. People would often look at her sideways, wondering if this was on purpose or if Mom was beginning to lose it. The truth is, Mom relishes being playful and unapologetically being herself—two qualities that I try to emulate in my own life.

These days, Mom is dedicated to making the life of our dad more colorful. For years, our wonderful, amazing dad has filled our lives with unimaginable adventures and opportunities. He always included us in his well-lived personal and professional life. He has been the leader of the free world, the leader of our family, and we adore him. Because of Parkinson's disease, he is now confined to a wheelchair, though he never complains. While his memory is fading, his love of others, especially my mom, is powerful, and Mom does everything she can to color his world. She makes sure Dad gets together with friends and family. She takes him to the theater or to the Houston Texans football game. She lovingly fills him in on the happenings in the world. She sits by his side when he is hospitalized and makes sure he is comfortable and cared for. Through this, Mom has taught me to lead with love because that is what really matters. She has taught me the importance of being present for one another, no matter how difficult the circumstance.

Ultimately, Mom has taught me to make the world a better place. My mother brings color to the world each day with her imaginative comments, her authentic style, her passion for literacy, and her unwavering loyalty. She is our very own Miss Rumphius.

—Doro Bush

Preface

I have loved writing this book and know that it is a story of a life of privilege—privilege of every kind. If I didn't know it before, I certainly do now. No man, woman, or child ever had a better life.

Lisa Drew, my editor with Scribner's, passed a message to me after reading five chapters that said she would only allow me to use one "wonderful" a page and one "precious" a chapter. Later Jean Becker added "close friend" to that list. "Nobody has that many good and close friends," she said.

Not bad to have had a life that was filled with *wonderful* people and happenings, *precious* family, and many *close friends*. That's the life that first my family, and then for much longer, that wonderful, precious, close friend, George Bush, have given me and I'm grateful for it.

I wrote every word in this book myself from copious diaries, tapes, letters, and a very selective memory of the early days. It is the truth as I see it.

It might amuse the reader to know that I wrote in my diaries about more good meals that I have eaten (and am wearing today) and that many pages were filled with resolutions not to eat so much and remorse over my lack of self-discipline. I have spared you that.

I also note that we seem to weep a lot in this book. We are an emotional group and rather like a good tear or two. Please also notice that we cry when we are glad *and* when we are sad. Love brings a tear. Friends bring a tear. A smile, sweetness, even a kind word brings a tear. In a life of privilege there are lots of tears.

I have left out so many friends and happenings, but I hope they will forgive me. Time and space have run out. I hope you know who you are and how much we love you.

I want to thank lots of people for putting up with me, especially Jean Becker, who not only researched this book but also reassured me, did the first editing, checked me on truth and spelling, and laughed in all the right places. I certainly want to thank Lisa Drew, my editor, for her third attempt to make a writer of me. (She was there also for *Millie's Book* and *C. Fred's Story*.) I suspect that Lisa wanted more from me, but she applied no pressure to write about things I did not feel were appropriate or things that might make a book sell, but also might hurt.

I also want to thank everyone at the George Bush Presidential Library Center, especially Mary Finch, for helping us track down the facts.

And to the hero of this book, what can I say? George Bush knows how I feel. He is the hero. Incidentally, at my request, he read the book before it went to print. I wanted him to save me from myself, as I would not knowingly hurt someone. He made no deletions and the only additions he made were so typically George. He added many complimentary adjectives, often added praise for a fellow worker or shared the credit with others. I, of course, gave it to him alone. He is my hero.

Barbara Bush
March 1, 1994

BARBARA BUSH

A Memoir

$\mathrel{\mathop{\sim\!\!\!\!\!\nearrow}}$ I

Prologue

January 20, 1993. We were going home. For four extraordinary years, home had been the White House, but when we woke up that morning, it felt like a foreign place. Our bed, along with our tables and chairs, already were in Texas. George had been telling people that I almost had gone, too. He was right. Once we lost the election, I had tried to ignore the hurt and turned my mind toward Houston and a new life.

George, on the other hand, was presidential until the very last moment. He worried about the staff and where they would go. And he had to cope with the larger problems of Iraq, Somalia, and Bosnia.

We started that day as we did every morning, waking up about 5:30 A.M., ringing the bell for the butlers, and drinking coffee in bed while we read the papers. Our phone started ringing almost immediately with our children checking in to make sure we were okay.

Later in the morning, George called me from the Oval Office and asked if I wanted to walk around the South Grounds with the dogs just one more time. It was a glorious, sunny day. The dogs ran and chased squirrels and dashed around looking for who knows what. The pleasure George got from his dog Ranger taking flying leaps over imaginary logs cannot be described. We talked about the ducks that had been nurtured in the South Grounds fountain the past spring and summer and wondered if they would all come back to roost that spring. If they did, how would the White House groundskeepers cope with all those little families? We walked past the tennis court and the horseshoe pit, where you could always hear the clink of shoes at lunchtime. We wondered if Bill Clinton would keep up the White House horseshoe tournaments. It was a great way to get to know the ninety-three people who kept the People's House in such beautiful shape. We walked hand-in-hand by the swimming pool and the cabana, the Oval Office and the Rose Garden, sharing happy memories. Even writing about that day, the house, and the very thoughtful staff brings a warm feeling to me. We always have lived in happy houses, but nothing matched this special place. The problems George faced there were unbelievable, but the staff surrounded us with goodwill, warmth, and caring. They gave the President of the United States exactly what he needed: a happy, tranquil home.

We had put off the good-byes to the residence staff and groundskeepers as long as we could, but at 10:00 A.M., it was time. We had been dreading it. Chief Usher Gary Walters, head of the household, led off with a funny, warm essay about all the new phrases they had learned from George. It read in part: "We thought that 'Pops' were either soft drinks or a breakfast cereal, but we found it to be a term of endearment. We also thought that 'Eeooooh' was something you said when you hit your thumb with a hammer—not 'Where's Ranger?' We learned that the real name of the presidential retreat in the Catoctin Mountains was Camp Marvin, not Camp David, and that a six-pack does not necessarily refer to beer, but is the means to becoming the horseshoe king."

Ron Jones, a houseman and a great horseshoe competitor, presented George with a trophy made in the carpenter shop. The staff also gave him the flag that was flying over the White House on January 20, 1989, and one that had been flying there that morning. Nancy Clarke, the genius in the flower shop, gave me a beautiful doll in a large Lucite case—a reminder of all the beautiful dolls and other decorations her staff had made for Christmas each year. We had so much fun together decorating the house for formal state dinners and holidays. (I should say she and her shop worked; I admired.) We were too choked up with emotion to say what we felt, but I think they knew the affection we had for them all.

Vice President Quayle and Marilyn and George's chief of staff, Jim Baker, and Susan arrived, along with my outstanding chief of staff,

Susan Porter Rose. We talked for a few moments, and then right on time—at least I thought it was right on time—the Clintons, Gores, and the other guests arrived. I say that because I read in the paper that they were late. I don't think that was true. The ladies looked great and both wore hats. It reminded me of how critical everyone had been about Marilyn Quayle's hat four years before, and I wondered if Hillary and Tipper would get away with theirs. The time probably dragged for the newcomers, but it raced for me. When we were told we must leave for the ceremony, I rushed around, through the Red Room then back into the Blue Room, to hug the butlers, out of sight of everyone else. How dear they had been to us and our family.

From then on, it was all downhill. The hard part for me was over. I rode to the Capitol with Hillary, and the conversation was relaxed and easy as we talked about the long day ahead. It could have been an awkward time, but I think we were both determined it would not be. People waved at the new First Family, as they should have, and everyone looked very happy.

Then came the moment when the mantle was lifted from the back of my superb husband and placed on Bill Clinton's. It will come as no surprise that I felt a lesser man by far had won the election, but that was behind us now. The speeches were fine. Bill Clinton's was short and sounded very familiar—like John F. Kennedy's, but not quite as eloquent.

We said good-bye to Senator Bob Dole and Elizabeth, Senator Alan Simpson and Ann, the Clintons, and the Gores. The loyal Quayles flew with us to Andrews Air Force Base, where we hugged good-bye. After a great send-off from staff and supporters, we flew to Houston on *Air Force One* surrounded by friends. From my staff we had Susan Porter Rose and Laurie Firestone, both remarkable women who had been with us for twelve years. My great and dear friend Andy Stewart was there along with Richard Moore, the former ambassador to Ireland, and so many others. Every person on that plane was someone we hold very dear.

The press complained bitterly to me that they were not being allowed to send a press pool. That amused me, and I told them that any one of them who had voted for George should speak up then or forever hold his peace. The silence was deafening.

During the flight we watched a film put together by Dorrance

Smith, a Houston childhood friend of our children, and more recently George's communications director and tennis opponent. It was very funny, very tongue-in-cheek. He had interviewed many of George's staff, and two of our children, Marvin and Doro. It poked fun at us, and it lightened the day.

We arrived in Houston to a great airport rally and immediately saw so many old friends. We said good-bye to the people who had flown down with us, as most of them were going back to Washington with the plane.

Our new life began.

We did not expect the welcome we received. Everywhere we looked were yellow ribbons. Stores and motels had WELCOME HOME on their marquees. There were billboards with WELCOME HOME, GEORGE AND BARBARA. There were even homemade signs on the backs of pickup trucks. People stood and waved flags along the entire route.

When we pulled up to our rented house, the neighbors were all out to give us a big welcome. It was so sweet, and made everything look brighter and better.

There were even more surprises ahead. We walked into a house that was unpacked and filled with plants and flowers. Paula Rendon, our beloved housekeeper; dear Don Rhodes, who had been with us for years; and our friend and neighbor Jack Fitch had worked like dogs sorting out what should be stored and what should be opened. Jack's wife, Bobbie, organized the neighborhood to put flowers in the house and in the garden. What a wonderful way to come home.

January 21, 1993—What a difference twenty-four hours make. We awakened at our usual time of 5:30 a.m.—but we had no bell to ring and no butlers. We got up, walked and fed the dogs, picked up the papers, and carried coffee upstairs to read in bed.

So here we are—almost full circle—taking care of ourselves again and loving it. How did we get here, and where are we going . . .

2

Growing Up

Where to start? I was born in New York City in 1925, the daughter of Marvin and Pauline Pierce. Our family had just moved out of the city to Rye, but my mother returned to the same doctor and hospital where my sister, Martha, five, and my brother Jim, three and a half, had been born.

Rye was a wonderful place to grow up. It was tiny in those days, and we knew most of the eight thousand people who lived there. It had a bakery, a meat man, a greengrocer (no supermarket), a movie theater, and a library which we visited often. We went to the movies almost every Saturday afternoon, usually children's adventure stories.

It was then, and still is, a bedroom community to New York City. Daddy worked for the McCall Corporation (he became president of the company in 1946), and every day he walked fifteen to twenty minutes to the train station for the commute into the city. He loved the ride. In the morning he would read his paper, and in the evening he'd ride in the Club Car, where the men had a drink and played bridge. We didn't know him at the time, but George's father commuted on the same train, getting off two stops farther down in Greenwich, Connecticut. Some of my happiest times were walking with Daddy to the station in the morning, and then I would take the bus to school.

Everyone in Rye knew everyone's business. I remember one humiliating incident when I was ten years old. I had walked downtown, bought a can of Marshmallow Fluff, and happily ate it all the way home. By the time I got there, my mother already had received three phone calls from people saying they had the cutest thing to tell her: Barbara was walking down the street covered with Marshmallow Fluff, eating right from the can with her fingers. Mother did not think it was quite so cute. To add insult to injury, I was violently ill. I haven't eaten it since.

Indian Village—the name of our section of town—was a true neighborhood. We knew everybody and all their families and dogs. The houses were modest by Rye standards, but I know our house seemed enormous to my parents after a New York City apartment. Years later when I visited the house with my brother Scotty, I was surprised how much smaller it was than I remembered.

The bedrooms and bathrooms especially were squeezed into a small space. Once, when George and I were visiting after we were married, Mother asked him not to go to the bathroom at night because he woke her up when he flushed the toilet. George, already inventive at twenty-one years of age, went out the window! That would have killed Mother, but her request was outrageous.

My memories of that lovely little house are only good ones. Our living room was full of bookshelves, and although I do not ever remember Daddy with a hammer in his hand, he was a graduate of MIT and claimed he made those shelves. He always said he had trouble making them even, so he tucked in a match someplace and all was well. There was a set of "My Book House," the *Encyclopaedia Britannica,* and several other collections. We were a family of readers, and many evenings were spent with everyone enjoying a favorite book or magazine. I also believe we had a radio in that bookcase which we listened to a lot in those days. I especially remember "The Shadow."

The best food in the world came out of our kitchen. I don't remember that Mother cooked, but she knew good food and trained the helpers very well. Thursday and Sunday afternoons were their days off. I don't remember what happened on Thursdays, but on Sunday evenings we picked up dinner. We ate a big meal at lunch, usually a baked chicken with the world's best stuffing and mashed potatoes. On Sunday night, we would have graham crackers and cream. What a glorious dish that was. Even talking about it puts on weight. Everything we had was rich and, I now know, bad for us. Daddy and I were the only ones with a weight problem; Scott and Martha were really skinny.

I remember my mother saying, all in one breath, "Eat up, Martha. Not you, Barbara!"

We ate meals as a family in those days—a wonderful tradition few families now enjoy. My mother sat at one end, my dad at the other, and Martha, Jimmy, Scotty, and I fell in on either side. Daddy always took the gravy spoon and made a little bowl in the mashed potatoes and then let the gravy fill it. Mother would scold him for very bad manners and for eating so much potatoes and gravy. On Friday we always had fish just in case one of us brought a Catholic friend home. (In those days, Catholics were not allowed to eat meat on Friday.) Scotty got lamb chops because he did not like fish, and since he was sick as a child, he got away with it.

Being kept home from school was fun. Sometimes we got to lie in Mother's bed and listen to the radio. There were all sorts of great, sort-of-forbidden programs like "Stella Dallas" and "Helen Trent." If you were getting over a tummy problem (probably from gorging on something like Marshmallow Fluff), which your mother mistook for the flu, you got milk toast. It was delicious. You toast some white bread, butter it while hot, sprinkle it with white sugar, and pour hot milk over it. Then you eat it immediately. It was just as good for you as graham crackers and cream, I'm sure.

⌒⌒ My dad was a smiling man, about six feet tall. He had a great sense of humor and everyone liked and respected him. He was the fairest man I knew until I met George Bush.

Daddy worked hard his whole life, starting in high school. His father, Scott Pierce, was born in Sharpsville, Pennsylvania, where the very wealthy Pierces had the big houses and had started the churches. They lost all their money in the 1890s, and my grandfather never recovered. He sold insurance in Dayton, Ohio, but the family lived humbly. Daddy and his sister, my Aunt Charlotte, supported Grandfather and Grandmother Pierce financially for years. They did it willingly and with love. My mother did not feel quite so loving about it. She would tell the story about how during World War I, when Daddy was serving in Europe, my grandfather took up golf and wrote Daddy all about his golf game. That irritated Mother no end, but I never heard my dad criticize his father.

Daddy was really bright and graduated Phi Beta Kappa from Miami University in Oxford, Ohio, while at the same time waiting tables and tending furnaces. He also earned nine letters playing on all the athletic teams. Toward the end of his life, he was made Miami's first "M" man, a very special occasion attended by all his children. Miami is where Daddy met and fell in love with Mother, who was studying to be a teacher. It's also where he became friends with Colonel Red Blaik, who went on to become Army's great football coach. Red was Daddy's friend for life, and years later, I was thrilled to be at the White House when President Reagan honored Red with the Medal of Freedom.

When I was about four or five years old, my father would take me with him on business trips to Dayton, the site of a McCall plant. We would catch the overnight train from the Harmon, New York, railroad station. In those days, the sleeper had a female attendant who would undress me and put me to bed. In the morning, Grandfather or Grandmother would meet me and take me home by bus. I don't ever remember them owning a car. In the summer the house was so hot my funny little grandfather would sleep in the basement to keep cool. The rest of us died of the heat. My grandmother, Mabel Marvin Pierce, was a country girl and both she and my Aunt Charlotte put up with no nonsense. They called a spade a spade. Aunt Charlotte, who never married, taught school around the country. In later years, she would sometimes stay with our children when George and I went on a trip, although they didn't like her very much because she was too strict. One night, our boys apparently were misbehaving badly at the table, and in desperation my bright schoolteacher aunt told them if they didn't stop she would leave the table. So of course, they just got worse, and she left. They still laugh about that. I know she was a wonderful teacher, because many people over the years have told me she taught them fifth grade, and they loved her.

When she died she left each of Daddy's children $6,000. That was a great gift to me. We had five children at the time, and we could only afford necessities for the family. But George said, "This is for you alone. Do not spend it on groceries or something for the children." I wonder if he regretted saying that. That $6,000 really spread itself thin, because whenever I wanted something for myself I'd just think, Aunt Charlotte would want me to have this . . . and this . . . and this . . .

* * *

⟡ My mother was a striking beauty who left the world a more beautiful place than she found it. She grew lovely flowers, did the finest needlepoint I have ever seen, and knew how to keep an exquisite home.

I understand her better now than I did then. I certainly did not appreciate all the pressures she must have felt until I also became a mother. She taught me a great deal, although neither of us realized it at the time. Probably her most important lesson was an inadvertent one. You have two choices in life: You can like what you do, or you can dislike it. I have chosen to like it.

My mother, on the other hand, often talked about "when her ship came in" she was going to do such and such or buy such and such. She was a lucky woman who had a husband who worshiped the ground she walked on, four loving children, and a world of friends. Her ship had come in—she just didn't know it. That is so sad.

She was a wonderful gardener and was, in fact, famous for her green thumb. Our house had an unfinished basement that would often flood in heavy rain (it also had rats), but one year Mother grew endives—that wonderful white vegetable that grows in damp, dark places—down there. Another year Mother sent off for tons of earthworms and nurtured them in our basement, using them to aerate her garden soil. She also had a compost heap—although not in the basement. My sister Martha tells the story of when she took Mother up to Greenwich to meet her future mother-in-law and aunt, two very stylish older ladies, and a woman rushed up to Mother and exclaimed, "Oh, the compost and worm lady!" Martha was humiliated. I suspect Corinne and Madeleine Rafferty thought she was charming. Mother was very active in the Garden Club of America and was the conservation chairman for a while.

She grew up one of four children in Marysville, Ohio. Her father, James Robinson, was a lawyer who served on Ohio's Supreme Court in the mid-1920s. Her mother, Lulu, was a tall, thin woman who changed after my grandfather died. Up until that time, she was a very sweet, sedate lady who baked bread and looked after her husband. After his death, she learned to drive and with several friends drove a small trailer around the United States, Canada, and Mexico. My mother and her sisters complained about their driving and safety. I only knew her after her husband died, and I loved my Grandmother Robinson more than my other grandparents.

Mother was close to her sisters but her only brother, Jim, was an alcoholic who caused nothing but heartbreak. At one time he was married to Aunt Peggy, and they had a son, Jimmy. After my uncle ran away with his secretary, Aunt Peggy left with Jimmy, and we have absolutely no idea where she went or what happened to them. My uncle surfaced off and on, always in trouble and often drunk.

~ Mother did most of the scolding in the family. My brother Jimmy got the most spankings. Yes, my mother spanked us and pretty hard with either the back of a hairbrush or a wooden clothes hanger. I bet that Jim would agree with me that we were never spanked without deserving it. I know I deserved my spankings. And we were never really hurt—mostly hurt feelings and probably a little mad that we had gotten caught. I spanked my own children, but not as hard as my mother did. On the other hand, they were not as naughty. I can't remember anything I ever did that was really bad, but I suspect I baited my mother and was rude and sulky.

My older brother and sister fought a lot. Martha was thin but tall, and Jimmy was feisty. She would kick him, and he would pick up the child's chair by our fireplace and fend her off like a lion tamer. I must have been a real pill, for I either told on them or called my friends to come and watch.

Our neighborhood had few children Martha's age, and she grew up somewhat of a loner. She was a great student and a raving beauty in her teenage years. The boys all adored her. She used to compete in the Manursing Island swimming and diving meets, and we were very proud of her. People wore rubber bathing suits in those days, and those suits had to be handled with care; I seem to remember her bathing suit ripping during a Fourth of July or Labor Day meet. She has been a great sister and shares my love of reading. She once told me that she got one of those college reunion questionnaires, and one of the questions was "How many books do you read a year?" Well, she figured she read probably close to 260, but felt that would be bragging, so she knocked off 110 books. The reunion newsletter reported that the average number of books read was eight a year. There was a footnote that said, "One liar claims to have read 150!"

I both was terrified of Jimmy and looked up to him—he was, after all, my older brother. My friends and I followed him around constantly, which drove him crazy. I was such a pest. Once, on my eighth birthday, he told me he was going to kill me, and I believed him—probably because I deserved it! I spent the entire day hiding under the front porch. He grew up to be a great athlete, and Daddy was very proud of him at the Saturday football games at the Taft School in Watertown, Connecticut. He loved fishing and hunting and was well known in that world.

Scotty was born when I was five. He broke his arm at age two, and the family discovered he had a "cyst" in his arm. That started some five years of operations. The surgeons took bone chips from his hip and both shins and implanted them in the arm. He spent forever in the hospital after the operations, and then months in bed at home with one cast, or sometimes two casts, on. I really don't know what he had, but it was an enormous worry for our parents, not only emotionally but financially. Mother really carried the load. She commuted to the hospital in New York City daily and was worried to death all the time. I don't remember ever being told that we couldn't do this or have that because of Scott, so our parents must have done a great job of sheltering us from their worries. I remember Mother reading the Wizard of Oz books to him, and eventually he learned to read them himself. One of the presents he got was multicolored strips; we made paper chains and hung them from the four posters on his bed. I seem to remember armies of soldiers all over his bedspread, too. I'm sure he complained, but I don't remember it at all. I only remember him as being a great pleasure. Finally, the last operation succeeded, and Scott also went on to become a great athlete. If the four of us voted on "Who do you feel the closest to, who's the kindest, etc.," I suspect we all would say Scott.

I had five good friends in our neighborhood: Lucille School-field, Posy Morgan, Kate Siedle, June Biedler, and Joan Herman. We played all the time. Twice a year Daddy would bring home an outdated McCall's pattern book, and my friends and I would have such fun. We would choose a mother, father, and a family and cut them out and play paper dolls by the hour. Lucille and Kate were a year older and a grade ahead. Lulu was clearly our leader. She decided what games we would play and who would play what part, although she never made herself the heroine. She had a glorious imagination. The Schoolfields' house was bigger and quieter and always open to us. We would play the Victrola and sing sad cowboy songs. To this day I can sing "The Red River Valley" and "Jesse James." We also listened to many of Joe Louis's fights on the radio in Lulu's basement.

The Schoolfields were originally from Knoxville, Tennessee, and often served southern dishes. I remember on their dining room table they had a silver basket with a handle. The basket was filled with flowers or fruit. Lulu insisted her mother give me one as a wedding present, and I still have it. In the backyard they had a rope tied to a tree, and we would jump for hours and chant: "All in together girls, never mind the weather girls, etc."; or "Teddy Bear, Teddy Bear, touch the ground. Teddy Bear, Teddy Bear, turn around. Teddy Bear, Teddy Bear, walk upstairs. Teddy Bear, Teddy Bear, say your prayers. Teddy Bear, Teddy Bear, get into bed. Teddy Bear, Teddy Bear, lay down your head. Teddy Bear, Teddy Bear, turn out the light. Teddy Bear, Teddy Bear, say good-night."

When Scotty had his operations, we had to be careful he didn't catch any diseases. So when I got sick with the usual childhood ailments, I moved in with the Schoolfields. It was so great to be sick there. Mrs. Schoolfield, who died while George was vice president, was like a second mother to me.

꿈 It was a very carefree childhood. One of my first memories of something really awful happening was when Charles Lindbergh's baby was kidnapped and killed in 1932, and that really frightened us. I can remember being thrilled whenever we spotted Amelia Earhart, the first woman to fly the Atlantic solo, at the Manursing Island Club. She lived for a time in Rye and was a huge celebrity, so we were devastated when she disappeared in 1937. Likewise, we couldn't believe it when the *Hindenburg* exploded that same year, especially since we had loved watching the huge blimp fly over Long Island Sound. Many years later George told me that he had seen the *Hindenburg* the day it went down.

As we grew up, we all went to Miss Covington's Dancing School. She was a formidable, well-corseted woman who carried a clicker and spoke in a commanding voice. A Westchester County phenomenon, she went from Scarsdale to Bronxville and other cities nearby. In Rye we met in the Episcopal Church Activity Center on Friday afternoon and evening. The younger you were, the earlier you went. So Friday was wash-your-hair and put-on-your-party-dress day. I remember owning one silk dress during those years, maybe two, bought strictly for those Friday afternoons. I was one of the tallest girls in my class and probably should have been corseted myself. Miss Covington had us all line up in rows, and we practiced for half the lesson what we learned last week and the step we were going to learn that week. Then the dread moment would come when Miss Covington clicked her clicker. The boys would be seated on one side of the room and the girls on the other. "All right," she would yell. "Cross your feet and put your hands in your lap." Every now and then she would slip up and yell, "Cross your hands and put your feet in your lap." She would be furious and click away at our giggles and snickers. She then announced in her loud voice that there were several more girls than boys and she needed two or three girls to volunteer to take the part of boys. Most of the boys hated dancing school. Some of them got sick on dancing school day or hid in the bathroom until their parents came to pick them up. I always raised my hand to play the part of a boy. That way I avoided being the last girl chosen, or rejected altogether. Finally, Mother absolutely forbade me to raise my hand again. She used to come and sit in the balcony with the other mothers and watch the lesson. She was by far the prettiest woman there, but she was the only mother who didn't wear a hat and that humiliated me. I would ask her to please wear a hat and be like other mothers. I must have been the biggest pain in the world.

⁓ I went to the Milton School, a public school, through the sixth grade, then Rye Country Day School through the ninth grade, and Ashley Hall in Charleston, South Carolina, for the tenth, eleventh, and twelfth grades. My mother, who grew up in Ohio, always felt that East Coast people thought everyone from west and south of the Hudson River was a hick. That offended her, so my sister and I went south to Charleston for school. I also believe it was cheaper than some of the eastern schools, but that was never discussed. Although my family certainly was much luckier and better off than so many others at that time, I know we pinched pennies during the Depression. But Daddy left his business problems at the office, and family worries were kept behind bedroom doors.

I loved going to school at Ashley Hall, where I grew up quite a bit. I was a true square, making good marks and never breaking the rules. I swam a lot and acted in school plays, which I loved. I was so shy at the time and never could have gotten up and given a speech, but somehow, acting was different. George still teases me that as the angel in the Christmas play, I had the only speaking part.

✎ Ninth grade was the year I discovered that doing things with boys was just as much fun as doing them with girls. My friends and I eased very gently into traveling in a group with both boys and girls. It was so much easier then than it is now. Drugs, sex, and violence were not constantly thrust at us by television.

All during my fourteenth year, we rode bikes every Saturday afternoon to somebody's house or just rode around picking people up and then dropping them off again after a fun and exhausting day of bike riding. I had no special beau in those days, but was part of the group.

When I came home from Ashley Hall for my first school break, I started going to vacation dances. Our little group went from dance to dance, sometimes with dates. I had several boys whom I liked, who had written me from their schools, and who were kind enough to take me to dances. We were still too young to drive, so our fathers or theirs took us to the dances and drove us home. I honestly think we had much more fun than our children did at the same age. We did not stick with just one person. We danced with anyone who asked us, and there were boys who cut in and we danced away. Eventually I had a special boy whom I liked, but we were very shy and certainly never kissed. I think one reason I liked him was that my mother and older brother thought he was a jerk. He was, but a sweet one.

One thing I rarely did during my teenage years was drive. We had only one car, and with two parents and two older siblings, I never got the chance. My mother was so smart. She would let me have the car if I would do a few errands, and the list always included a personal female item. I hated asking the druggist or clerk for such things, so therefore did not want to use the car very much.

* * *

෴ Just before Christmas vacation in 1941 the Japanese bombed Pearl Harbor. Although fighting had been going on in Europe for several years, war seemed very far away. This astonishes me today, but then it was true.

It wouldn't be too long, however, before I realized how closely the war would touch my life—and how important this particular Christmas vacation would be.

3

Love and War

It was the Christmas when I was sixteen—1941—and I was having a wonderful time. I was at a vacation dance in Greenwich, Connecticut, seeing friends I hadn't seen since summer and wearing a pretty, bright, new red-and-green dress. Jack Wozencraft, a boy I had grown up with, cut in on my dancing partner and took me to meet a wonderful-looking young boy he said wanted to meet me, a boy named Poppy Bush. We danced a little, and it was fun talking to him. He asked if I'd mind sitting out the next dance as it was a waltz and he didn't know how. He told me he was a senior at Phillips Academy Andover, and I told him I went to school in Charleston. I honestly cannot remember any more of our conversation than that, but we did chat for about fifteen minutes. He asked me what I was doing the next night, and I told him I was going to a dance in Rye.

I went home and sat on my mother's bed, answering all her questions about the dance. We always had to go into Mother's room and talk when we got home. Otherwise, she could not sleep and, I believe, she was smart enough to know that in the night, you are willing to tell all. If she waited until the next day, she knew she'd get one-syllable answers. Always from Daddy's bed we would hear, "Can't this wait until morning?" Mother knew it couldn't.

On this night I told her I'd met the nicest, cutest boy, named Poppy Bush. By the time I got up the next morning, Mother—who should have been an FBI agent with her superior intelligence network—

knew that Poppy was a wonderful boy who came from "a very nice family." That was enough to almost do him in!*

The next night Poppy did show up with his sister and several friends. He asked me to dance, and my older brother cut in almost immediately, saying: "Aren't you Poppy Bush? Please go over and wait on the side. When I get rid of her, I want to talk to you." I could hardly believe it! Jim barely tolerated me on good days, and here he was dancing with me when I would much rather be dancing with my new friend. And he acted like I'd be difficult to "get rid of." Jim wanted to ask Poppy to come to Rye on the following Thursday night and play in a basketball game between prep school boys and the local Rye High School championship team. Pop said he would love to. Then he asked me for one more dance, and also asked me to go out with him after the game. To my horror, the whole family turned out the next Thursday for the basketball game. I was absolutely sure it was to look over my new friend.

The Rye championship team won the game, Pop met my family—all of them—and we went out. Poppy told me later that he had begged his mother to let him use the Oldsmobile that night because it had a radio and their other car did not. He was so afraid we would sit in stony silence and have nothing to say to each other. For years he has teased me that there was no silence that night and I haven't stopped talking since. All I know is that I liked him a lot.

He went back to his school, and I went to mine. We wrote letters all winter. Only one day of our spring vacations overlapped, and he and a friend took me and a houseguest of mine out to a movie.

I was so excited when he invited me to come to his senior prom. I stayed with Prissy and Pen Hallowell, a house master and his wife, who were great friends of my sister, Martha. Poppy walked me all around the campus and introduced me to his friends. The other girls seemed so sophisticated to me—they obviously had been to a senior dance before.

---

* I should explain the name "Poppy." George was named after his maternal grandfather, George Herbert Walker. He had four very young uncles who called their father "Pops," although maybe not to his face. So they called their nephew "Little Pops," which soon became "Poppy." Poor George hated it as he got older, but it was hard to break such a long-standing habit. We had been married some seventeen years when a man told me he thought it was so cute the way I called George "Poppy" when we had so many children. That cured me—almost. You'll see "Pop" in some of my diary entries throughout the book.

I hadn't and had just turned seventeen that very week. "Sweet Sixteen and never been kissed" has been written about me, and it was true. But after the dance, Pop walked me home and, in front of the world, leaned down and kissed me on the cheek. I floated into my room and kept the poor girl I was rooming with awake all night while I made her listen to how Poppy Bush was the greatest living human on the face of the earth.

Pop graduated and joined the Navy on June 12, 1942—his eighteenth birthday. Most of his friends waited for a year or two, but Pop wanted to go right away. He went to basic training, and I had a summer job working at Lord & Taylor department store in Greenwich. We wrote letters back and forth. On the way back to school that fall, I stopped off for a few hours in Chapel Hill, North Carolina, where he was training. Travel was curtailed in those days, and I was very lucky to get on a train that stopped at North Carolina. Before I went, he wrote and asked me to please tell everyone I was eighteen years old. He was the youngest man in flight training school and got teased all the time. As we walked around campus, we met a few of his friends and not one of them asked me how old I was, although I tried to work it in several times. After that visit, Pop wrote my mother and asked her to please send him a picture. She sent one that was several years old and featured my cairn puppy, Sandy. Poor Poppy. That picture made it look like he was dating a twelve-year-old. Shortly afterward, I had a graduation picture taken and at least it was without the dog.

George got his Navy wings in Corpus Christi, Texas, in June 1943. At age eighteen, he was the youngest pilot in the Navy at the time.

I graduated that same June and was accepted at Smith College. None of my family came to my commencement because travel was "unpatriotic"; most trains and planes were reserved for troops and military personnel. Much to my mother's distress, I worked that summer in a nuts and bolts factory in Port Chester, New York. I rode my bike to work with a boy I knew, and both of us were "gofers," doing the most menial of jobs. Yet, we were constantly told we were helping our country as the company did some war work.

By this time, my sister, Martha, had graduated from Smith, married Walt Rafferty, and had a baby girl. Walt had joined the Marines and was in Camp Pendleton, California, waiting to be sent overseas.

Martha had gone out to say good-bye, and they had been in a holding pattern for several months. They missed their baby, who had stayed back east. The baby's German nurse was afraid to go on the train to California alone—she thought people would think she was a spy—so I was tapped to accompany them. I was very excited, as I had never been west of Dayton, Ohio. What I remember most was body-surfing in the Pacific Ocean and being terrified of the big waves. Walt eventually shipped out to the Pacific and landed on Guadalcanal. Many of his friends died in the war, and his brother Kevin, a pilot, was lost in Europe.

Pop was due home on leave for seventeen days. His mother invited me to come to their home in Maine and stay with them throughout the leave. I guess Mrs. Bush had all sorts of reasons to invite me, but I suspect they wanted to see as much of their son as possible before he went off to war. By having me there, it meant Pop would spend less time going back and forth. That was my first trip to Kennebunkport, Maine, and my first glimpse of our beloved Walker's Point.

All the way up on the train, Poppy kept telling me about his wonderful family—and scaring me to death. I knew, of course, they would hate me. George is from the biggest, closest family. His grandmother and grandfather were alive, and all six of their children were there with spouses. George's family lived next door in a considerably smaller house than it is now. About eight of us shared the only bathroom.

Because of gas and tire rationing, the Bushes had a horse-pulled wagon. The horse's name was Barsil. George's brother Pres used to tease me and call me Barsil, and that is how I got my nickname, Bar.

It was a wonderful visit, with lots of undercurrents. First, we knew Pop soon would head overseas—either the Atlantic or the Pacific. And there was the budding romance. Did they like me? Did I like them? I know the answer to that one—yes. But they were overwhelming. The teasing was enormous from everybody, except George's mother. She was the most wonderful woman and had an extraordinary ability to see good in everyone without sounding insincere or like a Pollyanna.

When she told my mother I was a great cook, I thought I'd die laughing. My mother said something like, "Oh?" Mrs. Bush recounted the story of the night she and her husband were going out for dinner and she didn't have time to make dinner for Bucky and Johnny, Pop's brothers who were about four and ten at the time. According to Mrs. Bush, I stepped right up and said I'd take on that little project and made the most delicious peanut butter and jelly sandwiches for all. My mother's face was worth seeing.

We rode bikes, went to the beach, played tennis, collected sea glass and seashells, and had marvelous picnics. At night, Poppy and I walked on the rocks and watched the moon come up, and we were finally alone. I can't speak for George Bush, but I fell madly in love. We got secretly engaged.

The time came when Poppy had to go back to his ship and I went to Smith College. George wrote and he called some, but not much. Telephone use was limited because of the war, although servicemen had priority.

Smith then had around two thousand women undergraduates, and it was the first time I had been in a racially mixed school. I had some very exciting times just finding my way around campus. It must have been a lean year, because I not only made the freshman soccer team, I was captain. I lived in Tyler House with my great roommate, Margie Boyce, and many other girls who quickly became good friends.

However, in the fall of my first year the most unpleasant thing happened. A pretty little sophomore came to me and said, "I've looked the freshman class over and have chosen you to go with me on a blind date to Amherst." I made some excuse and thanked her. I wasn't the least bit interested in going on a blind date. I was in love with George Bush, but it was a secret. This happened several more times, and then she stopped asking me. My roommate, Margie, came to me and told me my secret was out. She said that nasty sophomore decided I didn't like men and told everyone that Margie and I were lovers. To protect herself and me, Margie told everyone that George Bush and I were engaged. I was shocked by all of this. What a protected life I had lived. As far as I knew, I had never been the victim of gossip before. It was a lesson then—and now—that you shouldn't believe everything you hear.

Poppy and I decided to announce our engagement at Christmas. When I called to tell my family I had a surprise—and to ask permission—they said, "So, you're going to marry Poppy. How nice." I couldn't believe they weren't surprised. "You fool," my brother Jimmy said. "Anyone within a mile of you two knew you were in love."

I went with George's mother to the Philadelphia shipyards for the commissioning of George's ship, the U.S.S. *San Jacinto*. The *San Jac*, a converted cruiser, looked enormous at the time, but compared to today's aircraft carriers, it was tiny. George flew a Grumman Avenger, an awkward plane compared to jets now. How he landed that big thing on that tiny deck is a wonder. He gave me my engagement ring on that trip, before he headed for the Pacific.

I went back to Smith, where I drifted through the rest of my freshman year and summer school. I was hoping to graduate in three years, but I did not put my heart and soul into my studies. I'm not too proud of that, but it was true. My poor dad spent a lot of time explaining to Miss Corwin, the freshman dean, that my marks were bad because my fiancé was on a ship in the Pacific. I'd like to say that was true, but I also just did not work. My dear father, who had worked his way through high school, college, and graduate school, must have suffered.

I certainly did miss George (for his sake, I'll quit calling him "Poppy"), and I was really worried about him. We listened for every piece of news from the Pacific, and rumors ran wild. Edward R. Murrow had a radio report that we all listened to and it almost made us feel like we were there. Well, we certainly weren't there compared to today's news reporting. Every word he said was censored, and we heard lots of "This is Edward R. Murrow from someplace in the South Pacific" or from some other theater of the war. No names and no places. The reporters in those days were much more careful than they are now about not giving away too much information in combat situations.

George wrote faithfully; sometimes I would receive many letters in one day, and sometimes a month would go by with no word. All mail was censored. No hints were allowed as to where they were. We all read between the lines as best we could. He received mail in the same fashion. (Unfortunately, in all our moves over the years, I've lost his letters.)

George was due to come home in the fall of 1944, and I was leaving Smith to get married. The plan was for me to return to college when George returned to his fleet. We heard nothing from him that September, but that was not unusual. Mail was slow. Then one day I got a letter from Doug West, a pilot in George's squadron, who told me George had been shot down off the island of Chichi Jima in the

Bonin Islands. Doug said he had buzzed overhead and had seen George swimming toward the raft. (I later learned it was thanks to Doug that George had even found his raft; Doug buzzed it with his plane, pointing George in the right direction.) Doug also said that he and another plane had strafed an enemy boat that had set out after George from the Japanese-held island.* I called Mrs. Bush, who had just gotten the same notice and was calling me. We were frantic, but Doug's letter held out hope that a submarine had been alerted and might have rescued George. I really don't remember the next three days—they are just a blur—but the Navy got a message to the Bushes that George had in fact been picked up and was in Hawaii for some R&R before being returned to the *San Jac.* His two crew mates, however, had been lost. George could have gotten home leave if he wanted, but he was anxious to get back to his ship. Of the original fourteen pilots in his squadron, four were dead.

I continued making wedding plans, addressing the invitations, and buying my trousseau. Mother begged and borrowed shoe coupons from friends since shoes were rationed during the war.

One might well ask why our parents would sign permission slips for us to get married at the ages of nineteen and twenty. I know that our children have asked that question. The answer: In wartime, the rules change. You don't wait until tomorrow to do anything.

Just before I was married, Daddy invited me into New York City for lunch. This was an enormous treat for me. I rarely went into the city, even though we lived so close, and I hardly ever got to be with my dad alone. I will never forget that luncheon. He talked to me about marriage and the commitment it meant. He told me the largest cause of divorce was money or the mishandling of money. That shocked me, for my dad absolutely idolized my mother, and yet she constantly spent more money than Dad made. I got up my nerve and asked him about that. He said Mother was different. He budgeted the money that he could afford for her allowance, and then gave her half. Then twice a year—at Christmas and at their anniversary in August—he bailed her out and she thought he was a hero! I think that he learned the hard way that no matter what he gave her, she was going to spend twice as

---

* We later read in *Life* magazine that the Japanese had committed acts of cannibalism on this same island.

much. The top drawer of the nightstand next to Mother's bed was full of unpaid bills. I thought she kept that a secret from Daddy, but he knew. He had just given up trying to get her to live within her budget. Several years later, when Mother died, vendors from around the country came to Daddy with unpaid bills. Thanks to her example, I have tried to pay my bills as they came along.

He also told me that the three most important things you can give your children are: the best education, a good example, and all the love in the world. He certainly lived by that rule and gave us all that and more, including trust. George has done the same with our children.

George's return date kept being put off. We eventually scratched December 17 from our wedding invitations and wrote in January 6. He finally called from Hawaii to say he was on his way home, waiting for a military flight. On Christmas Eve, he called from New York City, and I met him at the train station in Rye. What a Christmas present!

On New Year's Eve, we went to Miami Beach for his brother Pres's wedding to a wonderful girl, Beth Kauffman, which began a life-time friendship between the two of us. Then it was our turn.

We were married January 6, 1945, in the First Presbyterian Church in Rye. Aunts and uncles and cousins by the dozens came on both sides and as many friends as possible. Needless to say, there were many more women than men at the wedding. My brother Jim was not there as he was in the service and couldn't get leave. It was a lovely, cold day, and I remember standing in the back of the church with my dad. The bridesmaids were just about to start down the aisle when the church door blew open and there stood Gerry Bemiss, a childhood friend of George's, in a Navy uniform. He said he was in the wedding, but my dad said that he wasn't, that it was too late. Wrong. Gerry whipped out of his winter gear and was racing down the aisle before the bridesmaids. I was told that George's smile when he saw Gerry was wonderful. We had a lovely reception, and then headed for New York City for the night. Before leaving town, we saw *Meet Me in St. Louis* at Radio City Music Hall and then took the sleeper to the Cloisters in Sea Island, Georgia. We had such a nice time there. Most of the people were older, but we did meet some other honeymoon couples. We swore that we would return often. So much for resolutions. We finally went back to that lovely place in 1991 for a wonderful weekend.

For the next eight months we moved around the country while

George's new squadron formed and trained. Sometimes I could go with him and sometimes I couldn't. We went to Grosse Ile Air Base in Michigan and lived in rooms in Wyandotte and Dearborn. The first room we rented was dark, and the landlady took great pleasure in my mistakes. I made many. I heard her say one day to a friend on the phone, "You should have seen what she did today. She washed all her silk underwear and it shrank." I did, and it did, but how mean of her not to tell me how to wash it. We moved over to Dearborn and stayed with the dearest family, Joe and Grace Gorgone and their children. We have stayed in touch all these years, until Grace died in March 1993. She taught me some of the things my mother thought I should be able to pick up by reading—things like how to cook, clean, and wash clothes.

We were moved to a base in Maine and lived in several rooms in the Lewiston-Auburn area. George's mother came to see us and told my mother we lived in the red-light district. Rooms were hard to find in base towns. We had a small, one-room efficiency apartment with a kitchen in a closet and a Murphy-in-a-door bed. It smelled of other people's cooking, and there was really very little to keep me busy all day. So I wandered the streets and read a lot. I'll never forget the day George came home early because Franklin Roosevelt had died. We were sick. Neither one of us had ever voted—we were too young—and we probably would have voted for the other fellow, but Roosevelt was our President, the Commander-in-Chief of a country at war, and we joined the world in mourning. We felt truly lost, very young and alone. Who had ever heard of Harry Truman?

The next time I joined George was in Virginia Beach. I had been warned by an older friend from Rye that I should go down early to get a place. She also suggested that we try to join the Princess Anne Country Club, which had several very inexpensive service memberships available. We ended up with a tiny basement apartment in a really big private home right across the street from the club, and for six dollars, we became members of this little gem of a place. The food was good, and the golf course was beautiful. The woman we rented from, a Mrs. Grandy, was an absolutely crazy woman. We had a tiny bathroom across the hall from our little room. Mrs. Grandy rented out space on her living room floor and said that our bathroom went with it. So I instantly became the cleaner of a public bath. She had wild, dyed red hair and wandered around that big house in her nightgown. There were hundreds of stories about her, and I believed them all. The one I liked best was the fact that she hated hairy men and made her late husband sit in a bathtub of Neet hair remover. We never heard how he died, but we guessed it was a very painful death.

It was a fun summer. We sat on the beach, partied, and entertained guests. George's sister, Nancy, came to visit and lived on the beach. We warned her about the sun, but she said she didn't burn. Famous last words. We sent her home on the train with a burned face and closed eyes.

George took up golf with Max Moore, another young pilot, who has remained a friend for life. The boys would send me into the fairway about three hundred yards ahead. Then one of them would hit, and I'd hear a yell: "Left." Then I'd charge into the woods to the left and try to find the ball. Those two lost more golf balls than you can believe. We laughed our way through the summer with Jacquie and Doug West, Milt Moore, Jack and Bea Guy, and Max Moore.

But again, the undercurrents were strong. George and his new squadron, VT 153, were getting closer and closer to going back overseas, probably to be involved in the anticipated invasion of Japan. By now I realized that what my dad had told me before I married was true. He said that every day you stay married, you fall more and more in love with your husband or wife. It was certainly true in my case, and I did not want George to return to the war. Many of our friends were dying. V-E Day came and went, and yet the Japanese fought on. Then the atomic bombs were dropped on Hiroshima and Nagasaki. Horrid as those bombs were, they saved many, many American and Japanese lives. I've always respected Harry Truman for making that courageous decision. I was also very grateful.

V-J Day arrived in August, and the rejoicing on the streets in Virginia Beach was loud, wild, and fairly liquid. And why not? There was a lot to cheer about. Before the day ended, George and I went to a little church to thank God for ending that war and to pray for all who had not lived. What a waste of so many good men and women, including many friends.

❧ Because George had been in for three years, and had served overseas in combat, he was one of the first in his squadron to get out of the service. He had two air medals, a Distinguished Flying Cross, and a wife, and he was headed to Yale University.

George had been accepted into Yale his junior year in high school, but his family felt he was too young. So four years later, in 1945, George and I moved to New Haven, Connecticut, for his freshman year of college. The GI Bill paid for his tuition, and he had some savings from his years in the Navy.

We went to all the football games and joined his family and friends at tailgate parties in the stadium parking lot. George played his beloved soccer his freshman year, but did not continue as it took too much time. He became a member of Delta Kappa Epsilon fraternity and was chapter president for a short time. He really worked hard.

I, on the other hand, played bridge and went to movies with some of George's more frivolous friends. I did work half a day at the Yale Co-op and audited a course (nicknamed Pots and Pans by the students) given by John Phillips, an authority on American furniture and silver. I did not go back to Smith, and Yale did not take women at the time. I could have commuted to Connecticut College, but I hated to ask my dad for the tuition. I had every opportunity to finish my education, both then and in later years. George would have been very supportive. I chose, instead, to have a big family.

We lived in three different places the two and a half years George was at Yale. The first was a shotgun apartment on Chapel Street, a tiny, adorable place we loved. The front faced the avenue, with the trolley going up and down our street. Two doors down was a funeral home. Somebody has to do it, I know, but I have been a little cynical about funeral homes ever since. We often saw the men standing in the back of the building in shirtsleeves, kicking the hearse's tires, chewing, smoking, spitting, laughing, and joking. Five minutes later, these same men appeared in the front of the building with the hearse with their Digger O'Dell suits and long, funereal faces.

On Thanksgiving, George invited ten of his best friends at Yale from Andover days to have dinner with us. Travel was still difficult, the boys could not get home, and rationing was still on. I do not remember too many of the details, but I know we had a turkey and we did not have a dining room. We sat on the couch, chairs, and the floor. I remember pulling out every pan we owned and getting every dish, piece of silverware, and glass dirty. After dinner, they went home and we fell into bed exhausted. It took me three days to get those things washed. Today, I can clean the kitchen up after feeding fifty in less time than it takes to say "Thanksgiving."

We had a wonderful black standard poodle puppy named Turbo. We were devoted to him. He was a great dog and went to work with me. He would stay behind the counter until George's last morning class, then George would pick him up and take him on to his next activity.

George played baseball for Yale and was a great fielding first baseman. There are lots of jokes about his hitting ability, but the truth is, George hit when the chips were down. I should know—I kept score. He never missed playing in a game the three seasons we were there, and his team won the Eastern Championship for two of the years. I sat behind third base, with family members of the other players and some faithful Yale baseball fans. Finally, one game, Ethan Allen, the Yale coach and a former big league player, asked me to sit behind home plate, where they had a safety net. I was huge and weighed more than a Yale linebacker. Yes, I was pregnant with our first child. The Chapel Street landlord liked dogs, but not babies. So we moved to Edwards Street, where they did not like dogs, so Turbo went to live with George's mother and father in Greenwich. The baby did not come and did not come. George's mother finally gave me a good dose of castor oil and that baby came all right—I'm tempted to say covered with glory. The baby was a lovely little boy, but sad to say, he did not weigh sixty pounds. That is what I had gained and that was what I had to lose. George and I were mad about our baby, whom we named George Walker Bush. My mother said she hated to be in the room with the baby, for if she took her eyes off him, George looked hurt.

In the fall we moved into our third and last New Haven home, on Hillhouse Avenue. The president of Yale University lived next door in a tremendous old Victorian house. The houses on either side belonged to the university and had been converted into housing for students who were married and former military. George and I shared the first floor with two other families. We were so lucky, for we had three tiny rooms and a tiny bath. That was the key—our own bath! We shared a kitchen with the other two families. There were two of everything, and since the other two families did not speak to each other for various reasons, George and I had a third of one refrigerator and a third of the other. They scheduled their mealtimes so they would not be in the kitchen at the same time. And the communal bath was a source of great contention. It was fairly amusing. I think there were nine families and eleven children living in that house. Longtime friends Bill and Sally Reeder lived on the third floor with their twin sons, Boots and Shack. Our second year in the house, we lost one of our kitchen mates, thank heavens, and we had some peace. In their place came Patsy and Jack Caulkins with their little boy, Corky. They have been very dear, close friends for the last fifty years. Communal living has its ups and downs, but since I'm a people person, I loved it. It was hard for George to study there, but he certainly managed. He won a number of awards and was Phi Beta Kappa his senior year. It was during George's Yale years that we began a lifelong relationship with Bill Trent, then head of the United Negro College Fund (UNCF). George was involved with the school's annual charity fund drive, and UNCF was one of the beneficiaries. George brought Bill home after one of the meetings, and a friendship was born.

Bill and his wife, Vi, invited us to come to their home in Harlem for dinner following a baseball game between Yale and Columbia University. Most of George's family was at the game; I sat with Bill and Vi. The family all looked us over, but George's Ganny Walker—who truly was a dear woman—said in a loud stage whisper as she walked by, "It's all right. They look like Indians." I was embarrassed, but Bill and Vi understood; they had lived a life of segregation.

This very special man died in November 1993 after spending a lovely Thanksgiving at home surrounded by his wife of fifty-nine years and his children. He truly was a great American.

⤳ Recently, I learned my father was just as proud of George then as I was. I came across a letter Daddy had written a childhood friend, updating him on the Pierce family. He wrote about us:

> My second daughter, Barbara, went to Smith College for a year and a half and then married in January 1945 a young fellow named Bush, to whom she had been engaged for two years while he was flying a torpedo bomber in the Pacific. He won the Distinguished Flying Cross and altogether is

a great guy. They are still living in New Haven where he is attending Yale until his graduation in June. He is by all odds the biggest man on the campus, having been the last man tapped for Skull and Bones and having been awarded a faculty prize for having done the most for Yale. He is captain of the baseball team and a hell of a good first baseman. They also have a baby and I hope I live long enough to see George Bush [our baby] playing one end for Yale and Kevin Rafferty [Martha's baby] on the other.

4

Striking Out on Our Own

Geeorge interviewed for jobs all winter and spring of 1948. We had spent most of his savings from Navy days, and we needed to get on with real life and make a living.

It was very important to George that he like his work. He told me he had thought about it a great deal while standing night watch on the submarine deck after being rescued. He had decided he did not want to work with intangibles; he wanted a product he could see and feel. I think that meant he did not want to be in the investment or banking business like so many of his family. His dad was a partner with Brown Brothers, Harriman and Company, and his grandfather was the founder of G. H. Walker and Company.

We looked into farming briefly and read some books by Louis Bromfield. Thank heavens we did. It saved us from racing off into a life we were unqualified for and which is hard work. Bromfield made farming sound very romantic and idealistic. But he also made it clear that in order to be a success, you needed a lot of money to invest, which we didn't have. So realism overcame idealism, and we looked elsewhere.

Numerous companies came to New Haven to interview Yale graduates, but there were many applicants for every job. The country was gearing down in peacetime, military plants were cutting back, and there were many out-of-work servicemen. I do remember that Procter & Gamble interviewed George, and they turned him down.

George had several good choices, but ended up accepting an offer from Dresser Industries, a holding company that had several oil-related subsidiaries. The CEO was Henry Neil Mallon, a classmate of George's father and a dear family friend. I had heard stories about "Uncle Neil" almost from the moment I met George. He and Prescott Bush were certainly about as different as two men could be. George's father was six feet four inches tall with a full head of black hair and a take-charge attitude; Neil, a bachelor, was about five feet nine inches, bald, and a modest, quiet man. Yet, both men were very successful in their own fields and were the best of friends. Every family should have an "Uncle Neil." The most thoughtful man alive, he always seemed to have time for everyone.

One story will explain why the Bush kids loved this dear man. When they were about ten or eleven years old, George and his older brother, Prescott, were playing catch as Neil watched. One of the boys threw a wild ball, and it shattered the car windshield. George's father came charging out the door, bellowing at Poppy and Pressy that they knew better than to play ball near the house. Neil quickly stepped up and took the blame, saying he was the one who threw the ball!

Neil's excitement about George coming to Dresser was contagious. He wanted George to have experience with all the various companies, starting with Ideco (short for International Derrick and Equipment Company) as Dresser's only trainee.

So the day after graduation, George headed for Odessa, Texas, in a little, two-door, red Studebaker, a graduation present from his mom and dad. He stopped on the way in Birmingham, Alabama, to see his Yale baseball teammate, Frank Quinn (who had signed with the Boston Red Sox for $100,000) play minor league ball.

Our son, Georgie, and I went to Maine and stayed in "the big house" with Gampy and Ganny Walker. As always, they spoiled us to death. It was a happy time—except I missed George. He promised me he would send for us the moment he found a place to live. I remember he wrote his grandparents to thank them for putting us up. He also told them he was so happy he had gotten a great education at Yale, because he was putting it to good use. He knew this for a fact, because his boss, Bill Nelson, told him he was the best warehouse-sweeper-outer he had ever seen. He also was very good at painting oil field equipment in temperatures that reached 105 degrees at noon. As you can tell, George started at the bottom.

Odessa was a boomtown and there was little or no housing available. Midland was twenty miles down the road, but that's where the white-collar workers lived. The blue-collar workers, like us, lived in Odessa. A week after his arrival, George finally called to say that he had found a tiny place and we should come down. He said it was a sorry little house—and it was—but Georgie and I were so excited about being with him. This was an adventure the three of us had signed up for together.

We stepped off the plane—after a twelve-hour flight in those days—to a whole new and very hot world. Odessa is flat as a pancake and as different from Rye, New York, as any place imaginable. Nothing comes easy to West Texas. Every tree must be cultivated, and every flower is a joy.

As far as my mother was concerned, we could have been living in Russia. Who had ever heard of Odessa, Texas? She sent me cold cream, soap, and other items she assumed were available only in civilized parts of the country. She did not put Odessa in that category. I loved being given all that stuff, but eventually had to write and tell her we had big, beautiful supermarkets, which Rye did not have at the time.

George had rented a two-room apartment on East Seventh Street. We first shared a bath with a very nice couple from Oklahoma, Valta Ree and Jack Casselman, who had a similar apartment on the other side. When they moved out, three females moved in: a grandmother of thirty-eight, a daughter of twenty, and a three-year-old. The two older women had questionable occupations, and we saw very little of them, day or night. To use the bathroom, we walked in and locked the door on their side; then when we were done, we unlocked their door before going back to our own room. The big key here was remembering to unlock the other door as you left. Our neighbors' many gentlemen callers had a hard time remembering that, which caused a small amount of friction. We would be locked out of our own bathroom! Otherwise, sharing a bath did not seem strange to us—we had done it most of our married life. We also felt lucky, because most of our neighbors did not have bathrooms at all, just outhouses. The family two doors down not only had an outdoor toilet, but mules and some other livestock. The overwhelming smell drove the neighborhood wild. We also had the only refrigerator on the street. As life is relative, we lived pretty well.

Speaking of smells, I still blush when I remember awakening soon after our arrival to the strong odor of gas. I woke up George, Georgie, and the Casselmans and made everyone leave the house before it blew up. The Casselmans were dear and patiently explained to me that the wind had shifted and I was smelling fumes from the nearby oil-related plants.

✐ Some wonderful things happened in Odessa, and we certainly grew up a little more. George and I learned a whole new outlook on life. Texans are apt to think that the "Texas way" is best. One day at work a man said to George, "Say, you're a college grad, aren't you?" When George told him he had gone to Yale, the man thought a minute and said he'd never heard of it. He mumbled something that sounded like "Too bad." George got the distinct impression he felt sorry for him. So much for eastern elitism. It didn't count much in West Texas.

Texas was "high and dry" then—literally. You could not buy liquor by-the-drink over the counter. You either belonged to a private club or bought a bottle and "brown-bagged" it. Some counties were absolutely dry—you couldn't even buy a bottle. Nearby Midland County was "dry," and Ector County was "wet." So people drove to the Ector County line to Pinky Roden's liquor store—a rather profitable business. It wasn't until 1970 that a liquor-by-the-drink bill passed, much to our dismay, which I'll explain later.

We drank little or nothing, but I remember one night when George brought home a man named Smitty, an Ideco salesman from Oklahoma. Smitty was a real good ol' boy, and when George offered him a drink, Smitty picked up our one bottle of bourbon and took a big swig. He then passed it to me. Out of the corner of my eye I saw George watching to see what I'd do. He had a big grin on his face. I let the men pass the bottle. Poor ol' Smitty eventually was "run off," caught by the boss for having very light fingers, and George poured him on the train for Oklahoma after emptying his pockets of Ideco supplies.

We had another very interesting visitor in the fall of 1948, whom I wrote home about:

> Friday Pop did not come home for lunch as he had to meet a man who was coming in from Dallas—a Mr. Rabacheck from Yugoslavia. He does not speak English. Just "hello," "okay," "good morning," etc. We find some West Texans are

not only Eastern-prejudiced, but also "furiner"-prejudiced. No one in the store wanted to have anything to do with Mr. R. He has visited all the Dresser Companies and has been wined and dined by the presidents and vice presidents of these companies. He gets to Odessa and they act like he has a disease. Consequently, Pop has been with him constantly since Friday. He is an excellent engineer. Pop says Mr. R. was very apologetic that he couldn't speak better English so he could talk to Bill Nelson. (This was all with the help of a dictionary and the hands.). Pop looked up the word "shy" and told him that Bill was shy, but the truth of the matter was that Bill did not want to have anything to do with a "furiner" and a "commie."

Mr. R. wanted to know how to skid a rig from well to well without breaking the derrick down, moving it and reassembling it again. This is a very complicated process, and Pop had to ask for answers to almost everything that Mr. R. asked. Something gets lost in the translation. It has been good for Pop, but not so great for Mr. R.

Friday night we took him to the football game. He was fascinated and a charming guy. Last night he wanted to see "cowboy," so we took him to see a western movie. He loved it.

He and Pop went out to different rigs Saturday, Sunday and Monday and today, and will probably go out until he leaves on Wednesday.

He came back here last night after the movie and we had a very interesting talk. It was rather like playing The Game. [We would guess what each other meant, using our hands, facial expressions, and the dictionary.]

Both George and I really liked this man a lot. It broke our hearts when he said good-bye to us, clutched his heart, and said "Friends." George and I felt sad that because of his country's policies, we could not really be friends. As I write this in 1993, his beautiful country is under terrible civil strife, and I think of this warm man and his family.

*   *   *

⤳ My letters home during this period are boring, filled with stories of Georgie—a much beloved and slightly spoiled little boy. They sound lonesome for family and family news, although the people we met both at church and at work were very nice to us. One of the many things we have learned in all our travels is that it's the people who count. West Texans were the best. Most people everywhere are interesting, and if you can't find a friend, then maybe there is something wrong with you. For our brief stay on East Seventh Street, the Casselmans were friends. And our housemates from Yale, Bill and Sally Reeder and their twin boys, lived in Midland and we saw them several times.

We had our first Christmas away from family. We got many packages from home and decorated our new little apartment on East Seventeenth Street—still considered on the wrong side of the tracks, but we had our own bath.

On Christmas Eve, Ideco opened the doors to its shop and had an open bar for all its customers. George and another fella were put behind the bar to pass out Christmas cheer. Each "good ol'" boy had a drink, and you had to have one with him. George started sipping early, and at dusk Christmas Eve, store manager Leo Thomas drove up to the house in a pickup truck and dropped George off—literally. He opened the back of the truck, dumped George in the yard, and drove away. It was a long time before I let George forget it. Maybe that's why my letters to my family were so boring. I left out the more interesting things happening to us!

⤳ In the spring of 1949, George, Georgie, and I moved to California, where George first worked as an assemblyman at Pacific Pumps, and then became a salesman for Security Engineers Company, a manufacturer of drilling bits. Both were Dresser companies. We lived in a motel in Whittier, the beautiful Pierpoint Inn in Ventura, a rented house in Bakersfield, and finally came to rest in an apartment in Compton. By this time I was very pregnant with our second child.

That fall my brother Jimmy married Margie Dyer in Cleveland, Ohio. I went east for the wedding and had a great time with my family and friends. She was a lovely bride, and we were all so happy that my precious, funny, slightly wild brother had found the rock of Gibraltar to settle down with. She has remained a great beauty and a great wife.

At that time, George was working in the Pacific Pumps factory seven days a week, eight-hour shifts. A week or so after the wedding, George came home early one day and had the terrible job of telling me that my mother and father had been in an automobile accident. My beautiful mother had been killed immediately, and my dad was in the hospital. After much discussion with my sisters and brothers, we got the message from Daddy that I was not to come home. He did not want the baby endangered. What a lonely, miserable time that was. I was so glad I had been home for the very happy family wedding. Sudden death is a terrible shock—but then all death is a struggle and a shock. My younger brother, Scott, a freshman at Yale, heard the news on a car radio. Jim and Margie came home from their honeymoon, moving in with Daddy for several years until he remarried. My sister, Martha, and her great husband, Walter, took charge of all funeral plans. And I sat in California.

George was wonderful. His bosses gave him the next day off, and he called several friends from Yale and Smith who were living in the Los Angeles area. Margie and Dick Jenkins, David and Suzy Grimes, and Barbara and Bill Mannon were marvelous to me, and all have remained friends for fifty years. Certainly, George and I could not have lived the life we have without friends.

We had a lovely little apartment, living near a couple with four small children. They seemed so very nice. She agreed to keep Georgie when I went into the hospital to have the baby. About a week before the baby was born, we heard screaming, banging, and shouting. Then four little children came tumbling out of that apartment and said, "Call the police. Dad is killing Mother." We brought the children in and called the police. They arrived, knocked on the door, and the noise suddenly stopped.

In a few minutes the wife came to the door bleeding, with a blackened eye and a red, tear-stained face. She said there was no problem and became angry with us because we called the police. It was so ugly and awful. The police finally went away, and we tucked the children in for the night. Eventually the husband drank himself into a stupor and the wife's father and brothers came, put the drunk on the floor, and moved the family out. George and I grew up a little more.

For prenatal care, I was going to a clinic where you saw whichever doctor was on duty. So I didn't meet the doctor who delivered our little girl until the night of her birth, December 20, 1949. I can't remember his name or what he looked like, but I remember thinking he was a knight in white armor, a prince, and a saint. Any woman in labor feels all that and more about the doctor who delivers her baby.

We named our daughter Pauline Robinson Bush and called her Robin. We were considering calling her Pauline Pierce Bush until George's mother said the poor child would go through life as P. P. Bush and that would never do. That was so unlike Dotty Bush—it's funny the things you remember.

George brought Robin and me home Christmas Day. You can't ask for more than that. Daddy gave us a Hoffman television set—a big, heavy rectangular thing with a tiny little yellow screen—and our friends came over for Milton Berle, which was fun. My sister, Martha, visited us for a few days that Christmas, which was wonderful. Daddy and Scott went to a fishing lodge in Florida for the holidays, and Scott told me that they were very lonely. We all missed Mother as she really loved Christmas.

Fortunately, Scott wasn't lonely for long. He married his childhood sweetheart, Janice Chamberlain, when she graduated from Mount Holyoke College and he from Miami University in Oxford, Ohio. They have been a team for some forty years and have four wonderful children.

And there is another happy footnote: In June 1952, my father found a wonderful woman named Willa Martin, a writer with the Associated Press and an artist of some renown, from Greenville, South Carolina. She brought many good things to the family when they married, not the least of which was her niece Patty, who eventually married George's youngest brother, Bucky.

In 1950 George was transferred back to West Texas, but this time to Midland. He was back working for Ideco as a city salesman, calling on oil companies mostly located right in town. I was glad, as he had traveled a great deal in California. At first we stayed in George's Courts, a motel right on Main Street in downtown Midland. The first morning, George went out to get some milk for the baby, but he came rushing back into the motel and changed his clothes. He had on Bermuda shorts, and the truck drivers were whistling at him. I don't believe he wore shorts ever again, except to play tennis.

We stayed there until we were able to settle into our very first house. It was located on East Maple Street in a section of town called Easter Egg Row. Every brand-new, identical house was painted a different wild color and cost just under $8,000. We loved that marvelous little home.

Many Easterners had come to Midland to get in on the oil boom—John Ashmun, Toby Hilliard, Dottie and Earle Craig, Hopie and Jimmy Ritchie. There were Texans, too, like John Overbey, Marion and C. Fred Chambers, Steve and Anne Farish, Liz and Tom Fowler, and Betty and Murphy Baxter. There were Oklahomans like the Liedtkes—Betty and Hugh, and Bessie and Bill—and Jimmy and Jocie Hewgley, Marian and Bill Bovaird, and many more. We all had been uprooted; we all had young children; and we all were having a lot of fun. The women joined the Midland Service League, and the men played touch football in the Martini Bowl. We all worked in the Little Theater and the YMCA and volunteered at the hospital. Most of us were active in church; George was an elder, and we both taught Sunday School at the First Presbyterian Church. We took turns having cookouts on our tiny patios or in backyards and watching each other's children. When the chips were down, all of us were there for each other.

George was working very hard trying to support his growing family. After several years of working for Dresser, he decided to go off on his own. He went to see Neil Mallon, and in his usual supportive fashion, Neil said that if he were young again, he'd do the same thing. So in late 1950, our neighbor across the street, John Overbey, and George went into business together, forming Bush-Overbey Oil Development Company, Inc. George's wonderfully loyal Uncle Herbie Walker helped him finance his part of the deal.

George worked even harder and spent a lot of time traveling, looking for good oil deals and financing. A few years later, in 1953, Bush-Overbey joined forces with the Liedtke brothers, Hugh and Bill, calling their new company "Zapata." (They took the name from a Marlon Brando film playing in downtown Midland at the time, *Viva Zapata!*) It was truly an exciting time, a life filled with risk and hope.

We moved again, into a slightly bigger house, on West Ohio Street, and we all had more babies. For us, it was John Ellis Bush, born in February 1953. We called him Jeb.

Life seemed almost too good to be true.

5

Robin

So I am glad not that my loved one has gone,
But that the earth she laughed and lived on was my earth, too.
That I had known and loved her,
And that my love I'd shown.
Tears over her departure?
Nay, a smile
That I had walked with her a little while. *

Jeb was just a few weeks old when Robin woke up one morning and said, "I don't know what to do this morning. I may go out and lie on the grass and watch the cars go by, or I might just stay in bed." I didn't think that sounded like a normal three-year-old and decided she must have what my mother called "spring fever." I took her to our excellent pediatrician, Dr. Dorothy Wyvell. She examined Robin, took some blood, and told me she would call me after the test results were in. She suggested I might want to come back without Robin, but with George. That sounded rather ominous to me, but I wasn't too worried. Certainly Robin had no energy, but nothing seemed seriously wrong.

Dr. Wyvell called, and George met me at her office in the late afternoon. Dorothy was not one to pull any punches. She told us Robin

---

* Sent to us by a friend after Robin died.

had leukemia. Neither of us had ever heard of it, and George asked her what the next step was; how did we cure her? She talked to us a little about red and white blood cells and told us as gently as possible that there was no cure. Her advice was to tell no one, go home, forget that Robin was sick, make her as comfortable as we could, love her—and let her gently slip away. She said this would happen very quickly, in several weeks. We talked a little more, and George asked her if she would talk to his uncle, Dr. John Walker, at Memorial Sloan Kettering Hospital in New York City. She readily agreed. Uncle John also thought Robin had little chance to live, but he thought we should by all means treat her and try to extend her life, just in case of a breakthrough.

I drove home, and George had to return to the office for just a minute. On the way, he stopped at Liz and Tom Fowler's house and asked Liz please to come over to be with me. By that evening our living room was filled with close friends, all offering to help. I remember being so surrounded by love that I did not really believe what the doctor had told us was true. She just had to be wrong. But either way, we knew we had to do everything we could to save our beautiful child.

It's funny how you remember such unimportant things at moments of stress. Our minister, Dr. Matthew Lynn, and his wife popped in. They were offered a drink, and I will always remember his answer. He said, "Not *now*, thank you, George." Tommy and Matthew Lynn would no more take a drink than fly, but by saying "now," he made everyone feel comfortable. Such a silly, small thing to remember.

The very next day George and I flew to New York City, leaving Georgie and Jebby with different friends, and checked Robin into Memorial Sloan Kettering on Sixty-eighth Street. At first, no one there believed that our little hospital in Midland had done the testing correctly. Robin's white blood cell count was just too high—the highest they had ever heard. Unfortunately, it was correct, and they immediately put Robin on medication. We moved into Ganny and Gampy Walker's beautiful apartment on Sutton Place in New York and stayed there off and on until October 1953, when our little one passed away with both of us standing by her side.

It was an extraordinary experience, and in a strange kind of way, we learned how lucky we were. We met people there who had only one child. We had three. We met people who did not love each other. We loved each other very much. (I learned later that 70 percent of people who lose a child get divorced. I suspect this is because their love for each other was found wanting and they did not communicate.) We had the most supportive family, and we shared. We had friends who helped us. Financially, we were very lucky, as our insurance covered almost everything.

And last, but not least, we believed in God. That has made an enormous difference in our lives, then and now.

I became very close to the parents of the other patients. Not only did we spend hours together, but we understood each other. So many of them had serious financial problems, which made the ordeal even tougher. Sloan Kettering did not charge those who couldn't pay, but there were so many other expenses involved. I remember one precious little boy named Joey, whose mother had a big family in upstate New York. Her husband was a laborer and was trying to cope with schools, bills, and meals. She worried all the time. She had no Ganny Walker to put her up nine blocks from the hospital, and no Mom Bush to help with the children. (Mrs. Bush had sent one of her boys' childhood nurses, Marion Fraser, down to Texas to take care of our boys.) Joey's mom had a cheap room out in the Bronx and commuted every day on the bus and subway in her bedroom slippers. She had the face of an angel, a big warm heart, and enormous faith in God. As Joey's time drew near, I met her one day in the parents' room and asked about her son. "Joey's bad, Barbara," she said, adding: "Do you remember in the Bible where it says, 'Let the little children suffer and they will come unto me'? Joey is really suffering." I loved that courageous lady, and I loved Joey. God bless him.

Years later, when I did a little work for Ronald McDonald Houses, I always thought of Joey's mother and how much they would have helped her. Ronald McDonald Houses not only provide inexpensive rooms and transportation to and from the hospital for whole families, they also allow parents who are going through the same thing to be together, to support and care for each other. It's a wonderful program that really helps families in need.

George was just getting started in business, so he rushed back and forth between Midland and New York. He came east whenever he could, and we talked on the phone every evening. I missed my baby Jeb and Georgie at home, but George was with them as much as possible.

Friends and family made such a difference. There were so many who cared and helped. Lud Ashley, George's classmate and great friend from Yale days, was a bachelor then living in New York City. He quietly checked in all the time. I did not know just how much until very early one morning a night nurse said, "What does your husband do, Mrs. Bush? I meet him every morning around 2 A.M. when he comes in to check on Robin before going to bed." I said that it couldn't have been my husband because he was in Texas. It was Lud Ashley.

One day, when Robin was very ill, I remember going out onto the cold roof off the parents' room to be alone for a tear or two. I found Lud huddled outside, freezing. He hadn't wanted to intrude, but he wanted to be there if needed. Lud went on to be a Democratic congressman from Toledo, Ohio, and has remained a great friend.

People really wanted to help. One friend of George's, Jimmy Markham, felt so bad that he appeared with his most valued gift—a beautiful, pedigreed, tricolored collie pup. With "Mark" came a list as long as your arm of things that this dog needed. Needless to say, the last thing on my mind was the care and feeding of this big, gawky puppy. We got the basics and put Mark in our backyard in Midland. When we returned in October, we had the world's most beautiful gentle dog. We all loved him. He was dognapped several years later, breaking our hearts.

Back in Midland, George dropped by church every morning at 6:30 A.M. and prayed for Robin. He said at first only the custodian was there. Then one morning he felt a presence, and our minister, Matthew Lynn, had started joining him. They never talked, just prayed. That meant a lot to George.

One day George got several phone calls from friends who had heard radio personality Paul Harvey talking about a doctor in Kansas who had a cure for leukemia. George spent the day following up, and after about five hours, he finally got the doctor on the phone. The poor man was distraught. He did not have a cure—just another medicine they were testing. He had spent the day talking to other parents who were desperate to help their loved one. He did tell George that Sloan Kettering was a great hospital and if there was a breakthrough, they certainly would know it. I'm sure Paul Harvey, whom George now knows and respects, had no idea what anguish he caused a small group of parents. He raised our hopes only to have them dashed.

Robin was wonderful. She never asked why this was happening to her. She lived each day as it came, sweet and loving, unquestioning and unselfish. How we hated bone marrow tests. They were so agonizing for all ages. She had many painful blood transfusions, and family and friends quietly slipped into the hospital and replaced the blood supply. Several times I was called to come pick up my sister or a friend who had passed out while giving blood. The hospital asked people to try to get replacements for the blood that was used, and thanks to many dear people, I honestly think we fulfilled our obligation.

Robin would go into remission, and once in a great while, we were able to take her as an outpatient to Ganny Walker's. Gampy Walker was a scary old man, but he was putty in Robin's hands. He taught her to play a simplified game of Gin Rummy, which she misunderstood to be Gin Mummy. She then changed it to Gin Poppy, after her beloved father.

Sometimes we went to the Bush house in Greenwich, and in the summer, we went to Maine for a brief period and Robin got to see her brothers. She had their pictures taped to her headboard at Sloan Kettering and every single doctor and nurse heard about those "superman" brothers of hers.

We took her home to Midland for a short stay. That was the farthest the hospital had ever allowed a patient to go, but the doctors knew Dorothy Wyvell could take care of Robin. Still, it was scary to be so far from the hospital. Hugh Liedtke and George were building their new business, and George must have been exhausted with work, worry, and travel, but somehow he managed to do it all. Hugh's wife, Betty, who had children of her own, saved my life. She spent hours each day with us, thinking up ways to get Robin to eat and make her laugh. She was loving and funny and no matter how bad it got, she came. I don't know how she knew, but if I got frightened, she was there.

Leukemia was not a well-known disease. Many people thought it was catching and did not let their children get near Robin. In those days, cancer in general was only whispered about, and some people just couldn't cope with a dying child. It was not an easy time for our friends or us.

I made up my mind that there would be no tears around Robin, so I asked people who cried to step out of her room. I didn't want to scare our little girl. Poor George had the most dreadful time and could hardly stand to see her get a blood transfusion. He would say that he had to go to the men's room. We used to laugh and wonder if Robin thought he had the weakest bladder in the world. Not true. He just had the most tender heart.

Rightly or wrongly, we did not tell six-year-old Georgie that his sister was dying. We hated that, but we felt it would have been too big a burden for such a little fellow. On the other hand, there could be no more roughhousing since leukemia patients easily hemorrhage, so we had to keep a close watch on them when they were together.

One day, back in New York, George's father asked me to go with him to the graveyard in Greenwich. He wanted me to see where he would be buried. The lot he picked was lovely, on a nice hillside with trees. He was such a dear man, and he picked out a modest headstone that said BUSH—about three feet tall and four feet wide. On one side of the headstone was a freshly planted lilac bush; on the other side, a dogwood tree. It was a sunny, bright day, and Dad pointed out some enormous mausoleum-type buildings or large headstones. Then he said, "I knew old so-and-so. He certainly thought highly of himself, didn't he, Bar?" That darling man bought that lot so Robin would have a place to rest.

Eventually the medicine that was controlling the leukemia caused other terrible problems. We called George, and by the time he got there after flying all night, our baby was in a coma. Her death was very peaceful. One minute she was there, and the next she was gone. I truly felt her soul go out of that beautiful little body. For one last time I combed her hair, and we held our precious little girl. I never felt the presence of God more strongly than at that moment.

We loved our doctors at Sloan Kettering and have kept up with them. Joe Burchenbal, Lois Murphy, and Charlotte Tan were so bright, caring, and dedicated. Lois and Charlotte were Robin's doctors and became dear friends of ours, although they tried to stay detached. They just could not get too involved emotionally. At that time no leukemia patient had recovered. Today, if caught in time, recovery is fairly common, thanks to many dedicated doctors and researchers.

The nurses also were very special to us. I wondered at their ability to put in day after day with sick and dying children, and then go home to face all the problems that come with raising a family. They were, and are, exceptional.

❧ We called our families and told them the news and went to Greenwich for a memorial service. (There would be no funeral; we had signed papers giving Robin's body to research.) Those few days are a little vague, but several things come to mind.

The day after Robin died, George and I went to Rye to play golf with Daddy, at his suggestion. As we drove out on the parkway, I was shocked that the leaves were at the peak of their fall beauty. I remember realizing life went on, whether we were looking or not. I also remember changing my shoes in the ladies' locker room and seeing a childhood friend, Marilyn Peterson. We talked briefly, and I did not mention Robin. I wondered later if she thought it was strange that we were playing golf the day after our baby died. I, for one, was numb.

The next day there was a memorial service for Robin with family and only a few dear friends. Upstairs in our bedroom, I could hear the family gathering below and told George I did not think I could face all that. He was so dear and special and became the rock of our family. For one who allowed no tears before her death, I fell apart, and time after time during the next six months, George would put me together again. He looked out the window, and seeing my sister, Martha, and her husband, Walt, walking up the driveway, said, "Sure, and with the O'Raffertys, it is going to be a grand wake." Sounds dumb now, but believe me, it did the trick. I giggled through my tears and went down.

The minute the service was over, George and I raced home to Midland. (George's mother and Lud Ashley laid our little Robin to rest several days later when the hospital released her body.) We wanted to be the ones to break the news to Georgie. As we drove up to his school, Georgie was walking down the covered walk carrying something into his classroom. He ran and asked his teacher, "My mom, dad, and sister are home. Can I go see them?" We felt devastated by what we had to tell him. As I recall, he asked a lot of questions and couldn't understand why we hadn't told him when we had known for such a long time.

We picked up Jebby at Betty and Hugh's, and George made us all go by several friends' houses just to say hello and get over that first awful moment of seeing each other after a death. That started the most painful period of adjusting to life after Robin.

We awakened night after night in great physical pain—it hurt that much. I hated that nobody mentioned her; it was as if she had never been. I know now that it was because our friends did not want to hurt us, but you don't think too clearly after a death. Several times Georgie helped break the ice. At a football game George had taken him to, Georgie suddenly said he wished he were Robin. George told me all his friends stiffened with uncomfortable embarrassment. When he asked Georgie just why he wished he were Robin, he said, "I bet she can see the game better from up there than we can here." Another time, he asked his dad if we had buried Robin lying down or standing up. Again, shocked silence. George said that he wasn't sure, but why did Georgie want to know. He said he had just learned that the earth rotated, and he wanted to know if she spent part of her time standing on her head, and wouldn't that be neat? He made it okay for our friends to mention her, and that helped us a great deal.

Midland was a small town, and many, many people called on us. It was exhausting, and once I complained to George about it. People I hardly knew came by. I caught one friend practicing in front of a mirror her sad facial expressions and what she was going to say to me. I backed out of the living room and came in again. She struggled through something that came out like this: "At least it wasn't your firstborn and a boy at that." I was speechless. George pointed out that it wasn't easy for them and that I should be patient. He was right. I just needed somebody to blame.

I wanted to get back to real life, but there is a dance that you have to go through to get there. When I wanted to cut out, George made me talk to him, and he shared with me. What a difference that makes. He made me remember that the loss was not just mine. It was his, Georgie's, and Jeb's, our friends' who loved her, and all our family's so far away. He did it subtly, but with love. Many times he held me in his arms and let me weep myself to sleep. In those days there was no Hospice program, which I certainly needed. Thank heavens George was always there for me.

Hugh Liedtke came up with the brilliant idea of setting up a foundation for leukemia research in Robin's name, which helped me enormously. We called it the Bright Star Foundation.

I devoted my time to our children, spending every single moment with Jebby, and then with Georgie when he came home from school. One lovely, breezy day I was in our bedroom when I heard Georgie talking to a neighbor child who wanted him to come over and play. Georgie said he wanted to, but he couldn't leave his mother. She needed him. That started my cure. I realized I was too much of a burden for a little seven-year-old boy to carry.

For a year I devoted my time to starting a little woman's exchange shop for the Junior Service League. I worked at that project night and day, and everyone helped me. We made very little money for the league, and when I retired in 1955 to have yet again another baby, the store closed. I think the shop was just another way that our supportive hometown helped me cope with death.

We named our beautiful, smiling little boy after Neil Mallon. Less than two years later, in 1956, Neil was followed by Marvin, named after my dad. Just as an observation—men are funny. We wanted to name the other boys after Daddy, but he always said that we should not because Marvin was a dreadful name. Well, when George and I called and told him that in spite of him, we were going to name the baby Marvin Pierce Bush, he cried. He really had not meant it when he said no.

᠁ George and I love and value every person more because of Robin. She lives on in our hearts, memories, actions, and through the Bright Star Foundation. I don't cry over her anymore. She is a happy, bright part of our lives.

After George's mother died in 1992, I was given an envelope with George's name on it. It contained the following letter, which George had written his mother several years after Robin died and which she had saved all these years:

> Dear Mum,
>
>   I have jotted down some words about a subject dear to your heart and mine. It is fun to fool around and try in one form or another to express thoughts that suddenly come up from way down deep in one's heart. Last night I went out on the town and on my way home—late—I said to myself, "You could well have gone to Greenwich

tonight" . . . this thought struck me out of the blue, but I felt no real sense of negligence. The part I like is to think of Robin as though she were a part, a living part, of our vital and energetic and wonderful family of men and Bar.

Bar and I wonder how long this will go on. We hope we will feel this genuine closeness when we are 83 and 82. Wouldn't it be exciting at that age to have a beautiful 3½-year-old daughter . . . she doesn't grow up. Now she's Neil's age. Soon she'll be Marvin's—and beyond that she'll be all alone, but with us, a vital living pleasurable part of our day-to-day life. I sometimes wonder whether it is fair to our boys and to our friends to "fly-high" that portrait of Robin which I love so much; but here selfishness takes over because every time I sit at our table with just our candlelight, I somehow can't help but glance at this picture you gave us and enjoy a renewed physical sensation of closeness to a loved one.

This letter . . . is kind of like a confessional . . . between you and me, a mother and her little boy—now not so little, but still just as close, only when we are older, we hesitate to talk from our hearts quite as much.

There is about our house a need. The running, pulsating restlessness of the four boys as they struggle to learn and grow; their athletic chests and arms and legs; their happy noises as the world embraces them . . . all this wonder needs a counterpart. We need some starched crisp frocks to go with all our torn-kneed blue jeans and helmets. We need some soft blond hair to offset those crew cuts. We need a doll house to stand firm against our forts and rackets and thousand baseball cards. We need a cutout star to play alone while the others battle to see who's "family champ." We even need someone . . . who could sing the descant to "Alouette," while outside they scramble to catch the elusive ball aimed ever roofward, but usually thudding against the screens.

We need a legitimate Christmas angel—one who doesn't have cuffs beneath the dress.

We need someone who's afraid of frogs.

We need someone to cry when I get mad—not argue.

We need a little one who can kiss without leaving egg or jam or gum.

We need a girl.

We had one once—she'd fight and cry and play and make her way just like the rest. But there was about her a certain softness.

She was patient—her hugs were just a little less wiggly.

Like them, she'd climb in to sleep with me, but somehow she'd fit.

She didn't boot and flip and wake me up with pug nose and mischievous eyes a challenging quarter-inch from my sleeping face.

No—she'd stand beside our bed till I felt her there. Silently and comfortably, she'd put those precious, fragrant locks against my chest and fall asleep.

Her peace made me feel strong, and so very important.

"My Daddy" had a caress, a certain ownership which touched a slightly different spot than the "Hi Dad" I love so much.

But she is still with us. We need her and yet we have her. We can't touch her, and yet we can feel her.

We hope she'll stay in our house for a long, long time.

Love, Pop

6

Oh, the Glamorous World
of Politics

In the years that followed we moved into a slightly larger house, near McCall Park, where we could watch Georgie play Little League baseball. We got a puppy named Nicky—a "gift" from Saint Nicholas—who lived to be nineteen years old. He was sold as a poodle, but as he got older, we discovered he was a mixed breed. He looked like a lamb.

Every other summer we went to Maine. It was just too far and too expensive to take the whole family every year, and several times I was pregnant. George went more often, if even just for a day or two, to talk to his biggest investor, Herbie Walker, or to attend a family wedding or funeral. George has made it to Maine at least one day every summer of his life except for a year during the war.

Georgie started our children's tradition of going to Camp Longhorn in the Hill Country of Texas for a month in July. Now George's twins go, too. They all became "aterwaytogoers"—short for "That's the way to go!"—which we all shouted on Parent's Day.

One summer, George's brother Buck and his friend Fay Vincent, who later became Commissioner of Baseball, came to Texas and spent their college vacation working in the oil fields.

In 1957 we rented the Pierce house (no relation to my family) in Kennebunkport for a month. It is a wonderful house that sits on the rocks just past St. Ann's Church on Ocean Avenue. Our boys were eleven months and two, four, and eleven years old. George wisely thought it would be no vacation for me without help, so he hired two young black women to go up with me: Julia May Cooper, who already helped me part-time, and a woman she knew, Otha Fitzgerald. Six of us—Julia May and Otha, the three younger boys, and I—drove cross-country. George, who was going to fly up later with Georgie, had planned very carefully the places where we would stop at night to avoid any racial incidents. Fortunately, we had no problems and the trip east was painless.

We had a great month, and then since Georgie's school started early, he flew back to Texas with his dad and Julia May. Otha, the three little boys, and I would drive. We planned a fun trip, with stops in Niagara Falls and several other places. I learned to tuck the boys in the back of the station wagon asleep around two A.M., stop for breakfast when they woke up, and then drive until about noon. I would check into a motel with a pool, the boys would spend the afternoon swimming, and after an early dinner, we all went to bed to start again at two A.M. It may sound crazy, but that way, we usually missed traffic and the boys didn't get too restless. All went well until we got to the South. The racial showdown in Little Rock, Arkansas, over school desegregation had erupted, and tension was high. Otha was not welcome in any restaurants, motels, or hotels. That dear woman insisted I take the children into restaurants alone and leave her in the car. That was unacceptable to me, so we all picnicked together from food bought at 7-Elevens. Sleeping also was a problem, and again, she insisted we go ahead and check in and she would sleep in the car. I wouldn't go in without her. Finally, we stopped at a Howard Johnson's between Tulsa and Oklahoma City and found that they would both feed us and let us spend the night. It just so happened that one of their restaurants between New York City and Washington had refused service to a black man, and when he turned out to be a diplomat, it caused an international scandal. From that moment on, Howard Johnsons across the country were integrated.

Otha and I had very long, interesting conversations on that trip. Once again, I grew a little more—a lot more—and my eyes were opened to an aspect of life that was inconceivable to me. I was so ashamed of our system that could tell this fine woman she was not equal. When we got home, Otha moved to East Texas to take another job and we lost touch. Twenty years later, when George and I were attending a National Federation of Republican Women's Convention, I was told there was a delegate by the name of Taylor who wanted to speak with us. It was Otha, now married. We have stayed in touch ever since.

Looking back, I'm not sure if I really appreciated how protected my life was—and always had been—from such ugliness. I thought I was very much aware of what was going on in the world. For example, during the early 1950s, I can remember the terrible "Red Scare" going on in the country. We were convinced there were Communists everywhere (there were some legitimate spies), and everyone was glued to the TV and radio listening to Senator Joseph McCarthy conduct his hearings. But seldom did I have to deal with such issues personally. I was much more concerned with my family and keeping house.

By this time, George was president and CEO of Zapata Off-Shore Company, a subsidiary of Zapata Petroleum. Their venture into offshore drilling was exciting and new. The rigs they ordered were a revolutionary tripod design by R. G. LeTourneau, weighing about nine million pounds and costing up to six million dollars. Before you could borrow money in those days for something that big, that expensive, and that risky, you had to prove you had a certain number of contracts lined up. (By way of contrast, George and I recently saw several eighty-million-dollar rigs in "mothballs" in Galveston, Texas, built with no contracts at all.) So George and Hugh Liedtke worked very hard, nationally and internationally, getting work. They were very successful and had four to five rigs operating.

In 1959, Zapata Petroleum Company amicably split, with George taking over Zapata Off-Shore. There was only one problem: landlocked Midland is nowhere near "offshore," and it only made sense for us to move to Houston. When George first mentioned it, I felt a sinking feeling. I loved Midland and our friends and did not want to leave that cocoon of warmth and love. Midland had been home for almost eleven years. We—especially George—had been such a part of the community: raising money for the church and the little theater; helping establish the first Midland YMCA and starting a bank; building the Republican party, including twice heading the Eisenhower/

Nixon campaigns; working for the cancer drive; serving on the United Way Board. How could we leave?

George and I also had one other very small problem: I was pregnant again. How could I leave the wonderful doctors, Walter Parks and Garland Lang, who had delivered Neil and Marvin?

But George couldn't work three hundred miles from home, so we headed for Houston to look for a house.

We stayed with Baine and Mildred Kerr, who certainly made our life easier and were to become great friends. A lawyer, Baine had done legal work for both Zapata companies. He found 1.2 acres of marvelous wooded land just around the corner from their new house. We bought the lot, contracted with their builder, and went back to Midland to await his blueprints. Sitting with the boys one day, we planned what we wanted. George told young George to go measure Jeb's bedroom. When he came back with the measurements, George said, "Write down 'four rooms twelve-by-twelve.'" We went through our whole house that way and sent the measurements down to Houston. The builder sent word back that our proportions were a little off: The first floor would have filled a half block; and the second floor was about the size of a pinpoint. That's why you hire professionals.

George moved first to set up his office, and I stayed in Midland until he insisted I join him to supervise the new house, meet my new doctor, and find new schools. The boys would finish up the school semester in Midland with our wonderful baby-sitter, Mrs. Lois Rogers. She and her husband later moved to Houston for three months to help out with the move and the new baby. I was hoping they would stay with us forever.

Once in Houston, I awakened several times feeling almost nauseated over leaving Midland, yet I was too busy to be really homesick. Anyway, what a waste to miss what you can't have.

George and I moved into a "swinging" apartment house built around a swimming pool. Most of the residents were young working people, and we could hear them partying all night long. I got to know them very well when I sat at the pool. What a different world it was from ours. It actually was a lot of fun, and once again, we made new friends. Marion and Dave Arnspiger, who attended our church, were living there while waiting to get settled into a house, and a young Al Vargo, who now owns and runs one of the best restaurants in Houston, lived nearby.

The house and the baby got finished at the same time. On August 18, 1959, Dorothy Walker Bush—named for George's mother—was born, weighing in at nine pounds, eleven ounces. We called her Doro. Aunt Charlotte, who had come down for the birth, told me that when George went to look at Doro in the nursery, she found him with his head against the window, tears of joy running down his face.

George moved us into the new house while I was in the hospital. When I came home, I found very neat rooms with no clutter. Mrs. Rogers, who had just arrived from Midland, said that she didn't know Mr. Bush could do housework. He certainly could, and he had done a great job. Except that it took months for me to find everything. George had unpacked by putting things in the nearest closet, with no regard for what the item was or what room it would be used in.

The Rogers family did finally leave, and we answered a newspaper ad to sponsor a lady from Mexico to help with the housework. That was one of the best things ever to happen to the Bush family. A tiny woman named Paula Rendon came to live with us, and she's still here! She started out as Doro's nurse and is now our housekeeper and a member of the family. She has a tremendous family of her own, and she rules them and us with an iron hand. (Although she spoils George to death.) She has been just as at home in the Waldorf Towers, the Vice President's House, and the White House as she is in Houston.

That fall, the boys went off to their new schools—Georgie to the Kinkaid School; Neil and Jebby to Grady Elementary public school—and Marvin and Doro were home with me. One night in November, I went to bed exhausted as I had played golf for the first time since Doro was born. George stayed awake a little later reading *The Caine Mutiny*. Georgie was not home; our four youngest children were asleep in their rooms on the second floor; and Tom Devine, a friend visiting us from New York, was asleep in the guest room on the first floor, where our room was. George heard a tiny cough on the intercom and decided he'd better check the baby. A "blue norther" had blown in and we had turned our heat on for the first time. Something had been put in backward, and the whole upstairs was filled with smoke. George yelled for me, put Doro in my arms, and ran for the other children. He got them all out, breaking a window for air as he carried them downstairs. Groggy and asleep, they did not awaken until George put their feet on the icy cold pavement. We were told that if George had been fifteen minutes later, our four youngest children would have been dead from smoke inhalation. Thank God he heeded that tiny cough. After that, we put ladders on the outside of our house on both ends so that our children could get out and, if need be, we could get in. People thought we were crazy to invite burglars like that, but we were never robbed and we certainly slept better after the ladders were in place.

The boys all became very active in Little League and school activities. I spent half of the next ten years doing what every mother in America does: taxiing children to the doctor, the dentist, birthday parties, baseball games, tennis matches, and so on. When I look at my date book entries from those years, they're all baseball games and what fields they'll be played on. The boys were good players, and I felt torn in two, racing from game to game. When they weren't playing organized ball, they were in our backyard. We had a pool, a small baseball field, trees to climb, and tires hung for all the children to swing on. The Kerrs had three boys and, much to our great pleasure, a little girl named Mary a year younger than Doro. The boys played in the nearby bayou and had several hair-raising experiences, most of which ended with trips to the emergency room for stitches.

For several Christmas Eves, all these little wild men turned into angels when the Bush-Kerr children put on a Christmas play for the adults. Those are the wonderful memories you just never forget. Fortunately, the grandchildren have continued the tradition and entertain us every year.

And of course the children got all the childhood diseases. It was during a siege of the chicken pox that Neil, who was about six years old at the time, was in my bed one day, and I asked him to read to me. I discovered that not only could Neil not read, he didn't have a clue. Yet, he was getting all A's at school, including in reading. I spoke with his teacher, who told me I was dead wrong; Neil was one of her better students. So I went to his class to see this "great little reader." It was a fascinating study in manipulation. The teacher had the children read a line or two, and when she got to Neil, he flashed that great smile of his and paused. A student helped him with the first word, the teacher the next, and so it went. Neil had been faking his way through reading—not uncommon for children with reading problems—and nobody had noticed.

Neil was diagnosed as having dyslexia. Grady Elementary had no courses for children with this problem, but Kinkaid had a wonderful reading teacher who was willing to help Neil. Marvin hadn't started school yet, but we had been told he was more than ready for first grade, so I enrolled both boys in Kinkaid. Then I learned you get a discount for a third child, so I enrolled Jebby also. While all this was happening, George was in some far-off place trying to find work for his oil rigs. He came home and he couldn't believe it: four of his children were in private school. My math confused him; I was convinced we were saving money.

For the rest of his school days, Neil had to work very hard. We spent hours reading together as he struggled with every word. But thanks to wonderful teachers, and a little boy who refused to give up, Neil eventually earned his undergraduate and master's degrees in business administration at Tulane University—and in just five years.

By this time, Georgie had followed in his father's footsteps and was attending Phillips Academy in Andover, Massachusetts. How we missed him. Every day I walked down the driveway to meet the mailman to see if he had written. I was homesick, but the child obviously wasn't. Finally, the mailman, John Taylor, rang the doorbell and thrust a letter into my hand with a big smile on his face. He knew how much I missed Georgie. Fortunately, he didn't hang around to see me open the letter. It started out, "Last weekend was the greatest in my life . . ." I burst into tears. Our boy had the "best weekend of his life" without us! How silly that seems now and just a tad selfish.

If I had any complaints in those wonderful early days in Houston, it was that George and I didn't have time to do a lot together. He was busy building a business, which involved a lot of travel, and we had five young children and a new house, which meant a lot of expenses. Needless to say, we rarely went out.

One of the reasons I fell in love with George was that he was so kind and nice. He always thought of the other fellow. Sometimes that caused me some pain and jealousy, which I'm now ashamed to admit. I just didn't think there was enough time for us.

I remember one incident that for years made me feel guilty and now I think is funny. We had a friend whom we both adored and admired, a smashing, bright young widow. George and I both worried about her, so he decided that the next time he was in New York City, he would round up all the eligible bachelors he could find and give her a dinner at the "21" Club. For weeks before the trip, George reported to me the progress of his dinner plans as he lined up ten attractive available men. I must confess that I was so jealous that he was giving this splendid dinner at "21," where we could never afford to go and I, for one, had never been. Of course I never said a word but just listened to his planning, getting more and more envious.

The morning after the big dinner, he called me heartbroken. Our widow friend had breezed into the dinner quite late, with a date, and stayed barely long enough for a drink before rushing off to the theater, leaving George with a large dinner bill and his bachelor friends. I told George I was sorry his plans were for naught. Deep down, I was thrilled. I'm not very proud of that, and George didn't find out until recently just how jealous I had been.

It was during this period of our lives when George decided to get more involved in politics. He always had been interested: His dad was a United States senator from Connecticut at the time, and George had been politically active in Midland. In February 1962, just before Doro and I left to visit Mom and Dad Bush for a week in Florida, George asked me how I'd feel if he became chairman of the Republican party of Harris County. He said he really wanted to do it, and I said fine. So off Doro and I went for a great little vacation, and when we got back, George was in the meanest political battle of his life. I was so naive; I had assumed that he had been invited to be chairman. It never occurred to me that he had to run. I can't really remember who the opponent was—maybe I'm purposely forgetting—but it was ugly. Harris County, with 210 precincts, is one of the largest in the country. George, usually with me along, managed to visit all of them. The evenings could be long and tedious. That's when I took up needlepoint, just to keep from looking and feeling bored to death. After all, I had heard George's speech two hundred times! Not only did needlepointing do the trick, it was a good icebreaker. Fellow stitchers always wanted to know about my project and tell me about theirs.

George was elected, along with our dear friend Nancy Thawley as vice chair. The county executive meetings were a circus, and George was like a ringmaster. We went into each one with fear and trembling, and he always pulled it off. The party even took on the old courthouse crowd and won a redistricting suit that would have great impact on our lives in a few years.

In 1963 George decided to make a run against incumbent U.S.

Senator Ralph Yarborough, who was up for reelection in 1964. Texas Democrats were very divided at that time. Yarborough was battling with Governor John Connally, and polls showed that Vice President Lyndon Johnson was at an all-time popularity low. It looked like a long-shot opportunity for a Yarborough upset.

Eventually four people got into the Republican primary race: Jack Cox, who had made a good run against Connally in the last governor's race; Dr. Milton Davis, a thoracic surgeon who claimed to be "grass roots"; Dr. Robert Morris, who was originally from New Jersey; and George. I hate primary campaigns, as you are fighting people in your own party. George appeared all over the state debating these men or joining them on the speaker's platform. My blood boiled at half the things they said about George. There was some discussion about making George wear a cowboy hat to make him more "Texan." George rejected the idea, saying he didn't want to resort to gimmicks.

I remember one meeting at a Republican picnic in Fort Bend County. We had a great chairman there, Mary Ann Napier, who requested we get there early and mix and mingle before the speeches. With five-year-old Doro along, we worked the crowd and ate the barbecue. Jack Cox appeared with great fanfare just as he was being introduced for his three-minute speech. Some celebrity had died that day, and Jack dramatically praised the man and called for a moment of prayer. Before we could even bow our heads, he said, "Thank you," and started his harangue. He certainly wasn't going to waste any more of his precious three minutes on that poor dead soul. That always amused me.

I was not so amused, however, on another evening, when we were sitting in a darkened auditorium listening to candidates for every conceivable office. Someone gave me a stack of papers and said, "Take one and pass it on, please," which of course I did. When the lights came on, I had a handful of hate literature about George, calling him a "tool of the Eastern establishment"; a "Rockefeller plant largely financed by the Eastern group who are leading the 'Block Goldwater' movement"; and "a stockholder in Brown Brothers, Harriman." That was the name of George's father's firm, but they were referring to Ambassador Averell Harriman, a liberal Democrat. No doubt, this was the world of the ultraconservative John Birch Society, who thought George was way too liberal.

One day we received a flyer in the mail that said I was the daughter of Marvin Pierce, president of the McCall Corporation (true), which published *Redbook* (true), and everybody knows *Redbook* is a tool of the "commies." Huh? I countered by reminding people that McCall also published *The Blue Book*, the John Birch Society's handbook. Another flyer, addressed to all Republican voters, said I was "an heiress who spent all her time on the Cape"—meaning Cape Cod. I wrote my dad that to my knowledge I had never set foot on the Cape and to please write immediately if I was an heiress. He sent my letter on to Aunt Charlotte with the note that she must never let it be known she voted for FDR! He added that they had given up publishing *The Blue Book* because it was losing money.

Several times we had hate letters under our door in the morning. That was scary since the person who put them there had to walk up a long driveway.

During the campaign I went east to visit family, who quickly let me know George was too conservative. What a world: George was too conservative for the East and too liberal for Texas. I always have been proud of the fact that George thought each problem out separately and did not take a party line. If I had to label George, I would say he was a fiscal conservative and a social liberal. I know that others might disagree. As for George, he says "Labels are for cans."

On November 22, 1963, George and I were in the middle of a several-city swing. I was getting my hair done in Tyler, Texas, working on a letter home. Here are some excerpts:

> Dearest Family,
> Wednesday I took Doris Ulmer out for lunch. They were here from England and they had been so nice to George in Greece. That night we went to . . .
> I am writing this at the Beauty Parlor and the radio says that the President has been shot. Oh Texas—my Texas—my God—let's hope it's not true. I am sick at heart as we all are. Yes, the story is true and the Governor also. How hateful some people are.
> . . . Since the Beauty Parlor the President has died.

We are once again on a plane. This time a commercial
plane. Poppy picked me up at the beauty parlor—we went
right to the airport, flew to Ft. Worth and dropped Mr.
Zeppo off (we were on his plane) and flew back to Dallas.
We had to circle the field while the second presidential
plane took off. Immediately Pop got tickets back to Houston and here we are flying home. We are sick at heart. The
tales the radio reporters tell of Jackie Kennedy are the
bravest I've ever heard. The rumors are flying about that
horrid assassin. We are hoping that it is not some far right
nut, but a "commie" nut. You understand that we know
they are both nuts, but just hope that it is not a Texan and
not an American at all.

I am amazed by the rapid-fire thinking and planning
that has already been done. L.B.J. has been the president
for some time now—2 hours at least and it is only 4:30.

> My dearest love to you all,
>
> Bar

Certainly this was not the world's most brilliant letter, but it
reflects a little of my feelings at that time. George canceled all his
political activities for the next few months.

In a letter I wrote on November 30, I complained to my family that all the press talked about were fanatics on the far right, even
though word was out that Oswald was playing games in both Cuba
and Russia. They just couldn't stand the thought that the assassin was
someone leaning left.

George eventually won the hard-fought primary contest,
and we formed the greatest team for the general election. Locally, I
joined a group of supporters, organized by our friends Jack Steel and
Bobbie Fitch, who went door-to-door handing out literature. I'll never
forget one night when I was teamed up with Jack, working what could
be called a "redneck" neighborhood. I didn't want people to know I was
the candidate's wife—we wanted honest reaction from the voters—so
my name tag just said BARBARA. Everyone assumed I was Jack's wife
and called me Mrs. Steel. One lady spit in her flowerpot the whole

time we tried to talk to her; one man answered the door in his underwear and didn't seem to mind one bit. Jack and I got so tickled it took everything we had not to laugh until we got back out on the street. That same night, the "Bush Bandwagon" bus, which was supposed to go around and pick everybody up, couldn't find us, and we sat on a curb under a streetlight waiting and waiting. Oh, the glamorous world of politics.

Another time when George and I were at a reception in San Antonio, I heard several times, "Would the lady in the red dress please get out of the photo?" I suddenly realized they were talking about me! They didn't have a clue who I was.

That was the year of the famous mushroom cloud TV ad, where the Democrats were trying to play off people's fear of nuclear war. Locally, I heard our opponent say something like, "George Bush doesn't care if our small children are exposed to leukemia." I can't remember if I heard this on TV, or if maybe I heard it while driving by an outdoor rally. You can't imagine how shocked we were by that. In the speaker's defense, I'm sure he didn't know about Robin.

With or without such campaigning, Kennedy's death drastically changed the political world, and with Johnson at the top of the Democratic ticket, we did not have a chance to beat Yarborough. After we lost, George called and wrote thank-you letters to console the fabulous people who had worked so hard.

He went back to devoting his energies to Zapata, and the company continued to grow. In September 1965, disaster struck: Hurricane Betsy ravaged the Gulf of Mexico, and a rig the size of a football field completely disappeared never to be seen again. Luckily, the workers were evacuated by boat and helicopter and nobody was hurt. Several days later George came home and told me his eyeballs hurt from looking for the rig all day by helicopter. He also described the small towns in Louisiana he had flown over, saying they looked like those playing card houses we used to build, then push one card and they all fell down. I don't know if he hurt more from the devastation he saw in those little towns or the devastation his company felt from such a mammoth financial loss. But he rallied the troops; they dug their heels in and rebuilt. As usual, George put more stock in the people than the equipment. He wrote in Zapata's annual report that year: "We are lucky to have the finest offshore drilling crews in the business. This year 23 more men completed their fifth year with the company, a record of which we are very proud."

Houston got a new congressional seat in 1966 and, thanks to George's redistricting suit, there was a chance a Republican could win. George decided to make another run at elected office. His chief opponent was the very popular district attorney, Frank Briscoe, a conservative Democrat. He ran as a native-born Texan and tried to paint George as a carpetbagger. It really worried me until George told me that three fourths of the people living in the new Seventh Congressional District were newcomers, too. Besides, by this time, we had lived in Texas nearly eighteen years!

I'll never forget driving Doro and one of her friends to school one day, listening to the two of them talk in the backseat. Doro's friend said something like, "I saw your daddy on TV last night." To which Doro very nonchalantly replied: "Oh, you know, it was about that erection that he's going to have."

Frank was actually a very nice man and well liked, but thanks to a lot of hardworking volunteers, friends, and George Bush, George won. This was quite a win for us. George was the first Republican elected to Congress from Harris County, and one of just three Republicans in the entire Texas delegation: Bob Price had been elected in the Texas Panhandle; and our dear friend John Tower was one of Texas's U.S. senators. Jim Collins of Dallas eventually would become the fourth, after winning a special election.

The night of the big win, Jack Steel and Sarah Gee came to George and asked him if he would do them a big favor. They had been the most extraordinary volunteers, and George certainly would grant them anything. They asked if they could continue to run his office as volunteers. What a favor! They lined up some of the very best people, and for years this little army has helped George over and over again. They did such a great job, along with a superb Washington staff, that George was unopposed when he ran for reelection two years later. Many of these same people are volunteering in George's office today, helping him answer his enormous stacks of mail. Jack, who personifies the very definition of "best friend," comes in every day, at age seventy-five. I do not know what we would have done without these dear friends (see Appendix A).

Once again, we had hundreds of decisions to make. Would I move to Washington? Would the kids move? Would we see more of George if we stayed or moved? Would we keep our big Houston house or move into something smaller? What about Washington; houses were so much more expensive in Washington than Houston. If we moved, where would the children go to school? How would George organize his office? What about Zapata? These are problems that all new congressmen and congresswomen face, and today, I think it's even more complicated with so many two-career families.

As for Zapata, George already had resigned as head of the company to devote himself to the campaign. It had been a tough call to make, but the one he thought most fair to the company and the campaign. Now he decided it was best to get out altogether. We also decided the entire family should go to Washington. So we sold our house, bought a lovely town house as a home base in Houston, and headed for Washington.

7

A Different World

We bought a house in Spring Valley, a lovely section of Washington with lots of trees and houses built in the 1920s and 1930s. George bought it over the phone, sight unseen, from Senator Milward Simpson of Wyoming, Al Simpson's father. It was a really old house—such a change from our home in Houston where everything worked. One day I came downstairs to find George sitting in the living room under an umbrella. A bathtub had leaked right through the ceiling. I would have laughed, except that's how the whole house was. Only three of the children were with us: George W. was at Yale and Jeb stayed at Kinkaid in Houston, living with Baine and Mildred Kerr, before going on to Andover.

George's campaign manager, Jimmy Allison, helped set up the office. Aleene Smith, who had worked at Zapata and the Republican party of Harris County office, moved to Washington with us, and George hired Rose Zamaria, who had headed the office of Houston Congressman Albert Thomas, the powerful Democratic chairman of the House Appropriations Committee until his death. Rose knew The Hill and George's constituents, and Aleene knew George Bush. These two amazing women, both used to ruling the roost, worked very well together and became best friends. Aleene is retired and lives in Florida with her husband, Hargrove; Rose moved to Houston with us and ran George's office there until March of 1994 before returning to Washington.

Eventually, Don Rhodes, a volunteer during the campaign, moved from Houston to Washington to become part of the team and has been with us ever since. Like Paula, he has become part of the family.

❧ Washington was a whole different world for us: exciting, overwhelming, intimidating, interesting, exhausting. Looking back on my diary entries, I'm not sure when we slept. Here's some of what I wrote that very first month:

January 3—Drove up to the house and there were the moving men shoveling the snow. Moved in all day. House was frozen. Piano didn't fit in the living room. House without carpets seemed tiny and cold. Moving men invited to spend the night by G. He cannot stand an empty bed! Only had sheets for two beds and so had to race to Sears to buy sheets, etc. before it closed. BOYS ACCEPTED AT ST. ALBANS!!!!

January 4—Up at 4 a.m. for me. From 7 to 10 moving men and George and I unpacked boxes and there was no damage. George and I left at 10:30 for two days of briefings for new Republican congressmen and wives (or husbands). Invaluable for me.

January 5—Wives had a panel the second afternoon telling us what to expect. I now expect to be without a husband most of the time!!! Mrs. Les Arends, Betty, a great beauty, spoke on protocol and was lovely to look at. Her speech was ridiculed in the papers and although she claimed later to have been misquoted, it caused great excitement among the ladies. She gave calling cards a great play. All this surely went out with the horse and buggy. She also told us that she "tagged" her gowns so she wouldn't wear the same thing with the same people twice. She told us that she took out all the hems from store-bought clothes and hemmed them by hand. Talked about long gloves, etc. I must confess that we were worrying about schools and making ends meet, etc. [This same dear lady wrote me a note in 1993, enclosing a copy of a letter she sent to Ross Perot. It said: "Dear Ross, I hope you are happy about what you did to your country. You ASS. Love, Betty." I guess she decided to heck with calling cards and white gloves!]

January 9—TV connected. Went to Yarborough reception . . . met the Vice President (Hubert Humphrey). Jack Steel killed us by going up to the Vice President and saying to him, "Mr. Vice President, you remember me? Jack Steel?" The Vice President gave him the biggest jolly and a two-handed clasp. I later said to Jack, "I didn't know that you knew the Veep." And of course Jack answered, "I didn't, but you saw the welcome he gave me."

January 10—Ate with GB in Capitol Dining Room and went on into the State of the Union Address. Great thrill to see all the dignitaries. Sat in far left corner and therefore could not see the speaker or the President, but could see the Congress . . . G and I loving all the excitement!

January 12—I took a cab to the Capitol with evening clothes over my arm. G and I rushed over to the Capitol Hill Club. We were just getting settled, talking to nice people when George grabs my arm and says that we are at the wrong reception and so we race to the Rayburn Building to the reception the 89th Congress was having for the 90th! BOTH receptions very nice.

January 15—Walked in the afternoon and attacked by strange dog. He followed us for hours and G finally returned him to address on his collar. Belonged to the new Secretary of Commerce. They were thrilled to get him back.

January 25—ANNOUNCEMENT MADE OF G'S APPOINTMENT TO WAYS AND MEANS!!!

January 26—Kids like Washington. Already have many friends. That night we went to Rolly and Kay Evans' house for a black tie dinner. We were crowded into a dining room with round tables. I sat next to Senator Ed Muskie from Maine. We had a lovely talk about Kennebunkport where he has a house . . . George and I were the only Republicans. Also at the party were Ambassador and Mrs. Harriman. He spoke so well of Mom and Dad. Mrs. Harriman, when the ladies were having coffee, said to me, "I've known many Republicans. Now let's see . . . there's John and Lorraine Cooper. Everyone likes them, and oh, yes, that man who died, Chris Herter and his wife, and I remember Dotty and Pres!!" She was so proud to be able to think of three Republican couples . . . also at this party were Joan and Teddy Kennedy. She is a very lovely-looking person. I found her very friendly, a bubbly type person. I like her. Teddy, in fairness, I did not talk to, but also wasn't charmed by. He had much more of Bobby and less of Jack.

January 29—Still cold. We all get dressed for church and then can't find it.

February 2—GB and I were at The Shoreham at 7:30 a.m. for our first Presidential view. The Congressional Wives Prayer Breakfast. G went to the men's breakfast where 1,100 men gathered. He says that he was not impressed because the TV lights and cameras took away any spiritual meaning to the breakfast. 500 ladies gathered on our side and it was lovely. Mrs. Humphrey, VP's lady, read a text, and Mrs. Johnson gave a truly meaningful short message. Last night G came home in the rain to pick me up. I have given up on these unending receptions, but this one given by the President of the American Bankers Association was supposed to be filled with Texans just dying to see G. We arrived . . . to find thousands of people and the only Texans we saw were other Texas congressmen looking for Texans!

I tried everything once. I went to briefings at the State Department, Republican meetings, Congressional Wives meetings, luncheons, and dinners. Texans came to visit at the drop of a hat. George and I decided early on that we should not go to any embassies—there were no votes there. Considering our later life in the diplomatic world, that's funny. But you have to learn in Washington that you can't do everything. Like all of life, you have to set your priorities, and it took me a while to discover that.

At a dinner party one night, when we were still sorting out which parties to attend and which to skip, I sat next to a man who almost immediately started talking about how sad it was I had missed the "Days of Camelot." I listened while he criticized the Johnsons for every known fault until he said, "I hate all Texans." When I told him I was a Texan, he said something like, "Well, you know what I mean. You were born and brought up in the East." I said that he was right, but that he was talking about my children, who were lucky enough to be born Texans. I turned my back and never spoke to that whining, pompous man again. Looking down on the Johnsons was a favorite of this particular group. As part of the clique who had hung around the Kennedys, they viewed the President and First Lady as "gauche outsiders." George and I cut "inside Washington" dinners off our list.

Because George was the first freshman in this century to be put on the prestigious House Ways and Means Committee, we were on everybody's "list." I was flattered to be invited to small lunches with the cabinet's and other leaders' wives. We would have cocktails and lunch, then I would have to race for one of my many car pools. After about three months I told George I didn't think I could do these luncheons; they were just too time-consuming. He laughed and said that they were given by lobbyists' wives—people who were trying to get to him through me—and of course I didn't have to go. So I cut out lunches. Several of my friends didn't and at least one became an alcoholic.

One of the groups I did join was the International Club II, of which George's mother had been a founding member. The club was made up of twelve congressional ladies: six from each party, which were evenly split between the House and the Senate; and ten embassy wives whose husbands were all ministers, the rank just below ambassador. The club was started to make foreigners feel at home in our country. I liked this group a great deal for several reasons. Most of the other clubs took ambassadors' wives only; we took the number twos. Also, our club let the women whose husbands retired, died, or went on to other jobs stay in the club as associates. Some of the other current or former members were Abigail McCarthy (Eugene), Bethine Church (Frank), Betty Ford (Gerald), Helen Jackson (Scoop), LaDonna Harris (Fred), and Lady Bird Johnson. We must have had more people whose husbands were running for president than any other club, and three eventually made it. We would eat one month at a congressional home, and then the next at a diplomat's home. I tried hard never to miss one of these meetings. In later life, I met many of the embassy wives in their homelands where their husbands were foreign ministers, protocol chiefs, and so on.

George went home almost every weekend that first term, but the children and I could go only during school vacations. It was a strange life, but an exciting one. I decided the children should see all the sights. So every single weekend, I dragged those poor young people around Washington, taking hundreds of pictures. It got so bad that Neil and Marvin begged not to go, and I took pity on them. Doro was not so lucky. I remember one Sunday the two of us took a Park Service tour around the White House. We stood at the foot of the South Lawn with our faces pressed against the fence while the guide told us some interesting fact of history. At that moment the door opened and people came out. We strained to see who was lucky enough to have been in that glorious house. Years later, whenever we walked down to the fence on the South Grounds with our dogs, I thought about little Doro and me on the outside looking in.

All those pictures I took came in very handy later. I put together several slide shows and raised money for different causes by showing them to schools, garden clubs, civic groups, churches, and so on. It certainly was an easy way to give a speech. The slides were almost a protective shield, something you could hide behind—just like writing a book with a dog.

✑ We lasted in that old house for only a year and then bought a wonderful new, four-story town house right across the street from Supreme Court Justice Potter Stewart and his wife, Andy. Through the years Andy and I became very close, and she is absolutely the best friend anyone could have. She and Potter would walk down the street every single Sunday for soup or whatever on our back terrace or in the basement playroom. George always gathered the most interesting group of people of all ages for Sunday lunches. One such couple was columnist Bill Safire and his wife, Helene. Unfortunately, when George became President, Bill turned on him with a vengeance.

We loved that house and our new neighborhood. Congressman Jerry Pettis from California and his beautiful, bright wife, Shirley, lived right next door. She is one of the most beautiful women I have known. Even when she is sick, she manages to look lovely and glamorous. In spite of that, we also became the best of friends. Since George and Jerry were elected to Congress at the same time, Shirley and I took in many meetings together.

We made so many other new good friends during this period of our lives. Among George's closest colleagues in the House were Sonny Montgomery, a Democrat from Mississippi; Lud Ashley, a Democrat from Ohio; John Paul Hammerschmidt, a Republican from Arkansas; Bill Steiger, a Republican from Wisconsin; and Tom Kleppe, a Republican from North Dakota. There were so many others, but these men stand out in my mind.

George also thought highly of Wilbur Mills, chairman of the House Ways and Means Committee. Other new congressmen told George their committee chairmen never let them talk or left when they presented their thoughts. However, Wilbur listened to the lowest-ranking member, Democrat or Republican, and stayed until the end of the most boring hearing and made sure every member could question the witness. Our shock when Wilbur Mills did all those crazy things with that burlesque queen cannot be described. How could this fair and decent man be such a Jekyll and Hyde? As it turned out, he was a closet drinker. He and his darling wife, Polly, overcame their problems, and we were so proud they were our friends.

An informal group of wives of the 90th Club (our husbands were members of the Ninetieth Session of Congress) got together to study issues. All of us were brilliant, of course, but Janet Steiger—who later became the first woman chairman of the Federal Trade Commission—seemed to understand the issues better than most and would usually lead the group. We eventually filtered down to eleven women, remaining very close, dear friends and trying to stay in touch all these years. The other "ladies of the club" are Shirley Pettis Roberson, Olga Esch, Louise McClure, Loret Ruppe, Joan Winn, Antoinette Hatfield, Carol Vander Jagt, Dee Collins, and Mary Jane Dellenback. Some of these women went on to do some pretty impressive things on their own.

There were so many other dear friends, but these people have remained such an interesting part of my life.

The year 1968 began with me taking a very important step: I gave up smoking. I had been a smoker since age eighteen and knew I should quit but just never did. A few months earlier, I had gone into the hospital for a small operation and woke up several times in the middle of the night alone. I can remember really wanting a cigarette, and although I was still groggy from the medication and had an IV in my arm, I made it into a chair and lit up. At that very moment, a tiny nurse came into the room, got me back in bed, and before charging out of the room, informed me she'd be back to talk to me in the morning. True to her word, after she got off duty, she took the time to come in and read me the riot act. She told me that I was addicted and a disgrace. Addicted? Me? I couldn't forget that nurse, and on New Year's Day I quit. It was terrible. For about six weeks I would wake up in a cold sweat. Sometimes I dreamed that I was having a cigarette and would awaken in panic. I had trouble staying in one place and was restless. I'm not trying to show how brave I was, but how addicted I was and how hard it is to wean yourself off a bad habit. I'll always be grateful to that little nurse. George Bush never smoked, but he never complained about my bad habit. I am very antismoking now; in fact, George says I'm a bore about it. He's right. I am only critical of the people I care about.

This was a very interesting time to be living in Washington. The Vietnam War was debated at all the dinner parties, and the whole country worried about racial and student unrest. Here is part of my diary entry from April 5, 1968, to show a little of what it was like then:

In truth I cannot begin to write the horrors of the day. Memphis, Tennessee, has been having the most awful garbage strikes led by Dr. Martin Luther King, Negro Nobel Peace Prize winner . . . Standing on a balcony last night Dr. King was gunned down by an unknown man. The reaction to this killing may turn out to be very bloody. A newsman at 11:30 called from the Houston Post. I asked about Houston and he said, "Small stone throwing and small groups wandering around the city." I am frightened.

Took children to school. Worked in tiny garden getting the flower beds ready for plants. I took Neil to his knee doctor only to discover that the entire city was rioting about 5 blocks away. We could see smoke, etc. It took us an hour and a half to get home. George called from Texas to see if we were all right. . . . All day our lovely city burned, and all night. A curfew was put on, no liquor sold, no gasoline unless in cars and no guns. We went to bed in shock.

Later that month, Congress passed the civil rights open housing bill, the most controversial bill George voted on while in the House. He voted yes, despite the fact that mail from his constituents ran heavily against it. What made him feel particularly strong about this was that so many young black men were fighting in Vietnam for the cause of freedom, yet were denied freedom when they came home.

I was proud of the stand he took, but upset by how personal and mean his mail was, including from supporters who said they were shocked and disappointed. I remember that we went to a Peter Sellers movie the night of the vote, just to be able to laugh.

I was even prouder a week later when George flew to Houston to face a hometown crowd. He was introduced to loud boos, but at the end of the speech, during which he told them he "put human rights above property rights," he had won them over and they gave him a standing ovation. Still, I was very relieved he had no opposition for reelection that fall; it would have been a tough campaign.

*   *   *

〜 We had settled into a nice routine in Washington. In between carpooling the children to school, I took care of the house, attended various lunches and meetings, tried to lose weight, and even took to coloring my hair.

One of the funnier luncheons I attended was at the White House. I discovered that most of the attendees were world-renowned doctors and nurses, all women, in all different fields of medicine. Several people asked me what I did, and I began to wonder myself. You can imagine my surprise when Mrs. Johnson got up and said that there were twenty nurses among the congressional wives, including Mrs. George Bush of Texas. I got to attend this fascinating luncheon under false pretenses! I learned later that a computer had mistakenly identified me as a nurse. I'd like to add here that Mrs. Johnson was a very gracious First Lady and a wonderful hostess. This particular luncheon was just a few days after President Johnson had shocked the nation with the news he would not run for reelection, and I marveled at her composure.

That summer was filled with presidential politics, including the National Republican Convention in Miami. Here are some excerpts from one of many letters I wrote that year to George's cousin, George Walker, who was serving in Vietnam:

Dear George,
     It was my first convention and very, very exciting for me. We stayed at The Barcelona Hotel on Collins Avenue at about 42nd Street. The world's rudest people work there, but the location was just great . . . I loved seeing all the big GOP names at the Republican Gala the night before the Convention opened. We sat at a table right next to the Nixon girls, David Eisenhower and his Mom and Dad. The girls were darling and the minute I introduced myself they quickly said they'd like to meet Pop . . . I had flown down in a plane load of Reagan supporters and they were so eager for me to meet the Reagans. Since we sat near them, I took advantage and went over to meet them. I found them both very attractive. She is tiny and really a very lovely natural beauty. I thought that he should get a lot of credit for hanging in there after losing on the first

ballot. He kept his troops very happy and allowed harmony to prevail . . .

Bill Steiger decided his first morning there that GB had a good chance of being the VP candidate and so turned all his attention to this one project. He spent the rest of his time lining up delegates on the floor, making telephone calls, etc. A very few people put out a great deal of effort and the long and the short of it was that although this may never seem possible to you, your cousin almost became the candidate for Vice President. . . . I must confess that up until the last morning I thought it was such a long shot that I didn't worry. I'm sorry for Pop for he would have loved it so. I am glad for the five little Bush children. . . .

> Love,
>
> Bar

Since George was unopposed in 1968, he worked hard for the Nixon-Agnew ticket. I sat in Washington with the children, biting my nails while George traveled all over the country campaigning. I certainly was glad when it was over and Nixon had won.

During George's second term, I began writing a monthly newspaper column called "Washington Scene" for the Houston newspapers. It was lots of fun, and although the writing was not brilliant, the columns gave people back home a glimpse of life in Washington. Here's a column dated March 1969:

Early March saw the annual White House Congressional Reception. I cannot describe the excitement we felt from the moment we drove in. George, at my request, parked on the circle and we walked across the lawn to the diplomatic entrance hall where the Marine Band was playing. Can you picture the setting? The men looking SO handsome in black-tie and the ladies in long gowns and the Marines in their red uniforms!

We gathered in the East Room, bright and gay with the flags of the 50 states, visiting with friends. The excitement when President and Mrs. Nixon were announced was electric! There was an Honor Guard, "Hail to the Chief" was played, and they walked slowly through the room to the receiving line followed by Vice President and Mrs. Agnew.

There was a large buffet in the State Dining Room, but George and I did not linger there. The whole beautiful house was open to the guests and we took advantage of the opportunity to look around. The rooms were filled with lovely flowers and each room had a large crackling fire in the fireplace. Every room has well passed the test of time since James Hoban designed the house 170 years ago. I kept thinking of the feet that had walked these same steps before us: every president since John Adams, foreign kings and queens, great world statesmen, outstanding men and women in every field and walk of life.

The gifts given to the President on his trip to Europe were on display upstairs. We did NOT try out the Lincoln bed as I read another guest did, but we did look at paintings and at the Gettysburg Address written in Lincoln's hand. We did see the magnificent Yellow Oval Room, the Treaty Room, and the family living and dining rooms. We, as Americans, can all take pride in this beautiful house for it belongs to us all.

March saw Neil and Marvin Bush confirmed in the magnificent Washington Cathedral with 26 of their classmates by Bishop Paul Moore. The size of this cathedral and the glorious voice of the all-boys choir must surely add to the awe and beauty of any confirmation. Happiness for a mother is seeing her boys confirmed!

March saw our son George home for a weekend from flight school in Valdosta, Georgia. Happiness for a mother is also having a boy home from the service!

March saw George going home to Houston for two weekends and spending the week days in the Ways and Means Committee hearings as they struggle through the tax reform legislation. . . .

The end of March—best of all—saw the Bush family home in Houston for Easter with four of their five children!

That summer, the Bushes almost missed the main event of the year, on July 20, when man landed on the moon. We had spent the day boating on the Potomac River and had stopped to eat dinner on the way home. When we came out of the restaurant, we had locked our keys in the car. We eventually got the car unlocked, raced home, and with the rest of America, watched with pride and awe as Neil Armstrong made that first historical step.

One last note on 1969: After several years of failing health, my father died. During the last months I spent a great deal of time traveling between Washington and Rye to be with him, and it was very difficult to watch him slip away. He truly was a hero of mine; a daughter could not ask for a better father.

∝ The year 1970 began with George considering another run at the Senate against Ralph Yarborough. George found being a member of the minority party in the House very frustrating. As head of his own business, he was used to making decisions. In the best of times, things moved very slowly in the House and almost never for minority members. So at the urging of friends and supporters, he decided to get into the race.

With all of that going on, the last thing on my mind was our twenty-fifth wedding anniversary in January. You can't even imagine my shock when George managed to pull off an enormous surprise party at the Bayou Club in Houston with so many of our friends and family. Even when we got there and I saw many people we knew walking in, I thought it was just a coincidence.

George's schedule that whole year was unbelievably busy, with him trying to run a Senate race in Texas and be a member of the House in Washington. We were both very disappointed when he was going to be out of town on April 4 for the wedding of Mildred and Baine Kerr's son to the daughter of William S. White, a well-known and highly respected newspaperman who was a close friend of Lyndon Johnson. It was to be a small wedding in the Whites' Washington, D.C., apartment with many festivities planned around the day. We offered to do anything we could—George W. was a member of the wedding party— and Mildred and Baine asked if we could have a buffet luncheon the day of the wedding for all the people coming from back home.

George had to be in Texas that day for an event that he just could not cancel. I hated having a party without him, but these were our dearest friends and I really wanted to help. For the first time I hired a caterer, filled the house with flowers, and actually was beginning to feel ready.

At the last moment we got a message from Jack Valenti, President Johnson's former aide and now head of the Motion Picture Association, that ex-President Johnson would love to come to the lunch—if invited. That put a whole new light on the party. I panicked and called George, saying he couldn't invite the Johnsons, or if he did, he should cancel his event and come right home. George laughed and said that of course we should invite the Johnsons—after all, they had been so nice to us when they were in the White House—but that he couldn't possibly come home.

A former President coming to our house for a buffet luncheon and no George? I was terrified.

The day of the big event arrived, and the Kerr party came in enormous black limousines that they had hired to taxi their friends around Washington. This caused big excitement on our little Palisade Lane. By the time the former President arrived in his big limo, our neighbors were out in full force, led by Andy Stewart sitting on the curb in her gardening clothes watching all the cars go by.

Lyndon Johnson held court in our little library and could not have been a better guest. Years later, after *Millie's Book* came out, Jack Valenti sent me a picture of the former President scratching our dog Nicky's ear, with a note that said, "Millie is not the only Bush dog who has been a confidante of a President."

Doro and little Mary Kerr were awestruck and followed the Johnsons everywhere. They were in deep shock, however, when they saw the former President take our newspaper from the front yard as he was leaving.

The day still was not over. George got home that night just in time to throw on rented white-tie dinner clothes so we could race over to the White House to meet the Duke and Duchess of Windsor. We had not been invited for dinner, but had made the second cut, for after-dinner drinks and entertainment.

All went well until George looked for the shirt. The aide who had rented the outfit had forgotten to get one. So George, who certainly wears some strange clothes at times, said that it did not matter, put on a plain white shirt, and away we went. All night long we could see men studying George's neckline with interest, amazement, and some jealousy, I believe. Could they have thought they were outdated? George couldn't have cared less. We were amused that although he was eyed strangely all night, no one mentioned the outfit.

As for me, I had bought a new dress for the occasion—at that time, the most expensive dress I had ever owned. The entertainment was Bobby Short, and his date had on the very same dress! My, what an impression the Bushes of Texas must have made that night.

At one point during the evening, President Nixon came up to us and said, "George, you and Barbara know the Duke, don't you?" Before George could answer, he went on, "He has asked about you. Go talk to him." I believe that the President had exhausted his "small talk," of which he had a limited supply, and just wanted to share the load. We had met the Duke and Duchess once at a small dinner at Lloyd Smith's home in Houston several years before. We were equally sure that the Duke did not remember or ask for us.

I remember at the Smith dinner being surprised by how tiny the Duke and Duchess were and how charming she was. The ladies retired upstairs for coffee and the men to the salon for cigars. (I'm not really sure what the men did, but that sounds like what one would do if you had a Duke for dinner.) The Duchess of Windsor held forth upstairs in a very warm and amusing fashion. I was charmed.

But back to the White House event. On the way to the car, George fell ill and got sick all over his rented cutaway. (Shades of things to come?) What a day it had been.

On May 4, 1970, the terrible confrontation took place in Ohio on the campus of Kent State between students and the National Guard, with four young people being killed. The tragedy rocked the country and lit a fuse on campuses everywhere. I was driving home from a meeting late one afternoon and ran into a large traffic jam on the Key Bridge. As I sat patiently in my car, I realized a frenzied gang of students was working its way down the bridge. When they got to my car, one of them yelled, "We got one here," and before I knew what was happening, my car was rocking and what seemed like a hundred mean faces were leering in the windows at me. A young man thrust a microphone in my car window and said, "What do you think about Nixon who killed the students at Kent State?" I was scared to death and started to speak, "I don't t-h-i-n-k . . ." and then burst into tears. The young man with the mike took one look and quickly told his friends that I was crying and to back off. They did and moved on. The faces all suddenly looked like young, caring kids instead of the mean-faced monsters I had seen one second before. I honestly think they all pictured their own mothers in the same situation. They had picked me out of the crowd in the first place because my Texas license plate said "House 7."

I was spending as much time in Texas as possible helping George campaign. I will never forget one memorable day. First, as I was getting off the plane in Marshall, Texas, my heel caught on the steps and I literally fell off. I'm sure that made quite an impression on our supporters who were kind enough to greet me at the airport.

The day only got worse. I recently had decided to do something with my hair, which to me looked dead. So I tried a new hair color product, a rinse called "Fabulous Fawn." Well, as the day got hotter, and when the air-conditioning quit working on the plane, "Fabulous Fawn" began to trickle down my back. All day I looked like I had a dirty neck. I think that was the last time I ever colored my hair, and I decided to let nature take its course.

I remember another slightly more glamorous day on the campaign trail when we traveled with the Agnews. I was amazed that during the long flight between Texas and Washington, the Vice President never once read, wrote, or worked. He played gin rummy. I liked them both very much. They were very relaxed and absolutely put on no airs.

Once again, lightning struck to completely change the political picture. This time, our friend Lloyd Bentsen ran against Yarborough and beat him in the Democratic primary. This hurt us badly, but we still thought we could win. Then those smart Democrats put a liquor-by-the-drink bill on the ballot, and the Democrats who otherwise would not have voted turned out in record numbers. Losing is not fun at all, and this was harder than ever. Election night, as we were walking out of the hotel where George had spoken to his loyal supporters, Doro burst into tears. We tried to tell her it would be okay, but she sobbed, "Oh, no, it won't. I'll be the only girl in the fifth grade whose Daddy doesn't have a job."

The next day I went to play tennis with several of my close friends, but every time I thought of George Bush sitting at home calling people and thanking them, I'd start weeping. We finally gave up and went in to have coffee and lunch.

Incidentally, no more brown-bagging it in Texas. We could now buy liquor over the counter by the drink.

The United Nations

8

After the election, George and I returned to Washington to finish out his career as a congressman. George was very disappointed. He always had wanted to be in the Senate, especially since the days when his father had served there. Now the big question for us was: What next?

Many people felt President Nixon owed George, because he had asked him to give up his safe House seat to run for the Senate. George did not feel that way. It had been his choice to get into the race. Nevertheless, rumors flew all over Washington about who would get what jobs, including George. The President once hinted that maybe George should move to Connecticut and run against Senator Abraham Ribicoff in 1972. That had zero appeal. I was ready to suggest we go home to family and friends and live happily ever after.

However, George knew exactly what job he wanted: Ambassador to the United Nations. Family friend Charley Bartlett had suggested it once, and after much thought, George decided it was where he could serve the President and the country best. He discussed it with White House Chief of Staff Bob Haldeman and many others, but not directly with President Nixon.

Finally, the call came for George to come to the White House, and the President offered him a job as special assistant to the President. George said he would do whatever was asked of him, but added he was sorry that the President didn't like the UN idea. He said he felt he could have served the President well there, especially since incumbent Ambassador Charlie Yost was a liberal Democrat and really didn't represent the administration's views. A few minutes later, President Nixon called George back into the Oval Office and said, "I've thought about our conversation—you have the UN job."

This story tells you something about the presidency: Very often the people around the President do not present the case for someone else very well—or maybe at all.

It also makes one wonder: In light of what later happened in the Nixon White House, were we not the luckiest people in the world?

At the time, I knew nothing about the United Nations other than what was in the newspapers. So I looked it up in the children's World Book encyclopedia, and once when I was in New York City, I cruised by in a cab. I didn't dare go in, since George had not yet been confirmed.

In late February, our friend and neighbor Associate Justice Potter Stewart conducted the swearing-in ceremony at the White House, with Mom and Dad Bush in the audience. While we were waiting in the Red Room, Potter told me President Nixon always said the same thing when he saw him: "Of course, I know the Justice. He is the youngest Justice on the Court." Just then, President Nixon walked in and said, "Oh, Justice Stewart, how are you? Barbara, did you know that the Justice is the youngest Justice on the Court?" It was hard not to laugh. In later years, Potter would swear George in as Director of the CIA and as Vice President of the United States. That lovely man died before George became President.

Shortly before the swearing-in, we went on an orientation trip to Europe to visit some of the UN agencies and world organizations. The U.S. government would pay first-class for George and an aide, Paxton Dunn, but George would have to pay for me. There was lots of teasing about how we would go. George said he and Pax would send me back messages from first class to coach, or maybe I could come up and visit first class once in a while. They also told me not to worry: They would wait for me to get off the plane.

Of course, we all flew coach class. Paxton was a very good sport about it, and was also a great guide through the State Department maze. All went well until we arrived in Austria on a tiny European plane. As we exited from the rear with the other coach passengers, we saw a band playing at the front of the plane, along with a small delegation headed by a very official-looking mayor. At first we wondered who was getting such a grand welcome. Then George spotted the American ambassador among the welcoming party. What a dilemma! Do we leap back on the plane and get back off through the first-class exit, or do we creep up on them from behind? We bit the bullet and chose the latter course. Ambassador John Humes was kind about our unusual arrival. He kept mentioning how great we were to save the government so much money. Although we always were concerned about saving government dollars, I must admit we were more worried about saving our own!

In Paris, we stayed with an old Bush/Walker family friend, Ambassador Dick Watson. While there, I went with a darling young woman, Eva Prohme, whose husband worked at UNESCO (United Nations Education, Scientific, and Cultural Organization), to my first couture house; I have forgotten the name. The room was crowded, but it quickly became apparent that the others were straphangers and the whole show was for me. They must have been told I was a rich Texan who certainly would buy out the place. Three beautiful models were in and out of some eighty dresses in just about an hour. It was so embarrassing for me and certainly for my young guide. We did not know how to get out of there. Finally, when the high-pressure saleslady turned her back, Eva and I slipped away in giggles—and feeling very guilty, I might add.

It was a fast, exciting trip for me as we whipped through many of the European capitals. But I soon realized that trip was just the beginning of two wonderful years for us. I will leave the politics to George and tell you instead about the personal side of being at the United Nations.

Our first look at apartment 42A in the Waldorf Towers—the UN ambassador's official residence—was slightly frightening. The Towers was a formidable place to live. Ambassador and Mrs. Yost had just been relieved of their post in a cruel, awkward fashion. They very kindly invited us for lunch, but I remember them as dour people. He later did the unforgivable: Not only did he stay in New York, but he wrote anti-U.S. policy articles for *The New York Times* op-ed page. Soviet Ambassador Yakov Malik would wave them in George's face in Security Council meetings and say, "See, George, just how wrong you are. Your colleague says . . ."

The residence is a large, roomy apartment with five lovely bedrooms. We used one of the large bedrooms for a study/dressing room for George and often tucked one of our boys in there when they came for a visit and we had a crowd. One bedroom was a guest room (we had lots of guests), and Paula and Doro had the other two. Doro was an adorable, chunky twelve-year-old at the time. She missed all her friends from Washington, but Paula kept her from being lonely, and her older first cousin, Peggy Pierce, often came for the night to keep her company. And of course she had lots of friends from the United Nations school. At that time, it was in an old warehouse on Fifty-fourth Street, and I could walk her there if the weather was pleasant. Our three younger boys were all away at school, but they visited often with friends.

The apartment had a lovely front entrance, a small octagonal room with one of what seemed like hundreds of original Gilbert Stuart portraits of George Washington (he must have turned them out like rabbits!), a lovely den with a fireplace, and a mammoth living room that was forty-eight feet long. The Yosts had their own furniture in the apartment, and when they left, it left also. The hotel sent up some sorry replacements: white satin couches and chairs and two large round mirror-topped coffee tables. They cannot be as ugly as I remember them, but they were hideous. At the first of our many receptions, these coffee tables caused no end of excitement. Women's skirts that year were just shorter than the coffee tables, and to my horror, I realized that you could see right up the ladies' skirts if you were standing across the table from them. The tables left the very next morning.

I worried about furnishing an apartment that big and making it look warm and inviting. I borrowed some beautiful paintings from the Metropolitan Museum: *Tennis at Newport* by Bellows; a lovely Mary Cassatt; a glorious, small John Singer Sargent of two ladies lounging on a very green lawn; and many others. Much to everyone's dismay, I returned two beautiful Monets. I would love to be surrounded by Monets, but felt that since we do not subsidize our artists as so many countries do, the least I could do was display American art. When criticized, I would answer, "When the French start hanging American artists, I'll think about hanging French paintings."

Mildred Kerr came to visit while I was worrying about furnishing the living room. She noticed all the beautiful glass objects (supplied by the Steuben Glass people) and told me she had seen a big Steuben bowl filled with eggs that looked very cozy. Maybe eggs would add color to that cold-looking room. So out we went and bought seventeen colored stone eggs, put them in a bowl, and stepped back to admire them. Well, in a room that size, they were absolutely nothing. They looked like a grain of sand on a big beach. However, as a result, people thought I collected eggs and brought them to me as gifts, which I thought was rather funny. But at the same time, people also would "borrow" an egg every now and then, so I remained pretty constant—eggwise.

As I mentioned earlier, living at the Waldorf could be intimidating. At the time, it was home to Mrs. Douglas MacArthur; actress Carol Channing; former Senator Bill Benton; former postmaster general and confidant of Franklin Roosevelt, Jim Farley, with whom we shared several fun dinners; Mrs. Edwin Hilson, a great friend of the Eisenhowers; benefactress Mrs. Charles Engelhard; and many others. The first time I went to the grocery store and brought back bags of groceries in my arms, I felt a slight panic. Would they lead me to the service elevator? Would somebody tell me that their clientele did *not* carry groceries up in the tower elevators, much less through their lobby? They did no such thing, and by the time we left after two years, I felt that everybody in that sumptuous hotel was a friend. I mean everybody—the permanent residents, doormen, elevator operators, the manager, and on and on. George and I grew very fond of Jean MacArthur, Mildred Hilson, and Jane Engelhard, who was a great supporter of the White House Endowment Fund and remained faithful twenty years later when I revived it.

You'll be happy to know that Jean took us to the "21" Club several times—the source of my great jealousy years earlier. She had her own table, and when we arrived, she would be there to greet us. Always in front of her would be a stem glass with a pale liquid and an olive in it. It seemed so amazing to see this tiny little southern lady drinking a martini straight up, and even more amazing when she would request another. After we got to know her quite well, we discovered that she was having water with an olive. She wanted her guests to feel free to order whatever they wanted.

Apartment 42A also was the place where the Secretary of State entertained when in New York City, and Secretary William Rogers used the apartment several times. I remember being told about many things that the Secretary did or did not like. So you can imagine my surprise one night when Bill and Adele Rogers took us out for dinner and he ordered lamb. I had definitely been told that the Secretary hated lamb. I mentioned this to Bill, and he laughed and asked what other things he "disliked." When I repeated the list, he really laughed. Not a bit of truth in the list! That is so typical of getting information secondhand.

One luncheon the Secretary gave at 42A will always remain indelibly—maybe I should say "pressed"—in my mind. It was in the fall, during the busiest time. I had arranged the flowers, chosen the menu, and gone gaily off on my own schedule. George told me the luncheon had gone well. Paula, close to tears, had a different story. Just before the luncheon, the chief of protocol came in and announced the tablecloth looked wrinkled. So the waiters pressed it right on the table. After the lunch was over, and the dishes and cloth were removed, we saw marks left by a hot steam iron on our beautiful table. But we were told that if you rubbed the table with ashes and camphor, the marks would disappear. So Paula and I collected ashes from the ashtrays and took turns rubbing with ashes and Campho-Phenique. I really don't know if the mixture did it, or if we did by rubbing so hard and long, but it worked.

We loved Bill and Adele Rogers. Later, I did a little work with her in the literacy field. She volunteered in public schools in both New York City and Washington, D.C., as they commuted back and forth for many years.

One thing we learned to hate at the United Nations were the words "We don't do it that way." An example: Immediately after we arrived, all the ambassadors from other countries wanted to pay a courtesy call. When George got the call that one was on his way up the elevator, he would start down the hall to meet him. An aide said, "Oh, no, Mr. Ambassador, we don't do it that way. I meet him at the elevator and bring him to you." George met every ambassador at the elevator, whether he was from Great Britain or Ceylon (now Sri Lanka). They fast learned that George does things differently and his own way. And they loved it. There were eleven floors of State Department people at the U.S. Mission—for the most part, very able and dedicated people. George brought Tom Lias, Jane Kenny, and Aleene Smith with him from his congressional office. Our dear Don Rhodes went to work for Congressman Charles Sandman of New Jersey.

At the time, New York City's mayor was John Lindsay, who was married to George's childhood friend Mary Harrison. We both loved Mary, but grew to think that John was the most conceited, arrogant man ever born.

The Mayor of New York and the U.S. Ambassador to the United Nations often co-hosted events. John came late to everything—and sometimes did not come at all. Then he would look at anyone—Mary, me, a member of his staff, or a member of George's—and say "Get me coffee" or whatever without a please or thank-you.

John's slogan for New York was "Fun City." Aleene and her husband, Hargrove, had fun with that. For instance, one day walking to work, a car came very close to the curb and splashed filthy water all over them. They would say, "Welcome to Fun City." Tom Lias judged his days in Fun City by whether it was a "one-dog day," "two-dog day," and so on—depending on the number of dog piles he stepped in on his way to work.

꿈 George loved to entertain and came up with some extraordinary and fun ideas. Sometimes, however, they would backfire.

When the movie *The Godfather* came out, people were waiting in lines for hours to see it. George thought it would be fun to have a private showing, so he rented a little theater and invited around one hundred people. They were thrilled—until the movie came on.

Sitting through this bloodthirsty film, showing the worst of America, I suddenly saw it through the eyes of our foreign guests. They already thought our streets were unsafe, and here we were showing them a film that seemed to prove them right. After the movie, I assured them that this kind of thing didn't happen anymore. As we walked out of the theater, the early-morning editions of the newspapers were already on the street, with screaming headlines: MOB KILLINGS IN NEW JERSEY!

Another time, during the Security Council meetings in the fall when many heads of state and foreign ministers were in town, George woke up on a Sunday morning with the idea that British Foreign Minister Sir Alec Douglas Home and Lady Home might like to get out of the city and go to Greenwich for lunch and a nice walk. I quickly said that he could not call their Ambassador, Sir Colin Crowe, at six A.M. Not only was it too early to call, it was certainly too late to extend a luncheon invitation to a very popular foreign minister. He called anyway, although he did wait until seven A.M. The Homes and the Crowes loved the idea. So George got on the phone and arranged for us to have lunch with his aunt and uncle, Mary and Herbie Walker, followed by a walk through the beautiful Audubon Society Park.

Well, we forgot to find out if it is open on Sundays in October, and when we got there, it was closed tighter than a drum. That didn't stop George. He hoisted Lady Crowe and Lady Home—skirts and all—over the fence, along with the rest of us, and we took a glorious walk through the park. That is until the park manager challenged us with his dogs. George quickly ran ahead and explained who we were, and we finished our walk—leaving by the proper gate this time. One of the Foreign Minister's security men from Scotland Yard later told George this was "a first" for him. Well, I guess so!

One August weekend, I invited the French and Italian ambassadors and their wives, whom we liked very much, to come to Maine and get away from the ghastly summer heat. George loved the idea, especially since they all played tennis. Later George came home laughing, saying his office had seen a cable about the improvement of the relationship between France and the United States. The proof the cable cited was the fact that the French ambassador and his wife were visiting the U.S. ambassador in Kennebunkport!

This story might answer a question I'm asked all the time: Did anyone tell you what to do, or give you any guidelines, when your husband was in government? The answer is no. Certainly I was given advice on protocol, and occasionally on what to wear or not to wear, but, for the most part, I just depended on the manners my mother taught me.

George's Uncle Herbie was a small partner of the New York Mets baseball team, and we occasionally took some ambassadors and wives to dinner and a game at Shea Stadium. Baseball is not an easy game to explain to foreigners, but peanuts and hot dogs were a refreshing change from all the black-tie, six-course meals.

Speaking of six-course meals, we usually served four, and I would worry whether we were doing enough. George just would not put up with any more, and he said there was a direct correlation: The poorer the country, the grander the meal. So we weren't surprised when Burundi served a seven-course meal.

Once we took a group of ambassadors and their wives for a briefing at NASA and dinner in Houston. We also hosted a Texas barbecue on the eleventh floor of the U.S. Mission and took them around Manhattan Island on a boat.

George's biggest party success was one he had for "The 10 Most Overrated Men in New York City"—at least according to *New York* magazine. George promptly invited all ten men—well, the nine others—to come to a reception in their honor. He asked Dick Schaap, the author of the article, to join us, along with quite a few ambassadors and their wives. I can't remember the others, but I do know that Senator Javits was on the list, and although he was a fine man, he had no sense of humor about his selection. He said he "wouldn't dignify the article by attending." At the party, George jumped up on a chair, called us all together, and gave out some funny awards. Our Russian friend, Ambassador Malik, confused by the party, was overheard asking another ambassador more familiar with the West, "Vat is dis '*overrated*'?" George loved that.

Dick Schaap was brave enough to attend. George said in his little award ceremony that "only modesty kept Dick himself off the list." Dick later wrote that he came to the party in fear and trembling and believed that his worst fears had been realized when the first people he saw, being a man of Jewish faith, were ambassadors from Arab nations!

George wasn't the only member of the family who enjoyed entertaining. I invited several of my Washington groups to New York for a day. They were to take the train, tour the residence, have a light lunch, and get a briefing and tour of both the U.S. Mission and the United Nations. The first group came, about forty in all.

Since the kitchen in our apartment looked like an L-shaped Pullman train kitchen, I decided to have the Waldorf serve a light lunch: chicken salad, lobster salad, hot rolls, white wine, and then some sort of yummy dessert. The whole day went well. Several weeks later, George asked me how it had gone—and then told me that the bill from the Waldorf was $900. I burst into tears and told him I had two other groups coming. He said I shouldn't worry. But I did, and Paula and I worked up a light lunch for sixty people in that tiny little kitchen that cost considerably less and tasted just as good.

Although we entertained a lot, we also were entertained a great deal. We went to several receptions every evening, many dinners, and quite a few lunches. I loved all that. In fact, I was born to the job: I love people and adore eating. For George, these social functions were work. At the ambassadors' level, much of the real work of the United Nations was conducted at these social functions. Especially if there was a problem between two countries, the only communications the ambassadors had with each other were "after hours." Your guest list often was composed of people who wanted to meet but couldn't on an official level.

We were on the reception circuit one December evening, racing from party to party. As it was close to Christmas, I had on a bright red suit—really bright red. Suddenly we pulled up to a building that looked different, and I asked what reception this was. George grabbed my arm and said that this was a call we had to make. As we ran up a flight of stairs, he explained that a brand-new ambassador, a former president of a Central American country, had died shortly after arriving at the United Nations and was lying in state here until arrangements were made to send him back home. At that moment, we literally ran into a room filled with people dressed in black and clearly mourning. We were led right up to the open coffin, where people were posing for pictures with their fallen leader. Yes, posing for pictures, putting their arms around the casket and putting their heads near his and having their pictures taken. Tears were everywhere—and so were TV cameras. It never occurred to George that I might not have been appropriately dressed in my bright red. To him, being there is what counts, not one's clothes.

I cannot tell you how many times during our UN years I wished I spoke French or Spanish. I had studied French as a child and learned some Spanish after moving to Texas, but was proficient at neither. I've decided people who are musically inclined are also better at languages. I am tone-deaf and can't carry a tune, so that was my excuse. I did find that the Spanish-speaking people were thrilled when I tried to speak their language, but the French always acted like I was attempting a language they had never heard. George didn't care. He went right ahead using his schoolboy French.

I learned that a touch, many smiles, much interest, and lots of honest affection were a universal language.

Being the host ambassador kept George very busy. When the elderly ambassador and his wife from Cyprus were attacked, robbed, and had their shoes thrown in the Central Park lake one evening, it was George's fault for not making the park safe. When a bomb was placed next to the embassy door of a small African country, it was George's fault. And when the Soviet Embassy had a shot fired into it from a nearby rooftop, just missing a Russian family, it was George's fault. He spent hours working on these housekeeping, rather than policy, problems.

I volunteered one morning a week at Sloan Kettering Memorial Hospital—not with the children but with adults. I loved it. The hospital had the most marvelous staff and an esprit de corps that made being there a joy. My job was the Art Cart—hardly a big job, but worthwhile. The cart had many pictures, classic and modern. We were assigned a floor and told what rooms to call on. Then you asked the patients what they liked and if they wanted the art changed in their rooms. All of this was really a cover. Mostly our job was to get to know the patients, see if they were happy or lonely, and generally to spread good cheer. I became very attached to many of the patients and even taught one sweet military wife to needlepoint. Many times I would bring the patients souvenirs from dinners and other UN events.

One day the hospital asked me to call on a lady who was very much in the dumps. They confessed that the only spark they had seen was when they told her that the wife of the U.S. Ambassador to the United Nations was working at the hospital. I called on this lady many times and dropped names and events like mad. She loved it.

I felt very guilty and disappointed when I had to miss my Thursday morning at Memorial. Often I would race from the hospital to a luncheon. Our foreign friends found volunteer work really strange, but certainly commendable. They always said "it would never work in our country."

In those days, about 80 percent of the people who were treated at our hospital went home either in remission or cured, never to return again. Several times we had friends come through the hospital. The saddest for us was when George's wonderful dad got a persistent cough and was sent to Memorial. He was in the hospital about three weeks as I remember, being tested, operated on, and then sleeping away his life. He died October 8, 1972. He was a magnificent man who brought great pleasure to his family. He and Mom had been married fifty-one years and were a great team.

Dotty Bush planned his funeral with their children. I remember several things about that service. First, she told us to wear color. Death was a beginning and not an ending. She wrote the eulogy herself, and it was so loving and hit the mark. She made her children sit with their own families. She said she wanted their friends to see what grand families Pres Bush had. She sat with the pallbearers, who were their grandsons. Several of our boys were pallbearers—maybe all of them—but the one I remember was Jeb. He was a student at the University of Texas, nineteen years old, six feet four inches tall. Remember, this was the early 1970s. He, of course, did not have a dark suit. He told me not to worry—he'd borrowed one. I should have kept worrying. It was black corduroy. He is the most handsome man (at least according to his mother), and that saved him. Otherwise, he would have looked like a card shark from Las Vegas.

After the church service, we all walked over to the cemetery and buried Pres Bush next to our little Robin. George and I felt very fortunate we were living in New York during the last year of Dad's life.

So much of what we did during the United Nation's years was fascinating, but a number of events or periods stand out in my mind.

The fall of 1971 was not to be believed. Witnessing the election of new Secretary General Kurt Waldheim, the China vote, and the constant meetings of the Security Council were extraordinary.

The Dual Representation Policy (some erroneously referred to it as the Two China Policy) was a very difficult time for the U.S. Ambassador to the United Nations, but it was interesting. The United States wanted Taiwan to keep its UN seat despite the entry of the People's Republic of China into the United Nations. We lost by a narrow margin—59 to 55—but it was a major setback for the United States. The night of the vote, I was seated with a few other American wives in the General Assembly. Once it was clear that we had lost the vote, the room went wild. Seated right in front of me were some people from the Tanzanian Mission. They turned and jeered and spit at me. I truly was shocked by the hatred they felt for us. It was so sad to see the lovely foreign minister from Taiwan walk out of the United Nations, his back straight and head held high. It was equally dramatic to see the new ambassador from the People's Republic of China walk in that first time.

The very next day, I was scheduled to attend a luncheon the African wives were having for me. I told George I didn't think I'd go. He insisted that I go and said they would be nice. How right he was. The wives were so sweet and lovely and we even shared a tear or two, although for the most part they were on the other side of the China issue.

The People's Republic of China delegation was the rage of New York. They lived in a hotel and their every move was reported. What they wore and what they ate became front-page news. The fact of the matter was they were very nice people just trying to feel their way along.

Shortly after George's dad died, he asked his mother if she would mind including the Chinese in one of our family Sunday lunches. Although still in mourning, she was a dear and immediately agreed. She would have a buffet and let the grandchildren help as usual. At that time, the Chinese men and women all dressed alike in Mao suits, so Mrs. Bush greeted us in black pants and a black sweater. She wanted the Chinese to feel at ease and at home. We were late getting there, and her dinner sat for a little too long in the warming oven. When our lunch was served, I heard the foreign minister ask Mrs. Bush what something was. Her answer: "Minute Rice." We had a hard time explaining to the Chinese what that was—and why we were giggling. Poor Mom. The rice was so overcooked that even the Chinese did not recognize it. I never loved that courageous little woman more than that day.

✑ Another outstanding, very educational experience for us was a trip to Africa in February 1972. George went first to Somalia and then on to Ethiopia, where the Security Council was to meet. I joined him there.

The altitude in Addis Ababa was devastating to many of us. Sleep was impossible at eight thousand feet. The Security Council met all day and half the night. During the day we visited the marketplace, and it was teeming with poor-looking people who thrust things at you to buy. The pressure was enormous.

From there we went on to Khartoum, Sudan, where we caught

up on our sleep. Since we did not have relations with the Sudan at that time, we had to deal through the Dutch Embassy. We stayed in our chargé d'affaires's guest house. Curt and Sally Moore were truly wonderful people. She was the principal of the American School—according to her, because they couldn't find anyone else, but I doubt that. She was a very bright, strong woman. We did take a lovely boat trip up the Nile and saw where the White Nile meets the Blue Nile. We saw an oxen water bucket routine that was exactly as it was done in 1500 B.C. The irrigated land around the river was green and fertile. All the rest was sand. The Sudanese are very beautiful people. At that time, the Sudanese ladies were circumcised, which was common all over Africa. It was a very depressing country. We saw many dead or starving animals. I don't know how these people eked out a living.

There is a tragic footnote to this visit. We eventually normalized relations with the Sudanese, and at a going-away party for the Moores in March 1973, the Black September Terrorists took incoming Ambassador Noel and outgoing Chargé d'Affaires Moore hostage and eventually killed them both. George and I attended their joint funeral on March 7 in Washington, D.C.

We went on to Kenya for a lovely visit. We drove out of Nairobi through beautiful rolling residential countryside, past tea and coffee plantations and into the mountains. Suddenly, far below us, we saw the Rift Valley spread at our feet. Nairobi is about five thousand feet high. We climbed to eight thousand feet and then dropped about three thousand feet into the valley. We saw many deer, monkeys, impala, the yellow-billed stork, those tiny little deer called dik-diks, and giraffes eating those marvelous thorn trees. But the most exciting part of this day trip was Lake Nakuru, where we saw the most fantastic sight. Nakuru is an alkaline lake filled with green algae, on which pink flamingos feed by the millions. From a distance, it appears the lake has pink beaches. Not true—just miles of beautiful flamingos, moving like ballet dancers.

On to Lusaka, Zambia, where we immediately took a side trip to Victoria Falls and got soaked. We walked out on a bridge that formed the line between Zambia and Rhodesia (now Zimbabwe). Since our government had asked us not to go into Rhodesia, we stopped in the middle of the Knife Edge Bridge and looked at the glorious falls.

We were then taken to the Quadrapoint, where Namibia, Rhodesia, Botswana, and Zambia meet. We jumped on a very primitive river ferry, which was really a small converted steel barge. As we approached Botswana, we could see a welcoming party of officials waiting and, twenty feet away, another kind of welcoming party behind barbed wire: Rhodesians with guns and cameras. Fortunately, they shot only the latter. We nervously took pictures back.

We spent the night at the Chobe Game Preserve. We took a boat trip looking for hippos, saw none, but loved the extraordinary river. We drove through the preserve and saw many families of baboons and hundreds of elephants bathing, rolling in the dust, and squirting their young. We passed a baby rhino with parents and friends and saw some waterbucks. The Zambians had gotten their independence in the 1960s, but were still struggling when we visited. At the time, the country had only one hundred college graduates and one Zambian doctor.

Next was Zaire, where we visited a space satellite station funded by the Export-Import Bank. This was our first visit with President Mobutu, who wears a leopard skin hat and carries a tribal stick. He is very flamboyant, but charming. Years later he visited us for dinner in Maine one night on his way to a meeting in Montreal. He speaks no English, and we speak little French. George's mother came for dinner with us and enchanted him and her grandchildren as she reached way back to her school days and spoke French very well.

Next stop: Libreville, Gabon. Our embassy was a lovely, modern home with nice gardens on a tall hill looking down on all sides at native huts and shacks. I found it fascinating, but felt uncomfortable in a "Marie Antoinette" way, watching the women trudge by carrying tremendous loads on their heads.

Our entry into Lagos, Nigeria, probably influenced my feeling about that country. The traffic was horrendous. The city was filthy. The river was polluted. There were no closed sewers, no water, and sometimes no electricity. The streets were teeming with people—some dressed, some half dressed, and some relieving themselves. The roads were lined with shacks. I saw beggars, people sleeping on the streets, and garbage everywhere. Never had I seen such filth. The very worst was that a lady gave birth on the street outside our car and no one seemed to care. People just stepped over or walked around her.

Chad was more of the same—poor. The minister of health told

me they could keep the clinic open with a mere $100. The capital, Fort Lamy, was a dry, dusty city. We ate lunch with President Tombalbaye, who was assassinated several years later in a coup.

We left that fascinating continent thinking Africans were the world's warmest, friendliest people who had more problems than we could believe.

~~~ We met many world leaders and interesting, exciting people during the two years we were at the United Nations. Ali Bhutto, then deputy prime minister of Pakistan and later prime minister, made an enormous impression on George when he spoke before the Security Council. Ambassador Toukan from Jordan was a very dear man. We became close and George even helped his daughter, Alia, who was in her early twenties, get a job at American Express. I think she was in the secretarial pool and sat in the fifth desk from the back. The ambassador and his family were recalled to Jordan after a year. The beautiful Alia went on to become the third wife of King Hussein. On a state visit to the United States, Queen Alia told George that right after her engagement, the women she had worked with at American Express all chipped in and called her in Jordan.

During this same period, we went up to the Rockefellers' country place, Pocantico Hills, on the Hudson River for a luncheon David Rockefeller gave a visiting dignitary. It was a lovely day, and we ate outside around the pool. Sitting at our table was Najeeb Halaby, who at that time was CEO of PanAm, and his daughter, Lisa. A child of the 1970s with long hair and sandals, she stood out in this crowd of older, well-dressed people. But she grew up to be a beautiful young woman who went to work in Jordan and became Queen Noor, the fourth wife of King Hussein, after our little friend Alia was killed in a helicopter accident.

I have to tell you another story about that lunch. I distinctly remember that Pat Patterson, whose husband was head of Chase National Bank, was at my table. She sat next to a man from a South American country who spoke with a heavy accent. I heard him say to Pat, a gorgeous redhead, "Do you like New York?" She immediately went into all the virtues of New York City. When she finished telling him about the opera, the theater, museums, and so forth, he said, "And sex?" Pat, a normally sophisticated woman, looked nonplussed, but before she could answer, he added, "Sex Fifth Avenue; don't you like shopping?"

⌒ Toward the end of our United Nations days, and shortly before the 1972 election, George and I were in Austin, Texas, where he was speaking. As we were getting ready to fly home in a private plane to Houston, George decided to call President Johnson to see if we could make a courtesy call. He told me he didn't want to give him any warning. That way the President could say that he was sorry, it was too late to make plans. Instead, he said to come ahead.

Besides being President when we arrived in Washington, Lyndon Johnson had served in the United States Senate with George's dad. Pres Bush used to say, "I rarely agree with Lyndon on anything politically, but he always kept his word to the Senate and he was a great majority leader." We landed right on the LBJ Ranch landing strip. There were Lady Bird and Lyndon in a big white Lincoln. He immediately asked us if we'd rather go to the ranch house or drive around the ranch. Before we could answer, he chose to ride around the ranch. Lady Bird and I were put in the backseat and the men got in the front with Lyndon at the wheel. We charged over hill and dale without any thought to trails or roads. I decided that it must be a manicured ranch, for we hit no potholes or rocks as we raced through the tall grass spotting and chasing deer. George and the President talked a mile a minute about domestic successes and problems. The President told George that he had resigned all the boards he was serving on and put Lady Bird on some. He talked at length about the LBJ Library and invited George to speak there. He told us that he was thrilled that Barbara Jordan was there, or was going to be there. He knew that George had great respect for Barbara and had served with her in Congress. At one point we stopped on a hillside and looked at a great Hill Country scene. A man appeared at our car window and asked what we would like. Drinks appeared for all and we were off again. It was a marvelous experience. When we got back on our plane, both George and I felt that LBJ knew he did not have long to live and was paving a smooth way for Mrs. Johnson.

*   *   *

⟋⟍⟋ George worked very hard at his UN job and was superb. We went to the UN as critics and left as critics—but much less so than when we arrived. The United Nations has done so much good in fields like drugs, population, health, and environmental problems. And I guess that we will never know the wars that didn't happen because of the United Nations.

I take great pride in the fact that twenty years later, the United Nations came into its own when Iraq invaded Kuwait, and the world formed a coalition to protect one country from being invaded by another. George worked long and hard to form that coalition and to keep it together during the months before UN troops freed Kuwait. George Bush taught us how to keep the peace.

9

Surviving Watergate

President Nixon easily won reelection in 1972. I campaigned with other cabinet wives and had a very good time doing it. Sometimes we went out in teams, and I was fortunate to campaign in Texas with Jill Ruckelshaus and Lenore Romney, both women of great stature and knowledge. Jill's husband, Bill, had run for the Senate from Indiana and was head of the Environmental Protection Agency. Lenore's husband, George, was Secretary of Housing and Urban Development and had been Governor of Michigan. Lenore herself later ran for the United States Senate. Jill and Lenore did the heavy lifting, with me usually introducing them to Texans and our wonderful Texas to them. I take no credit—but get lots of joy—from the fact that Jill and Bill Ruckelshaus eventually moved to Houston.

Sometimes the reelect committee sent me out alone, and that was not as enjoyable. I respected the President, but he did not make it easy to like him. He just did not know how to deal with small talk. I like him much more now twenty years later.

I loved Pat Nixon, who was a sensational, gracious, and thoughtful First Lady. She was personally involved in acquiring some of the White House's most treasured and historic possessions, including original furniture from previous administrations. It was her idea to have the White House lit at night, and she also started the annual Spring and Fall Garden Tours. She worked tirelessly promoting volunteerism, a cause she believed in deeply.

Immediately after the election George attended a cabinet meeting in Washington. The President thanked them for all their hard work and left the room. Then Chief of Staff Haldeman, speaking for the President, asked the entire cabinet to have their resignations on the President's desk as soon as possible. They were shocked. Eventually there would be a total of eight new cabinet members.

George Shultz, who remained Secretary of the Treasury, talked to George about being his number two, an idea George liked a lot. However, it had been rumored in the papers that President Nixon was going to ask George to be chairman of the Republican National Committee. When the call came for George to meet with the President at Camp David, I sent him off with the strong urging not to accept the RNC post if offered. I just felt it would be a terrible experience. Party politics are very dog-eat-dog, and I knew he would have to travel a great deal. Of course, that's exactly what the President asked George to do, and of course, he took it.

Our diplomatic friends' reaction was very interesting. They thought being chairman of the RNC was not only a great job but a step up. I could understand the Chinese thinking that, since Chairman Mao's title was head of the Communist party. But several other ambassadors told me that leading one of our two great political parties was an honor. Several lectured me on the fact that our country's strength comes from having two strong parties. In contrast, many of their countries had many parties, resulting in coalition governments. In retrospect, I agree with them and understand their envy of our party system. I strongly believe people should pick the one that most closely fits their political philosophy and then try to work within the party. So many people criticize our system of government or the people who run it; yet, they never would think of attending a precinct meeting. They complain that the party has gone too far left or right and then announce that they are Independents. I think that is a cop-out.

In December, George went to Washington for a meeting and had lunch with our friend Congressman Bill Steiger of Wisconsin. Bill suggested they wander over for an informal visit to the Republican National Committee headquarters. What a shock. Not only did no one welcome them; they were ignored. Many people had their feet on the desks, and the building seemed filled with staff with nothing to do. The offices were messy and dirty. George realized he had an unpleasant task ahead, but he excelled at this kind of challenge.

So after a round of going-away parties in New York, we headed back to Washington. Our house was rented and the tenant did not want to leave until his lease expired in six months. Once again, I went house-hunting, and found a great furnished house on Cathedral Avenue convenient to the children's schools.

The Republican National Committee met on January 19 and unanimously elected George its new chairman. As we visited with the committee members, they all seemed to have the same complaint: unhappiness with the Nixon White House staff, whom they found arrogant and inaccessible.

On January 20 we attended the second inauguration of Richard Nixon and Spiro Agnew. We sat with the cabinet and went to the luncheon in the Capitol Rotunda with the President and Vice President and their families, and the House and Senate leadership. Then we sat on the presidential platform to watch the parade. At that point life seemed challenging and very exciting.

George and I dropped in at the RNC to get warm for a moment, and we were surprised to find that it was almost closed. We couldn't believe it. Not only was a Republican president being sworn in, the city was teeming with party members, including all the committeemen and -women. We had heard that the morale was low, but so was the service they were giving. Life was getting more exciting and challenging by the minute.

That night we attended a dinner given by Ross and Margot Perot for the three Texans serving in Washington: Anne Armstrong, a counselor to the President who later became Ambassador to Great Britain; Bill Clements, an Assistant Secretary of Defense who later became Governor of Texas; and George. It was an extraordinary dinner attended by the Joint Chiefs of Staff, many senators and congressmen, Billy and Ruth Graham, a Medal of Honor winner, an escaped POW, a Vietnam widow, the son of a general killed in Vietnam, Governor and Mrs. Reagan, Supreme Court justices, and many friends. It opened with a blessing, which is unusual for a Washington dinner, and the entertainment was the Naval Academy choir. Ross Perot certainly knew how to put on a party, and it will come as no surprise that he gave a little speech.

George and I then went to the Inaugural Ball at the Kennedy Center, where we were supposed to be hosts. Our only role was to greet the Nixons and the Agnews when they arrived and lead them to the stage. We never could work our way through the crush that night and were so far away that we barely heard the President's remarks. It taught me a good lesson: Don't buy new clothes for that event. (Okay, I did break that rule in later years.)

It immediately became a busy year. President Johnson died suddenly on January 22, Neil's eighteenth birthday. We were so glad that we'd had that nice visit at the ranch in the fall.

On January 23 President Nixon spoke to the nation at ten P.M. and announced that we had peace at last in Vietnam. It was a very emotional time for our country. The war had lasted such a long time and in the process, had torn us apart. Finally, our servicemen and servicewomen could come home. I wrote in my diary:

January 23—It seemed so ironic that President Johnson died some 28 or 30 hours before the peace announcement. It would have pleased him so. No man wanted peace more. I think back to the United Nations. Vietnam hung over our head. It affected every talk, every negotiation. For so many reasons we are thrilled about the peace. Think of Sybil Stockdale . . . knowing that her (husband) Jim will be home soon. [George and I had gotten to know and like Sybil Stockdale through George's involvement with POWs and MIAs. In fact, I wore her husband's POW bracelet. We were disappointed in 1992 when Jim agreed to be Ross Perot's running mate.]

January 25—Mrs. Johnson was absolutely magnificent. She smiled at everyone, thanked everyone. She was quoted as saying that she was sure she would have those great waves of sorrow, but right now she was just grateful for 38 years. They really laid Lyndon to rest in great style.

February 12—THE FIRST POWS ARE OUT!!!! OUR MAN JIM STOCKDALE LIMPED OFF. THANK GOD.

There is one more diary entry from this time period I must share with you, if only because it amused me when I came across it in 1993:

February 1—First time I had my hair blown dry. It was very easy but I'm not sure it will catch on. Didn't do much for my hair.

* * *

〰 As much as we loved our stay in New York, it was great to return to Washington. Doro was happy to be back at her school with friends, and although the Waldorf was an elegant place to live, we loved being in a house again. Neil, who had boarded at St. Alban's while we were at the United Nations, moved home and became a day student, and Marvin was just a short distance away at Woodberry Forest School near Orange, Virginia. He absolutely loved that school and it started a lifelong love affair with Virginia, where he still lives with his family. George W. was at Harvard Business School and Jebby was at the University of Texas in Austin.

I should note that as close as Marvin was, 1973 was the year of the Arab oil embargo and we suffered through long, long gas lines. It made going to see him almost impossible. Several times I barely made it home; my gauge was right on Empty. It was an inconvenience for almost everyone but absolutely devastating for those whose livelihood depended on the availability of gasoline.

We were especially thrilled to be with Neil that year. Everything was coming together for him. He was elected a prefect (class officer) at his school, and through much hard work, he made the honor roll and was named all-city second string in basketball—quite an honor in a city like Washington. Neil had overcome his learning disability and now could read with the best of them.

Dotty Bush, George, and I were in the audience on Prize Day when Neil won a coveted award. No child ever worked or tried harder to please, so this was truly a joy for us all. And we were all thrilled when he was accepted at Tulane University. He had come a long way from the day when we discovered he could not read.

After graduation, Neil took a group of four girls and four boys to Maine for a house party. Thank heavens I am too old to chaperone another one of these. It was agony. They were good kids, but the sloppiest, messiest children I have ever seen. Maybe since they had done the wonderful thing of graduating for us, they felt they could be rude. I put up with it for as long as I could, but when they didn't stand up when George's mom came into the room, I said, "Up, up!" and gestured with my hands. Later I overheard the girls imitating me, and I must say, I must have sounded pretty bad.

One of the children was the daughter of Spiro and Judy Agnew. The Vice President was going through a dreadful time in the press and the rumors about him were running wild. I was so touched by the way the other children protected Kim; politics can be brutal to children.

Agnew finally resigned in October, and President Nixon appointed Jerry Ford Vice President. He was a popular man with House and Senate members of both parties and a reassuring, healing choice for the country.

◠ In June, on my forty-eighth birthday, the family surprised me with a month-old blond cocker spaniel. After much thought, we named the puppy after C. Fred Chambers, a dear friend of George's. Our dog Nicky had gone to live with Paula's family in Texas when we moved into the Waldorf, and I really needed a dog. It was Marvin's idea, and George asked our friend Don Rhodes to take him dog-shopping. Don said Marvin looked deeply into the eyes of dozens of dogs until he finally found the perfect pup—C. Fred. It was an absolutely perfect birthday present.

I was keeping very busy. I had rejoined my International Club; saw a lot of my 90th Congressional friends; spent day after day with Andy Stewart; had twelve to twenty-five people over every Sunday after church for cookouts; carpooled; and worked as a volunteer at the Washington Home, which was a nursing home. And of course I worked for the party. Although I was one of the founding members of the Republican Forum, which educated party members on the issues, I can take very little, if any, credit since others did all the work.

Once a month Andy and I attended the Washington World Affairs Council luncheon, where Mrs. Virginia Bacon, widow of a New York congressman and an old grande dame, invited fascinating speakers to tell us about the world. They were very informative luncheons, but the thing I remember most was the fact that Mrs. Bacon put her head back and slept soundly and noisily through every speech. It was amusing to watch the speaker when he or she realized that Mrs. Bacon was asleep and then tried to act like it didn't matter.

I also joined the Theater Group, which I continued off and on throughout all our Washington days. It was an interesting group of eight or ten women made up of Supreme Court justices' wives, ambassadors' wives, historians, Democrats and Republicans, small business owners, and a housewife or two thrown in, all active in the community and all bright women. In those days we attended matinee performances and saw some wonderful plays, including *Macbeth* and *The Day After the Fair.*

Once a week in the early morning, I played tennis with Meredith Homet, Milly Dent, and Ann Buckley. I also played with Barbara MacGregor, Joanne Kemp, Martha Bartlett, and many others. All of our husbands held various positions in Washington.

Meanwhile George was keeping the most extraordinary schedule. In the first eleven months after taking over the party, he traveled 97,000 miles in thirty-three states, giving one hundred and one speeches, conducting seventy-eight news conferences, and making eleven national TV appearances. Watergate haunted him and permeated absolutely everything. Scores of Republicans were deserting the President. It got so bad that my childhood friend Milly Dent, whose husband, Fred, was Secretary of Commerce, became my only tennis partner. We couldn't find two others who did not think President Nixon was lying. It was a very unpleasant time for everyone.

Top Nixon aides Bob Haldeman, John Ehrlichman, and John Dean, and Attorney General Richard Kleindienst resigned April 30. George told me that the morning of the announcement, Bob said something to him like this: "I'm all right, George. Jo and I were sitting around the breakfast table this morning, reading our lesson from the Bible, and we came across the passage where it says [again I am paraphrasing], 'If *you* know that you have not sinned, then nothing else matters.'" I mention this because after twenty years, I have come to the conclusion that none of these people think they did anything wrong. It certainly is a different way of thinking.

Fortunately for George, his counterpart at the Democratic National Committee was Bob Strauss. He was a worthy opponent who played fair. We have counted Helen and Bob Strauss as dear friends for many years. When George was President, he sent Bob to the Soviet Union as ambassador at a very crucial time. He was the right man in the right place to help protect American interests as the Soviet Union fell apart.

Our household was jumping during Christmas vacation that year. All the children came home, including Jeb with the news that he wanted to marry a young woman he had met during a high school program in Mexico. This came as no surprise to us as Columba was the only girl he had ever dated. I remember one episode that made it clear to me that she certainly was a great influence on Jeb. We were notified that because of his academic record, Jeb had made Phi Beta Kappa. I called to say how thrilled we were, and he told me he had done it for Columba because he wanted to prove he was serious. She thought he was a rich man's son and a playboy. That vacation I went with Jeb when he bought a tiny engagement ring. I wrote in my diary:

> Jeb and I went in the afternoon to Boone & Sons and bought a ring and had my Grandmother Pierce's wedding ring fitted to Columba's size. When he has a wedding date he'll then get it marked. I am praying that he'll be as happy as Grandmother Pierce was and I am . . . How I worry about Jeb and Columba. Does she love him? I know when I meet her, I'll stop worrying . . . I am praying to be like Dotty Bush but it will be hard.

Jeb and Columba were married February 23, 1974, in a small family wedding in the chapel at the University of Texas. Only Columba's mother and sister, George's mother, and our immediate family plus Paula, our housekeeper, were there. Jeb was our first child to get married, and he and Columba reminded me so much of George and me. Jeb was just twenty-one, a year older than his father had been, and Columba was my age, nineteen, and they still had college to finish.

We were not an easy family to marry into. I had found the big Bush family a little overwhelming twenty-nine years before, so I could imagine Colu's feelings! To complicate things, she spoke very little English then, although she became fluent very quickly. She was a superb campaigner in Spanish and English in all our presidential campaigns; has helped with the Mexican Ballet Folklorica, Mexico's national ballet company; and has sponsored Mexican artists in this country. She also has given us three of the most attractive, bright grandchildren. She has made Jeb very happy, and we love her dearly.

⁀ The wedding was a happy interlude in a year dominated again by Watergate. On January 14, I wrote in my diary: "I am worried about George as he does not love his work. How could he? All this scandal."

I will never forget those marvelous Nixon daughters and how

hard they worked for their dad. Julie called George once and asked him why he wasn't defending her dad more. She didn't realize it, but she had caught him, exhausted, in an airport going from city to city doing just that. He told me that she sounded just as frustrated as he felt.

Of course I thought George did a terrific job keeping the party out of the mess while still defending the President. He told me that the White House asked him to do things he just wouldn't do. They weren't illegal; they were just wrong. For example, they asked him to send out strongly worded letters he didn't believe in. He got memos from White House aide Chuck Colson saying, "The President wants you to . . ." George would ask Chuck to have the President call him. President Nixon never did, and George never did what Chuck asked. White House staff often quote the President, and one would do well to be sure that the President wants what the staffer wants. This is not a partisan statement. Both Democratic and Republican staffers have the same proclivity: a desire to appear on the inside track close to the President.

Certainly Chuck Colson was not alone in outrageous requests. I remember him because he totally turned his life around and has done the most remarkable job helping felons discover new and productive lives.

George wrote President Nixon a letter in August saying that he regretfully had to tell him that he felt the President must resign for the good of the country. The President continued to insist to George in private that he had done nothing wrong and asked George to help raise money so he could buy television time and take his case directly to the American people. On August 8, I was in Maine with the children when George called me from California, where he was fund-raising, and told me President Nixon would announce to the nation he was resigning and asked me to meet him in Washington the next morning. He flew all night, and on August 9 we met Dean Burch, a counselor to the President, and his wife, Pat, at the White House mess for breakfast. At ten A.M. we joined the White House staff and cabinet members in the East Room. The Nixon family came in, and the President told us good-bye. It was a sad moment in our history. One of the brightest men of our time was brought down by a stupid cover-up. The buck does stop with the top man, and President Nixon and the country paid the price. Tears flowed down all our faces. We went down to the helicopter pad on the

South Grounds and awaited the First Family. Who will ever forget that moment when the President turned and gave that final wave?

We went back into the White House to attend the swearing-in of Gerald Ford as the thirty-eighth president of the United States of America. We had lunch with the Burches, after which Dean went to President Ford's first staff meeting. He later commented on the difference between it and President Nixon's. President Ford asked each person in the cabinet to stay on and told them he was grateful for their help.

I will never forget that day: We saw a president resign and a new president sworn in. It was amazing how gently and quickly the executive branch switched gears. As we were walking to lunch, we noticed that even the White House pictures had changed: Photos of the Nixons were gone and the Fords already were on the walls. We are a great country, and the wonder of the smooth transition will stay with me forever.

⟋⟍ 10

China

After the change of presidents in 1974, George felt Jerry Ford needed his own spokesperson at the Republican National Committee. I also suspect he was exhausted. George always said dealing with Watergate was like dealing with a centipede: The other shoe kept dropping.

He had worked hard to keep the party away from the scandal and the scandal away from the party. In a letter he wrote me from Denver in the fall of 1974, he said: "I can't do this job much longer, if it is to be done well. It will need new blood after the elections." He suggested to President Ford that the RNC co-chair, Mary Louise Smith, be appointed. She was, doing a great job as the first woman to head a national party.

George had worked closely with Jerry Ford during his years in Congress and as chairman of the party. So when he went to Washington to talk to President Ford about the future, the President kindly offered him just about any job he wanted. We were vacationing in Maine at the time, and when George returned, he told me he hoped I would understand, but he had turned down all the stylish embassies (including London and Paris) and asked for the post in the People's Republic of China—if I agreed. He'd had all he wanted of constant receptions and dinner parties at the United Nations, and felt the People's Republic was where the action was, where one-fourth of the world's population lived.

To say that I was speechless is an understatement. Evidently President Ford told George he would give him that job, but he must be ready to stay for two years. The more George talked, the more excited I got. I missed being with George—he had traveled a great deal as RNC chairman—and the thought of having him to myself sounded like the answer to my prayers.

Besides that, it was a new adventure for us both. I remember as a little girl digging in the sand on the beach and being told that if we kept digging, we'd go right through the earth and come out in China. And there we would find little Chinese boys and girls digging in the sand trying to find the United States. That beach in Rye, New York, was the closest I ever thought I'd get to China!

The United States and the People's Republic of China had a special relationship in 1974. Although Richard Nixon had opened the door a crack on his historic visit in 1972, we did not have formal diplomatic ties. There was no embassy, but a liaison office. George's title would be Chief of the U.S. Liaison Office to the People's Republic of China.

As we sat with our children on the porch of the gray house* in Kennebunkport, George told them he had a new job, but they had to guess what it was. We would still be on that porch if George hadn't given them some heavy hints!

I was so grateful that Doro, who was fifteen, already had decided on her own to go to boarding school. At first, I didn't want her to go away—she was my baby! But now it was for the best, because there were no classes for foreign children her age in China. I was glad she was going to boarding school because she wanted to, not because she had to.

That fall was very busy. We got Doro and the boys ready for school. I studied very basic Chinese language at the State Department's Foreign Language School, and we were briefed by the State Department. The Chinese based in Washington gave us a party, and we gave them a party. And then there was the packing. We sent two shipments, one by sea and one by air.

Earlier, George had broken the news to me that C. Fred could not

---

* I'm referring to a house that we owned for about ten years. We did not buy Walker's Point, our current residence in Kennebunkport, until 1980.

go to China. I asked the State Department people, and they said there were American dogs in China. Then I asked the Chinese, and they said there were many foreign dogs there. That settled it—C. Fred was going! I shipped seventeen cases of his special dog food—then George had to let him go; he had too big an investment in dog food not to. We never regretted taking him. There were lonely times, and both George and I enjoyed curling up with a good book and C. Fred at our side.

Finally, in early October, the big day came. George and I took off for China via Alaska and Japan. C. Fred, who had traveled many times to Maine in the bowels of an airplane, was in his little box in the luggage compartment. I walked him in Alaska on the tarmac and never saw him again until he was delivered to me in China.

In Japan, we were met by our ambassador and his wife, dear friends, Marie and Jim Hodgson. We were told that C. Fred was to go into quarantine while we were there, but not to worry, he would be exercised daily. We spent two wonderful days in Japan and then flew off to Beijing,* stopping briefly in Shanghai.

We had read in all the books about the great cleanup in China and the fact that we would see no insects. The first thing I saw in Shanghai was a fly—but I must admit I saw very few after that first stop. In Shanghai we were isolated from the Chinese people in a special room until we flew on to Beijing. This was a sign of things to come.

George had told the liaison office staff not to come to the airport, but he invited them instead to come to a reception at our residence—within an hour of our arrival! Who but George Bush would have done that, but it was just the right thing to do. So over they came with their wives and children—fifty-three in all. They were an amazing, brave little army of Americans. Most of them had come with David Bruce, George's distinguished predecessor, to open the office. Now many of them were leaving, moving onward with their careers. C. Fred was brought in with our luggage, and you have never seen a happier little dog. After looking at him and his cage, I suspected that he had spent five days locked up without any care. He was very dirty in an equally dirty cage and soon had the first of many baths in China.

After the reception, George and I had dinner at the home of

---

* Beijing was then still spelled Peking, but for the sake of consistency, except in diary entries, I'll call it Beijing.

John Holdridge, the deputy chief of mission, and his wife, Martha. They had an apartment in one of the buildings set aside for foreigners. Mr. Guo, our driver, honking the horn the whole way, wove through a crowded, poorly lit street, barely missing pedestrians and people on bicycles. George said to me, "You studied Chinese. For heaven's sake, tell him to put on his headlights. We're going to hit somebody." My two months of Chinese didn't teach me to say anything even close. We quickly told the Holdridges of our hair-raising drive, and they told us it was against the law to use headlights. Everyone in China drove with one hand on the horn and one foot on the brake.

John and Martha were real pros. I was so lucky to have this bright woman as a friend and a guide. They went on to a brilliant career with the State Department.

Our residence and George's office were inside the same, small compound. We had an apartment upstairs consisting of a large sitting room/dining room, four bedrooms, and two enormous baths. The toilets had "The Victory" written in English on their sides. The Chinese tend to name all their goods, but sometimes you wonder just how they think these names up.

The staff consisted of Mr. Yen, the head of our household; the number two, Mr. Chen; two ladies who did the dusting and ironing; and two cooks. Not one spoke a word of English. Thank heavens Mr. Yen was replaced by Mr. Wang after several weeks. He was a fine young man who spoke some English. He was also politically very correct— he always carefully touted the party line. The cooks were excellent, although the one who knew how to cook Western food didn't do it very well, so George and I ate Chinese food and loved it. The first time we ate in our upstairs dining room, we had a beautiful meal. I think the cooks were trying to please us and show off. At one point we were served some delicacy that almost did us in: rubbery, gray-looking things about two inches long with slippery-looking spikes all over them. George and I debated what to do with them. Should we eat them so that we wouldn't hurt their feelings? Should we flush them down the toilet when the cook was out of the room? After much discussion, George said that we better just leave them on our plates so they wouldn't think we liked them and serve them again. We later learned they were sea slugs, or sea cucumbers, and the Chinese believe they are a great treat. Whenever we had Chinese guests, our chef insisted we serve them. To add insult to injury, sea slugs cost $25 a pound. When we were served them at banquets, we bit the bullet and ate them.

Although we ate what seemed like a lot of food, we both lost weight. I believe that was because the Chinese eat a low-fat diet and no dairy products, which only made sense since they had no refrigerators or iceboxes. We did have delicious yogurt and fresh milk delivered to our residence daily. The yogurt came in blue Chinese jars, and the unhomogenized milk came in bottles just like we used to have in the United States in the 1920s and 1930s.

The household staff arrived at eight A.M. and left at four P.M., unless we had a party in the evening, and then they were paid overtime. The Chinese prided themselves—in fact, boasted—about having no unemployment. Judging from our household, we could see why. They had two or three people doing something one person could have done. As head of the household, only Mr. Wang had any incentive to work hard and see that the job was well done. The cooks worked hard, but only prepared one meal a day. The rest did the minimum. We heard story after story about three people vacuuming at the Peking Hotel: one to plug the machine in, one to turn it on, and one to push the darn thing. I know for a fact that when I went to the government bank to cash a check, two people made the calculation on abacuses. The result was passed on to two other people who counted out the money and passed it to me. And peering over all of this was a supervisor.

The household staff rode bikes to work from great distances and through all kinds of weather. Several days a week after work, they all had to attend block meetings where they heard "the party line."

The Chinese were bombarded with propaganda wherever they looked and wherever they went. There were billboards that sent some pretty strong and strange messages: DIG TUNNELS DEEP, STORE GRAIN EVERYWHERE AND NEVER SEEK HEGEMONY. Sometimes they said charming things: BEWARE OF THE IMPERIALIST DOGS WHO INVADED VIETNAM. Since George and I did not read Chinese, the signs looked rather pretty to us.

The propaganda continued on trains, parks, and often on the streets. A loud, shrill voice would come bellowing out of microphones placed high on light posts, exhorting people to work hard for the Chairman. The first week we were in Beijing we went to the Western Hills for a long walk with the Holdridges. When we were close to the top, the loudspeaker came on and really shocked us. You just can't get away from it. Evidently, a little boy quite far down the path felt the same way: He put his fingers in his ears.

It didn't take us long to fall into a routine. George, C. Fred, and I awakened at six o'clock or so. One of us walked the dog and picked up the yogurt. That was breakfast. We listened to the Voice of America, which drifted in and out, and sometimes BBC. That was the most frustrating experience. We would hear: "Today, tragedy hit . . . [fade out] . . . this well-known American was beloved by one and all." We would worry until George saw the cables, hoping it wasn't one of our friends. When something bad did happen, we would get phone calls. I especially remember when our former next-door neighbor and friend, Congressman Jerry Pettis, was killed in an airplane crash, and we felt bad for his wife, Shirley. And when a good friend of our children's, Lisa Rimmer, was killed in a car accident, how we ached for them. Those were the times when home seemed far, far away.

George walked over to the office around seven-thirty. He came home at eleven A.M. for our Chinese lesson with Mrs. Tang, whom we liked very much. Like so many Chinese, she had a warm personality and a good sense of humor. Half our lessons were spent laughing at each other's terrible accents and mistakes.

We had lunch right after our lesson, then George went back to the office. If we weren't going out to one of many marvelous restaurants, the cooks left our dinner in a thermos. We might have soup, hard-boiled eggs, and sliced bread. We would spend the evening reading unending books about the history of this massive country, or George would read cables from home.

Every night I set out about ten P.M. with C. Fred on a leash and walked around several large blocks. I was never afraid. We walked by the embassies of Cuba, North Vietnam, Romania, Great Britain, Egypt, and others. Incidentally, all of the embassies had People's Liberation Army guards outside their gates. Never in fourteen months did those bright-looking young men ever relax, smile, or speak to us. In fact, no one did. There was a constant swishing on the streets of the bicycles going silently by all night long. An occasional truck or car went by. There were absolutely no privately owned Chinese cars in the country when we lived there.

But we would get lots of looks—all at C. Fred. There were dogs in the country, but not many. In the 1950s, the Chinese had killed most of the dogs because they were considered scavengers and thieves, stealing food from the people. The Chinese especially had never seen a dog like C. Fred, who had beautiful blond curls. Sometimes we would hear them say something that sounded like "mao." We realized they thought poor C. Fred was a cat—an insult he found unbearable. I learned to say in Chinese: *"Ni bu pa. Ta shi shau go. Ta bu yau ren."* ("Don't be afraid. He's a little dog. He doesn't bite people.")

In the spring, we would see a lovely sight on our evening walks: young men and women standing close together in the park, sometimes holding hands. The need to have a little privacy must have been intense.

The first full day we were in China, George took me to the Friendship Store, where foreigners and high-ranking Chinese shopped. We bought two "Flying Pigeon" bicycles. As Beijing is flat as a pancake, it is the only way to go. I was also lucky enough to find a new friend named Lois Ruge, an American married to a German reporter. She not only played tennis, but had taught herself Chinese and knew Beijing like the back of her hand. We played tennis and explored the city on our bikes. She made my life so much happier. I would retrace our bike trips with George on his afternoons off. We would take our bikes to the Forbidden City or the old theater district to browse through shops or markets. We would park our bikes and some very old lady would give us two wooden tags with the same number. One went on the bike and one you kept. I often wondered as we rode along with hundreds of Chinese if we were the only people riding for fun. I'm sure they thought we were crazy.

One thing I noticed as I rode around Beijing: There weren't many white-headed people around. I asked the wonderful beauty parlor man if there was something in the water or diet that kept their hair from turning white. He laughed and told me there was "something in a bottle that kept them from going white." He went on to say that "one bottle serves all," meaning every head in China was black and there were lots of dyed heads around. That really surprised me, for this was in the days when everybody looked alike in baggy Mao suits. Thank heavens—they were human.

George rapidly found people to play tennis with and had games with the Chinese at the International Club. It was their job to play with us, and it was also a rare opportunity to mix with the Chinese. The ambassador from Canada played fairly well, but George was the best among the diplomats.

On Sundays, George and I attended church above the old Bible Society Building. We loved that dear church. There were only seven Chinese who attended, three of whom had been pastors in other Protestant churches in the old days before the Communist takeover. The service was held in Chinese, but we all had our own Bibles and could for the most part follow the service. I especially loved the hymns. We all shouted out our songs in our own language—French, English, and Chinese. With the exception of Easter, when the church was packed, we were a small army of Christian soldiers, maybe twenty on a good Sunday.

In the summer of 1975, Doro was christened in that little church in the most beautiful service. Due to deaths, politics, long distances, and floods (literally), her baptism had been put off four times. This was hard to explain to ourselves, much less the Chinese. So Doro became the first American to be baptized in China since 1949. Marvin stood in as a proxy for her godparents, Spike Heminway and Mildred Kerr.

We revisited our church on a trip back in 1989, when George was president. The congregation had moved into a big church and was crowded with Chinese people who even stood in the street. It was an emotional homecoming.

And as incredible as this would have seemed during our China days, our three ministers from that church visited us at the White House. We all certainly had come a long, long way.

One of the decisions George made soon after our arrival was that we should socialize with the Chinese as much as possible. Up until then it had been U.S. policy not to attend the various National Day receptions, since we did not have formal diplomatic relations. George disagreed, feeling that any contact we had with the Chinese—and representatives from Third World countries—was important. He felt we should not isolate ourselves. The first reception we attended was given by the Algerians in the old section of the Peking Hotel. We created quite a stir when we walked in.

To describe this reception is to describe them all. The reception had four waves. Wave number one was a group of sixteen chairs which remained unoccupied until the top Chinese guests appeared. The minute they did, our hosts stepped out of the receiving line and sat down in the chairs, alternating every other one with the eight Chinese. The most enormous amounts of food were served and consumed.

Wave number two consisted of diplomats and ambassadorial rank, and wave number three were diplomats of lesser rank (like us). Waves number two and number three watched the action of wave number one, with everyone analyzing how high the Algerians rated, based on the rank of the Chinese who had shown up. Wave number four was the most interesting. In marched a large group of Chinese who looked like a rent-a-crowd. In the back of the room were forty food-filled tables. The Chinese immediately surrounded the tables and did some serious eating. We tried to talk to them, but they did not come to talk. They came to eat.

Our receptions were not too much better. We gave many for visiting American delegations, and George worked out a system where the Americans came early so they could ask us questions and tell us a little about home. Then the Chinese would appear and it was business as usual.

We also gave many receptions for various Chinese groups who were headed for the United States. In our first month we had back-to-back receptions for the Chinese Plant Photosynthesis Study Group and the Pharmacological Theory Study Group of the Chinese Medical Association. If these men spoke English, I might have found it pretty heavy sledding. But since they didn't, you can imagine what fun it was.

How we loved our "responsible person," Mr. Wang. One evening after a deadly reception for two groups going to the United States—the Chinese Solid Physics Investigation Group and the Chinese Art Delegation—I spoke to Mr. Wang. First, I told him the food was beautifully presented. But didn't he think we had just a few too many canapés? The table had been loaded with food and, although our guests ate and ate, we had lots of food left over. Mr. Wang thought over my suggestion of "a few too many canapés" and came back with "No, I think we just had too few guests." I couldn't argue with that.

When we first got to China, our colleagues told George the Chinese accepted only one out of ten invitations. So George, the great entertainer, thought up a million reasons to invite them to the residence, so they actually ended up coming over quite a bit. Our diplomatic corps colleagues, not knowing George's trick, complained about the number of times we had the Chinese.

⌒ We barely had arrived in the country when it was time to get ready for a visit from Henry Kissinger. A trip by Henry Kissinger was a thing of wonder. He traveled with an enormous staff, and both he and they were very demanding. He is a brilliant man with a large self-proclaimed ego, and therefore one put up with some nonsense. He also was and is very entertaining and great fun to be around.

He came three times while we were in China. Later, when George visited foreign countries as the vice president or president, he kept the Kissinger demands in mind and tried to make it easy on our embassies.

On the first trip Henry brought not only Nancy, but also his two very attractive and bright children, David and Elizabeth. Nancy is a fascinating woman—such a series of contrasts. When we visited a hospital or commune, followed by her large press contingent, she certainly did not look the part in her long mink coat, glamorous hairstyle, constant cigarette smoking, and very bored look. When we got the inevitable lecture on productivity of the commune, always ending with the glories of Chairman Mao—the "line"—Nancy would look up and ask the most intelligent questions. She was clearly very interested and interesting.

During our commune visit we saw a dairy farm, and I was appalled to see their milk cows had horns. We city mice in Rye, New York, did not know our farmers dehorn their milk cows so they won't get hurt or hurt each other. I was really proud of Nancy, for while we were viewing the cows, with the TV cameras whirring away, we saw a number of them being mounted. Nancy never flicked an eyelash. That's savoir faire. We finally got to the last part of the briefing—the cows who were producing. The Chinese told us their cows were such good producers that they had to be milked three times a day. I have never seen such full bags. Several of the poor old girls were literally on their knees. I wouldn't put it above the Chinese to have put off milking those poor cows just to prove they had upped productivity. Every place we visited, whether it was the engine factory in Harbin, the Peking Duck farm outside Beijing, or the rug factory in Tientsin, they all had increased productivity thanks to the glorious leadership of Chairman Mao.

To our great pleasure, the Kissinger family joined us for Thanksgiving lunch. We had not been there long enough for a turkey to arrive, so we pretended the chicken course was a turkey. It was a happy lunch, even for C. Fred. For every five candied nuts Secretary Kissinger ate, he gave C. Fred one. George teased me about that, saying I would kill him if he did that. True. If poor C. Fred were here today, he would tell you he was always on a diet.

Several things happened during the Kissinger visit that confirmed our suspicions we were being spied on. Our first week there, I could tell that one of the household staff, because of the information he knew, had read a note on my desk from George. That did not worry me, but it helped me decide not to keep a diary. So for the fourteen months we lived there, I wrote long letters home to our families and several friends and sent them in the diplomatic pouch, being careful to never leave them sitting around. These letters were saved for me.

But during the Kissingers' stay, the spying was even more evident. Nancy told me she had said to Henry one afternoon in their room, "I wish the Chinese would let the children be in the car with us. It would be more relaxing, and we are not seeing them enough." When they went out for dinner that evening, the Chinese greeted them with: "We have put David and Elizabeth in the car with you. We thought you might enjoy that."

George and I also were staying in guest quarters near the Kissingers, to cut down on the commuting time. The thoughtful Chinese had supplied our rooms with absolutely everything a person could want: slippers, bathrobes, every kind of nail polish made in China, facial creams, perfume, toothbrush, toothpaste, face powders, and on and on. The tables were filled with cigarettes, matches, candies, nuts, fruits, postcards, writing paper, ink, and stamps. While waiting for the next event, I sat down to write some postcards. I mentioned the one thing they had forgotten was glue to affix the stamps to the cards. When we returned to our rooms after the event, there was the glue!

Another time, while riding my bike with Lois, I left my glasses in one of the many shops we had visited. I had no idea which one. My glasses were back at the residence before I was.

When the Kissingers went home, I left with them to be with our children for Christmas. Although this was planned for months, I was heartsick. I had never been so far away from George and could hardly stand saying good-bye to him. On the other hand, we both missed our children, and George could not leave the post so soon after arriving. So I went without him, spent a day or two in Washington, and then went to Houston to check on our newlyweds, Jeb and Columba. Friends called from all over, and many invited me out. I especially remember a lunch with Rogers Morton, the Secretary of the Interior, who invited me to have lunch in his private dining room. I thought he wanted to hear all about living in China. But he showed no interest and led the conversation toward politics. In the course of talking, it came out that George had written Rogers and asked him to please give me a call. He told him that we had never been apart for Christmas or for such a long time. It also turned out that George had written all those nice people who had invited me for meals, the theater, and so on. And here I thought I was incredibly popular!

George also had written our children: "Take care of your mother at Christmas. If she seems down once in a while, hold out your hand to her. Make her very happy . . ." There has never been a nicer, more thoughtful man.

Meanwhile, George's mother and his Aunt Margie Clement went to stay with him for Christmas. They had a wonderful visit and wowed everybody. Dotty Bush, at seventy-three, rode my Flying Pigeon all over Beijing. George took them on a trip south to Nanking, among other places.

When the children went back to school, I went back to China. We had our first of many, many houseguests, Neil and Anne Mallon. Everybody wanted to come to China. It was all so new and exciting. But in all honesty, it was easier to get a dog into the country than a person. One could come only if invited by the ambassador to stay in his residence. So from the Mallons on, we had wall-to-wall houseguests, and we loved it.

Back in the States, Don Rhodes helped people get their visas and arrange their trips. He must have told people we needed cheese and tennis balls. Well, that was true—but not for long. Soon, we were up to our elbows in both. It made us pretty popular with our diplomat friends from other countries who needed either or both.

There were certain things you had to show your houseguests, such as the wonderful Forbidden City. To do the city justice, you really needed several visits. I went so many times that I took to sitting on a wall in a lovely sunny spot and reading Chinese history or just people-watching while our guests toured. The Forbidden City has to be the most fascinating, most beautiful, and the largest museum in the exact middle of a city in the world. Once, when I told an exhausted guest that it covered 250 acres and included 9,000 rooms, I quickly added that all the rooms weren't open. I overheard her say to her husband, "Thank God, I thought she was going to make us walk through them all." My enthusiasm apparently had outlasted her feet.

The ceremonial palaces were spectacular. I found the little ones where the empresses and the concubines lived the most interesting. Some of them were filled with period furniture; others were little museums that housed jades, jewels, embroidered costumes, and porcelains. They also had marvelous gardens filled with tree peonies, lilacs, and fruit trees, depending on the season. The pomegranate plants in huge pots are a very clear memory.

But I especially remember the people. The Chinese walked around the Forbidden City staring not only at the signs but also at the Westerners—sometimes two feet from your face. There is no Sunday "day off" in China, so one-seventh of the people are off every day, walking through the parks and, for a few pennies, around the Forbidden City or the Temple of Heaven.

Another great favorite and a must-see was the beautiful Summer Palace. It was about twenty minutes out of the city, close to the Western Hills. In the winter the lake froze, and people ice-skated.

And, of course, there was the Great Wall of China, which was about forty minutes out of town. Our favorite thing to do was to go to the Great Wall and stop on our way home for a picnic at the Ming Tombs. I loved this, for we could take Freddy with us. He would sit in the car with Mr. Guo while we charged up the Wall. It was quite a hike and sometimes scary as the angles are so steep. Our guests usually went up the left side, which was steeper, but gave a much better view. The wall is about sixteen feet across with a four-foot stone wall on each side. There are stopping places along the way where you can get some great pictures. The guests I remember with the greatest affection were those who did not carry too much luggage in the way of cameras and other equipment. I remember one houseguest who insisted on wearing high heels up the Great Wall as I was to take their Christmas picture at the top. George and I were fairly amused to see when their card arrived I had cut the picture off at her knees—not on purpose.

How I loved the tombs. With Freddy on a long leash, we would walk by the famous Avenue of the Animals—glorious statues of huge animals, seated and standing, and wise men or guardians who lined the road. This was a great "photo op" for our guests. We'd climb back into the car and drive to the only tomb that had been excavated, the Ding Ling. (Honest, that is what it was called. *Ling* means "tomb" in Chinese.) That was where all the tourists went. First we would explore this wonderful tomb, visit the museum, and see the artifacts buried with the emperor. Next, we would go off to one of the other twelve tombs that had not been touched. Many times broken pieces of tile from a fallen altar or the tomb would just be lying around on the ground. One of our more famous houseguests went out to the tombs and brought back some large pieces of the tile. This was reported to me, and I hardly knew what to do. So at lunch, I made up an awful story of the British houseguest who was stopped at the airport for trying to carry out some antiquities—to be exact, pieces of a monument. I went into detail of how embarrassing this had been and just how long the Chinese had detained him. After the guest left, we found a bag of the yellow tiles in the guest room, and I sneaked them back to the tombs.

All our guests wanted to visit schools, communes, and one of the beautiful areas of China outside Beijing. Some got to go, and some didn't. We had a twenty-mile limit as to where we could travel without permission, and sometimes I think the Chinese decided who could travel and who couldn't on a whim.

Even the Chinese could not travel without passes, and there were checkpoints at every village. That's how you controlled 800 million people. (Today, their population is estimated at 1.2 billion.) They were taking no chances after the violence and upheaval of the Cultural Revolution.

Pat Moynihan and two of his children came to visit on his way home from his ambassador's post in India. Pat is a fascinating man and very good company. One afternoon, George invited our little embassy family to come hear Pat tell us about India. I remember two things about his talk. He spoke exactly fifty-five minutes, the length of a college class, and he felt very strongly our foreign policy was ignoring India and that was a mistake.

One morning during Pat's stay we went to visit a Revolutionary Street Committee. Among the many things we did there was visit a home where there was a young teenage girl about Maura Moynihan's age. The two girls quickly got to be friends and ended up holding hands as they sat side by side on the bed. They did not speak the same language, but they certainly communicated. They examined each other's clothes and discovered they had the same socks. They giggled over the bulge under the Chinese girl's socks—long winter underwear. It looked home-made and very warm. On looking around, I found that everyone had a bulge under their socks. No wonder I was freezing. The two girls from such different backgrounds sitting there holding hands was very sweet.

We also visited a schoolroom that day. Quoting from a letter written home:

> We visited a nursery where there were children up to the age of 3. The room was divided in half. One half was a raised platform covered with a blanket and had a railing to keep the babies from falling—rather like a giant playpen. Tucked in that nursery were about 20 babies and three old crones, probably my age. The other part of the room had a few baby cribs with sleeping babies, or babies nursing on mothers who had rushed in from the fields. When we walked in, several of the older babies were standing at the railing and applauded. To save time, let me just say that we were applauded over and over again.
>
> We went on to a kindergarten where about 35 children, age 3 to 5, were sitting in the barest room on three crude long benches about 6 inches from the ground. There were two young teachers and absolutely no teaching props. Up they jumped, applauded, and then a tiny little thing with her hair in two black pony tails said something like our "a one and a two" and all 35 belted out a song that would have done Judy Garland proud . . . when she was 16! You have never seen anything like it. Then the little leader sang an unending song about a happy little worker and the glories of the Chairman, and we were dragged away from those lovely looking children. Their teeth are good, their smiles broad. You can't fake that.

We visited several more classes that morning and it was more of the same. The art class was made up of 40 little fourth-graders copying line for line a picture drawn on the blackboard of a happy little worker tilling the fields for Chairman Mao.

When we got home Pat Moynihan said the school visit depressed and frightened him.

It was a depressing morning, but old China hands will tell you that these same children would not have even been in school 25 years ago.

At Easter, our dear friends John and Betty Rhodes—John was Minority Leader in the House—came on a trip with the Leader of the House, Carl Albert, and his wife, Mary. It's no secret Carl had a drinking problem in those days, which I understand he overcame. More power to him. At a banquet for him and his party, Carl argued with the Chinese and was really insulting. At one time during the evening he was told he would meet the next day with the foreign minister. This was not a high-enough ranking official for Carl, and he explained to the Chinese that the whole U.S. government was controlled by the Congress and that made him one of the most important men in the country. What a frightening thought! He went on to say that he should be seeing some "big" Chinese leaders. (I guess they believed him: He saw Vice Premier Deng Xiaoping the next day.) As the toasts went on, his mood shifted and he was soon ignoring the high-ranking Chinese and flirting outrageously with Nancy Tang, the charismatic interpreter who became well known during the Nixon visit. You could tell she was very embarrassed. (Having said that, I should say that Carl and Mary are dear friends, and Carl subsequently overcame his drinking problem. He served his country with great distinction, and we respect him very much.)

Both couples stayed in the former Indian Embassy in the old Legation Quarters, which the Chinese had reclaimed and turned into offices or guest houses. Looking at old maps of the city, it was easy to see why these places had irritated the Chinese. The foreign community had made its own rules and acted as though the natives were visitors, keeping them out of large sections of the city. That probably explains why when we lived there, the foreign embassies were surrounded by

Chinese apartments and hovels. Yet, the Chinese were careful to never let us know where they lived or let our children play together.

∽ Weather-wise, we thought we were the best prepared people to live in Beijing. It is hot and humid in the summer—the so-called rainy season—and cold and dry and dusty in the winter and spring. It sounded very much like Houston and Midland to me. But then spring arrived and I realized even I wasn't prepared for this. The Chinese pulled out all their grass to keep down the insect population. But it also created a big dust problem. Then you add a cold wind from the Gobi Desert, and you are talking dust storms beyond anything Midland ever dreamed about. It was really bad. We could not keep clean, and poor old golden Freddy became a gray dog. He had more baths than any dog ever had to suffer, but he was our bedmate and we had to draw the line someplace.

Shortly after Easter we went to Canton to visit the Trade Fair and then went on into Hong Kong. It was exactly like going from a black-and-white movie into Technicolor. We returned to China on the famous train that drops you at the bridge at the border. You detrain, walk across the bridge, go through a checkpoint, and climb on the next train. For years this was the only way you could enter Red China, and it was dramatic. As we were crossing into the People's Republic, we could hear singing voices and, "just by chance," there was China's greatest asset: schoolchildren marching home for lunch being led by a child carrying a red banner. They all belted out a welcoming song. A lot of poverty and broken windows were disguised by these precious little children.

Both trains were comfortable, and the roadbeds very smooth. But the bathrooms on both cars were beyond belief. Really bad. All through the station we were followed by the loud singing and music of the revolutionary opera at a very high pitch. Much to everybody's horror, it was piped into the train as well. The next hour and a half was spent viewing the most beautiful truck gardens, rice paddies, tree-planting and irrigation projects, and spotless little compounds. I was a little cynical as everyone we saw was really hustling. This was just not true elsewhere. As there were only two trains a day coming from the border, I wondered if the Chinese didn't pick up the pace just a little around train time.

Marvin was going to graduate from high school that spring, and as the date drew nearer, I got bluer. Marv understood it was a long way, and he and his brothers and sister were coming to China in June. Yet, George and I were having a problem with letting him graduate without one of us being there. I can't tell you how happy I was when George said I must go home for a week and surprise him. Don Rhodes told Marvin to go to the airport to meet a good friend of ours. I walked right by both him and Neil, who were scanning faces for our friend. Suddenly I heard, "Mom, what are you doing here!?"

The children and I left for China about the same time, but I flew back as I came, and they took the slow route: first to Houston to see Jeb and Colu, and then on to Hawaii for a day or two, then finally Beijing.

We had a great time exploring China together. We all had bikes. The children thought the public baths smelled and that some of the food was "gross." I'm afraid I had romanticized just a little. I especially remember one day when we rode our bikes through a commune, on our way to the Summer Palace. Those loudspeakers were blasting away at the happy little workers in the fields. George drove out to meet us and treated us to the best lunch at "The Pavilion for Listening to Orioles." Either the eighteen-mile ride out had gotten to Doro or she just wanted her father to herself, for she tucked her bike in the trunk of his car and rode back to town with him.

One evening we drove out to the Ming Tombs and had a picnic at the Mao Ling, a lovely old fallen-down tomb. The diplomatic choral group sang before and after dinner to about one hundred friends tucked here and there among the ruins. It was lovely as the sun set, with the Ming Temple set back among the pines. A dear young Mexican couple ended the evening by singing some plaintive Mexican songs, and we all hummed along. It was our nicest evening in China, I believe.

George took us all to Beidaihe (spelled Pietaiho then), a large seaside resort that grew up at the turn of the century for the missionaries and Western diplomats. It is on the Bo Hai Sea, just southwest of Qinhuangdao, a large seaport. We were given villa number 12, which turned out to have four bedrooms and four clean baths, which is not a given in China. The cottage had a large veranda, and a lot of time was spent reading in the lovely wicker furniture for which the town is famous.

George had brought several Frisbees with him, and we all threw them on the beach. The Chinese gathered to watch this and got as close as they could, but would not enter in. So sad.

We had a very nice young man assigned to our house who, we discovered the hard way, slept two feet from our bedroom and bath. We literally could hear him breathing. He also practiced the violin in the bathroom, which had a nice, close, damp quality to it. I think several ladies slept off our courtyard. I saw them several times shoveling coal into a furnace that George thought heated our water.

About fifty feet from our house, between us and the sea, was a twenty-four-hour manned guardhouse. We were ever conscious of being observed. The question was: Are we being guarded or watched?

Young George ran for miles every day until he came to signs that said: NO LOITERERS BEYOND THIS POINT. This translated meant: "This is the beach for our foreign friends" or "No Chinese allowed." The diplomatic world hates being segregated. It's so odd: Before the Communist takeover, the Chinese were not allowed on the beach by the foreigners, and in the 1970s they didn't allow the foreigners to mix with them. Therefore, we are still segregated. We have been told that Beidaihe is now used by the Chinese as a rest place for workers and many of the villas are now owned by factories and communes.

We also took the children to see where the Great Wall rises out of the sea and starts its meandering trip across the north of China for 2,000-plus miles.

On the third of July, we had the usual agonizing reception: Guests stood around until the Chinese arrived and sat in the only chairs and ate; our top-ranking staff talked to theirs; and their rent-a-crowd ate us out of house and home. On the actual Fourth of July, we all were up early, decorating the whole liaison office with red, white, and blue bunting and paper streamers. It was the hottest day, and all day long a storm threatened, but it held off. George had all four Bush children out working, along with the Thayer children. By this time, Harry Thayer, who had worked with George at the United Nations, had replaced John Holdridge as deputy chief of mission at the liaison office. Those great kids manned the hot dog and hamburger stands in the most unbearable heat, and the diplomats came en masse, along with the Chinese, for great American food and fun. George had spent months getting all the right ingredients together for this big day and it was a smashing success. The next morning, the same little army of "volunteers" came back as the cleanup squad.

* * *

◠ Traveling through China was always an adventure. The children and I took off late on the fifth of July for a trip to Nanking, Wuxi, and Shanghai. It was a hot, sweaty but wonderful trip. We visited all the usual things and laughed our way through these marvelous historic cities. We discovered that our Chinese guides usually knew much less of their history than we did. We also discovered that Beijing was China's window to the world, and the quality of life goes downhill outside the capital city.

The Chinese say "Women hold up half of the world." That means that women are equal. I would say their women were equal to men on the ditchdigger level. In 1975 you saw many women laying pipes, sweeping the streets—in fact, doing heavy work. But how many women did you see ruling the country? None. Well, maybe one. Chairman Mao's wife, Jiang Qing, was said to wield great power at this time.

Family planning in the cities was fairly successful, but less so in the countryside. We were told at a commune that they gave incentives for male and female sterilizations. A woman was offered forty days with pay and extra rice and brown sugar rations. A man was offered fifteen days with pay and no extra rations. You can imagine the family pressure on the woman to have the more serious operation.

George and I and a houseguest, Greg Petersmeyer, who later did a wonderful job heading the Points of Light Foundation for George, and dear Bill Thomas, our economic officer, took a great trip as guests of the Chinese to Dalien, Harbin, and Daqing. The Chinese had created Daqing by arbitrarily picking up people—some with their families and some without—and putting them down in this godforsaken, brutally cold place. The residents told us they could see their families two weeks out of the year.

Our friend Jack Steel from Houston, Bill Thomas's wife, Sarah, and I took a trip to Datong on the northern border and visited the caves and tunnels where they stored grain. This pathetic little underground city would not have withstood a conventional bombing, much less missiles. We went by train and slept together in a tiny compartment. We panicked that a fourth would be put in the car with us, but it didn't happen.

I took another train trip, to Loyang and Sian, with two women who worked in the liaison office. There in Sian, by the old Bell Tower, we saw miles of eighteen-year-olds being lined up to "go to the countryside." We asked our interpreter if they looked forward to that. He said no. They knew they had to go and they also knew most of them would spend the rest of their lives there. They could come back only if they were voted back by their peers—whatever that means.

Out the window of our train we saw carts being pulled by camels, donkeys, oxen, and people. We saw people riding their bikes with terrified, wiggling little pigs tied to the sides—shades of "this little pig went to market . . ."

It was interesting to see how everyone's impressions of China were so different. In May 1975 we had two couples visiting at the same time. One morning, one of the women said to me: "Bar, you know the thing that I notice in China? I don't see the children playing. They seem so sad to me." That very afternoon, the other wife and I were walking home when she said, "Do you know what I find so surprising about China? I didn't expect to see such happy children!" These two ladies saw the exact same places, but through different eyes. Remember that my memories of China are through my eyes.

⌒ In October, George and I took part in one of China's big national celebrations—Liberation Day. (The other big day there is May Day.) Here are parts of a letter written to the children on October 2, 1975:

> Another exciting day or two in our life in the PRC, the 26th Anniversary of the Liberation. For days we have seen activity in the parks. The Temple of Heaven has been closed. Disappointing for our latest houseguests. Our celebration started with an invitation from Chou En-lai to a banquet on September 30th. As we do not attend the banquets for visiting heads of state as our colleagues do on a weekly basis—a welcoming banquet and a farewell banquet—we were really looking forward to the evening. Our buddies dread them for they have little notice and are expected to cancel any other plans, and also because they are seated by protocol and sit with the same people week after week, whether they speak diplomatically or personally or not, and because the speeches are long and very often dull.

We were told to leave a little ahead of time, for on this evening the crowds would be large. George's driver has to be a genius. He maneuvered us through more cars, more people on bikes, more standing pedestrians, more buses than we had seen in our whole stay in the PRC. By the end of our drive we were driving through a human tunnel. We could hear people saying *"Meiguo Ren,"* meaning Americans. We saw nothing but warm, friendly faces or faces filled with curiosity. Thank heavens that we feel absolutely no fear and have no reason to.

How to describe the city? Oh to be a writer, for it was lovely. As we passed the Friendship Store, the International Club and the tall apartments built for foreigners, we got our first hint. The buildings were outlined from head to toe, from stem to stern, and balconies in-between, with white light bulbs. As Peking is a flat city, these buildings can be seen for miles. The Railroad Station was particularly spectacular as it has twin pagoda-like towers. A plain square building becomes a thing of splendor when draped in white lights. Some of the buildings had gentle swags, some designs around the roof line and some red stars. The Peking Hotel, for instance, went from three rather different, rather ugly sections (one section built by the Russians, one by the French, and finally a tall new Chinese section) to a fairyland building with the two outside sections outlined, and the French middle section covered with swags and designs. It was lovely.

To understand the scope of what we are talking about in Peking, one must know that Tiananmen Square is 98 acres big. On the north, outlined and lighted, is the Gate of Heavenly Peace that leads into the Imperial City and on into the Forbidden City. Chairman Mao's tremendous picture dominates this gate. On the south can be seen the southern gate that is all that is left of the Tartar Wall, a tremendous building that is four or five stories high. It has a lovely roof line. Also on the south is the Marco Polo Shop and several other buildings, all with the bright white light outline. On the east is the National Museum, which has not been opened since we have been here. On the west is the Great Hall of the People, where we had our banquet. I believe that all the street lights were on when usually only two of three layers are on. The first is a big globe; the second has five globes; and the third—the one they use on special days—has nine globes. Also, there were large characters in red lights. As we can't read Chinese, these look very beautiful, such lovely shapes and all. The five big, and I do mean big, pictures on Tiananmen Square are Chairman Mao facing south, and Lenin, Stalin, Marx and Engels, two on the left and two on the right, facing north. For these few days only, a sixth big picture is put up right in the middle of the southern part of the square, that of Sun Yat-Sen. If this year is like past years, he will disappear in a few days. I still can't understand the great love for him, even though he was the first president of the republic. But he also was the man who tapped Chiang Kai-shek (who opposed the Communist takeover of China) to succeed him.

On to the banquet . . . 4,500 people. There were some tourist delegations in the darndest outfits. Of course some were fine, but some were outrageous. Just because the Chinese aren't dressy does not mean that they aren't the neatest, cleanest people you have ever seen. I was thrilled to hear people in front of us speak French. What a relief. They had on filthy, frayed clothes, tangled hair, tight pants over female rumps, run-down heels on their shoes, dirty toenails showing through their sandals, etc.

Every inch of the room was taken up. There were two orchestras in the balcony instead of the back of the room. We were about three-fourths of the way back and therefore could not see the Head Table guests, as it was not raised. The betting was that the Premier would not attend and he didn't. Deng Xiaoping was the top ranking man. Prince Sihanouk and wife, as visiting Head of State from Cambodia, were the guests of honor.

The room itself cannot be described. It is really tremendous, has spectacular lighting, including TV lights that look like part of the wall decoration when turned off.

I counted 27 chandeliers on the three balconies, 90 lights that were three feet across in the three sections of the room under the balconies, and heaven only knows the number of lights in the main center section. The room must be four stories high.

The National Day was a joy. Very much a repeat of May Day. It did seem to me that there were more exhibits, more decorations, many more of the masses let in. We had tickets allowing us to go into eight parks. As I understand it, the Chinese needed tickets to get into a park and certainly we saw many people standing outside the parks watching the foreign guests go in. We went to the Summer Palace in the morning.

We got home at 1 p.m., picked up our lunch, had a quick nap and then rode our bikes down to the parks on either side of the Forbidden City. Many children dancing, acrobats, magicians, stand-up comics, adult ballet and opera singers, plus exhibits galore. We wandered around and made the mistake of staying until 6 p.m. when it suddenly ended. We were two of hundreds of thousands who rode our bikes home. It is quite a sensation to find yourself riding 10, 20 and 30 abreast like that. The worst place is at the street lights. Those little Chinese ladies who ride on men's bikes have trouble getting on and off at the stop. Their feet do not touch and so they fall off and swing on in a very set fashion. We were too tired to ride to the Workers Stadium for more acrobatics last night and that really is sort of dangerous at night in a crowd that size.

All summer long we had seen sunflowers growing on every available inch of space around the hovels and homes. Fall was the season when their heads were cut off and they were put out to dry for the oil from the seed or just for the seeds themselves. They were dried on rooftops, and it looked like a van Gogh painting. It was also the season of harvesting that long, wonderful Chinese cabbage. For a few weeks in the fall, the streets were packed with mule- and horse-pulled wagons, three-wheeled bikes with a platform on the back, hand-pushed wheelbarrows and trucks, all coming in from the countryside filled with cabbage. It was then piled high on the streets before being toted to the different homes, often to be dried on roofs or on a small apartment balcony to be used during the cold winter months. I wondered how much soot and dust there are along with it.

The pomegranates were on the enormous potted plants in the Forbidden City and the persimmons were ripe at the Temple of Heaven. And the leaves were turning red at the Western Hills. There was a sign that said: DO NOT PICK THE RED LEAVES. And the Chinese came down the hill with their arms filled with red leaves.

On November 2, George got a "for eyes only" cable asking him to come home and head the CIA. We were riding our bikes home from church when he was notified. What a shock. The CIA! What would our high school and college-age children think? At that time, the CIA was going through a very unpopular period and was highly criticized for abusing its power. We talked it over at length and then decided to call our oldest son, George, and ask him to feel out his brothers and sister very discreetly. He called back and said, "Come home." I often have wondered if George really asked for their opinions or if he just waited a reasonable period of time and called back with his opinion. Let me add that George Bush, the dad, was thrilled. He had the utmost respect for the CIA and the men and women who served so valiantly there. I was torn. I missed the children and home very much, but I was enjoying our China experience. However, I knew it was always smart to leave a place while still wanting to stay.

Before heading home, we had President Ford's visit on our plate. That meant an enormous advance team came for Thanksgiving, which was fun. The trip itself went well, mainly because the Fords are such nice, generous, easy people. The logistics were fascinating, for the President had agents, Betty Ford had agents, Susan Ford had agents, and Henry Kissinger had security. The motorcades often came from different directions and caused traffic jams beyond belief.

Another thing I remember from their visit was how rude our press was to the Chinese. Mrs. Ford and I, accompanied by several high-ranking Chinese women, visited the Forbidden City. The American press pushed and shoved, trying to get at Mrs. Ford. They especially pushed the Chinese out of the way, not realizing their rank since everyone in China dressed alike, regardless of who they were. I was embarrassed.

There were many going-away parties before we left. Because of the isolation from the outside world, there was a special bond among the foreigners who lived in China during that period. I especially remember the Russian ambassador teasing George about his new "spy" job. You're tempted to think of that childish taunt "It takes one to know one!"

On December 10, we left this fabulous, fascinating country with few regrets. We had been privileged to live there, and now we were looking forward to home, a new job, friends, and especially our precious families.

Keeping Secrets

Dear Pres, Buck, Nancy, John,

Pardon the joint message. It occurs to me that my controversial new job may cause concern—if not to you, to some of your kids. No I can't see (5-year old) Billy bitching about the CIA to his peers, but for the older ones, it might not be easy.

I did not seek this controversial job. It came to me— one week ago—short fuse reply.

It's a graveyard for politics, and it is perhaps the toughest job in government right now due to abuses of the past on the one hand, and an effort to weaken our capability on the other. Besides, it's not always a clean and lovely business.

I am convinced it is important.

I know we will be thrust into ugly controversy—my intentions and character will be questioned.

But overriding all this is what I perceive to be a fundamental need for an intelligence capability second to none. It's a tough, mean world and we must stay strong. My year here has given me a chance to think and to observe. We have got to stay strong.

When the cable came in I thought of "Big Dad"—

what would he do, what would he tell his kids—I think
he would have said, "It's your duty."
    It is my duty and I'll do it.
    I love you all.

Pop

George wrote this letter to his four siblings from China, explaining how he felt about his new job. As you can see, he expected tough times ahead.

We hadn't been home one week when the Senate confirmation hearings began on George's appointment. I sat and listened and of course was furious at anyone who spoke against him. The final witness was a young man who was a member of the Socialist Workers' Party. The TV lights were turned off, and Senator John Stennis of Mississippi was the only member of the committee who sat through the testimony. In fact, the only people in the room were me, Senator Stennis, George, the witness, and some TV technicians. The young man was against George, and I fumed as I listened to his untrue and irresponsible accusations. Then suddenly I found myself thinking: What a great country we live in. Here is a United States senator giving this man a chance to say exactly what is on his mind. This couldn't happen in China.

During the debate on the Senate floor, Senator Frank Church led the attack against George (really against the CIA); and Texas Senator John Tower led the charge in his favor. Our friends Bill and Janet Steiger went with me to watch the vote. I hated it as "Nay" after "Nay" resounded across the floor. The minute enough votes were cast to confirm George, John Tower turned and gave me a thumbs-up. And a minute later my friend and fellow International Club II member Bethine Church rushed over, gave me a hug, and said that she wanted me to know Frank did not mean it personally. I don't think the average American understands that in Washington you can be friends with your political opponents. Bethine and I remained close, even when she moved back to Idaho after Frank's death.

George was to replace William Colby, who had been a controversial director. However, he and his wife, Barbara, could not have been nicer and even gave us a dinner party before George took over. On January 10, 1976, our much beloved friend and neighbor, Potter Stewart, once again swore George into a new job, this time with President

Ford looking on. George also was very pleased that his former boss on the Ways and Means Committee, Wilbur Mills, and his wife, Polly, attended. They had been through their own personal hell, and George insisted they be invited.

The news coverage was something else: *The Washington Post* ran a front-page, above-the-fold picture of me kissing Jerry Ford; *The New York Times* ran a front-page, above-the-fold picture of me kissing Potter. For months, every time I saw Potter, he sang "I Wonder Who's Kissing Her Now?"

George was thrilled with his new job, despite the fact that the CIA was under fire and morale within "the community" was at an all-time low. There also was a great deal of fear. Richard Welch, the CIA station chief in Greece, had just been assassinated on the front steps of his house. This gentle Greek scholar's cover had been blown, along with many others', by a traitorous, tell-all book written by former CIA agent Philip Agee.

George and I went on a morale-boosting trip to Europe shortly after his confirmation, and security was unbelievably tight. We traveled commercially with an assumed name—I believe we were the "Rushes." When we landed in Munich, Germany, we disembarked before the plane taxied into a ramp and were immediately put into cars and driven to the hotel, skipping Customs. It amused me that after all this secrecy, as we marched into the lobby, we heard loud and clear bellowing across the lobby: "It's the Bushes! Hello there, George Bush." It was Sir George Weidenfeld, a British publisher and the husband of our friend Sandra Payson. So much for all that subterfuge.

Several times we stayed in the private homes of CIA employees because the security was better. Because of Agee's book, the houses had to be heavily guarded. I came to love these courageous people and their brave families, and George came to believe that CIA employees were the most dedicated and brightest in the government. Their main job was to collect information, evaluate it, and pass it on. They certainly did not do all the things you see in cloak-and-dagger spy movies.

Back home, I threw myself into life in Washington. I resumed my volunteer work at the Washington Home, a nursing home where I had worked previously, and especially enjoyed getting to spend time again with my dear little friend Frances Hammond. She had broken her body in a dive into a swimming pool many years before, leaving her a paraplegic, and although every inch of her hurt, she never ever complained. She thought only of others and was an inspiration in courage.

Her one relative was a son who had gone to the Naval Academy and was stationed quite far away. I often took C. Fred to sit on the terrace with Frances. All of the residents loved Freddy. We forget that people in homes miss children and animals, and I'm so glad many institutions today have "pet" days. Anyway, I used to do Frances's fingernails and we'd sit and visit. She had many other friends, but none who loved her more. She remained an important part of my life until she died in November 1983.

I also put together a slide program on China and traveled around the country showing it to civic groups, schools, and churches; at fund-raisers for different charities; and at political gatherings. China was still a "hot" item. I tried to have a fast-moving program with *no* pictures of George, me, the children, or even C. Fred. I wanted to be completely nonpartisan so civic groups would feel comfortable inviting me to speak.

I rejoined my International Club, met with our 90th Club congressional friends, played tennis, entertained many, many houseguests, and kept very busy. Although the children were scattered at various schools and jobs, they came home often to visit.

Yet, I was very depressed, lonely, and unhappy.

It still is not easy to talk about today, and I certainly didn't talk about it then. I felt ashamed. I had a husband whom I adored, the world's greatest children, more friends than I could see—and I was severely depressed. I hid it from everyone, including my closest friends. Everyone but George Bush. He would suggest that I get professional help, and that sent me into deeper gloom. He was working such incredibly long hours at his job, and I swore to myself I would not burden him. Then he would come home, and I would tell him all about it. Night after night George held me weeping in his arms while I tried to explain my feelings. I almost wonder why he didn't leave me. Sometimes the pain was so great, I felt the urge to drive into a tree or an oncoming car. When that happened, I would pull over to the side of the road until I felt okay.

Years later, I did tell my doctor, and he asked why I hadn't sought help. He said that there are several treatments for people with problems like that—in many cases quite easy ones—and it could have been caused by a chemical imbalance.

It seems so simple to me now: I was just the right age, fifty-one years old, for menopause; I could not share in George's job after years of being so involved; and our children were all gone. I was a classic case for depression. My "code" told me that you should not think about self, but others. And yet, there I was, wallowing in self-pity. I knew it was wrong, but couldn't seem to pull out of it. I wish I could pinpoint the day it went away, but I can't. All I know is that after about six months, it just did. I was so lucky.

But I do not consider those miserable six months lost or wasted; I became much more sympathetic of people with emotional problems. I used to think that you could control your emotions, that you just needed to think of others and not yourself. I still think that is one of the secrets to happiness, but I also realize you cannot handle everything alone. And when things go out of control, you should seek help. Certainly if I could do it over again, I would.

While all of this was going on, the 1976 primary season was swirling around us. We were completely out of it, since George's job was not political. I wrote in my diary that spring:

The primaries seem insane at times. The words get so mean and bitter. Then I say to myself, Don't ever complain about a free election. This couldn't happen in China.

On February 24, I wrote in a letter to Mrs. John Sherman Cooper, wife of our ambassador to East Germany:

The Democrats are having a fascinating political season. I wish you could have heard them this morning, the morning after (the New Hampshire Primary), on the tube. (Jimmy) Carter, having come in first, was "elated." (Mo) Udall, having come in second, was "ecstatic." (Birch) Bayh, who came in third, was "joyful." (Fred) Harris, who came in fourth, "couldn't believe the friends he had made." And lastly, Sarge (Shriver) was "overcome by the good feeling he had gotten from all the good people in New Hampshire."

Jerry Ford had his own tough fight with Ronald Reagan in the primaries, and although he won the GOP nomination, he lost in

Life has barely begun, age one. (Family photo)

I guess they forgot to tell us to smile. I'm the chubby little girl standing in the middle, with the Peter Pan collar. (Family photo)

One of my favorite pastimes—eating. I'm at the far left, with Susan Kennedy, Wease McDowell, and Shirley Ayres.

One of the first dogs in my life, Sandy. My mother sent George a copy of this photo when he was in the Navy. (Family photo)

Playacting with friends Posy Morgan and Kate Siedle. I'm on the far left. (Family photo)

With Father and Mother on
my wedding day, January 6,
1945. (Family photo)

The bride and groom.
(Family photo)

With Yale housemates Jack and
Patsy Caulkins and David Grimes.
Patsy's chocolate chip cookie recipe
was destined to become famous.
(Family photo)

Easter 1948 with my family. Standing
behind the couch are my brothers Jim
and Scott. Sitting on the couch are,
from left, George, me holding George
W., Mother, Daddy, my sister Martha,
and her husband, Walt Rafferty, with
their daughter, Sharon. (Family photo)

This was taken not too long
after we moved to Midland,
Texas. (Family photo)

Holding Robin with George W.,
October 1950. (Family photo)

Robin with her daddy,
1953. (Family photo)

Playing golf with the world's best
in-laws, Dorothy and Prescott Bush.
(Family photo)

George in his very first political campaign, the 1964 Texas Senate race. With him is our good friend Will Farish. (Family photo)

The boys think they're being funny, imitating their father on the campaign trail, 1966. From left: Doro, George, Jeb, Marvin, George W., Neil, and me. (Family photo)

The Ambassador to the
United Nations and Mrs.
Bush. (Family photo)

The Great Wall of
China. (Family photo)

In Tibet in the fall
of 1977, drinking
the horrid tea.
I love the child
peering at us from
behind the quilt.
(Family photo)

Welcoming the hostages home from Iran, January 27, 1981.
Tip O'Neill is on the far right. (White House photo)

Something
certainly has Lady
Bird Johnson
and me tickled,
September 1981.
(White House
photo)

Our dinner with the Ceauşescus in Romania, September 1983. Not exactly what you would call a cozy evening. (White House photo)

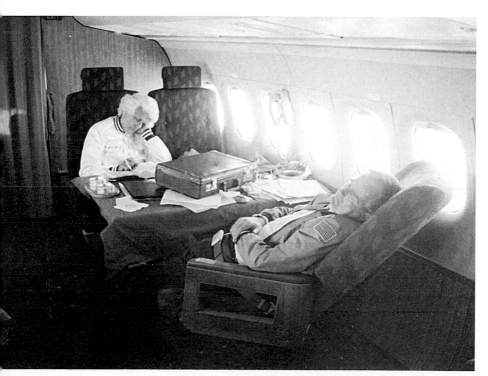

Sneaking in a nap during the 1984 campaign. (White House photo)

Doing a little garden work in Kennebunkport while taking a break from the 1988 campaign. (David Valdez)

The Reagans meet our grandchildren George P., Noelle, and Jebby as they leave the 1988 Republican National Convention and we arrive. (White House photo)

Addressing the 1988 Republican Convention. (White House photo)

Kicking off the inauguration festivities with the Quayles. (White House photo)

Granddaughter Barbara Bush shares a secret during the inaugural gala,
while twin sister, Jenna, and Gampy watch. (David Valdez)

I get the first kiss from the new President of the United States. (Susan Biddle)

Walking the parade route. You can tell it was cold and windy. (David Valdez)

Would you have guessed the shoes underneath cost $29? (Mike Sargent)

Everybody wanted their picture taken on the Lincoln bed. Here George does the honors for then Congressman Edward Madigan of Illinois and his wife, Evelyn. He later became secretary of agriculture. (Mike Sargent)

Holding an AIDS patient at Grandma's House in Washington, D.C., March 1989. Looking on are the heart and soul of Grandma's House, Joan McCarley and Debbie Tate. The baby died a few weeks later. (Carol Powers)

Watching the
President give a
press conference from
the Ushers' Office in
the White House.
(Carol Powers)

I was thrilled to be honored
along with George and
(not pictured) President
François Mitterrand and
Chancellor Helmut Kohl
at Boston University's
commencement in 1989.
(Carol Powers)

The Harlem Boys
Choir lights up
the East Room.
Betty Ford is
sitting behind me.
(Carol Powers)

One of my best friends, Andy Stewart. What you don't see are all the people gathered for her surprise birthday party on May 9, 1989. (Carol Powers)

Doing a little play-by-play during a Texas Rangers baseball game. (Carol Powers)

Millie and the children
on the South Lawn
of the White House.
(Mike Sargent)

George and Ranger
bonded early on.
(Carol Powers)

November to Jimmy Carter. A day or two after the election, George said that I better head down to Houston and house-hunt yet again. Typical George; he already had invited guests to a home that didn't exist! The recently widowed King Hussein of Jordan was going to be in Houston for his annual physical in March, and he had accepted George's invitation to dinner.

I looked at about thirty houses and fell in love with one on Indian Trail. George flew down with me on the first of January to sign the papers—*then* he went to see the house. He could barely hide his shock at discovering that it had no garage and needed to have the kitchen gutted and completely replaced. I found a fantastic man, Bob Wilson, who agreed that he would have the house finished in time for our dinner party, and he did.

That didn't prevent the evening from being a borderline fiasco. First of all, it had to be kept a secret in order not to compromise His Majesty's security. As I made plans for the evening, I kept reading all the things that His Majesty was going to be doing at the exact same time of our party. I would ask George, "Are you sure the King is coming here?" He assured me that he was.

So I hired a caterer, had an instant garden put in our backyard, bought new terrace furniture, had the pool cleaned, and sat back to enjoy the dinner.

George had invited guests from all over the country whom he thought the King might enjoy seeing. Before anyone arrived, the heavens opened up with a fierce storm. My new garden washed right into our clean pool, along with the garden furniture. Meanwhile, the plane from Washington carrying our very important guests, former Vice President Nelson Rockefeller and his wife, Happy, and Ambassador Henry Catto and his wife, Jessica, was circling over our heads, trying to land. Of course His Majesty would appear early. Thank heavens for Jessica's lovely mother, Oveta Culp Hobby, who arrived on time and entertained us. Just to make it a perfect evening, the food was cold, not very tasty, and poorly served. I was talking to Nelson (who had finally arrived an hour late) on my left when I heard a little commotion on my right. I caught Nelson's eye and he said, "Don't look now, Barbara." Sissy that I am, I didn't. The waiter had dropped a steak in the King's lap. His Majesty was very kind, but I'm sure he put it down as an evening to be gotten through.

Although we missed our Washington friends, we loved being home in Houston again. The most exciting thing to happen to us was becoming grandparents: George Prescott Bush had been born in April 1976, and Noelle Lucila Bush was born in July 1977, both to Jeb and Colu, who were living in Houston at the time. How we loved having those two darling little babies around.

I still did some traveling, showing my China slides and raising money for various charities, and George had joined several corporate boards and worked for a bank. Mainly, he traveled around the country making speeches and consulting with friends, laying the groundwork for a presidential race. You could say he was "testing the waters."

At one point during this period George and I found ourselves in a most unusual situation: We were alone. Paula had gone on her month's vacation, and the children were either grown up or away at summer jobs. I must confess it was like a second honeymoon, and we were loving our quiet, relaxed time together.

He went away on an overnight fishing trip with his friend Fred Chambers, and they came home as excited as two little kids, showing off a cooler full of redfish. I told George I would fix it for dinner. Well, I knew nothing about scaling, cleaning, or cooking fish, so I got out *The New York Times Cookbook* and set about following the instructions for baked stuffed redfish.

I chopped, seasoned, and stuffed this awful-looking thing half the afternoon. I set the table with our finest, including candles, and when George came home, I was feeling pretty happy with myself.

The big moment came for our main course, and I had a dreadful time getting the smelly, slippery thing on the platter. George, not knowing I had spent hours on this project, took one look and said with a twinkle in his eye, "You don't think I'm going to eat this sh-t, do you?" I burst into tears. My sense of humor had deserted me.

That was almost twenty years ago, and he has raved over everything I have cooked ever since. That expression has become a password between us that always brings a giggle.

〜 In the fall of 1977, George and I returned to China as guests of the Chinese government. Also in the delegation were our good friends and George's former business partner Hugh and Betty

Liedtke; Dean and Pat Burch; our friend and Texas state Representative Chase Untermeyer; Jim Lilley, who had served with George in China; our friend James Baker, who had just headed President Ford's reelection campaign; and David Broder of *The Washington Post* and his wife, Ann. But the most interesting member of the delegation was Lowell Thomas, the eighty-seven-year-old broadcaster and world traveler, and his new bride, Marianne. (I should note that Susan Baker stayed home with their new baby girl, Mary Bonner Baker, who is George's godchild.)

What a grand trip: Beijing, Chengtu, Chungking, a boat trip down the Yangtze River through the gorges, and Kweilin. But the highlight was visiting Tibet in the company of Lowell Thomas. In 1949, Lowell and his son were the seventh and eighth Americans to visit this remote country, and for years he was called "the last American out of Tibet." On that journey over the Himalayas, he fell from his horse and broke his hip and had to make a seventeen-day trip by litter to India and safety. China annexed Tibet two years later and closed the door. The next group of Americans to visit was a group headed by former CIA Director and Secretary of Defense James Schlesinger in 1976—and now us. We were told I was the third American woman ever to put foot on Tibetan soil.

We were all so excited about visiting this remote, mountainous country, home to the exiled Dalai Lama. Unfortunately, in my case, that didn't last long. The 12,800-foot altitude of the city of Lhasa was difficult to handle. I wrote in my diary on September 30:

I had such a sick headache that I wanted to die. Dean Burch slept. He is not at all well. Lowell, at 87 years of age, seems to be in better shape than any of us. In the morning we all walked as though we were walking on egg shells, being given oxygen off and on . . . We took off for the Norbu-Linka Park (Pearl Park), the summer palace of the Dalai Lama, 360,000 square meters, built by the 7th Dalai Lama in 1755. . . . We were given a choice of barley beer or Yak butter tea. (The former looked and smelled like urine and the latter like tea with some rancid fat on the top.) Both were nauseating. Our old friend, the sea slug, has appeared again. When feeling well, they are dreadful; sick, they are revolting.

. . . I am beginning to believe Lowell when he says that Tibetans don't bathe all winter long. I just wonder, "Do they bathe in the summer?"

On October 2, I wrote about our visit to the Potola, the Dalai Lama's hilltop palace:

It was a beautiful day and we all set off looking forward to seeing this wonder of wonders that sits on a lone hill dominating this whole city . . . There are 13 floors, 178 meters high—two-thirds as high as the Empire State Building (Lowell's offering). 420 meters east to west, 330 north to south. 130,000 square meters, wooden and stone structure, walls 3 meters thick, built in conformity of the hill. Most ancient and well-preserved building in Tibet, started in the 7th Century.

. . . The weather in Tibet is crazy. It is cold in the shade, and the sun is the hottest that I have ever felt. I got sunburned. The air—what little there is of it—is the clearest I have ever seen.

. . . This is the only place that I have ever been in where I felt the people were oppressed. I felt that we were in an occupied country. It is not a comfortable feeling.

As the plane left Tibet, most of the party missed the clear, crisp air. Dean Burch and I got steadily better as the cabin became pressurized, thank heavens. For those who also suffer the same "altitude sickness," I have discovered recently that pills from your doctor, lots of fluids, and moving slowly really do help.

The trip down the Yangtze River was marvelous. One evening George invited Lowell to tell us about his first trip with his son, Lowell Jr., to Tibet. He took us around the world, dropping famous names as he went. We were fascinated. I'm not sure he ever got around to telling us about Tibet, but the tales of Indian maharanees who wanted to marry him; Franklin Roosevelt, a friend and neighbor near Hyde Park in New York; Lawrence of Arabia; and kings and queens he knew were marvelous. Incidentally, one by one, our Chinese hosts, not the least interested, got up and crept out.

Another night we had a musical evening with David Broder organizing a song-and-dance group. It was pretty bad. The Chinese took on this challenge, and different members recited some heavy poetry and one sang an aria from a Chinese opera. It was a highlight as we cruised down that magnificent river that for so many years divided the country. (The first bridge across the Yangtze was built after the revolution in 1949.)

Another time we were sitting in the stateroom when we looked out, and there was Lowell jogging in *very* slow motion around the wet and slippery deck. He was an amazing man and knowing him was a treat. We kept up a wonderful correspondence, and we loved his letters and notes that continued right up until his death. George and I attended his funeral in 1981, and I was amused to see that his coffin was draped not with a flag but with some exotic cloth that he must have received from a king or emperor. He was a true adventurer!

The day after we got home from our China trip, George W. came to Houston with a beautiful young woman and announced they were getting married. Laura Welch and George had been grammar school classmates in Midland but had not been aware of each other. They were married in November, right in the middle of George W.'s campaign for Congress. The next year, he would win his primary fight, but he lost the general election.

Laura is a very special person, and I always thought that being an only child with few cousins, she was amused by us. In our very competitive, large family, she does not compete. She walks, reads a lot, has great taste, is excellent company, and like Columba, was a fine addition to our family.

⌒ As we entered 1978, it became more and more apparent that George would run for president in 1980. On March 3, I wrote Frances Hammond at the Washington Home:

> What a man is my great George. He is getting better about "blowing his own horn," a thing we were taught as children to never do. But a thing that you must do if you want this job. He is uniquely qualified, and I am more than willing to tell people why. The one thing that he has done that none of the rest of them have done is he founded and made a success of a company that has business around the world. He knows what it means to meet a payroll, work with all government rules and regulations, and he also knows how to wrestle with tough problems and make it work. You don't need a lecture about my George, but when you add his business experience to his many government

jobs that he did well, it just adds up to the right person at the right time for the job.

We had a late summer meeting in Kennebunkport with Bill Steiger, Dean Burch, Jim Baker, and others where the possibility of a George Bush run for the presidency was seriously discussed. Strategy and timing were debated. It was decided that if George was going to make the run, he must step up his travel and start lining up teams in every state.

One of the questions people asked George was how he could run with no constituency. He would answer that he had "a big family and lots of friends." I know people laughed, but how did George eventually win? He has a big family and lots of very loyal friends who know George is the best friend someone can have.

That fall George suggested that since he would be on the road, I should accept Bill and Sarah Thomas's invitation to visit them in China, where they still served in the U.S. mission. I invited George's sister, who lives in Massachusetts, to go with me. As I sat in a New York City airport waiting for Nan Ellis to join me, I began to think: What do I actually know about her? We meet at big family gatherings, but how do I know I will be able to share a room with her for three weeks and end up liking her?

Almost as soon as she arrived at the airport, she asked me the time. My heart sank as I thought: My gosh, she does not wear a watch! For three weeks she'll be asking me "What time is it?" Nan could tell that I was appalled and quickly assured me, "I will never ask you the time again and I will never be late." She didn't and she wasn't. She then announced several rules that she felt very strongly about. I remember two. "Never use my hairbrush. You may use my toothbrush, but never the hairbrush." And: "Wash out the bathtub after your bath." I agreed to the rules and added: "Never ever use my toothbrush."

She was the best traveling companion and went from being my sister-in-law to a dear and close friend.

꙳ On January 5, 1979, George filed his intention to form a Presidential Search Committee. It wasn't as strong as actually announcing he was a candidate (he would do that in May), but it meant he was very serious about running. We were on our way.

12

Hitting the Campaign Trail

It didn't take long for me to find out just how frustrating this campaign would be at times. On March 9, 1979, I was asked to participate in a national press conference at the Waldorf in New York with the other candidates' wives. A better name for it would be a "Cattle Show." We were not going to be allowed to speak! I had the best candidate, but in a beauty contest or best-dressed competition, I didn't have a chance. The other wives were Nancy Reagan; Joy Baker, wife of Senator Howard Baker; Jackie Fernandez, wife of Ben Fernandez; and Elizabeth Dole. We were asked to pose together over and over. Crazy!

Campaigning was exhausting. George was flying from one end of the country to another and then back. He was getting advice from everywhere. Some friends were telling him to smile more; some were saying to smile less. I remember one day thinking I would love to fix his hair, but I didn't want to join the chorus of criticism!

The receptions, lunches, and dinners were endless. Some would be wonderful and lift your spirits. But there were many others where we were told 400 people would come and maybe 150 would show up. I was never sure what to do at many of these affairs, and I often felt like I attracted the people who had been drinking too much. It also seemed that the worse the day was, the better the chance our motel room that night would smell of stale cigarette smoke or we would take a bumpy plane ride to the next stop.

We still found lots to laugh about, though. One night, we were awakened at four A.M. by our message light flashing on the phone. We immediately thought of the children, picked up the phone in fear and trembling, and found instead that some unknown couple in room 210 wanted us to come down for a drink. The hotel had forgotten to pass on the message until the wee hours of the morning. I lay in bed thinking about calling and telling them we accept, or just getting up, getting dressed, and appearing at their door. I fell asleep giggling.

Another night, I awakened to hear George answering the door. There was this tiny little girl asking if he was Mr. Jones and had he sent for her? George sent the poor little thing away and told me she was a hooker. Later someone suggested that it might have been a setup.

On Ash Wednesday, we were in Mexico to speak to the Young Presidents' Organization. We were very excited to find that Billy and Ruth Graham were there and invited them to take a boat trip with us. While picnicking on a military beach, Billy saw his hotel down the way and decided to jump ship and work on his speech. He was wearing George's borrowed bathing suit and no shoes. He ran into military police who would not let him walk up the beach, and Billy Graham had to walk down the burning hot highway barefoot and in swimming trunks.

In July 1979 we took a brief break from the campaign trail and traveled to the Middle East. President and Mrs. Sadat of Egypt were absolutely charming and invited us to their lovely home in Alexandria on the Mediterranean, sending a helicopter to Cairo for us. In conversation, he took us around the world and gave George his evaluation of what was happening. He spoke in a soft, clear voice and we were spellbound.

In Israel, we met with Prime Minister Begin, who was pleasant but not forthcoming. I believe he didn't think George had a future. However, we did have a glorious tour of Jerusalem and met with the mayor, Teddy Kollek, in what was to be the first of many meetings George had with this respected leader.

Long before the campaign began, I had put some hard thought into what my role would be. I knew people would ask me what my cause was, and I still wasn't sure about that.

Rosalynn Carter was interested in mental health; Betty Ford, arthritis; Pat Nixon, volunteerism; Lady Bird Johnson, the beautification of America. I had to know exactly what my cause would be. For many years I had volunteered in hospitals and nursing homes, such as Sloan Kettering Memorial Hospital in New York City and the Washington Home in Washington. I loved doing that, but I felt there was now a real opportunity to pick a cause that would involve a larger group of citizens. During the summer of 1978, while jogging in Houston's Memorial Park, I thought about all the things that worried me: the environment, the homeless, teenage pregnancies, hunger, crime, and on and on. I felt the subject I chose should help the most people possible, but not cost the government more money and not be controversial. A president has enough troubles—he does not need a wife to stir up more controversy for him.

Sad to say, there were plenty of problems filling those criteria. Finally, after much thought, I realized everything I worried about would be better if more people could read, write, and comprehend. More people would stay in school and get an education, meaning fewer people would turn to the streets and get involved with crime or drugs, become pregnant, or lose their homes. It seemed that simple. I had found my cause.

So the campaign was told that literacy was my interest—but we forgot to mention I knew absolutely nothing about the subject, at least not yet. One day, my traveling companion, Becky Brady, and I took off for a swing through the Midwest, including a stop at Cardinal Stritch College in Milwaukee. We were met by a Sister Camille, who led us into a meeting saying, "We are so excited about your visit. I have collected literacy experts from all around Milwaukee, some forty-five of the most informed people, and they are waiting to hear you. We are just thrilled!"

At that moment I could have killed Margaret Tutwiler, who had just come on board to do George's scheduling and who had sent me off on this trip. (It certainly was unfair to blame her, but at the time, she was the only candidate.) All the experts sat in two large rows, forming a semicircle around two chairs in the middle. Sister Camille and I plunked ourselves down, and she introduced me by saying, "Well, here she is. We can't wait to hear what you have to say."

I was lucky, for it suddenly came to me what to do. After saying a very few words, I asked them a question: "If you were married to the

President and had the opportunity to really make a dent in the field of illiteracy, what one thing would you do? How would you go about it? We'll start on the right and go around the room. Each person, please tell me how you'd approach this."

Well, you can guess the rest. They started talking, and by the time we got halfway through, Becky told me it was time to go on to the next event. I thanked them all, and we were out of there. We got back in our minivan and laughed ourselves silly. As wife of the Vice President, I went back to Cardinal Stritch College to give the commencement address and receive an honorary degree. I'm not sure I deserved the degree, but I certainly did learn something there: People would rather hear themselves talk than someone else. So when in doubt, keep quiet, listen, and let others talk. They'll be happy, and you might learn something.

By the way, the Margaret Tutwiler I mentioned is the same marvelous woman who went on to become the spokesperson at the State Department during George's presidency. She was a great scheduler for us during the campaign, although George used to tease her unmercifully for being the world's worst speller.

In a campaign you came to expect the unexpected. One time, George and I were together at a rather unusual fund-raiser: a dance, where the top prize was dancing with us! Thank heavens I danced with a gray-haired gentleman. What if I had gotten a rock-'n'-roller? George joked with the audience that he had heard first prize was dancing with him; second prize was dancing with him twice; and third prize was dancing with him all night. Then he introduced me to give a few remarks. I could have killed him; I had absolutely nothing prepared. Then it hit me. I went to the microphone and said: "I hope I win first, second, and third prize," and sat down.

You also learned how to keep a stiff upper lip when things didn't go as planned. I remember one tough day in Massachusetts traveling with one of our local campaign workers, a young man named Ron Kaufman. The "crowds" were pitiful; we rarely hit double digits. Poor Ron was trying to keep my spirits up, and he promised that the last event would have probably 150 people. There were exactly four, three of whom were staff. Nevertheless, the four people saw my entire China slide show.

Ron Kaufman, by the way, was one of the many young people we met in the 1980 campaign who became a friend for life. He headed up the Political Affairs Office at the White House and guided us through many political mine fields.

⌇ One of the real joys of the campaign was our children. They all put their own lives on hold to campaign for George. George W. was just coming off his run for Congress in West Texas, and although he needed to get on with making a living, he campaigned as much as he could. Jeb and Colu were living in Venezuela, where he was a branch bank manager, but he gave up the job to come home and work full-time in the campaign. It was an enormous sacrifice financially, and an enormous gift to his dad. Neil campaigned hard in New Hampshire and Marvin in Iowa, both boys taking time off from school.

Doro told her dad she wanted to leave Boston College and work in the campaign. George, who adores her and could deny her nothing, surprised me and asked her what she could do; what could she bring to the ball game? He said she must have a talent and therefore should go to typing school so she could really help and not just be the daughter of the candidate. To our amazement, Doro enrolled in a nine-month course at Katherine Gibbs, certainly one of the finest, toughest secretarial schools. I know that George only meant for her to go to a three-month school to learn a little typing. So off came the blue jeans, on went the stockings and skirts, and she gave up summer vacation in Maine. I wonder if Doro ever realized she did way more than her father had in mind. When she finished the course, she worked in the Bush for President headquarters in Boston and did an outstanding job.

One very good thing came out of that campaign. The children treated me like an adult for the first time. Before that, they asked me all the "peanut butter and jelly" questions and George all the "steak and potato" questions. Then they discovered I could campaign with the best of them. My thinking about them changed, also. They no longer were children. They were able, bright, loving, loyal young men and women. They still are. They have been tested time and again, and always have made us very proud.

Cousins, nieces, nephews, brothers, and sisters from both sides of the family were involved in the campaign, which was wonderful. Sometimes, however, it could be very misleading. While driving through Massachusetts early in the campaign, I was so excited to see a George Bush for President bumper sticker. I drove up to catch the car, and there was the husband of one of George's cousins. Another time, driving through Iowa, I was listening to a radio talk show when a young man called in and said he was for George Bush because he was a great man and had a great family. Again I was so excited—until I recognized Marvin's voice!

ご One thing I had to get used to during the primary was being followed by press. The "Today" show was planning features on each wife and asked permission to follow me. They came along one whole day through New Hampshire, attending coffees and other political events. I wore an open mike on my belt, so everything I said and everything said to me was on tape. I constantly pointed to the open mike, telling people they were on tape. Nevertheless, people said dreadful things I otherwise would have ignored—but I certainly did not want, by keeping silent, to leave the impression I agreed with them. Although the TV technicians assured me they turned off the tape when I went into the bathroom, I still ran the water in the tub or sink.

It was an exhausting day, climaxed by a half-hour interview with Jane Pauley. She was so pretty and sweet-looking—and managed to absolutely devastate me. We had a polite little interview until her last question, which went something like this: "Mrs. Bush, people say your husband is a man of the eighties and you are a woman of the forties. What do you say to that?"

Why didn't she just slap me in the face? She was darn lucky I didn't burst into tears and say that was the worst question I had ever heard! I was speechless and heartsick. I finally answered: "Oh, you mean people think I look forty? Neat!" I went on to say, "If you mean that I love my God, my country, and my husband, so be it. Why, then I am a woman of the forties." The interview was over practically before it started. After she left, while I was still rocking from the question, I told Becky I was sure I hadn't understood her question. It was so hurtful. A crew member spoke up and said, "Oh, you understood her okay." He conveyed the impression that it was not unusual for her to be so ugly.

To add insult to injury, we got a phone call saying the whole day's tape had been ruined and they'd like to spend another two days with me in Illinois. Since the other wives' interviews were "in the can," the office felt I must do it.

So we started over again with fear and trembling. The first day was an unbelievably bad one. Nothing went right. It snowed, and we traveled all day in a tiny plane, landing in small airports that usually closed immediately after we took off. Because of the weather, the people who were supposed to meet me were often late or didn't show up at all, so the cameras got pictures of me trudging through the snow alone. During a college visit, I was asked all the tough questions and harangued for not speaking out on the issues myself. It was the worst possible day. Jane flew in and met me at a high school to redo the interview. She started out by saying something like, "Mrs. Bush, some days on the campaign trail everything seems to go wrong . . ." I waited for a real zinger, but surprisingly, the interview was all sweetness and light. Several weeks went by, and then it was my morning on the air. I was very nervous, sitting alone in a California hotel room. Although the interview began with the footage of me walking alone through airports and Jane asking her "everything goes wrong" question, the next seven minutes were spent with the "Today" show allowing me to say in every way possible just how great George Bush is. It was amazing. The man who edited the tape really did me a favor. I honestly feel he did it on purpose. I think he felt we had bonded on those bumpy, scary flights through the storm; that we had been good sports by spending two more days with them after their tape had been bad; and that Jane had been cruel in that first interview. Who knows what he thought or why it turned out so well. When the seven minutes were over and the show went back to New York, Bryant Gumbel said, "The Bush campaign should have paid for that segment." Lucky me.

About this same time, I had a very hurtful conversation with a very loved sister-in-law who told me she had attended a dinner where some of the family had talked about "What are we going to do about Bar?" Huh? That really hurt. They discussed how to make me look snappier—color my hair, change my style of dressing, and, I suspect, get me to lose some weight. I know it was meant to be helpful, but I wept quietly alone until George told me that was absolutely crazy. He has always made me feel loved and just right for him. I certainly did not expect all the personal criticism when he announced for the presidency.

On this same note, one day after speaking at a New York City luncheon, I went to see a well-known speech consultant who was going to critique my speaking. I was very hesitant about all of this. The consultant greeted us kindly and truly gave me a pretty fair mark on the public speaking, but she had a dress consultant with her. That very young woman had on hideous pink tights and an off-colored weird dress; wild, long, frizzy hair; not to mention a very made-up face with emphasis on lavender eyelids. She started in: My clothes were all wrong; I should color my hair . . . I stopped her there. People had gotten to know me with white hair and it would be fake to change it now. She then said that if I wouldn't tint my hair, I must shave my dark eyebrows—they did not go with my hair. While I was still rocking from that ridiculous suggestion, Becky said we had to leave that very moment because we were late for our next meeting. We hardly got out of there before we doubled up with laughter.

Becky and I often got the giggles. Once we were touring the Springfield, Massachusetts, area with a large entourage, and I had just spoken to a group of GOP women and done a couple of press interviews when a tiny lady came up to me and asked if she could "read" my wrinkles. She counted six wrinkles on my forehead and said: "You've had six traumas and handled them well." Looking at the sides of my eyes, she counted five wrinkles and said: "You've had five children." Then I knew she had read my biography, and I knew the next thing in it was the line "The Bushes have lived in twenty-seven homes in seventeen cities." Unfortunately, Becky managed to drag me away to the next event and I never got to hear the rest of the wrinkle-reader!

Becky was the first of many aides who have become so dear to me. She was followed by Nick and Kitty Brady's daughter Kim. (No relation to Becky, who was the granddaughter of our longtime friend and former RNC chairwoman Mary Louise Smith.) Kim could head a company anytime she wanted, she is so organized and certainly a considerate, thoughtful young woman. She was followed by Elizabeth Wise, who looked like a Botticelli painting and was so smart I felt like the dog was being wagged by the tail. We loved that tiny, dainty, smart young woman. Casey Healey from Oklahoma came next and was beloved by all ages, and she was followed by Peggy Swift, who has all the above abilities, plus is a great beauty. At this writing, Nancy Huang has been my aide for six months, and I don't believe I've ever seen her frown, she is always so upbeat. Beside all her other talents, she is a computer genius and has saved me from disaster several times writing this book. I have shared everything with these young women, and they know more about us than anyone else in the world. Not one has betrayed our trust and friendship. They traveled around the world with me, held my hand throughout sickness and many a terrible faux pas on my part. We have had unending days and many funny times. They have remained loyal and even-tempered throughout—heaven only knows how. Both George and I love them and would do anything we could for them.

    ❦ One of the best things about being on the campaign trail was seeing old friends along the way. I especially remember spending two days in Michigan with dear Patsy Caulkins—one of our house-mates from Yale—and her sister in-law, Chrissie Finkenstaedt. They were helping out with the trip, although neither one of them had orga-nized a political event, or attended one to my knowledge. The "pros" said that the trip would be a failure, since they did not know how to raise a crowd, and so forth. So we spent two days going from town to town attending some of the best coffees and receptions we had in the primary. These young women didn't know that what they planned couldn't be done, so they just did it! Incidentally, we won the Michigan primary, which, in all honesty, was due to George Bush, a very popular Governor Bill Milliken, and many other hard workers, including the present governor, John Engler.

    In reading my notes on the primary season in 1980, I am once again reminded that the more things change, the more they stay the same.

    In the Republican primary, a candidate must always prove just how conservative he is. George has always been accused of being a lib-eral in conservative clothing in the primary, and a conservative in lib-eral clothing in the general election. I was always so proud of George. He stuck with what he believed, whether or not it was popular. He never paid attention to the polls.

    Also during that campaign, I was quoted as saying about John Anderson, who lost the GOP primary and went on to run as an Independent: "I think being an Independent is a cop-out. The strength of the United States is in the two-party system. You pick the party that is close to you philosophically and try to change the things about it you don't like." Like I said, the more things change, the more things stay the same. A three-person race does not give the winner a clear mandate.

One of the big issues in the 1980 primary campaign was abortion. It seemed that's what we were asked most about. Just how committed was George to being anti-abortion? Very committed. He did believe, however, that abortion was acceptable when it came to rape, incest, and the health of the mother. His views were not acceptable to the true believers on either side of the issue. One of the public misconceptions about George was that he changed his opinion on abortion. He never did. He was always opposed. I think the misunderstanding came from the fact that as a congressman he had been very active in promoting family planning and had supported Planned Parenthood before abortion became their battle cry. That's where he parted ways with them.

In all our years of campaigning, abortion was the toughest issue for me. Everyone, it seemed, tried to make me say how I felt about the issue, hoping to catch me disagreeing with George. I honestly felt, and still feel, the elected person's opinion is the one the public has the right to know.

I never questioned George's conviction and certainly shared his concerns about abortion being used as a contraceptive. There is no question in my mind that the law permitting abortions has been abused. We both agree that the estimated 1.6 million abortions performed in the United States every year is unacceptable.

For me, abortion is a personal issue—between the mother, father, and doctor. If a minor is involved, you can add parents to that list also.

It should be allowed in the first trimester only.

Abortion is not a presidential matter.

Education is the answer.

Morals cannot be legislated.

On the campaign trail, abortion met us everywhere. We were greeted outside the first primary debate in New Hampshire with large pro-Reagan signs and signs that said: GEORGE BUSH—MURDERER. Reagan supporters also took out many ads saying George was for abortion and Reagan was against. It was very untrue and unfair.

Once, when I was campaigning in Maryland with Helen Bentley, the tough but very nice congresswoman from the Baltimore area, the press asked her: "You are a well-known advocate of women's rights. How come you are anti-abortion?" I loved her answer, although I never saw it in print. She said simply, "It's against my religion." George Bush could give the same answer.

Both George and I felt strongly about our positions but respected each other's views; there was no point in discussing it every time it came up.

❧ By the end of the primary season, it was evident 1980 was not our year. After the high of an upset win in Iowa, we lost New Hampshire, and although we rebounded to win several more important primaries, Ronald Reagan was well on his way to winning the nomination.

During the campaign, Neil had met and fallen in love with a darling young schoolteacher from New Hampshire, Sharon Smith. He not only won her vote, but thank heavens, her heart, too. In the summer of 1980, they got married in Kennebunkport at tiny St. Ann's Church, where George's mother and father had been married more than sixty years before. We had the reception on the lawn at Walker's Point with family and friends. It was a very happy time, and they left for Europe on their honeymoon having been assured by us we were going to the Republican Convention to bow out of politics with style, and then go home to Houston.

❧ We went to the convention with the plan of asking George's delegates—he had the second-highest total—to get 100 percent behind Ronald Reagan. I dreaded the trip, but must confess it was fun. I joined a team that went from delegation to delegation speaking well of Ronald Reagan. I remember that Cap Weinberger, later Secretary of Defense, was on the team. He was a gentle, kind man who made it very easy for me. Maureen Reagan was also on the team, working very hard for her dad. She was a piece of work who came on like gangbusters.

I truly began the convention thinking, Hurrah, no more politics! But as the week went on, I found myself getting very competitive.

George was by far the best man for vice president. Groups were forming for Jack Kemp, Paul Laxalt, Howard Baker, and, of course, Jerry
Ford. The next thing we knew, George was in the running, too.

The keynote address at the convention was to be given by our
dear friend Guy Vander Jagt. Guy and Carol had come to Congress the
same year we did and we are good friends. His speech was being highly
touted. Guy is a great orator and prides himself on using no notes. He
was fast becoming a dark horse candidate, and a lot was riding on his
speech. The night he was to speak, the convention ran overtime, so the
keynote address was put off for one day so it could be in prime time.
This built up expectations even more. George was to follow Guy, so he
was put off twenty-four hours also.

I remember walking over to the convention hall that night with
Susan Baker and Pat Burch and discussing the interview we had just
heard with Walter Cronkite and Jerry Ford. Jerry hinted he would
consider being the vice presidential candidate, under the right circumstances. We were confused about what was happening. We walked past
people working for Jack Kemp, who were handing out Kemp posters
and yelling "Stop Bush." What was happening?

Guy started his speech with that beautiful, strong voice and he
talked and he talked and he talked. He recited from memory parts of the
Bible and some poems, and he talked very movingly about his forebears.
When he got past the thirty-minute mark, I knew that George's speech
would be well received, for it was short. I don't know how long Guy
talked, but it was very, very long. With each word he helped George.

George's time finally came. The whole convention hall seemed
blanketed in homemade BUSH signs, which our friends and supporters had spent the whole night painting. George gave a fine speech. I
learned later that just before he spoke, he had been told Jerry Ford was
Reagan's choice for vice president.

We went right back to the Pontchartrain Hotel and our whole
floor was filled with many close friends and family. It was like a funeral.
George found Jeb in our bedroom really upset. "It's not fair, it's not
fair," he said. George and I put on old clothes, and I urged him to
let us pack up and get out of there. George gave both Jeb and me a
talking-to: "We came to this convention to leave politics with style and
we are going to do it." Almost immediately, the phone call came to our
room from Ronald Reagan and the rest is history.

By the way, the next day in Austria, a honeymooning Neil and Sharon saw George's picture on the front page of a local paper. Neil excitedly grabbed a paper and tried to figure out what it said. When the owner of the newsstand realized the man in the photo was Neil's father, he translated the article. That's how Neil and Sharon found out it wasn't over yet.

On September 3, 1980, my first day of campaigning for Ronald Reagan and George Bush, I flew to New Orleans under the protection of the Secret Service. This began a twelve-and-a-half-year relationship with some of the world's finest, most professional men and women I have ever met. Over the years, people often would ask us if we didn't get tired of being constantly under surveillance. We never did. In fact, it amazed me whenever I heard someone complain about these brave people. Their only job is to see that you are safe. They are ready to risk their lives—and many of them have—for whomever they are protecting.

I wonder if many people know that the Secret Service also investigates financial crimes, such as counterfeiting and credit card frauds. Protecting presidents and vice presidents and their families, presidential candidates, and visiting heads of state is only one of their roles. I often felt it almost was insulting for these highly dedicated and trained people to follow me around. They surely were bored.

Becky and I soon realized it embarrassed the Secret Service to see us struggling through airports with our luggage. Their job was to protect me, not wait on me, and they certainly could not carry bags. I told Becky that from now on, the advance people (the campaign workers who went out ahead and set up events) should have someone meet us who could help with luggage. That made such a difference after all those months of carrying our own bags.

Getting back to that first day on the campaign trail—it was very different. I knew everything about George Bush and very little about Ronald Reagan. For quite a while there were "Reagan people" chaperoning George and me, to be sure we were toeing the line. I am not sure that they knew us well enough yet to realize that loyalty, decency, and honor are George's code. I believe that for the most part, they came to respect George.

What made it easier for us was that our primary campaign manager and dear friend Jim Baker was now a senior adviser in Reagan's campaign, and ours was being run by Dean Burch. Dean was very smart and had such a great sense of what was right. The two campaigns were in perfect sync.

I campaigned twenty-seven days in September alone, touching down in sixteen states and thirty-seven cities all over the country. Sometimes I campaigned with George and sometimes by myself. I met Nancy Reagan on the trail only once, campaigning with her in Baltimore. People wanted to see, meet, and touch her. She was more than nice to me.

I was asked over and over again about what Reagan felt about this or that. Since I really did not know the Governor, this was difficult for me. But it was fairly easy to talk about Jimmy Carter's inflation, Jimmy Carter's interest rates, Jimmy Carter's unemployment, Jimmy Carter's failed foreign policy. However, I was used to campaigning for George Bush, which was a cinch, and not against the opponent. I certainly prefer the former.

When it came to being interviewed, I was always afraid that I was going to hurt, rather than help. One day I was going on a radio call-in show, and the topic under discussion that day was a statement made by the head of a large Protestant church group. He was quoted as saying: "I never get over how strange it is at political meetings. We have a Catholic priest, a Protestant minister, and a Jewish rabbi pray, when everybody knows that God doesn't hear Jewish prayers." I panicked. What a terrible thing to say, and I didn't want to get involved in any way. If asked, I would say how outraged I was by that kind of bigotry. I thought that I might give a Helen Bentley answer—"That kind of talk is against my religion"—which it is. But the wonderful talk show host, a man named Mike Miller, not only did not involve me in the discussion, he did not take phone calls while I was on the air. I went back to the hotel relieved, but almost sick with rage at a statement like that.

There is sort of a pattern to campaigning you fall into. When something doesn't follow the schedule, you remember it. One day I raced into a meeting where I was told absolutely no speeches; just mix and mingle. I was met at the door, led right up to a standing mike, and handed a card. It read: "1. Thank hostess. [No name on card.] 2. Thank party chairman. [No name on card.] 3. Party line. [That I could wing.]" Not my finest hour.

Another time I was expecting to speak and was greeted at the door by a nice-looking man who said, "Did they tell you to speak well of Apple?" I looked at my notes—no Apple. He said, "Apple is our one hope and bright light. Rave about Apple." Well, I added Apple and gave him a big plug. After the reception, one of our people asked me who Apple was. I sought out my man and asked him and he, of course, said, "Me."

You do meet all sorts of people on the campaign trail. As George and I stood in receiving line after receiving line, having pictures taken with supporters, I often thought about Rosalynn Carter, who once innocently had her picture taken with Jim Jones, the man who led the cult to Guyana and forced them to drink poisoned Kool-Aid. As I shook people's hands, I would think, Is this a good guy? Is he a mass murderer? It could happen.

≈ We campaigned in backyards, ballrooms, courthouses, bowling alleys, at a cider and doughnut farm, hot dog plants, high schools and colleges, retirement homes, and hospitals. You name it, we were there.

Jeb and Columba stayed active in the campaign, but our college-aged children had gone back to school, campaigning on the weekends only. I called Doro one morning to check in, and she told me that nobody at Boston College was for Reagan-Bush. She had joined the campus campaign and was doing all the work. However, when the Reagan-Bush campus chairman had asked her "Where's your Reagan-Bush pin?" she answered him, "Are you crazy? I'm trying to make friends on the campus!" She is such a warm, funny child.

≈ I remember the day that I knew Ronald Reagan was going to win. I was in Detroit with a couple of free hours, waiting for George to get into town. I had the evening news on and saw Jimmy Carter denying he had called Ronald Reagan a racist. Then the news showed a tape of President Carter in a black church saying Ronald Reagan was a racist. For the first time I saw the "dark side" of Jimmy Carter. One of the things he had going for him was that he was a good, decent man, but for that one moment he also was a man who told a lie and felt hate. He had an indefensible record, so his people ran an underground smear campaign about Ronald Reagan. They said he was a racist, and pulled out another old campaign threat: Ronald Reagan would do away with Social Security. In truth, he and George actually strengthened the Social Security system while in office.

On Election Day we gathered our family and friends in Houston to wait for the results. I went running in Memorial Park and came across members of our traveling press corps playing softball with some of our staff. Several press people told me that the election was over; the exit polls were showing that Reagan-Bush was going to win big. I still couldn't believe it. We had worked so hard—yet it seemed so sudden. In May, we had bowed out of politics forever; six months later, I was the wife of the Vice President-Elect of the United States of America.

13

Around the World and Back

The next two and a half months were spent hiring a staff, getting ready to move yet another time, deciding what to do about our homes in Texas and Maine, and celebrating Christmas.

I have read that Nancy Reagan considered me lucky because I was not a newcomer to Washington and knew what to expect. That is very true. But I also knew enough to hire the most perfect person to be my chief of staff, Susan Porter Rose. Susan knew Washington and knew her way around the White House. I met her when she was a very young woman working for Pat Nixon. She went on to be Betty Ford's scheduler and then worked in the Justice Department during the Carter years. Susan has the most extraordinary sense of what is right and thinks things through with great care. I don't. Therefore, we made a great team for twelve years. Susan saved both George and me from many mistakes, and for that we are both eternally grateful. She also ran the very best office and hired the very best staff, many of whom would stay with me for the next twelve years. Susan is married to Jonathan Rose, whose father, Chappy, was a friend of George's dad. Both Mr. Rose and Jon were highly thought of by all.

The day after the election, Joan Mondale called me in Texas and couldn't have been nicer. She offered to show me the Vice President's House any time I wanted to see it, and she received me with great kindness several weeks later. My wonderful friend Andy Stewart went with me. Andy is one of those people who pull out a tiny camera to record moments of history. She humiliated me during the visit by insisting that Joan and I pose shaking hands upon arrival and several other times during the tour. That's when I knew Joan was sincerely a nice person— she agreed to pose over and over.

Joan is a great supporter of the arts, and the house was filled with the most modern work. Andy would back us up to some amazing piece of neon art that she (and I) thought was hideous and insist that we pose. She knew that George would last about five minutes with most of the pieces in the house. Let me add as a footnote that we know absolutely nothing about modern art, so this should be taken as a knock at our ignorance rather than a slap at Joan's taste. (I should also add that you rarely see any of the pictures Andy takes; she keeps them in drawers or under beds.)

⟶ The moment the election was over, George generously suggested I go to New York City and buy some "designer" clothes. He didn't want me to have to hear about how "dowdy" I was. So I took Laurie Firestone, the magical young woman who was our social secretary for the next twelve years, and bought some clothes from Bill Blass and Adele Simpson (both of whom had visited China while we were there), and Diane Dickinson. Later I would meet Arnold Scaasi, and for the next twelve years I bought my clothes from these very talented people. I never was criticized, but I didn't draw raves either. Nobody noticed what I wore. All I know is that I felt terrific. All these designers were very kind to me, but Arnold became a close personal friend and a supporter of my literacy causes.

On that first visit I bought a great purple dress and a red coat to wear to the Inauguration, a pretty bright blue coat with a white dress, and several other things. Thank heavens Nancy Reagan slipped the word to me that she was wearing red. In my excitement I had forgotten that I was not the "mother of the bride" and never thought to ask! So I wore the blue coat instead and it was fine. All our children had to buy long evening clothes, and we had great fun doing it. They looked beautiful.

That red coat and purple dress gave me a good laugh later in the year. In May, the Archbishop of Canterbury visited Washington, and George and I attended a service at the Washington Cathedral with His

Royal Highness the Prince of Wales. An unusual cold front had come through Washington, and I decided to wear that outfit one more time before putting it away for the summer. As we were standing for the procession, young Prince Charles leaned over to George and said, "Your wife, sir, is very appropriately dressed." We turned and looked, and there came the bishop followed by twenty-eight primates—all gowned in purple vestments with red overrobes.

Inaugural Week could not have been more exciting and fun for us and our children. Of course everything did not go perfectly. At the Texas Ball, held a few days before the Inauguration, I tripped and hit my leg as George and I were announced onstage. It stunned me for a minute, then I was okay. While George was speaking, I noticed that something felt slightly funny. I turned sideways and looked down, and I was standing in a nice little pool of blood. The military aide who had been assigned to me for that week only, a Navy lieutenant named Todd Bruner, looked like he might faint. (Todd's parents were not only our good friends in Kennebunkport, but his dad, Laman, was our minister.) The minute the speeches were over, the Secret Service quietly took me into the nearest ladies' room. As the women came out of the stalls, they were slightly taken aback to see men in their room and rushed out gasping. Dr. Bill Hughes, ABC News reporter Ann Compton's husband, came to my rescue and sent me to the emergency room at Georgetown University Hospital. The Secret Service really didn't want George to go for fear rumors would start about his health. I insisted he go, and he was the rage of the nursing staff. It was Saturday night, and they had a full load of stabbings, but all was momentarily forgotten while they sought autographs. And no rumors started, thanks to the big Band-Aid I wore over my fourteen stitches throughout the Inauguration. When we went to the star-studded Inaugural Gala, we sat across the room from the Reagans in great thronelike chairs. The doctor had told me to put my foot up, but I couldn't. I was afraid I'd look like Henry the Eighth.

We began Inauguration Day at St. John's Episcopal Church for a service with the Reagans, our joint families, and friends. The minister, John Harper, and his wife, Barbie, were old friends of ours as we are Episcopalians. Every president since James Madison has worshiped at St. John's, located across Lafayette Park from the White House.

Then it was on to the White House. Fritz and Joan Mondale met us at the North Portico entrance and were warm and gracious.

They had been most helpful during the transition, despite the fact this couldn't have been an easy time for them.

The Reagans arrived, and it was a long, tense forty-five minutes. We did not sit down, but just "hung around" waiting for the trip to the Capitol. Rosalynn Carter spent the time telling the White House staff good-bye. Nancy and I discussed that when we faced being in her position—in four or eight years—we would not drag it out like this. And we didn't. However, twelve years later, I would be much more understanding of Rosalynn. In 1993, although we had already said our good-byes to the staff, I was still much more concerned about them than the incoming administration.

I rode to the Capitol with Joan Mondale, driving past crowds of cheering people. For the first time, the Inauguration was to be held on the west side of the Capitol, looking out toward the Mall and the monuments. With thousands watching, and surrounded by family and friends, our dear friend Potter Stewart swore George in as the forty-third vice president of the United States, and Chief Justice Warren Burger swore Ronald Reagan in as the fortieth president. We were especially grateful that George's mother was there to see him sworn in, as she would be in 1989 to see him become president. To add to the excitement and the drama, we got word that the fifty-two American hostages held in Iran were released while President Reagan was giving his Inaugural Address.

George saw our house for the first time when we drove up after the Inaugural Parade. We arrived exhausted, and were about to host 150 family members for a light dinner! However, we found C. Fred and Paula in the house, our clothes all unpacked, and a great buffet supper on the dining room table. Laurie Firestone, Paula, and a group of volunteers had performed this miracle.

After the dinner, and after every family member had had their picture taken with the new vice president, George and I climbed into bed for a nap. We awakened and looked out our bedroom window to see lighted on the horizon the Capitol and the Washington Monument with fireworks over the Mall. It was magical. That view, which we had only in the winter, never failed to thrill us. In the summer, we looked out over a carpet of green, and when it rained—summer or winter—the colored car lights on Massachusetts Avenue looked like a shimmering jeweled necklace winding up the hill.

For the Inaugural Balls, I had a glorious new gown—bright blue, made of the most heavenly silk with big puffy, long sleeves. I felt like a bride in all my new finery. I still blush when I think of this, because when the pictures came back, they were not so glorious. The light hit that silk in all the wrong places, and I had two big shiny balls on the top and a big round tummy—highlighting my finest points!

Our very first week in office, President Reagan asked George to meet the hostages at Andrews Air Force Base and escort them to the White House for their official welcome home. The entire route into town was lined with people waving flags, cheering, and even weeping. The strangest assortment of people were hugging each other—all ages, all shapes, all sizes, all races—all Americans whose prayers had been answered. Inside the bus was a quiet disbelief. The hostages just couldn't believe that we had prayed and cared for them; that we had counted "Day 1, Day 2," up to the last day, "Day 444." As we got closer to the District, the hostages were overwhelmed by the yellow ribbons and growing crowds. Their leader, Bruce Laingen, wrote "thank you" on a tiny piece of paper and held it up to the window. I found a bigger piece and gave it to him, and he taped a big "thank you" on the window. He left it on the bus, but I took it and mailed it to him a month later, thinking he might like a remembrance of that historic day.

⁓ Once the excitement died down, I turned my attention to the house. It had been built in 1893 at a cost of $20,000 on the seventy-seven-acre U.S. Naval Observatory grounds for the in-resident admiral. In July 1974, it became the official residence of the vice president.

Virginia Senator Harry Byrd, who was on the congressional committee charged with finding a house, told me that Admiral Elmo "Bud" Zumwalt was the occupant when they decided this would be the perfect home for the vice president. Harry said Zumwalt did not seem too thrilled with the idea that the Navy's house was going to be confiscated. However, Harry didn't realize just how strongly the Admiral felt until his next election. Bud Zumwalt ran against him. Incidentally, Harry was one of only fifteen or twenty people who told me that they "personally" were responsible for getting that house for the vice president's residence. Must have been a big committee.

I first saw the house when Nelson Rockefeller was vice president (they did not live there but used it for entertaining), and I remember thinking it was nice but small. It was actually bigger than I thought, and I loved it. "It's a house that sort of talks to you," I wrote in my diary. But it also needed a lot of work. Everything was off center—the fireplaces, chandeliers, windows, arches, and so on. And there was a terrible conglomeration of furniture and artwork. It had been perfect for Joan Mondale's purposes. She used it very much as a museum and sponsored American art and artists. I was into literacy. She had teen-aged children. Mine were all grown and living away from home. Our needs were different. However, we both shared a great love of books, and there was one addition to the house the Mondales made that I loved: a library of books by and about vice presidents, their wives, and later, their dogs.

I got lots of help with the redecorating. I was especially grateful to the outstanding decorator Mark Hampton and Dottie Craig, an old friend from Midland days. Mark not only found some beautiful rugs and furniture for us, he donated his time and profit. He is great fun to work with as he uses what you have, and he and his wife, Duane, have become good friends of ours. Mark also has served on the Committee for the Preservation of the White House, worked on Blair House (the president's guest house), and helped us redo the Oval Office and the family rooms at the White House. At this writing, he is helping Ambassador Pamela Harriman with our embassy in Paris and with our new home in Houston.

Dottie Craig's part in the redecorating really was almost a gift from God. George had been asking me just how I was going to pay for all this, and I told him not to worry, that I knew it would all work out. One day my phone rang and it was Dottie. "Bar, I know from George W. that you are redoing the VP House. I am without a project and would love to help raise money." I don't know what I would have done if she hadn't called, and I certainly don't recommend this kind of financial planning to others. Dottie raised all the money we needed (she'd be the first to say she did it with lots of help), and then eight years later, helped me resurrect the White House Endowment Fund. Dottie and Earle are presently serving on the Board of Trustees of the George Bush Library Foundation.

After the house was redecorated, I wrote in my diary: "The rooms say, 'Please come sit down,' rather than, 'Please stay out.'"

We lived in that graceful, charming house for eight years—the longest we have lived in any one home in our forty-nine years of married life. We especially loved the large veranda that wrapped around the front of the house. We ate many meals there, watching grandchildren swing or C. Fred, and later Millie, chase squirrels and explore.

Talking about redoing the house does bring up a subject that I have wanted to comment on. Nancy Reagan got lots of criticism for redecorating the White House when we all should have been on our knees thanking her. She raised the money privately and not only redecorated but restored the White House, including modernizing the bathrooms and fixing faulty wiring. As her successor, I was eternally grateful to her for that.

~~~ March 30, 1981, began as a fairly typical day—even quiet compared to most. My schedule read:

FYI	Cherry Blossom Festival
11 a.m.	Washington Performing Arts Society Volunteer Reception (&NR)
12:30 p.m	Cabinet Wives Lunch, National Trust Historical Preservation (&NR)
3 p.m.	San Antonio Art Institute Tour/Tea

After lunch, Nancy Reagan ("&NR" on my schedule means it was an event with Nancy) went back to the White House and I went home. Working at my desk with the TV on mute, I looked up and found myself looking at a newscast: a lot of racing around; a shot of the President being pushed into the car; someone lying on the ground. I couldn't believe what I was seeing. My heart ached so for Nancy. I knew that the best thing I could do for her was to stay away; what she needed was a best friend. Dear Andy Stewart came right over to be with me. George was in Texas and called me several times during his flight home. I really needed to be near his voice, and he must have sensed that. The TV kept saying that after he landed, he was going to take the helicopter right to the White House. He told me that was not true; he was going to land at our house and then drive to the White House. George felt strongly that only the President should land at the White

House in a helicopter. There are exceptions, but George knew that he needed to send the message that Ronald Reagan was still responsible in every way to run the country. Ed Meese, one of the President's senior staff, stopped by the house before he went up to the helicopter pad to meet George. He was obviously worried sick and yet took time to stop by the house to reassure me. I especially remember the hug he gave me with tears in his eyes. We walked up to the helicopter pad together to wait for George. When he landed, he gave me a hug and then left with Ed for the fifteen-minute drive to the White House.

George was asked over and over again what he felt and thought when he heard about the assassination attempt. His answer: "I worried about my friend who was hurt."

⁀ There were two big weddings that summer: Prince Charles married Lady Diana, and on June 13, Marvin married Margaret Molster in Richmond, Virginia. Margaret is from a large, loving family— not as large as George's, but few are—and she and Marvin attended the University of Virginia at the same time. They both had many mutual friends and have shared them with us. We watched the royal wedding at a breakfast at the British Embassy. Ours looked like much more fun. Betty Molster, Margaret's mother, worked really hard before we all arrived, and then when we got there announced that if it wasn't done, it wouldn't get done. She was going to relax and enjoy it. She taught me a good lesson: Everyone has more fun if the hostess is enjoying herself.

⁀ Early during the vice presidential years, I got a letter from a woman saying she had read that I did needlepoint and played tennis. She then asked: "Do you also sit home and eat bonbons?"

It probably seemed that way to some, but the eight years George was vice president were, I believe, the busiest of my life—more so than the White House years in many ways. I hate quoting statistics. I agree with Mrs. Robert Taft, Sr., who once said: "All statistics are hard to swallow and impossible to digest. The only one I can ever remember is that if all the people who fell asleep in church were laid end to end, they'd be a lot more comfortable."

But I'm going to chance it anyway. In the 2,923 days of the vice presidential years:

- 1,629 days were spent out of Washington traveling, including visiting all fifty states and sixty-five different foreign countries, many of them more than once.
- George and I traveled an estimated 1.3 million miles, which is about fifty-four times around the world.
- When I was in town, I hosted 1,192 events at the Vice President's House and attended 1,232 other events in Washington.

Whew! Lucky for you, I'm not going to describe every single mile or share every speech. But it was an extraordinary eight years, and I would like to share with you some of the people we met, some of the places we visited, and some of the wonderful experiences we were lucky to enjoy.

June 30, 1981—At President Reagan's request, George and I attended the inauguration of President Marcos of the Philippines. Clare Boothe Luce and Efrem Zimbalist, Jr., and his wife were in the delegation. We were all amazed that Clare never slept on the entire seventeen-hour trip. She talked—maybe entertained is a better way to describe it—the whole way over and back. George and I had a private cabin, but we all took turns listening and enjoying her. What a remarkable woman: a famous beauty and seductress; wife of legendary Henry Luce, founder of Time/Life; author of *The Women*; congresswoman; ambassador to Italy; and a delegate to the United Nations. Clare, whose tongue was finely honed, was very opinionated, generous, charming, and amusing.

We arrived late on a Sunday night and left at six A.M. Tuesday, our visit cut short by a typhoon in the forecast. Imelda Marcos, a charmer in her own right, met us upon arrival and took us straight to the famous Malacanang Palace (home to Imelda's 1,060 pairs of shoes), where we were staying. Before being allowed to go to sleep, she said she had two dresses for me and asked if I'd try them on to see if they fit. Neither dress would have gone over my thigh, much less my body. Imelda said not to worry, a seamstress would fix that. She must have worked all night and the next day, because just as I was getting dressed for the ball the next evening, the dress Imelda insisted I wear was delivered. I certainly didn't want to wear it, but felt that I must. It was a disaster. It was a long sheath of a dress with a slip top, which was covered by a capelike overtop. Every time I raised my arms to eat or dance, this cape thing rolled back up my arms to expose my slip. The dress did not move when I moved, so I had to turn my whole body with every gesture. To add insult to injury, the dress was about two inches too long and my every step looked a little like a goose step—a kick and a scoot.

Among the other guests were many friends from the United Nations days who were there representing their countries. I asked one of the ladies if Mrs. Marcos had given her a dress, and she assured me that she had, but of course she hadn't worn it. My only comfort was that when I told Nancy Reagan about the dress, she told me that the same thing happened to her. I don't mean to sound ungracious; I know Mrs. Marcos was just being generous.

It was a well-known fact that she was a compulsive shopper; it certainly was obvious from our rooms. There were several dozen large baskets of food stacked on the floor, all wrapped in cellophane. Much to our horror, they were put on our plane when we left. They were filled with stale chocolate, cans of diet food, popcorn—you name it, we had it.

While we were there George praised Marcos for lifting martial law, which we had been pushing him to do for years. The press crucified George for this because of continuing human rights violation charges. But they neglected to mention why George felt he must praise Marcos: to encourage him to continue moving in the right direction; and because, at that time, it appeared Marcos was the only person standing between his country and a Communist takeover. I guess the reporters' parents never told them that the "sin of omission" is as bad as a lie.

We had a great visit while we were there with General Carlos Romulo and his wife, Beth, dear friends from our UN days. Rommy was a great hero in World War II, along with President Marcos, and was a compadre and friend of General Douglas MacArthur. I think in light of the later troubles in the Philippines, we forget the enormous courage of these people and the losses they suffered side by side with our own troops.

However, as Imelda escorted us around, we would pass high wooden fences behind and through which we could see abject poverty. I wrote in my diary: "I have a feeling that I'm looking at a Marie Antoinette. Someone who is living pretty highly while others are suffering . . . I fear that they will have another Iran or Nicaragua here."

I take little credit for predicting Marcos's overthrow; it did not take a rocket scientist to see it coming.

The actual inauguration was held early in the morning because of the immense heat. Thousands of people were bused in, and the square was packed. The visiting dignitaries were on a stage overlooking a large crowd held back by security men holding hands. On the right, in the middle of the crowd, I noticed one of our tall Secret Service agents. In that group, he literally stood out in a crowd. During Marcos's address, a man suddenly broke through the hand-holding security line and charged across the square waving a tube. He got within five feet of Marcos before our tall agent, jumping over twenty or so people, managed to put both arms around him and carry him off. It must have embarrassed our hosts that their own men hadn't responded. Considering the fact that Imelda had been slashed by a machete several years before in just such a situation, their security should have known something could happen. We were so proud of our brave, disciplined agent. As it turns out, the tube held only a petition, but no one could have known that at the time.

We came home from that trip to our new summer home, Walker's Point in Kennebunkport, which we had purchased after George dropped out of the presidential race in 1980. George's Uncle Herbie Walker, a great friend and business backer in earlier days, had died and the Point was for sale. It had been in George's family since the turn of the century. Several commercial groups wanted to buy it, but George's mother would not sell her little acre that sits right in the middle of the Point. On a government salary we felt we couldn't afford it, but in June 1980, we were out of politics, so George bought it. Suddenly, in August, we were back in politics. So to meet our financial commitments, we sold our dream house in Houston and bought a small lot, and we also sold the gray house in Kennebunkport where we had summered for ten years. As it turns out, the Point was a smart buy for us as our happy gray house would have been impossible to protect. It was right on the street, and people often walked up on the porch and looked in the windows.

We are so lucky in Maine to have great friends who also are great builders. Longley Philbrick had worked on Walker's Point in 1925 when the porch was incorporated into the house as a living room. In 1981, Longley and his son Danny restored Walker's Point and helped us make many changes in the structure of the house. At this writing, Danny and his son Terry are restoring Mrs. Bush's bungalow.

Longley is gone, but the family, headed by his wife, Mary, represents everything that is great about America. They love their country, their God, and their family. They are fair, honest, and hardworking.

Walker's Point always had been an important part of George's life. For the next twelve years, it would be the perfect refuge from our high-profile lives and is now our summer home.

During the vice presidential years we had several terrific Memorial Day house parties in Maine. They were great fun for us as we gathered some of our favorite people, many of whom had not met each other before but are now friends. Political party affiliations made no difference in this house party. Among the many people who came were Louisiana Senator Bennett Johnston and his wife, Mary; Wyoming Senator Alan Simpson and Ann; Ambassador Fred Zeder and Martha; Betsy and Spike Heminway, from Kennebunkport and Greenwich, longtime friends of ours and our children; Malcolm Baldrige, Secretary of Commerce, and his wife, Midge; Pat and Dean Burch; Bobbie and Jack Fitch and Daphne and Bob Murray, all from Houston; former Houston neighbor Charles Neblett, a brilliant brain surgeon, and his wife, Sally; and Dick and Sally Novetzke (she later was named ambassador to Malta). These are all people that George and I love and enjoy.

One Memorial Day weekend, Mac Baldrige and George spoke at the First Congregational Church service on Sunday. Mac told about when he was a soldier during World War II, holding a hill on an island in the Pacific. During the day, a group of Japanese women started up the hill with water jars in their arms. Mac, as the leader, had to make the decision: Were they really women, or were they armed men? They got closer as dusk came, and Mac decided that he couldn't take a chance, so they opened fire and killed them. The next morning the Americans rushed down the hill and found that they had made the right decision—they were fully armed Japanese men.

Mac then skipped to several months later when he was with the occupation troops in Japan. They saw pictures of Americans as villains with long noses and mean faces—just as we saw Hirohito in our country. Worse, he saw that the average person was afraid of him and other Americans. He suddenly saw the Japanese as human beings. He ended his very moving talk by saying that we must learn all people are the same, and wars must end.

Several years later our dear friend Mac suffered a massive heart attack while taking part in a rodeo. Every Easter, our friend Annie Cluff gives an Easter lily in Mac's name at the First Congregational Church, and just recently we found two new hymnals in our pew given by Annie: one in Mac's name and one in ours.

September 10, 1981—I went to Sandra Day O'Connor's Senate hearings on her appointment to the Supreme Court, which was very exciting since she was the first woman nominated. Potter Stewart had resigned from the court after serving twenty-five years. When he was sworn in in 1956, he said that he would resign after that period of time and he did. I believe that he hoped that other older justices would do the same, but they didn't.

Sandra is everything that I admire in a woman. She and her husband, John, have three fine sons and have struck a balance in their two careers that is enviable. I was very happy to attend her swearing-in on September 25.

There are several stories that I love about Sandra. One concerns a graduation speech that she gave. She said that she never thought that she'd be a Supreme Court Justice. She just tried to do the best she could in everything she did: the best student, the best daughter, the best wife, the best mother, the best lawyer, and so on. I rather liked that because I have always felt that's what George Bush did. He just did his best at everything he took on. The mountain seems easier to climb if you take one hill at a time.

The other story I love about Sandra has to do with golf. She took up the game so she and John could enjoy it together. She took lessons and hit balls on the practice tee for several years before she ever played a game on a course. What marvelous discipline.

I played tennis with Sandra at seven A.M. once a week during both the vice presidential and White House years. She was always on time, a good sport, very competitive, and played a much better game than I did.

One morning I noticed that her hair was causing her great trouble. It was too long, and she kept poking it up. As with many busy women, she had a sense of priorities and her hair was not on that list. I mentioned to her that she badly needed a cut and my hairdresser had a shop near her on the Hill. I told her that I would call her office and give her secretary the number.

She called me that afternoon and said, "I had my hair cut, and I feel like a new person. Thank you so very much."

Several days later I got a note from her husband:

Dear Barbara,

I married Sandra 27 years ago, and once, the year after we were married, she had her hair styled. She's never done it since. When I came home, I said: "Wow. What happened?" She said: "Barbara Bush told me to have my hair cut." If I ever find myself in trouble with Sandra, may I call on you?

John

In spite of the hair story, Sandra and I have remained friends. I only wish that my children and other friends were as obedient when I make suggestions.

October 4, 1981—I came home to find George in the living room talking with a very nice man, the vice president of Egypt, Hosni Mubarak. A few days later, he was president of his country. On October 6, Anwar Sadat was assassinated, shot down during a military parade. That brave, courageous man was one of the heroes of the twentieth century, and the two or three times that I met him were very special. President Mubarak has been a great leader for Egypt, and he and his wife, Suzanne, have become dear friends of ours. Their job has not been an easy one, and the stand that he took years later during Desert Storm showed great courage.

It was thought too dangerous for the President or Vice President to attend Sadat's funeral, so President Reagan invited the former presidents to go, and they all accepted. The Reagans very kindly invited me to join George and the President's top three aides, Jim Baker, Mike

Deaver, and Ed Meese, at the White House when President Reagan symbolically gave the presidents a letter to carry to the funeral. We watched from a window as President Reagan and Nancy greeted the helicopter on the South Grounds. It was certainly a historic moment. There stood the four living presidents of the United States. It all rather amused me. I don't really think they liked each other very much. Ronald Reagan had challenged Jerry Ford in a nasty Republican primary fight in 1976. Jimmy Carter was beaten by Ronald Reagan in 1980. Jimmy Carter had beaten Jerry Ford in 1976. Many people believe Jerry Ford lost the election because he pardoned Richard Nixon. And there they all stood together. Rosalynn came also, and I don't believe that she and Nancy liked each other very much. Those tense fifteen minutes were up fairly quickly, and the helicopter took off for Andrews Air Force Base.

I was especially curious about who sat in the President's cabin. I was further amused to discover that it was "none of the above." Al Haig, who was Secretary of State, and Cap Weinberger, who was Secretary of Defense, did. And to be truthful, I don't think they liked each other very much either. Henry Kissinger was also on the trip. Now Henry and Al Haig had worked for Presidents Nixon and Ford, and, of course, Al worked for Henry. I don't know how much they all liked each other, but it was fun to speculate. And speculation it is—and a little fun I had.

October 17, 1981—President and Mrs. Mitterrand of France came to the United States to celebrate the two hundredth anniversary of America's—with France's help—victory at Yorktown, ending the Revolutionary War. George and I were asked to have a dinner for the Mitterrands one evening of the visit. The inn where we were holding the dinner sent us three menus to choose from. They sounded great, but all were French cuisine. I sent back a request that we have American food, and they came back with a delicious menu of pumpkin soup served in pumpkins, turkey, and other uniquely American foods. I was very pleased. You can't out-French the French, and we do very well on our own.

The next evening the Reagans had a sensational dinner with all the pomp and ceremony one could imagine. We made a dramatic entrance through men and women in colonial costumes, with flares to light our way. I never tried to out-Reagan the Reagans, either.

This was the beginning of a warm relationship George had with Mitterrand. For some reason, President Reagan and Mitterrand did not strike up a friendship, and it is pretty hard not to like Ronald Reagan.

November 19–23, 1981—Loret Ruppe, the able director of the Peace Corps and my dear 90th Club friend, invited me to go to Ghana to help celebrate the twenty-fifth anniversary of the corps. We had the most marvelous trip. Before we went, I called an old friend from our UN days, Shirley Temple Black, and asked her for any advice she might have since she had served there as ambassador. She came up with the same suggestion as others: Get some wedge-heeled shoes, as many of the parties were outside and the ground at this time of the year was soft from the rain. In regular heels, you would sink into the ground. So Becky, my aide, was sent out on a search, and after much looking did find some beige patent leather shoes with a wedge heel. What a laugh. All the ladies in Ghana wore the highest heels. We also were there during the driest, hottest time of year. The ground felt like rock, and not only did I look really dowdy, the patent leather cooked my feet.

One day we went out into the countryside, where we met with an *asantehene,* who is a chief of a tribe. This gentleman was a great big man with a very cultured voice; he was dressed in tribal robes and covered with gold toe and hand rings, chains, and other finery. (I also saw pictures of him in his white wig and barrister robes.) Then the ceremony started. Very dramatically we were led in to sit under an awning, then the tribes came in, dancing and singing to beating drums. The women came first, followed by the children and finally the men. It was hotter than one could believe. Finally the Asantehene was carried in with much pomp, and he sat opposite me under another tent. Little boys shimmied up long poles, teetering above our heads, and men and women did strange dances.

Out of the middle of all this came a man covered with white powder. The crowds parted, and he took center stage, dancing around and around in a frenzied fashion and swinging a feathered thing over his head and down on the ground. I'm not sure when it came to me that the feathered thing was a live chicken. I think it was just before this crazy man put its head in his mouth and bit it off. He then rubbed the blood on his body as his followers threw more white powder on him. Yuk. He got closer and closer to me until someone yelled at him, and they led him off. Becky almost fainted from the heat and disgust.

During all this I sat next to the governor of the state. He had on the darndest costume. He told me with pride that he had gotten the material in Europe. It was a simulated leopard skin that was made of something like oilcloth. He wore it like a toga, and it was dripping wet. I can't think of a more miserable outfit to wear—or to sit next to—in that kind of heat.

Another day we visited several villages where we saw the work our Peace Corps volunteers were doing. They were all ages, shapes, sizes, and colors. What extraordinary men and women. They are the very best aid that we give, I believe, for they teach people to do for themselves. It is not a handout, but a hand up. George and I have visited Peace Corps workers around the world. They sometimes live under the most destitute conditions but they always do a great job. I hated leaving them so far from home and tried to either write or call their relatives when I got back to the States. I will confess that I didn't always tell their families that their child or parent was living under the most primitive of conditions.

꿈 *December 1, 1981*—I was invited to put the star on the top of the national Christmas tree on the Ellipse in front of the White House. I went up in a cherry picker with a dear man named Joe Riley, who was and still is the chairman of the Annual Pageant of Peace. This ceremony is not to be confused with the annual lighting of the Christmas tree. The tree is the same, but the events are two weeks apart. The President has the honor of doing the latter. For the eight years George was vice president and the four he was president, up I went in that cherry picker. It was a wonderful, fun event. Over the years, Joe and I took many of the grandchildren—Jenna and Barbara, Sam and Ellie, Walker and Marshall, Lauren and Pierce—and several schoolchildren to help us. Some years were bumpy and some smooth; we went rain or shine. Sometimes I felt a little like Mary Poppins.

It struck me that I worked so hard all year long for literacy and got little or no press coverage, and then I would do something frivolous like going up in a cherry picker and my picture is seen around the world. So one year I took Rita and Rex Saurus, two puppets who encourage children to read. I had met Rita and Rex at a Reading Is Fundamental (RIF) event, and then saw them several times around the country. I am a huge fan of RIF and believe it is a very effective way to put books into the hands of children, many of whom never had the joy of owning a book. You can find RIF in schools, migrant workers' camps, homeless shelters, and soup kitchens, just to name a few. Although it gets some federal funding and many grants, it's largely a volunteer effort.

My dear friend Anne Richardson took over the leadership from its founder, Margaret McNamara. It has grown from Margaret taking her children's old books to a public school into a nationwide effort that gives away an estimated ten million books a year.

April 23–25, 1982—During a visit to Japan, George and I had lunch at the Imperial Palace with Emperor Hirohito. While waiting for him to appear, I remember standing in front of some closed double doors and thinking that behind them stood the man we thought of as the devil when we were growing up. This was whom, rightly or wrongly, we blamed for Pearl Harbor. When the doors opened there stood a tiny, gentle-looking being.

During that most memorable lunch, I sat next to the Emperor and found the conversation pretty heavy sledding. I would say, "I went to the school your grandchildren attend this morning." He would smile and say, "Yes." He had a "yes" or "no" answer for everything with an occasional "thank you" thrown in. We were sitting in the glorious, relatively new palace, so, desperate for something to talk about, I said that the new palace was lovely.

"Thank you," he answered.

Then I tried, "Is it new?"

"Yes."

Finally I tried: "Was the old palace just so old that it was falling down?"

He turned with a charming smile on his face and said, "No, I'm afraid that you bombed it."

I turned to my partner on my left.

* * *

◇ *September 1, 1982*—Doro, who had graduated from Boston College in June, married Bill LeBlond on a cold, rainy day in Kennebunkport at little St. Ann's Church. This is our summer church in Maine, open only from the Fourth of July to Labor Day. George's parents and Neil and Sharon were married there, several of our children were christened there, and various other family functions have taken place in this beautiful stone church.

We were to have a reception under a big tent on the lawn at Walker's Point. We awakened that day to not only rain, but a fierce rain that came in at an angle. I will never get over being grateful to Jane Weintraub, formerly Jane Morgan, a Kennebunkport friend and neighbor and a marvelous entertainer. She came by that morning around nine A.M. to see if she could help. I was suffering over just what I should do. Should we move the party into the Boat Club? Should we take a chance and stick with the tent? George was calling the Coast Guard for weather reports on the hour when Jane said: "Make up your mind at ten o'clock. We move to the Boat Club or we don't and then sit back and enjoy it." We did just that, moving to the Boat Club. We stopped the florist from decorating the tent, and she and my boys moved the tables and chairs and the flowers. It was a day of hard work for all.

I was amused because many "Bush-watchers" had gathered across the bay with chairs to see the Vice President's daughter get married. They did not get the word and watched the empty tent for hours in pouring rain.

In spite of the weather, it was a happy wedding. Bill's parents are dear friends, and we love Billy. Sad to say, the children did not stay married. They had two very beautiful children, Ellie and Sam, and have behaved in a way that should be a manual when that awful thing, divorce, happens to others. The happy ending is that they both have remarried lovely people, and Sam and Ellie have two sets of parents, siblings on both sides, and more grandparents who love them than any other children I know.

◇ *October 3, 1982*—George and I had the great pleasure of dedicating the Betty Ford Center in Palm Springs, California. George said in his speech what we both felt:

In 1978 Betty Ford discovered that she had become dependent on alcohol and drugs. I can state the case plainly because Betty has already had the courage to do so.

. . . She transformed her pain into something great for the common good. Because she suffered, there will be more healing. Because of her grief, there will be more joy.

. . . Our nation has produced great men. It has also produced great women. Our gracious First Lady stands among them.

November 9–24, 1982—George led a delegation on an African trip, including Dr. Ben Payton of Tuskegee and Dr. Louis Sullivan of the Morehouse School of Medicine, representing two prestigious, predominantly black schools. We had some funny things happen on that trip. At one luncheon, our hosts wanted to make us feel at home so they played American music—"Ol' Black Joe," "Carry Me Back to Old Virginny," and some other gems. I caught Louis Sullivan's eye, and he winked at me.

In Zaire, both men went with me to visit a literacy program at a university. A lady named Alice Anderson had come to Zaire for a short visit, saw a great need, and stayed on for the next twenty years to teach people to read. We attended a graduation, where I gave a small talk and handed out certificates. Then some of the students read a short story telling us what reading meant to them. Their reasons resembled what I heard from adult literacy students in our own country: They want to get a job; they want their children to be proud of them; they want to read their Bibles, and so forth. Then one woman got up and said: "I needed to read. My husband kept getting letters. He said they were business. Now I can read . . . now I know." She left the clear impression that her husband had been up to no good, and she had put a stop to that!

Shortly after we returned from that trip, Dr. Sullivan invited me to join the Morehouse School of Medicine Board of Directors. I accepted and spent six very happy years with some of the finest men and women I have ever met. Although I was concentrating most of my time on literacy, there is a very good argument that a healthy child is a better learner, so there was a definite connection.

It is not easy trying to start and support a medical school. Louis Sullivan did and did it well. It was a constant struggle, especially when we had no alumni to draw from. I traveled with Louis and fellow board member Bob Froehlke to many cities across the United States to fund-raising lunches. The need for a school like Morehouse is very apparent. There are many rural and inner-city areas in our great country that are medically underserved or not served at all. Morehouse doctors are being trained to go into these areas.

Although I went off the board when George was sworn in as president, I certainly didn't lose interest. I went back in October 1989 to give the convocation speech, which said in part:

> Compared to white children, black children are twice as likely to die in the first year of life; three times as likely to have their mothers die in childbirth; and five times as likely to become pregnant teenagers . . . boarder babies, throw-away kids, crack babies. It doesn't sound urgent enough to call these children the "medically underserved." The children George and I have seen at Covenant House, Grandma's House, Martha's Table, and at D.C. General Hospital are literally fighting for their lives. Their fight is our fight . . . and that fight is the mission of Morehouse.

It always amused me that I got credit for Louis's being asked to join George's cabinet as Secretary of Health and Human Services. George introduced me to Louis, and I got invited to join his board because I was George Bush's wife. They certainly got that one wrong, but I was always glad to get the credit. Lou and Ginger were a great addition to the Washington scene, and he was an outstanding HHS secretary. Lucky for the school, he has returned to Morehouse.

In the middle of our trip to Africa we got the word that Soviet leader Leonid Brezhnev had died. There were many cables sent back and forth about who would go to the funeral. We heard that all the former presidents and secretaries of state wanted to go with George. There was so much pressure being put on the White House and State Department that it was decided "none of the above"; Barbara

Bush would go and then nobody could gripe. What a break for me. The fact that I had only summer clothes with me and this was November in Moscow made no difference. We called Laurie Firestone and she bundled up boots, gloves, dresses, and a winter coat along with George's clothes and saw that they were put on Secretary of State George Shultz's plane.

We left most of our traveling party in Africa and flew off to Moscow for the most extraordinary day or two. On our arrival, Secretary Shultz boarded our plane with our winter coats, which we put on over our summer clothes, and we went right away to view the body, lying in state at the Kremlin. We walked up a glorious, winding staircase with the most haunting music wafting downward. Above our heads were large wall sconces, all wrapped in black net. Russians were standing about four deep. I will have to confess that I saw no people weeping for Brezhnev, in contrast to China, where the people kept their heads down and looked mournful at Chou En-lai's funeral. The people we saw were all types, some very well dressed and some not so well dressed.

Suddenly we were at the top of the staircase, and there in a bier directly in front of us, slightly tilted upward, was the body of the former chairman. To our left was a symphony orchestra all dressed in black and the source of the plaintive music. The whole casket was covered with a blanket of flowers, and his medals were displayed at the front. To the right sat a sweet, sad little group, and George rightly judged an older lady to be Mrs. Brezhnev. He told her that he was an American expressing the grief of our people, and she answered back something about our two peoples wanting peace. It was amazing that before this funeral, we Americans were not even sure that there was a Mrs. Brezhnev.

The next morning our ambassador's wife, Donna Hartman, bundled us up, and George, George Shultz, Ambassador Arthur Hartman, and I went off to the funeral. It was the most beautifully orchestrated event I have ever attended. I wrote in my diary:

We got to Red Square, got to a certain spot and were let off. We came out behind Lenin's Tomb and the next thing I knew, they came up and said: "This is the place where you stop." They let George Bush through and then there was some discussion as to whether or not I could go through. Finally they said: "Yes, because she is part of the delegation."

And Secretary Shultz was sort of pulled through. They cut off Arthur Hartman and my Secret Service, but they had a better view than us, to be honest. They could see Castro, Arafat and the rest. They had put on the left all the countries who were sort of friendly to them, and on the right countries like us and Great Britain, Italy, Australia and Ireland.

In the middle of the square was an orchestra that stood at the ready without moving or playing for an hour. Directly in front of us stood the most elite, Aryan-looking troops I have ever seen, all facing us. I was amazed. This in a country that prides itself on having some forty minorities.

As we stood talking with our friends from Great Britain, Ireland, and Italy, we heard a great commotion in the crowd, and pushing by us went Imelda Marcos. She had on the most extraordinary floor-length mink coat with a herringbone pattern. Very soon after she passed an aide came back and said, "The First Lady of the Philippines would like the Vice President of the United States to join her in the front row." George thanked him and turned him down. George Shultz and I told George that was lucky for him. Had he accepted, it would have been the end: George Shultz would not have let him back in the country, and I certainly would never have let him back into the house. How we later laughed over that.

The funeral started on the hour, and in came the casket drawn by a tank, solemnly followed by Brezhnev's family, who were walking. The orchestra started playing the most beautiful lugubrious music. The casket was turned to face the tomb, where the hierarchy of the Soviet Union was standing. There were no women near the top. We saw Gromyko, that great cold warrior, and Andropov, the former head of the KGB and the newly designated leader of the USSR. There were many speeches, and we all huddled around an interpreter with the Irish delegation. The speeches said very little about Brezhnev and lots about the future. The casket was taken around behind the tomb, followed by family and then the diplomats. I was cut away from the men and led toward the cars, where Arthur Hartman and I waited for the two Georges. The minute the casket disappeared, the whole tone of the day changed. The music was one of victory and jubilation. One of our Western friends rather cynically said, "The King is dead, never to be mentioned again."

Much to his surprise, George saw Mrs. Brezhnev lean over the coffin and make the sign of the cross. After the funeral was over, both Georges were led up a staircase into a great hall in the Kremlin where they shook hands with the top leadership of the country, including Andropov.

Just fourteen months later, George would attend Andropov's funeral and meet his successor, Chernenko, and then a year later, he would go to his funeral, where he met Mikhail Gorbachev. George developed a friendship with Gorbachev and to this day has enormous respect for this thoughtful man who really changed our whole world for the better.

It was shortly after the Chernenko funeral that people started introducing George as the man with the motto "You die, I fly."

I was amazed recently to read that Vice President Gore announced that he didn't do funerals. I really feel that is shortsighted. George met with many current or future heads of state at the funerals he attended, enabling him to forge personal relationships that were important to President Reagan—and later, President Bush.

July 10, 1983—George and I hosted a clambake at Walker's Point for the governors and their families who were attending a governors' conference in Maine. (Many years later, Bill Clinton would remind Chelsea that she had met us that day.) There were so many governors and family members that we had to make a rule that no straphangers—meaning staff members—were allowed. Those with babies under age two could bring nannies, but that was it.

Our children helped with tours of the Point, and then we had a typical Maine clambake with clams, lobster, fresh Maine corn, coleslaw, salad, ice-cream bars, and of course hamburgers and hot dogs for those who can't face shellfish.

George's mother joined us on the lawn for lunch and met all the governors. Governor George Wallace came with his new, very sensual third wife, I believe. (I know that she was sensual; it's which wife she was that I'm unsure of.) She had on a very tight dress, was very well endowed, and had her hair pouffed up with much teasing and hair spray. By comparison, the rest of us looked a little underdressed in pants and cotton shirts. The Governor was in his wheelchair, pushed by an Alabama state policeman. They both were very pleasant and polite to Mrs. Bush. After the lunch, when we were alone, Mrs. Bush said, "George, I just can't see what that nice man sees in that woman." George didn't have the heart to tell her.

George liked and felt a lot of sympathy for George Wallace. Whether or not you agree politically with a person is certainly no excuse for taking the law into your own hands.

August 6–8, 1983—In the middle of a trip to the western states, George decided that we should go camping in Glacier National Park in Montana. I was thrilled as I had never visited a national park. George also decided that we would sleep in a tent in the woods. The others in our party had a choice of a tent or a camper with running water, indoor plumbing, and air-conditioning. Not for us. We wanted to be communing with nature. So our little tent was set up quite a way from the others; we zipped ourselves in and climbed into our sleeping bags with many giggles. It didn't take long for us to realize that for security reasons, our tent was ringed with lights some thirty feet away. We felt like we were sleeping in the middle of Times Square. Then the roots under our sleeping bags started to torture our backs. It was very hard to sleep. Finally George got up to go to the bathroom in the woods to discover that behind every light and tree was a Secret Service agent. It was one of the most miserable nights of our lives. The next night two tiny mattresses appeared under our sleeping bags, and a jar appeared for George's nocturnal use. I walked half a mile to the camper, followed by an agent. I was tempted to stay.

Nevertheless, that was really one of the most fun trips we took. Wyoming Senator Alan Simpson and his wife, Ann, were with us, and as always, they were great fun to be with. The park was beautiful, and the National Park Service people were splendid.

September 11–21, 1983—George and I took an amazing ten-day trip to northern Africa, visiting Morocco, Algeria, and Tunisia, and then went on to Yugoslavia, Romania, Hungary, and Austria, refueling at Ireland on the way home. In every country we were received graciously by the leaders of the country. We had dinner with King Hassan in Morocco, lunch with President and Mrs. Bendjedid of Algeria, and an unusual

luncheon given by President and Mrs. Bourguiba of Tunisia. He was a
national hero who many years before had been the "father of his country."
By 1983 this fine man was very old and senile. His doctor had put him
on a diet, so all during lunch he ate from my plate. When it came time
for his toast, with the TV cameras running, he fumbled and yelled. His
glasses slid down his nose, and he shouted that he was going blind until
his wife leaned across the table and pushed them up. When George got
up to give his toast, this poor man interrupted, ranting and raving until
he was quietly pulled down. It wasn't funny, just sad. What was amazing
was, on the evening TV news, he looked perfectly in control.

In Yugoslavia, Kim Brady, my personal aide, became very ill and
ended up having her appendix out. Luckily, it was a very good hospital and her doctor had been trained in Houston. How I hated to leave
her there, but her mother was en route to be with her and the ambassador, David Anderson, and his wife, Helen, were wonderful. Before
leaving, we had dinner with the Foreign Minister, Lazar Mojsov, and
his wife, old friends from the United Nations.

Then it was on to Romania for an unbelievable twenty-four hours.
We were warned that President and Mrs. Ceauşescu were very strange
people. We weren't surprised, then, to find that the plans for meeting with them were loose and different. Our events in Bucharest were
few and very limited. I visited a pleasant outdoor museum promoting
their handicrafts. We noticed that the streets were large, broad, and
very empty. The people were downcast, drab, and unhappy-looking.
In most cities around the world, you would see people walking around
outside after work enjoying life. Not here. It was a dreary place.

The tentative plan was for George to meet with Ceauşescu, then
there would be a dinner. The problem was that no one knew who was
invited. I was told early in the evening that it was going to be just
George and me and the dinner would be held at the Lodge, an informal place. So I dressed and settled down with a book. I waited and
waited. Then the word came that the plans had changed and we would
be eating at the official residence. So I changed into a short black taf-
feta dress with a little velvet trim. I was picked up by a sturdy interpreter with a nice smile and henna-colored hair, which finds such favor
in Eastern European countries. She took me to a large house where we
sat in the front hall for an hour and had a strained chat. The hour was
getting later and later. I could hear men's voices in the background

and recognized George's, otherwise I would have felt that I was in the wrong place. At about 8:45 P.M., a plain-looking, very informally dressed woman walked down the staircase and was introduced as Mrs. Ceauşescu. We sat in the stiff front hall and talked. She had no small talk, spoke not a word of English, and did not initiate one word of conversation. After forty-five tense minutes, the door opened and out walked George and President Ceauşescu, thank heavens. At ten o'clock we went into a magnificent dining room with a long table that probably seated sixteen or eighteen people. Down one side were four place settings with about three feet separating each one. I sat on the end, followed by the President, then George, and finally, waaaaaaay down on the other end, Mrs. Ceauşescu. No sooner had we gotten seated than the press were led in for pictures. I looked down the table and saw George smiling and the two of them looking grumpy as if they smelled something bad. So all the pictures that appeared in the papers reflected that we were having fun and they were not.

A seven-course meal followed, starting with bowls of caviar served by four men in lavender livery. There were plates of bread, butter, fruit, and cheeses at each place. At one time during the lavish meal, a London broil was served, and after I took a tiny piece, my lavender-liveried waiter said: "Oh, go on, take some more, it's good," in an obviously Brooklyn accent! What in the world an American was doing serving our dinner I never did find out. I couldn't believe all the grandeur in a country where people were lining up for every bite they ate and where we had been told the shortages were almost overwhelming.

All during the dinner Ceauşescu talked and talked and talked and George listened. When George tried to answer or talk, Ceauşescu interrupted. We were stunned by his ego. She spoke once only, and he turned and said something that was not interpreted, but the tone of voice led me to believe it was something like "Be quiet!" Years later it would be clear that we had been with two of the most evil people in this world.

The visit to Hungary was very typical of the many trips we took during the vice presidential years. I visited schools, hospitals, museums, and met with the leading women of the country while George met with the heads of state.

*   *   *

〜 *October 23, 1983*—Tragedy struck when 241 of our Marines, who were part of a multinational peace-keeping force, were killed in Beirut by a kamikaze terrorist attack. The country was stunned. George was going to make a top-secret trip to the war-torn country to boost the remaining troops' morale. He told me he would go to the office and leave from there, taking only Admiral Dan Murphy, Shirley Green, and Jennifer Fitzgerald of his staff. We were supposed to go to the Pakistan Embassy that night for a dinner given for us by General Zia. George asked me to go alone and told me to sidle up to the General and explain just how sorry he was and that he would know the next morning why he wasn't there. Thank heavens that I did not have to go to the Embassy. The nice Chief Justice Warren Burger went in George's place. I could never ever have kept from showing how frightened I was.

George told me that his trip was very safe and that I must not worry, but that for the sake of security, I must be very, very discreet and not tell another living human.

Several times during the day I got calls from the White House switchboard asking me if George was home. Each time I said no. The operator mused once, "Well, we show him still at the office, but he isn't answering." I kept my regular schedule and went to a Ronald McDonald House event and later to a Daughters of the American Revolution tea where they very kindly gave me a medal for my work with literacy. I felt funny not saying a word to Susan Porter Rose or Andy Stewart, to whom I tell everything—almost.

That night I sat at home alone doing needlepoint, worrying and praying. The phone rang, and it was Steve Rhodes, a wonderful man who worked for George and who also was a friend. He said that he had been trying to reach George all day. I lied and hated it. I told him that George was in a very important meeting and I expected it to run very late.

The next morning when I awakened, I saw George in Beirut on TV. One minute later he called. He had told me that he would call the minute the plane left Beirut, and he did. I called his mother immediately so she would not worry when she saw him over there. I was so grateful. I will confess that keeping secrets is an enormous burden for me. Having George in danger is almost unbearable.

*   *   *

⚬ *February 11–12, 1984*—We went to England and stayed at Winfield House with our wonderful Ambassador Charlie Price and his wife, Carol. Carol is the person in the world that you would most like to stay with. She is the best hostess, very thoughtful, and runs the most comfortable household. They hosted a glorious black-tie dinner, including on the guest list many Americans who came to England especially for the evening and some who were in Europe for a vacation or business. One of our more stylish friends wore the darndest dress for a thin, over-thirty—well, maybe over-fifty—socialite. It was a green chiffon sheath with a bib top and spaghetti straps. The side view on an eighteen-year-old would have been provocative; on an aging lady who was prone to flamboyant gestures, it was embarrassing.

The next day, Margaret and Denis Thatcher gave a large lunch at No. 10 Downing Street, the home of the prime minister. George sat next to Denis, and I noticed they were sharing a big laugh. George told Denis to tell me the joke, which he did immediately. "George asked me if I hadn't enjoyed the dinner at the U.S. Embassy the night before," Denis said. "And I replied that I had; but that I had sat next to [the woman in question] and quite frankly, I got awfully tired of looking at her left tit." I was so surprised that I burst out laughing; not a small giggle, but a loud laugh. At which time Margaret turned to George and said, "Isn't it nice that Denis and Barbara get along so well?" That got the three of us really laughing.

On that same visit the Thatchers invited us and the Prices to Checquers. It was a joy to see this exciting country estate, which is the British equivalent of Camp David. We were greeted by our host and hostess, given a cup of tea, and led to our rooms. Margaret made sure that I was comfortable and had plenty to read; gave me the guest list for dinner, saying that she had picked dinner partners that she thought I would enjoy; then rushed off to discuss armaments and other issues with George. Amazing. I remembered being very moved and touched by her thoughtfulness and thinking that she combined all that was good about being a woman in public life. She was proud of both her ability and of being a woman.

While they talked, Denis squired Carol Price and me around, showing us, among many things, trees that foreign heads of state had planted. Although I later went back to Checquers with Norma Major, George never went as president and so did not plant a tree there. On

Sunday morning while the leaders worked, Denis, Carol, and I went to a lovely tiny church that sat on top of a hill and that had a spire that was taller than the church was wide or long. Denis told me not to worry—the service would not be too long. And believe me, it wasn't. The poor minister had barely gotten into his sermon when Denis made a loud "Ahem," raised his arm, and looked pointedly at his watch. It worked. The sermon drew rapidly to a close.

Every time I saw Denis, I loved him more. When George and I first met the Thatchers, George was still in Congress, and Margaret came to Houston to give a speech. I was so impressed with her knowledge and presentation. But Denis I found rather rude, especially when he made several disparaging remarks to me about Americans. But I learned over the years that he has a wonderful sense of humor and is steady as a rock. Plus, he's a good sport. Many times he found himself the only male in a roomful of "spouses."

April 3, 1984—C. Fred officially became a famous dog and an author with the publication of *C. Fred's Story.* I don't know who was more surprised—him or me.

It all started many months earlier when we were having dinner with Nelson and Sandy Doubleday at the Vice President's House. Nelson backed into C. Fred, and George said, "Don't kick that dog. He is writing a book." Nelson took George seriously, and several weeks later asked me to talk to Lisa Drew, an editor at Doubleday. I certainly did not know when I met this bright, feisty, funny lady that she would edit three books for me, help me with a foundation, and become a good friend.

Up until this point, I really just had been *talking* about writing a book with Freddy. I wanted to raise some money for literacy, and that was just one idea that I had. Lisa came to call on me when she was in Washington, and we were on our way. I'm not sure that Lisa ever had a handwritten manuscript sent to her before, but I do know that after she saw mine, she requested a typewritten one. Thank heavens, our dear friend Jane Kenny typed it for me. We had a lot of fun with that book and raised around $100,000 for Literacy Volunteers of America and Laubach Literacy Action, the two national programs I had been working with.

About half the money raised came from donations people sent in. One day George called and asked if I was seated. He knew I'd fall down otherwise when he told me that he had opened a letter from someone whom we had never met, a Mr. Joseph Uihlein of Grafton, Wisconsin, but who was a friend and classmate of George's uncle, Dr. John Walker. He had sent a check for $25,000 for LVA along with a letter saying he liked the book. In my wildest dreams I never thought the book would make $25,000, so the whole experience was very happy for me. On a smaller scale, quite a few other people sent in checks and contributions.

We had several book parties in public libraries, including the kickoff at the New York City Public Library. I am a big supporter of libraries, which play such an important role in our educational system. Many of them sponsor literacy classes and programs to get children hooked on books early in life. Sad to say, if there is a money crunch, the libraries are the first to feel it—just when their services are the most needed. Many city libraries have numerous programs that can really help, such as English as a Second Language classes, seminars on job hunting, coffee kitchens for mothers, story times for children, art appreciation classes, and on and on.

In conjunction with the book parties, I also went on a media tour to talk about the book. I didn't mind doing that as I really wanted to talk about the problems of illiteracy in this country. I wanted people to know that we had a literacy problem and to urge them to be part of the answer, whether they donated money to local programs that worked, volunteered their time, or just made darn sure that they were reading aloud to their children and grandchildren. It gave me an opportunity to urge people to support their public libraries and to take an interest in their children's schools by volunteering, running for the school board, or just attending PTA meetings. My mission was to make literacy an important value in every household.

So the day after the first book party, I appeared on the "Today" show to be interviewed by my old friend, Jane Pauley. She raced on the set, and as she was putting on her mike, she said something like, "Let's make this fun and not talk about literacy." Not talk about literacy? No way. That was what I was there for. Her first question was, "Mrs. Bush, why would a dog write a book?" Knowing that this might be my only chance, my answer was that he was worried about illiteracy in our country, and then I got in as many facts as possible before I let her get another word in edgewise.

～ *May 7–20, 1984*—George and I took a fascinating trip to Japan, Indonesia, India, and Pakistan.

In Japan we lunched with Prime Minister and Mrs. Nakasone, a very attractive couple, and their children. We also had a reunion with Mike Mansfield, a former senator and our ambassador to Japan, and his wife, Maureen. I believe that when they thought up the word "gentleman," Mike was the model.

In Indonesia our host was Vice President Wirahadikusuma. I just put this in because I loved thinking about saying to a store owner: "Just charge it to Umar Wirahadikusuma, please." We called on President and Mrs. Suharto, and most important, we saw our former colleagues from our days in China, Martha and John Holdridge; John was now our very able ambassador in Indonesia.

In India, George and I had dinner with Indira Gandhi at her house. Also in the group were Mrs. Gandhi's son, Rajiv, and his wife, Sonja. I wrote in my diary:

The Prime Minister's house was modest, really nice. Rajiv and Sonja live with Mrs. Gandhi. Sonja runs the household and Mrs. G. pretty much tells her what to do. They have a staff of servants. A lovely garden with many lilies out the window in full bloom. Sonja, who is from Italy, tells me she has vegetables growing in the back of the house. The minute we arrived Mrs. Gandhi and George went to another room to talk privately. Sonja and Rajiv have been married 16 years and have two children, a boy age 13 and a girl 12. The boy was with us briefly. Mrs. G. seems very affectionate towards him. We keep hearing that she is gearing this son to succeed her. Seems very hard for me to believe. He seems soft to me . . . just a little overweight and elite and effete to me. He also seemed feminine in that he was interested in gardens, schools and things I was interested in. He was educated in a public (our private) boarding school in India where his son is now, on to Cambridge where he met this very beautiful Italian girl. They are very attractive, very compatible, very easy to be with, loving, a gentle kind of man . . .

The five of us had a very pleasant dinner talking of many things. I was surprised to hear that Mrs. Gandhi's husband was not related to Mahatma Gandhi; I knew that she was Nehru's daughter. We discussed the awful dowry system that was causing such a scandal in India at the time. Then we learned that all the Gandhis had chosen their own mates. (Unfortunately, she was divorced.) After dinner George and Mrs. Gandhi retired again, and the young couple and I returned to garden talk.

Back on the airplane I was asked by the support team to give my impression of Rajiv because he was little known to Americans. His late brother, who had been killed in a plane accident, had been the apple of his mother's eye and had been the one being trained to take over. I told them my thoughts. To this day I blush about that. I could not have been more wrong. Several months later his mother was assassinated by some of her own guards, and Rajiv took over. From the moment of her death, he was strong, brave, and wise. He didn't just reach into thin air and find strength when he had to; he had it all along, and I was just too naive to see it. Later, when they were in the United States, we were thrilled to escort Sonja and Rajiv to Houston for a visit to NASA. The tragedy is that this fine young man was assassinated by a fanatic. George and I felt a personal loss.

We then went to Pakistan, where we were guests of President Zia. He had the most beautiful eyes I have ever seen, and was very sweet to a very nice, but very plain, wife and a retarded daughter he took many places with him. He also had put to death our friend, Prime Minister Bhutto. Just ten years before we had been guests of Bhutto, stayed in the same guest house with the same household staff. What a strange world. Not too many years later, Zia himself would die in a plane crash under very suspicious circumstances. What to believe? Was he a good man or a devil? I remember thinking after he died that I hoped someone took care of his wife and child. Bhutto's beautiful daughter, Benazir, then became prime minister and visited us while we were in the White House. She now also is embroiled in political problems involving her own family.

Next we visited the Khyber Pass, which historically had been the gateway into India. History tells us this was where Alexander the Great and, much later, Genghis Khan came through the rough and impassable Hindu Kush mountains to conquer India.

Now it is the border between Pakistan and Afghanistan, and at the time of our visit, a very dangerous place to be. We were eye-to-eye with Soviet and Afghan Communist troops, and we were told not to put one foot over the border or we might be shot. We visited a forward base for the Pakistani forces who were defending against possible Afghan aggression.

From there we went to one of the largest camps for political refugees from Afghanistan, located between the pass and Peshawar. The land was barren, with no trees or grass in sight. We were told that men and women lived in separate sections—almost separate worlds. Theirs is a male-oriented society where the men take care of the women, and we were told that the first thing the Communists did when they attacked a village was to kill males of all ages and rape the women and girls. The women often fled over their mountains with improper clothing, dragging or carrying their children with them. Many died, and many others buried their babies along the way.

George went to an enormous tent where he addressed thousands of men, and I was led into a smaller tent where about one hundred of these "women without men" were seated. I looked carefully around the tent and saw empty faces and dead eyes. To my horror, I was introduced to speak.

I fumbled around, telling them that we had brought them food and medicine. I put my hand over my heart and told them that President Reagan and the people of the United States were thinking about them and cared. I smiled and stepped back. Nothing. Absolutely no response.

Then someone whispered in my ear to keep talking because George was still speaking. We could hear roars of cheering coming from the men's tent. So I tried again. This time I asked them to tell us about themselves. The first woman told us a hideous story of death and destruction. Again, I told her we sympathized and cared. Those dead eyes came alive, her voice got strident, and she was screaming at me. I asked the Pakistani interpreter just what the woman was saying, and she said in a soft voice, "She says she is grateful to you and thank you." The next woman and the next and the next all told similar tales and looked beseechingly at me. Again they would scream at me and wave their arms. And again the interpreter would tell me they were saying things like, "She wants to thank the generous people of the United States for their kindness."

Finally it ended, and when we got into the car, my American interpreter told me the women really were saying things like, "We don't want your sympathy. We want guns. Our lives are worth nothing. We want weapons to go kill the Communists. We want to go home."

I have thought about these women a lot, and sometimes I think being told that you can never go home again must be the toughest thing in the world.

⌒ *June 12, 1984*—For George's birthday I invited the Reagans to come by for a surprise drink with us. They had just returned from the annual Economic Summit meeting in Europe and, as usual, the President was full of marvelous stories. He told one about how rude Canadian Prime Minister Pierre Trudeau had been to Margaret Thatcher. When President Reagan mentioned it to her, she said: "Don't worry. We women are used to men who don't mature."

14

The Poet Laureate (Retired)

The campaign in 1984 was a relatively simple one for the President of the United States. The economy had recovered with a bang, and Ronald Reagan was riding a great high.

It was not so easy for the Vice President. George had been the butt of the liberal press's frustration over Reagan's popularity, and he was running against history in the making: Geraldine Ferraro, the first woman to be a candidate for vice president for one of the major parties. I'm sure that we will mature as a country when it comes to a woman running against a man, but in 1984 it was very difficult. There seemed to be a double standard: one for her and one for George.

Case in point: One of the nicest events in Washington is the Italian-American Dinner, held every fall. Either the president or vice president usually attends, and in an election year, so do the candidates. It's a black-tie event that draws a very large crowd from across this country and from Italy. In 1984, George and I arrived first, soon to be joined by the President and Nancy in a holding room. Normally the president arrives later, so we should have been able to go right into the dinner. However, we were told that Mrs. Ferraro's dress had been left on the plane, and we would have to wait. After about twenty minutes, the President and George decided that two thousand people should not be kept waiting any longer, so we went in. Not too much later, the Mondales and Geraldine appeared—the women, I might add, in short silk dresses although the rest of us were in formal clothes. Had she been a man, she would have come in her suit and apologized and explained that her bags were lost. Everyone has lost bags and would have understood. She then proceeded to talk throughout President Reagan's speech. She was playing by women's rules. By the way, she got a polite hand and the President brought down the house.

That night was the first time I had seen Geraldine in person, and I wrote in my diary: "It was good to see that she didn't have wings and a halo and her feet were on the ground."

Another case in point: George was campaigning in the shipyards the day after their debate. He was working his way down a group of longshoremen when one man held up a sign saying: GEORGE, YOU KICKED A LITTLE ASS LAST NIGHT! The man followed George all along the line, and as George was getting in the car, he leaned over and repeated what that longshoreman said in a low voice. This was picked up by a TV boom mike and made a big splash for days on the news. Geraldine and her followers claimed that it was a sexist expression. Baloney. I will say that it is not my favorite, but as the mother of four competitive boys, I know what that expression means and, I suspect, so does Geraldine.

I campaigned all over the country for the ticket with great pleasure until one fateful day when George and I were flying to New York City. I was in the press section of the plane laughing and joking with Terry Hunt of the Associated Press and Ira Allen of UPI about the debate the night before between the President and Fritz Mondale. Fritz had needled the President about his elite, rich vice president. It really had burned me up because we all had read that Geraldine and her husband, John Zaccaro, were worth at least $4 million, if not more. The press were teasing me about it, and I said something like, "That rich . . . well, it rhymes with rich . . . could buy George Bush any day." It was not a nice thing to say. But we all laughed and went on with a jovial give-and-take.

George and I did a joint event in New York and then parted ways. I was on my way to the airport when Kim Brady told me that my statement was running every few minutes on the radio and would shortly be on TV. We arrived at the airport, went into a holding room, and I immediately called Geraldine and apologized. She was very gracious about it. I certainly wasn't lying about being sorry. I would rather die than hurt George Bush in any way and what I had said in jest was ugly.

I called George to confess. He was so dear, saying that he had heard it, but not to worry. Worse things had happened. As we were talking, Kim came into the room and told me that there were press waiting for me outside the boarding gate for our flight to Buffalo. Then I was really upset. I told George, and he said that I should call him back in five minutes, that he was with Dick Moore and they would think of something. When I called back, he said he was on an open phone, but that Dick's advice was to "remember Halloween." So I marched out smiling and said that I had talked to Ms. Ferraro, apologized for calling her a witch, and that she had graciously accepted my apology.

Everything said on the campaign plane was supposed to be off the record unless specified otherwise. It was dumb of me to believe that. I do not blame the press for reporting it because I should have known better. But they should know that I never again felt free to be relaxed with them. The other reason I regretted saying it was that it was not nice and I choose to think that I am not like that.

I can laugh about this incident now, but at the time it was agony. For several years I thought it would be engraved on my tombstone. My family teasingly called me the "Poet Laureate" of our household.

Another torturous event of the campaign for us was marching in the annual Columbus Day Parade in New York City. The sparsely attended Labor Day Parade had been a large embarrassment to the Democrats, so this time they bused people in. The streets of New York were filled with their supporters carrying Mondale/Ferraro signs. They yelled and jeered at George and me. We were saved by the beautiful Sophia Loren, who, as grand marshal, marched right in front of us. Nobody would dream of booing her.

At one time during the parade we were told that we shouldn't worry, "our people" were "up around Fifty-second Street." When we got there, we saw one Reagan/Bush sign carried by our cousins, Debbie and Craig Stapleton, with their daughter, Wendy, on Craig's shoulders. Those dear, loyal people ran up and appeared on every corner as long as we stayed in the parade. It was so bad that one of the organizers felt sorry for me and came back and said, "Mrs. Bush, don't worry. George McGovern won the 1972 Columbus Day Parade."

Because Geraldine was the first woman chosen to run for vice president, the national media assigned many women to cover both her and our campaign. It was a hostile press on our plane, and the camaraderie of earlier campaigns was gone. A CBS reporter told George that was not true of the Ferraro plane, where, according to him, women reporters often went to the front and helped with strategy. At one of the debates, the women of the press cheered when they thought Geraldine had scored a point. Another time they gave her a standing ovation. After the debate, the press reported that she won; the polls said George won.

So the 1984 campaign was not much fun for us. But it wasn't any better for the Mondales and the Ferraros/Zaccaros either: The former because he was running against a very popular president, and the latter because they were plagued by ugly rumors. Our personal experiences with both of them and their families were extraordinarily nice.

More important, we won another four years.

Once again we got ready for an Inauguration, and once again I was destined to sport a bandage with my fancy clothes. In early January, while George and I were in Florida visiting his mother, I got hit by a car while taking a walk. For some reason, the driver tried to pass another car on the right, driving up on the grass where I was walking with a Secret Service agent. Of all the people in America to hit, she picked the wrong person! I was surrounded by law enforcement officials. However, I begged them not to arrest her because I did not want to make a scene. Because of my black-and-blue and bandaged arm, I could not wear the short-sleeved red gown I had for the balls.

The 1984 Inauguration was unique in several ways. First of all, January 20 fell on a Sunday, so there were two swearing-in ceremonies. The Sunday ceremony was a small, very moving family affair at the White House. Both the President and Vice President took the oath on the steps of the Grand Staircase on the State Floor surrounded by family and friends. All the cabinet, Supreme Court, and top staff members were invited. It was a marvelous treat for our family as they also stayed for a buffet luncheon served in the glorious State Rooms. At one time the President came over and sat with Mrs. Bush and me, which was a very kind thing for him to do.

The big outdoor swearing-in was going to be held the next day, but Mother Nature intervened with a record cold spell. The ceremony was moved into the Rotunda of the Capitol and the parade was canceled—a huge disappointment for the high school marching bands. However, their lips would have stuck to their instruments.

Each congressman and senator was given two tickets, and only our families and very closest friends were allowed in the room. I was amused to see that some of the members of Congress had wedged in their wives and several children. It was jammed.

Two of our grandchildren, George, eight, and Noelle, seven, were going to see their grandfather sworn in. The winter weather didn't bother them one bit. Born in Texas and now living in Florida, they had never seen snow, and we had great fun watching them slide down the hill behind the Vice President's House.

Noelle watched the video *Annie* six times that week and knew every song and dance. The day of the Capitol ceremony, we went to St. John's Church with our adult children and the Reagans. The plan was for Paula to bring George P. and Noelle straight to the Capitol. Columba had bought a darling dress for Noelle and asked Paula please to comb her hair and tie it with a bow. The little group got to the Capitol, but we noticed Noelle had no sash on her dress and no bow in her uncombed hair. We later learned that Noelle had been in the middle of her seventh viewing of *Annie* and refused to leave before it ended. She locked herself in the third-floor bathroom, and poor Paula was desperate. The military aide assigned to bring the children to the ceremony had to take the door off the hinges. They got her out in the nick of time and raced to the Capitol, dressing her on the way.

✐ With the campaign and Inauguration behind us, it was back to business as usual—if that's what you can call life when you hold public office. Anyway, once again, I'd like to share with you some stories about George's second term as vice president.

✐ *January 30, 1985*—George and I attended the annual "Salute to Congress" dinner, which honors the new members. One of my dinner companions was Sam Donaldson, whom I wrote about in my diary: "Much to my shock I really enjoyed him. He seems like such a devil and such a mean guy (on the tube). He was a very interesting partner."

Sam told such a funny story, which was verified by my partner on the left, Senator Alan Cranston of California. At one of those deadly receptions before the dinner, Jay Rockefeller, the newly elected senator from West Virginia, came up and introduced himself to Sam. He then went on to say, "Sam, tell me about yourself. I want to get to know you. Are you from humble beginnings?" Sam's answer: "Compared to you, Senator, I guess you could say that I came from humble beginnings."

During our presidential years, Sam and Diane Sawyer did one of their "Prime Time" shows live from upstairs at the White House. At one point, Sam and I were touring the Yellow Oval Room with Millie at our heels. Sam asked me how Millie liked living in the White House at the exact same moment she decided to clean up a little. I gave her a gentle nudge with my foot, and the White House switchboard immediately lit up with people saying: "Who does Sam Donaldson think he is, kicking Millie?" Poor Sam, he does have an image problem.

After we finished the show, George invited Sam and Diane to have a glass of wine while their crew removed some of the tons of equipment they had brought in. The most amazing conversation followed. One said to the other: "I thought I handled the Lincoln Bedroom well, didn't you?" Back came, "Yes, but didn't you think I was good in the Long Hall?" Back and forth they went, complimenting each other and themselves for several moments. The other "spear carrier" and I were amused and thought to ourselves: Who says that politicians are egotistical? I very much would like to add that Diane has always been a favorite of ours and still is. She and Sam are just human—very human.

George and I went to hundreds of dinners during our political years. Typical of many of them was one I went to one night when George was out of town. This had been sold to me as an early evening with few speeches. The man who gave the invocation set the tone. He prayed for the whole world, person by person. I sat next to the ninety-year-old man who was being honored that night. I discovered that he had taken a taxi to the dinner and told him that I would give him a ride home. After a long dinner, the chairman stood up and gave a longer talk. The hour was getting late, and both my partner and I were getting very restless. When the chairman called on his committee heads to give their annual reports, we moaned and settled down for a miserable additional hour. Just then a Secret Service man slipped me a note: "Mrs. Bush, we have to go. Our job is to protect you and you are being bored to death. Let's go." It was signed "USSS" (United States Secret Service). I made my apologies, grabbed my new ninety-year-old friend, and left. Lest I leave the wrong impression, the note was written by my aide, Kim Brady, not the Secret Service.

March 3–12, 1985—George and I went to the Sahel countries in Africa to take food and medicine to drought victims. Much of the aid we took was gathered by AmeriCares, and Bob Macauley, its founder, accompanied us on our plane. This amazing man had gotten tired of fighting red tape and had organized the most comprehensive program that brings immediate relief to those in need around the world. He sees a problem; begs, borrows, or steals the food, medicine, doctors, nurses, planes, or trucks that he needs; and takes off for whatever part of the world needs help. George and I are AmeriCares' biggest fans.

On this trip we visited large refugee camps in Sudan where they were trying to save the lives of drought victims and refugees from Ethiopia. There were so many unforgettable impressions: everything and everyone covered with dirt and flies; a seven-year-old who weighed twenty-seven pounds, the same as our grandson Sam LeBlond, who wasn't a year old yet; a four-pound baby whose mother had died shortly after the birth and who now was lying at the feet of her dying grandmother on a filthy mattress. I held that little baby and was told that she had no chance of living. The newcomers to the camp were so thin and malnourished that it was like looking at X rays instead of bodies. Five times a day relief workers would spoon a mush made up of milk, sugar, and oil into these people's mouths, and we were told that in several weeks, many of those listless blank-eyed children would be running and playing. The dedicated volunteer nurses, doctors, missionaries, and Peace Corp volunteers who worked surrounded by filth and the dead and dying were the most giving group of people I had ever met.

We also went to Mali, taking food and medicine to drought victims there. Lala, the wife of President Moussa Traore, was my hostess. She really touched me. She was a large, smiling woman who'd had nine children, the first when she was thirteen years old. She was caring and so sweet. I sat next to her at a banquet and watched her stuff three morsels of beef surrounded by at least an inch of pure white fat into her mouth. To her, it was a treat. I really loved her and have thought of her often.

After Africa, we went to Switzerland, where George made an impassioned appeal at a United Nations Famine Relief Conference. That evening we met up with a congressional delegation at a reception given by our close, dear friends, Katy and Sadruddin Aga Khan. Texas Senator John Tower and his wife, Lilla, were there. She told me that she thought George was all wrong: "I don't believe in feeding those people. They should learn to take care of themselves." I have to confess that I had been so moved by what I saw that I just said, "Lilla, go away." Starving babies and we shouldn't feed them?

July 1, 1985—We were in the middle of a swing through Europe when the President asked George and me to go to Germany to meet the hostages from the TWA hijacking incident. The entire world had watched as that plane had been held captive on a runway in Beirut. What joy it was for them and their families they were finally free.

Sadly, however, George and I also had gone to Andrews Air Force Base to meet the body of Seaman Robert Stetham, who had been killed in cold blood by the hijackers when they discovered he was in the service. His family had a rich military tradition, and I'll never forget his mother and father and siblings standing there on the tarmac at Andrews with us. They were grief-stricken, yet proud. As the casket came off the plane, his younger brother, in his dress Navy uniform, saluted his hero brother as tears ran down his face

July 13, 1985—A few weeks later, we were in Kennebunkport for a weekend when George got a call saying the President was going to undergo surgery to remove a polyp in his colon. George decided to return to Washington in spite of opposition from Chief of Staff Don Regan, who thought it might hype the public's perception of the seriousness of the operation. I wrote in my diary:

We wondered, of course, all day about how things were going in Washington. Pop called several times and told us the President came through the operation. And a very historic thing happened and, thank God, George went down there because the President signed a paper transferring the power to the Vice President, and I think it held true for the seven hours that he was being operated on. Evidently Don Regan went in and talked to him and decided he was in total control, no more effects of the anesthesia, thus rescinded the power after seven hours. Pop played tennis, stayed out of sight, and tried to keep a low profile. But he was president for seven hours.

We stayed glued to TV the whole weekend. After we knew that the President was fine, Marvin and I got the giggles. The descriptions of the bowel and all its processes were on every station with graphic drawings. What I didn't know was that Marvin was getting more and more frightened. Every symptom that was described was exactly what he was going through, although he hadn't told any of us. So thanks to the very personal press coverage and Ronald Reagan, he went to see Dr. Tabb Moore, an excellent doctor and a former neighbor of ours. Marvin got temporary relief from his problems, then went his merry way, pretty much ignoring all Tabb had told him.

Marvin was diagnosed as having colitis, a devastating autoimmune disease. After a miserable winter of cramping, racing to the bathroom, and bleeding, he went into the hospital in the spring of 1986 to try to control this dreaded illness. He continued to lose weight and to lose ground. Margaret spent night after night at his bedside. No man ever had more friends and, if there was an up side to this ailment, it was then that both children surely learned how loved they were. I knew that Margaret and Marvin really loved and valued their friends; now we learned that their friends felt the same.

After weeks in the hospital, a forty-five-pound weight loss, and consultations with specialists, our doctors told us that they were going to reevaluate Marvin at the end of the week. On May 7, 1986, I was on my way to Santa Fe, New Mexico, to do a charity fund-raiser for my dear friend Marion Chambers. I would be back in twenty-four hours. We had an interim stop in St. Louis, and after the plane doors had already closed, the Secret Service told me the Vice President was on the phone and needed to speak with me right away. They reopened the door, and my heart sank when George told me that Marvin's vital signs were failing and I should come home. No trip was longer. I tried to pretend that I wasn't afraid. Nothing could happen to our precious boy. I was praying that he would be all right. I was so afraid that I would see George at the steps of the plane, because that would mean something awful had happened. He was not there. I raced to the hospital to find George sitting at Marvin's beside, with his hand on his arm. Marvin told me later that he knew he was dying when two things happened: His dad spent the day by his side, and Jeb called to just pass the time of day. He ended his call with "I love you, Marvin." My boys don't say things like that to each other. They just know it and act it. That day, Jeb said it.

Marvin had several blood transfusions to give him enough strength to go through an operation. The next day he had a temporary colostomy. That is a terrible shock to anybody, but to a very athletic young man it is a bitter pill to swallow. The other choice was death. I suspect that sometimes in those next few days Marvin thought that he would have preferred the second choice. The pain was bad, and he was depressed. Thank God for Margaret, who was so strong and very supportive.

They had a double worry as they were also at the end of a long period of trying to adopt a baby. They were so eager to adopt. Anyone who has ever been through that process will tell you that the strain of all the interviews and then the waiting is so hard. To have gotten this far and to lose the baby would have been such a disappointment.

Ten days after the operation Marvin's doctor brought in an attractive young man who talked to Marvin about his similar operation and the fact that he'd just run in a marathon. Marvin later told me that this man really helped him see that life was not over. Another person who was very helpful was NFL player Rolf Benirschke, later the day-time host of "The Wheel of Fortune," who had had a similar operation. His calls meant a great deal to Marvin and to all of us.

The convalescence was long because he had lost so much weight and blood. I never saw anyone work harder at getting strong. At first he joined me in long six-mile walks at the Naval Observatory. His good friend Jeff Austin hit tennis balls right to him so he wouldn't have to run. Dorrance Smith, who then was producing David Brinkley's show on ABC and later came to the White House with George, kept him supplied with good and interesting books. Other friends helped in different ways.

Within the year, it was decided that Marvin could not do away with the colostomy, so back he went for more surgery to remove what was left of his colon. Again, we were worried.

About this time, the Pope came to visit the United States. President Reagan welcomed him in Miami and we were to bid him goodbye in Detroit. George invited the family to join us there and as many as possible came. We also urged our housekeeper, Paula, to come with us. We were puzzled when she said no, especially since she's a devout Catholic. Finally, one day I had an idea, and said to her that it was too bad we only would be able to shake the Pope's hand instead of really talk to him. Suddenly, she decided to go. I think she was afraid he was going to quiz her about her religion!

The day finally came and we all waited anxiously for the Pope to arrive. One by one we walked up to meet him, all of us sounding tongue-tied. He is such a charismatic man and so gentle-looking that we were in awe. After the receiving line it was suggested we have a group photo taken. When that was done, Paula broke ranks, went right up to the Pope, and said in Spanish, "Papa, the Vice President's son is going to have a very serious operation. Will you pray for him?" He put his arms around her, calling her "Little Mama," and assured her that he would. At that, he and George left to talk in private. The rest of us closed ranks around Paula, just like a football huddle, tears spilling down our faces. This dear little woman had overcome her fear to speak up for Marvin. It was so sweet and touching.

The prayers must have worked. Marvin came through the operation fine, and although he suffered through a lot of pain, he got back in shape quicker than before. Today, his tennis game is superb, better than ever, and he's improving at golf.

But more important, Marvin is trying to use his experience to help others as the spokesman for the Crohn's and Colitis Foundation of America. Through humor and sensitivity, he has helped people of all ages learn to live with the "bag" which replaces your bowels. The late Tip O'Neill, a truly dear man and former Speaker of the House, underwent this same surgery, and every time we saw him, he let us know in his wonderful Boston accent how much a phone call from "your Mahvin" helped him recover.

And there's more happy ending. In June of 1986, Marvin and Margaret adopted a baby girl, Marshall Lloyd Bush. She and her little brother, Walker, who joined our family in 1989, are special children and have brought such joy into our lives. I never see them that I don't thank God for Marvin and Margaret, who are loving parents. I might add that I'm very grateful to the Edna Gladney Home in Fort Worth, Texas, where they adopted their children.

*   *   *

⌒ *October 10–20, 1985*—En route to China and Hong Kong, we stopped to refuel on Saipan in the Mariana Islands. George loved revisiting the islands that he had flown over during World War II and seeing the relics left behind by the Japanese.

During our stay, I dedicated a hospital, the Commonwealth Health Center, which certainly was not an uncommon event for me. But this particular occasion really touched me. I wrote in my diary: "It's kind of a funny feeling knowing that there'll be a plaque somewhere in the middle of the Pacific with your name on it, Barbara Pierce Bush. It's stretched my life a little and made me feel very humble."

⌒ *January 6, 1986*—I would just like to share with you my diary entry for that day:

Sunday and Monday I worked around the house, trying to get rid of Christmas . . . Monday we were going to the NBC dinner. First I was told that I was to wear a daytime dress, then they revised the schedule to a cocktail dress. I talked to Doro in the morning in Maine. Just sort of spent the day getting things together and getting back into regular life . . . I put on a black skirt and brocade top. Did not wash my hair . . . Just as we were going out, Marvin called and said that the stole that was left at our house did belong to Ulla Wachtmeister (the wife of the Swedish ambassador) and could we drop it by her house as she was leaving town the very next day. George said that was easy as we were dining right across the street. He said as he got into the car, "Gosh, I have to call the office. This is the annual NBC Dinner, there is some news breaking and before I get there I better be briefed." So he tried to call the office and the line was busy. Meanwhile the Secret Service got on the phone to tell the police escort that we were going to make an interim stop at the Swedish Embassy. Just as we pulled up, George's phone call came through, and he asked me if I'd mind running the stole up to the door. I rang the doorbell. They opened the door and . . . I looked up and there were Jeb and Colu. I couldn't believe that they knew the Swedish Ambassador. Then I saw Doro with tears running down her face . . . it was a 41st wedding anniversary surprise party! And in all honesty it was the biggest surprise in the world. George Bush was so thrilled as were Ulla and Willie . . . That morning George had called Doro and said, "Call your mother before you leave. Otherwise, you know your mother, she'll call, and the baby-sitter will tell her that you are on your way to Washington." So she did call me. During the day Libby Crudgington (Doro's friend) had called me and asked for Doro. She said the baby-sitter had told her that Doro was in Washington. I had said, "Dumb baby-sitter. She has gone to a hockey game in Boston." . . . Andy came by for tea . . . I just called Marion Chambers (in Texas) to see how she was just as she was rushing out the door to come see us. She said that she was afraid that I was going to make her miss her plane.

. . . There were all those people, Bob and Georgette Mosbacher, Bobbie and Jack Fitch, Mildred and Baine Kerr and Hugh and Betty Liedtke . . . I mean there was the most extraordinary group of people . . . Bob and Marion Blake from Lubbock, Marvin and Margaret, Doro, Jeb and Colu. Neil, Sharon, George and Laura didn't come . . . it's a long way and too expensive.

There were many many more friends there: the Drapers, Nan Ellis without Sandy and Betsy Heminway without Spike to just name a few. And my dear Andy. I couldn't believe that she didn't tell me. She said that she knew that I didn't know because I had not washed my hair.

. . . Jack Fitch had brought up lots of blown-up pictures and Marvin had gone over on Sunday and helped with the seating . . . there were poems, slide shows, songs and on and on. It was one of the loveliest evenings of my life.

A lot of people couldn't believe that I was surprised. I did joke about it and say, "Wouldn't you be surprised if it was the second time in forty-one years of married life that your husband had remembered?" But the truth is we have never needed parties to celebrate.

George really had worked hard with the marvelous Wachtmeisters to pull it off. (There wasn't even such a thing as an NBC dinner!) I could write a book about the parties and nice things he has planned for others. Maybe that is what I am doing right now.

᠆᠊᠍*July 4, 1986*—It was a very special July Fourth celebration that year for our entire country. I wrote in my diary:

The Statue of Liberty celebrated her 100th birthday. The Bushes and the Jim Bakers with (their daughter) Mary Bonner and our Noelle spent the 4th in Kennebunkport and then flew down to New York City for the closing ceremonies. 55,000 people at Giants Stadium (The Meadowlands). The whole week had been an extravaganza beyond belief. They had fireworks, lit the Lady and Tall Ships.

The finale, which we attended and George took part in, was unbelievable. They had 350 Elvis "look-alikes." More like impersonators as there were men and women, black and white. We were all given a light and a separate lens. At the given moment we all turned on our lights and we turned into a red, white and blue flag with stars, and LIBERTY was spelled out. Dancing girls came out by the thousands, and when they flipped their capes, they were the American flag and they made the flag wave to the cheers of the crowd. Liza Minnelli, Shirley MacLaine and John Denver sang, backed by a cast of thousands. Our two little girls were not the only ones who loved that show.

After the evening was over, the pilots of the helicopter flew around the Statue of Liberty at 11 p.m. It was so beautiful. We could see the New York skyline outlined in lights and the Tall Ships in the harbor. One of those magic moments in life.

July 25–August 5, 1986—I will never forget my visit to the Wailing Wall in Jerusalem during our trip through the Middle East. George was led off to the men's side of the wall, and I was taken to the women's. We both were touched by the sight of people praying and tucking notes into the wall. I left a note: "Please, dear God, let us have peace. Protect my little family. Your devoted servant, Barbara."

January 19, 1987—Just as we were going to bed, C. Fred seemed to have a horrible spasm. His little legs went out from under him and he looked awkward. He couldn't move. His beautiful brown eyes looked so trustingly at us. George moved our loyal little friend onto a blanket and we brought him in by my side where we could comfort him. He didn't move all night. Whenever we turned on the light to check on him, his eyes were open and he was looking so puzzled. It was almost as though he expected us to make it all right. Eventually we both fell asleep for a few hours. In the morning we awakened and there was our little friend sleeping normally. He jumped up for his morning walk and all seemed well. In the middle of the morning Laurie called and said it had happened again in the garden. We went straight to the vet's, where he told me that Freddy was having a stroke. He said that he might come out of it and maybe would have several more months experiencing these strokes intermittently. I could not let my best little pal suffer, and with tears running down my face and the doctor's, I held Freddy in my arms and the doctor gave him a shot. It was very peaceful and that twisted, tormented little body relaxed and rested.

I was devastated, but reminded myself that the loss was not just mine, but George's and Don Rhodes's, too. It was also an opportunity for me to prove what I always have said: I value all people more than dogs. I may sometimes like the dog better, but people are and should be more important.

I came home and called George to tell him what I had done. He said I'd made the right choice. I also called Susan Porter Rose about something else, burst into tears, and told her what had happened. She advised me not to tell people that I had put him to sleep. She said that we would get letters about how mean I was. I did it because I loved him.

We cover sadness in our family with humor sometimes. I was just giving myself a real talking-to about not being mournful when the door burst open and our son, George W., arrived from Texas for the night. He had been forewarned not to mention Freddy, so he rushed in saying, "Mom, I'm so sorry, doggone it!" Funny. Even I had to giggle.

George immediately called our friend Will Farish and asked him if he had a puppy or knew where we could find a young dog. We had fallen in love with Will's black-and-white springer spaniels when we had visited Will and Sarah on their Beeville, Texas, ranch after Christmas. Several days later he called and said they had a perfect dog for me, but there were several problems. For starters, the dog was a girl. We'd never had a female dog, but that seemed fine. Then came the zinger: She wasn't black and white; she was liver-colored. She was a little over a year old. Will said that she had been trained as a huntress, but that she was such a loving dog they thought she'd be a better house dog. She sounded perfect.

We had a small problem with Don Rhodes. He truly was C. Fred's best friend. I loved Freddy best, but he loved me second best. Don was his first love. George told Don that we were getting a new dog. I suspect that Don thought I had not let enough time pass between dogs, because he came to my door one night, leaned in, and asked, "Let me ask something. If the Vice President died, would you get a new husband?" And I answered, "You bet, if I could get one just as good." Don did not think that was funny, stomped out, and did not speak to me for several days.

On February 13, Will delivered Millie to the steps of *Air Force Two* after a speech George had given. Millie turned out to be my dog in about five minutes. Don Rhodes likes her, but not like Freddy. He did forgive me—I think.

All this reminds me of another dog story. It sounds so silly, but it was about to cause a real family disagreement.

One early morning in Maine I was sitting in my bed reading the morning paper and having a cup of coffee when the bedroom door burst open. George's wonderful Uncle Lou Walker was standing there looking really upset. He said, "Bar, we have all agreed that you will make the final decision on a family argument. I know just how much you loved C. Fred and so I will accept your words. You alone understand how much I loved my dog, Gilbert, who died this past winter. Grace and the girls say that I can't give flowers in her memory this Sunday in church. Don't you think that is all right?" My heart sank. Of course he couldn't give flowers in her memory in church. I could just hear Laman Bruner saying, "The flowers this morning are given in loving memory of John Smith, adored father of Betty and Jim Smith, and Gilbert Walker, most beloved dog of Grace and Louis Walker!" The whole congregation would laugh us out of church or be insulted and furious. Grace and the girls would be humiliated. I said, "Lou, just tell me one thing. Did Gilbert accept Jesus Christ as her savior?" That seemed to end that.

September 24–October 3, 1987—We visited Poland during a fascinating time in their history, when Lech Walesa was becoming a national hero and Solidarity was becoming known worldwide. I wrote in my diary:

I got in the car with Mrs. Jaruzelski. She is very nice and about 59–60. Very friendly. She has a trim little figure and wore a pale green dress. She has very blond hair and speaks English . . . better than we thought. She teaches German at the University. She told me that without her job she could not exist because he is gone so much. He, of course was (General Jaruzelski), now head of country and chairman of the (Communist) Party . . . She told me that she was reading in English, through her interpreter. (I noticed that she didn't really need her.) She told me that she'd just finished "Home Front." I said that I'd never heard of it. She said, "You know, it was written by Mrs. Reagan's daughter. Is it true?" It was that horrible book that Patti Davis had written. I said no, that it was a novel. It was not true and it was not a success in our country. Ye Gads! I asked her how she had seen it, and she said that a friend had sent it to her. Some friend.

I had another strange encounter with another wife of a Polish official. I told her that the American people really like the Polish people. She returned with: "Why?" (Hardly encouraging to a long conversation, but I persisted.) I reminded her that there were so many Poles in America that Chicago is the second largest Polish city in the world. Her response was "You only got the peasants and ignorants." So much for composer Ignace Paderewski, baseball greats Carl Yastrzemski and Stan Musial, Duke basketball coach Mike Krzyzewski, Maryland Senator Barbara Mikulski, Illinois Congressman Dan Rostenkowski, and many others.

It was on this trip that we met with the courageous Solidarity leaders, including Lech Walesa, at a dinner given by our talented ambassador, John Davis, and his wife, Helen. Many of the men had spent years in jail as political prisoners and yet they fought on. The next morning George went to lay a wreath at the grave of the martyred priest Father Popieluszko. As we were getting ready to leave, Lech Walesa slipped into our car, and right behind him, wedging into the front seat with our driver and agent, came an enormous man that only Hollywood could have cast to be a spy. Lech said that this man followed him everywhere to keep watch on him. The day before, Jaruzelski had told us that the Solidarity movement was almost dead. Well, the ride to the church was lined with thousands upon thousands of people waving Solidarity and American flags, cheering Lech and George.

*   *   *

∽ *December 8, 1987*—It had been a very tough year for Nancy Reagan. She had a breast operation in the fall, and her mother died three days after she got out of the hospital. Two of her husband's Supreme Court nominees had been rejected, and the Iran-Contra investigation was in full swing.

On top of all this, Mikhail and Raisa Gorbachev arrived for their first visit to the United States. Excitement ran high. Since the men's meetings were closed to the press, the ladies' activities became a big news item. The press had noted an antagonism between the two First Ladies. There was some truth in that. It was what I call a "chemical thing," plus a cultural difference.

I recorded the following on my tape recorder as I walked Millie around the Observatory grounds on December 11:

The arrival ceremony was very exciting. You could certainly tell whose husbands weren't running for president. I wore a very Republican cloth coat, and Nancy wore her mink. Mrs. Gorbachev, who had stepped off the plane the night before in what the press described as an "indescribable" fur, had on a very long, very chic, brown or liver-colored broadtail coat . . . belted in the back, collar turned up.

, . . We went right into the Green Room, where we were offered tea and coffee. Under her coat she had on a beautiful white wool suit. Her feet were demurely crossed at her ankles. Her coloring is marvelous . . . paper says "henna" hair, but I'd say much softer. She is a lovely looking creature, smaller than the size twelve we are reading about, more a six or an eight. She is a prettier package than the pictures show. I don't know how old, but think the paper said fifty-three or fifty-five. That's funny, for we really don't know if Nancy Reagan is sixty-five or sixty-seven and she won't tell. I guess Raisa won't tell either.

Mrs. G. never said (to Nancy), "I hear you have been sick. How are you?" Or, "I was sorry to hear about your mother." She started right in on, "We couldn't understand why you didn't come to Iceland" (where the husbands had met recently). Nancy started to say, "But I thought that only men were going . . ." She never had a chance because Mrs. G. interrupted and went on, "You would have liked it. People missed you." Nancy tried again, but Mrs. G. interrupted again, "It was so interesting," and on and on.

Mrs. G. moved immediately into their twenty-year housing project or program and told us there were no homeless in Russia. (Several days after the G's left town, our papers were full of stories about the thousands of homeless in Russia.) She said everyone had a place to spend the night in Russia. Clearly a jab at us.

She then went into the Civil War—yes, the Civil War—and slavery. Evidently Russia had freed their serfs about the same time.

From there she moved rapidly into the homeless widows caused by World War II, hoped we would never experience a war in our country. I was tempted to tell her that we had seen many widows and orphans in Afghanistan refugee camps in Pakistan . . . RECENTLY.

At one time Obie Shultz leaned over to me and whispered, "Nancy doesn't like this conversation." I whispered back, "Who would?"

Mrs. G. took over the whole conversation.

Finally Nancy said, "I'm afraid that I am keeping you from your schedule." Mrs. G. said, "Oh, that's all right." That should have told us how little staying on schedules meant to them. They were late to almost everything on that first visit.

. . . George and I went to the East Room on the State Floor for the signing of the INF (Intermediate-range Nuclear Force) Treaty. I was flattered to be included. Nancy, Mrs. G. and I were the only spouses there. Everyone else had worked on the treaty. We were packed in like sardines. It was thrilling.

On that first visit we were all impressed about how well briefed the Gorbachevs both were on all of us. At the receiving lines, both at the State Department luncheon and the White House Dinner, they had something personal to say to each guest. That's pretty impressive. It also made the receiving line take hours. Jane Muskie told me that she and Ed got to the State Department at 12:30, lunch was served at 1:45 and she got home at 5 p.m. Wow.

On December 9, I wrote:

The Russians had the return dinner for the Reagans at the Russian Embassy on 16th Street. The embassy was built around 1909 by Mrs. Pullman, the railroad king's widow, for her daughter and son-in-law. The latter was a congressman. It was sold to the Russians in 1913 and they moved in around 1930. It is very ornate and has grand, gilded chandeliers, mirrors, etc.

They had 72 people and served 9 courses: caviar to start with (it came around twice), crab, fish soup, suckling pig, baked fish, maybe veal, sherbet, fruit and blueberry pie . . . It was a lovely, but very long dinner. Then they had entertainment . . . a rather formidable (stands for large-chested) young opera star who sang song after song, popular romantic songs—maybe well-known is a better description than popular. George said that he took a chance, and after quite a few songs said to Mrs. G. while looking at the singer with a twinkle in his eye: "I think I am falling in love." The interpreter struggled through the translation and Mrs. G. thought a minute and then said with a perfectly straight face, "I think you better not. This is an election year. Remember Gary Hart." George says that she didn't have a twinkle in her eye. It was a flat statement. She certainly was well briefed and knew a lot about us and our politics.

. . . I went to the going-away ceremony on the South Grounds in the pouring rain. The Reagans were smiling and the Gorbachevs looking straight ahead and very serious . . . for home consumption?

. . . I drove to the airport that evening with Mrs. G. She had been well briefed on me and had me down as a housewife. She asked me if we ever served pies? I said that we did and she then gave me her recipe for blueberry pie: "You take a cup of flour, a cup of cream and a cup of blueberries and mix 'em up and you have a pie." Even I know that will not make a pie. I put my hand on her knee and said, "Mrs. G., I am not a great cook. I can feed 50, but no one would ever rave over my food. Tell me about your average day." She did.

After that we had the darndest conversation. I asked her if she knew that Nancy Reagan had a serious cancer operation a month ago. She said yes, but that in her country they would not talk about it and the doctor would be in trouble for mentioning it . . . that it was very difficult for a woman to have a breast removed. I said that in our country the press would know if the First Lady disappeared for several weeks and would want to know her whereabouts. That brought about a big discussion about the press's right to know personal things . . . like Gary Hart's personal life. It was hard to explain that Gary Hart invited the press to follow him and examine his life. And they did. I found myself defending the press and finally said, "We get so angry with the press for their probing personal questions but would die for their right to ask them." She then asked, "What if the First Lady had an abortion?" I said that the First Lady wouldn't have an abortion and that breast cancer and an abortion were certainly two very different things. I then said that we felt that Nancy

Reagan had been very courageous, and that by going public she had saved many lives by influencing women to have mammograms. We arrived at the airport before we could pursue this anymore.

It occurred to me later that women in Russia do not have the machines that we have to cope with mammography or delicate radiation. Therefore encouraging women to go for these procedures is not a part of their lives.

We had many more visits with Raisa over the years, and I grew to like and respect her. She was the first wife of a Russian leader to surface into the public eye. It was not easy for her. She was a pacesetter. She once asked me why Nancy Reagan didn't like her. I said that I was sure that Nancy did like her. She said that she had read otherwise in Nancy's book. I was hard put to answer, but she almost answered her own question by saying that she did not know our customs and that she was trying to learn. She did dominate the conversation, but maybe she thought that was what she was supposed to do. Who knows?

I never saw her in such stylish clothes again. I was amused to note that on that first trip her skirts got shorter and shorter to match Nancy's. They must have had a seamstress working late at the embassy.

I believe that the Russian people did not like the wife to be front and center. We heard that she got off the back of the plane at home, and I read that when NBC's Tom Brokaw interviewed Gorbachev, before the Russians showed it on their TV, they deleted the part where Gorbachev said that he discussed everything with his wife.

This is an interesting subject. A spouse has a fine row to hoe. Denis Thatcher played it just right, in my eyes. He was supportive of Margaret always, and yet had a life of his own.

I am not too sure that the American public likes the spouse to be too front and center. The jury is still out on this, but in January of 1994 when I am writing this, Hillary Rodham Clinton is certainly very much a part of her husband's decision-making process. She seems much the stronger of the two. Does it make him seem weaker? I am afraid that when problems or controversy occur, and they will, the finger will be pointed at Hillary. I am not saying this is right or wrong. It just occurs to me that the American people also are going through an adjustment.

* * *

⤫ One last note on 1987: George became an author, writing his autobiography, *Looking Forward,* with the help of our great friend Vic Gold. George donated his share of the profits to the M. D. Anderson Hospital for its work in the field of leukemia, and the United Negro College Fund.

⤫ Before I talk about George's last year as vice president, which was dominated by the 1988 presidential race, I'd like to make a few general observations about that eight-year period.

The 1980s was the decade that televangelists truly came into their own. I am not going to attempt to pass judgment. So many of them bring hope, love, and God into American homes. We all have aging shut-in relatives who are nourished by these people. But we also know that there are some greedy charlatans out there who take advantage of vulnerable people and who seem to put self above God and the people they say they are hoping to help.

I bring this up because we had a reception for a group of televangelists during the VP years, including Jimmy and Tammy Faye Bakker and Jimmy Swaggart. I wrote in my diary: "I'm offended when they think they are the ones who discovered God when He has played such an important part in our lives. I was amused when Jimmy Swaggart said on that visit that whoever likes country music was immoral. GB's response: 'Well, that does me in.'"

It hurts me when I see Billy Graham grouped in with these fakes. George and I have known Billy and Ruth Graham for many years, and they have had a very positive spiritual influence on our whole family. We have had several wonderful evenings where our extended family has sat around Billy and asked him questions that worry us about death, life, and the Bible. We have learned a lot about each other in these sessions, and more important, about God and our relationship to Him.

Religion has played such an important part in our lives. It's a very personal thing with us, but I know we could not have survived the difficult times without our faith and the support of our religious family. Whether we were worshiping in our enormous church in Houston, St. Martin's; our two tiny churches in Kennebunkport, First Congregational Church and St. Ann's; the tiny little chapel at Camp David; or

St. John's Church, across from the White House, we always have felt we were a part of a very special community.

◯ One of my greatest pleasures during the 1980s was getting involved with the literacy cause and witnessing firsthand the exciting things beginning to happen. People began to see the potential problems of an uneducated work force, and businessmen and politicians began to be aware of the problem. This did not just happen. It took men like Harold McGraw, retired CEO of McGraw-Hill, Inc. Harold and his wife started the Business Council for Effective Literacy, seeded with a million dollars of their own money, and for ten long years he stood on the literacy soapbox. He talked many companies into having on-site continuing education classes or supporting literacy programs in their communities. He made the point that it would save them money in the long run. He also lobbied Congress hard. With no personal agenda, Harold played an invaluable role in making people aware of our silent, hidden problem.

I was lucky to work with so many people who understood the problem and wanted to help make a difference. One of my favorite literacy stories is about a gentleman named Gary Stein who works with the Houston Food Bank. We met while I was taping a public service announcement for a food drive, and he wrote me the following in his thank-you note:

> Illiteracy should also not be allowed to occur in America. I know that eliminating this terrible condition is your personal battle. I would like to offer a suggestion which has resulted in a win-win situation for our company, a Houston-based steel distributor with about 100 employees, and an illiterate individual.
>
> Recently a slip-up occurred in our hiring procedures, and a totally illiterate man—we'll call him "Tim Jones"—was hired. (Someone else had filled out his job application.) Ordinarily a false application would be grounds for immediate dismissal.
>
> However, I intervened and told our plant manager that we would allow Tim to stay employed *if* he would

enroll immediately in a reading program at Houston
Community College. He would be required to bring regular progress reports and report cards to his foreman. Tim
accepted our offer.

The results after several months were:

1. The company has gained a motivated, loyal,
extremely hardworking employee.

2. Tim Jones has gained some literacy in school and
on the job and is eager to learn more. In fact, he informs
us he is saving to hire a private tutor.

3. A man was taken off of the welfare rolls and now
has a well-paying job with a future.

But best of all, this was accomplished by individuals without government involvement or special programs.
Just a simple concept under which everyone wins—the
company and individual . . . imagine how much impact
could be made in working for greater literacy if more companies would try this with only *one* new employee.

Many states were establishing literacy councils and I worked
with some wonderful people, but I particularly recall working with
the present governor of Illinois, then the secretary of state of Illinois,
Jim Edgar. He and his staff were very able and eager workers in the
field. Three Secretaries of Education also were most helpful: Ted Bell,
Bill Bennett, and in George's presidential years, Lamar Alexander.

Perhaps the biggest success story was Project Literacy U.S.,
known as PLUS. A private/public partnership between PBS and ABC,
it was an unprecedented coming together of public and commercial
TV. Margot Woodwell of PBS's WQED in Pittsburgh and Jim Duffy,
Anderson Clark, and Jack Harr of ABC were the prime movers behind
the extraordinary project. PLUS launched a major public awareness
campaign on literacy and helped organize communities to deal with
their individual needs. It also set up a referral network which brought
together all the different groups working for literacy.

ABC also started sponsoring the Reader of the Month, many of
whom became real success stories and went on to join national literacy councils. One Fourth of July, I left my family in Maine to fly to St.
Louis to take part in their annual celebration under the Arch. Attract-

ing a million or more people, it's considered one of the biggest Fourth of July events in the country. ABC was going to broadcast the celebration live, so millions more would see it this year. I had agreed to a walk-on part where I would introduce a darling Reader of the Month. "Mr. Smith" was a retired truck driver who had driven for forty years although he was illiterate. He decided to learn so he could read his Bible. On this particular show, he was going to read the Preamble to the Constitution. We had a little practice session in the afternoon, and although it seemed to me that he could not read at all, I was assured by the production people that he was just nervous and that by that night he would be able to read. He didn't seem nervous to me. In fact, he seemed very relaxed. That night he sat having refreshments and laughing with the many actors, singers, and dancers who were entertaining this huge crowd that spread as far as the eye could see. Our big moment came around eleven P.M. I went out on the stage and said my words, which I had put to memory just in case I couldn't see the cue cards. Then this lovely old man came out, smiled, hugged me, and we waited, arms around each other. Nothing, absolutely nothing, came out. He did look adorable. So after an agonizing standoff, I said: "Let's all join Mr. Smith in saying the Preamble to the Constitution," and we did, all one million of us. It truly was a magic moment.

We encouraged all sorts of literacy programs. We visited senior citizens' homes with reading classes. We supported English as a Second Language programs for immigrants who wanted to learn. We visited Head Start and Even Start classes. We tried to help alternative school programs for kids at risk like Cities in Schools. We encouraged programs that worked with mothers who had dropped out of school. We tried to help programs that taught new mothers not only parenting skills but the importance of reading to their children. We supported the March of Dimes Reading Olympics, which I liked for it not only encouraged children to read, but to help others. We went to schools to try to motivate reading, and spoke to civic clubs to encourage people to volunteer. Nothing is sadder than an adult student getting up the nerve to come to a class and finding no tutor available. We visited homeless shelters and food banks, such as Martha's Table in Washington, where they not only feed the body, but they feed the mind by reading to children. We wrote articles for newspapers, newsletters, and magazines trying to raise awareness and encourage volunteerism. We answered enormous amounts of mail and became somewhat of a clearinghouse for literacy. In the eight vice presidential years, I participated in 537 literacy-related events and another 435 events related to volunteerism. At times it was exhausting but it was always exhilarating. I always felt like I got more out than I put in.

I have saved the most important highlight of our VP years until last. Our family grew by leaps and bounds—two new in-laws, whom I've already mentioned, and eight new grandchildren: George and Laura had the twins, Jenna and Barbara, in 1981; Jeb and Columba had their third child, Jebby, in 1983; Neil and Sharon had Lauren in 1984 and Pierce in 1986; Marvin and Margaret adopted Marshall in 1986; and Billy and Doro had Sam in 1984 and Ellie in 1986.

Each of the grandchildren has a letter from their Gampy, written when they were born. Following is what George wrote Lauren on June 28, 1984:

> Dear Lauren,
>
> You're just a few days old. Already you have made your old grandparents very, very happy. We saw that picture of you in the Daily News and in the N.Y. Post. That's pretty good coverage for a 3 day old.
>
> You are a lucky girl. You have a loving Mother who is always thoughtful and nice; and you have a Dad who his brothers and sister named "Mr. Perfect."
>
> Anyway, Lauren, we can't wait to see you. We want to see you smile, to hold you, to love you.
>
> It's a funny thing—when you get older, even if you have an exciting life surrounded by interesting people and having the chance to meet all the world leaders—even with all that—what counts is family and love.
>
> We love you more than tongue can tell.
>
> Devotedly,
> Gampy

15

The 1988 Campaign

The 1988 campaign started, I believe, January 21, 1985, the day after the Inauguration. As early as May 30, 1986, I wrote in my diary: "George is obviously the most qualified person for the job. Do I want him to run? Absolutely not!"

I am surprised that I wrote that, but there it is. I may well have been tired that day, or maybe that's truly how I felt. Thank heavens I didn't feel that way very often. I do feel that campaigns are too long, but how are you going to keep people from running? I don't care if it is for dogcatcher, city council, governor, or president, someone will start early and then the others have to jump in. I am writing this in January of 1994, and about ten Republicans are running for 1996. I suspect it won't be long before we have eight Democrats.

For the first couple of years, the campaigning consisted of getting out and meeting as many people as possible and attending receptions and dinners. By 1987, it was in full swing. That was the year our son George moved his whole family to Washington to work in the campaign, which was such a gift to us both.

Finally it was 1988, which started off with a bang. On January 25 we went up to the Capitol to have dinner with our houseguests, Bud Wilkinson and his wife, Donna, and then to attend the State of the Union Address. George was scheduled to have an interview with Dan Rather before the President's speech. It was billed as a political profile, which they had done on all the other candidates and which had been benign stories devoid of controversy. However, CBS opened with a six-minute "exposé" on George's alleged role in Iran-Contra that was filled with false assumptions. It was just plain ugly. Then came nine minutes of Dan grilling George. There were raised voices on both sides. At one point George said: "You have impugned my integrity . . . if this is a political profile for an election, I have a very different opinion as to what it should be." George rarely gets angry, but Dan kept on about Iran-Contra with the most vicious slander, never listening to an answer. At one time George interrupted Dan and said: "It is not fair to judge my whole career by a rehash on Iran. How would you like it if I judged your whole career by those seven minutes when you walked off the set in New York." (He was referring to an incident several years earlier when Dan had done just that, resulting in dead air.)

After the interview each side accused the other of an ambush. Our campaign felt CBS purposely misled them on the content of the interview; CBS said that the Bush campaign deliberately planned an attack. I do believe we came out the winner: CBS reported getting complaint calls; ours were of support.

I was there and, believe me, there was no plot or plan to attack. But you can just take so much. I really do feel that CBS news programs often start an interview with an unflattering opener, and in this case, an untrue one. This puts many interviewees on the defensive. George often has to remind me of that when I see an interview featuring a political opponent and I'm taking some comfort in their unease. George forgives to a fault, but he will never trust Dan Rather again.

The year 1988 was so different from other campaigns, mainly because George had a full-time job in addition to being a candidate. The vice president, despite all the jokes, has many duties. At least George did. Not only was he President of the Senate, but President Reagan put him in charge of regulatory relief, narcotics interdiction, and antiterrorism, to name a few.

Although I had no official job, I had certain responsibilities that continued, campaign or not. We were very busy. I can't even find a diary for the primary season, which maybe is my excuse for a sometimes faded memory.

I do remember that the field of candidates was enormous on both sides, which is typical of a year when there is no incumbent running. There were eight major Democratic candidates, four of whom were members of the U.S. Senate. The one I knew best was Paul Simon from Illinois. He shared my interest in literacy, and we had attended several breakfast meetings together at the Department of Education. I'm not sure if he remembers, but twenty years earlier we had worked together as volunteers in a public school. On a personal basis, I thought he did a great job. We disagreed on the means to solving the problem—he wanted to pump more money into everything—but his heart certainly was in the right place.

Then there was Gary Hart. Since I was the president of the Senate Ladies, I had known his wife, Lee, although she had not been an active member. Lee was always polite to me and seemed very nice. She went on television several times defending her man, and I was sorry to see her put in that position. They have disappeared from public view—I hope, to live happily ever after. I had met Senator Hart many times. He was a very attractive man, and he was certainly the front-runner on the other side. Behind every candidate there is an army of believers who work their hearts out, and his must have been very disappointed in him. He threw away a good shot at being president.

Senators Al Gore and Joe Biden made a try and ran into problems—Joe's self-inflicted, and Al just died for lack of attention. I ran into Al's father on the campaign trail and had a nice visit with him on a plane. He had served with George's dad in the U.S. Senate.

Congressman Dick Gephardt from Missouri ran. He won Iowa and was a "flash in the pan," although I'm sure that he thought he had what was called "BIG MO." We certainly knew that feeling from 1980.

Two governors ran: Bruce Babbitt of Arizona and Mike Dukakis of Massachusetts. Neither of them seemed to have a chance either—in the beginning.

And then there was Jesse Jackson. Jesse is a big man who fills a room. He must be a chore for the Democrats. He has his own agenda and has never missed a funeral, a strike, or a march. He certainly must be the man they wrote the joke about: "Where is the most dangerous place in the world? That spot between Jesse Jackson and a camera." That being said, Jesse could charm the paper off the wall. His wife, Jacqueline, is a lovely woman, and he has very bright, articulate children. It always amused me that with all his talk, he sent his children to private schools. And it always saddened me that Jesse did not get out of politics and use his charismatic talents to turn kids off drugs and into school. We have seen what he can do; he had and has the ability to really make a difference. With his golden tongue and pied piper quality, kids listen to him. George has told me over the years that when Jesse gave him his word, he kept it. I must confess to liking him.

On our side of the political aisle, it was not so simple, at least from our viewpoint. Certainly Kansas Senator Bob Dole and televangelist Pat Robertson were the main competition, but former Congressman Jack Kemp, former Delaware Governor Pete DuPont, and Al Haig were right in there for every debate. It is always unpleasant to run against members of your own party, and this election was the worst. Because George was considered the front-runner, the others all took dead aim at him and hit the target hard. Much of it was ugly, and rumors ran wild.

The debates were a nightmare, but then they always are. The very first primary debate that took place in Houston in the fall of 1987 is especially memorable. That "man of the people," as Pete DuPont called himself, especially went on the attack, accusing George of not having an agenda. George turned to answer him and said, "Well, Pierre . . ." and that was the end of that. But then it was the others' turn to take a swipe. Al Haig went ballistic on George. All in all, it was hard, as Joanne Kemp was and is a great friend, and I have the utmost affection for both Elizabeth Dole and Pat Haig. I just hate Republican primaries and love Democratic ones!

The first big contest was the Iowa Caucus, where we had upset Ronald Reagan in 1980. What a difference eight years make. The farm economy was faltering, and as we drove through town after town, we would see boarded-up stores and farms that needed paint. As in so many businesses across the country, people had borrowed heavily with no collateral, so when the economy took a natural, cyclical downturn, they could not meet their obligations. So the climate in Iowa was not great for George Bush. We could understand Bob Dole's victory; he was "the farmer's senator." He also is a tough opponent. He has a razor-edged tongue and wit that is better aimed at someone else.

However, Pat Robertson's second place finish to our third was a shock. With his religious overtones, Pat brought a whole new dimension into the campaign. In fact, after his surprising showing in Iowa, he said, "God deserves credit for the victory." I had the same reaction to that as I do to televangelists in general: God is important in our lives, too; it's just more personal. Anyway, with the "700 Club" appearing daily on TV and radio, Pat already had a national following, and he is a personable, soft-spoken man who appeals to many people.

We left Iowa before the count was in, but we knew what was coming. The plane trip to New Hampshire was awful. Lee Atwater, our very bright campaign manager, was down in the dumps, as was the rest of the staff. I finally said that they must cheer up. How could they expect George to campaign with so many people around him singing the blues? George was looking forward, not back, although how he kept so stable, I'll never know.

We landed at the airport, and there was Governor John Sununu. What a man. He gave me a hug and whispered in my ear, "Don't worry. He'll win New Hampshire. 'Mr. Fix-it' will see to it."

The next week I asked and received permission from George never to sit in on a meeting or watch television. So after a full day of campaigning, usually on my own, I would join George and the others for dinner and then retire into our bedroom to read "no-think" books. I believe that I read six or seven that week. I could hear the others talking in the living room night after night, but I stayed away.

One evening as I was returning from an exhausting schedule, ABC's Carole Simpson stopped me and said, "You know your husband is losing the state, don't you?" I said that I didn't—and didn't she know that nobody was allowed to talk to me about the campaign? She apologized and scooted away. I have always laughed about that. Of course she didn't know, but I can't campaign with all that doom and gloom. We had the best guy, and I knew it. And so did many others. That marvelous baseball great Ted Williams campaigned with George, and he loved that. Longtime friend Nick Brady was there, and family and friends came from all over once again to stump the state. In a mall one day, trudging through the slush, was Barbara Franklin, carrying a BUSH sign and handing out literature. Barbara had held a key position in the Nixon White House as well as sitting on many prestigious corporate boards, and here she was carrying a political sign for George. This very able woman was the Secretary of Commerce at the end of George's administration.

On Primary Day I went from polling place to polling place to thank our supporters who were carrying signs and handing out literature. I saw tons of young people with Dole signs and ran into Pete DuPont and his family doing what I was doing. How I worried that day. I just knew we were going to lose. In the early afternoon George called me and said, "Come back to the motel. We are winning!"

All week John Sununu had been winking at me, saying we were going to win. We did, but it was not without a lot of bitterness from Bob Dole. The polls had showed him closing fast, but when the votes were counted, George got 38 percent and Bob got 28 percent. A year or so later I told John just how much his enthusiasm meant to me. He laughed and said that he was faking, that he never dreamed we were going to win.

New Hampshire had some real problems for us. Former Governor Hugh Gregg, father of then-Congressman Judd Gregg and now Senator Gregg, had been our campaign manager in 1980 and was our dear friend. The Greggs and the Sununus had a lot of personal animosities that I didn't understand. That put us all in a very tense situation. We liked them all so much and still do, particularly John and Nancy Sununu, who went through hell for George later on. John is a hero of mine. He's such a bright man, such a funny man. Unfortunately John does not suffer fools gladly and is sometimes his own worst enemy.

We spent the day after New Hampshire in Washington, and then spent the next three weeks crisscrossing the country, usually apart. George was great about calling, so we stayed in touch. The Super Tuesday primary took on enormous importance. I bumped across the country visiting some eighteen states, and George did more. We all spent long hours.

But it paid off. On March 8, George took all sixteen states and 57 percent of the votes cast, winning more primaries on a single day than any U.S. politician ever. The press called it a "knock-out blow." And it was. We coasted through the rest of the primary season, watching as Michael Dukakis emerged as the winner on the other side.

During the Democratic Convention in July, George and Jim Baker went fishing in Wyoming, where George finally rested. He was in heaven: fishing with a friend and no TV. I was in Kennebunkport with family and for some reason settled down to watch Ann Richards's (she's now the governor of Texas) ugly, devastating attack on George. I watched about ten minutes and turned off the tube with a sick feeling in my stomach. How naive of me to think that I was going to enjoy watching people trash George for three days! It hurt. What was worst, by the end of the convention, the Gallup Poll had us trailing Governor Dukakis 55 to 38 percent.

We headed to New Orleans to our own convention with no known vice presidential candidate. George whispered to me on the plane that he was going to ask Dan Quayle to be his running mate, but he had not told anyone else. He had looked over a field of very well qualified men and women and after much thought, felt Dan had much to offer. He was highly respected by members of the Senate. He had co-sponsored with Senator Ted Kennedy the Jobs Training Partnership Act, which was helping unemployed and laid-off workers get back into the job market. He was bright and, George felt, the right age. Some of George's closest advisers had worked with Dan and recommended him highly. I might add that some of those advisers developed a little amnesia when the going got tough.

Upon arrival we were greeted by the Reagans, who had been at the convention and were flying to California. We then went right away to a private home, where George got on the phone to all the potential candidates and tried to find Dan Quayle, which he eventually did. No one else was allowed to use the phone; George didn't want anyone letting the word out before the official announcement.

I can't resist saying a word or two about "leakers." All politicians are blessed with them, I don't care who they are. A leaker is a person who puts self above the candidate or boss. Leakers think they will get better treatment by the press. Maybe they do, but they get no respect from me.

In direct contrast to a leaker is someone like Craig Fuller, George's chief of staff during this period. He did not travel with George all the time, but I loved it when he did. Craig always put George first. He did not react to every little bump in the political road; instead, he stayed calm and seemed relaxed and confident. I liked him before the campaign and absolutely loved him during it. He quietly did his job and did it well. I thought that perhaps he deserved to continue on as chief of staff in the White House. I don't know if he wanted the job, but he carried on well after he knew he wasn't going to get it and agreed to head the transition team. Now a highly successful businessman, he and his wife, Karen, have remained really good young friends of ours.

New Orleans was a great place to have a convention; almost

everything is within walking distance. We made a grand entrance on a riverboat, where George announced Dan as his running mate. I heard later that Dan and Marilyn had trouble getting to the platform because they looked too young and no one realized why they needed to be up there. I wonder if they had anticipated the beating they would take for the next four years if he would have accepted the job. I hope so.

My memories of the convention are kind of a blur. Our dear friend Jane Morgan Weintraub sang at the luncheon honoring me. She came out of retirement to sing as she had long since concentrated on being a wife and raising her three little girls. Her voice always reminds me of honey or velvet, it seems so pure and easy to listen to. She and her husband, movie producer Jerry Weintraub, have a house in Kennebunkport, and we have been friends forever.

Doro introduced me at the tribute lunch and looked absolutely perfect to her old mother. George came as a "surprise" and teased me unmercifully. I recall asking him to please sit down and look at me with the same adoring eyes I had for him when he spoke. There were always innuendos that we were not lovey-dovey enough in public. That is not us. We don't need to be public about our affection; it's just there. I know that perception is very important in public life, but I also know that people can spot fakes. It may take a while, but eventually they do. We both resisted the "handlers'" request that we hold hands or whatever.

The whole convention was a happy family time. All our children and brothers and sisters had worked hard for George, so the night of the big roll call vote, our family was very well represented. First, Colu gave the second nominating speech for George. She had not eaten a thing all day and really was nervous, but she did it with style and, as I remember, partly in Spanish. When it came time for the roll call vote, all five of our children represented their states: Neil, Colorado; Jeb, Florida; Doro, Maine; George W., Texas; Marvin, Virginia. In addition, George's sister, Nancy Ellis, announced Massachusetts. Several states passed so that our Texas could put George over the top, which meant poor Marvin, when he announced Virginia's vote, gave it long after the celebrating and hoopla were over. He claims only the janitors were left to applaud him. Colu's role especially was a surprise. Earlier that year, she had quietly gone off and become an American citizen without a word to us. We never would have asked her as she has a great love for her native land, Mexico. It was a very touching gesture on her part.

On the last night of the convention there was a lot of pressure being put on George to make "the speech of his life," since we were behind in the polls. I don't know how he does it, but George seems to be able to stand the heat and even enjoy it. He did look so handsome and gave a magnificent speech.

The next day, the polls showed us almost in a dead heat. On to the next leg.

∽ The official kickoff for the general election campaign was Labor Day, the beginning of the end of months and months and months of campaigning. Both Kitty Dukakis and I had agreed to write a weekly column for *USA Today,* which forced me to keep scrupulous notes. So probably the best way to describe the frantic pace and nervous energy of the next nine weeks is to share with you excerpts from my diary.

September 4—How to pack for these long trips where you spend every night in a different bed? Well, first of all, at the age of 63, I announced that I no longer carried bags through the airport. I learned this from George. At the age of 60, George had announced that he no longer ate broccoli.* So I decided that I no longer carried luggage through airports and my life was much happier. The advance people took care of it.

. . . First I pack books; second, needlepoint; third, toiletries; and fourth, clothes. I am trying to go all black, or blue or brown, thus cutting down on shoes and handbags.

Labor Day—Packed all the wrong clothes. We did four outdoor events in record heat wave from San Diego to Los Angeles with a stop in between at Disneyland. Should have worn picnic dresses to all four.

(Went to) Chesapeake Bay Fish Company. Two attractive young owners, third generation proud. After touring the plant where GB got a lesson in filleting, we went to an outdoor rally. Stood on a stand with maybe eight workers, men and women, with ships of all sizes in the bay

---

* This became public knowledge several years later, and the National Broccoli Growers delivered two tons of the stuff to the South Grounds of the White House. Millie and I were the designated receivers. Some we kept for the White House mess and the rest we sent off to homeless shelters and soup kitchens.

behind us with balloons and large BUSH FOR PRESIDENT banners. The "Good Duke" was with us all day, a quiet and decent man. [George Deukmejian, governor of California. I'm afraid that in my mind the "Bad Duke" was Mike Dukakis. This was nothing personal—I had never met him. But in politics, the opponent is always the bad guy.] A few protesters. Bob Grady, a speech writer, noted that he recognized some of Dukakis' paid workers among the protesters. . . . It was hot, hot, hot. After the rally we heard that a man was picked up with a stun gun on his back.

. . . We went to an enormous rally at Disneyland (built-in crowd, of course) to send off the American Olympic Team to Korea. They are all shapes, sizes and colors, and they are all the best in their field . . . George gave a very moving speech . . . full of pride and love.

An amusing note: Sheila Tate told me that they did not want the picture of the week to be GB and Mickey Mouse, the Disneyland logo. They wanted George and the athletes. So I stood on George's name tape to keep two people between G. and Mickey, and several times George moved to my other side. Not an easy man to control.

On to the Los Angeles Police Academy annual picnic. A young policeman named Pratt had just been killed in the line of duty. His wife was pregnant with their fourth child. I hate to hear the police abused when you think that they risk their lives daily for us.

September 6—Awakened at 4:15 Los Angeles time (7:15 EDT), so I guess you could say we slept in. Read papers. Good pictures of GB. Was thrilled to see that the N.Y. Times is running three articles, PRICE OF ILLITERACY TRANSLATES INTO POVERTY AND HUMILIATION, on the front page. Left at 7 a.m. and flew to Oregon, where we were met by Antoinette and Mark Hatfield.

. . . We went to the Northwest Ironworks, where George toured the USNS *Andrew J. Higgins* and then on to a staging area to address the workers. I would have to give this a mixed review—at best. Big organized labor force with a large loud Dukakis cheering section. The press loved it, *BUT* so did George. His adrenaline flowed, and he kept on top of the situation. We heard from some workers and members of the press that he was gutsy to speak to people who were not for him. Some even asked if the campaign had planned it that way so it would show just how good George was. Well hardly! But he did a great job and went in to have lunch with some workers who invited him to join them.

. . . Flew on to Everett, Washington, where we visited the Fluke Plant. There we got away with a classic campaign boo-boo. At one point GB spoke with the word "Fluke" right above his head. I am sure that when the advance "how-to" book is written, this will be featured as "how-not-to."

. . . (Went to) airport rally where George gave a Distinguished Flying Cross to a Mr. Harry Lewis. It had gotten lost and he'd never received it. He was in the same task force as G.B. in WWII. I got weeping because he looked so moved . . . talk about unsung heroes.

September 7— . . . Flew last night to Louisville, Kentucky, arriving hotel at 11:45 for bed. No windows to open so it was either cold or stuffy. There is no happy medium. Walked almost three miles in a nice residential community called Hurstbourne. A darling young woman rushed out of her house with a camera, BUSH sticker, and a young daughter by the hand. She said that it was her daughter's first day of school and could she take her picture. Then the car pool arrived with six little girls, and the young woman got all their pictures. It brought back memories of putting five little Bushes in school the first time. I could hardly wait for them to get home to tell me about it. I can even remember my mother taking me to the Milton School for the first day of the first grade. Suddenly I looked around and she was gone. No good-byes, and I felt abandoned. But I had such fun and truly loved school that I had forgiven her by the time I got home. I think in our own children's case they never looked back.

. . . To the American Legion, where George got a great reception . . . he gave a very moving speech, but in the middle of it, got off the track on Sept. 7th being the anniversary of Pearl Harbor Day. We all got confused, and he could hear a titter run through the audience and quickly said, "Did I say September 7th? I meant December 7th." But for a while the press made so much about it. He recovered and all was well.

. . . On to a Victory '88 fund-raiser . . . to a G.O.P. Headquarters . . . back to a late lunch . . . flew to Baltimore. Airport rally . . . George spoke to a B'nai B'rith, enormous convention in Baltimore Convention Center . . . home to meetings for GB at the house. SPR (Susan Porter Rose) came by to tell that I was going to be followed by Dave Montgomery (Fort Worth Star-Telegram) on the morrow. I miss the good old days when (my aide) Casey and I just took off.

September 9—Met George in York, Pennsylvania, for a rally. There was a woman picked up the night before who said that she had a friend who told her that he was going to shoot George Bush at the rally. They ran his name through the computer, found his picture, a man with a gold tooth, and I was told that the spotter on the rooftop with a telescopic lens had spotted him with his gold tooth and a red shirt in a crowd of two to three thousand people. The Secret Service had followed him for several blocks, picked him up only to find they had the wrong man. They were back trying to find him again.

. . . Finally we were introduced and it was thrilling. I wish I hadn't known about the man with the gold tooth. [I've been asked if I worried about this kind of thing a lot. The truth is, no—not unless we knew something specific. You just can't let yourself think about it.]

. . . There were thousands of people, lots of BUSH signs and, of course, a few for DUKAKIS or a few anti-Bush signs. Lots of press, lots of color. Big American flag on Court House, flags, cheerleaders with pompoms, bands, football captain, balloons, etc. George gave a fired-up speech, they barely let him talk with cheering. Steve Studdert (with the campaign) was in front like Cecil B. DeMille directing, "take a pompom," "move the Senator," "get behind George," etc. Lee Greenwood sang his song, "I'm Proud to Be an American"; the crowd went wild. Steve was wildly trying to get my attention to get me to move George next to Lee and then to move me and the Senators next to him . . . You just have to have a sense of humor, not to mention nerves of iron.

September 11—We asked the Quayles for lunch with their little people, three very nice children. They have a boy about 14, Tucker; a boy Ben, 11; and a daughter Corinne, 9 . . . it is so different for Marilyn than it is for Kitty Dukakis, B.A. Bentsen or me. She still has to worry about riding lessons, homework, dentists, etc. Quite a juggling act.

September 12—Northern Kentucky Senior Citizen Center . . . welcomed by a kazoo band playing "Yellow Rose of Texas." Adorable. One man with thimbles on all his fingers playing a metal washboard, antique bottles, etc. . . . One elderly citizen to another:

"Which one is Mrs. Bush?"

"The one with the white hair."

"They all have white hair."

"Which one *is* Mrs. Bush?"

[This reminds me of a funny story that happened after George became President. He was talking at a Veterans Hospital about health care reform when an elderly gentleman in the back kept yelling, "What's all this crap? When is Ike coming?"]

. . . Hyatt Regency, Chicago. Biggest suite I have ever seen . . . George got in from a big rally in Illinois and a full day. I could barely speak to him I was so tired, but I loved showing him the bathroom in our suite, sauna with seats for four or more, Jacuzzi for two to four and every fancy soap you have ever seen and lotions. I filled the "lake" as I called the tub and took a hot bath. George took a sauna. I was asleep before you could say "Jack Robinson."

I am torn over the soaps and lotions. Do I want the hotel people to think I need soap, shampoo and lotions? Not really. But do I take them? Yes, I do. I have a nice collection at home right now, and every now and then I send them down to the shelter in Washington. I keep thinking that a clean piece of soap all your own must be nice.

September 13—Executive Club of Chicago breakfast. Sat one away from Johnny Johnson, the publisher of *Jet* and *Ebony* and founder of a cosmetic company. He grew up in Arkansas, the son of a widowed black woman. He told me his mother worked as a domestic and saved her money to move her family to Chicago so her son could go to school. Arkansas was not educating teenage blacks 55 years ago. He started a *Black Digest* on a shoestring that grew into *Ebony* and *Jet* and, I guess, a lot of other things. He reminded me of Frederick Douglass. If you want to do something badly enough, it can be done. A great man. It does show what a positive influence a good parent can have on a child. His mother set an example and instilled a work ethic in him that money can't buy.

We drove through Illinois . . . listening to country music, reading and occasionally looking out at miles of rolling countryside. Whenever we went through a town there would be people with homemade signs or just plain waving, standing on the street or running out to greet the Vice President. At one place we passed a graveyard, and there stood a young woman with her head bowed putting flowers on a grave. Even in the middle of a big campaign, life does go on. That young woman somehow or other put things in perspective.

September 14—How George loves the West Coast because he can call anybody he wants when he wakes up. I have to hold him at bay on the East Coast. By the time we left our rooms (in Los Angeles) at 7:40 he had called his office, his mother, his sister, and Nick Brady who had gotten through the Senate confirmation committee 15 to 0.*

. . . I took my soaps, lotions, shampoos, etc. (to Christian Mission) and dumped my filled purse on the table. They all laughed at me. Evidently a hotel does supply them with all the above, but they said they could use all they could get.

. . . George didn't sleep well because he was worried about his speech before the San Francisco Economic Club, thought it was too negative about Dukakis. I urged him to rewrite it. George got up at 5:30 and did rewrite his speech. I heard him tell Jim Baker that he just had to be himself. I know that George got where he is today by trusting his own instincts and he usually is right. Let others knock Dukakis. Dukakis is knocking Quayle a lot. I don't think George has mentioned Bentsen once. Frankly, we are not hearing much about Lloyd either.

September 16—Cleveland, Tennessee . . . There I ran into Kids-on-the-Block again. They are a great group of puppeteers who teach kids about the handicapped, drugs, sex education, etc.

Chattanooga, Tennessee . . . We met with PROJECT READ volunteers and students. They were a good group of 225 tutors teaching 280 students . . . they have a waiting list. This always saddens me. Imagine, people get up their nerve to ask for help and we can't help.

Home to stacks of mail.

. . . On the way home in a light rain we spotted those cardboard figures that people have their pictures taken with. There was the President, Dukakis, George, Nancy and the latest, I believe, Tom Selleck. We stopped the car, jumped out and had our picture taken for $5 with "George." It caused lots of excitement among the tourists. I took a picture of the vendor and his pretty little wife with the real George. Back in the car, as the picture developed, we saw why people were so surprised that George is so tall. He just towered over the cardboard George by at least 4 inches.

---

* When Jim Baker resigned as Secretary of the Treasury to be George's campaign chairman, President Reagan appointed Nick to replace him.

. . . George called the two former presidents to see if they had any advice for the debates. President Nixon said, "Just be yourself." Jerry Ford said, "Take your time before you answer a question. Take a deep breath and think and then answer." Both good advice.

All through the campaign I read to relax . . . "Lilly: Reminiscences of Lillian Hellman," by Peter Feibleman. Amazing just how much I dislike her lifestyle and still like so much of her writing. She is like Truman Capote in that respect. I hated his lifestyle and yet thought "In Cold Blood" absolutely beautifully and chillingly written.

. . . Doro called late Tuesday night. She was *so* upset. She'd been to a big GOP dinner and the entertainers were so vicious that John Engler (our Michigan chairman) had taken her from the room. She said that they said ugly things about Dukakis and GB, but they were really mean about me and Kitty. They had someone in a white wig debating Kitty. In the debate I used not only all the four letter words, but also made an ugly hand gesture to K.D. Doro was so upset, but I must confess to laughing. It reminded me of a night in Indiana recently. I was the guest speaker at that tremendous fund-raiser they have every year. I was one of five speakers, so why they felt they needed to hire a comedian, I will never know. This man was so tasteless and just plain crude that I got the giggles from embarrassment and from catching the eye of my dear friend Mary Jo Bradley. It was horrid, so very bad and the worse he got, the worse I got . . . almost hysterical giggles. I had to put my head down. I know that 1,500 Indianians thought I thought he was funny and liked him.

. . . Jim Baker and I were talking about how you can't control some things. He told me that when Susan Baker and Tipper Gore were exposing the dangerous, sick, ugly words that were hidden in the rock and roll music that the kids are listening to, *Hustler* magazine had a picture of the two of them as "A—h-l-s of the Month." Apparently they have one every month. That is too much. Can you imagine lovely Susan Baker or Tipper Gore being treated that way?

September 23—Woke up at 6:30. Went down in my bathrobe to walk Millie. Got caught. There were press all lined up for George's breakfast with (Soviet Foreign Minister) Shevardnadze. Then later they were moved from the front gate to the front lawn with a direct view into my dressing room. I crawled to the closet for my clothes. What has happened to my usually peaceful private home?

. . . Lots of questions about debate coming up on Sunday. "Was I nervous?" "Was I giving George advice?" The answers were all the same— "No" and "No."

. . . Lots of phone calls wishing GB good luck in the debates. They have been hyped to a make-or-break situation. Polls showing GB slightly ahead after being *WAY* behind. They are expecting a hundred million people to watch this debate. Amazing. I do not envy GB.

September 25—We slept until 6:30, which is pretty good for us.

On board the plane the press had a gift for George. Everyone had signed a Christmas card. Pearl Harbor on September 7th—therefore this was Christmas Day. All signed with funny messages. GB loved it.

. . . Walked through the Convention Hall (in Winston-Salem, N.C.), where the debate was to take place. There was the Dukakis podium three inches shorter than George's. When the big moment arrived the Dukakis people carried in a carpeted thing that looked like a pitcher's mound, making Dukakis now 6 inches taller in perception—a 3-inch shorter podium and a 3-inch riser. I am amazed. He is shorter and it ought not matter. They clearly think it does. (When the two candidates were announced from different sides, they both walked across the stage to shake hands. George tripped over the hidden box!)

September 26—I thought that George won hands down. The polls, pundits, commentators, etc., seem to feel that no one made a knock-out punch, but the undecideds leaned slightly towards George. "Too close to call" was the consensus. One reporter wrote, "I went to bed thinking Dukakis had won and woke up to find that the American people thought that George Bush had won."

September 28—George P. and Noelle joined us in Bloomington, Illinois, on a bus tour. The three sisters, our dear friends Loretta Lynn, Crystal Gayle and Peggy Sue, were with us all day to sing and warm up the crowd. It was such fun because they sang in the bus.

. . . We were told to move over to the window and wave as the press truck pulled up for a "photo op." So we all moved over to the right side of the bus, opened the windows and leaned out smiling and waving. The truck moved up and as they got alongside us, the press said with one voice, "Pardon me, sir, do you have any Grey Poupon?" We died laughing.

September 30—Last day of the month. 40 more days to go, but who's counting?

October 3—Hardly slept knowing that we had a long day ahead, flying to California to welcome the shuttle home. This will be an exciting day. It will end for me in Yakima, Washington, at 9:20 p.m. (12:20 EDT). Arrived at Edwards Air Force Base in California. Driven immediately to Shuttle Landing viewing area on lake bed, an immense 50-mile space, flat as a pancake, hard clay bed . . . On the exact moment that we should have, we heard Discovery break the sound barrier twice and then we saw the shuttle. It circled the sky and then came down at a 27-degree angle that looks like it is going to crash into the earth . . . with perfect timing the plane "flared" and set down exactly where they wanted it to. When you consider that the shuttle has no power, it is on glide, it is a miracle. Some of that same feeling of pride that we felt at the Olympics. The USA certainly got a gold medal on this flight. There was great rejoicing among everyone here. It had been 2½ years since the Challenger blew up. (This was the first shuttle flight since Challenger.) A promise kept, I felt. "Back to the Future" pins were handed out.

. . . George and I went into a holding room, really a men's locker room. He went into a tiny back room and promptly fell asleep. I read my book, "The Duchess of Windsor: The Secret Life," by Charles Higham. Fascinating, but not fascinating enough to keep me awake. She certainly was a racy, determined devil!!!

Reading, California. Big rally, streets lined to and from with warm cheering crowds. George Deukmejian told us in the car going back to the airport that he felt *VERY* good about the crowd reaction.

October 5—34 more days to go!!!!
Slept like a baby, but awakened with clenched teeth and a headache. This will be a tough day. Dan Quayle will be debating Lloyd Bentsen. The latter is so confident, saying things like, "Day I'll be eating Quayle," etc.

. . . New NY TIMES poll. Gap is closing. GB 3 points ahead, down from last week.

. . . Flew home, getting home in time for last hour of the V.P. debate. Lloyd got in one, really telling shot at Dan on JFK. He was lying-in-wait for him. Rather interestingly, I wonder just how well Lloyd knew JFK. The Kennedys hated Lyndon, and surely Lloyd was for his fellow Texan. Ah, well, it does not matter. He got his shot in.

October 8—During the morning our house was really buzzing. First a CIA briefing. Then, to action. Our dining room had to be seen to be believed. Two podiums set up, cameras, TV monitors, table for questioners, red, green and yellow lights for timing and warning on answers. It was set up just as it will be on the night of the debate, TV lights and on and on. In the living room there were 14 people with pads on their laps, all watching the monitors and the simulated debate. (Richard) Darman is the "Bad Duke" and George answering the questions put to him by Margaret Tutwiler, Craig King, Jim Pinkerton and Bob Goodman (moderator). Amazing production. The next debate is on Thursday or Friday . . . depending on the World Series . . . let's get first things first!!!

. . . Finished "Breathing Lessons" by Anne Tyler. Loved it. Started Eric Segal's "Doctors."

October 10—New Atlanta poll out today. Showing George ahead in the South by 12%–49% BUSH, 37% DUKAKIS. Showed 14% ahead in Texas and Florida. Now that is good news.

A week of interviews   I wonder if Kitty Dukakis feels like I do—so sick of talking about myself.

One good thing happened from all the interviews: Maeve Binchy, the Irish author, read that I loved her book "Light a Penny Candle" and sent me "Firefly Summer."

. . . I have never seen anything like the trashing of Dan Quayle. He is a fine choice, but I honestly believe that the liberal press are so eager to beat George that they are beating Dan to death. He is certainly as well qualified as Geraldine Ferraro, Spiro Agnew and I could go on and on. I might even suggest Mike Dukakis! The real truth is that Harry Truman, who will go down as a great president, was thought to be a "little man from Missouri." Some people rise to the occasion— others don't. Harry did. I cannot watch the tube. The leaning towards the "Bad Duke" gets me down.

. . . ABC Poll: 50% BUSH—47% DUKAKIS

. . . *The Scholastic News*—never wrong in last 25 years—57% BUSH—43% DUKAKIS

. . . Tulsa, Oklahoma. Went to Children's Medical Center for emotionally disturbed, abused, drug recovery children—ages from babies to 17½ . . . started out the door and there were the little 11- and 12-year-old boys I had read to. One child, Dudley, who they said suffered from lack of self-esteem, asked me if he could hug me good-bye. Another little voice said, "Don't forget me." I was so touched, and the next thing I knew I had an armload of little boys. Willis, my (Secret Service) agent, mumbled as we walked out, "They can forget all those expensive programs and just give them a little love." But sad to say, we can't forget all those expensive programs because they don't get the love.

. . . Boarded a commercial plane for Los Angeles. Had a little nap. At one time during the flight was awakened when the pilot announced that "If we looked out the right window we could see the four corners. If you got down on all fours, you could be in four states at one time." So, of course my traveling companions suggested a campaign stop. What a photo op!!

October 12—Anniversary of Robin's death—or was it the 11th? Time does soften death. It was 35 years ago. Hard to believe that our little angel would be 39 years old!

October 13—Awakened early. The pressure mounting on the debate this afternoon. George seems relaxed. 26 more days to go. Awakened to a new ABC–*Washington Post* poll: BUSH, 51%; DUKAKIS, 45%. If the election were held today it would be a landslide for George, but we all know that numbers go up and down.

Dan Quayle announced this week: "No more handlers." I am thrilled as the handlers have gotten too important (as if it is perception that counts, not substance)—as have the press (how many times we see the press interviewing each other?)—as have the spin artists (why not let the viewer decide what they just heard or saw?) I read that one station is now claiming that this is a "Bush ploy," getting Dan to speak out. I can vouch for the fact that this was a surprise!!!

I was led into the (Los Angeles) debate surrounded by friends: Governor Sununu, Gloria and George Deukmejian, Henry Kissinger, Gayle Wilson, the Darmans, Mosbachers, Bobby Holt, Al Simpson and on and on. I sat between Neil and Jeb. On they came. Same podiums, same mound. Incidentally, this time Kitty, looking beautiful in a bright red dress, came right over to shake my hand. I met her before she got to me. (At the first debate, I had asked Pete DuPont to take me over to her and introduce us.) Then the debate started. George was relaxed and confident and funny. The questions were asked by Bernard Shaw, Ann Compton, Margaret Warner and Andrea Mitchell. Jeb got so excited over his dad's answers. Neil, as always, was thrilled. All, if not almost all, gave GB a big win. George was a clear winner. We'll see when the national polls come out.

. . . Drove to a large rally at Loyola University. Drive was long and so we called George W. to see how he liked the debate. (He is the son who pulls no punches and tells it like he thinks it is.) He confessed that he and Marvin had gone to the movies as they couldn't stand the pressure. Marvin told me that George sent him out about 12 times to call friends and ask them how it was going. They then went home and were watching a taping when we called. George W. said that the late evening news was good.

October 14—Visiting California School for the Deaf . . . A warm welcome. Big crowd that all wanted to touch me. They were such a gentle group, tiny little noises to get my attention. They touch. It was like walking through a bunch of butterflies. I loved them. Some are also slow. Many of them are truly beautiful. I walked through the school where they live 5 days a week and go home for weekends. Each child grows up literate and with a vocation. On into a TV station where a precious girl interviewed me. She was part of a team: cameraman, director, lights, etc. All children, all without words. I was put in a chair, with an interpreter, and interviewed live. Michelle had moved into the house when she was 12 and for the first time in her life "felt important." So sweet. Imagine being in a regular school and not hearing a word. She was articulate, bright and warm—very strong in her beliefs. She asked me not to forget people like her, and I won't. When we got through, the whole crew rushed together and said: "You did it, you did it!" to each other. It was their first live interview. Michelle shone like a light. Her mother and father were there to share this glorious day with her. I left full of love.

. . . Flew back to George. We walked over to Chasen's with Tommy Lasorda and Jerry Weintraub. We were joined by Jane Weintraub, Tony Danza and wife, Tommy's wife, Jo Lasorda, Peter O'Malley (owner of the Dodgers), and Jerry's lawyer. In the next room, Gloria and Jimmy Stewart, Barbara and Frank Sinatra, Jane Dart, and Stevie and Iris Dart (Iris wrote the book that I so adored, "Beaches"; Jane's husband, Justin, had been a member of President Reagan's "kitchen cabinet") were dining with Fleur Cowles. We had a nice visit. Fun, relaxed evening. Polls all day look good for George.

October 15—Dodgers won in the 9th!

October 16—(Denver) GB read the papers. Darling front page picture of Neil with Lauren and Pierce . . . Endorsement by *Rocky Mountain News*. I finished my diary and called Jean Becker of *USA Today*. It is hard to write for a week and then pick out a few incidents to put in the weekly news article. I keep a daily diary, pick out what I want to use for the week, talk to Jean, she sends the final back, I okay it and off it goes. I had to tell her that I would not write one after the election. She says that Kitty has agreed to write one. I think it would be too hard on the loser, and the winner will be too busy. Either way, I said, "No." (When I was approached about writing the column last summer, I was told that Kitty had agreed to it; therefore my office felt I should, too. I wonder if the same gimmick was used to get Kitty to write one?)

October 17—George and I didn't sleep well at all. Highway too close to room. At times thought that trucks were coming into window. I think we are both beginning to believe that he might win—and then there will be so much to do. George is not letting himself think that way, but you can't keep your mind from churning. So we got up at 5 a.m.

On plane flying home . . . a lovely black lady who worked for United Airlines came up and said: "I want you to know I made up my mind to vote for your husband this weekend. Let me tell you what decided me. It was the death penalty. We must stop this killing. People just have to pay. It may be a deterrent." She also said that she never thought that she would say that. I feel the same way. We just have to stop these killings.

October 18—55% to 38%, new ABC–*Washington Post* poll. 17 points ahead. Too good to be true. Do we believe it? No. We are scared to death that people will stay home. The Teamsters endorsed George yesterday, but not Dan Quayle.

October 19—Spent day in Missouri. Then flew to NYC and was greeted by news the Stock Market went wild with rumors about an exposé The Washington Post was doing on George's "romance" with Jennifer Fitzgerald. The market plunged. Ugly campaign tactics. How do you defend against that which isn't, wasn't and never will be? It got so bad that Ben Bradlee (Washington Post) put out a statement that no story was coming out or being worked on. We must be doing better than I thought for this kind of ugliness.

October 20—AL SMITH DINNER in NYC
. . . Mike Dukakis came up and apologized to George for something a "low level" staff member had said about George. He should have. [This refers to Donna Brazile, who had made a crack to the press about the above rumors. She was fired.]

October 22—Marvin Bush's 31st birthday.
. . . Chase Untermeyer, John Sununu, Jim Baker, George and I had lunch outside in the garden in the sun (a little crisp, but our last chance.) These men are working on the transition team. Very interesting. *Both* parties are working on transition. The day after the election, the transition team must be in place and ready to go, about 95 people that first week.
. . . George spoke to Jim Baker about being Secretary of State and John Sununu about Chief of Staff. I am assuming that Jim said yes. George told me that John said he wanted to talk with (his wife) Nancy. Two very big jobs. Ridiculous to talk about jobs when you haven't won, but very necessary.
. . . Nap
. . . Walked
. . . We went to the annual Italian American Dinner. They honored former Prime Minister Craxi, Liza Minnelli, Peter Rodino who is retiring after 40 years in Congress, and an Olympic skating star—all from Italian backgrounds. George passed me a note during the evening saying that the M.C. was "dangerous near the mike." How true! It was a very long evening. I sat next to our old friend PM Craxi, who is a very big man. He suffered under the TV lights and kept moaning about the heat. He was right. The speeches went on and on. I finally showed him George's note, and he laughed. I talked Spanish and he spoke Italian and we did pretty well. At one time in the evening, as a speaker was going on and on, he leaned over and said very clearly in English, "Very dangerous man."
The "Bad Duke" came during the dessert, sat through the speeches and then gave his talk (well done) and then GB (better), and we went home.

October 24—George was in Connecticut, Maine and Vermont. He saw Doro. I asked him if Doro was upset by all the protesters. He said there weren't many and why would I ask? I told him that the evening news had said that there "were more of them than us" at the meeting. George was surprised and said that was just not true. No wonder we feel down on the press. Mike Dukakis called George a liar and a racist today. Nice campaign.

October 25—In Illinois . . . met President Reagan's teacher. That's right, President Reagan's teacher, now Mayor of Jacksonville, Mayor Helen Forman. I said that could not be as I just went to his 77th birthday party. She taught Ronald Reagan when he was at junior high school, and it was her first year of teaching. She is 84 years old and fit as a fiddle. She also told me that she taught him English—not government—and she thought he was very good at English.

October 26—13 more days to go. Decatur, Illinois. I awakened in the middle of the night. Can't keep my mind from racing over problems. I probably even make up some problems in the middle of the night . . . new polls show George with a double digit lead, but I just can't believe them.

October 27—California . . . Jim Baker called and said the polls are showing a little slippage to MD.
. . . Lots of speculation over who will hold what job in the Bush administration. Hard not to begin to believe that we are going to win. But "It ain't over until it's over" is very true. You can go down just as fast as you go up. Mike Dukakis is blitzing the airways with talk shows and media. It may be paying off.

October 28—California, Nebraska.

October 29—Call in the middle of the afternoon that my brother Jim Pierce had an emergency operation in Orlando, Florida. Tried all the numbers that I was given and finally after dropping G.'s name, I got his nurse. He was in great pain, but they had given him medication. Margie must be very worried. I am.

October 30—One of the nicest days of campaign '88. First of all, the overnight tracking looks good . . . We flew to Philadelphia with George P. for church with retired Cardinal Krol. We were very touched when George P. fell in behind the Catholic nuns and took communion.

. . . George and I went to Bob and "Big Z" (her name is Teresa but no one calls her that) DeAngelis' house in Norristown for lunch with their pregnant daughter, Paula, and son-in-law. This was a campaign tradition that we started in 1980 and have loved. They are a great family and besides that, "Big Z" is the best cook ever. Their neighbors were on the street, and I found Tommy Lasorda's three brothers in the crowd and brought them over to meet George.

October 31—(Halloween)

Nervous time . . . Barbara, Jenna, Laura and George W. went to South Bend with George. The girls went in costumes. Jenna was a package of Juicy Fruit and looked just like it, and Barbara was a vampire, or "Vampora," some character they all seem to know.

. . . This is the last week of the campaign. It has been ugly. Dukakis, or his supporters, have called George a racist, liar, and adulterer, silly and effeminate. I truly believe that George has run on his record, and Dukakis has run away from his. When George talks about Dukakis' record, they cry foul.

[The best example is the now infamous Willie Horton incident. Under Governor Dukakis, Massachusetts allowed weekend prison furloughs. One weekend, convicted murderer Willie Horton raped a woman and stabbed a man in Maryland. George used this heinous incident to illustrate that Dukakis was not tough enough on crime. Then a pro-George independent committee—not our campaign—decided to turn the example into a campaign ad, using the image of a sinister-looking Willie Horton, who was black, as the focus. We got blamed for dirty politics and racism. Baloney. The ad was not ours, and the truth of the matter is, Willie Horton should not have been out of prison. The victims' families campaigned for George, they were so angry with Dukakis. Roger Ailes, who was in charge of our ads and did a great job, was unfairly blamed for the controversy. He had nothing to do with it. I still miss seeing Roger on the "Today" show, where he was brilliant yet devastatingly funny while knocking the Democrats.]

The negative ads on both sides are bad. We ran one on defense weapons that ends by saying that (Dukakis) thinks by riding in a tank he can make us forget what he is against, all the while showing that silly scene of him riding around in a tank with that silly enormous helmet on his head. Poor man, he looks ridiculous. Some staff person must be cringing. They thought this would be a marvelous photo op!

. . . How do we cope with the pressure? I guess George is right. "Faith, family and friends." All have helped.

. . . Lots of mail.

. . . Lots of people want to redo me. My favorite so far was the lady who took the LIFE magazine picture gave me a new haircut, new earrings, necklace, clothes, makeup, and sent me a slide she had taken of her work of art.

. . . Lots of people want to pass advice on to George.

. . . Lots of people have requests.

. . . Lots of resumes.

. . . Lots of people with ideas for projects for me. A large, orchestrated one for mental health. I sympathize with them all. And if George wins, I wonder, if while working to make America more literate, could I highlight some others?

November 1— . . . On plane Casey told me that she had gone to Williamsburg to hear Crystal Gayle, Peggy Sue and Loretta Lynn sing. She went to both concerts, 2 p.m. and 5 p.m. At both concerts she said that Loretta and Peggy Sue campaigned for George, and they were booed at the five o'clock concert. Crystal told the audience, "No matter who you are for, be sure to vote." How right she is. It makes me sick when I read the percentages of Americans who do not vote.

November 2—Flew to Rye, N.Y., for a Barbara Pierce Bush Day. It was fun. My family greeted me in the old family drugstore we used to go to, McCullough's, and then we marched the length of the village. So much has changed since I bought that Marshmallow Fluff and walked to the movies. A Hunan restaurant! When I was growing up we hardly knew where China was . . . The old movie theater is now the Town Hall. The mayor, Mary Ann Ilse, is a woman!

. . . On to Rochester, N.Y. . . . went to bed "too tired to think. Too fat to like myself."

November 3—Took off for Arkansas. When we return to VP House, we will know if we have won or lost.

. . . On to Baton Rouge.

. . . Bumpy plane ride to Cincinnati.

November 4—Raining off and on all night. Amazing volunteers worked all night setting up for a big rally. They hung painted sheets out windows, great political signs, built big platforms and stands for press and performers.

Big rally. George and Doro came in on a fire truck, covered with confetti. On stage with George Voinovich [now governor of Ohio] and baseball great Johnny Bench. George spoke to hundreds and hundreds of people who had been standing in the rain for 2½ hours. The rally ended with Moe Bandy singing "Americana."

. . . On to a big rally in Michigan.

. . . Newark, New Jersey.

. . . The sadness is that no matter what happens on Tuesday we lose our Secret Service. They go to other details. If we win, ours go to Dan Quayle and Marilyn. These have been wonderful men and women whose only job has been to keep us safe. They have been very much a part of our life during the past eight years. They know our children and grand-children. They have worked, run, fished, laughed, driven with us. On the whole they are the finest, most decent men and women I know, and I will hate to say good-bye to the VP detail. I'll never forget the day when George was singing in the car, and just as we were getting out of the car a quiet voice from the front said: "If I were you, sir, I wouldn't give up my daytime job."

. . . I also have kissed my four advance ladies good-bye and thanked them: Nancy Pilon, Suzanne Rich, Andrea Raiford and Karen Gossett. What a job they did.

November 5—Did an event with (Governor) Tom and Debbie Kean in New Jersey.

Philadelphia . . . met by our most wonderful friend, Elsie Hillman, and our state chairman, Tom Judge. Elsie had been the most devoted Republican worker in the state and knows everyone. She also knows the joy of life. How they have worked.

. . . Great rally at Immaculata College. Both Senator John Heinz and Arlen Specter were there. John Heinz's polls show him at 80%.

. . . Flew off to Illinois, met by the governor, Big Jim Thompson. He is a fun campaigner, loves the push and the pull of a crowd . . . Enormous crowd in Chillicothe, Ohio.

. . . Flew to Colorado City. Doro and I hopped on a plane and flew
to Los Angeles.

November 6—Casey brought me coffee at 5:30. Doro came in right
after that, dressed with washed hair. She looked so beautiful. At 6:40 Jeb,
Doro and I went to the studio to do "Face the Nation" with Lesley Stahl.
I'm not sure Lesley knew what hit her. She went negative and attacked,
but Jeb and Doro were superb. Back to the hotel and we called in our last
USA Today column. Then to a 50-year-old church, St. Nicholas Church,
in Encino, California.

. . . 20,000 people at a rally where we met up with GB.

. . . 2nd rally in Los Angeles, 10,000 people.

. . . Flew to Detroit, exhausted. Bed about 12:30.

November 7—One day to go! Polls look like they are holding. Nervous time.

. . . Can't watch TV. Dukakis ads are so bad.

. . . Big rally, Southfield, Michigan.

. . . Ashland, Ohio.

. . . Flying to Missouri. Cautious optimism on the plane.

. . . St. Louis rally at headquarters. Elizabeth Dole and Bucky Bush
met us. Governor and Mrs. Ashcroft (John and Janet), and Senator and
Mrs. Danforth (Jack and Sally) were at the rally. Get out the vote. LAST
RALLY OF THE CAMPAIGN!!!

. . . Flying home to Houston. The "handlers" are all on the plane.
They want George to do six television shows via satellite. He put his foot
down. 4 big rallies in 4 big cities are enough. We are all tired, but George
is dead.

. . . Lee Atwater is quiet. Thinks it will be 53% of the popular vote
for GB. I wish he was making more noise. His quiet bothers me.

. . . Craig Fuller has been superb. Good and thoughtful. Not full of
gloom and doom.

Jim Baker has been superb. George loves and trusts him.

. . . Houston arrival was great. George, Laura, Phil and Wendy
Gramm at the foot of the steps. The Gramms have been so great, so supportive. They were so excited. We, because of the gloom and doomsayers,
were very nervous. They were almost high!

The rally at the Galleria was unbelievable. Crystal, Loretta, Peggy

Sue, Moe Bandy, wife and children were there. Marvin, Margaret and Doro were also there.

> *November 8*—This is the day.
> . . . Voted at 8 a.m.
> . . . Went to GOP Headquarters, made a few calls.
> . . . Went to Memorial Park to walk 5 miles. It occurred to me that they had closed the park to all car traffic for George.
> . . . Lunch at Center Court with my great buddy, Marion Chambers.
> . . . Got a massage, did mail, washed hair and went over to the Nebletts'. They had a perfect dinner, a repeat of Super Tuesday.
> . . . In the late afternoon Jim Baker had walked in our room and told me we had won. A few minutes later we were down again. We walked into the Nebletts' feeling pretty shaky. At one time in the evening Jim bet Lee $5 that we would get under 53%. Lee paid him off halfway through the evening. All our friends thought we had it in the bag.
> At 8:16 CBS reluctantly announced George the winner. We went back to the hotel with our family. We watched the news and we went from a "squeak" to a big victory—42 states and 54% to 46%. We continued to watch the tube. First Lloyd Bentsen came on, congratulated George and said he was honored to serve as the senator from Texas again. He raved over Mike Dukakis and that was that. Mike Dukakis called George and then went public. Funny that Lloyd went public before Mike. I thought that was a breach of protocol.
> . . . Down to the Convention Hall, where thousands and thousands of Texans and friends from all over the country were cheering my George. It was so touching. George gave a healing speech.
> . . . G talked to the President, Margaret Thatcher, the King of Saudi Arabia and others.
> . . . All five of our children's states went for George. We were so happy for them as they worked so hard.
> . . . We went to bed in shock. Think of all the people who should have been here, who would have been so proud and said: "I knew it all the time." Neil Mallon, Marvin Pierce, Herbie Walker, Pres Bush, Bill Steiger and Jimmy Allison, for starters.
> Well, it's over. How do you thank the people for all they've done? The advance people who literally worked all night and day? The staff who stayed in Washington and worked with none of the fun? The staff who

traveled, who not only had the fun, but lost their luggage, slept five hours a night if they were lucky, constantly were asked to change speeches and survived on junk food; volunteers, the backbone of the campaign, who give hours and hours of time, who gather votes and money, spend hours on the phone, drive motorcades and on and on? How do we thank our brothers, sisters, and cousins by the dozens? And, especially, how do we thank our children and grandchildren for putting their own lives on the back burner for us? We will never be able to say thank you adequately, but will try our darndest to do right and be honest, good, caring people.

November 9—I awakened this morning with the President-elect of the United States of America.

16

"Please Guide and Guard Us"

George wanted to begin his first day as President-elect by going to church. It seemed the natural thing to do since we both were fortunate enough to grow up in families where God played an integral part.

So at 7:45, before we left Houston for Washington, we went to St. Martin's Church for a service of thanksgiving and guidance. Our present and past Houston ministers, Claude Payne and Tom Bagby, offered prayers, and Bishop Ben Benitez read the lesson. They were all wonderful, but the prayer that our son George W. gave touched us deeply:

Our Heavenly Father, we thank you for your many blessings:

We thank you for our health and safe passage during the past months.

We thank you for our country and the freedom to exercise our free will.

And we thank you for our greatest gift of all—your Son.

We ask, Lord, that you open our hearts and minds to you:

Many of us will begin a new challenge. Please give us strength to endure and the knowledge necessary to place our fellow man over self.

We pray that as we face new challenges, we understand that through you we can clear our minds and seek wisdom.

We ask that you open our hearts and minds to prayers so we can feel the solace of your gentle love.

Please guide us and guard us on our journeys—particularly watch over Dad and Mother.

We pray that our lives be beacons to you by remembering the words of David:

May that which I speak and that which I have in my heart be acceptable to thee, oh Lord.

The plane back to Washington was jammed with exhausted but happy staff and family. George's twins were wild. At one time they stuffed the toilet with paper, and I was up to my elbows pulling it out. I couldn't help but wonder if any other First Lady–elects had spent their first morning unstuffing the toilet.

It all seemed so sudden—the election was over and we had won. I can't explain it, but there was a difference in the air; a difference in how George—and I—was treated. Everything had changed.

After a big rally at Andrews Air Force Base, we drove to the White House, where President Reagan and Nancy greeted us. George, Laura, the twins, and Marvin's wife, Margaret, were with us, and the girls were thrilled to have their pictures taken with the President and Nancy in the Oval Office.

George then went to his office and I went home. Laurie Firestone and the stewards had decorated the house with WELCOME HOME signs; red, white, and blue bunting; and balloons. Paula and Millie were there waiting, too, and we all had champagne. It was so touching and warm. George came home that night absolutely exhausted.

A few days later we flew to Gulf Stream, Florida, and stayed with our dear friends Sarah and Will Farish. Will Farish was George's very first aide when he went into politics, and twenty-eight years later, before we left the White House, his son Bill also would serve in that position.

On this visit, their children stayed in a motel down the road to make room for us, which was pretty amazing in itself. It should have embarrassed us, but didn't, we're such good friends. I think it was there I learned just how different things were going to be for us. The press was everywhere, and even walking on the beach was impossible. At one time I dove off a boat that was a half mile off-shore and saw a picture of the dive in the paper the next day. But we still managed to relax. George played some golf, and I read, answered mail, and swam. We went to church at Hobe Sound with Mom Bush on Sunday and had lunch with her and our great friends and supporters Elsie and Henry Hillman. We saw Nancy and Sandy Ellis, George's sister and brother-in-law, and John Sununu came down to fly back with us. George soon was going to announce his selection as chief of staff.

One of the first things on my agenda was a literacy conference that Susan Porter Rose had organized to be held November 15 at the White House, followed by an honors dinner that night. I had been bugging Susan about some money that had been given me for literacy, and I was worried about not having a place to put it. She finally had to tell me that this money was going into a new foundation—which was supposed to be a surprise—and that the dinner was not only to honor seventeen "learners of the month," but also Barbara Bush. "What if George had lost," I asked Susan, "and we had to go through an evening of being brave?" Susan said then it would have been a celebration of eight years of literacy work. Believe me, it would have been hard.

For the conference, Susan brought together literacy leaders from across the country. To be fair, I'll quote from my diary:

Bill Clinton from Arkansas (Governor) was a star, Mayor Wilson Goode of Philadelphia was terrible. I think I felt that way because under his leadership, Philadelphia was actively working to be a more literate city. I had expected him to be a better speaker, but I should judge by actions, not speaking ability. Robert Winters, CEO of Prudential, was the best. Harold McGraw, Peter Waite (of Laubach Literacy), Jinx Crouch (Literacy Volunteers of America), Jim Duffy (ABC), etc., all good. Susan Porter Rose gets all the credit for putting together a great conference.

The dinner was put on by ABC, PBS, and Prudential. There were so many stars that evening: Peter Jennings was the host; Pearl Bailey and a group of beguiling children sang a song about teaching children to read; our close friend Loretta Lynn sang "Coal Miner's Daughter" and then shared with us the fact that she had had four children by the time she was seventeen and reading had not been easy for her. There was a sensational film about the seventeen "learners of the month," all of whom had worked hard to learn to read.

It also was the birth of the Barbara Bush Foundation for Family Literacy.

The next day Susan brought over a very high-powered group of people, all concerned with the problems of illiteracy and all willing to help form a foundation. It was decided that the focus should be the entire family, to try to break the intergenerational cycle of illiteracy. We wanted to make literacy a value in every single home in America. The foundation officially was announced in March 1989 and to date has awarded fifty-two grants totaling $2 million to literacy programs all over the country. I'm especially proud of the foundation's extraordinary volunteer board of directors, all of whom are busy professionals and leaders in their fields, and of Susan Porter Rose, who was so instrumental in putting the foundation together and has now joined the board (see Appendix B).

꩜ This was a very busy period for us, for making new plans and saying some good-byes, too. At the end of November, the Ladies of the Senate had an informal luncheon for me, ending a happy time in my life. I loved those women and had faithfully tried to attend their Tuesday morning meetings. They gave me a beautiful gold watch from Tiffany that I will wear to the day I die.

Our house was constantly buzzing with many friends and politicians calling on George. Tip O'Neill came by one morning, and George invited him to be our ambassador to Ireland. We all got a little teary when Tip told us that he had always wanted this post, but just could not say yes at this time. He was so sweet as he told George that he and his wife, Millie, were now of an age when their health was not so great and they wanted to spend time with their grandchildren. Eventually, George offered the Irish post to our great friend Dick Moore.

Tip also gave George some good advice. He reminded him that Jim Wright, the new Speaker of the House, had greatly admired former Speaker Sam Rayburn, who had been very nonpartisan, and that George should remember to remind Jim of that whenever the two had problems. I thought it was also interesting that Tip said the three brightest men he had worked with were Tom Foley, who became Speaker of the House when Jim Wright was forced to resign on ethics violation charges; John Brademas, a former Democratic congressman from Indiana who had been Majority Whip; and Wilbur Mills—all three men whom George respected. We both admired and loved Tip. He may have been on the opposite team politically, but he was a decent, fair man. We were thrilled when he agreed to serve on the Board of Trustees for the George Bush Presidential Library Center. The nation suffered a great loss when he died in January 1994.

We spent a quiet, restful Thanksgiving in Kennebunkport and saw Doro and her family. George had talked to Mike Dukakis and offered to drive down to Boston to call on him, but Mike was not ready for that yet. However, he did come to Washington in early December for a visit. He and George had a pleasant talk, and then George called me down to say hello. I told Mike that Millie was going to "write" a book to raise funds for charity and that she had a chapter on famous people she knew. Could we get their picture together? He said yes but didn't move, so I picked Millie up to bring her to him. I heard him mumble something like "I never liked dogs" just as the picture was taken. He must have realized how ungracious he sounded and went on to explain that as a child he had delivered newspapers and every dog in town attacks the paper boy. I could certainly understand that. Dan Quayle also met Governor Dukakis during that visit and was very gracious, considering the awful things that had been said about him during the campaign.

Campaigns *are* hurtful, and George already had started the healing process by having a small dinner at the house with Lloyd and B. A. Bentsen, Nick and Kitty Brady, Helen and Bob Strauss, Bob and Betsy Teeter from our campaign, Kansas Senator Nancy Kassebaum, and Alec Courtelis, one of our National Steering Committee members. It could not have been an entirely comfortable evening for the Bentsens, but Bob Strauss made everything easier. He is absolutely the most amazing politician. He is everybody's friend and, if he chooses, could sell you the paper off your own wall. This was the second time that Lloyd and George had faced off; we had been opponents in 1970 when Lloyd beat George for the U.S. Senate. Both he and B.A. are nice people, and my admiration and affection for her knows no bounds. She is a great lady.

On December 6 we had a "December 7th" party for the press, in honor of George's Pearl Harbor gaffe. We had become quite fond of our traveling press corps during the campaign. However, I believe that 1988 was the beginning of great discontent on both sides of the political spectrum with the press and their "pack mentality," and if there had been a three-way vote among Republicans, Democrats, and the press, the press would have been the big loser. The Capitol Steps sang and were very funny. This is a group of young men and women who work on Capitol Hill and get together to sing very clever songs that poke fun at one and all.

All this time George was working hard at putting together his cabinet and the rest of the administration. Although my job was less daunting, I also had a staff to hire. I felt very lucky, for I already had a nucleus, tried and true for eight years, headed by Susan in the office and Laurie Firestone in the house. Both women agreed to continue on, thank heavens: Susan as chief of staff and Laurie as social secretary. Julie Cooke had been my number two in the Vice President's Office; she took a leave of absence to be a full-time mom, and then came back for the campaign. She agreed to be my director of projects, which included overseeing my involvement in literacy and numerous other interests. Julie is a very conscientious, thoughtful person who has great judgment. We still call to ask her advice.

Shortly after the election Susan asked me about hiring a press secretary. I had not had one for the eight previous years, although Sondra Haley of my staff had stepped in and acted as press secretary during the campaign. I wasn't sure I needed one now. Obviously I had not yet realized how much had changed and that everything I said and even thought would be news.

For as long as George had been in politics, he had asked his chief of staff or office manager to hire minorities. Although neither of us believes in quotas, we believe strongly in equal opportunity. So I asked Susan, who was in charge of putting my team together, to look for someone who qualified. As Yogi Berra once said, we found ourselves "with insurmountable opportunities." There were many attractive, bright, experienced people to interview. Early in the search, Congressman John Miller from Washington called to say he had the perfect person, a woman named Anna Perez. "Hurrah," I said, "a Hispanic." He said he didn't think so; he was fairly certain she was African-American.

I told him it didn't matter; just have her call me. (As it turns out, her grandfather was Venezuelan.) Anna became not only my press secretary, but also my constant companion for four years. She is bright as a whip, tough, fair, fun to be with, and has great judgment. She now works at Creative Artists Agency in Los Angeles, and like all the others, we stay in touch.

Susan did a great job of putting the team together, and for four years they all worked long hours—whether they traveled or stayed home in the office—to keep up with a very busy agenda. George used to tease me that I was a chauvinist—no men in my office. Not true. We had one very good man, Jay Suchan, who had worked with Anna on the Hill and I suspect deserved credit for keeping Anna organized and on time (see Appendix A).

In the middle of the transition, Christmas plans and packing, the Gorbachevs came to New York for a summit meeting. Once again I was struck by how much things had changed. I wrote in my diary on December 7:

Flew to NYC on the biggest plane—discovered that it was Nancy Reagan's. She had gone to NYC the day before for a dinner party that was being given for her, and the plane was going back for her. It was such a treat as I normally went on commercial flights. I went with Sondra Haley (SPR thought that I needed a press person), so there were the two of us and four Secret Service men. Silly. They did have the best pictures of George and our family in the picture-holders. Before I got off, I suggested to the flight attendants that they change back to Reagan pictures. Somehow or other I did not think that Nancy would be amused by Bush pictures all over the plane. We got to NYC very early, and the traffic was not bad at all. People had been warned not to bring their cars into the city and evidently they believed the warning . . . I asked to go by Tiffany to have the band on my new watch adjusted, and Mike Young (head of my new Secret Service detail) said that was fine, and we buzzed right over to the store. There were rope lines everywhere and people were dying to see Raisa Gorbachev and the General Secretary. They had arrived the night before and he was to speak at the U.N., lunch with the President, Secretary General of the United Nations and George and then sight-see. The crowds were kind and seemed to recognize me. I went into Tiffany through the crowd and found the watch repair department, and never have I seen people so accommodating. I asked if I could leave my watch and they could mail it to me. They said, "But what will you wear today?" (Showing me that they all knew that I was having lunch with Raisa and Nancy.) I assured them that I could go "naked-armed" to the lunch, but they said that the watch would be finished in fifteen minutes if I had the time. So I walked downstairs to window-shop to find that we were surrounded by people watching us ogling the diamond and sapphire necklaces. It was a little scary when I realized that they might think I was really shopping! So up we went to the repair department and signed about fifty autographs. I am beginning to realize that George is going to be President of the United States and that my window-shopping days are over. On to the luncheon with my beautiful watch fitting just perfectly!!

. . . Marcela Pérez de Cuéllar, wife of the Secretary General, met me and took me upstairs. I was greeted by an old friend who said, "We did it, Barbara darling, we did it! We've worked so long for this." I did not remind her that she was for Ronald Reagan in 1980 and that I'd read in the paper that she had supported Dole, Kemp *and* Bush financially in 1988.

. . . Guests were Barbara Walters, Carol Sulzberger, Estee Lauder, Matilda Cuomo, Drew Heinz, "Suzy" (the columnist), and many others including those wonderful henna-haired East Europeans or Soviet Satellite ladies who stand around and look uncomfortable. Mrs. Gorbachev arrived early, so when Nancy arrived on time she seemed late and rude. This is a small game that Mrs. R and Mrs. G play. So far the score is Mrs. G—2; Mrs. R—0. (In Russia she had Nancy in the wrong part of the museum and then told the press that her guest was late!) They barely spoke before the sparks were flying between the two ladies. Nancy felt that Raisa was being critical of the openness between our two countries because she kept saying, "I thought we were open," and Nancy would say, "What do you think we are doing now?" (I asked Nancy on the plane about this and she told me that President Reagan's speech was all about our new open relationship.) Barbara Walters came over and repeated the conversation and asked me what it meant. I had no idea. These two ladies just have a competitive thing. Mrs. G is or has been rude, and Nancy just plain does not seem to like her.

We did lots of pictures . . . they do want me in the pictures. What a difference an election makes!

We went in to lunch, many round tables. Marcela sat between Nancy and Raisa, then me, Maria Pia Fantani from Italy, Matilda Cuomo, Obie Shultz, the wife of the President of the General Assembly, and back to Nancy.

There were three courses, the first being a crepe filled with a poached egg and mushrooms all tied up to look like a sachet. It looked pretty, and Marcela cut into hers and I cut into mine and, of course, the yellow yolk ran out. Mrs. G took one look and put her fork down and never even pretended to take a bite. The second course was red snapper and Mrs. G waved the waiter away and finally Nancy said, "Aren't you going to eat anything?" Raisa answered, "I would, but I don't know what it is." We told her, she took some and ate not a bite. She did eat some of the dessert, a raspberry dish. Nancy said to Mrs. G after she had had two bites of dessert, "You are like my husband. He loves desserts." At that Mrs. G put down her spoon and fork and that was that.

Matilda Cuomo (wife of the governor) saved the day. She had been to Russia and spoke of the day-care centers that she had visited and the different ladies she had spent time with. Raisa would give a rote answer: "Oh, yes, Madame So-and-So is one of our national treasures." Although Raisa does speak some English, all the conversation comes through an interpreter. [I remember feeling so sorry for Marcela Pérez de Cuéllar. She had planned such a nice luncheon and it resembled a sparring match.]

At 2:10 Mrs. G got up, announced she had an emergency and rushed off. That was the day of the tragic earthquake in Armenia where some 24,000 died (final death toll was estimated to be 55,000) and the G's cut their trip short to rush home.

The stories continued to come out of Armenia about the thousands of homeless people in the freezing cold. On December 23, Jeb and his son, George P., flew to New York City, helped load a plane with food, toys, and medicine, and then flew on Christmas Eve to Armenia on a cargo plane with AmeriCares. They toured the totally wiped-out city of Spitak and went to a hospital in Yerevan, where George P. gave out toys. I wrote in my diary:

We saw them on TV. At one time Jeb was trying to comfort a woman who had lost her husband and two of her children and was trying to save a remaining child that they saw in the hospital. We also saw Jeb and George in a church praying. When our precious Jeb stood up he wiped a tear from his eyes. [Several years later Mikhail Gorbachev told George that tear did more for Soviet-U.S. relations than we ever will know. It showed the Russian people we cared.]

Jeb called from NYC on the 26th and said that George P. was wonderful . . . I think it was just too much pain for a 12-year-old to see and feel. The stories were horrifying. One mother or grandmother fed her child by pricking her finger and the child sucked it for eight days. They saw the child.

In retrospect, I think it was probably very good for George P. We all take family, medicine, food, and water for granted. I was very proud of our Florida family—not only those who went, but Colu and the other children, who willingly had a lonely Christmas at home without their dad and brother.

George went on his annual post-Christmas hunting trip. He used to tease me about packing my bag early. This year he was so excited he was packed a week ahead of time.

We spent New Year's Eve at Camp David thanks to President Reagan's generosity. George finished Edmund Morris's book about Theodore Roosevelt; I read Ishbel Ross's *Grace Coolidge and Her Era,* and eventually read Morris's wife Sylvia's book about Edith Roosevelt. George met with quite a few people, and we both talked to our good friends Penne Korth and Bobby Holt, who had taken on the enormous task of putting on the Inauguration. We were trying hard to keep it as open as possible and stay within budget. Not only did we not go into debt, but the Inaugural committee had some donated money left over. Bobby was kind enough to ask me for some charitable suggestions, and one of the things we did was donate $5,000 to two libraries in each state, chosen by the American Library Association. The letters we got back were very moving. Most of these libraries were in small communities with very tight budgets and the donations made a real difference. In one New Mexico town, the amount of the donation was higher than their entire annual budget!

After Bobby and Penne left, I wrote in my diary:

(They) have organized an extraordinary five days, starting with a big Mall opening for thousands on Wednesday and ending with an ecumenical church service on Sunday at the National Cathedral. We hope that churches across the country will ring their bells at twelve noon after a service of prayer for our nation. This is symbolic of our belief that we are truly one nation under God. We must get back to faith, family and values. Our children need food, shelter *AND* love, faith, stability, family—they surely need someone who cares—they need God.

I also want to give credit to Senator Wendell Ford of Kentucky, head of the Inauguration at the Capitol. He and his staff not only did a wonderful job, but were very easy to work with.

At one time during the campaign I had given George a list of things I really wanted to do someday when he got out of politics— things like take a barge trip with all the family through the French wine country, go on a cruise, and so on. Since we had won, the only one we could tackle now was to have puppies, so shortly after the holidays we sent Millie off to Will and Sarah Farish's Kentucky farm, where she married "Tug."

With everything else going on George managed to plan a surprise for me on our forty-fourth anniversary, a small dinner at a restaurant in Washington. I met him there to find Andy Stewart, Dick Moore, and Johnny Bush. The weather was so bad that other guests were stuck in airports and couldn't make it, but we had a great evening, ending with a play at the Kennedy Center.

On January 11 I did see the upstairs at the White House. Of course I had seen it many times before, but this was a complete tour of all the rooms, giving me an opportunity to decide where to put some of our personal furniture. Unlike past (and future) years, the visit was not covered by the press—Nancy met me upstairs instead of outside. That may have been why the media assumed Nancy had not shown me around. Actually, she showed me everything, including the laundry rooms and upstairs kitchen after I asked. I needed to see them so I could tell Paula about her living and work space. I was lucky that Nancy had redecorated the White House so beautifully. We needed to do very little. We turned one room into our family room, bringing our own furniture from the Vice President's House and the curtains that matched, although we had to add some material so they could fit the huge windows. I was amused four years later when I was informed that I could not take those beautiful drapes with us because "they belonged to the White House." Well, half was theirs and half was mine and I couldn't help but wonder who would want chintz curtains that matched my chairs and couches?

On January 18, we moved out of our home for the last eight years and into Blair House. Saying good-bye to the stewards—Rommy Cruz, Rudy Arca, Angel Paroan, Herman Capatti, and Danny Ibanez—was hard, and I drove off in tears. I also was sad to say good-bye to Mike Xander, Beth Becker, and Barbara Marshall, who had taken such good care of the Vice President's grounds. As we drove up to Blair House, there were Betsy Heminway, Sandy Doubleday, and Doro and Neil cheering from the Inaugural Parade viewing stands. They must have sensed that leaving would be hard for me.

The Inaugural festivities opened with a ceremony at the Lincoln Memorial, just as they had in 1980. It was a wonderful night. Grandchildren Sam, Ellie, and Lauren danced away to the Gatlins, Sandi Patti, the Beach Boys, Up With People, and others, ending with Lee Greenwood singing "I'm Proud to Be an American," fireworks, and thousands of people lighting small flashlights representing a Thousand Points of Light. Our little children went to bed and our big children went off to one of three dinners. George and I went to all three briefly.

The next day was the Tribute to the First Lady at the Kennedy Center. Since the tickets to this event are fairly inexpensive, it is always well attended and they have to use three theaters. Mr. Scaasi insisted that I have a new suit for this, and I loved it. It had a pretty flowered blouse, and the jacket was lined in the same silk. Now that is the height of luxury because you can only wear one blouse with a suit like that—the matching one. Marilyn Quayle introduced me in each theater, which was nice. There were many, many entertainers. At one point we got slightly behind schedule. Our Noelle, age twelve, and her first cousin, Alexandra Schmitz, sang with a mariachi band in one of the theaters. Everyone was told the exact number of minutes they could perform, but the bandleader got carried away and each time they ended, they'd start the whole thing over again. Noelle and Alexandra would start in singing, dancing, playing the violin and guitar one more time. Nobody dared "put the hook" on the grandchildren of the President-elect. The girls looked adorable, dressed in high red boots,

Mexican costumes, and enormous hats. I must add that I was mightily surprised that Noelle could do all that.

On Thursday night we went to a dinner that Kitty and Nick Brady had for our family and very close friends. We never would have seen anyone if they hadn't done that. Then we all raced off to the gala. Our four oldest grandchildren were allowed to go, and that made it even more special for us.

Finally it was Friday, January 20. It was a lovely, sunny day. We got up early, and I tried on my hat. It was dowdy-looking, and I decided it was my big day—no hat! We began at St. John's with a family church service with Tom Bagby from our church in Houston; John Harper, rector of St. John's; and the Quayles' minister taking part. We were surrounded by family and a few friends.

Then it was time to go to the White House. The atmosphere was much more relaxed than it had been eight years earlier. It was, after all, a "friendly takeover." I suspect it also was easier for the Reagans in 1989 than it would be for us in 1993. They were leaving the White House under very different circumstances. George and the President rode together, and I rode with Nancy. The streets were lined with people waving, smiling, and cheering.

It was so exciting with George's mother and so many of our relatives there, including five of the older grandchildren. To this day, my impressions are very vivid: lots of friends, beautiful singing, miles of people. It was thrilling.

Billy Graham gave the invocation and the benediction. I got many phone calls about this, people telling me that Inaugural ceremonies always included a man representing each faith. I explained that this was not true. We had researched this; plus, we considered Billy to be representative of all religions, a man of God. It wasn't just friends and strangers who got into the prayer act. One of our very distant relatives who had just been ordained let it be known to my office that she would come only if she could give a prayer. We turned her down and guess what? She came anyway.

Alvie Powell, a soldier in the U.S. Army who had performed for us before, sang "The Star-Spangled Banner."

Then it was time. Justice Sandra Day O'Connor swore Dan in, and Chief Justice William Rehnquist swore George in. (Although we considered Bill and Nan close friends, we badly missed Potter Stewart.) I held two Bibles: the one George Washington had held two hundred years ago when he was sworn in, and the one the House and Senate prayer group had given George, opened at the Beatitudes. I have used a different Bible at each of George's swearing-ins—one for the United Nations, one for the CIA, two for vice president, and one for president—so each of the children may have one.

As the oath was given, I felt as if we were standing still in time. In one awesome moment George Bush became President of the United States of America.

As I sat listening to his speech—which I had not read ahead of time—I remember thinking it covered many of the same concerns I had, things like education, the welfare of our children, and other issues. I was never so proud of him or what he stood for.

Then suddenly it was over and we were leading the Reagans to their helicopter. It was sad telling them good-bye, although he should have felt great, leaving with a very high approval rating and the affection of the nation.

After a marvelous—but too long—lunch, the parade began. George and I got out and walked at different intervals during the trip down Pennsylvania Avenue to the reviewing platform outside the White House. It is amazing how many of your friends you see along the route. I spotted Willard Scott and ran over and gave him a kiss. Unbeknownst to me, he was live on the air at that very moment. I think I left him speechless! How he has teased me about that ever since. The parade went on and on—a record three hours, forty minutes—but George and I stayed until the end. Our children and grandchildren ran in and out of the White House, and by the time we got there, they had reported on every room. George's mom was comfortably settled in bed in the Queen's Bedroom and had already had a visitor, Billy Graham.

We all dressed in our best new ball gowns and black ties, and one by one went by to see Mom and be inspected in our finery. I had a beautiful Scaasi blue velvet dress with a satin skirt, a stole, and a glorious Judith Leiber blue satin bag made of the dress material with a rhinestone clasp and shoes dyed to match. Knowing that I would wear the shoes only once, I bought a pair for twenty-nine dollars. They were absolutely the most uncomfortable shoes I ever owned, in addition to which, the blue dye came off on my feet and was almost impossible to get off. The dress, the stole, the bag, the shoes (good riddance to bad rubbish), and the pearls later went to the Smithsonian. That night, after fourteen balls, every inch of my body ached, as did George's.

This is what I wrote about the next day in my diary:

Saturday the 21st we opened the house to the public at 8 a.m. People waited all night long. Amazing. Some people said: "I saw you come in last night!" After a half an hour, George went to work and I went upstairs to start finding things. (Our bags had been unpacked but who knew where things were?) Imagine this house had all 10 of our children, all 10 of our grandchildren, Mom, a doctor, a nurse, Paula and two nannies. All during the day we saw tourists streaming through the White House and out the front door. Once Jenna and I went to check on Mom and found her sitting up in a chair at her window waving at the tourists who were looking up and waving. When they saw Jenna and me they yelled "Come on out." We waved and said we couldn't and tried to look sad so they'd know just how badly we felt. (When we tried going downstairs, the tourist line came to a standstill. It just didn't work.) There were about 85 people out by the North Portico and spontaneously they started to sing "God Bless America." We couldn't help but weep. So tender. [By now you've discovered we weep more for joy than sorrow.]

Later in the day we went to check on Mom again and she was outside shaking hands with the tourists in her wheelchair. She was such a sweet lady. Several of the children spent a lot of time shaking hands also.

At noon that day we had all our relatives and our children's in-laws for lunch. As the group was growing by leaps and bounds I made a rule that no girlfriends or boyfriends, just fiancées. George said that I was going to cause many engagements. The office had called one day in a panic and said that one of our relatives had called and said that she wanted to bring her fiancé and *her* name was so-and-so. The office asked what they should do. I said: "Say yes." Then there were those who asked us if they could break the rule and bring their best friend. The answer was: "Sorry, no." There are more last minute things to solve at a time like this. After all was said and done, about 250 family came to lunch.

That afternoon the children, girls and I went to Constitution Hall to see a play, "George to George." It was fine, a little too old for the really young ones, but they behaved.

Back to the White House and dressed for yet again another Ball, in fact two. The Texas State Society Ball was jammed and filled with friends.

The Young People's Ball—Marvin and Lee Atwater in charge—was loud R and B. Lots of fun. Dreadful music. It was like being at an aerobics class.

We ended Inaugural Weekend by attending a service at the Washington National Cathedral on Sunday. It was truly beautiful. That cathedral has special meaning for us: Neil, Marvin, and Doro went to the cathedral schools; the boys were confirmed there; George's mother had made one of the needlepoint pillows; we had said the final good-bye to many of our friends there; it was one of my favorite places to bring visitors; Bishop John Walker was a friend. So we felt very much at home.

Memories of the weekend are many. I think we sat down to eat together only once, and as I looked around at the table, Barbara and Jenna were not anywhere to be seen. I mentioned it to their mother, and one of the butlers spoke up and said that they had just telephoned the kitchen and ordered sandwiches to be delivered to the bowling alley. The bowling alley! We put an end to that before it started, and they ate with us.

One of the sweetest sights of the week was Marvin and Margaret's little Marshall asleep on the Lincoln bed. She looked big as a minute. Neil and Sharon's son, Pierce, learned that if he rolled over on his back at the top of the ramp by the solarium, he could slide to the bottom. He would pop his hands over his head with his stuffed monkey and buffer his stop.

Then one by one our children left, leaving George and me alone in that wonderful house with literally the weight of the world on his shoulders.

17

The First 100 Days

That first Monday George went off to work at seven A.M., and I set about getting settled in. I especially wanted to unpack some of our personal pictures to set around on the tables so this great big house would feel more like home. One thing I did not have to worry about were paintings for the walls. The White House has the most glorious collection of art, and I pretty much got to choose just who I would like to spend the next four years with: Glackens, Twachtman, Winslow Homer, Cassatt, Monet, Cézanne, Potthast, Lilla Cabot Perry, Remington, Russell, Thomas Sully, Metcalf, George Healy. We also brought with us from the Vice President's House a borrowed painting from the Houston Museum of Fine Arts, *Passing By,* by E. Martin Hennings, a Taos painter. I even found a Grandma Moses to go in the room I set aside for visiting grandchildren, not that those little monkeys ever would notice.

Every day I was struck by how much things had changed in our lives. I expressed a desire to use a smaller car rather than a big black limousine, and on out-of-town trips, to travel by train or commercial airline. Susan Porter Rose and Mike Young, head of my Secret Service detail, agreed to the smaller car, but they said I really could not travel commercially since the number of threats against the First Lady is higher than that for the vice president. That's just the nature of the "job." But what really persuaded me was learning that if I flew commercially, the flights sometimes would be delayed while the agents thoroughly checked out the plane, luggage, and so on. I reluctantly also gave up on the train. To inconvenience so many others was not reasonable. We nicknamed the plane I flew on "Bright Star," for the leukemia foundation George and Hugh Liedtke founded after Robin died.

Another big change occurred when Millie came home to her new life. We were so glad to see her, but there was a big difference between opening the door at the Vice President's House (where there wasn't a soul around) in your bathrobe and letting the dog out at six A.M. and throwing on your warm-up suit at the White House (where the morning crew already was hard at work), waiting for the elevator to take you down two floors, racing down a long corridor through the Diplomatic Reception Room and out to the South Grounds. Gradually the butlers took over that job. I really enjoyed those morning walks, but it also was nice for George and me to be able to enjoy coffee in bed and share the newspapers. We read all or parts of five papers every morning, discussing the news as we went. This is still my favorite time of day.

On February 1 we had our first big formal White House party, a white-tie reception for the Diplomatic Corps. This had been a tradition of many years which the Carters stopped, the Reagans reinstated, and we continued. For many ambassadors and their wives, it provided their only opportunity to see and speak to the president. It was always a colorful event for they came dressed to the teeth, often in native costumes. As for me, I decided to wear my Inaugural gown one more time before sending it to the Smithsonian.

I wrote in my diary about the evening:

Just before we were to go downstairs, George suggested that we invite Willie and Ulla Wachtmeister, dean of the Diplomatic Corps and our very close friends, to come up and march down the Grand Staircase with us. They were followed by our Chief of Protocol, Joseph Reed, and his wife, Mimi. Millie bounded up to her friends, the Count and Countess. Ulla was in a glamorous black velvet gown, soft and feminine, with a lovely diamond tiara. She looked like the fairy godmother in Cinderella, if not Cinderella herself. As they leaned down to pat their old friend, Millie turned her back, walked a few feet and quietly threw up. George led the horrified guests into the living room saying, "She has never done that before. It must be *evening* sickness!" Joseph Reed kept saying, with hands fluttering, "Perfectly natural, perfectly natural," in his very eastern accented voice. What an introduction to the Diplomatic Corps for Millie.

I might add that it was certainly an interesting start for wonderful Joseph, who turned out to be a fine protocol chief.

Almost every day we experienced a "first." On February 9, George gave his first State of the Union Address, and although I had been to many, many before, this was very different. I wrote in my diary:

It is so funny not being the wife of the Vice President. I used to sit in a single seat on the side, sort of like a step-sister. I invited Marilyn Quayle to sit with us, no closer, but just not isolated. I had Marvin, me, Doro, Marilyn, Ann Simpson and Corinne Michel. When I walked in, I got a nice ovation. It is customary, but it still pleased me. I felt that they had great affection for George who, after all, had worked with many of them. He walked in to much applause. I thought he gave a wonderful speech. He was interrupted some fifty times. He showed warmth, caring, wisdom and humor. So much to do!

The day after the speech we went to Canada for a meeting with Prime Minister Mulroney, stopping on the way home for a weekend in Kennebunkport. There we discovered yet another change that is true to this day. When we walked from Walker's Point to downtown one morning, the crowds around George were enormous. A large press corps kept asking questions, and the people in cars almost drove off the road because of rubbernecking. After I left one of the stores, the press went in to ask what I bought and how much I'd spent.

It wasn't much better back in Washington. I wanted to show our friends Don and Adele Hall from Kansas City the newly renovated Blair House, which is right across Pennsylvania Avenue from the White House. As we started to cross the street we found ourselves surrounded by the press asking questions, which gathered a crowd. At first George and I tried walking to Blair House or to church, but it was just so disruptive, bringing traffic to a standstill. We decided it would be more thoughtful to ride, thus giving up one of our great pleasures— another fact of life that took a while to accept.

* * *

〜 It wasn't long before George was earning his nickname, "Perle Mesta" (she was a famous Washington hostess during President Truman's time), which had been given to him during his UN days. I had known for years about George's flair for entertaining—after all, he had brought ten Yale classmates home for our first Thanksgiving dinner—but the White House staff was in for a shock. I wrote in my diary on February 16:

Yesterday was a great funny day. George awakened full of it—whatever that means—and decided to have a dinner party that night. He decided on fourteen. Laurie (Firestone) told me that the chef said, "I am used to having two weeks notice." How funny. We were lucky that he had given us twelve hours notice.

The next day I flew to Denver to visit the Food Bank of the Rockies, which worked with Second Harvest. This is a marvelous national program that feeds many hungry people with food that ten years ago would have been dumped—cans that were dented but perfectly good, two-day-old bread, and so on. Then I went to visit grandchild number eleven, who had been born February 7: Neil and Sharon's Ashley Walker Bush. She is a beauty. I had a quick visit with her older sister and brother, Lauren and Pierce, and was then going to go by Lauren's classroom. The Secret Service suggested that I not go as that would highlight where she attended school, creating a security risk for Lauren. It was another tough change we'd have to get used to—and our children and grandchildren, too.

I got home that afternoon to discover that George must have felt "full of it" again: He had forty coming for an informal, light buffet supper upstairs and a movie downstairs in the White House theater.

〜 A week later we left for our first major trip abroad. First stop: Japan, to attend the funeral of Emperor Hirohito, followed by quick visits to China and Korea. I wrote in my diary:

I am so confused about the time we spent in the air. I know we left from the White House at 5:45 a.m. (Wednesday) and arrived in Tokyo at 1:10 p.m. They say it is Thursday here. Who knows?

. . . We drove straight to our residence, absolutely *NO* cars on the road. (Roads cleared for foreign arrivals.) George went right to bi-laterals with other foreign heads of state, starting with lunch with President Mitterrand. During the talks George invited him to visit us in Maine in June when Boston University, celebrating its 150th birthday, was giving both Presidents (and me) honorary degrees. [Later that year, BU also gave Helmut Kohl of Germany an honorary degree. I was in mighty fine company—which is the world's greatest understatement.]

. . . We were waiting to hear about John Tower's confirmation hearings from Washington. The FBI says he is clean and yet allegations continue to come. I guess we'll know tomorrow. George told me that John asked to see him alone on Tuesday and said he was grateful to George for standing by him. George said that he had tears in his eyes as he told GB that "he would be the best Secretary of Defense that this nation ever had."

February 24—Today is the funeral for Hirohito, now known as Showa. (As in China, the emperor's name changes after death.) So the last 60 years are now known as the "Showa Era."

. . . It is raining.

. . . Dressed in black shoes, stockings, dress, coat, hat, veil, gloves and even black earrings and pearls. Pretty grim and ugly. George and Jim Baker in their rented morning suits. (National Security Adviser Brent Scowcroft and John Sununu did not don theirs.) Off we went in a big black limousine with American flags flying in cold, drizzly weather. We arrived in about ten minutes and were led immediately to a front row seat. I sat next to President Kaunda of Zambia, a darling man whom we had visited in 1981 or so and who had returned for dinner with us at the V.P. House. At our dinner he and his lovely wife sang a love song duet that I will never forget. He also played the guitar. I remember that he was a Christian and that they had a picture of the Last Supper over their dining room door at his palace. George sat next to the President of the Federal Republic of Germany, and next to him was François Mitterrand. Down the row from us sat many "royals," the King and Queen of Belgium, the King and Queen of Sweden, the King and Queen of Spain (we had a private dinner with them at the Okura Hotel, seated on the floor; I am not sure His Majesty enjoyed either the food or the seating arrangement, but we laughed a lot—they are delightful people), the King and Queen of Togo and many others. I did not see any of the top Russians or, for that matter, the Chinese. [All in all, fifty-five heads of state, eleven premiers, and fourteen members of royalty attended the funeral. For some, including George, attending the funeral was somewhat controversial because of Hirohito's role in World War II. However, George and the other heads of state felt strongly it was part of the healing process. And certainly most Americans trusted their president's judgment on this: After all, he had been shot down during the war by the Japanese!]

. . . In front of us was a black cloth curtain. We were seated in a big black and white tent and were given small lap robes and there were small heaters. In spite of all that we were cold. I enjoyed seeing all the ladies in their fur coats and hats (can't touch fur if you are an American politician's wife.)

. . . After several announcements and quite a little time, the curtains opened in the middle and the procession came marching in, monks carrying the bier, and then the delicate little royal family walking slowly, the ladies in black coats and gowns to the floor and veils that came way past their shoulders. The new Empress walks like a ballet dancer, and she reminded us of a beautiful black swan with her graceful posture and lovely long neck. The men in morning suits and top hats in their hands. The Imperial family paid homage to the fallen Emperor, bowing quite a few times. The new Emperor spoke as did the Prime Minister, the heads of the Diet and the Chief Justice (a cold damp wind blowing all the time).

. . . There was much carrying of (the Emperor's) personal effects, including his microscope. They were carried in and out of a tented, draped pavilion. Reminded me of the Egyptian or Chinese Tombs where treasures were buried along with the body. Some very weird chanting, and the curtains closed and opened. This all had to do with the separation of church and state, I believe. It ended with the foreign dignitaries going up to the bier, bowing to the Showa, turning and walking towards the royal family, stopping, bowing again and walking out. The whole ceremony took about two and a half hours and was really freezing. Having said that, I wouldn't have missed that for anything.

. . . A word of praise for the Japanese protocol. Everything went like clockwork. There was no waiting. That is amazing when you think they had to orchestrate 120 motorcade arrivals and departures.

. . . George had bi-laterals all during this visit, including one with Cory Aquino that was set up at the last moment. She at first said that she had no time for a meeting. I couldn't believe it. No time to meet with the

President of the United States, but she had a change of heart. I sat quietly in on the short meeting with GB, Jim Baker, Brent Scowcroft and John Sununu. Cory had four people. One of the things she mentioned was needing the name of someone to talk to to facilitate the AID (Agency for International Development) money they needed. What nerve! Too busy to meet, but not too busy to ask for money! She is an attractive-looking woman. (George said in the car that we had to understand that she had enormous pressures from the left. There were also rumors that she held the Reagan/Bush administration responsible for her husband's death and this attitude was a holdover from that.)

Next stop was China, where I couldn't believe the changes:

We drove past thousands of people and many, and I underline many, new buildings. Many brighter winter clothes including several children in bright fur coats! Still thousands of people on bicycles, still people pulling loads on bikes, but so many more cars, buses and trucks. People say that the traffic jams are enormous! (The roads were all cleared for us.) When we got to Tiananmen Square there were hundreds and hundreds of people. We stopped and had pictures taken. We waved to the people and they all waved back. They used to just stare. Chairman Mao's picture still over the big outer gate, but Lenin, Engels, Stalin and Marx gone. The trees have grown around the Great Hall of the People. The Chinese and American flags on telephone poles or light poles everywhere. And the wonderful red and white banners hung across the road for visiting heads of state. I certainly never thought when we lived in the PRC that we would see this welcome for George. It was great to be back.

. . . President Yang Shangkun hosted a banquet. He did the nicest thing and gathered many of our old Chinese friends at a reception before the dinner.

. . . We went to our old church to discover that they had moved into a much bigger church and the crowds were overflowing. We did see the three ministers who had led our services 19 years before. They gave us such a warm welcome back to our Peking church family. It was very moving.

. . . Deng Xiaoping hosted a warm, intimate luncheon. This fascinating 85-year-old man was just as sharp as he could be and looked very well. He only smoked one cigarette during lunch. That was amazing as in the old days he chain-smoked.

. . . We gave our return dinner at the Great Wall Hotel. George thought that it would be fun to have a Texas barbecue for the Chinese. It was not one of our better ideas for the Chinese didn't seem to understand ribs and beans, and the beef and chicken in the PRC is not the same as ours. But the idea was fun and the room looked pretty with red-checkered tablecloths and flowers.

Usually when our president goes to a foreign country, he will meet privately with the dissidents or opposition. Both George and I believe strongly in human rights. But our ambassador, Winston Lord, invited dissident Fang Lizhi to our banquet, which made it almost impossible for the top Chinese leadership to come. This caused a big flap even before we arrived. For a smart man (Lord), this was an amazing act, and hours were spent trying to find a solution to this gaffe. The night of our banquet we still did not know if the leadership would attend or not. After quite a wait, they did arrive. During the dinner, George, thinking that dissident Fang was in the banquet hall and fearing that there would be a scene, mentioned that he hoped this had not caused too much of a problem. The answer he got was very noncommittal. It wasn't until the next day that we discovered that Mr. Fang had been prevented from attending the dinner. He had been stopped twice by the police and buses were kept from picking him up.

. . . The other unpleasant thing that happened was that the Chinese security got way too rough with the press on a visit back to my beloved Forbidden City. I should have stopped the tour and told our hosts that unless they lightened up, the tour was over. It wasn't until Carol Powers, the superb White House photographer who had been assigned to me and a true friend, got socked so hard that her jaw was dislocated, that I did stop and lay down a few ground rules. To her extraordinary credit, she did not make a scene, and it wasn't until we got back to the guest house that she went for help. [To save money I had not let the office send a press advance person on this trip and so I must take the blame. I tried so hard to save money and was rarely, if ever, successful.]

In Korea we were entertained by President and Mrs. Roh, and George addressed the National Assembly. The two things that pop into my mind about that trip are the beautiful ladies in their glorious pastel-colored dresses, which one of the men in our party said made them all look pregnant (I thought they were lovely), and the tight,

tight security in the country due to a strong anti-American sentiment at that time. We went everywhere by helicopter instead of motorcade.

On the plane coming home I wrote in my diary:

> The whole trip has been overshadowed by the Tower vote. The committee finally voted on a partisan basis: 9 for; 11 against. George is on the phone talking to Joe Biden, Chris Dodd, Lloyd Bentsen and others, asking them to please not make up their minds until he gets back and talks with them. We have just seen Bob Dole on CNN and he says he cannot understand Sam Nunn. No proof that the innuendoes are true. This is truly a character assassination.

The accusations against John ranged from alcoholism to questionable dealings with defense contractors—none of which could be proved and none which George felt were true. The Senate eventually voted in March, 47 for and 53 against. We were heartbroken for John and thought it was unfair.

By the way, the Tower hearings marked the end of any "honeymoon" period between George and the Democratically controlled Congress, and the press heralded it as a major political setback for the new president. That certainly sounded familiar as Bill Clinton struggled with many of his appointments.

⤳ All during this time I was trying to determine exactly what my agenda would be. I had told Susan Porter Rose and others in the office that each day we should do something to help others. I didn't want to waste the great opportunity before us. Julie Cooke, in charge of projects, took this to heart. I trusted her judgment on everything, and she scheduled many events that either highlighted a need, helped encourage volunteerism, or focused on literacy.

We didn't waste any time. On January 31, I visited Martha's Table in Washington, where they have enormous soup kitchens, staffed in most cases by volunteers, and also a highly professional team of child-care staff to tutor and love homeless children after school. I had visited this remarkable place before, and would return several times in the next few years. Three days later we visited the United Community Ministries in suburban Virginia, which also feeds and clothes the homeless. During the next four years, I sent them many boxes of clothes—always anonymously. I wasn't sure how they would feel knowing they had the President of the United States's clothes!

We did literacy programs in Philadelphia, Chicago, and the Bronx. There we visited a multigenerational program that was in the heart of a tough poverty area. The Secret Service were concerned because several of the students had criminal records. I said not to worry; that was the whole point of the visit, to encourage them to get their lives back on track. When we arrived at the top of ninety stairs to visit one of the classrooms, there was the lovely Brooke Astor. She was bordering on her nineties herself and was concerned about *my* having to walk up so many stairs. She is a great supporter of libraries and literacy, and I am her greatest admirer.

We helped celebrate Black History Month in Anacostia, a poor area in Washington. We hosted Reading Is Fundamental on the South Lawn for their annual celebration of books, and I attended and spoke to both the United Way and American Newspaper Association conventions about literacy.

We went to the hundredth anniversary of the National Zoo, and Doro and I welcomed to Andrews Air Force Base the Armenian children, victims of the earthquake, who were brought here by PROJECT HOPE to receive medical care.

But of everything I did, my March visit to Grandma's House in Washington certainly received the most attention. This is a wonderful place where babies with AIDS are housed, treated, and loved by a fine professional staff and caring volunteers. There I held a precious baby who later died. Unbelievably, this photo made news because, even then, people still thought that touching a person with the virus was dangerous. Along with Burt Lee, George's doctor, I also met with a group of adults with AIDS. It was a wrenching visit. Besides having trouble finding housing and medical care, they all had personal problems. I especially remember a young man who told us that he had been asked to leave his church studies when it was discovered he had AIDS. His parents also had disowned him, and he said he longed to be hugged again by his mother. A poor substitute, I hugged that darling young man and did it again in front of the cameras. But what he really needed was family.

* * *

I always felt George took a bad rap on the AIDS issue. He closely followed the progress being made at the National Institutes of Health through Dr. Tony Fauci. During the Bush administration, funding for AIDS doubled to nearly $5 billion. Of course, it was not enough. But there also is not enough money for cancer, heart, stroke, or many other kinds of research either.

I took some pleasure from the fact that the AIDS virus was isolated through leukemia research. Money spent for cancer research affects AIDS and other autoimmune diseases, and when we find the cure for one problem, we find the cure for others.

Every year we put candles in the White House windows to commemorate AIDS victims, and George and I both visited various hospitals and clinics involved in the fight against AIDS—but it never was enough. Members of Act-Up, a radical gay group, hounded George during his presidency, after drowning out the more reasonable voices speaking out about AIDS.

This is a sickness that can be helped by education. We have got to teach the young that there is no such thing as safe sex, although maybe there is safer sex. I also think there's nothing wrong with reminding our youth of the moral aspects of promiscuous sex and drug use. Certainly we must teach them they are not invincible.

The best way to explain how I felt about my "job" as First Lady" is to share with you a letter I wrote during my first year in the White House but never sent. Donnie Radcliffe of *The Washington Post* had written an unauthorized biography about me which was very kind. But Liz Carpenter, who had been Lady Bird Johnson's press secretary, wrote a scathing review—not really of the book, but of me. She felt I was letting women down by not speaking up on issues, even if it meant disagreeing publicly with my husband. I said I didn't care what she said, but obviously that was not true, for I woke up one morning and wrote a letter to Liz, whom I knew and liked:

Dear Liz,

I read with interest your review of *Simply Barbara*. I know how you feel about me. How did you like the book? Well, I know how I liked the book and I also know that I

like you, and I thought that just for fun, and because I am
learning how to use a computer, I'd write you a *personal*
letter explaining just how I see life these days.

Long ago I decided in life that I had to have priorities. I put my children and my husband at the top of my
list. That's a choice that I never regretted. If I had any
regrets, and who doesn't, I wish I'd taken more time to
listen a little longer, look a little deeper and spend even
more time with our children. Having said that, they all
grew up and "my turn" came and I did the same thing.
Unconsciously at first, and then with great purpose these
last few years, I set priorities—my priorities.

After spending several months pondering over
exactly what cause I would take on if George got elected
to "high" office, I realized that a more literate America
would benefit every single thing I worry about: crime,
unemployment, pollution, teen-age pregnancy, school
dropouts, women who are trapped into welfare and therefore poverty, etc. You name it, I worried about it. Incidentally, we hadn't heard about AIDS, the homeless or
hunger at that time as major crises. So I made my major a
"More Literate America," with several minors all related
to better education. I have not regretted it for a minute.
Abortion, pro or con, is not a priority for me. ERA is not
a priority for me, nor is gun control. I leave that for those
courageous enough to run for public office. Educating a
young girl early that she has a choice to wait before she
has a relationship with a boy is a priority for me. Teaching
that all people are equal is a priority for me. Feeding the
hungry and housing the poor is a priority for me. Keeping
kids in school is a priority for me, and I could go on and
on. I do not want to defuse or confuse my top priorities.

Incidentally, I may have learned this from one of my
heroines who said not so long ago:

"It would be sad to pass up such a bully pulpit. It's
a fleeting chance to do something for your country that
makes your heart sing . . . and if your project is useful,
and people notice it, and that reflects well on your hus-

band . . . heavens, that's one of your biggest roles in life."
(Lady Bird Johnson from an article in *USA Today* on First
Ladies.)

Even though I never mailed the letter, I sure felt better after I
wrote it, so I really owed Liz Carpenter a thank-you.

☞ I tried hard to stay out of George's business for all of the
above reasons. Needless to say, I did not succeed. George barely had
gotten into office when I agreed to do some press interviews, and Terry
Hunt of the Associated Press got me again. (He's one of the reporters who got me into trouble over the Geraldine Ferraro incident.) He
asked me if I favored enactment of laws banning the sale of military
assault guns to the public. I, of course, answered "Yes," never dream-
ing it would make big news. But the press interpreted this to mean I
disagreed with my husband! It seemed so clear to me that there was
absolutely no need for anyone to have an assault weapon, and frankly,
I assumed it already was against the law. Apparently it was not. My
wonderful brother Jim and my husband were both against gun control.
Among their reasons: There already are many laws on the books that
only law-abiding people keep, and gun control would be one of them.
We had an honest disagreement about gun control and probably still
do. However, in March, George did expand the ban against importing
assault weapons, including the AK-47, which had been used in California to kill five schoolchildren.

About that same time I also hosted a luncheon at the residence for
several members of the White House press corps who had been asking
for interviews. This was the first of several I would hold over the next
few years, and I enjoyed them very much. For the most part, I liked
the reporters and found the lunches stimulating and fun. But I never
got off scot-free. I always made news even though I swore I wouldn't. I
must say, however, I found it was interesting that the fact George and
I agreed on 99 percent of the issues never made the news!

☞ All during this time George and I were discovering the
wonderful pleasures of living at the White House. Even the simplest

daily routines could suddenly become almost magical. On January 30 I wrote in my diary about, of all things, lunch:

I ate in the West Hall Sitting Room at a little game table. I ate off President Cleveland's white china with touches of navy blue and gilt, made in England, I believe. It was lovely. Duck soup, smoked trout, delicate salad and peaches and passion fruit! Glorious. The food is so special that you cannot believe it.

The butlers loved trying to make me guess whose china I was using. Imagine being served a meal on dishes that Abraham Lincoln ate from! For a while my favorite was the china of Rutherford B. Hayes. It was so ugly. Each serving looked like the food that was to go on it: a plate shaped like a fish for the fish course; oysters for oysters; and snow-shoe-shaped dessert plates.

The White House staff constantly amazed me. By this time I had lived or visited many places but never had seen a household where every living human's only concern was to make us, our children, and our guests happy. Actually, that's not entirely true. Their first concern was taking care of the People's House—your house—and they do it with great pride. I also was impressed with the fact that they do not gossip about previous tenants.

I decided to make the tiny sitting room next to our bedroom into my office. It is a lovely sunny room on the southwest side of the house with the magnolias that Andrew Jackson planted right outside the window. However, in the spring, I moved to the north side of the house into the beauty parlor. The southwest corner was really too hot in the summer sun, and I needed a room that I really could use as an office. The other room was just too pretty. But this one, with its wonderful northern light, was perfect. Pat Nixon had made it into the White House beauty parlor, and I know that it always irritated Nancy Reagan that she "got credit" for putting it in. I don't care who did it— it was a needed addition to the White House and all First Ladies used it. The carpenters made a nice little desk for me and I could spread out my papers, computer, and printer and be right at home. And yes, I also had my hair done there.

There was one problem with the office: My window overlooked Pennsylvania Avenue and Lafayette Park—a great, fun distraction. I would like to share with you some of the observations I would record in my diary in the coming months:

It truly is like looking at a Norman Rockwell Saturday Evening Post cover. It gives me a seasonal view of Washington. Much of what I see is for my eyes only as I alone am the only observer. The people on the first floor have too many barriers (trees, etc.), and most rooms on the second floor look over the South Grounds. How disappointed the protesters would be to know that only one person sees them.

. . . This past Friday a small, but persistent protest was held across Pennsylvania Avenue. For the first time I could really read the signs held up by a small hard knot of people. On two long banners stretched out and held through drizzle and rain was writing that said: *STOP MADMAN MILO SEVIC NOW* and *STOP GENOCIDE IN KASOVA.* There was a small group of people marching up and down carrying both the American flag and a red flag with a black figure or seal in the middle. Now that is sad. My own little protest and I don't know what it is all about. I, the only observer, did not know who Milo Sevic was. [Little did we know then how newsworthy Milosevic, a Serbian leader, would become as the painful breakup of Yugoslavia dominated world news.]

. . . I saw a school bus pull up the other day and a group of school children got out holding cardboard signs, made in school, I'm sure, and then one group holding a large sheet on which was written *SAVE OUR RAIN FORESTS.* They marched up and down and after twenty minutes reboarded the bus and took off for school. These children are being taught "peaceful protest." Pretty nice.

. . . In the winter I often see people come and feed the pigeons and squirrels. There is one person, I have never figured out whether it is a man or woman, who comes and dances with the birds. It is a modern kind of crazy dance as he or she flings out seeds to the birds and darts around throwing arms and legs in odd gestures. It always amazes me that passersby seem to take it all for granted and do not look surprised.

. . . This morning I was talking on the phone to Arnold Scaasi when I looked out the window and saw a bride and groom posing across the street for a wedding photo with the White House in the background. I was flabbergasted to see the bridesmaids dressed in black. The bride—in white, thank heavens—had a big bustle on her back and a great floppy hat. I loved it and called Doro, who was visiting, to come and take a peek. Arnold told me that he is often asked to design black bridesmaid dresses!

. . . I love looking out. I know that eventually I'm going to see every-thing. The other day an extra long white stretch limousine drove up and stopped on Pennsylvania Avenue in front of the White House. The top was slipped back and slowly a big cowboy hat appeared and then a head. The head turned our way, a picture snapped and the head and hat slowly disappeared again. The car rolled off as the trap door, or whatever you call those things on the top of the car, closed.

I worked at my desk (when not looking out the window) about three hours a day. Wonderful Chris Emery in the usher's office became my computer guru, and after years of keeping handwritten or audio diaries, I turned high-tech. Like millions of Americans, I quickly developed a love/hate relationship with my laptop, but without it I'm not sure this book would exist.

The mail especially was brutal. In the first hundred days alone I received more than 30,000 pieces of mail, and my yearly average was roughly 100,000 letters. Most of the mail was positive, which was very nice, and sometimes it was about the silliest things—such as George not liking broccoli! I also heard from many people hoping I could help solve their problems, which personally I could do very little about. But we referred more than 12,000 letters over the years to various govern-ment agencies that possibly could help. Fortunately, I had the wonder-ful Joan DeCain, in charge of my correspondence, and her staff to keep my head above water. On the other side of the White House, Shirley Green was doing the same for George, whose mail volume averaged 3.4 million pieces a year. Shirley was a good friend who had been with us for years; she was the prefect person to trust with the mail.

Neither during the vice presidential or White House years did I have an office in the Old Executive Office Building (part of the White House complex) or the East Wing, traditionally where the First Lady's staff works. As it was, my staff was jammed in on top of each other, including our marvelous volunteers, without whom we could not have gotten through the work load. I always suspected my staff appreci-ated my staying out of their way. Lucky for them, I couldn't even do a "surprise" drop-by: Millie always preceded me by about two minutes, announcing my arrival.

Another thing I loved about White House life was having George so close by. If he needed a break, he'd call and say, "Do you want to take a spin around the South Grounds?" or "Can you pop over to the Oval Office to say hello to so-and-so?" Sometimes he would suggest that I give the guest a tour of the residence. I suspected at times he just wanted to get rid of them and get back to work. Or he might call and say, "How about joining me for lunch?" or "How about me joining you for lunch?"

One day very early in the administration he called and said, "What are you doing? Look out your window, you'll see a friend." I walked over with the phone in my hand and there looking out of the Oval Office was Danny Rostenkowski paying a courtesy call on the new president. We waved. He and George had served together on the House Ways and Means Committee, and although they had many political differences, they were good friends.

Right after Millie's son, Ranger, moved in with us, Danny and his wife, LaVerne, came to the White House for a visit. We were sitting in the West Hall Sitting Room, and Ranger got so excited that he promptly wet—just a little—on Danny's shoe. We still remained friends.

Another time Danny sent me some shampoo that he said was made especially for people with white hair. A well-known cosmetics firm is based in Danny's district, and he often passes out shampoos to members of Congress and other friends. The first day I used it, several people mentioned my hair looked different but I thought nothing about it. When George came home, he not only mentioned it, he suggested that maybe I'd added a little color. We went out in the light and, lo and behold, I had a definite platinum blond look. It was not a shampoo for me and, as it turned out, it was not for Millie either. When I shampooed her with it, she became a brown and slightly yellow-haired dog. I never dared tell Danny that he had given me the wrong shampoo.

At this writing Danny is under fire, accused of financial wrongdoing. We certainly wish him well. With George and me, friendship counts and we always will remain Danny's friends.

✏ By March Millie's expected pups had become big news. One of the local Washington papers had a "Millie Countdown," and my press office was getting calls from all over the world. One Australian reporter insisted on a full report on how Millie felt. He apparently didn't understand he was inquiring about a dog.

The White House carpenters made Millie a large nest with a presidential seal that fit in my office/beauty parlor/birthing room. We were hoping that she would have her babies there. Even I was amazed at how big she was getting. Her veterinarian predicted a large litter, scaring me to death about all the bad things that could happen. I asked him over and over again for his night number.

The vet taught me how to take Millie's temperature, explaining that when it went down two points, the puppies were on the way. What he did not tell me, however, was that a dog's normal temperature is 102 degrees. So when Millie was at 98 degrees on March 17, I was very disappointed because she seemed to be trying to nest, both in and outside the White House. Temperature or not, I was sure the time had come. That night we were hosting a group for dinner and a movie, so Paula sat with Millie during the meal and I skipped the movie. Around 9:15, Millie sat up, panted several times, and lay down to deliver her first of six babies. I wondered if Dr. Lamaze watched animals give birth before he came up with his natural birth concept involving panting and relaxing? It was a miracle to me. Millie knew exactly what to do and so did the pups. They were nursing almost before they were cleaned by their mother. I called George at the theater to tell him the good news, and he asked me if it was a boy or a girl. I told him that I didn't know as it was too soon to tell. He slipped out of the movie to see the third pup born. We stood watching our little Millie deliver and got quite teary. She had five girls first and then had her only boy, Ranger. They weren't too young after all to tell the difference.

Millie's puppies were a joy. They were absolutely the dearest, sweetest little ones and a pleasure to the whole White House. My office had more visitors and drop-in trade than I could believe. Millie was a perfect mom. She knew exactly how long she should sleep with them, and after about a month she moved back in with us. I have wondered so when I read about parents abusing their children: If a dog's natural instincts are to protect her young, why, oh, why wouldn't we humans do the same?

*   *   *

꙰ Not all the animals at the White House were quite so beloved. One Sunday in April we were having a relaxing family afternoon, and I decided to swim laps. This was one of the great habits I had gotten into during the first hundred days, to take advantage of the White House swimming pool and do laps every day, rain or shine, summer or winter. I swam with a snorkel and mask, and it was very relaxing.

On this particular day I first had to shoo away a pair of mallard ducks who were having a little rest and swim. Millie was beside herself with excitement, barking and running around the pool. I finally got started and had just swum half a mile (twenty-four laps) when a great big rat went right in front of my face mask. Believe me when I say that this fella did not resemble Mickey Mouse. There was nothing cute about him. I flew out of the pool screaming all the way. George and Don Rhodes, who were throwing horseshoes at the time, came running to my rescue and took care of that nasty little devil. I was through swimming for the day and had to force myself to go the next. You can believe I checked every drain before entering the pool.

In addition to swimming, I played tennis at the crack of dawn several mornings a week with friends. It took a while to learn to concentrate on my game, the view was so awesome: either the White House or the Washington Monument was in the background.

George immediately had a horseshoe pit put in and opened it by inviting about twenty world champion players to the White House to inaugurate it. They and their spouses were so excited to be there.

That was the beginning of the White House Horseshoe Tournaments, which started with sixteen teams from all different departments and eventually grew to thirty-two, I believe. Marvin and George teamed up, playing the nurses, the groundskeepers, electricians, housemen, military aides, and on and on. At lunchtime we often would hear the clink of shoes as people practiced. Although women were certainly welcome, only two played—one was a nurse who beat almost everyone, and Nancy Mitchell from the usher's office. It was such a good way for us to get to know the folks who made our lives sing. The finals brought some of the families together for soft drinks, or hot chocolate if it was cold.

* * *

⌒ Soon after taking office George called a meeting in the Oval Office that included the Vice President; Boyden Gray, a trusted friend and George's chief counsel for twelve years; the Chief of Staff, John Sununu; Burt Lee, good friend and the President's doctor; Susan Porter Rose; and myself. The purpose of the gathering was to discuss the Twenty-Fifth Amendment to the Constitution: what would happen if George got ill, what the law was, and what we all should do. It is a dreadful thought, but one every president must think about and face. George led the discussion, and I remember two things very clearly: Dan Quayle sitting quietly, saying not a word; he was in a most sensitive position. And Burt Lee saying that the people in that room would be the most likely to notice a change if George were ill and must be ready to declare him unable to continue to be in charge. What an awful burden for a friend—not to mention a spouse. I am glad that we never had to face that issue. I think George wanted this meeting early on so that the performance of the Wilson administration would not be repeated, when the President's illness had been hidden from the public for months. We all promised George that we would be honest and responsible, no matter how hard. Boyden explained the legal side to us. That settled, we decided that we would never talk about this meeting since any discussion about the president's health starts rumors.

A few weeks later I read a small squib in the paper about the meeting, and the unnamed source said that Marilyn Quayle had spoken up a lot. She was *not* at the meeting. It was so unfair to her. Probably someone in the meeting innocently discussed it with a spouse or a friend, who then told someone else, and so on. This is how many leaks happen, through thirdhand sources, and the facts almost always get twisted in the retelling.

I don't think the average American realizes just how important the president's health is to the whole world—or maybe I was the only one who didn't. If the president of the United States hiccups, the world trembles.

When George had his annual physical, the press wanted to know absolutely everything. George is very healthy, and I always questioned the press's right to know things about his body that had nothing to do with his ability to govern. We all remember the grim and minute details of Jimmy Carter's hemorrhoid operation. We were told more than we wanted or needed to know about that miserable, painful procedure.

⟶ As for me, I had never felt better and I was thrilled because I was losing weight—easily. I convinced myself that was because I was eating smaller portions and working so hard. However, I was having some problems with my eyes, and Dr. Lee insisted I get some tests run. I wrote in my diary on March 20:

I am now driving back from Walter Reed Hospital having had all sorts of tests and drinking some radioactive stuff that makes all the alarms go off at the White House. All this testing has to do with my eyes. They started acting up the week before the Inauguration. I thought it was a makeup problem, allergy to makeup, etc. But it didn't stop. They are red, sort of tearing all the time, itch, are puffy and I see double. After a visit to Bethesda and Walter Reed hospitals, they think I have a thyroid gone berserk. Frankly, it is a little scary. I don't want pop eyes.

Eventually I was diagnosed as having Graves' disease, caused by a dysfunctional thyroid. (It doesn't mean you'll go to the grave; it's named for the doctor who diagnosed the ailment.) As it turns out, it was the disease causing me to lose weight, and once we started treating it, that ended. Since it is not life-threatening if treated, we decided to go public immediately.

Needless to say, the press made a big deal of it and there were endless articles about Graves' disease, which probably was good. However, I didn't realize just how seriously some people were taking my illness until April Fool's Day.

George and I were going to attend the annual Gridiron Club Dinner, an evening where members of the press put on little skits at the expense of politicians but all in good fun. Their motto is "We often singe, but never burn." It's supposed to be off the record, which means you can count on reading it in *The Washington Post* the next day.

When I saw the dinner on my schedule, I decided I had to play an April Fool's Day joke not only on our hosts, but also George. So I came out of our bedroom that night dressed to the nines for the black-tie dinner, and wearing a strawberry-blond wig. So much had been made of

my white hair, I thought this was the perfect joke. George was flabbergasted, saying, "You are not going to wear that thing, are you?" I loved
it, however, and away we went. But it really almost backfired. Several
people asked George if I was really sicker than what was reported and
was I wearing a wig to cover hair loss, etc. Some people thought that
I hadn't come at all and wondered who the woman with George was.
Some people just never even mentioned it when they talked to me. That
was one April Fool's Day joke that many people just did not get.

    Later that month we hosted three black-tie dinners for for-
eign visitors; the Mubaraks from Egypt; the Shamirs from Israel; and
King Hussein and Queen Noor of Jordan. Interestingly enough, the
Israeli ambassador and his wife came to the Egyptian dinner and the
Egyptian ambassador and his wife came to the Israeli dinner.

The Mubarak visit was the first, and George took Hosni and his
son over to Baltimore to see the baseball Orioles' home opener and
throw out the first pitch. So when Prime Minister Shamir came several
days later, George felt that he should do something special, and they
went to see a film at the Air and Space Museum. Then of course he
couldn't let our old friend, King Hussein, be without a special event,
so he took him to Mount Vernon. George told me that sometimes these
private trips really allow for a more informative, relaxed exchange of
ideas than the official talks.

Audrey Hepburn attended the Israeli dinner and came to call on
me the next day to talk about her work with UNICEF. I had met her
once before in Rome at a luncheon when George was vice president.
Audrey felt passionately about two things, both of which mattered to
me also: She loved children and became an advocate for young people in distress around the world; and she adored dogs. She had read
C. Fred's Story, and after that first lunch she disappeared and returned
in a few moments with her two small dogs in her arms. I loved that; it
was so human. When she came to call in 1989 she played with Millie's
puppies, and I was slightly surprised that Millie let her pick them up
without even a small protest.

How the world admired that lovely creature! She was famous as
an actress—who will ever forget *Breakfast at Tiffany's?*—but I think
she will live forever in the minds of the world as a lover and protector

of children, for whom she traveled to the most desolate spots in the world. Shortly before her death in January 1993, George awarded her the Medal of Freedom, but she was too ill to attend the ceremony.

The dinner for the King of Jordan and Queen Noor caused a small crisis in the kitchen. We had checked with the State Department for any special menu requirements and were told no shellfish or red meat. (The King probably remembered that we had dropped a steak in his lap in Houston.) So we settled on duck. They had been marinating for some time when we got the word that the Queen would prefer white meat. Laurie called and asked what we should do: Should we change the menu? I said absolutely not. After all, the Queen was, in truth, just an American girl (Lisa Halaby) who married a king and she certainly would understand. I am glad to report that His Majesty wolfed down all his duck.

He is such an extraordinary man. I remember years ago attending a state dinner for His Majesty that Richard Nixon gave. In his toast President Nixon said something like: "Your Majesty, when you took over the throne, there were many people who said that you would not last. Well, sir, you have outlasted three American presidents." Well, that was six presidents ago and he is still going strong despite the many problems he faces. In spite of major differences of opinion during the Iraq crises and Desert Storm, George and I both respect and have genuine affection for Jordan's King.

During the next four years George and I would host thirty-two state dinners, most of which were part of an official state visit that always began with a very impressive, formal arrival ceremony. Both this event and the dinner gave the visiting heads of state an opportunity to be seen in their homelands with a world leader; both events had so much dignity; and both gave the leaders and their aides an opportunity to talk with Americans they might want to see. For example, people who do business in a particular foreign country often were invited to that state dinner to encourage more exports. The dinners also were a wonderful opportunity to showcase American hospitality, cuisine, and entertainment.

All the dinners were special, but one that stands out in my mind was for Australian Prime Minister Bob Hawke. To begin with, Bob and Hazel are warm, open people and great fun. We had invited Leontyne Price to sing and were so lucky that she was free for that night. During dessert, she gave us a little preview of what was to come later in the evening. While the strolling violins were playing "As Time Goes

By," we suddenly heard the most beautiful sound. It was Leontyne at George's table singing along, low at first and then louder and louder. It was so special and sweet—a magic moment of pure beauty.

Of course not everything always went perfectly. There certainly were gaffes here and there, but at the dinner for the Antalls from Hungary, almost everything that could go wrong did. I wrote in my diary:

George said during the music after dinner that we needed to tighten up a bit. I'd say so! . . .

1. There was nobody waiting at the door to take her coat.

2. When we got to the top of the stairs, the door leading into our private residence was locked.

3. Nobody kept us on schedule.

4. Nobody told us what positions to be in for the flag ceremony.

5. Nobody gave us names in the receiving line.

6. There were four blank seats at the P.M.'s table because of the storm. (The weather was so bad that several guests from the New York City area were still sitting at the airport. I had to signal somebody to bring others over to our table.)

7. Violins came in too late and George thought they were too long.

8. (Concert pianist) Van Cliburn was superb, but considering our guests' jet lag, too long.

9. When George glanced at his cheat cards so that he could thank our talented good friend Van, he noticed that they had Frank Liszt on his cards. He caught it and so did say Franz Liszt (Hungarian composer) and not Frank. Yikes, could you see the next morning's papers if he had gone with what they had on the card?

We almost had a real crisis during the dinner for the new president of Mexico, Carlos Salinas. The pastry chef had described the dessert on the menu as "Mexican Fantasy." Just as the platters were leaving the kitchen to make a dramatic entrance into the State Dining Room, Laurie noticed that the chef had constructed an adobe house out of edible sweets, filled with ice cream and surrounded by a fence and flowers. It was stunning. BUT, leaning against the wall of the house was a little candy Mexican boy taking a siesta with a sombrero over his eyes. Just the unfair image that this young bright Harvard graduate was trying to (and has) erased about Mexico. So as each platter went by, Laurie plucked off the sleeping boy. It would have been insulting. She saved the day for her country, but the next morning had to face the pastry chef who had labored so long over that glorious dessert.

Then there was the dinner when the popular and talented Harry Connick, Jr., was to perform. He was very unhappy (to say the least) to discover that his date, model Jill Goodacre, was not sitting with him at dinner. I should explain that we never put couples together at social functions; we always split them up. To complicate the situation, Mr. Connick wanted us to change the seating when most of the guests already were in place.

Still unhappy after dinner, he threatened not to perform and went to his dressing room. It wasn't until he walked into the East Room and sat down at the piano that we were sure the crisis was over. That said, he gave us a knockout performance.

Certainly one of the people who always helped smooth out such problems was Laurie Firestone's very able assistant, Cathy Fenton. She is truly a beautiful young woman whose gentle touch made every crisis seem not so bad.

On April 25, I wrote in my diary:

Monday was George P.'s 13th birthday. Imagine having a teenage grandchild!

. . . George and I were up at the crack of dawn and flew by helo to Andrews Air Force Base and from Andrews to Norfolk where we went to the memorial for the 47 crew members who died on the Iowa.* It was the most moving ceremony and made more so by the audible sobs of the wives, children, families and friends of the dead. The ceremony was held in a large, damp hangar. The captain of the ship spoke and I thought he was very moved and moving. George spoke and was wonderfully comforting. He cracked at the very end and just barely got through it. We walked down the line and spoke to the immediate families. Almost impossible to know what to say to a young woman who has lost her husband or to a mother or father who has lost their only son. You can just hope that they believe in God and that they know that God loves their child, husband, brother and loved one even more than they do.

---

* An explosion in the U.S.S. *Iowa*'s gun turret had killed forty-seven sailors on April 19 while the ship was participating in naval exercises near Puerto Rico.

We were so very busy those first few months but always made time for friends and family. Our children and grandchildren were in and out of the house and made life seem more normal. My friends were pretty good about calling. I say "pretty good" because most friends don't want to impose. My advice is to impose, as it can get to be pretty lonely in that house. Thank heavens for Andy Stewart, who spoiled me by calling or coming over every day. I was so lucky to have her.

For the most part weekends were spent at Camp David. George and I worked out a wonderful schedule. He had his office at the lodge called "Laurel," and I had one in the president's cabin, "Aspen." We both got up very early and worked all morning. We did this whether or not we had guests, giving each of us time to answer mail, think, work on speeches, and generally get caught up. (Although the president *never* gets caught up.) Our guests were on their own with a world of things that they could do, and then all of us would meet at lunchtime. In addition to family members, "Perle Mesta" invited people from all over the country to spend the weekend, and sometimes aides or advisers would come up to brief George and then stay for lunch before heading back to Washington. We also had a number of foreign visitors, including Prince Charles, who had dinner with us. Women always oohed and aahed to me when they heard that, which I found so funny. After all, he was the age of our oldest son, although I liked to tease George W. that the Prince was much better dressed and considerably more polite!

∽ The first hundred days ended April 30. It's a term made up mainly by the media to "judge" whether the new president is doing a good job. Quite honestly, I don't remember what they said about George. What I do remember is that it was an unbelievable but exhilarating whirlwind. As close as I can count, I hosted either alone or with George: eighteen receptions, sixteen dinners, twenty-four coffees or teas; nineteen lunches; and two breakfasts. I visited nine states and four countries, conducted twenty-four press interviews, and participated in forty-two "doing and caring" events and forty-one other types of events. We had fifty-one different overnight guests and fed 5,825 people.

And it was only the beginning.

18

Whirlwind First Year

B y this time I knew one thing for sure: I had the best job in America. Every single day was interesting, rewarding, and sometimes just plain fun.

In May George W. invited me to Dallas to see the grandchildren and throw out the first pitch for a Texas Rangers baseball game. He had been part of a group of investors who had bought the team and was chosen to be one of two managing general partners.

I had another important task that trip: deliver the first of Millie's pups to leave the nest to Jenna and Barbara. The girls named her after their favorite baseball payer, Scott Fletcher. Fortunately, they named the dog "Spot Fletcher," for "Scott" was traded to another team shortly thereafter.

George W. had planned the best evening for me, and I was really touched. I wrote in my diary:

We started with a reception for the wives of the players, wives of the owners and some key women in the management. We had pictures taken and everyone was darling. On to the game and I was so excited. George knew every living human, almost seemed like all 38,000! He introduced me to the "best groundskeeper in the major leagues"; the "finest ticket-taker in any park"; and the "fastest hot dog vendor." He knew them all.

(George W.) had Reading Is Fundamental posters everywhere and on everything. Jimmy Dean was there, and they ran our RIF (public service announcement) on and off during the whole game. George gave away 1,000 tickets to kids participating in the RIF program and handed out bookmarks with Texas Rangers on one side and RIF on the other to every single person who came. The ball I was to throw out had been signed by all the players and by the coach. Below their names they put their favorite books. I was crazy about Bobby Valentine, the coach. While waiting in the dugout, he and I talked. He told me that he always thought the greatest thing that could happen to a man was to throw a ball to his son. Then he said that was not true. "The greatest thing that could happen to a father is to sit with your arm around your son and read." He went on to tell me that he and his son, Bobby, are reading The Wizard of Oz series. He tells me that he rushes home after practice and reads to his 5-year-old before the game. I loved that talk.

There is a footnote to the story about the signed baseball. Several weeks later I attended the Literacy Volunteers of New York's annual fund-raiser. One of the participants was Larry McMurtry, and his *Lonesome Dove* was one of the books that had been written on the baseball (by a baseball player whose last name also was McMurtry, I might add). I had planned to make a little game of this and throw the ball to Larry during my speech, but when I saw his Coke-bottle glasses, I thought better of it! I handed it to him instead.

∽ One of the greatest pleasures of my job was the luncheon the Ladies of the Senate give the First Lady at the Capitol every spring, and the reciprocal luncheon she gives at the White House. I missed my friends on the Hill and really looked forward to this event every year. The first year, the whole enormous Caucus Room was decorated like a schoolhouse and filled with children's books, which later were donated to District of Columbia schools. Nothing could have pleased me more.

The next year they decorated the room as a Maine seacoast city because they knew how I loved Kennebunkport. Everyone received an autographed copy of Anne Morrow Lindbergh's *Gift from the Sea,* and mine had a personal inscription. I was thrilled. The next year the theme was "Texas," which they knew was our real home, and the last year, it was a "Secret Garden," as they had seen pictures of me working with my flowers. They were all happy occasions, and I have never lost my affection for those marvelous women, Democrats and Republicans.

My first luncheon for them was June 5, just as China was in turmoil over the brutal put-down of protests in Tiananmen Square. We were very upset over the suffering on a personal level, and officially, it was a huge concern for George. A day with my friends was just what the doctor ordered. And to make it even more special, Betty Ford and Lady Bird Johnson, former presidents of the Ladies of the Senate, attended. After a lovely lunch, the Harlem Boys Choir sang—the first of several times they would entertain for us at the White House. They are thrilling singers and excellent students as well. In future years I would have the New Visions Dance Theater perform, young handicapped children who were beautiful and graceful; the two-man comedy act Greater Tuna; and the cast from *Conrack*.

When lunch was over, Betty had to rush off, but Lady Bird and her daughter Lynda, married to Senator Chuck Robb of Virginia, accepted my invitation to join me upstairs:

The reminiscing was fun for me. (Lady Bird) remembered the Mary Cassatt, the Winslow Homer (Proutt's Neck) and several other paintings that friends of theirs had donated to the White House in their name . . . when Lady Bird got to the Thomas Eakins portrait of little Miss Ruth Harding,* a grumpy little girl with a big bow on her head and a turned-down mouth, she told the story of showing off the White House to a small group. When she got to the Eakins, she said: "Have you ever seen a grumpier little girl?" A voice from the back of the group said, "You'll be glad to know that she grew up to be a grand person. I married that little girl." Lady Bird was always a joy, and she brought the White House to life even more with her happy stories.

I continued to be spoiled by life in the White House. One wet morning when I was supposed to play tennis, I got up at 6:00 A.M. to walk Millie around the South Grounds. I noticed that although the rain had stopped, the tennis courts were soaked and had puddles of standing water, so back to bed I went to read awhile. At 7:30 I got a

* Ruth Harding was no relation to President Harding. She was the niece of Jennie Dean Kershaw, the fiancée of Samuel Murray, who was Eakins's favorite pupil and closest friend.

call saying that my tennis-playing friends were waiting at the court. I couldn't believe it, but threw on my clothes and ran down. There, in a wet world, was a bone-dry court. The groundskeepers had squeegeed the court and then blown it dry with giant blowers.

Another time I was not so lucky. During the whole four years we were in the White House, the exterior was undergoing renovation, which included being scraped down and painted. That first spring the south side of the house was wrapped with a canvas covering with only small openings for the windows. One morning I got up and walked Millie at 4:45 A.M. under leaden skies. I was dressing for tennis as George left for the Oval Office and at 7:00 A.M. was on my way out the door when George called and suggested I look out the window. It was pouring. Because of the wrapping around the house I hadn't noticed. To everyone's amusement and amazement, I went out and swam instead. My theory is that you can't get any wetter than wet.

I was having a tough year tennis-wise, and after my matches, the ushers and other members of the staff would ask how I'd done. Each time I had to confess that I had not been on the winning team. Until . . .

On the 25th I played tennis with Jean Douglas (Mrs. Leslie) against Andy Stewart (Mrs. Potter) and Aileen Train (Mrs. Russell). For once I was on the winning side. Of course, my partner, Jean, is really good. Having lost so many times I came into the house dancing. When I sat down for lunch that day I had a bouquet of flowers on the table with a small tennis racket and a note tucked in the center of the arrangement, "Congratulations from the White House Staff." No wonder I am so happy in this house.

But with the good came the bad. My trip to Kennebunkport later that month, always a cause for joy, began with much heartache instead. Security had to be tightened at Walker's Point, which included adding a large chain-link fence; a helicopter pad was put in; and a small house was built where the doctor and military aide could stay. To accomplish all this, they had to cut down a number of trees, which really hurt since Walker's Point is built on a rock ledge and every tree had taken years to grow. Suddenly we looked like a prison instead of a beautiful summer home. It all made me cry. I'm not too proud of that, but it hurt to see a ten-foot-high fence when we rounded the drive instead of the ocean. (The security people eventually agreed, and forty feet of fencing came down.) In retrospect, the Secret Service and everyone who worked on the Point tried their hardest to keep George safe and to respect our wishes and privacy. But that first view was a shock.

We were especially eager for the Point to look pretty and be ready for the visit from François Mitterrand and, at the last minute, his wife, Danielle. Many preliminaries go into a visit from a head of state, and Doro agreed to meet the French advance team and show them the rooms where the two Presidents would meet; where Jim Baker and their Foreign Minister, Dumas, would meet; and where the enormous support staffs would sit and wait.

It had been decided that the Mitterrands would stay in George's mother's bungalow. This wonderful little house had been given to her as a wedding present some seventy years before and enlarged about thirty years later. I don't believe that other than being cleaned and used hard every summer, it had been touched since. Doro said all went well on the walk-through until they got to the bungalow. Even the most beautiful summer cottage that has been unopened for eight months looks dirty and feels damp; Doro said Mom's looked even worse. Her tiny little hospital bed especially seemed shabby, but Doro told the French not to worry: We would rent a large bed for the President. The advance people were so kind, but even they looked shocked when they glanced into the bathroom and there was a "riser" on the toilet for Mom. One man turned to Doro and said in total horror, pointing with a disdainful finger, "Wat is dis?" Poor Doro. She lived through it, but said it was so embarrassing.

Several days before the visit I arrived with a small army to open the big house and Mom's. We cleaned morning, noon, and night. My aide Casey, Paula, even Carol Powers the photographer pitched in, and by Friday we were ready. I must say that when the rented bed appeared it was horrible, and what's worse, I think the rental people bought the ornate brass monstrosity especially for the visit. It would have looked more at home in a French bordello. I wonder what François thought? Maybe better not to know.

On Friday George had Secretary of Defense Dick Cheney and the Joint Chiefs of Staff for a working lunch on our deck, and in the afternoon, Walter Curley, our Ambassador to France, and his wife, Taitsie, our close friends, arrived along with Jim and Susan Baker, Brent Scowcroft, John Sununu, and Jody Bush, who is George's brother John's wife. She came because she speaks fluent French, we love her, and George thought it would make François feel more at home. Dinner that night was such fun as we were surrounded by dear friends.

It had been decided that during the visit I had to take the ladies sight-seeing since every inch of the Point would be used for meetings. At the last moment I called Doro, who worked for Maine's Department of Tourism, and said, "You are Mrs. Tourism. Please find a restaurant in Portland with a view of the harbor, tell me what boats are available, and see about dropping in on the museum."

I was so touched by the job she did. First of all, there was no moaning on her part. She was so burdened by her own life—holding down a full-time job with two young children—and she took this on with joy. She quickly called me back and said, "No such restaurant. But Mom, Betsy Hunt has a wonderful house on the bay that overlooks the islands and she is eager to have you. We have a great boat, and the museum is ready." All this with three days' notice.

On Saturday, May 20, we awakened to a lovely, bright Maine day, walked down to the new helicopter pad, and met François and Danielle and their party. Quickly the men went into meetings, and shortly the ladies took off for Portland. Danielle and I had with us an interpreter and the French ambassador's wife, Hélène de Margerie.

Danielle is a fascinating woman who has an agenda of her own. We no sooner got in the car than she started talking about her foundation and the plight of the Kurds. For forty-five minutes she talked and we listened. She talked about the Kurds' flight from Iraq and Iran and also a lot about the Turks. I confess I began to feel a little drowsy, which is not too surprising considering our five days of hard work and late nights combined with the warm car ride. I found myself praying that I would not fall asleep or, worse, say something like, "Tell me more about the Turds." Fortunately, I didn't, and Danielle certainly opened my eyes to the suffering of these poor people, which continues on today. I was and am impressed by her fervor and passion.

Dinner that night was at two round tables of eight in our dining room with a roaring fire. I wrote in my diary:

George's table had a rather lively conversation about religion. I wasn't there, but I understand that Danielle told them that she did not

Playing pool with the boys at Cranston Senior Center in Rhode Island. (Carol Powers)

Please notice that no one is driving the boat while George points something out!
(Susan Biddle)

Watching *Marine One* land
at Kennebunkport was too
much for granddaughter
Ellie LeBlond's ears.
(Carol Powers)

Three of my boys:
George, George W., and Jeb.
(White House photo)

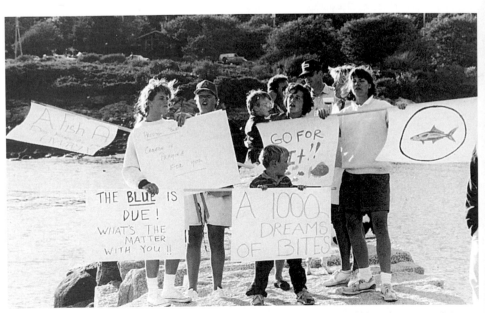

George gets some ribbing from family and friends about his inability to catch a fish.
(David Valdez)

Forty-five years after dropping out of Smith College, I finally get my degree, even if it is just honorary. (Carol Powers)

Making a new friend during International Literacy Day at the United Nations, September 1989. (Carol Powers)

Goofing with the grandchildren outside the White House. (Carol Powers)

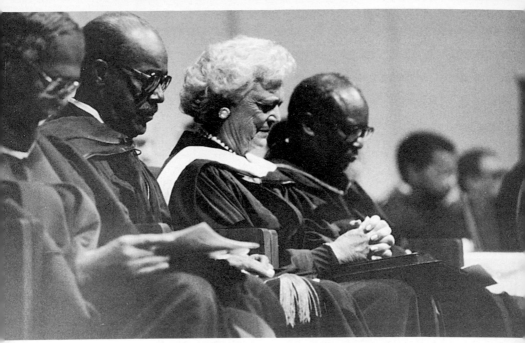

Attending convocation at Morehouse School of Medicine in Atlanta,
October 1989. (Carol Powers)

One of the many friends I made while First Lady. (Carol Powers)

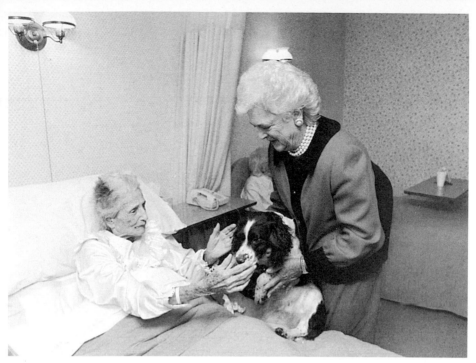

You can see who's getting all the attention during this visit to a nursing home in Washington, D.C. (Carol Powers)

Reading to a group of children in New York City. (Carol Powers)

One of those moments in the White House you never forget—showing Rosa Parks the original Emancipation Proclamation in the Lincoln Bedroom. (Carol Powers)

Sorting through a new shipment of books for the grandchildren. (Carol Powers)

At Wellesley College with Raisa Gorbachev, June 1, 1990. (Carol Powers)

Millie and Raisa Gorbachev get acquainted while I drive the
golf cart at Camp David. (Carol Powers)

Horseshoe diplomacy between George and Mikhail Gorbachev, May 1990. (David Valdez)

Taking a break from a working weekend at Camp David. From left: Secretary of State James Baker; Barbara Bush; George Bush; Raisa Gorbachev; Mikhail Gorbachev; Soviet Foreign Minister Eduard Shevardnadze; Brent Scowcroft, head of the National Security Council; and Marshal Sergei Akhromeyev of the Soviet Union. (David Valdez)

Stumping for
Millie's Book in
September 1990 on
the "Fox Morning
News" with anchor
Lark McCarthy.
(Carol Powers)

George gives Margaret
Thatcher a taste of
the Wild West at the
Economic Summit in
Houston, July 1990.
(Carol Powers)

Hard at work,
August 1990.
(Carol Powers)

Welcoming
President Gampy
to Kennebunkport,
August 1990.
(David Valdez)

Can you believe this
outfit someone sent
Millie? (Carol Powers)

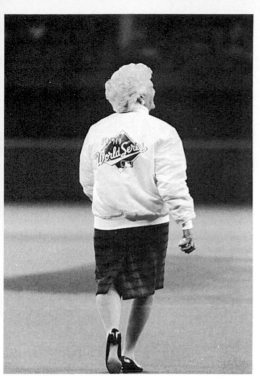

One of the perks of being First Lady, throwing out the first pitch during a 1990 World Series game. (Carol Powers)

I can't remember the story I was telling Prince Fahd bin Salman of Saudi Arabia, but he was nice to laugh. (Carol Powers)

Thanksgiving Day 1990 in the Saudi Arabian desert with our troops. (Carol Powers)

Katharine Hepburn gets a standing ovation at the Kennedy Center Honors, December 1990. From left: Katharine Hepburn, Dizzy Gillespie, me, our daughter-in-law Margaret Bush, and Dan and Marilyn Quayle.

Rubbing noses with a young cancer patient at Children's Hospital in Washington, D.C. (Carol Powers)

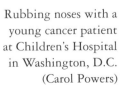

George (second from right) and Secret Service agents pull me back up the hill after I broke my leg, January 1991. (Carol Powers)

You can see how worried everyone was—George and Arnold Schwarzenegger back on the slopes. (Carol Powers)

Getting a free ride from my aide, Peggy Swift, in the Oval Office. (Carol Powers)

Watching George tell the nation that Desert Storm has begun, January 16, 1991. With me are our daughter, Doro; my press secretary, Anna Perez; Millie; and Billy Graham. (Carol Powers)

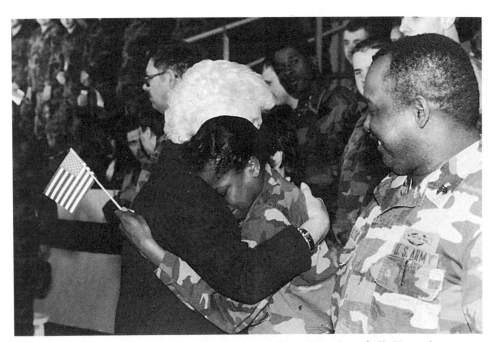

Sharing a tender moment with a young soldier at Fort Campbell, Kentucky. (Carol Powers)

George takes a "power walk" with the omnipresent media in Kennebunkport. (Susan Biddle)

Caught sleeping again, this time on *Air Force One* with grandson Sam LeBlond. (Carol Powers)

Acting very silly with some of my staff and Secret Service agents during a late-night flight home. (Carol Powers)

Queen Elizabeth and the "talking hat," on the White House lawn, May 1991. (Steve Purcell)

A royal White House evening. (Susan Biddle)

A little quiet fishing in the Black Hills of South Dakota with the President. (Carol Powers)

believe that intellectuals believed in organized religions, life after death, etc. Susan Baker and George defended strongly. I guess that it got a little heated at their table. Our table, on the other hand, was fun and François was amusing and warm and cozy. I never saw him after that that he didn't mention the fact that we had had him in our home. I believe that 24-hour visit was the beginning of a great relationship between the two men. George was and is devoted to François.

After the dinner ended I announced that our little church was having an early morning service for us and that the vans would leave from both the Point and the hotel at 7:45. I thought that it was funny that George was trying to shush me and Jim Baker, who was at my table, was asking me to repeat the announcement. George thought that Jim and I were needling Danielle. Not at all. We just hadn't known that their table had had that strange conversation.

The next morning many of us, without the Mitterrands, went to our First Congregational Church for an early morning service. They kindly put the service ahead an hour to accommodate our departure for Boston University to celebrate their 150th year.

It was a relaxed yet productive visit and the beginning of many heads of state coming for informal visits to Maine. Brian and Mila Mulroney and their four marvelous children came from Canada several times, and John and Norma Major of Great Britain, to whom we felt very close, came with their two children. The Kaifus came from Tokyo with their son and a charming, bright interpreter. We were thrilled when the two later married. They said the romance started on that trip, so I guess more than foreign affairs were advanced on those Kennebunkport visits. Our old friend Poul Schluter, the Prime Minister of Denmark, came on his honeymoon. His new wife, Anne Marie Wessel, was a lovely former ballet dancer and director of the Royal Danish Ballet.

One summer the King of Jordan and Foreign Minister Saud of Saudi Arabia came by for separate meetings (more about that later), and the Rabins came from Israel and spent a weekend in the summer of 1992. Yitzhak and Leah had been friends for many years as he had been their ambassador to Washington during our early years in the capital.

Shortly after the Mitterrand visit George and I took a quick trip to Italy, Belgium, Germany, and England. Our main destination was a NATO meeting in Brussels, but we stopped on the way in Italy to celebrate Memorial Day at Anzio, where so many Americans gave their lives in World War II. George gave the most beautiful speech and had me in tears. The streets were lined with hundreds of cheering people, and it was interesting to note that many of them were older and obviously remembered the sacrifice that so many Americans had made for them.

In Belgium, Queen Fabiola and I made a lovely visit to a village where mentally disabled people live independent, productive lives. The Queen and I had met several times before, and she is such a caring, spiritual person. She and her husband, King Baudouin, were childless and seemed to have such a gentle, close relationship. It is hard to know what other people are feeling and thinking, but I truly felt that this quiet lady had an enormous faith in God and a strong drive to help others.

The reports in the papers about the NATO meeting were stunning. They raved over George—his knowledge, his ability to persuade, just everything about him. George told me that Jim Baker and Brent Scowcroft deserved a lot of the credit because they had been through some very difficult negotiations on nuclear weapons and other matters. Even the papers at home were very kind and called the meeting a great success.

We flew from Brussels to spend a day or two with the Kohls in Germany. Hannelore is an old friend and a bright, charming lady, so it was an easy visit. We did many things, but the most fun was flying over much of Germany in a helicopter. I couldn't get over just how clean West Germany was. There were absolutely no old used cars or farm equipment left around to rust and no garbage. Where did they send it?

We also took a beautiful boat trip on the Rhine River from Oberwesel to Koblenz. I wrote in my diary:

Listened to a great men's singing group, went by the famous Lorelei Rock and finally at 2:30 or 3 o'clock went into a marvelous buffet lunch. All the time we were passing castles and lovely old towns, great looking trains went by, people waved from windows and streets, boys rode bikes down the bike path waving all the time, people waved American flags and flags hung from their homes and we went by old forts and on and on. It was a joy. The day was bright and sunny, a dream day. I sat next to Helmut

Kohl. It was here that Helmut made my day by saying: "It's great to see a lady with a lusty appetite." Now why doesn't George Bush say something romantic like that?

. . . We flew on to London on a crest of good feeling over the great success in Brussels.

. . . Went off to Number Ten Downing Street to meet up with George. He was talking with Margaret (Thatcher). Denis met us at the door and kissed my hand. The press asked him to do it again. He didn't, so I picked up his hand and kissed it on the spur of the moment. Yikes. Will I never learn? That picture went around the world. George and Margaret appeared, and we went to Buckingham Palace for lunch with Her Majesty and Prince Philip.

The Queen and Prince Philip greeted us, and while the Prince and George reviewed the Scots Guard, Her Majesty and I chatted. She had just returned from a visit to Sarah and Will Farish's farm, Lane's End, in Versailles, Kentucky, and said that she'd had a lovely time. I asked her if she had seen my little puppy. (The second of Millie's pups to leave the nest went to Will and Sarah.) She said rather coolly that we'd talk about that later, and I thought, "Oh my, you are not supposed to ask the Queen a direct question or something."

. . . After lunch Her Majesty led us over to a table with her picture and his in lovely, silver frames. She presented them and then turned over a leather frame and gave it to me with the biggest smile. There was a signed picture of Her Majesty with "Pickles." I was so thrilled that I almost cried. There was our sweet little puppy. She looked so big. Nothing could have made me happier.

One other funny thing happened at that lunch. On the gift table was a small silver bowl with three little feet. George looked at it and asked what it was. The Queen answered: "I don't know. *You* gave it to *ME.*"

That spring our grandson George P. spent some time with us in Washington. He showed no enthusiasm and seemed to have lost all energy, and I worried about his attitude. I shouldn't have wasted the time. He is a marvelous, bright, serious young man. But at the time I worried. I guess that it showed, because after he went to a Baltimore baseball game one night with George, and Dick Darman and his son, I received the most marvelous thank-you letter from Dick. It put everything in perspective and explained my thirteen-year-old grandson to me:

Your grandson is, of course, a great kid. Like boys of all ages he's part of the mystical brotherhood bound together across the generations by bubble gum cards. But what's most remarkable is this: You know how a child's face can seem totally blank at times—and then all of a sudden, it can switch to an open, bright smile that not only transforms the child's face, but seems to capture the very heart of life at its best. It's almost a trap. Just as one is wondering how to get through the blank stare, one is totally drawn in and engaged with spirit transformation.

Our kids have perfected the blank face and the transformation—and I am always vulnerable to the trap, surprised and delighted each time.

But the most dramatically delightful version of the transformation I've ever seen is that of George P., when he goes from the essence of non-communicative blankness to that fantastically engaging smile. I bet it gets you every time. It sure got me.

I have read over the years some not-too-nice things about Dick Darman, who was George's budget director. I also have read that he won me over. He certainly did. I also loved his wife, Kath, and I loved his relationship to his own boys. Like John Sununu, he does not suffer fools gladly either and that does not serve him well. But among the many nice things he did was to remind me that thirteen-year-old boys live a life of their own. How could a mother of four boys have forgotten so soon?

Thursday was my 64th birthday. I swam a mile as I did every other day this week . . . It is a well-known fact that I detest birthdays (mine, that is). If you are in public life everyone feels they have to remember. That darn Willard Scott mentioned my birthday on the "Today" show—and I'm not even 100—so I spent the day thanking people and answering the phone. I did talk to all our children, including Jeb from Indonesia. I sat down to a quiet lunch with a book, and when my dessert came in, it was an adorable little chocolate present, wrapped in a candy ribbon, sitting in a sauce. Below the present were some musical notes and when hummed:

You got it—Happy Birthday to you! So sweet. I could kill myself. I was too dumb to take a picture!

Every year we were in the White House something happened on our birthdays to make them hard to ignore. The next year, I got a phone call that really amused me. The White House operator told me that she had a call for me from a Mr. William Wright. Normally if I didn't know someone, I would not take the call and ask her to transfer it to the office. However, I decided to take this one as his name sounded familiar. This nice voice said that it was his birthday, too, and he just couldn't believe that I had accepted his call. He said that he was a history teacher who called the White House often, only to be told that "the First Lady and the President were busy." I thanked him for calling and wished him a happy birthday. Once again he said that he could not believe that I had accepted his call. I explained that normally I wouldn't have, but I wanted to wish him a happy birthday. He said, "You're kidding." I repeated, "Happy Birthday," and hung up. I'm afraid that I left a very confused man.

I believe that was the same year that George gave me the most unusual present. I had mentioned in passing that although there were hundreds of different kinds of athletic shoes, it was really hard to buy Keds, the old-fashioned sneaker. The next time I'm going to say diamonds, for on my birthday George dragged in a bag of twenty-four different styles, colors, and patterns of Keds. He had written the company president and asked him to send what he had. So, just to tease George, I divided them into three lots for Camp David, Kennebunkport, and the White House, but did not match up the pairs. So I now wear the purple with the black or the pink with the orange, and so on. I love watching children's faces as they poke their mothers and point.

In July we celebrated a truly important birthday in Maine: George's mother's eighty-eighth. Mom seemed so much better. She was stronger than she had been and came to us from the bungalow for cocktails. The family—all forty of us—sang "Happy Birthday," and then George, who was sitting next to his mother on the couch, reached over and said, "Mom, you've had eighty-eight birthdays. Tell us about the best." And she said, quick as a wink, "Well, of course, today, George. I am sitting here holding the hand of my son, the President of the

United States of America." That was a precious moment; one that you want to hold on to forever.

         A few days later we left for our first G-7 Economic Summit, held that year in Paris. First, however, we stopped in Poland for a thrilling visit. We could not have chosen a more exciting time to be there.

The Solidarity party had just won an overwhelming victory in the first free elections under Communist rule. Two years earlier, General Jaruzelski had told George that Solidarity was dead. Now they were on the verge of taking power. The General himself seemed more relaxed, and his wife, Barbara, seemed much thinner than I remembered and spoke better English.

We hosted a lunch at the ambassador's residence in Warsaw that was memorable for several reasons. First, it was hot as the dickens and was held outside. George immediately suggested that coats be removed, and everybody seemed thrilled with the idea. When General Jaruzelski arrived and was told to remove his coat, he seemed hesitant. But then he retired into the back room and came out in his shirtsleeves. Later, when they insisted that he give a toast, he confessed that he had removed his suspenders and was afraid to give too long a speech in fear that his trousers might fall.

The second thing I remember is sitting between the General and a Solidarity leader, Janusz Onyszkiewicz, who had spent many years in jail. Tension seemed at a minimum, considering the circumstances.

Also, the Polish people, men and women, smoked all the time. It smelled terrible.

The next day we flew to Gdańsk, where we first visited Bishop Goclowski. He gave us a quick tour of the six-hundred-year-old Oliva Cathedral with its beautiful panels of the kings and an amazing organ that has extraordinary carved wooden figures that move.

We went right from there to the home of Lech and Danuta Walesa, which was new for them. Before the election they and their eight children lived in only half of the house; the other half was headquarters for Solidarity. Now they would have both halves of what was a rather small duplex. They were so excited. We were led into a small room with a table that could hold eight people. Each place was set with six different glasses, and we were fed enormous amounts of food and drink while Lech talked a mile a minute through an interpreter:

He is bewitching. For starters, he began this monologue with all the things George had been going to say to him: that they must have economic reform, etc. During the course of the conversation he talked about his responsibility as a Nobel Peace Prize winner, an obligation to do something for his country. I also remember him saying that when this all started he couldn't have dared ask for free elections, an elected Parliament, etc. He said that they just started by asking for bread and it went from there.

. . . Danuta is shy and quiet, but when she smiles it is a joy.

After lunch the four of us drove to the shipyard. The roads were jammed, and as he looked at the crowds, Lech spoke his only English, saying over and over, "Oh, my God, fantastic." As we got closer, he said, "Ten times more than Margaret Thatcher." The Polish estimated the crowd at 250,000. I looked out over an ocean of people and saw ABC's Peter Jennings, up on a press platform, surrounded by people as far as the eye could see. Imagine my surprise when I read in the White House press summary that he had started out his program that night asking, "Why has President Bush had such disappointing crowds?"

We left Poland on a real high. It was so exciting to see democracy coming—slowly, painfully—but coming.

From there we went on to Hungary, where we were met in Budapest by Interim President Straub and his wife, Dr. Gertrude Szabolcsi. They were both charming scientists who spoke English well and were familiar with the United States. He was an interim president only because the Hungarians were in the middle of trying to write a constitution and deciding what kind of government they wanted.

Although we arrived in a terrible thunderstorm, the streets were lined with waving, cheering people. We arrived at Kossuth Square to find 25,000 soaked people. They had spent hours waiting. I am terrified of lightning and could not believe that these dear people braved that storm to see the President of the United States. That was the only thing that got me out on the platform as the storm had returned and lightning and thunder were raging again along with torrents of rain:

A Secret Service agent took off his coat and made George put it on. (I had an umbrella.) President Straub gave quite a long speech and when it came time for George to speak he tore up his talk and spoke briefly from the heart. Then George plunged into the crowd to shake as many hands as he could. There was an elderly woman in the front who looked cold and was literally dripping wet. George whipped off his coat and put it around the woman.

When we got back in the car, I scolded him for giving away the coat. He looked offended and said, "We have so much, Bar, and she looked so cold." Right he was, but he had just given away someone else's coat! He looked shocked and then we all burst out laughing. He sheepishly confessed to the agent and later replaced the coat.

The next day I visited a home for blind retarded children, run by nuns whom I consider close to saints. I then joined George for a fascinating discussion with a group of students, and then went to the Transylvanian Refugee Center at Tahitotfalu. This was a marvelous camp where the community had taken 110 families into their homes and now were helping them build their own on donated property. The refugees came from Transylvania, which was being brutalized by Romania. I visited one of the finished houses and thought it looked like a small Swiss chalet. To them, it looked like heaven. This was the most positive, hopeful refugee camp I had ever visited.

That night our able ambassador, Mark Palmer, and his wife, Sushma, a biochemist, had a large reception at their residence for George. We had a receiving line at the top of the garden and our dear protocol chief, Joseph Reed, stood and greeted the guests and then passed them on to George, saying in the most formal way, "Sir, let me introduce you to the President of the United States and Mrs. Bush." George and I got the giggles. We knew our names. It was theirs he was supposed to pass on. So we shook hands with a stream of officials and never ever knew a name.

After the receiving line, we were about to walk down some stairs into another part of the garden to join an even bigger group when the announcer said, "Ladies and gentlemen, the President of the United States and Mrs. Bush." At that very moment, the Palmer's dog—a big bulldog named Fred, if I remember right—slowly started walking down the stairs. The timing could not have been more perfect. The Palmers were so embarrassed; everyone else loved it.

The next morning we left for Paris and the Economic Summit, which had been planned to coincide with the French Bicentennial Celebration. We went immediately to Place du Trocadéro for the simple but very elegant opening ceremony, followed by a full afternoon:

. . . The spouses lunched in the beautiful heretofore unseen Morny Apartments. About sixty wives of Chiefs of State or Heads of Governments attended this luncheon, so I saw many old friends from around the world. I sat next to Madame Mitterrand and a bright young man who is in charge of the big ceremony on the 14th. He is praying for good weather. So am I. I ate every bite and Danielle nibbled—as she did at every meal. I'm afraid that I didn't change my pattern either, but it is all so good!

I opened the new wing at the American Hospital and back to the embassy to change quickly into a short cocktail dress for a night at the Opera. This was the opening of the new Opera House. I didn't like the building at all, but certainly it had many pluses. The acoustics are marvelous; every chair I am told has a full view of the stage (there are 2,000 seats); the depth of the stage gives amazing versatility to the producer. The minuses to me were that first of all it is ugly, and the stairs going down from the balcony are shallow, steep and there is no hand railing. I found them frightening. The pluses outweigh the minuses. We went on to the newly redone Musée d'Orsay (the old railroad station and now a 19th century museum). We had a great, but slow and late dinner. Home late . . . long after we were in bed we heard fireworks. Danielle Mitterrand told me that they went by to see the people dancing in the streets. After all, they were celebrating 200 years of independence—we know how that feels.

The next morning, July 14, was relaxed, and I had a good visit with Taitsie Curley. Then we went to the Bastille Day Parade and I sat with the spouses. Protocol put me with France, Bangladesh, Egypt, Ivory Coast, Zaire, Mali, Greece, and Uruguay for almost every event:

I sat next to Mrs. Bangladesh and her 6½-year-old little boy who never left her side. There were three of us and two seats. As the parade went on and on he got very restless and bored. He sat on my lap half of the time which was okay with me as, frankly, I got bored also.

We went to the Ministry of Foreign Affairs building for lunch where we stood around for almost an hour and a half. Hannelore Kohl, Margaret Thatcher and I were talking when we noticed that there were hundreds of people outside in the garden having a great time. We saw loads of our friends like Carlos Ortiz de Rozas and his wife Carmen from our U.N. days, and so the three of us escaped to the outdoors to visit. We enjoyed the breeze and friends. I went back to get George, but (someone from) Protocol grabbed me. I think they were panicked that all the captives inside would rush outside—and they were right!

Another great meal. The French certainly live up to their reputation. However, the lunch was 1 hour and 5 minutes late. The number of people being accommodated at all events is amazing—32 different motorcades with police escorts. This of course will end tonight and then the Economic Summit starts.

The leaders from the G-7—the United States, Japan, Great Britain, Italy, Germany, Canada, and France—all went to a working dinner, and the rest of us went to the Hôtel de la Marine for supper. After dinner we all came back together to watch the celebration, a very big dramatic show that we could hardly see through the bulletproof glass and certainly could not hear. We turned up the TV monitor and that helped a lot. The highlight of the evening was when Jessye Norman came out dressed in a flowing blue, white, and red gown, like the French flag, and belted out "La Marseillaise" as you have never heard it sung!

I found all of this very interesting: Jessye was born in Georgia and now lives in Westchester County, New York; the new Opera House was designed by a Uruguayan who now lives in Canada; I. M. Pei, an American, did the Pyramid; and a New Zealander restored the Musée d'Orsay. I think this shows the French have a lot of confidence. I believe that we would feel that we must have an American do all these things.

The minute Jessye finished we took off for our beds. George was exhausted. He had been running from meeting to meeting for two days. When we got into bed, the skies exploded, and I got up and watched the most beautiful fireworks. George never heard a sound.

Here are some of the things I wrote in my diary about the many people we saw during the French Bicentennial:

. . . I had a nice visit with Benazir Bhutto, who truly looks pregnant.

. . . Mila and Brian Mulroney are surely the most attractive couple. She is tall and wonderful. Speaks English, French and some Slavic language. Everyone loves her. Very chic. He is warm as you get to know them.

. . . I am very fond of Suzanne and Hosni Mubarak. She had a Welsh mother and is truly a lovely looking woman, 47 years old, trim and happy looking with two grown sons. He is a dark, handsome man who had a hard time following Sadat, but now seems secure and respected.

. . . I am very fond of Hannelore Kohl, she is bright and full of warmth and outspoken.

. . . Margaret Thatcher seems to be out of sorts with the men both at NATO and the Economic Summit. She is having trouble at home. She is kind to me and I like her and have enormous respect for her.

. . . I really enjoyed President and Mrs. Hillery from Ireland. He has a wonderful job   goes to all the ceremonies and doesn't have the worries of a Head of State. He is a fine, warm, funny person and so is she. Both are medical doctors.

. . . We have enjoyed President and Mrs. Sanguinetti of Uruguay. She has sat at my table and is charming.

. . . Sally Mugabe of Zimbabwe and her husband, President Robert Mugabe, seem to be warm, nice people. They have had many sad suffering times. Both sons died and she had a bad kidney problem.

. . . Elizabeth Diouf of Senegal and her gentle seven-foot-tall husband, Abdou, are highly respected.

. . . Mário Soares from Portugal is charming, very chic.

. . . Corazon Aquino was one of three women who were heading their delegations. She was in France on a state visit on the 12th and 13th and just stayed on. On this visit and all succeeding visits she was warm and friendly.

. . . Marie-Thérèse Houphouet-Boigny of the Ivory Coast was a large, friendly woman.

. . . I was sorry that I didn't get to visit with either of the Gandhis. They both look well. Rather amazing that both India and Pakistan are now headed by the children of assassinated leaders. They are neighbors and enemies and now, getting better, I hope. I like them both so much.

. . . The Greeks, Efrosine and Christos Sartzetakis, newly elected, are unknown to me. I sat at his table, but far away and he hardly spoke.

. . . Mrs. Cameroon, Jeanne Irene Biya, very dignified, quiet and I did no more than greet her and smile at her.

. . . I don't know the name of the President of Bangladesh, but I sat with one of them at every meal. She became a challenge to see if I could wipe the frown off her face. Her little boy appeared at 11 p.m. to see the parade . . . he let us all know he was tired, irritable and couldn't see.

I read a great deal on the trip. This time it was *Foreign Student* by Philippe Labro, suggested to me by Virginia Governor Jerry Baliles. I loved it. I also read *The Dinner Party* by Howard Fast.

I spent a lot of time in Maine that summer. George's mother was frail and I wanted to be nearby, and although I was feeling wonderful, I still suffered from double and sometimes triple vision and had popping, watering eyes, a result of Graves' disease. George came when he could, but he had a lot of problems:

August 3—G. started out west on a three-state visit, but came home after one stop in Chicago. Lt. Colonel William Higgins, who has been a hostage for months, was rumored to have been executed yesterday. It is very complicated, but the Israelis kidnapped a sheik last Friday because of a terrorist Arab attack on Israel which they claimed was because of an ambush attack on the Arabs earlier, which they said was caused by etc. The extremists say that until the sheik is freed they will kill a hostage daily. Poor Pop has the weight of the world on his shoulders.

The children came and went with their children, and they all were wonderful and continued to be a joy. Noelle at twelve years old took painting lessons and was producing some pretty sweet watercolors. She was wonderful with her younger girl cousins, who looked up to her at all times. One of the younger girls found a mini sanitary napkin and asked Noelle what it was. She didn't know what to say and, thinking fast, said that ladies put them under their arms to stop perspiration. The little girl then wore them under her arms the rest of the day—until she ran into her mother.

Noelle struck up a great friendship with her cousin Wendy Stapleton, and when George and Laura's twins arrived, they dogged the two older girls all the time. Noelle and Wendy spent some time trying to hide from their seven-year-old cousins. Then Neil and Sharon's Lauren arrived, and she wanted to do everything that Jenna and Barbara did and they tried to hide from her. It never changes.

All four of the older granddaughters slept in the dormitory, a large room on the third floor of our house that has five beds.

One night I went up to put the little girls to bed and hear their prayers. As we all knelt, Barbara said the Lord's Prayer, and Jenna made up a sweet personal prayer. Five-year-old Lauren thought very carefully and finally thanked God for flowers and little animals. So cute.

George finally came to get some R&R and spent a great deal of time on his boat fishing. With our boat, the press boats, and the Secret Service and Coast Guard boats, we were a small armada. Unfortunately, George was not having much luck. One of the Maine papers ran a "Day 1—No Fish" column with a picture of a fish with a line drawn through it. The press showed up at the Bush/Mulroney press conference with the logo on their T-shirts, which George loved. We got up to "Day 14—No Fish." That day, as George and I left on the boat, a small delegation headed by Betsy and Spike Heminway and made up of our children, grandchildren, and the staff carried homemade posters encouraging George to catch a fish. They thought they were so funny—and they were.

September 4— . . . Now is truly our last day.

. . . it has been a great summer.

. . . George's mom has been a beautiful, uncomplaining wisp of a thing wandering around trying to dump her nurses and enjoying being with her children and grandchildren. She is the most selfless person and a joy to be with.

. . . On Saturday we had our big press picnic on the Point. We served only hamburgers and hot dogs with all the trimmings. They came with their families and it was loads of fun.

. . . On Sunday morning George went to the annual church breakfast, met us at church where he spoke and then with Marvin, Brent Scowcroft and I took off in the boat for Boone Island. We hadn't been out five minutes when George saw a lone gull diving and announced that we would slow down and troll for a minute. With Marvin at the wheel and three rods in, George announced that he had a fish and, lo and behold, he did! The press charged over on their four chartered boats and pictures were gotten by all. Then they all blew their horns. It was so sweet. I believe that they were all pulling for him.

Shortly after we got back I received an honor that had been a long time coming. I did not earn it, nor did I deserve it, but when Smith College gave me an honorary degree, I was thrilled. It meant a lot to me as my Dad would have been so pleased.

I did a lot of traveling that fall for literacy programs all over the country and was lucky enough to return to Midland to dedicate the George Herbert Walker Bush Elementary School, the first in the country to be named after him. How we teased George, for the school board vote was a "landslide"—three to two in favor. Now I must quickly add that they had to break the rules for George—you were supposed to be dead to have a school named for you in Midland County.

I soon got used to waking up in hotel rooms and sleeping in strange beds. One morning I was up early having a cup of coffee and listening to a local radio station for the news. Much to my shock the phone rang and it was the same "live" radio talk show. I said that Mrs. Bush was ASLEEP. They rang a little later and once again asked for Mrs. Bush, and I said, "Not available." I got the giggles, for I had gone out over the airwaves twice, both times sounding really grumpy. I suspected the bellboy who had brought the coffee had slipped his friend the room number.

I visited so many wonderful programs, from the restored Majestic Theater in San Antonio; to the Cal Farley Boys Ranch outside of Amarillo, Texas; to Eugene Lang's "I Have a Dream" classes, where a person, family, or group adopts a class and promises to help them go to college IF they will stay off drugs and stay in school; to WOW (Wider Opportunities for Women), a national program which helps get women off welfare and achieve economic independence. I attended the United Nations International Literacy Day, hosted a coffee for the Second National Adult Literacy Congress, and taped tributes for "Disney Salutes the American Teacher." I was on "Sesame Street" and "Oprah Winfrey" and marched in Chicago's Columbus Day parade—and much, much more.

One of the most important events of the fall was the Education Summit held at the University of Virginia in Charlottesville. It was attended by almost all the governors and many of their wives and George's entire cabinet. He had made education a top priority, and this meeting was an important step. They all divided into working groups, rolled up their sleeves, and came up with some very good guidelines which eventually became part of George's America 2000 program, his blueprint on how to improve education in our country and which is still being used today. I was very impressed to learn that Clinton's Secretary of Education, Richard Riley, decided it was not necessary to "reinvent the wheel."

As part of the summit, we hosted a dinner in Monticello, the home of Thomas Jefferson. What a house. Hours could be spent studying this extraordinary man and his home, where he lived with fourteen grandchildren. That in itself made him special. I wrote in my diary:

We had a reception in the house and then went to a lovely dinner in a truly beautiful tent. I sat next to Terry Branstad (Governor of Iowa and chairman of the National Governors' Association) and Bill Clinton (Governor of Arkansas) who went out of his way to be charming. I wouldn't be at all surprised if he runs in 1992. He is very attractive and seems to have analyzed both Carter and Dukakis pretty thoroughly.

The next morning the cabinet and governors split into three groups: "Choice and Restructuring"; "A Competitive Work Force and Lifelong Learning"; and "Post-Secondary Education: Strengthening Access and Excellence." We visited all three groups and heard their recommendations. George sat at the table, and I sat with the spouses behind them.

After the early morning session the spouses all retired to another hall, and I called on several wives who had said they would be willing to share with us projects they were involved with. It was fascinating:

One who had expressed an interest in sharing was Hillary Clinton from Arkansas, who gave us a good rundown on her program H.I.P.Y. [Home Instruction for Pre-School Youths]. This is a program that goes right into the home and works with families. She has modeled it after a program that was started in Israel and also is being used in Florida and a few other states. She is a lawyer and very bright and articulate. I noticed that they, the Clintons, were the last to appear for everything. [Shades of things to come?]

I called on Sue Ann Thompson from Wisconsin. She is a sixth grade teacher and read a wish list of things she wanted in schools. I noticed that people turned off pretty much over that. Typical. The only one who had practical experience and people were turned off. She is one really bright, nice lady.

Julie Mabus from Mississippi has put a lot of energy and focus on literacy in her state and done it in a very professional way. I liked her very much.

Martha Wilkinson from Kentucky has "Martha's GED Army." She has made it "chic" to get a GED.

Lynne Cheney spoke as a cabinet wife and as the chairman of the National Endowment for the Humanities and urged that we train teachers for the arts along with the sciences.

Then I asked Jeannie Baliles, wife of the Governor of Virginia, to tell us just how she set up her state's private-public sector foundation to work with literacy. She is a ball of fire and has done a real job in her state and shown great leadership in the field.

I spoke about the Barbara Bush Foundation for Family Literacy.

At the luncheon the sharing continued. Shirley Bellmon from Oklahoma told us about her Cottage Industries program that she started. Her project has allowed women to stay in the home, be with their children, continue their education, gain in self-worth and on and on.

I called on Susan Bayh from Indiana, wife of the youngest governor, Evan Bayh. Susan has taken literacy on in her state with a capital L. Evan was a classmate of Marvin's at St. Alban's. I knew his mother and father well.

Bea Romer from Colorado shared a brochure with us on The Year of the Reader, the Library of Congress initiative.

Matilda Cuomo also shared with us her mentoring program in New York State. It seems many states are getting into mentoring—a big brother, big sister concept.

Pat DiPrete talked about Rhode Island's plan to put all children through college.

This session gave us all a lot to think about.

I remember thinking what an incredible group of women they were, and I was impressed by their significant contributions to their states.

*   *   *

⤳ So many momentous things happen in the daily life of a president that it is hard to know what to comment on. The fall of 1989 was no exception:

George got a capital gains tax reduction—a victory.

Hurricane Hugo devastated several southern states.

There was a failed coup in Panama.

A tremendous earthquake rocked San Francisco. I found myself thinking: Does it ever stop?

And on a personal level, Bishop John Walker died. He was a friend besides being the bishop of the diocese of the District of Columbia. We went to the service at the National Cathedral, and when we got home, George sat down and wrote John's children the most wonderful letter. I was amazed and felt guilty that I hadn't thought of doing the same thing.

We took District of Columbia Delegate Walter Fauntroy to the cathedral with us, and while we were waiting in the car for George, he told me that he was mad at the President. His wife had seen George holding a drug baby and had said, "Walter, you spend your life going to foreign countries helping other people. From now on we are going to help Americans. You and I are going to adopt an abandoned crack baby." At the time of the funeral they were going through an eight-week indoctrination course and eventually they got their baby. At fifty years of age, that was quite a commitment for Walter and his wife, Dorothy. George and I were both thrilled by that story.

⤳ There also were dramatic developments in Eastern Europe as the Iron Curtain literally fell open. The world was changing right before our eyes, and every day George faced a new challenge. I wrote in my diary:

November 11—This has been the most extraordinary week. Turmoil around and across the world. Deng Xiaoping in the PRC has stepped down. The East Germans have opened their borders and people are pouring out. The Soviet Union, which is sitting on a time bomb, is not objecting. The longest ruling dictator in Eastern Europe (Bulgaria) has stepped down. "A new breeze is blowing" and the people of the world really do want freedom. Every now and then this week I have wanted to shout:

"Why are we doing our regular thing? Why aren't we dancing in the streets and singing and rejoicing?" I guess because as each new thing happens we also see so much to be done and we may well be looking at chaos. George certainly is President at the most interesting of times. His job seems to be putting Humpty Dumpty back together again without endangering the rest of the world.

. . . I heard him on the phone yesterday talking to Helmut Kohl. Helmut had been in Poland on a visit, but raced back home. Imagine people flooding into West Germany. Not just families being reunited, but food, housing and jobs to be found. Many people were overwhelmed, filled bags with oranges and rushed back over the border to East Germany. They had not seen an abundance of food like that for forty years. The stories were so moving.

We really got laughing for some people were not so pleased with the wall coming down. But the man we liked best was the guard at the wall. He said that he didn't like it one bit as that meant he'd lose his job. He has a point. No wall, no job.

Later that week we greeted Lech Walesa at the White House, accompanied by Lane Kirkland, president of the AFL-CIO, and Mrs. Kirkland. The East Room was jammed with the cabinet and members of the United States labor unions. These people had been supportive of Solidarity, the labor movement in Poland, and it was right and proper that they be there when Lech Walesa received the Medal of Freedom, the highest honor our president can bestow on a foreigner. This surely must have been one of the most moving ceremonies that we held in the White House. Lech stood there with tears in his eyes and gulped several times while George gave an inspired speech and the citation was read. Lech suddenly represented "every man" who ever had lived behind the Iron Curtain. There was not a dry eye in the room. Lech Walesa truly changed the course of the world. He said over and over again that he "couldn't believe that he was in this great land of the free."

We had a receiving line that took forever because everyone wanted to shake his hand. Unbeknownst to those of us in the line, there was a small drama happening in the State Dining Room. As this was a very special reception and was late in the afternoon, we had a heavily laden dining table covered with many trays of food, candelabras, and beautiful flower arrangements. One of our larger guests backed up to our lovely antique table and rested against it—well, really put a large amount of his rather large body on the table. The table broke in the middle and food, candelabras, and flowers crashed to the floor. The staff coped with it all and by the time the receiving line ended, all had been propped up and the guilty guest had slipped out never to be seen again. The table was gone for three months undergoing repairs.

George very kindly invited me to join him for four small, working dinners in November that gave me a front-row seat to everything that was happening:

One was with President Nixon, who had just returned from China. Nobody is more interesting when it comes to world affairs.

The second was a dinner with Henry Kissinger who also had just been in China. Deng Xiaoping told Henry that he still believed in all the things he believed in before—reaching out to the world, modernization, etc. Deng asked Henry why we were so shocked over Tiananmen when the Cultural Revolution was going on when we opened relations with the PRC. He pointed out that surely that was much worse. He had a point.

And the third dinner was with Lech Walesa. It was such a great evening. He is such a charming man. I truly felt that I noticed a big difference from last July. I think he is beginning to see the world as it is and not as he wanted it to be. He is also beginning to think of Poland as part of the whole. He mentioned that Germany must not be united again. (This did not come as a surprise because we found that most Europeans felt the same way. They remember German occupation and those memories are not pleasant.) Lech also mentioned that the stories of the East Germans being overwhelmed by all that fruit did not surprise him. He said that they were better off than most people in Poland. We Americans take so much for granted.

The fourth dinner was when our dear friend Prime Minister Brian Mulroney and Joe Clark from Canada came to debrief George after their trip to the Soviet Union. The fall of 1989 George was under criticism for not acting and for being "prudent" when it came to pushing for change in Germany and Eastern Europe. The dinner was fascinating. First of all they had spent hours with the leadership. They said 10 hours with one leader, 5 hours with Gorbachev and 8 hours with another man. They must have been dead tired as their whole trip was very short. Gorbachev asked many questions about George. He is scared to death of Germany reuniting. Brian quoted Gorbachev as saying several times, "One can be poisoned by eating unripened fruit." I think that meant: "Don't push us, we're not ready." Who knows? Gorby seemed to be sending a message to George that they were not going to be coming to the table with any flamboyant gestures. They all agreed that the Soviet economy is absolutely the worst. Amazingly enough Brian and Joe got the feeling that Gorby was relaxed about his future and his worries were Germany's reunification and not about putting bread on the table. Brian said that he acknowledged his domestic problems, but did not want a handout, but did want loans. Our side (Jimmy Baker, Brent Scowcroft, Bob Gates and our ambassador to Canada, Ed Ney) all agreed that the Soviet Union had to stop spending 5 billion dollars in Central America and Cuba before we could start giving them loans.

. . . The press is all over George for not taking immediate action. Gorby is getting a great welcome in Italy today where he and Raisa are on a state visit. She is also. George says to remember what our aim is—democracy to take the place of a dictatorship. Well, that's what's happening in Eastern Europe. We are getting what we want. They may not be yelling "George, George," but we are getting a freer world. He is so wise.

Just when I thought this life of our was going to overwhelm me, something would happen to remind me "real life goes on." I wrote in my diary on November 30:

Doro called and said that she went to a teacher's meeting and the teacher said that Sam (age 5) was a very bright boy, but that he was in cahoots with two other little boys. When the teacher asks a question Sam will raise his hand and when called upon will say, "Toilet," and then the two other boys burst out laughing. The teacher asked for help. She also said that Sam and the two other boys blow on their hands and make "fart" noises and then die laughing. Hard on the teacher, to say the least. Doro went on to say that Sam came home, opened the door and said, "Any calls?" Doro said, "Why would anyone call?" No answer. Then Doro said, "Sam, I won't scold you, but why would someone call?" He said, "I said a bad word." Doro tried to find out the word and he wouldn't tell. He finally said that it started out, "nnnnnnn." Well, finally Doro had to ask as she did not know any "nnnnn" words. It turned out that Sam said "naked body." Funny boy. History repeats itself every generation, doesn't it?

In early December George was scheduled to meet with Gorbachev on Malta, off the coast of Italy. We all agreed that it would be better if I stayed home. I had written Raisa and invited her to meet me in Florence while the men were in Malta. She very politely turned me down by saying that she had been to Florence. Sad to say, I hadn't and still haven't.

The men truly had a fascinating meeting. George tells me that it was pleasant with no friction. The earlier briefings by Andreotti of Italy and Mulroney of Canada made it easier. As George spoke first, he could make suggestions without Gorbachev having to ask. The suggestions were mutually beneficial to all of us. He had a short, pleasant visit with Mrs. G. . . . George said he adored his time on the ship rolling around out there. I would have hated it.

While George was gone the annual Kennedy Center Honors came and went. It is one of the most exciting, fun evenings of the year. The honorees that year were Alexandra Danilova, Harry Belafonte, Claudette Colbert, Mary Martin, and William Schuman. I wrote in my diary:

George, of course, would have done the honors, but it worked out very well. We would have all preferred to have him where he was—making a kinder and gentler *AND* more peaceful world . . . It was a star-studded evening: Helen Hayes, Dina Merrill and her new husband, Ted Hartley, Marvin Hamlisch and his new bride, Terre, Larry Hagman, Leontyne Price and her brother General George Price, Gloria and Jimmy Stewart, Sidney Poitier, Don Ameche, Lynn Redgrave, Isaac Stern, Kelly McGillis, Gregory Peck, Bernadette Peters, Van Cliburn and his amazing mother Rildia Bee . . . it was three hours of joy, great music and dance. The show opened with the Red Army Song and Dance Ensemble. It was a rousing opening and so appropriate with the "non-summit" that was going on in that rough Mediterranean at that very time. Bishop Desmond Tutu came to honor Harry Belafonte for his work with UNICEF and the oppressed in South Africa. That got a great ovation. The evening ended with the Soviets singing "God Bless America." It was so unbelievably moving . . . I raced backstage to thank them all before I left. There were such good vibes running around the room. It was a very special evening. We did not stay for dinner. Those other poor people had dinner at 11 p.m.!

Christmas in the White House was a joy. Planning had begun from almost the minute we moved in. I thought Nancy Clarke and Gary Walters were teasing me when they came to talk to me about the Christmas theme in February. But the decorations are all made inhouse, and the ribbons and other materials have to be ordered early. We settled on a Story Book theme, which seemed appropriate to my interest in reading. Down in the bowels of the first floor the flower shop worked all year. Often when I would drop by I would see figures appearing that looked like Aladdin with smoke coming out of his magic lamp, Babar and Miss Rumphius, a favorite of mine by author Barbara Cooney. Sometimes I met several women who were volunteering their time to make doll costumes, bows, and so on.

We started celebrating Christmas early, on November 27, when Marshall and I rode the cherry picker to the top of the National Christmas Tree to put on the star. After that, we did something almost every day:

December 5—I went to Mazza Gallerie in Washington to shop, but more to make a statement about the Salvation Army. I read in the paper that many malls across the country had banned the bell-ringers. Who can think of Christmas without the Salvation Army bell-ringers? So we let the press know that I was going shopping at the Mazza Gallerie because they permitted the Army to stand outside with their pots and bells. I dropped $11 in the pot with the press watching. The response was immediate and good. Georgetown Mall immediately permitted them in. [We later heard from the Salvation Army that that small gesture truly had filled their coffers.]

December 6—An 18-foot Fraser Fir from Spartansburg, Penn., was delivered on a horse-drawn wagon.

December 7—I flew to Houston to do many events and while there dropped by St. Martin's Church to pick up a crèche that they made for us. I went dreading it thinking that although it would be great to see our dear church family friends, it would be a homemade job. Not at all. What a surprise. It is absolutely magnificent. I have never seen such beautiful work. It is enormous, more than 5 feet. Along with the kings and shepherds there are some 50 pieces including C. Fred, Millie, Bevo (the University of Texas long-horned steer mascot) and an armadillo all done in the most beautiful needlepoint adoring the baby Jesus. I felt ashamed that I thought that I was doing a kindness to tuck in a visit to see my friends.

I was to fly from Texas to Andrews Air Force Base and then drive up to Camp David to join George, who was flying in several hours earlier from some other part of the country. We heard that the weather was closing in and that although George could fly in a copter up to Camp David, I might have trouble driving up later because of icy conditions. George opted not to go on the chance that I couldn't make it. Thus bad weather gave us one of the very nicest experiences we had in George's four years as President: watching the Christmas decoration go up.

When I got home at 1 a.m., Dennis Freemyer, a young White House usher, gave me an early morning tour of the State Floor and already it looked wonderful. George and Millie were sound asleep. For years volunteers had been invited to come help decorate. They arrive a week ahead of time, working in a warehouse and then moving to the White House the final weekend to put up all their finery. They decorate all the rooms and, of course, the big tree in the middle of the Blue Room. These wonderful people come during their vacations and at their own expense. Many of them have come every year and are an enormous help.

We awakened to discover our family tree was up in the Yellow Oval Room, a glorious 14-foot tree. It had been put up the afternoon before by some White House elves. It was covered with thousands of tiny white lights, decorated gingerbread Christmas cookies that Paula makes, and our own decorations collected over the years. George and I went down and met the volunteers and invited them to come upstairs to see our family Christmas decorations and the new crèche. I am constantly amazed at how little it takes to make other people happy. In any case, it made us very happy to show off our lovely house, Lincoln Bedroom and all.

Saturday night we sneaked off and took our children to our favorite restaurant, the Peking Gourmet, that Marvin had discovered in Virginia. When we came home, the staff and volunteers were putting snow on the 17 large trees in the front entrance and the grand cross hall on the State Floor and this had disintegrated into a snowball fight.

December 10—We attended the "Christmas in Washington" program that NBC puts on every year at the Pension Building. The stars were Olivia Newton-John, Diahann Carroll and her husband, Vic Damone, the flutist James Galway, Take 6, the Eastern High School Choir, the United States Naval Academy Glee Club and the United States Army Band Herald Trumpets. George invited the guests back for a drink and a preview of the decorations. We ended by singing Christmas carols around the piano in the East Room.

What a treat for us. Vic Damone told George that he had read that George yelled his name when he threw a ringer in horseshoes. True. George does yell "Vic . . . Vic Damone" when he throws a ringer. Short, of course, for victory. Olivia Newton-John is a lovely looking young woman and very nice.

December 11—We had the press preview of the first floor. The tree in the Blue Oval Room is covered with 80 storybook characters.

That same night we began two weeks of holiday receptions with the Congressional Ball. Every member of Congress is invited with his or her spouse. Laurie Firestone told me that any event with Congress was a hassle. They want to bring several guests or bring a staff member. When Laurie stood firm, they would try to appeal directly to us. Some just plain showed up with the uninvited. There are 435 House members and 100 senators, so the potential for this party is well over 1,000. George and I stood in a receiving line for several hours that night and almost all the nights following.

We held "eclectic" receptions, with a mix each night of cabinet members, the Supreme Court, the staff, the Secret Service, the press, and friends. It was much nicer for all, we felt, and we kept the tradition all four years. George and I would stand in front of the tree in a receiving line, have pictures taken with those who wanted them, go into the East Room to enjoy the entertainment, and then after several hours head back upstairs with aching knees and happy hearts.

During the public tours during the day, groups of singers, choirs, or bell ringers came from all over the country to entertain. We often would open the door to the private residence at the top of the Grand Staircase just to hear the music. As the grandchildren arrived for the holidays, they sat on the steps and listened. Neil often took his children down and talked to the tourists. It is such a special time.

On December 12 I had the Diplomatic Children's party, sponsored by THIS (The Hospitality and Information Service, kind of a Welcome Wagon for foreign dignitaries). It was a mob of little ones, each with a camera. We asked the cast of *A Christmas Carol* from Ford's Theatre to come and do a little scene. I was to sit on the floor surrounded by children, and I spent the whole program wondering how

I was going to stand up again, I could see the pictures of me crawling around trying to get up. As it turned out, a nice military aide stepped up and gave me his hand. Marshall Bush loved the whole afternoon and ran around being a little hostess.

On the thirteenth I went to the Central Union Mission in Washington to help give out Christmas bags to the children. The mission has a wonderful program where different groups—such as employees at the FBI—are given information about a specific child so they can fill a bag with toys, clothes, books, and other gifts for that child. I was supposed to read from Luke, chapter 2, verses 1 through 20, which is the story of the birth of Jesus. I took one look at those preschool children and realized that they were way too young and talked to them about the birth instead.

George lit the National Christmas Tree on the fourteenth. Willard Scott once again came to our rescue and dressed like Santa. Loretta Lynn and her daughter Peggy sang, and Tommy Tune sang and danced.

In the midst of all this activity George flew to St. Martin in the Caribbean for a brief meeting with Mitterrand.

Then our children and grandchildren started to arrive for our first Christmas in the White House and life became really wild.

The girls and I took the granddaughters to *The Nutcracker.* Ellie and Marshall were a little young. At one time one of the girls leaned over to the other and said, "Say peepee." Fortunately both girls were sitting on my lap, so I stopped that immediately. (Guess which little girl had picked up bad habits from big brother?) Sharon was not so lucky. One night she took the children to the President's Box at the Kennedy Center to hear carols, and in a quiet moment (one of the little boys) said in a loud voice, "My penis hurts." Sharon raced him out and brought them all home. Poor little guy, it turned out his suspenders were too tight. It makes me giggle just to think of that.

Then we had two parties that we had started in the Vice President's House that were really fun. On the seventeenth we had what we called our family brunch. This started out to be a few friends with their children and some of the Houston friends that our children had grown up with. Thank heavens we had moved to the White House, for by 1989 we had grown to 170 people. Our friends' children had gotten married, and grandchildren had gotten married and they also were having children. We loved that party, and had George been reelected, we might have had to rent a larger ballroom. We started out in the East Room, where we had entertainment for the children, and then moved upstairs to the second and third floors for a buffet lunch. (In case you're wondering who paid for this, the answer is "George Bush." It's a very good question. At the White House, if the event is business or official, you, the taxpayer, pay for it. If it is personal, the president pays for it. The staff is very careful about keeping track of which is which.)

Finally, for the last party, we invited all the household help and their families. It was fun to meet the spouses and children of all the people who worked so hard, not only at Christmas but all year round, to keep the People's House as near perfect as possible. We watched their children grow over those four years.

December 23— . . . Well, here we are at Camp David after a busy two weeks of Christmas parties at the White House. People raved over how the White House looked and it was true, but I have to say that every year I have gone away thinking "This year was the most beautiful." Well, *this* year was the most beautiful!

. . . We had catastrophe after catastrophe. I guess that happens when you have 11 children together. Little Jebby got a fever. George P. cut his chin while ice-skating and had to have five stitches. Jenna got the flu. Noelle hurt her wrist and had to go to the hospital nearby. It was not broken as Burt Lee was afraid, but was sprained. WOW!

. . . There was lots of action in our house all week, really from Sunday on. Brent Scowcroft, Jim Baker, Colin Powell, Dick Cheney, Bob Gates and John Sununu were in and out of the residence. On Tuesday night after our Christmas reception, the crowd gathered upstairs again and George told me after they had gone that we were invading Panama the next morning, December 20th, at 1 a.m. He stayed up until 4 a.m. He called many heads of state to tell them what we were doing.

. . . This past week has been a real history-maker. On Wednesday morning George sent troops into Panama for many valid reasons. #1. They had elections several months ago and Noriega was beaten three to one and yet he overturned the people's vote and took power. #2. He declared war on the USA and then a Marine was murdered. #3. His troops harassed a Naval officer, beat him and his wife and sexually threatened his wife. #4. We have thousands of American citizens in Panama. #5. They have violated our treaty. Sad to say, Noriega again was not caught, but his government is out of power and the duly elected government is now in power. We are praying that he will be caught right away. We lost 24 American men and are heartbroken about that. It is hard being president.

George reported to the nation the morning after the invasion at 7:15 a.m. The support is pretty universal across the country.

Then during the week there were rumblings in Romania and the impossible happened. Ceauşescu fled last night and at this moment chaos is in charge. The sad part is that Ceauşescu had really torn the country apart and there is no structure left. Their son is under arrest, but they escaped by helicopter to an unknown place. What a world. A new breeze is blowing. I was really shocked to hear that when Gorbachev announced the overthrow or the falling apart of the dictatorship, the Russian Congress cheered.

December 24—George flew down to the White House to have a press conference and back again. When he got back he went over to see the boys play Wally Ball. While there he got the phone call saying that Noriega had sought refuge in the Embassy of the Vatican. Finding Noriega made our Christmas.

December 25—We had 30 for lunch that first Christmas at Camp David.

December 26—We awakened this morning to see pictures from Panama showing the people cheering the Americans.

Ceauşescu and his wife were captured, tried, found guilty and executed on the spot. It certainly brought back many memories. Imagine people we had dined with not so many years ago are now dead.

After Christmas George made his annual trip to Beeville, Texas, to hunt. He called me from there to tell me that Sandy Ellis, George's sister Nancy's husband, had died. God bless him. He was a darling brother-in-law who after a series of strokes had faded away over the last few years. Sandy was the first of us to die.

I barely had hung up when George W. called me with the best news:

Charles Walker Bush had been born and was waiting for Marvin, Margaret, and Marshall to come pick him up. Marvin and Margaret had been wanting to adopt another child for some time and were thrilled. There was something sort of mystical about this, a death and a birth.

On New Year's Eve, the last day of the year and the decade, George and I flew to San Antonio to visit the wounded from Panama. We went immediately to a church service on the base, and then visited the troops:

We went on to Wilford Hall, where we saw about 21 or so of the wounded. There had been 200 in all to begin with, but so many of them had gone home or been transferred to hospitals nearer their homes. After Wilford Hall we went on to the Brook Burn Hospital and saw 11 more. It was one of the most moving experiences. First of all we were warned by the General who met us that they were an unusual group and it had been a privilege to doctor them. . . . They were all proud of what they had done and, he said, they all wanted to go back.

. . . They had horrendous wounds, from head wounds to the feet.

. . . They had members of their families with them. I saw several rooms where the mother, father, and stepmother and stepfather were all there together reflecting, I guess, the new world.

. . . There were mixed marriages . . . many. A very handsome black man with two beautiful boys and a lovely Filipino wife told George, "I couldn't have better care if I had all Donald Trump's money."

. . . In one room were two very young boys who had been in the same unit . . . they both had "fragment wounds," which I believe meant that something blew up around them. Both boys had families with them. The first boy had a tube in his nose and looked scared. We had been told that both boys had colostomies. . . . I said to the scared boy, "You know there is a life after a colostomy. Our son has one and plays wonderful tennis, jogs, and has a beautiful wife and a family." The mother from NYC whispered to me, "Thank you for saying that." The boy in the next bed was a 20-year-old with a mother, wife and fat little baby girl. He said that the first thing they told him was that our son had one. Marvin would be pleased to hear that.

. . . There were about six paraplegics, and they were amazing. One boy with a big loving Hispanic family had just heard that two of his buddies had died. He had read their names in a national magazine and was in tears when we walked in. He had the most awful head wounds besides everything else. I could tell from his mother's eyes that she knew what lay ahead for him. I felt so sad for her and for him.

. . . The most adorable Italian boy from New Haven almost jumped out of his bed when he saw George. "The most exciting day of my life." Since he felt he couldn't hug George, he asked if he could hug me and, of course, I hugged and kissed him and he kissed my hand. To think this darling boy will never walk again.

. . . The most moving moment came when a paraplegic said as we were leaving, "Sir, I wanted to give you this flag. It represents my buddies in Panama. We're proud of you and back you." [That flag was on George's desk in the Oval Office until we left on January 20, 1993, and is now on his desk in Houston.]

George told each of them that we were proud of them and that we wanted to thank them. Amazingly enough, many of them tried to stand for their Commander in Chief. Many thanked him for what he was doing, quite a few wanted to go back with their buddies. George asked each one where they had gotten their wounds, and they seemed pleased that he was familiar with the scene and the fighting in Panama.

This was one of the hardest days in George's presidency.

Finally, after the first of the year, it all ended. On January 7, 1990, I wrote in my diary:

The past few days have been dramatic to say the least. I am constantly amazed by GB's stability and ability to keep things on an even keel. All during the week after Christmas and early into the next week the press and the Congress were starting to get on GB's case about Panama. In fact, on January 4th, *The New York Times* had two articles on the editorial page suggesting that the Panama attack had been a failure as we did not have Noriega. They evidently put their paper to bed early as Noriega turned himself in to American authorities on the evening of January 3rd . . . the Vatican had sent a special emissary to negotiate with Noriega. Thousands and thousands of people had gathered outside the Vatican Mission in Panama City and were calling for the Vatican to give them Noriega. I overheard George telling Brent that anytime during the night he would be ready to hear the news if anything happened. I was working after dinner when George rushed through my office and said: "We got Noriega and I am going over to the office to make a statement." . . . We learned later that the Vatican had told him that he would be granted refuge until noon the next day and then he must choose between the USA and Panama. Had he chosen the latter, I believe that they would have torn him limb from limb . . .

Today, Noriega is in an American prison, and the people of Panama have a duly elected, democratic government.

19

Flying Chain Saws

Despite the excitement over Noriega's surrender, 1990 did not get off to a great start. On January 7, I wrote in my diary:

Pop (George) came into lunch today and said that Neil had called. He is worried to death. The group investigating the Savings and Loan scandal are investigating Neil because he was on the Silverado Board (as) an outside director. They came to Neil and said that if he'd sign a paper saying he'd never be on a bank board or have anything to do with a financial institution for the rest of his life, they would move off his case. He rightly said, "I've done nothing wrong. I am 33 years old and I won't sign that paper." His whole problem is that he is our son.

At the time, we thought that the fact they were investigating Neil was unfair but that it would come to little or nothing. How wrong we were.

Neil became the poster boy of the S&L scandal, despite the fact he was just one of literally hundreds of outside directors of failed savings and loans. He was investigated by the government *and* the press, who decided Neil was guilty before he even had his say. We particularly felt that NBC's "Dateline," hosted by Jane Pauley and Stone Phillips, took an unfair shot when they aired a piece on Neil in September 1992— long after Neil's case was settled but right in the middle of George's reelection bid.

Eventually, Neil did not have to sign that piece of paper, but he lost all his savings, his business, his house, and most important, for a while, his reputation.

The whole family suffered for Neil. Jeb told me a story that was so painful that when his partner, Armando Codina, tried to tell me again, I stopped him. It just hurt too much to hear it twice. Jeb and Armando were trying to put a business deal together, and the banker they were talking to said that they just couldn't work with the "Bush boy." Jeb and Armando, who had established a reputation in Miami for integrity and honor, were appalled. The bankers thought Jeb was Neil. Poor Neil. First, he was being judged guilty without an opportunity to defend himself; now his brothers were suffering because of name association.

Marvin told me a story of a friend of his getting in a verbal fight with two men he overheard talking at the airport. One said, "I hope they don't let him off just because he is the President's son." Marv's friend turned around and said, "I know him and there is not a dishonest bone in his body." Then a fight started.

George was heartbroken over what was happening but couldn't even talk to his son about it because a government agency was investigating him. He was especially disappointed in some members of Congress who professed to be friends, but who let politics get the best of them. Henry B. Gonzalez of Texas, whom George always liked, took out after Neil with a vengeance. (Henry later also filed impeachment papers on George during the early days of Desert Storm.) Congressman Frank Annunzio, who always told me how much he liked and respected George, suddenly found himself opposed in his Chicago district and attacked Neil unmercifully. And if Pat Schroeder from Colorado wasn't crying about some other cause, she always could use Neil as a daily kicking bag.

On the other end of this spectrum, we were touched, and so was Neil, by how family and friends rallied around him. Once more Lud Ashley, who had left Congress, came to the rescue and helped raise money to pay Neil's legal fees. When Neil moved from Denver to Houston, his longtime friends there welcomed him with open arms. And Neil's wife, Sharon, although she suffered horribly with her husband, stood by him like a rock.

In May of 1991 I wrote in my diary:

For the last few months George has talked privately like a man who is not running for office. I know he has the children on his mind. He is consumed with worry about Neil and a guilty feeling. He knows that Neil never would have been in this trouble if he hadn't been the son of the president.

I will say no more about this, but what happened to Neil took up more than its fair share of my diary for the remaining White House years. I couldn't help but think of former Secretary of Labor Ray Donovan, who, after being accused of wrongdoing and then exonerated, simply asked: "Where do I go to get my good name back?"

⌒ In early January we held the first of five Presidential Lectures, one of the best things we initiated at the White House. Nan Ellis suggested it after she heard David Donald, a Pulitzer Prize–winning author, speak about Lincoln. We loved the idea, and invited Professor Donald to kick off the series. Standing below George Healy's portrait of Lincoln in the State Dining Room, he chose to speak about the sixteenth president's life in the White House, rather than his role as politician, diplomat, or commander in chief. I wrote in my diary:

(The professor) was amusing, fascinating, warm, scholarly and so interesting . . . Boy, oh boy, we think we have problems. When the Lincolns moved into the White House, it was not furnished, there was oilcloth on the floor in the State Rooms because of the overflow from the spittoons, people could roam freely in and out of the house, there was no fence, we were at war with ourselves, Mrs. Lincoln had brothers and brothers-in-law fighting on the "other side" from her husband and government. Washington insiders thought she was a spy and a country bumpkin. They lost a beloved child while at the White House. Mary Todd Lincoln was depressed much of the time and hardly left her room. They had no friends. Their (political) party was new and so he had no proven party members to count on. The President's offices were on the same floor as the family residence. They had soldiers bivouacked on the South Grounds, etc. Professor Donald did a marvelous job and it was a splendid afternoon.

Through the next few years we had lectures on Theodore Roosevelt and Harry Truman by Professor David McCullough; Andrew

Jackson, by Professor Robert V. Remini; and George Washington, by Professor Gordon S. Wood. The White House came to life for us during these lectures and things were certainly put in perspective.

I think that we were aware of Lincoln's presence more than any of our other predecessors. His anguish was such that it almost could be felt, especially in the room he used as his office, now known as the Lincoln Bedroom. We could stand and look out the same windows he did. However, we never saw or believed in the famous ghost, nor did Ranger and Millie. (Winston Churchill and Queen Wilhelmina of the Netherlands were among the believers. During separate White House stays, they both reported seeing Mr. Lincoln. Also, the Reagans' dog, Rex, reportedly refused to go in the room.)

Some of the more interesting stories about life in the White House came from people who once lived or visited there. The little sitting room off the Queen's Bedroom had quite a lot of history. Lynda Robb told me that she served Chuck dinner there one night since they could not date in public and maintain their privacy.

Another night we had a small dinner for Susan Eisenhower and her nice fiancé, Ronald Z. Sagdeev. I couldn't help but think how much the world had changed: Imagine President Eisenhower's granddaughter marrying a Soviet! We had David and Julie, Anne and Susan Eisenhower, and a few others. I loved the reminiscing as we walked through the rooms that David sometimes stayed in from 1952 to 1960, and later, Julie and David stayed in during the Nixon years:

David told me that my little office–beauty parlor-puppy birthing room was the room his grandfather painted in. He said that he used to come into the room and talk to him while he painted and he always wondered if he was saying what his grandfather wanted him to say. I believe that Ike would be very proud of him. He has written a superb biography of President Eisenhower. Julie verified that the tiny sitting room off the Lincoln Bedroom was the room that her dad had chosen as his upstairs office. The Eisenhower ladies talked about riding their tricycles on the ground floor, and Anne told me that her grandparents had one of the first built-in-a-wall television sets in the West Sitting Hall and later sent me a picture of it. Pretty big and ugly. They are such a nice family and it was a relaxed, fun evening. David and Julie are truly thoughtful, nice, bright and easy.

Later in the year, Ed and Tricia Cox also visited us in the White House, and Ed told us that he studied for his bar exam in the White House solarium. I remember thinking at that time how sad it was that the White House had become almost a prison for the Nixon family during the difficult Watergate period.

∽ My diary entries from the first few months of 1990 reflect a wide range of activities in our lives—and thoughts in my head. I'd like to share just a few of them with you:

January 20—Just a year ago today George was sworn in as the 41st President of the United States. So of course this past week has been a rehashing of "The First Year" and marking George on his efforts. Doro called just thrilled by the *Boston Globe* poll: "In a nationwide poll of 1,002 people done for the *Globe* this week and last, more than 80% of those polled expressed a favorable view of the president, heady personal vindication for a man who just 18 months ago trailed Governor Dukakis by a wide margin in pre-election polling and was thought, even by some Republicans, to be virtually unelectable." I know and so does George that this is a very fragile thing. [Little did we know how fragile.]

February 2—Just back from the National Prayer Breakfast. Although it ran a little late, it truly was one of the best. Jimmy Baker was the reluctant main speaker and got me weeping a little as he shared his thoughts on faith and friends. He told a very meaningful story about driving to the White House one day and just as he was pulling into the driveway, he saw a former chief of staff walking all alone down the street—no driver, no security, no entourage—just all alone. He said that reminded him that all the trappings that go with power are fleeting. He went on to say that the only power that lasts is the power of God. He said, "Those people who didn't return my calls before I got these jobs, won't return them after I leave." He talked about the support that friends had given him. He certainly spoke movingly about his friendship with George. And, the thing I liked best was that he gave that near perfect Susan a lot of credit and showed his great love for her.

Jim did such a great job as Secretary of State that I suspect people are still returning his phone calls. He earned the respect of the whole world.

February 5—The hostages weigh very much on our minds. Not a night goes by that we don't pray for them.

February 14—One night several weeks ago George and I decided to walk Millie just before bed. We walked partway around the drive and saw two ladies looking through the Southeast Gate. George loves to visit with tourists and suggested that we walk over to say hello. The ladies kept saying, "Nobody will believe me when I tell them I met you" or "The others are going to die when they hear we talked to you!" One of the ladies told me that her grandmother was going to be 80 years old and would I drop her a note? I said, "Of course," and she gave me her name and address. The other lady asked me to drop her husband a note or otherwise he'd think she was lying. So I got her address. I did go right upstairs and write the two notes.

. . . Several weeks later I got a letter from Dottie Craig, who has taken on the task of raising money for the White House Endowment Fund . . . Among many things, Dottie's letter said: "You both made a friend who sounds as though she'd lay down her life for you when you talked with Betsy Sodano last Monday evening, the 22nd, through the W.H. fence, as I understand it. She is a cosmetician at a People's Drug Store in Maryland. I talked to her this morning because after she saw my name in a newspaper article about the fund, she called Earle's office to say that she wanted to help fund-raise in Maryland." That was so sweet. People are truly nice.

February 15—George, Jim Baker, Brent Scowcroft, John Sununu and Dr. Burt Lee left for the Drug Summit in Colombia . . . The dreaded trip was here. The press had been building up the danger for months. We got more letters and phone calls saying, "Don't let him go," from friends and strangers alike. I hardly slept at all the night before. George explained to me that we can't ask our Latin American friends to battle the drug cartel, risk their lives and then not go to the meeting because there were threats. He also explained to me that the security was going to be very tight. He was right, but it did not make me sleep any better that night or the next. GB called me when he left Colombia. I was so relieved. I cleaned my desk and then greeted George when he arrived at the South Lawn.

All during this time "the new breeze" of democracy was continuing to spread throughout the world, making it a very exciting time to be in the White House. One day in February, Jim Baker woke us up at

4:45 A.M. with the great news that Violeta Chamorro had upset Daniel Ortega in the Nicaragua elections—and by a pretty big margin. The press had been reporting that Ortega would win, which would mean a major defeat for George.

In March, the new President of Czechoslovakia, Vaclav Havel, and his wife came for a visit. When you realized that just four months ago this playwright-dissident didn't know if he was going to be jailed, exiled, or what, it truly was a momentous occasion. I had Olga Havelova for coffee and liked her very much. She had white hair and was a very chic, natural-looking woman. We had simultaneous translation as we visited, so I confess some of what she said was lost. But I did understand that she had been in jail several days and he for four and a half years. She told me that at one time they were given the opportunity to emigrate to the United States, but they refused. It would have meant not going back. I asked her if during the tough years, did she wish they had come. She looked shocked and gave a firm "No" answer.

Nancy Ellis came down from Boston to attend a dinner Katharine Graham of *The Washington Post* gave at her house for the Havels. All the Washington "in-group" were there and some administration types. Nan said that it was a good evening but that during dinner, Teddy Kennedy got up and asked Nick Brady to change places with him, thus putting himself between Nan and Kay, the hostess. The Havels gave Nancy a ride home to the White House since they were staying in Blair House, right across the street from us. She said as they were getting in the car, Teddy Kennedy came down and insisted that he get in the same car and take them to the Lincoln Memorial. They walked up the steps, and Teddy read the writings on the wall to them. Nan said that poor Mrs. Havel looked astonished and dead tired and clearly wanted to go home to bed.

We felt the "new breeze" again the very next day when we had a reception welcoming the National Symphony and especially its director, Mstislav Rostropovich, home from a glorious trip abroad. George had trouble speaking when he told the group about Slava having a chair brought up to the Wall in Berlin and playing his cello. It was so moving. But the highlight of the trip was Slava's return home to the Soviet Union. He had been exiled for sixteen years and had just recently had his Soviet citizenship returned to him. Evidently, when the orchestra played "The Stars and Stripes Forever" in Russia, the tears flowed on all sides. On top of all the other emotions at our reception, the symphony played "Linda Lou" for us, which really almost got us in tears again. Prescott Bush, George and Nan's father, had sung that song for years with his Silver Dollar Quartet. It was a wonderful hour.

Certainly one of the great privileges of living in the White House was meeting, seeing, hearing, and enjoying the best of the best our country has to offer. I know that for most people, getting to come to the White House and meet the president of the United States is an unforgettable experience, but many times we were much more in awe of our guests.

Another good case in point: In late February we held the annual Governors' Dinner, and the next day I invited the spouses to join me upstairs for lunch in the Yellow Oval Room. I had asked Helen Hayes to also attend and recite for us.

She started out by telling a story about two old ladies who met playing bridge at a club. As the party was breaking up, one said to the other, "I enjoyed being with you so much and would like to call you for a game sometime. I am so embarrassed, but I just can't remember your name. Would you give it to me?" And the other lady paused, thought, and answered, "Do you have to have it right now?"

Helen proceeded to tell us that she, too, sometimes forgets and therefore she had her glasses and a copy of the Benét poem that she recited. She only took a tiny peek. At almost ninety years old, she was amazing—a tiny, beautiful lady who stood straight as an arrow.

At the end of the lunch, Bill Orr, husband of Governor Kay Orr of Nebraska and one of our two male spouses, asked if he could give a toast. My heart sank, for it was time for the lunch to break up and I was afraid that his toast would be long and anticlimactic. Wrong—again! Bill told us that he and Kay had a ninety-eight-year-old friend. When they asked him why he looked so serene and untroubled, he said that he guessed it was because he had no peer pressure. Bill said, "Miss Hayes, you clearly have no peer pressure. In fact, you have no peers. You are the greatest lady of the theater." And then he made a toast to Helen Hayes and sat down. It was just so right and perfect, and another magic moment at the White House.

Both George and I loved Helen Hayes. Fifty-three years earlier I had gone with my fourth grade class to New York City to see a young, beautiful actress in *Victoria Regina*. That actress was Miss Helen Hayes.

She was a great lady. She campaigned for George, which was such a kindness.

✺ In March, while attending the funeral of Chappy Rose, Susan Porter Rose's father-in-law, George leaned over and said to me, "I'm afraid that I have done something that you are going to think is very bad." When I asked, "What?" he told me that he had invited the new Japanese Prime Minister, Toshiki Kaifu, to meet him at the Annenbergs' house in Palm Desert next week. I started to protest that he couldn't do that to Lee Annenberg, and he shushed me and said the funeral was starting.

Everyone was agog that George invited the Prime Minister with only seven days' notice and that the Prime Minister accepted. Usually there are months of preliminary meetings before the two principals meet. However, that just wasn't George's style.

Only the Annenbergs could have coped with a mini-summit with a week to prepare. George and I are very fond of both Lee and Walter. Lee was a former chief of protocol, and Walter was a former ambassador to the United Kingdom. They both did first-class jobs. There also was never a more giving couple. While we were at their house for the summit, George announced a gift of $50 million from Walter and Lee to the United Negro College Fund.

Their home, Sunnylands, was—and is—heavenly. At that time the main house was filled with the most glorious collection of Impressionist paintings, which they since have given to the Metropolitan Museum of Art in New York City. They hosted a beautiful dinner in the most spectacular dining room ever. But what impressed me the most was that Lee Annenberg herself made sure that all guests were well taken care of.

✺ One day in early March, Lee Atwater, who was doing an outstanding job heading up the Republican National Committee, fainted at a meeting. Eventually we learned that he had an inoperable brain tumor. We were stunned. This energetic, enthusiastic, bright young man was only thirty-nine years old, and he and his wife, Sally, were expecting a baby within the month.

Over the next few weeks I wrote about Lee in my diary a number of times:

. . . George W. came to Washington and had Lee Atwater for breakfast. They had a two-hour talk. Lee and Junior were great friends. ("Junior" was Lee's name for George W.)

. . . Lee's doctor gave him a fifteen-year reprieve. Burt Lee thought that he'd be lucky to have two years.

. . . Harry Dent came to Washington and spent the day with Lee. He is not only a hero of Lee's, but also is devoting his life to Christianity. Lee is seeking. (Harry, like Lee, is a native of South Carolina. He served in the Nixon White House.)

. . . I asked Lee how Sally was doing and he said that "she was as strong as horseradish." I reminded him to share with her and not to forget that she was frightened, worried and hurting also. He was sweet and said that he had awakened the other night and looked at her and realized that she was so vulnerable. The new little baby girl is due in two weeks.

. . . Bad news about Lee Atwater, went to NYC and doctor says he has 18 months to live.

Lee died March 29, 1991. He was one of a kind, and rose to the occasion in death as he did in life. He had nothing to apologize about, ever. George Bush truly loved him.

✎ There is another sad footnote to the spring of 1990: In April, Ryan White, the young hemophiliac who contracted AIDS through blood transfusions, died. He was at first ostracized by his school, but after a two-year court battle, won the right to attend classes. He devoted much of his remaining years to educating the public on how you get AIDS and how you *don't* get AIDS. He was a true hero.

Burt Lee and I flew to Indianapolis to attend the funeral. Burt had served on President Reagan's AIDS Commission and worked with AIDS patients at Sloan Kettering in New York City. He also had met often with Jeanne White, Ryan's mother, so he asked to go with me.

Many celebrities had taken up Ryan's cause, including Elton John and Michael Jackson, who had been supporters and friends for several years and attended the funeral. I was most touched, however, when some of his schoolmates, an all-girl group, sang "That's What Friends Are For." They stood in a semicircle, tears running down their faces, singing around the open casket where their tiny, eighty-five-pound, eighteen-year-old friend lay wearing his jeans and reflective dark glasses. It was so sweet.

∽ One of the hardest tasks for me during the White House years was to decide which invitations to accept. My scheduling office received on the average one hundred invitations a day for various events, ranging from second graders who wanted me to come read them a story to major national associations who wanted me to keynote their conventions. Often attached to the invitations would be comments or suggestions from Susan Porter Rose, Julie Cooke, Anna Perez, and every now and then, someone from George's office who had a special interest. Almost all of them were for causes or events I would have loved to support or attend but didn't possibly have time for.

The problem was never more acute than during the commencement season. Every year, out of one hundred or so invitations, we could accept only a handful. Many of the schools wanted to confer upon me an honorary degree. We tried very hard to select those that would represent a cross-section of schools and regions. In 1990, for example, we accepted invitations to speak at Southwest Community College in Cumberland, Kentucky; St. Louis University in Missouri; Wellesley College in Massachusetts; Kennebunkport High School in Maine; and Dunbar High School in Washington, D.C.

At the last moment Walter Annenberg asked me to do the University of Pennsylvania as a favor to him. I believe that they had invited Vaclav Havel, and he had to turn them down at a late date. For Walter I would do anything, so at the last minute we added the University of Pennsylvania, which was celebrating its two hundred and fiftieth anniversary.

My staff and I had been working on *the* speech off and on all spring. We asked Ed McNally from George's speech-writing department to help, so he joined our brainstorming sessions, which included Susan Porter Rose, Julie Cooke, Anna Perez, Susan Green, Jean Becker, and Sondra Haley. We sat around and talked about the things I wanted to say and tried to choose the theme for this year. They reminded me that I always say, "You have two choices in life. You can like it or not. I chose to like it." That, of course, is very simplistic. I know that there are people in life who have so many troubles that their choices are nil. But I was talking about people who waste their lives complaining about things that cannot be changed, who don't appreciate what they do have, and who spend time wishing for that which they cannot have. I read someplace that Oprah Winfrey said something like: "I have been lucky. But I made my luck." I believe that. Incidentally, I believe that most of us would not think Oprah was "lucky" when hearing about her difficult childhood. She overcame and is a real heroine to me.

We talked about my dad and the things he told me that you can give your children and about how important it is to give them independence. George has been wonderful about that, and I think it has added a lot to our children's lives.

I suggested that we end with the marvelous story from one of Robert Fulghum's books about "where do the mermaids fit into a world of wizards, giants and dwarfs." I wanted to make the point that we're not all alike and we have to respect each other's differences.

We also talked about my feeling that in order to be happy, one does not need to be married, and if married, one does not need to have children. But if you do have children, *they must come first.* They reminded me that I always say that I am "the luckiest woman in the world." I am.

Somehow, out of all these ramblings, a speech began to take shape.

In early April, the Gorbachev visit to Washington was announced for the end of May and beginning of June, conflicting with my Wellesley College address on June 1. However, rather than cancel, Susan Porter Rose suggested that I ask Raisa if she'd like to give a joint graduation speech with me. I asked George, and he thought that it was a brilliant idea.

Next I called President Nan Keohane of Wellesley to be sure that it would be okay. She sounded absolutely thrilled. I asked her please not to tell anyone because I didn't want to put pressure on Raisa to accept. I also warned her that judging from past experience, it might take quite a while before I got a definite answer.

I then hand-wrote Raisa a note, telling her that I was so pleased that a date had been set for the summit and inviting her to join me at the graduation. I told her that we could fly up to Boston together and that I thought it would give her a chance to tell a marvelous group about her great country and her great hopes for Soviet women. Foreign Minister Shevardnadze was gracious enough to hand-carry my letter to the Soviet Union for me.

A couple of weeks later, a handful of Wellesley girls began protesting my selection as their commencement speaker. According to them, "Barbara Bush has gained recognition through the achievements of her husband." Wellesley, they said, "teaches us that we will be rewarded on the basis of our own merit, not on that of a spouse." I should add here that the author Alice Walker was their first choice as a commencement speaker. When she declined, they invited me, the runner-up.

By the time my staff and I sat down for our second speech meeting, Wellesley had exploded into controversy. Although only 150 of the 600 graduating seniors had signed the petition, the protest had become big news. I told my staff that I did not want to make a special speech catering to Wellesley. I also did not want to complain, explain, or apologize in any way. By the end of the meeting, we had settled on three things I wanted the students to consider: You have to get involved in something larger than yourself; Remember to get joy out of life; Cherish human relationships. When I read my final draft to George, he suggested "Read to your child," and I added "Hug your child, love your child." Imagine my forgetting the most important and obvious things! We cut and pasted and were ready to start the graduation trail.

I gave a slightly different speech at Southeast Community College, located in Cumberland, Kentucky, the heart of the coal-mining country. These were truly a group of courageous students, many of whom were the first in their families to further their education beyond high school—and sometimes, elementary school.

Next was the University of Pennsylvania, where I gave *the* speech. I wrote in my diary about that occasion:

> I followed Bill Cosby into the stadium and there was a great deal of cheering. He is funny. He wore dirty sneakers or running shoes and a gray sweat suit. There was some worry when he arrived, but he quickly robed up and all was well.

Then came St. Louis University, where I basically gave the same speech with some local color added in. At neither school did the speech get any national attention. I think you need controversy to make news.

All this time the Wellesley situation was boiling. Here are some of the things I wrote in my diary during the month of May:

I got the darndest support from people like Ellen Goodman, Barbara Mikulski, Cal Thomas, etc. There were letters to the editor, and I received letters from friends and foes alike. Just yesterday *The New York Times* ran a front-page story about it and my phone rang off the hook. Richard Nixon called me and was outraged. My brother Scott Pierce called and wanted to know if I was all right. Jessica Catto called from London and wanted me to know that she had written an op-ed page article and faxed it to *The Washington Post*. George Bush thought the whole thing was dreadful. I have to remind myself that *THEY* invited me. I sometimes feel as though they think I invited myself.

. . . I must say that I felt for the President of Wellesley. She knew that I might just cancel the whole speech. There goes the graduation speaker and much more important, maybe Raisa's first speech in the USA.

. . . I can't go anywhere that I am not asked about it. So although I am not going to change my talk, it is not as much fun.

. . . That darn Wellesley flap has taken on a life of its own. There are more editorials, more talk shows, etc. It's putting too much pressure on. I read in the paper this morning that we had sent someone to Wellesley to ask the girls what they wanted me to talk about. FALSE. We did announce that Raisa Gorbachev was going to Wellesley with me and would speak. (That, of course sparked speculation that I had invited her so I could hide behind her skirts.)

On May 30, the day before the Gorbachevs were to arrive, I wrote my brother:

Dearest Scott,
A million thanks for your letter. Don't worry about your old sister . . . at least for now. The Wellesley thing has become a bore. We are tired of answering letters . . . almost all defending me. I feel for the college as

they are getting hate letters. I am trying to spread love, not hate, so this is not helping me any.

. . . This is the day before the big arrival and the papers are full of stories about things GB and I have done or thought. Funny how total strangers know what you are thinking. The truth about the invitation to Mrs. Gorbachev to come to Wellesley with me is that I wrote her long before the brouhaha, having sworn the president of the college to secrecy and gotten permission to invite her. I gave my note to Shevardnadze, their Foreign Minister, to carry home. Then a month or two went by with no answer. Now she has accepted and we are off the day after tomorrow for the speeches. It should be a fascinating three days. One thing I can promise you, I am going to love her in spite of anything she does or does not do. I am expecting her to be charming on this visit. She must have read Nancy's book. We have, of course, met before. The news about what is happening in their country is tough.

> Love to all,
> Bar

Also on May 30, I received a fax from Chris Bicknell, one of the young Wellesley women who objected to my being the speaker at the graduation. It was such a nice letter and really cleared the air. One of the things she said was: "I want to say thank you! *Thank* you for being the only one (it seems) to understand the reasons behind our debate— and thank you for saying so to the press."

I quickly picked up the phone and called Chris. I could hardly believe it, but the White House operator found her in her dorm room and we had a warm, nice talk.

The next morning we awakened to the most beautiful day in the world. I walked the dogs at 4:45 A.M., read the papers, swam, and got ready for the arrival ceremony.

Raisa looked so stylish and chic with her turned-up collar on a lightweight wool suit. After the receiving line, I walked her upstairs to have coffee in the West Sitting Room. My three "girls" came to join us—Neil's wife, Sharon; Marvin's wife, Margaret; and Millie. The latter seemed to bond to Raisa as we toured the residence. Raisa had interesting things to say about everything. At one point she gave us a small history of our previous meeting, what we said in the car, and so on. She told me that the Soviets think there are two great American Presidents: Roosevelt and Reagan. I showed her Ronald Reagan's portrait and said that we didn't like it. She, to her credit, said that she liked President Reagan very much. I quickly told her that we loved President Reagan; we just didn't like the portrait. (Neither did the Reagans; it later was replaced.)

The state dinner that night was lovely, with the beautiful Frederica Von Stade singing for us.

Then it was Friday, June 1. The day had arrived.

The funniest thing happened on the plane going up. I didn't know what it meant, but it sure shook me up for a minute. Raisa and I sat and talked through her interpreter for a while, and then I told her that if she didn't mind, I thought that I'd go over my speech just one more time. I moved across the aisle and started to work. After about a minute, Raisa interrupted me and asked, "Barbara, are we both supposed to be giving a speech?" I couldn't believe my ears. We had worked out all the plans in advance through the Soviet Embassy, and it had been agreed that we both would speak for six minutes. We even had told the embassy we would help with her talk, an offer they declined. I told her that we had hoped she would speak for six minutes. She pulled out a tiny piece of paper and started to write away. In a minute she got up and went into the ladies' room. While she was there, I asked the interpreter if I had understood her correctly—was she telling me that she didn't have a speech? How could there be such a misunderstanding? He smiled, patted his pocket, and produced the translation. Was Raisa being funny? Whatever it was, I was glad that she was prepared.

From the moment we got to Boston it was thrilling. Governor Dukakis met us at the airport, which was very kind. At every street corner there were people cheering. This caused no end of trouble as Raisa wanted to stop and shake hands and thank people. I made a deal with her: *After* the graduation, we could stop whenever she wanted, but I was determined that we would be on time. She was just not used to people at home cheering them, so the Boston welcome was especially nice. When we got to Wellesley, she did not put on a robe. I longed to join her as it was so hot, but President Keohane had gone to the trouble to get my hood from Smith College. Raisa told me that they didn't robe in the Soviet Union; therefore, she couldn't here. She was very conscious of the "home viewer." I think she got criticized on her last visit for being so stylish. This time she was wearing a lovely, long-skirted, light wool suit that I got to know very well over the years. Thank heavens that it was very becoming, for she wore it everywhere.

When Raisa and I walked into the tent, the young women went wild. Doro had come down from Maine to give me support, which really touched me, and Susan Porter Rose told me later that tears ran down Doro's face when we came in. The buildup had been so big that there were five thousand people in the tent, and five thousand standing outside. The TV networks carried it live. Thank heavens I didn't know that at the time. George saw part of it in Washington.

Chris Bicknell gave the first speech, I was next, and Raisa was last. She gave a very dignified, very poised talk. It was a good length and was translated as she spoke. I was very proud of her. I can't imagine giving a graduation speech in Russia! (See Appendix C.)

How did I feel when it was over? The truth is, I did understand what the girls who had protested were saying. I had quit worrying about the whole thing once the speech was written because I felt good about what I wanted to say to them. I will confess that I was thrilled with the welcome they gave Raisa and me.

One thing did bother me, however: One of the young women who had been so vocal against my selection was from a South American country. I thought she showed very bad taste criticizing the wife of the president of her host country. I'm not sure why, but I thought it was okay for American citizens to protest me, but not our guests!

After the commencement, we had a quick lunch with Doro, then headed for the Boston Common to visit with a group of elementary students at the *Make Way for Ducklings* sculpture, based on the famous children's story by Robert McCloskey. The entire route was lined by schoolchildren and people waving and cheering. We got out of our car three times to shake hands and wave. We were on a tight schedule, and I had trouble keeping Raisa going. We finally got to the ducks, and there we saw our nephew and niece, Jamie and Sue Bush, and their children, Sam and Sarah. They were adorable. Raisa said, "You seem to have family everywhere."

We had a small ceremony around those dear ducks with students from the Mather School, then talked to the press for a few minutes. They asked me how we were getting on, and I answered, "Just fine. We are having a great time." When they asked Raisa the same question, she gave the same answer, but took hours. George would say that she is the kind of person you ask the time and they tell you how to build the clock. (He says that about me, too.) As we had agreed that we *must* be back in Washington for the signing ceremony, we started back to the cars. I shook hands, said good-byes, and arrived at the car only to find that Raisa had gone back for ten more minutes with the press. We finally got her into the car and took off for the airport. I honestly think that since they did not have such openness with either their people or the press, she felt it would be rude not to shake every hand and answer every question. As we drove by many houses on the way to the airport, I found myself wishing that we could stop, go up to a door, and go in. I think she would have been surprised to see how gracious Americans are.

At six o'clock, we all met in the East Room of the White House to watch the two Presidents sign a series of agreements concerning arms and trade. It was quite a meeting. Imagine sitting in a room with the two Presidents of the most powerful countries in the world—and being married to one of them!

We were due at the Soviet Embassy at seven-thirty for dinner. Raisa and I had had a big discussion about what she was going to wear, long or short, and she took forever to finally say, "Short." So I wore my bright pink, very short dress from Scaasi, and she wore a long-sleeved, black velvet suit. It was so hot. She looked pretty as a picture, but must have died of the heat. If so, she never let on. We had a receiving line and went right on into dinner. They had seven courses, but the memorable one, as always, was the caviar, which they passed twice. We got home fairly early but I was dead tired. I bet she was also. It was tiring to spend a day speaking through an interpreter, not to mention giving a graduation speech where there had been so much controversy.

On Saturday morning we flew by helicopters, the men in one and the women in another, to Camp David. It was such an interesting day. We flew over miles of residential areas, and I could see that all the Soviets were impressed with the homes. One Soviet security man couldn't believe it when a Secret Service agent told him that he lived down below in one of the lovely subdivisions. The Soviets seemed amazed by our private lives.

The men were scheduled to work all day, so Raisa and I decided to go for a long walk. We went right to our cabins, changed our clothes, and were ready to take off when I looked at her feet. Although she had on pants, she also had on very high heels. I tried to persuade her to let me get her some walking shoes. She assured me that these were her walking shoes. (Her interpreter said that for photos, she wanted to have heels on.) I decided we should tour the camp in a golf cart instead. We talked of lots of things. She asked me if our children owned their own homes. I said that yes, they did. She asked if we had helped them buy their homes. I told her that we hadn't. I explained that we put them through college and since the age of twenty-one or so, they had been on their own. She asked how that could be, and I explained to her that both husbands and wives worked, they saved enough money for a down payment, got a loan for the remainder from the bank, and then paid monthly installments on the loan. I also explained that over the years some of them had been able to "trade up." She told me that their only child, a daughter, had a doctorate degree, was a researcher married to a surgeon, and that they could not afford their own apartment. So with their children, two girls aged three and ten, they lived with the Gorbachevs. She seemed genuinely interested in how much things cost in our country. For example, in the Soviet Union, all lipsticks cost the same—imported name brands and cheaper ones. The government subsidizes things at a great cost. She asked a million questions about the free enterprise system.

After a long golf cart trip around Camp David, we returned to the house for lunch. The men had been on the patio at the main cabin working all morning. It was fascinating as they were all wired up to two translators who were repeating every word as it was spoken. We had a very good lunch and then planned on a nap until three-thirty. But George's aide, Tim McBride (one of the finest young men we know), came running in early and said that the Gorbachevs were on the terrace, so we hurried out. I had noticed before lunch that Raisa's poor feet looked raw. We really hadn't walked at all and yet she had large blisters. She came back after lunch in black mules. The men went outside again, and Raisa and I talked in the living room. Later in the day Raisa and the men threw a few horseshoes. Mikhail threw a ringer on his first or second throw and was thrilled. George had it mounted and presented to him at our informal dinner that night.

It was during our long talks at Camp David that Raisa suddenly became a person to me and not just this woman who had done all her homework (although, as always, she had).

She was the first wife of a Soviet leader who was in the public eye. There were no rules for her. She had no staff of her own. People from the Foreign Office did help her with invitations, and people from another office helped her with the mail, but she was blazing a new trail and it was not easy. I think that she had been hurt by the criticism about her, and she asked me why I was so popular. I told her, as honestly as I could, that I felt it was because I threatened no one—I was old, white-headed, and large. I also told her that I stayed out of my husband's affairs. We both agreed that we put our husbands first above all else. I liked her a lot and felt very sympathetic. I also liked him. He was a strong, very able person and also quite charming. United Nations Secretary General Pérez de Cuéllar had said once: "He is either the world's greatest actor or is sincere." George and I agreed that he was sincere. He was smart, fast, and had a great sense of humor. We couldn't understand how he could keep his spirits up, there was so much turmoil at home. But he seemed confident. Someone said to me during the visit, "He's a small man, isn't he?" I was surprised. I didn't think of him as small at all.

⌒ We had another historic visit later in June, when Nelson Mandela came to call on George. I wrote in my diary:

On Monday morning I swam and was working in my office when George called and asked if I could rush over to the Oval Office. I said, "Yes," and raced into clothes and ran over, jamming on lipstick, pearls and earrings as I went. I had gotten the word from two sources that Mrs. Mandela would not be with him, but she had come unexpectedly. The minute I arrived, Nelson Mandela came right over to greet me. He is not as tall as I thought. He is in his seventies and stands straight as an arrow. He is a kind-looking man with a real presence. Winnie Mandela was in native costume. She is a big, smiling woman. Both were charming. After a few minutes of talking we walked out to a press conference and both men spoke. George did a beautiful job. Mandela spoke without notes. As I stood there next to her, I kept thinking that this smiling woman is the lady who allegedly has those "bully" boys who beat people and who ordered them to "necklace" people (pouring gasoline on rubber tires and putting them over people's necks). All done while her husband was in jail. I also had read that she built an enormous personal house. What to believe? [The Mandelas have since separated.]

. . . Mandela's welcome in this country, NYC, Boston and Washington, D.C., has been overwhelming. Jesse Jackson has stuck to him like glue. He attacked George in his introduction of Mandela. Much to my disgust, (Washington) Mayor Marion Barry, whose (cocaine) trial is ongoing, appeared with him last night and got a big applause. Is there no one to protect this fine man (meaning Mandela, not Barry!)?

Earlier that spring, another VIP visitor came to the White House—Michael Jackson. Now you might wonder why I would mention a pop star in same context as men who will be remembered for changing history. Because it always amused me what a huge ruckus the appearance of celebrities caused at the White House—sometimes more than the history-makers. You could tell from the number of staffers who left their desks to sneak a peek who was hot and who was not. Michael was definitely hot. I wrote in my diary:

He was honored this week as the Entertainer of the Decade by the Children's Museum. I went over to G's press conference announcing the Gorbachev visit and met Michael in the Oval Office, where he was talking to George and having a "photo op." He wears the darndest clothes, skintight black suit with at least two big medals on his chest, and this day he had on four belts, red leather with big silver buckles. One belt was around his waist and the other three were around his left leg, two above the knee and one below. He has straight, long black hair. You really have to listen to him as he has the softest voice, almost a whisper. He was very pleasant and genuinely wanted to see the upstairs at the White House, especially the Lincoln Bedroom. So I walked him over to the residence and was just amazed by the numbers of normally sophisticated people who suddenly appeared to be walking by, gaping and staring. He does like crowds, and I can certainly understand that. After we saw the Lincoln Bedroom we went across the hall to the Queen's Bedroom with Millie and Ranger at our side. The dogs jumped up on the window and looked out at the tourists leaving by the North Portico. This was a great fun thing to do because the tourists always take one last look back and when they spot the dogs and sometimes me, they wave and take pictures. This day I asked Michael to join us at the window. I have never seen such excitement. People literally jumped, laughed out loud and waved. I wouldn't have been surprised if they had done cartwheels and somersaults.

I was delighted when George asked me to head the U.S. delegation to the inauguration of the President of Costa Rica. So in early May, Nancy and John Sununu; Jeb (Columba was supposed to come but little Jebby got sick at the last minute); the former governor of Puerto Rico, Luis Ferré, and his wife, Tiody; and Roger Ailes, our great friend, who had run the successful campaign of President-elect Calderón, headed for Costa Rica.

A couple of things stand out from the trip:

The Calderóns were among the most gracious people you could wish to meet and had the most attractive, charming children. The morning of the inauguration, they had us over for a long relaxed breakfast as if they had nothing else to do.

At the inauguration, as our delegation walked into the stadium behind our flag, we got a standing ovation. I don't believe that anyone other than President Calderón got the same. The Costa Ricans love the United States, and we love them. I felt so proud knowing that the cheers were for the USA.

Of the 29,000 people there, John Sununu was probably the only person who wore tails. His comment: There were 28,999 badly dressed people there! I overheard him say to Roger Ailes, "You and I look as though we are going as two sofas." How I love John and his sense of humor.

⁓ While all of this was going on, I still was trying to keep my pledge to do something every day that would make a difference. I unveiled a literacy billboard in Miami, visited a library in Los Angeles and a veterans' hospital in Kansas City, attended a fund-raiser for an adult literacy center in Cleveland, played pool at a Boys and Girls Club in Washington, gave out books in an Iowa elementary school, and so much more.

The summer especially was very busy since George and I were

going to host the annual Economic Summit in Houston. One might question the wisdom of choosing our hometown for a summit in July. But not to be deterred, the city picked the summit slogan, "Houston's Hot," and went to work.

It was hot—and got hotter—but it also was wonderful. For six months a group of five thousand volunteer citizens worked on cleaning up our city. They didn't just clean the route that the delegates were going to use, but the whole town (and it's held up very well since then). George asked Jack Steel, who had been our loyal good friend since the first campaign in 1964, to sign on as special adviser, and Ben Love and Ken Lay coordinated the business community.

In Washington, Susan Baker, Kitty Brady, and I got together and talked about what we could do for the spouses that would be fun. We couldn't possibly compete with the canals of Venice or the castles in France, England, or Germany, but we did have one thing that, although not unique to the world, was pretty special: Texas hospitality. We decided to take them to San Antonio for a quick tour of that beautiful, historic city and to ask friends to host meals in their homes. Two very dear people came to our rescue: Betty Liedtke, wife of George's former partner at Zapata, agreed to have a dinner in Houston; and Joci Strauss said she would love to host a luncheon in San Antonio.

Such nice things happened. Everyone wanted to help. The Garden Club of Houston, to which I belong, planted the most beautiful giant pots around the university. Houstonians volunteered everything. For example, the press who came from around the world had free food in the convention hall, thanks to the hotels and restaurants.

On the evening of July Fourth, right before the summit, George flew to London for a quick NATO meeting. He is the strongest man. He arrived in England on Thursday morning, worked all day, had dinner with Her Majesty, spent the night with Henry and Jessica Catto at Winfield House, worked the next morning, and flew to Houston, arriving in time for dinner with me and then to bed early. I was tired just hearing about it.

I wrote in my diary about the week:

Saturday George had a one-on-one meeting with P.M. Kaifu of Japan. He is a new breed of Japanese. To begin with, he is young. He is tiny—not that that's new, but really tiny. He and his nice wife are happy-looking people. She, Sachiyo, is about 50, speaks English and is literally the tiniest little person I have almost ever seen. Mila Mulroney and I look like GIANTS next to her. They are both very agreeable. I think he is tough to deal with, but who isn't? I feel that all over America there is a big anti-Japanese feeling. Americans are very worried about the Japanese "buying up America."

. . . At 3:30 Saturday afternoon we took 6 Japanese, including the Kaifus, and Baine and Mildred Kerr, Marion Chambers, Charles and Sally Neblett and the President of Rice and Mrs. Rudd to the Opera House at the Wortham Center to see "Carousel." It was a glorious presentation and I got teary. I had forgotten what a sad play it is. There is not a bad song in the musical . . .

Sunday morning—Early 8 a.m. church at St. Martin's with Denis and Margaret (Thatcher). It was wonderful. Usually we have a smattering of people at that service. It was jam-packed.

. . . G. had one-on-one with Brian Mulroney. I swam and we had lunch with Mila and Brian at the Health Center.

. . . Raced over to the Rodeo. We got there early so that George could meet with Jacques Delors, president of the European Community. Then we had a reception which was attended by Japan, England, EC and Canada. All the Heads of State wore their big cowboy hats. I was sort of glad that Mitterrand had not arrived as it was a long evening for people suffering from jet lag. We went into a mini-rodeo and a mini "Grand Ole Opry," featuring among others, Minnie Pearl, the Gatlin Brothers, Loretta Lynn, Charlie Pride, the Judds. These friends have been there when we needed them over and over again. It was a fun evening. Like "Carousel," this was put on especially for the Summit. I am so proud of Houston.

July 9—George went to one-on-ones with Chancellor Kohl and President Mitterrand. In the middle of the day we went to Rice University to greet the delegates in reverse protocol order. The European Community came first, followed by Japan, Italian Republic, Canada, Federal Republic of Germany, the United Kingdom and France. We had a small reception and then were led out for the ceremony. It was hot. All seven anthems were played, the Colonial Fife and Drum Corps marched, cannons went off in salutes, etc. GB gave a two-minute welcome, and then the spouses went off to do their own thing. I came home and read Scott Turow's BURDEN OF PROOF.

George went to a G-7 dinner at Bayou Bend, Miss Ima Hogg's home in River Oaks, now a museum. The spouses went to Hugh and Betty Liedtke's house for a perfect dinner . . . the house looked beautiful, and all the guests said that they loved being in a private home. We had the spouses of the Heads of State, the Foreign Ministers and Economic Ministers. It is so much nicer to have Susan Baker and Kitty Brady with me. Betty had some little children playing chamber music during the dinner in the library and after dinner the most attractive young couple singing. It was just right. Because Denis joined us, Betty invited her husband, Hugh, Baine and Mildred Kerr, and her brother-in-law and our old friend, Bill Liedtke, to join us. Denis is a stitch. Suddenly, in the middle of a conversation about Russia, he says in a very loud voice and his British nasal voice, "Am I boring you?" The truthful answer is, "No."

Danielle Mitterrand sat on my right. She is a fascinating woman. Difficult, as she speaks not a word of English. She wears absolutely no makeup and is very good looking, I think. Protocol puts us next to each other at all times.

July 10—Hot, but not as bad as I feared. I went out to Ellington Air Force Base and met each group as one by one they arrived in their motorcades and we took off for San Antonio.

The spouses' side of the Summit was headed by Melinda Farris, her staff, plus many volunteers. They were efficient and calm and we did not have a hitch.

. . . We were met by Mayor Lila Cockrell and other dignitaries and put on a large air-conditioned bus . . . On the bus was a Mr. Henry Guerra, "the voice of San Antonio," who gave us the history of San Antonio as we drove to the Mission of San Jose.

. . . Lunch at Joci Straus's glorious cliff-hanging house with its bright colors, high ceilings and spectacular views. At my request Joci invited Flo Crichton, Patsy Light and the two Straus daughters, all of whom I love. On her terrace she had ladies making little tortillas which we filled with butter and cheese. There was music. The lunch was a delicious acorn squash soup, a plate of the best marinated beef and lovely tiny black beans, lettuces and other delicacies.

Back on the bus and on to the Majestic Theater that Joci had restored and I visited last year on the day of its reopening. They had about 900 children who are participating in a summer program in the audience and a half-hour program that reflected local talent.

On to the Alamo, where the Mayor made us all honorary mayors.

. . . We had our joint dinner with the men and many local Houstonians at the Museum of Fine Arts. It did us proud. The collection is superb and has grown so since we got into public life. They had a wonderful John Singer Sargent, a Mary Cassatt, a Bellows, a Frieseke, etc. in the reception hall. At the top of the stairs was the Remington that they had lent us at the Vice President's House. Speaking of the Vice President, he and Marilyn flew down for dinner bringing Nancy Sununu and Clayton and Jeanne Yeutter and others. The flowers were lovely. The food was delicious, and the tables looked spectacular. The entertainment was wonderful. Cicely Tyson was the M.C. A favorite of George's, Michael Davis, a juggler—now don't stick up your nose—was hilariously funny and François sitting next to me really roared. George was dying to get him to do his juggling act with chain saws, but nobody (except GB) liked the idea of buzzing chain saws flying all over a room with seven world leaders in it. Ricky Skaggs and his wife sang some country music and were followed by Marilyn McCoo, a glorious black singer who is a joy to behold and hear, and that darling Frederica Von Stade, the opera singer with the voice of an angel. It was a special night.

July 11—The spouses went early to the Texas Medical Center, where we had 19 different tours. We had asked the spouses their interests and sent them off on their own tours. We take second place to no one in the medical field. Dick Wainerdi, head of the center, arranged everything. We ended the tours with a very informal buffet.

We went to the Brown Convention Center, where we heard George read part of the joint communiqué, said good-bye to our foreign friends, toured the dining facilities for all the press, miles of free gourmet food, and George went to his press conference.

The last thing we did was go to the campus of the University of Houston, where we had a "Thank You, Houston" party to which everyone was invited. It was enormous and had entertainment and tent after tent of food. This was a small thank-you to everyone in the city who had made the Economic Summit of 1990 so very special. [Jack Steel later told me that after all the bills were paid, $600,000 was left over. The money was given to the Convention Center, the museum, the Houston Clean Committee, and other groups that helped us so much.]

In mid-July we flew to California for the opening of President Nixon's library. George invited Tricia and Ed Cox and their son, Christopher, to come to Washington and fly out with us. We gathered the White House staff who had been there between 1969 and 1974, about nineteen in all, so they could say hello to Tricia.

The library is a lovely, very bright, graceful-looking building surrounded by beautiful gardens, a reflection pool, and masses of flowers. President Nixon and Pat led us on a tour of the building and the grounds. The house that Richard Nixon was born and grew up in was a tiny house that was ordered from the Sears, Roebuck catalog. It had one bedroom on the first floor and one upstairs that was hard to stand up in. Dick showed us the fireplace and bookshelves that his dad added. I wondered what those grandchildren who are growing up on Park Avenue and in the suburbs in Pennsylvania were thinking.

The opening also was attended by President Ford and Betty and President Reagan and Nancy. Everyone was so excited and pleased to see Pat Nixon, who had suffered a stroke several years earlier.

The actual ceremony was outdoors, and the reports in the papers varied as to how many people were there, but it was large. I saw so many faces of old friends that I was dying to talk to and thought we would have an opportunity to afterward, but didn't. After everyone had said a few words, President Nixon spoke without a note and gave a very upbeat speech.

During the lunch, Ronald Reagan told funny joke after funny joke. I think that George was sort of glad. He had worked for all three of the former Presidents—and now here he was, the sitting President. It made for a rather strange situation.

⌒⌐ It amazed me when George was President how there was "always something." For example, on July 20, Justice Brennan resigned out of the blue from the Supreme Court. I asked George if they had been thinking about a new justice in case one resigned. He said: "Of course." In fact, he told me that within a month of taking office, he had met with a group of people and asked them for a list of qualified candidates. This was one of a million reasons why George was President and I wasn't.

A few days later George nominated David Souter for the Court. He came by for a quiet drink with us and became one of the people whom I liked immediately.

Also in July, George signed the landmark Americans with Disabilities Act, one of the pieces of legislation he was most proud of. For 43 million Americans, this bill meant an end to employment discrimination and access to all public buildings and transportation. More than two thousand people were on the South Lawn to witness the signing, making it one of the biggest events ever at the White House.

I'd like to share with you parts of a letter George received in 1993 from Evan Kemp and his wife, Janine D. Bertram, concerning this legislation. The letter touched both of us deeply.

> We are not sure that . . . you really take the credit for the great and revolutionary thing you did for this country when you fought [for] and then signed the ADA into law . . . as 43 million Americans become more integrated into society, you deserve all the credit.
>
> . . . On March 17, 1989, you first invited us to the White House for a small dinner in your residence . . . Each subsequent year, you invited us to a Christmas party. We were informed by the Secret Service that you had to personally approve Janine's attendance at these events because of her record . . . as you know, Janine was caught up in the Vietnam era, became an "urban guerrilla" and served 52 months in prison for bombing and bank robbery. Clearly, she wasn't your average Republican.
>
> . . . Your openness to include Janine gives her and others the knowledge that people can change, they can grow up. After they grow, the President and First Lady, the highest office holders in the land, may include and accept them.
>
> . . . (Evan) graduated at the top of his class from the University of Virginia Law School. Yet, after 39 job interviews, he could not get a job because of his disability. Fifteen years ago, Evan was told by the federal government that using a wheelchair made him incompetent to supervise two people. Yet, you, Mr. President, didn't bat an eye when you named him Chairman of the Equal Employment Opportunity Commission.
>
> You, Mr. President, encouraged disabled people, con-

victs and all other Americans to set aside our "victim" status. The ADA was one such policy. Your fight against quotas on the Civil Rights Act of 1991 was another.

Never forget what a great contribution you made to our nation.

That summer was a tough one for Millie, who had been limping and crying. At first her veterinarians thought she maybe had lead poisoning from the scraping of the paint off the White House walls. I was heartsick. It was obvious she was in pain, although she was, as always, undemanding and remained my shadow. Eventually she was diagnosed as having lupus and put on prednisone. She showed immediate improvement and has continued to take the medicine and to feel very fit.

When her illness became public, Millie received 382 get-well cards; then she received 122 notes on an article in *Good Housekeeping.* This was shades of things to come. Eventually, Millie had to have her own volunteer, Jean Richards, in the White House mailroom to answer her letters. She also got a tremendous amount of presents and even portraits.

The summer was worrisome for me, too. All year I still had been having problems with my eyes. They were puffy, swollen, teary, and I still saw double a lot of the time. (I still do when I'm tired, but am so used to it that I hardly notice it anymore.) By August I was weaning myself off the prednisone which I had taken for my eyes, and it was very painful. I also was taking therapy to try to strengthen my muscles. In layman's talk, it was explained to me that the prednisone I took killed something in my right hip and caused muscles to weaken, especially around my knees and hips. I confess I was in a lot of pain that would last through the fall. I couldn't wait for August to come and some R&R in Kennebunkport.

It was not to be, however, a very restful vacation.

On August 2, Iraq shocked the world when it invaded its tiny neighbor, Kuwait. At the time, George was in Colorado with Margaret Thatcher. Several weeks later, Margaret would say to George: "Now is not the time to go wobbly, George." George always loved that, and wobbly he did not go.

20

The Storm Before the Storm

August 7, 1990—George said this morning it has been the toughest week in his life. Fortunately he has kept the door open to world leaders and has talked to them often during the last year and a half. So when the Iraqis moved into Kuwait, George was able to get worldwide support. Earlier this week an amazing thing happened. Jim Baker and Shevardnadze denounced Iraq at a joint press conference. Who ever would have believed??? (George) had to send troops to Liberia to evacuate American citizens there this week to help them escape the escalating civil war. This morning troops were sent to Saudi Arabia. There are troops on the Saudi border. Based on gloom and doom reports all over TV, gas prices have soared. God bless my George.

There was much discussion about whether George should spend any time in Kennebunkport during the Gulf crisis. He felt strongly that he could stay in touch from Maine, and he didn't want to appear to be held hostage in Washington. However, it certainly changed the texture of our "vacation."

During one weekend he spent with us, I walked into the kitchen for a cup of coffee and heard *"Bonjour, François."* Other times I overheard "Good morning, Your Eminence" or "I just wanted to keep you abreast of what is happening and to ask your advice and assistance." Brent Scowcroft told me George talked to Hosni Mubarak while fishing out on his boat, *Fidelity.*

To show you just how difficult the balancing act between "real" life and worldwide politics was during this very difficult time, I'd like to share with you my diary entry from August 16:

This was an extraordinary day. Mrs. Bush's brother, John Walker, had an emergency operation in the night and George, knowing he was ill, went over to the hospital around 5:45 a.m. to check on him. He arrived a few minutes after he died. Johnny might be everybody's first choice as "the most remarkable person" any of us ever knew. He was a great athlete and a surgeon who around 1950 had polio and lost most of the use of his arms. The eldest of their five children died several years later, also of polio, and later they had two Down's Syndrome children, two little girls. That is almost more than any two people can bear, but bear it they did. Never a word of complaint from either John or his extraordinary wife, Louise. John had a great sense of humor, a loving heart, interest in everyone else, and always good advice *IF* asked.

George called me from the hospital and asked me to go over and tell his mother. The fact that he had gone to the hospital was sure to make the news and he did not want Mom to hear it on the radio or television. She looked so beautiful and seemed to understand very well. We shed a tear or two and both agreed that Johnny had been a saint. Later I went back to be sure that Mom was all right and to suggest that maybe she'd like me to push her down to see her sister, Nancy, also bedridden, who has a cottage on the other end of the Point, to tell her. She said that she had already done that and that Nancy understood. I could hardly believe her story and asked the nurse and, yes, she had done just that. Sometimes both ladies seem absolutely oblivious to all that is going on around them and at others, they seem really alert. They always rise to the occasion.

Meanwhile we had all the little kids cleaning out their rooms, straightening their drawers and then I had room inspection. We made a picnic lunch and sent Ellie, Sam, Jebby, Barbara, and Jenna to the beach for the day, I hoped.

. . . At twelve noon His Majesty King Hussein (of Jordan) arrived with an entourage at the helicopter pad. George and I walked down to greet him. He was an old friend and was very warm and friendly, although he had been anything but in the press. He softened his approach in the press later. The group of 12 had a lunch of half a lobster, chicken salad and muffins, blueberry pie and ice cream. George said that they ate it all.

Twenty minutes after the Jordanians left, another helicopter arrived with His Royal Highness, Prince Saud al-Faisal of Saudia Arabia, their Foreign Minister, with his entourage including our esteemed friend Prince Bandar, Saudia Arabia's very able ambassador to the United States. They stayed almost two hours and left.

Meanwhile the grands all came home from the beach. They were kept riding their bikes and playing down by the helo pad. They wanted to see and meet a real live King and Prince. We had a few lessons on shaking hands firmly, looking into the eye and speaking politely. This almost immediately disintegrated into "Good afternoon, Your Royal Hiney," and other such funnies. When the big moment came they all behaved.

We went in the evening to a fund-raiser for Dick Snelling, who is running for governor of Vermont.

We ended that very long day with the arrival of Laura and George. Their girls were glad to see them—and so was I. (The truth is their girls are so easy and fun to be with.)

George returned to Washington several times to brief Congress and consult with advisers, especially when the crisis would escalate. On August 20, for example, the Iraqis took thirty-five Americans hostage and placed them near key military or other strategic sites. The stock market plunged dramatically. We were on the verge of a war, a hostage situation, and a recession. It was an incredibly tense time for us and the country.

Once when he came back to Maine, George brought with him Cardinal Bernard Law of Boston and his assistant, Monsignor Timothy Moran. The Cardinal is very interested in world politics, and I remember he suggested to George that "some good just might come of all this bad," such as a solution to the Lebanon and Palestinian problem. At the time I didn't see how, but I certainly thought of the Cardinal's prediction on September 13, 1993, when the leaders of Israel and the PLO shook hands on the White House lawn.

Despite everything else going on, I managed that summer to read Kitty Dukakis's book, *Now You Know*. I wrote in my diary:

It was a shocking book as advertised, but not for the reasons I heard from friends. She writes with great frankness about being a manic depressive and an addict. What an enormous burden for Mike and herself. I am no doctor, but the agony they must have gone through was horrible. My gut feeling is that this book will be a comfort for people who have mental problems. They will certainly feel they are not alone and maybe it will encourage them to get help.

During the time that he was in Maine, George and I would go over to Mom's bungalow to catch the evening news. He would sit on the couch and hold his mom's hand as they watched together. She hardly ever said a word. I know that was very hard for him.

Billy and Ruth Graham spent the last weekend with us in Maine, staying in Mom's bungalow. He spoke at both our winter and summer churches, First Congregational and St. Ann's. It was such a comfort to have him there. He has been very dear to our family through the years, and we are grateful to him.

≈⊃ The very next weekend we flew to Helsinki, Finland, for a mini-summit between George and Mikhail Gorbachev. (Only George would consider a trip to Finland as a "weekend trip.") It was my first flight aboard the brand-new *Air Force One.* I wrote in my diary:

George told me that he couldn't wait for me to see the plane. He said that I wouldn't believe it and I don't. It is tremendous. The President's Suite has two rooms and a bath with a *SHOWER.* A large bedroom with oversized single beds at an angle like a ship's cabin. We can touch hands, but not feet. There is also a two-man desk with pivot chairs, a raised TV set, along with lights and shades that can be controlled from the bed. In GB's study there is a large partners table and a covered couch that would seat five very comfortably. And then there is a conference room down the hall a bit. Other planes this size hold 400 people. This plane holds 93. The galley is five times as big as Doro's kitchen. It is a very grand plane and a joy. We put on our night clothes and slept like babies. George got up and took a shower. I didn't dare for fear that I would soak my hair.

I spent the first day in Finland sight-seeing with Virginia Weinmann, wife of our ambassador, Jack Weinmann, who later in the administration became Chief of Protocol. She took me to Porvoo, a lovely old town filled with warm and friendly people. Imagine my surprise when

I heard someone call out, "How's Millie?" Don't ever underestimate the power of CNN.

That evening we dined in a restaurant while George had dinner with another old friend, Finland's President Koivisto. It was there that I discovered just how expensive everything is in Finland. I had been told that a Big Mac cost $8, a beer $5, and a massage $150. I ordered a delicious meal, trying to go by the lowest price, and it cost $70.

I wrote in my diary other observations of Helsinki:

It is the beginning of fall here, and the trees are beginning to turn right outside our window. Because we have been here on the weekend, we are seeing all the half million people who live here out on the streets. I am beginning to think the native costume is the running suit. Everyone, every age, has one.

The next day the spouses all met at the Koivistos' for tea. Raisa arrived wearing the exact same suit that she had worn for the Wellesley speech. I think she was sending a message home again. We sat around a round table: Raisa, Mrs. Koivisto, Rebecca Matlock (wife of our ambassador to the Soviet Union, Jack Matlock), Virginia Weinmann, myself, and several other ladies. Raisa did most of the talking, focusing on the problems that her country was having. You could tell she felt very strongly. From there we went to visit the library at the University of Helsinki, which had as much Russian history as Finnish. Hundreds of people were waiting across the street, and before the bus stopped, Raisa asked me to go greet the people with her. She took my hand and away we went. She made a little speech thanking the people on her behalf and my behalf. I now had a new spokesperson! I was very amused by the whole situation. Raisa could not pass up a crowd without making a little speech, and I was touched she included me.

After the library visit, we went to our separate embassies to freshen up and then Raisa was to host a tea at the Soviet Embassy. She appeared in a much more stylish outfit—it was closed to press and there would be no TV cameras. At the last moment we were told that except for me, all the other ladies we had spent the day with had been uninvited to the tea, including the wife of our host, the President of Finland. It was to be just the two of us and our interpreters. I wasn't sure why Raisa did that.

Although we had just finished lunch, Raisa served a full tea, starting off with both black and red caviar in a small pastry and some sort of
smoked fish on toast. We moved into kiwi soufflé (more like a mousse)
and a blueberry tart. This was served with a red wine, which both of
us drank just enough of to wet our tongues, and a red fruit drink that
tasted very much like cranberry juice. She talked at length about their
troubles again. She did ask me about how much two pounds of caviar
would cost in the United States. I told her that I did not know, that we
did not deal in two pounds when it came to caviar, but that I guessed
that it would cost around $500. Our interpreter said that she thought
that was correct. I told her that George and I both loved caviar, but
never felt that we could afford it. She was still very interested in how
much things cost. She had no inkling how the free enterprise system
worked, nor do I think she understood our work ethic. I asked her
about their politics and where their troubles were coming from. She
said that people were impatient. They had only one political party, but
that within the party there was competition. She said that shortly they
were going to have quite a few political parties. I told her that a two-
party system worked well, but more parties made it almost impossible
to get a consensus. (I confess this is not my field of expertise, but this
is what I told her.)

Each visit with Raisa made me like her more and understand her
a little better. She clearly loved her country and husband and wanted to
be a part of the solution. At times, their customs and traditions seemed
so different from ours that I felt we might as well be from different
planets; at other times, we were very sympathetic to each other.

Later, when we joined our husbands for their joint press conference, Raisa was back in her famous well-worn suit. Both Presidents
seemed relaxed. The communiqué was very clear and united on the
issue of Iraq. George came away from the summit thrilled with the
results: Now almost all the world was united against Saddam Hussein's invasion.

After we returned from our trip, *Millie's Book* had its official coming-out at the Pierpont Morgan Library in New York City,
followed by several weeks of a media blitz. One day I taped all three
network morning shows: the "Today" show with Deborah Norville;

"Good Morning America" with Joan Lunden; and "The CBS Morning Show" with Paula Zahn. I wrote in my diary: "All three ladies are beautiful blondes and I began to mix them up in my mind. They all three seem chic, stylish, bright and very nice. And they all three asked the same questions."

I also wrote in my diary about two magazine covers Millie and I appeared on: "In both . . . it looks as though I had forgotten to iron my face."

I had a wonderful time writing the book and was hoping sales would be good enough to raise a little money for my literacy foundation. What happened shocked everyone: It made its first appearance at number 1 on *The New York Times* best-seller list. All fall I signed and signed and signed books. My great friend Sally Neblett from Houston designed bookplates that I could autograph, which at least kept me and my staff from having to lug heavy books with us everywhere.

Over the years Millie sold more than 400,000 books and raised more than $1 million for the Barbara Bush Foundation for Family Literacy. Eventually the book came out in paperback and was printed in German and Japanese. Millie found out that being the President's dog had more than one perk. George liked to joke that it just wasn't right: He was President of the United States and his dog made more money than he did!

Also that fall, the very creative nonprofit Children's Literacy Initiative in Philadelphia invited me to read stories aloud on the radio. As a result, we launched "Mrs. Bush's Storytime," beginning with an ABC call-in program with Peter Jennings about literacy. For sixteen weeks, a host of celebrities, cartoon characters, and I read children's books, broadcast on ABC radio stations all over the country. The idea was to get families back to reading together and to spread the message about the importance of reading aloud to your children. The second year, the stories were made available on cassette tapes through Western Publishing Company, and we tucked into each one a how-to pamphlet with hints on reading aloud to your children. I often wondered if anyone listened, but as I write this in the fall of 1993, the fourth year of "Mrs. Bush's Storytime" is soon to begin on Thanksgiving Day and even will be broadcast to Shanghai, China.

Over the years people have told me just how much they enjoyed the stories. I usually ask if they listened with their children. They sometimes say yes, but almost as often would say, "Oh, no. My husband and I listen going to the market on Saturday mornings."

✑ The launchings of *Millie's Book* and "Mrs. Bush's Storytime" were nice beginnings to what otherwise was a difficult fall. For much of the year, George and his team had been working hard to get a budget through Congress that also would include a five-year plan to reduce the deficit. Finally, he almost had a deal with the Democrats when Newt Gingrich, a Republican congressman, got in the middle of it all and the compromise fell through. George agreed to raise taxes *if* the Democrat-controlled Congress would agree to cut spending. As a result, George was clobbered by members of his own party and the media. One New York newspaper ran the headline: READ MY LIPS: I LIED. Ugly. I wrote in my diary:

Everyone wants to pile on, but I don't worry. George IS doing the right thing. We just have to get the deficit down. I find myself in the funniest mood. I truly feel that George is doing what is responsible and right for the country and to heck with politics. There is a life after the White House and both of us are looking forward to it.

Eventually there was a compromise that seemed to please no one. I really felt it was a disgrace the way Congress—Democrats and Republicans alike—played politics with such an important issue.

George also was wrestling with Congress over a Civil Rights Bill. He did not want to veto the proposed bill, but the wording made quotas a possibility and that was not acceptable to him. George felt strongly about equal opportunity; he did not like imposing quotas. Again, it appeared they had an agreement worked out with Teddy Kennedy, the sponsor of the bill, but then the Democrats broke their commitment. It was apparent they did not want to give George a bill he could sign before the midterm elections, coming up in November.

And always hanging over George's head was the crisis in the Persian Gulf. I wrote in my diary on September 16:

Over the weekend George talked to François Mitterrand and told him how great it was that he had sent troops to Saudi Arabia. That dreadful man Saddam Hussein had sent troops into the French Embassy and scared their people to death. The more troops we get there from other countries, the happier I am. I love to hear George talk to his foreign friends: *"François, mon ami . . ."*

A wonderful, great thing did happen to George that fall: He got his own dog. Marvin and Margaret gave Ranger, Millie's only male puppy, back to us. George and Ranger had bonded early on, and for months he had been calling Margaret to invite Ranger up for the weekend at Camp David. Then he started suggesting that she bring Ranger over to the White House on Thursday nights so he would be sure to be there in time to leave for Camp the next day. Then he suggested that we return him on Monday morning instead of Sunday night. When he started asking that we keep him until Tuesday, Marvin and Margaret suggested that we keep him at the White House for Marshall, whose dog he really was. I was so glad for George to have that sweet and very amusing dog during these tough times. However, he immediately changed our sleeping habits: Ranger got up at five A.M., an hour before Millie.

But he was worth it. A big, bouncy puppy, he could leap straight up into the air and his handsome face made us laugh. He charged around Camp David in the snow and the rain, and he wandered the White House, knowing no strangers. He loved to curl up by George's side, and was everything in a dog George wanted.

Ranger made so many friends that we suddenly noticed that he was growing by leaps and bounds—out, not up—and George had to send out a memo requesting people *not* to feed Ranger:

IMPORTANT ANNOUNCEMENT
February 6, 1992
THIS IS AN ALL POINTS BULLETIN FROM THE PRESIDENT
SUBJECT: MY DOG "RANGER"

Recently Ranger was put on a weight reduction program. Either that program succeeds or we enter Ranger in the Houston Fat Stock Show as a Prime Hereford.

All offices should take a formal "pledge" that reads as follows:

"WE AGREE NOT TO FEED RANGER. WE WILL NOT GIVE HIM BIS-CUITS. WE WILL NOT GIVE HIM FOOD OF ANY KIND."

In addition, Ranger's "access" is hereby restricted. He has been told not to wander the corridors without an escort. This applies to the East and West Wings, to the Residence from the 3rd floor to the very, very bottom basement.

Although Ranger will still be permitted to roam at Camp David, the Camp David staff including the Marines, Naval personnel, All Civilians and Kids are specifically instructed to "rat" on anyone seen feeding Ranger.

Ranger has been asked to wear a *"Do not feed me"* badge in addition to his ID.

I will, of course, report on Ranger's fight against obesity. Right now he looks like a blimp, a nice friendly appealing blimp, but a blimp.

We Need Your Help—All hands, please help.

FROM THE PRESIDENT

We also were thrilled that fall when Doro and her two children, Sam and Ellie, moved from Maine to Washington. She got a job she loved at the National Rehabilitation Hospital, a state-of-the-art medical center where exciting things were happening in medicine. We loved having them so close that they could just pop in and check on us.

For me personally, it was an even busier time than usual. Besides campaigning for the midterm elections, I tried to keep up with my other causes and interests, which included both traveling and hosting teas and receptions at the White House. One reception that I especially remember was for the Craniofacial Foundation. This is one of Cher's favorite causes, and she arrived looking smashing. She is so trim and elegant and has the most beautiful complexion. I told someone how great I thought she looked and they said that she has had every kind of plastic surgery known to man. If that is the case, then we all should line up for the knife. She truly looked lovely. The wonderful part was that she knew all the kids by name. Many of these children were so deformed that it was hard to even look at them. She hugged them, held them, and played with them. I believe that Cher got involved with this group after she made the movie *Mask,* about a child with a deformed face.

Another distinct memory came during a trip to New York City, just after I had finished a visit to a day-care center for homeless children. I wrote in my diary:

As we drove up to the hotel, the Waldorf, I could not believe my eyes. There sitting in a wheelchair on the corner of Park Avenue and 50th Street was Jean MacArthur (wife of General Douglas MacArthur). I jumped out of the car to run over to give my dear little friend a kiss and say hello. That darling, chic lady said that she was just out getting some sun and air—as if she was out in the countryside instead of on a busy street corner in NYC. One of my traveling companions said, "Look at Mrs. Bush, kissing a homeless person." Some homeless person. Jean has made the Waldorf Towers her home for many years.

At the end of September we went to New York City for the United Nations General Assembly meetings. The reports coming out of Kuwait of rape and plunder were dreadful. We were very grateful that George's cousins' child, Sandy Clement, was in the United States with her Kuwaiti husband, Charles Haddad, and their five children when Saddam Hussein invaded. There was much hope then that the worldwide show of strength against Iraq and the air embargo would let our troops come home without firing a shot.

While in New York, I met with Queen Noor of Jordan. I wrote in my diary:

> She is a glorious-looking person, from a country that is overburdened with problems and has come out on the wrong side of the Iraq problem. They desperately need money for their refugees and it is hard to raise. She started out on her mission by saying that we must remain friends. I agreed. Then she talked about how we had made mistakes and that this was an Arab problem that must be solved by Arabs. I explained to her (which she already knew) that we had been invited into the region, as were 23 or 24 other countries, by Arabs. I also explained to her that if Jordan had been invaded we would have come to their aid also. She talked a lot about Israel and the weapons that they had that were illegal. I feel very sorry for their country, but must admit I was very glad to see the beautiful creature go. I like her so much, but truly feel that they are very wrong. The world can no longer sit back and watch one country, a member nation in the United Nations, invade and take over another, also a member state.

George spoke very movingly at the General Assembly and afterward we stood in a receiving line with Jim Baker and greeted several hundred people. We saw Eduard Shevardnadze from the USSR; our old friend Richard Akwei from Ghana, whom we knew both during our UN and China years; Ambassador Bishara from Kuwait; a delegate from Albania, which I mention because I don't believe that I had ever met an Albanian before, much less touched one; and the representative from North Korea, who looked George directly in the eye and said that he had listened carefully to George when he spoke about both Koreas being in the United Nations and he would pass his message on to Pyongyang.

During those several days George started early in the morning and went late into the night having bilateral meetings with other leaders. It took a tremendous amount of work to continue building, and then maintain, the coalition forming against Saddam Hussein.

The next night I had the great privilege of attending the opening of the Metropolitan Opera, with Plácido Domingo singing the leading tenor role. It truly was a glamorous evening:

The other honored guests were Prince Rainier and Prince Albert. The former was a dear, gentle man and the latter was the same. Very polite and kind. The Prince and I sat together the whole time and the minute the lights went out, the Prince went out. His head fell against his chest and he very quietly snoozed, awakening only when the audience clapped or his own snoring awakened him. Then he would clap away, saying, "What glorious tones. How marvelous, etc." as though he had heard it all.

I had another brush with royalty in early October when Princess Diana, in the States to raise money for several charities, came for tea. Just like when Michael Jackson came, I couldn't believe the number of staff who turned out to stare. And they had plenty to stare at. She is absolutely lovely-looking, and also bright and funny.

Margaret and Marvin had attended a gala dinner with her, and our dear friend Jenny Acland, wife of the British ambassador, put Marvin next to the Princess. They had great fun together, teasing and laughing, until Jenny asked Marvin to please invite the Princess to dance. He refused, saying that he had injured knees. All those years at dancing school gone to waste! Princess Diana told me at the tea—with a twinkle in her eye—that Marvin had behaved disgracefully. George later sent her a photo from that evening, which she signed for Marvin and sent back. He displays it with pride.

*   *   *

In early October, the budget crisis boiled over when both the Democrats and Republicans voted down the budget that had been worked on for months. George had granted a budget extension the week before but said he wouldn't grant another. So, without a budget, he was forced to shut down the federal government. Only people who were considered essential personnel could work, and no one was allowed to volunteer their time. The entire White House staff was let off except those crucial to the security of the government. And all the poor tourists who had come to Washington found the doors locked at the museums and monuments.

During the shutdown, we had the swearing-in ceremony for David Souter to the Supreme Court with 250 of his best friends. Standing in the receiving line, both George and I were impressed by the true affection people felt for David, and he for them. He gave us a very modest thank-you. I wish I could remember exactly what he said, but it was something like, "I will never be able to thank you all, but I can promise that I will pass it on to someone else." He said it so beautifully, slowly and with real feeling. We had no refreshments because we had no staff, but everyone seemed to understand.

During all this I was working hard for Republican candidates running in the midterm election. Without counting the days, I know I slept more nights in a hotel room than in my own bed, spending day after day on the road. I went from Connecticut to Texas to California, all the way to Hawaii, back to California, to Maine, to Florida, to Illinois, to Ohio, Kentucky, Georgia, back to Texas and on and on.

The funniest thing—at least we thought it was funny—happened to Jean Becker on the Hawaii trip. She and Sondra Haley were deputy press secretaries in my office and also advanced almost all my trips. They always had great stories of the things that happened to them on the road.

Jean was standing in a phone booth in Hawaii trying to talk to the office back in Washington when a pickup truck with a bunch of guys pulled up. They were playing the radio so loud Jean couldn't hear, so she politely asked them to please turn it down. A few minutes later Jean heard a funny noise, turned around, and one of the men was relieving himself on the side of the phone booth. She hung up and found another phone down the road. So much for the glamorous life of traveling.

We were traveling so much we didn't know where we were, and neither did anyone else. While I was in Maine I got a phone call from Jody Bush, my sister-in-law. She was calling from the cabana by the White House pool to find out if she could go for a swim. I said certainly—but where in the world did she think I was? It turned out she thought I was upstairs in the White House.

That reminds me of the great luxury of the White House operators. Besides being the world's nicest women, they can find anybody, anywhere, any time. But you had to be careful—you never knew where the person was you were calling. Once when George asked them to find Carla Hills, the U.S. Trade Representative, they woke her up in a Switzerland hotel room. I was in Houston campaigning when the phone rang at five-thirty in the morning and I heard that much beloved voice say, "How's the big guy?" I answered, "George Bush, I don't know how your dog is, nor do I know where you are, but I am in Houston, Texas, and it's only five-thirty!" He said, "Oh, my gosh, I thought you were in Washington. I'm in Minnesota."

The moral of that story is that we were working too hard *and* the White House switchboard could find us anyplace.

While on a campaign swing in Dallas, George W. asked me to go to the Institute for Aerobics Research Gala. Before I went, I told George (the father, not the son) that I was going to tell them that I bet I was the first speaker they ever had whose body was made up of 33⅓ percent fat. He bet me I wouldn't say it. I did, and there was sort of a stunned silence and then a large laugh. It was the leanest, trimmest, healthiest group I had ever seen.

A great bonus that night was seeing George and Laura's twins dressed up for their school's Halloween Carnival. I wrote in my diary:

Jenna went as Miss Halloween and looked so beautiful despite the fact that she had skeleton earrings and all sorts of ugly things on her costume. Barbara had on an all-green body suit and was covered with purple balloons—she went as grapes and won third prize. Both girls were heavily made up and I could see shades of things to come. They are truly going to be great beauties!

Another campaign stop was Portland, Oregon, which is one of the most beautiful cities in America and home to some of the finest, nicest people. Unfortunately it also seems to be the home training base for the state-of-the-art protesters. I went out to do a fund-raising breakfast for our friend Mark Hatfield, who was in a battle for his Senate seat. When Mark got up to speak, two protesters—one after the other in different parts of the room—started screaming very ugly things, making it impossible for Mark to be heard. The audience immediately stood and clapped and clapped until the protesters were removed kicking and yelling from the room. Antoinette Hatfield, Mark's wife and a great friend, is always so positive. Her response to all this was: "Look at it this way, Bar. They both paid to get in and the campaign can use the money."

In 1992 I went to Portland to do a fund-raising dinner for George. On the way to the hotel we passed some men and women in black body suits with masks on their faces. Some were holding signs that said: KILL THE PRESIDENT. Since George was elsewhere, that didn't bother me too much until I spotted a large poster that had a familiar-looking white-headed cartoon character with the words OFF WITH HER HEAD written in bold black letters. After the speeches had been given but before the dessert, the Secret Service strongly suggested we leave because of a bomb threat. We drove past a large crowd of protesters being held off by mounted police. By the time we got to the airport we heard via car radio that seventeen people had been arrested and some people slightly hurt in the fray.

Unfortunately, being the target of such things is a part of public life, but I'm not sure you ever get used to it. On a similar note, a friend sent me an article in which Joan Rivers quoted me as saying the most vulgar, disgusting thing I had ever read. When I let George see it, he said, "When did you talk to Joan Rivers, Bar?" He was just teasing, because he knew I had not talked to her at all. I distinctly remember forgetting what she said I said, but it was so ugly. Public life!

    I stopped campaigning long enough in October to fly to Ottawa, Canada, for the International Conference on Literacy and Corrections. Mila Mulroney introduced me, and I gave a speech that Susan Green, the wonderful, talented, funny woman (and closet Democrat) who had written my speeches for years, had worked on really hard. We all agreed that it did no good to keep men and women in prison and send them out having learned only how to be better criminals. I kicked off the conference, got back in the car, and flew home. I don't think I ever got used to in-and-out trips like that. On this particular day, I was home in time to have a 2:30 P.M. reception for the Victory Awards, which were sponsored by National Rehabilitation Hospital. Every year they honor people who have demonstrated great courage in the face of adversity.

A few weeks later we hosted the presentation of the Congressional Gold Medal to Andrew Wyeth in the Roosevelt Room. It was such a treat. He is a great painter and comes from such an amazing family— his dad, N. C. Wyeth; his son Jamie Wyeth, who designed his father's medal; and his sister, Wyeth Hurd, who painted Pat Nixon; all of whom are outstanding artists. His sons called him Daddy and kissed him, and I couldn't help but think that if more people did that, we'd have fewer problems.

∽ Unfortunately, these bright spots were rare. I had trouble reading the papers, so was thrilled to find Ken Follett's *Pillars of the Earth*. George also enjoyed it—although he didn't give up reading the papers.

I wrote in my diary on October 24:

Discouraging week for G.B. The budget talks have folded. The Civil Rights Bill had to be vetoed and the papers this morning are saying that "Republicans are running, not walking away from" George. He has worked so hard and he is right. It certainly is hard. Two more weeks until the election and G. says that it will get worse, not better.

I am having to work on myself to not be bitter about those members of Congress who are acting gutless, and there are so many on both sides of the aisle. What I should be thinking about are those valiant few, like Bob Dole and Bob Michel, Al Simpson, Orrin Hatch, Strom Thurmond and really so many more, who are helping George. I also have to remember that he will have to work with them all again.

. . . George has just called from Hawaii, where he was campaigning and attending a summit of 12 Pacific Island nations. It is 8 a.m. there and somebody has told him about a nice article in *The Washington Post* by Don-nie Radcliffe about me. How kind of him and how kind of her. He says that his trip is going well, that his budget has passed the House and will get through the Senate. Amazing! Finally!

Just before the election I joined the cabinet wives for lunch. I think we really needed each other that day. I wrote in my diary:

Kath Darman had been feeling very low and Nancy Sununu should have been for the press had been beating both these women's husbands up for a fare-thee-well. I had heard rumors going around that I was pushing George to get rid of both of these men. As Sam LeBlond would say: *NOT!* Tom DeFrank of *Newsweek* called Anna Perez and told her that he was going to go with that story and just wanted to verify it. I was so grateful to him for calling that I called him back myself and told him how much I admired both men and that I thought George was well served by his staff. For a reporter to check on a story is a pretty rare thing these days. *Newsweek* did not print that story.

There are always some mischief-makers in Washington who are try-ing to make trouble for reasons known only to themselves. Patty Presock (George's wonderful assistant) told me that two masked/voice-altered peo-ple appeared on Pat Robertson's program who claimed to be staff members fearful of reprisals who said that George was being taken over by liberals. That started rumors about just who they were, and that wasn't healthy. I believe that they were two recently fired staff members, but that doesn't matter. They didn't have the courage to let their faces show. They should not have been given air time.

In all honesty, George's administration was freer of rumors than most. Gossip and rumors are the food that Washington insiders live and thrive on. When reading a newspaper, you should suspect it's rumor if it reads something like this: "A high White House official, who spoke with the agreement that he would not be named, said . . .". or, "A source close to the President, who spoke off the record, said . . ." George refused to give off-the-record interviews, which did not always endear him to the press. I remember once when James Reston of *The New York Times* canceled an interview because George wouldn't do it "off the record." Many people plant leaks to get the word out or to send up a trial balloon to get public reaction. Some people do it feeling they then can get better press for themselves. That just wasn't George's style.

⤳ On my final campaign swing, I stopped in Salt Lake City for Genevieve Atwood, a bright, enthusiastic candidate for Congress who in her rally speech gave an unusual endorsement for George. She said that she was for George Bush "right down to his underwear." I don't think that is why she lost, but she did.

My staff and I were so exhausted when we finally got home November 1 that we cheered when the plane landed at Andrews Air Force Base. We had campaigned for thirty-three candidates in twenty states and twenty-nine cities. I wrote in my diary the next day:

I have just talked to Peggy (my personal aide) and she is feeling blue. I know the feeling. The press is so anti the GOP this morning. I think the hardest part of campaigning is the waiting. Now people need to get out the vote. They don't need me anymore, so I invited the children to come for dinner tonight. Andy (Stewart) will come for lunch. I give a literacy speech tomorrow and then fly to Texas to meet up with George and vote on Tuesday.

George and I went to rallies in Tyler and Waco, Texas, with Clayton and Modesta Williams. He was running for governor against Ann Richards and despite all the bad publicity he got, I liked him.

Election Day arrived and I sunk myself into some new reading thanks to Kath Darman. She had discovered that Rosamunde Pilcher, author of *The Shell Seekers* and *September*, had written several books before these best-sellers and they were now out in paperback. They saved my life and I read away. I just could not watch the news.

The election was something of a downer. We lost governorships in Texas, Florida, Nebraska, Rhode Island, and Kansas. We were thrilled when John Engler won Michigan; Jim Edgar, Illinois; Bill Weld, Massachusetts; Pete Wilson, California; and George Voinovich, Ohio. We lost Rudy Boschwitz's Senate seat in Minnesota, but Mark Hatfield won his seat easily in Oregon. All in all, it probably wasn't as bad as it felt. On an off-election year, the party who holds the White House traditionally loses twenty-four seats. We lost eight in the House, one in the Senate, and came out even on the governors' races. So it was not the wipeout that we kept reading and hearing about. My own track record was not great: twenty-three lost; ten won. While I sat and felt badly for everyone, George, naturally, was on the phone calling winners and losers alike.

  It had been an exhausting two months since Labor Day, but certainly there was no time to rest. George signed two major pieces of legislation in November. The first was the Head Start Bill, which gave this program its biggest boost since it had been founded in LBJ's administration twenty-five years earlier. George's goal was eventually to make Head Start—which gives low-income and at-risk children a running start at a good education—available to every eligible child.

  And he signed the landmark Clean Air Act, the first overhaul of that program since it was passed in 1970. He specifically targeted urban smog; acid rain; and cancer-causing emissions. Getting the bill through Congress had required some tricky negotiating between business interests and environmentalists. Bill Reilly, George's head of the Environmental Protection Agency, John Sununu, and many others had done a great job.

  Then, on November 16, we left on one of the most important overseas trips we took during George's presidency. Before coming home, we would visit six countries; George would join other world leaders for a historic summit in Paris; he would meet face-to-face with a man who long had been considered an enemy of our country; and most important, we would have our best Thanksgiving Day ever.

  I wrote in my diary the first day, as we headed for Czechoslovakia:

The trip over takes 8 hours and 15 minutes with a 6-hour time change. George has travel down to an art. We, of course, fly at night so that he will not miss a day's work. Now with this beautiful new plane it is so easy. (Before we left) George called at 4:30 and suggested a 6 p.m. dinner at the house. So smart, because if you wait until the plane, it takes at least an hour before they can get everyone settled and served after takeoff. So the ushers called Pierre (Chambrin) in for a light supper of eggs and bacon, a favorite of George's. What a laugh. We had the softest eggs in a wonderful puff pastry, bacon, and a side plate of smoked turkey and salsa. Pierre does not know light, but he does know good!

The ambassador's residence in Czechoslovakia, where we stayed, was a beautiful, graceful home with a fascinating history. It had been built in 1928 by a member of a very old wealthy philanthropic family, the Petscheks, whose members were spread all over Europe. In 1938 the family told the household staff they were going out to the country for a few days. They never came back. Other members of this great family did the same thing on the same day, leaving other European capitals. Imagine my surprise to find that my darling friend in Washington, Annelise FitzGerald, whose husband, William, succeeded Dick Moore as ambassador to Ireland, was one of those who left. She, her mother, and sisters escaped through England, Portugal, Argentina, Cuba, and finally New York City, where the entire family rendezvoused. Her dad came through Canada. Her aunt and uncle had built the residence we were staying in. At various times the house had been owned by the Nazis, Czechs, Communists, and now the United States, who obtained the house for debts owed us. And yet it still retained needlepoint pillows and other furnishings from the day the owners walked out.

The U.S. Ambassador was our old friend Shirley Temple Black, who with her husband, Charlie, worked as a very effective team for the United States.

Olga and Vaclav Havel met our plane, and she and I immediately went to visit a hospital for mentally retarded children. It was a grim institution and had "that" smell. The directress said they were hoping to enlarge the already huge place, and Olga spoke up immediately and said: "Oh, no. We want smaller institutions, more family atmosphere." In the car Olga told me that the directress was from the Communist regime, as are so many others, and that they will have to learn the new ways. Change is hard. She also told me that 80 percent of the women were in the work force and they would like to see that lowered. Like us, they worried about families staying together.

We stopped at a school, where the children came in just for the visit since it was a Saturday, and then we walked across the Charles Bridge, built of wood in the twelfth century and then rebuilt of stone in the fourteenth century. The view of Prague was spectacular. In fact, it was the best place to see the city, because close up, everything seemed dingy, gray, peeling, and crumbling. At one time during the day we were in the car with the Havels and passed the railroad station. George asked Vaclav how the railroads were, and Vaclav's answer will remain with me forever: "Like everything else in the country, George, old."

Later that day, we went to Wenceslas Square to celebrate the one-year anniversary of "The Velvet Revolution," so called because not a shot was fired. I wrote in my diary:

No words can describe this ceremony. There were one million people there all waving American and Czech flags. It was on this place that the revolution took place a year ago. Vaclav spoke and then George spoke. The response was overwhelming. . . . After the speech we walked out into the crowd to shake hands and then walked up on an unprotected platform to sing "We Shall Overcome," which has become the theme song for freedom around the world. It was so moving. I could not believe the crowd and the emotional feeling.

En route to Paris, we made a brief stop in Germany to visit the Kohls. When we got into a helicopter and flew over German forests and the Rhine River Valley, I couldn't help but think that it is still the cleanest country I have ever seen. I wrote:

The Kohls took us to Ludwigshafen, their home, where we indulged in the best and biggest meal anyone has ever eaten. It is so flattering to be taken to one's private home. The food was good, but the conversation was better. . . . Helmut agrees with George: We cannot allow naked aggression. He felt that Saddam Hussein does not understand the strength we have in Saudi Arabia and he felt people should tell him this. George felt that Saddam should be told himself and the message should not be relayed by one of his people. It is known that he has shot people who have told him things he does not want to hear. He is crazy. There was some discussion that he watches CNN and is getting a distorted picture of what our people are thinking at home. CNN, of course, shows the dissidents and not the supporters. The polls all show overwhelming support of George. Half the people who don't support him just think he isn't doing enough. I'd hate to be president!

On the way there Hannelore told me the problems of unification of the two Germanys. East Germany has no telephones (12 percent have phones), very bad roads, no idea of competition, no cars (now that they can buy a car, they don't know how to drive), no hospital beds, no social security, no health insurance and on and on. She was not discouraged, feeling that they can solve their problems.

We flew on to Paris, where George went to dinner with François Mitterrand and I had a cozy dinner with three dear friends: Susan Baker and our most able ambassador and his wife, Walter and Taitsie Curley. (I should note that Taitsie went by her given name, Mary, while living in France. Since our last two ambassadors' wives' names were Bootsie and Honey, she thought she'd make it easier for the French.)

We were to be in Paris for three days for the Conference on Security and Cooperation in Europe. It was a historic meeting of all the leaders of Europe and the United States and Canada, and many people considered it the official end of the Cold War.

The first day the spouses had a rather eventful lunch at the Trianon Palace:

It was a large lunch, and many wives of heads of state, heads of governments and international organizations were there. I was on Danielle's (Mitterrand) right; Poul Schluter's ballet dancer new wife was on her left. At the ends of the table sat Mila Mulroney and the directress of Le Grand Trianon, Madame Simone Hoog. Across from me were Hannelore Kohl, Mrs. Vassiliou from Cyprus and Raisa Gorbachev. The latter looked just fine. She did not take the tour and arrived a little late for the lunch.

The press came in before lunch with little or no discipline and in the shoving and pushing, one photographer's camera swung and hit Hannelore Kohl in the neck and she had to leave the lunch. We all worried about her.

The lunch itself was quite funny. Raisa made quite a few toasts. It seemed a little strange because no one else made a toast. (Obviously a difference in customs again.) Later, teasing, I told Mila that it was like an old Russian movie and it began to look like she was trying to drink us under the table. I heard Mrs. G. tell Mila that she had seen all the troubles that they are having in Canada with Indians and French-speaking people, etc. After she went on for quite a while about all the ills of Canada, to save my friend I said that the television often showed the controversy and very rarely the good. Mrs. G. said that they had a saying in their country,

"Where there's smoke there's fire." I said that we also had the same saying, but that sometimes the press made it into a forest fire when it was only a bonfire. She countered with, "There must be something there." Danielle Mitterrand said that sometimes you wondered if the press wanted to put out the fire or make it into something bigger. When Mrs. G. wanted to speak, she would interrupt Mila, who was talking to Anne Marie Schluter, and say, "Mila, excuse me, I'm talking," and then give another toast or start talking. She had a very good interpreter who spoke both French and English and, of course, Russian. Danielle Mitterrand, who is innately polite, realized that her luncheon was getting out of hand, and so she told a slightly risqué story to Mila and the rest of us. I watched Raisa's face as her interpreter struggled to explain the story to her. As it was a play on words, I guess it was difficult. We were all laughing and Raisa never cracked a smile. I was so proud of Mila. She never told Raisa that she had seen all *their* troubles on the tube. We all have and, even if the press is exaggerating, they are dreadful.

We were going to have one night off in Paris, and George asked Walter Curley if just the four of us could go out to a Paris restaurant and have dinner. Walter later told us that the Secret Service and the Paris police laughed at him when he suggested different places. If we had dinner on the river in a boat, they would have to close five bridges. The Eiffel Tower restaurant could be done, but we would have to walk up and down, and so on. In the end, George had President Gorbachev for a working dinner.

The next day the spouses went to see the magnificent Picasso exhibit. I wrote in my diary:

Neither Hannelore Kohl nor Raisa came. We have heard that the former hurt her second vertebra. The latter said that "She had seen a Picasso show before." We all had, but it was like visiting old friends—you always notice or learn something new AND our hostess had invited us. It was a fascinating tour. I was amused by Anna Perez, who had advanced the exhibit. The press was set up in strategic places around the museum for photo ops. Anna sidled up to me at one time and said when you get to the next room, just walk on through. DO NOT STOP and talk to the press. Evidently there were some pretty graphic pictures on the wall where they wanted me to stop.

The politics taking place while we were in Paris were almost unbelievable. For example, the French Premier, Michel Rocard, won a confidence test by just four votes. The very next day, Mrs. Rocard hosted a luncheon for the delegate spouses, which would have been very awkward if her husband had been ousted the night before.

But the major political storm was in England, where Margaret Thatcher—while attending the meeting in Paris—was in a fight for her political life. She also was facing a confidence vote that she had to win by a majority of votes plus 15 percent. She fell short by five votes of winning on the first ballot, so now we had to wait until the next week to see what would happen. She must have felt lonely away from her family at this difficult time, given this terrible insult by her own party. She had lost support mainly because of her poll tax and her opposition to a unified Europe.

On Tuesday night, President Mitterrand hosted everyone at a dinner at Versailles Palace. I wrote:

The arrival at Versailles was so beautiful. The palace was lit from top to bottom and the drive was lined with soldiers. The minute we got there we ran into Margaret. She is a gutsy woman. I gave her a big hug and told her that we had been waiting all day for the news. She said, "Not to worry," and went on to say that she'd get it on the second ballot. George and I took Margaret by the arm and ran the gamut of the press. The first person I saw after we went through the receiving line in the Hall of Crusades was Hannelore Kohl in a neck brace. She had been hurt.

After a short reception we were led into the Opera Hall, where we saw a very short selection from three ballets. The theater was exquisite. I sat next to George and President Gorbachev. Walt Curley said that he counted 520 seats. It seemed hard to believe. There were three balconies, one-person deep, I'd say. It was so nice.

Then we were led into the Coronation Hall, which was glorious, and had a refreshment and an opportunity to "wash our hands." (Stylish port-a-cans were brought in for the occasion.)

And then we went into the Hall of Mirrors, where I sat next to President Mitterrand and President Gorbachev. Thank heavens that I had Daisy Richardson to interpret for me. Daisy is married to a foreign service officer. She was born in Poland and speaks some Russian, beautiful French and, of course, English. President Gorbachev's interpreter spoke only Russian and

French. We were seated at a long, long table that held 200 people with mirrors lining all the walls. They reflected chandeliers, the candelabras and the beautiful flowers. We were all in our very grandest gowns and it was the most glamorous evening—a fairy tale evening. George sat across from me and next to Danielle and Raisa. I noticed several times during the evening Raisa and Mikhail raising their glasses to each other and exchanging affectionate glances.

The next day, after the historic signing of the CSCE treaty calling for the reduction of conventional weapons in Europe, we went on to Jeddah, Saudi Arabia, where we were met on arrival by a very gracious King Fahd.

While George had a men-only working dinner, I went to the Royal Palace for dinner with Princess Jawhara. It was a fascinating evening and gave the Americans a glimpse of the Arab culture:

The palaces are made of marble, they look well made and are very clean. We arrived at the Palace and there was a screen at the door—thus preventing the men from seeing the ladies. Princess Jawhara was inside the door to greet me and introduced me to several of her sisters and sisters-in-law and one chubby eleven-year-old niece dressed in a long elaborate gown. The Princess is a pretty lady with black hair and eyes . . . she had on a beautiful silk dress with a beaded jacket and the darndest pearl necklace and bracelets with diamond and emerald clasps. They were so exquisite and beautiful. We went into a large hall whose walls were lined with chairs. I stood and shook hands with every guest, 400 ladies. The first through the line were the King's sisters. They all looked like him and wore a black net or veil pulled tightly over their hair and several had covered faces. They all had on fabulous gowns and the most beautiful jewelry. Margaret Tutwiler* whispered to me that now we know who buys all that beautiful jewelry that we see in stylish ladies' magazines. There were many young women who were great beauties. Almost all the Arab ladies were related in some way. I had been well coached, and so I knew I was to drink the Arab coffee, which is slightly medicinal in flavor and quite

---

* Margaret was Jim Baker's spokesperson and usually attended working dinners, but could not, since she was a woman, so she came with me. There was "discrimination" at our dinner also: My Secret Service agents were left outside; a woman agent had to be brought in.

pale, maybe weak is a better word. I rather liked it. It comes in a tiny little cup, you drink it down, shake your cup from side to side and it is picked up. After the receiving line, the Princess and I sat and talked through an interpreter for a few minutes and then many of the women were led up to sit, talk and tell me what they do. And they do a lot. During the last 30 years the Arabs have started to educate their women. Quite a few of the women I met were married before they started college and got their doctorates. I met medical doctors, many university professors and some ladies who have formed a group to do good works (an Arab Junior or Service League?). They are very proud of their latest project, which is taking care of and working with Down's Syndrome children. Her Highness at one time leaned over and squirted my hand with scent that is pure essence and lingers on through many washings. She also gave me a great malachite and gold house. When I opened the double doors I found a lovely little working clock. This beautiful clock will be in the George Bush Library for all to admire. We did not go into dinner until 11 o'clock. The food was unbelievable and delicious. After dinner we retired back to the same room, where the coffee and incense came in again. I waved the incense towards me as is the custom and then to my shock my skirt was lifted slightly and the whole incense burner was tucked under my skirt. I was panicked. I was sure that my brand-new Scaasi gown was going to go up in flames and I with it! It was an evening never to be forgotten by me or any of the Americans who were lucky enough to be there. Besides the women who were traveling with us there were the wives of American businessmen and foreign service officers, mostly from the Consulate corps.

The whole evening did remind me that we have a lot of learning to do about the customs of our foreign friends and they about us.

Thanksgiving Day, 1990—The best we ever had.

Our day in the desert with our men and women in the military was a highlight of George's presidency. What a privilege it was for us to share their Thanksgiving Day.

That morning we slept until 6:45 and then had to race for a 7:35 departure from the guest palace. Our first stop was the air base in Dhahran, where we visited with the U.S. and Allied troops. George spoke, and then we plunged out into the crowd while somebody tried to keep order. Dhahran was the hottest stop. Every single serviceman and servicewoman seemed to have a camera. I was asked to sign pictures of their wives, husbands, babies, and dogs. We posed for as many pictures as possible and hugged and clasped hands.

We took a chopper to the Army Tactical Location, and repeated the speech and plunge. This time we also went through the chow line and got a Thanksgiving plate, which we then ate at two different tables with darling young people. A woman named Lisa at my table told me that her husband had gone last year to Panama and now it was her turn. They were so very young.

We choppered out to the U.S.S. *Nassau* for a short and very moving Thanksgiving Day service on the stern of the ship. We worked the crowd as best we could. The men were hanging from the rafters, and those on the upper deck were too far away to talk to.

Our final stop was the Marine Tactical Location, where we also saw the Seabees and the Brits. The spirit was amazing, and we spent quite a little time there.

Our guide for the day was General Norman Schwarzkopf, an amusing, big bear of a man. He was an expert on the Middle East and understood the customs of the Arab world. He was very deft at avoiding political land mines as well as military ones. He exuded confidence that day and expressed gratitude to George about having all they needed to get the job done, instead of having "his hands tied behind his back" as they did in Vietnam.

Flying over those miles and miles of desert we occasionally saw tracks that were made by trucks. We did see some roads that were bulldozed out of the sand. We also saw patches that were from underground water, and as the winter season comes on, they become boggy and impassable for cars and tanks. But for the most part you can drive anywhere in the desert. Every now and then we would fly over a pipeline that you can clearly see from the air. That worried me, as it seemed so easy for the Iraqis to blow up. The General told me not to worry, that our air power was so superior. We saw an occasional Bedouin tent, and if we looked hard, we could see camels in a two-mile radius of the tent. The camels dig down and find some root, and therefore graze in the sand. The General told me that every inch of the desert belonged to someone. Amazing.

The only disappointment of the day was that we learned Margaret Thatcher had resigned. This was quite a blow to us, although we were prepared for that possibility. Margaret had been such a rock. George called her from our last stop to express his regrets. After a hard fight, John Major from Margaret's Conservative party beat Michael Heseltine and became the new Prime Minister.

I hated leaving those brave men and women in the desert, and George and I both were thrilled when they got a special treat in December: a visit from none other than Bob Hope. At age eighty-eight, it was quite a feat that this remarkable man put together yet another USO show for American servicemen and servicewomen abroad at Christmas. George and I love Bob and Dolores, and they have been more than kind to us over the years.

✑ We went on to Egypt, showering on the plane to get rid of some of the sand and dust. While there, I visited the Egyptian Museum with a dear friend from our days at the United Nations, Eglal Abdel-Meguid, whose husband was now the Foreign Minister. Suzanne Mubarak, who has worked so hard raising money for neighborhood libraries, took me to visit the Children's Library of Cairo. I wrote about my observations of this great city:

. Cairo matches Prague when it comes to pollution. And Cairo is the only city that I have ever seen where the buildings seem to be crumbling from the top down. They have added a new overpass for cars, and as you drive over the city it is dreadful to see the tops of beautiful old houses crumbling. Our friends Sadri and Katy (Prince Sadruddin Aga Khan and his wife, Princess Katherine) told me a story of a friend of theirs who lives in an old restored house. She was sitting with her mother when they heard the most terrible sound. They thought that a bomb had been thrown. Then the air filled with dust and covered everything. They ran choking out on their balcony to see that the house next door had literally fallen down and was gone. No bomb at all, it just fell.

. . . As Suzanne and I were driving past all those crumbling houses, she said: "I don't know what happened to us, Barbara. Once we were the leaders of the world and look at us today."

She also pointed out to me that every other person we saw had a baby in their arms. She told me that they cannot get their people to cut the birth rate. Katy told me that Cairo was a city built for 1 million people and now 13 million live there. Katy was born in Cairo, and she and Sadri have a lovely old house in the old district that they have restored. Such a beautiful, old, crumbling city. The people look amazingly happy when you consider all their problems.

On the way back to the States, we made a nonscheduled stop in Geneva, where George was going to talk with President Assad of Syria. It was a controversial move on George's part. The papers were full of stories of the Israelis being upset by the visit, but George felt he must try for peace in every way he could. I wrote of Assad: "He looks like a warm friendly man for such a villain."

We got home very early in the morning on Saturday, November 24, and after a restful weekend, took a quick, marvelous trip to Mexico to visit with Carlos and Cecilia Salinas and their family. Carlos truly has been a great president for a country that has so many problems. I was shocked when Carlos told George that because of terrible pollution—a problem he is vigorously fighting—the children of Mexico City paint the sky gray, not blue, and without stars, which they've never seen.

Jeb and his family and George and I had a lovely visit with them in their family home in Monterrey, and they once spent an evening with us at Camp David, where Colu and her sister Lucilla joined us. At one time during the evening one of those very shy, quiet young women looked right at Carlos and said that she wanted him to know that he made them once again proud to be of Mexican heritage. It was said with such sincerity and feeling that I know Carlos was pleased and touched.

In December I plunged myself into getting ready for our second Christmas in the White House, but it wasn't so easy with the Iraq situation dominating everything:

December 2—This has been some week. Needless to say, the whole time, before, during, and since we returned from Mexico, has been spent worrying and thinking about Desert Shield and our troops there. Thursday the U.N. had their vote and they have given permission for any means to get Saddam Hussein out of Kuwait after January 15th. Then on Friday, George announced that he would meet with the Iraqi Foreign Minister in Washington and Jim Baker would meet with Saddam Hussein in Baghdad afterwards. This is not to negotiate, but to be sure that Saddam understands that we mean it and that we have the ability to wipe them out. The papers are full of urging for the latter move . . . the U.N. vote will make it much easier for George to deal with Saddam Hussein. As often is the case, the rest of the world backs George more than our own (Congress) or press. The House and the Senate have been having hearings. Many of the Congress members have plenty of criticism, but no solutions. We awakened this morning to Sam Nunn saying something like, "Of course, I am for stopping Saddam Hussein, just not in this fashion." We waited, but no solutions followed. Incidentally, I was amused to see that Sam resigned from Burning Tree Club because they have no female members, and I was told he also has changed his opinion on abortion. Guess who is running for president!

December 5—The Congress is hearing all sorts of witnesses on the Iraq situation. They are rapidly making it impossible for us to get Saddam to believe that we are serious. Oh, God, I feel sorry for George. Meanwhile Kuwaitis are being raped and plundered right and left.

December 15—Although we have done a million things this week the Iraq problem is still foremost in our minds. All the American hostages were released this week and we closed our embassy in Kuwait.

Many people are criticizing and prophesying that it will be a bloody war. There are stories about 50 thousand body bags that will be needed to bring our military home. This is very tough on the families that are left at home.

The message has come back . . . Saddam says that the first moment he can meet with Jim Baker is January 12th. He wants to get closer to the U.N. deadline and then who knows what shenanigans he will come up with? In a press conference yesterday George said that he found it difficult to believe that Saddam couldn't meet with Jim Baker for two hours when he met with people like Muhammad Ali, John Connally, Ted Heath and Ramsey Clark on the spur of the moment. Quite a few people let themselves be used by Saddam, but I did not expect it of John Connally, a fine former governor of Texas, who in contradiction to U.S. policy went to Iraq with (Houston businessman) Oscar Wyatt. He must have felt silly when he got there to find that it had already been announced that the hostages would be freed. He and Oscar brought back a half-empty plane of hostages and took credit. I could believe anything of Oscar Wyatt, but I found it hard to believe that John Connally would crassly put financial gain above honor. [I want to add here that we love John's wife, Nellie, and George had great respect for John when he was governor of Texas. George was very disappointed when he made the trip with Oscar, who had business dealings in Iraq.]

Amazingly enough, life went on. The Christmas season was fast upon us and we made all the usual calls on hospitals and schools, had all the Christmas parties, and took presents to Toys for Tots. This is one of my favorite programs. Marines collect new toys for underprivileged children and see that they are delivered. I went to help pack toys, but mostly to help get the word out that they were desperate for more new toys, plastic bags for packing, and volunteers. If you are reading this near Christmas, I hope you will remember the Toys for Tots program in your hometown.

Earlier in the month we also had hosted the reception for the annual Kennedy Center Honors. This year they honored Jule Styne, Katharine Hepburn, Dizzy Gillespie, Risë Stevens, and Billy Wilder. All were great stars, but Katharine Hepburn got the most attention for a lot of reasons. First, she is a great actress; second, she is slightly eccentric. She came to this black-tie event in a black turtleneck, a black trench coat, black pants, a white scarf, and black sneakers. Her marvelous hair was piled on top of her head in a rather helter-skelter fashion that was beguiling. She seemed feisty and immediately tweaked George on his antiabortion position. She allowed as how she wondered why she had come. Then having said that, at the awards ceremony itself at the Kennedy Center, she seemed very moved by her tribute, which showed scenes of her with Cary Grant, Henry Fonda, and Spencer Tracy, the love of her life. She stood with tears in her eyes and said, leaning over the balcony, "I never saw that scene with Spence before. They were all remarkable actors. I was lucky." She was lucky—*and* she was good. I was amused to see that after the intermission was over, she started back to her box and by mistake took the wrong door and ended up one box away. Instead of going back out into the hallway to come through the right door, she just climbed over the railing.

We also entertained visitors from England. The new Prime Minister of Great Britain, John Major, came up to Camp David with his wife, Norma, on the twenty-first. We found them both very likable, and we struck up an immediate friendship. George put great trust in John and valued his advice.

As always, the White House looked spectacular, this year with the theme "The Nutcracker." The parties were fun, but the one that stands out was when Sondra Haley and Ann Brock—my delightful director of scheduling—brought their "star dates." Since they are both huge fans of the soap opera "All My Children," they decided it would be fun to invite two of the male stars to be their dates to the Christmas party. They got "Yes" answers from "Tad Martin" (Michael E. Knight) and "Will Courtland" (Patrick Stewart). It wasn't too hard to tell who were soap fans at the party, and there were many. The girls and their dates brought the house down.

〰️ All our children came home. Their in-laws were marvelous about letting us have them every year George was president. I think that they knew that George needed them. He needed their support, their jokes, and their love—this year, more than ever. And we did have a wonderful Christmas, with all the usual noise, excitement, and constant motion of typical big families.

Nevertheless, 1990 ended on a tense note. It was as if the whole world was holding its breath.

21

Desert Storm

The line had been drawn in the sand and so we waited. An ABC/*Washington Post* poll showed that the majority of Americans backed the President, but of course there was still controversy. I wrote in my diary in early January:

> The Congress wants to position themselves on both sides. It takes guts to be George Bush . . . I asked George the other day how he could read the papers and listen to the news. It is so slanted and filled with things that didn't happen that I feel my stomach churning. He said calmly, "I know what I am doing, I know what I have to do and I don't worry about what they say." I wish I could feel that way. He is at peace with himself. That is not to say that he enjoys all this, but he can look at the big picture.
>
> . . . The press has a disproportionate part to play in this battle of waiting and nerves. As an example, Dick Cheney and Colin Powell came up to the Residence to see George after their trip to the Middle East and reported that we were ready for anything, everything was in place. Then a member of the press reported that they had said we were not ready. Think of the message that sends to Hussein, not to mention our allies! I could make a case that this might keep Saddam Hussein from obeying the U.N. Resolution and costing many Americans and Iraqi lives. Once this rumor got out, then every paper, TV station, radio, etc., picked it up as the gospel and it went like waves across the country.

We spent our forty-sixth wedding anniversary at Camp David with Nick and Kitty Brady. A friend told me once that if she could come back as anyone, it would be Kitty Brady. I can understand that. She is smart, laid-back, naturally nice, and sensational-looking.

We returned to Washington early Sunday afternoon and George went immediately into meetings with his military and diplomatic advisers. I invited the wives to come talk with me. We all needed to be together during such a difficult—and sometimes ugly—time.

Protesters constantly picketed the White House and kept up an incessant drumbeat. We could not hear them in our bedroom or George's private study upstairs, but I could from my office. Vietnam-era protesters Daniel Ellsberg and the Berrigan brothers resurfaced, and some of their group went through the White House on the public tour and tried unsuccessfully to throw red dye in the fountain. Another person chained himself to the fence.

The protesters were very much in the minority, but I hoped that all Americans realized their president did not want war. No one did.

We were all hoping for peace on January 9 when James Baker and Iraq's Minister Tariq Aziz met in Switzerland. After six and a half hours, Jimmy came out and told the world, "I regret to tell you I heard nothing" that would end the crisis. He said Aziz refused to talk about Kuwait, just wanted to talk about a Middle East conference. Hopes for peace were put off again.

I was trying hard to keep up my regular schedule. One morning in early January, for example, I met with members of the National Federation of the Blind. They were so fascinating I visited with them much longer than scheduled. Their spokesperson was a young blind woman who was a Yale Law School graduate and a court trial lawyer. She showed me how she took notes with a pocket Braille device that looked like a ruler. They told me that only 25 percent of our blind children are taught Braille; the other 75 percent are locked into second-class citizenry. The group was petitioning to have Braille education made available to all children. I had never thought about this before, but everyone must know how to read—whether it is by sight or by feel.

On January 10 I flew down to Charlotte, North Carolina, to do a public service announcement with the darndest group—several basketball players with the NBA's Charlotte Hornets. They ranged from

Tyrone "Mugsy" Bogues, five feet three inches, to Ralph Sampson, seven feet four inches. Together we visited Piedmont Open Middle School to help promote the NBA's "Stay in School" program. Mugsy, the shortest man in the NBA, told the students if he could attain his goals, so could they. The players also told the students that even if you're good at sports, the number of college kids who get on a professional team is so minute that if you don't have the backup of an education, you have nothing. Ralph Sampson told us that he was offered a professional basketball contract after high school and every year he was at the University of Virginia. Yet, he turned down the big money and stayed in school so he could have his diploma. What role models these young men were, and what a breath of fresh air in a world of worry.

On January 13 Congress was set to vote on whether George had the right to use arms in the Persian Gulf to back up the United Nations resolutions that had been passed against Hussein's aggression. There were many senators and representatives who wanted to usurp the powers of the President as Commander in Chief. This is a problem almost every president is forced to address. George feels strongly there are many times that the president must be able to act and not have his arms tied behind his back. In the end, after much debate and many dire predictions of hundreds of Americans killed in a ground war, the House and the Senate passed a joint resolution backing George. Regrettably, much of the Democratic leadership fought and voted against it. Can you imagine what Saddam Hussein's gleeful reaction would have been if Congress had not supported the President?

The UN Resolution gave Hussein until January 15 to get his troops out of Kuwait. The last hope for peace came when Javier Pérez de Cuéllar, the UN Secretary General, went to Iraq.

Again, failure. Saddam was rude to the Secretary General and kept him waiting for four hours. I remember feeling so frightened for our men and women who were there *and* for all the civilians in Iraq. George felt that if Saddam Hussein were to die, people would dance in the streets as they had in Romania when Ceauşescu fell.

All during this time we invited dear friends up to Camp David; people who had no agenda and with whom George could relax. George mostly worked, but the moments of exercise and rest helped. Betsy and Spike Heminway came one weekend, along with Arnold Schwarzenegger, Maria Shriver, their thirteen-month-old daughter, Margaret, and a nanny. Doro and her children and Margaret and her children came also, along with Marshall's close friend and playmate Abigail Meyer. I know it sounds like a crowd, but Camp David can handle it. It was tremendous fun as everyone in the group was very competitive and willing to try just about anything.

Maybe just a little too willing.

After a great snow, everybody got out the toboggans, saucers, and sleds. It was so much fun that unused sleds were at a premium. After church on Sunday, Betsy and I hurried and changed our clothes and raced out so we could get some sledding in before the crowd hit.

I wrote:

I jumped on the saucer and was the first down. During the night there had been a little thaw and then a big freeze. The hill had become thick ice and the ride was so different. I went spinning around and around so fast that I can still feel the fear that I felt. I knew that I should fall off, but I just could not seem to let go. Luckily, I hit a tree with both my legs and not my head, which might easily have happened. I was shaky, but not hurt—I felt. George had just come out on Aspen Terrace and was yelling "Bail out! Bail out!" and he and the agents rushed down that slippery hill. I said I could walk up, but was quickly forced to lie on a toboggan, and they pulled me up. That feeling of being out of control is the worst. The doctor insisted that I go to Hagerstown and be X-rayed. As Betsy and I were leaving in the ambulance we saw George, Arnold, Spike and Maria and all the grandchildren sleighing. They were smart enough to "bail out." The X rays showed that I had a thin fracture of the fibula. Minor, but a bore. Poor Arnold. For weeks afterwards I claimed in my speeches that the last thing I heard before crashing was Arnold yelling "Break a leg!" and therefore I was never going to invite an actor for the weekend again.

January 16—For the last twelve hours I have known something so dreadful that I can't even imagine it. I have the feeling that I'd like to go to bed and pull the covers over my head and stay there for six weeks, and then peek out and see if it is all over. If it isn't, I'd like to crawl under again. The day had a dream-like quality. George told me last night that they decided that it would start tonight. God knows they have given Saddam every chance.

. . . All America is praying and we are, too. George told me last night that it is always on his mind. As we said our prayers and as he read the message he is going to give to the American people tonight, his voice cracked and his eyes got misty. I know that those innocent children get to him. That darn Hussein, he is putting all those children at risk. George has been praying for the children all week, which led me to believe that unless Saddam met all the U.N. conditions we would have to attack and liberate Kuwait. I asked him over coffee in bed this morning as he read through tonight's message who wrote the speech and he said that he had. I had wondered how it could have remained a secret if it had been written by the speech writers. (This is not to cast aspersions on the speech writers, but once you tell a secret—it is no longer a secret. I had to bite my tongue all day. I wanted to share with Andy, my dearest friend, but I knew I couldn't tell. Too many American lives depended on secrecy.*) George told me that he might come home and have lunch with me and take a nap. I guess that sleep did not come too well last night.

. . . Susan Baker called. Neither of us said a word about the attack, but each of us knew that the other knew. We had a cozy, comforting talk and she told me something that someone had told her. "For Jesus, peace is not the absence of struggle, but the presence of love." That's nice.

We invited Billy Graham to spend the night with us because, unbeknownst to him, we wanted him to conduct a church service the next day. He did not know the war was to begin.

That evening Billy and I sat in our small sitting room watching TV. We saw Bernie Shaw of CNN talking from Baghdad. He said that CNN had given their reporters an opportunity to leave and though some had opted to stay, he said he was leaving on a plane that was being sent for him at three A.M. Baghdad time. I thought to myself: Oh, no, you are not leaving at dawn tomorrow, for in thirty minutes the bombing will start. I like Bernie and his wife, Linda, a lot, but I also must confess that I thought: Darn you for not leaving when your President asked you to. I know that Marlin Fitzwater, George's press

---

* I know that this is not relevant, but on the subject of secrets, for just the above reason, I am dead convinced that there was no one "Deep Throat" during the Watergate crisis. Had there been, it would have come out. Secrets, once known by one other person, come out eventually. I am not saying that Bob Woodward and Carl Bernstein made him or her up (although I wouldn't put it past them), but "Deep Throat" probably was a composite person, and I suspect they used a little literary license to make a better story.

secretary, called CNN president Tom Johnson twice to warn him to get his reporters out before the bombing started.

We, like the rest of America, watched the war begin on CNN. Three of their reporters were on the air for fourteen straight hours. They would say: "We hear planes, but can't see them and the anti-aircraft obviously can't either." The reporters described hiding under tables to get the news out. Because of our capability to have "surgical" bombing, our planes managed to avoid hitting any shrines and highly populated housing.

George slept fitfully and called the situation room off and on all night. The morning reports were great: no planes lost. Later in the day, it was not so great; We had lost three planes; the Brits, two; and the Kuwaitis, one. Saddam answered the attack by aiming SCUD missiles at Israel, hoping to draw them into the conflict, which might have resulted in Jordan's and Syria's entering on Iraq's side.

Congress and the vast majority of the American people supported George, but the protests continued outside. At one point they said we should expect 100,000, but the turnout was much smaller.

Nevertheless, when George talked to our allies, they all asked about the terrible protests taking place in America. George had to explain that they were seeing only the 20 percent who were against and not the 80 percent who were backing him. Incidentally, I want to emphasize that I didn't for one moment question the motives of the protesters. They were doing what they thought was right. However, I was very grateful one day when I heard a great cheer and looked out my office window to see about one hundred supporters of the administration marching. That was refreshing.

I could easily understand people like our friend Mark Hatfield and various religious leaders who are morally opposed to war in general. But I cannot understand sitting back and letting one country invade another and ravage its people. The reports coming out of Kuwait were so nauseating and brutal that after reading about ten pages of the Amnesty International report, I had to stop or get sick.

January 21— Several of our captured pilots have been paraded across the screen. Saddam Hussein says that they will be put in targeted strategic places, so if we bomb we will be bombing our own people.

January 22— Yesterday Bernard Shaw came home from Baghdad

and came by to see George. It was fascinating. My feeling is that he feels guilty about something and is not quite sure what. There seems to be some feeling that CNN is being used by Saddam Hussein. Whether it is true or whether it is jealousy on the part of the national networks, I don't know.

. . . the former PM of Singapore, Lee Kuan Yew, and Madame Kwa Geok Choo came by for tea. They are old friends from the UN days and both are bright, very interesting people. She had water with no ice and he had hot water . . . saying that tea was a diuretic to him. I had to laugh, for a few minutes later he was talking about some world leader that they both thought looked badly and he mentioned that "he had some small operation—piles," he thought. He can't be faulted for not telling it like it is! He reminded me of Sadat during our visit to Egypt many years earlier when he shared with us his views of the world. Lee Kuan Yew sat telling George, Brent Scowcroft and Bob Gates just how he saw the world . . . I was thrilled to sit in on such a discussion. He told George that he thought the coalition was brilliant and he hoped that George would share the glory when victory came.

January 23—I watched the war on CNN and saw Israel attacked by SCUD missiles and this time they hit. We watched people panicking. I thought of the children in Israel and the children here in our country. Recently Ellie ran into my room and said: "Ganny, we are being bombed. I'm scared." I thought, I hope parents are monitoring what their children are seeing on the television and helping them over this brutal time.

I had a call from Shelley Winters, the actress, who wanted George to make some war act that would forbid the press to "tell all." She was outraged about the way they talked to our briefing generals. She felt they were aiding and abetting the enemy. I tried to explain to this extremely agitated woman that if the President were to do as she asked and put a ban on the press, the hue and cry from one and all would be deafening. She was inconsolable and I sicced her on to the heads of the networks and big newspapers. Good luck, Shelley. I do know the frustrations that she felt. The press is just trying to do their job, although they are just making ours much harder.

. . . During the crisis I met with a Pentagon group who gives support to the families of the soldiers in the desert. I was amazed about how much had been put in place before the war. This military has thought of everything.

On January 28 I received a nice break from the tension when I flew to Boston to visit a Commonwealth Literacy Corps program at the United Electric Company. The new Massachusetts Governor, Bill Weld, met me there and we toured together. When this company discovered that 50 percent of its employees spoke a foreign language and were illiterate in English, it set up English as a Second Language courses right in the workplace. It also encouraged its employees to submit suggestions on how to make better use of time and space and how to make the plant safer and more efficient. Believe it or not, the company soon was saving hours of workers' time, making their work space more efficient and increasing the production rates with fewer errors. It also had happier employees and employers. By the way, it *exported* to Japan. I loved the great pride I felt at that plant.

That night I attended an I Have a Dream banquet sponsored by George's nephew Jamie Bush. He and his wife, Sue, had adopted a class of children, guaranteeing them a college education *if* they met certain requirements: stay in school, stay off drugs, and make reasonable grades. This is Eugene Lang's program which I've already talked about, which is popping up like mushrooms across the country. Jamie and Sue have proven that you don't have to be rich to accomplish this. But you do have to work very hard to get the money needed and to find people who are willing to serve as mentors and role models.

February 4—George got up early and flew to three military bases. We saw him live on CNN and I had tears watching him. He was speaking to home bases of some of the Desert Storm troops, and their families and buddies were there. The reception was great, flags and much cheering. He met with some of the wives and families of those who are missing. I could see it was tough. They kept saying on TV that he was fighting a cold. That was no cold. He was just so moved.

Every single event at the White House was affected by what was happening in the Middle East. At the annual Governors' Dinner, for example, Gary Morris was the entertainer, and he sang "Bring Him Home" from *Les Misérables,* and ended the evening with "Amazing Grace." It was so beautiful and moving.

The next day I was to speak at the spouses' luncheon. I teased them that when I was the host of this annual event, I provided entertainment, but when they were the host, they made me speak! However, this year, I had something very special to share with them, a telegram George had received:

> Dear Mr. President,
>   I am the wife of Lt. Commander Scott Speicher, the pilot of the FA-18 from the USS Saratoga which was downed last Thursday. I cannot pretend to know how it feels to commit our country to war. But it must have been a painful decision. I know you have an awful lot on your mind, but I want you to know that I feel the same way now that my husband and I felt when he was deployed last August. We supported you then, and I support you now with all my heart. Someday my children will be old enough to understand that their father went away to war because it was the right thing to do. Rest assured that all my children and I are well and I wish to maintain as normal a routine for them as possible, free of press and television cameras. The Navy is helping tremendously in that respect.
>   God bless you and all of our men in uniform.
>   Joanne Speicher and Antonio Salazar
>   Lt. Commander U.S. Navy
>   CACO CLAW 1 NAS CECIL FIELD
>   JACKSONVILLE, FLORIDA 32215

George's answer:

January 24th 1991

> Dear Mrs. Speicher, Dear Joanne,
>   You sent me a very moving telegraph. Barbara and I read it together and we shed a tear for your very noble husband. And we said a prayer that God give you the continued strength and courage that you have now.
>   I have read about Scott. He must have been "Mr. Perfect," for he was loved by all.
>   Sometimes God acts in strange ways . . . ways we do not understand right away.
>   The fact is your husband gave his life not simply to

a small country could once again be free, but so those kids of yours will have a better chance to grow up in a world more peaceful, more just.

Give your kids a big hug from Barbara and me. We know what family and faith can do to lift you up when you are hurt. And clearly those kids have a mother who loves them and whose courage will lead them.

I am proud of your wonderful husband and I will never forget him.

George Bush

George suffered over each and every casualty and their families. I love this woman for her telegram to him.

We received many wonderful letters before, during, and after the war. I want to share a few more with you that touched me deeply. The first came from a young woman in the Air Force, stationed in the Saudi desert. She wrote in part:

Today I sit outside my tent. I see a land I do not claim as my own, but out of respect and compassion for those who do, I am here. We share a common friend—peace. We see a common enemy—terrorism. When we speak in these terms, all boundaries cease to exist. I am afraid of what it might cost. But *far* more afraid of what it would cost if we elected not to invest at all.

I wanted you to hear that, for what it's worth, straight from me. A woman, a professional of 19 years, someone who is proud of what we, the United States of America, believe in.

The second letter is from a mother:

Dear Mrs. Bush,

This letter is from one who loves her country and wishes to express a few thoughts with someone who also needs our support.

I am a 38-year-old mother of two. My son, who
is 19, is serving in the Army Reserves in the Persian
Gulf. . . .

I just wanted you to be able to tell President Bush
that even though my only son is away, due to war, that he
has my support as well as that of our whole family.

I know that he feels deeply about God, country, and
family, as do we all. Sometimes people forget that he is
and was before he was President, a man and a father.

. . . We pray that God will give him guidance and
wisdom in these troubled times . . . I am proud to have
President Bush representing our country in the world's
leadership. May God Bless my son and our servicemen and
women; our country; and may God Bless our President
and his family.

February 8—The war drones on. It is the darndest war, fought over
the tube. CNN covers everything and tells us that they are only able to
show us what the Iraqis want us to see and hear. Then they show civil-
ian killings and residential bombings. (Although they have told us, we
believe our eyes and forget that we are only seeing what they want us to
see.) We know that Saddam has put weapons on residential roofs and in
residential sections. We have been hearing that they have five-story underground bunkers. Yesterday (former Attorney General) Ramsey Clark was
in Iraq with Peter Arnett saying that we were killing civilians and little
children and was beyond the pale. He is an outrage to his country and has
been for many years. (I can hear George saying: "Why don't you tell us
what you think, Bar.")

The White House has been closed to tourists since the beginning of
the air war. I miss the tourists. They bring the White House alive, they
make it truly the People's House. I am surprised that I feel this way.

. . . In early February we awakened to see a bomb shelter filled with
children and old people in Iraq that had been bombed. Saddam Hussein
is an animal. It was a command post and he put those old and young people there. He does not care about human lives. It is extraordinary to me.
This is a targeted war on our side and their SCUD missiles just hit helter-
skelter. I think we forget that war is not nice.

One of many side effects of the fighting was America's sudden fear of flying because of possible terrorism. On Valentine's Day, I was scheduled to fly to Indianapolis to visit a Veterans Hospital as part of National Veterans Hospital Week. George and John Sununu asked me if I'd mind taking a commercial flight to make the point that the airlines were safe. I said not at all. The press was alerted to the trip and came with me on the nearly empty plane. Fortunately, the trip got good news coverage, and the airlines said that people responded.

That morning as I got into the car to leave the White House, there was a little bag with a valentine in it and a Texas Instruments Thesaurus/Spell Checker (just the right size for my traveling bag) waiting for me on the seat. Although I say that George and I don't need to give presents, and heaven only knows that we have everything under the sun and more, I was thrilled.

After visiting the hospital I flew to Grissom Air Force Base, my second base visit in a week. (The first was Griffiss Air Force Base in Rome, New York.) First, I talked with the families of those who were in the desert—many of the spouses had been gone since August—and then walked out into a freezing cold hangar for a rally with about 2,500 men, women, and children connected to the base. It didn't matter what I said; they cheered. We worked the rope line and shook as many hands as possible. I was saddened to hear that quite a few of the young enlisted men held down second jobs so that they could support their families. The commander told me that when the men went overseas, this added income was lost and the families had to go on food stamps. That is dreadful! The same support group that I met with at the White House and that Joanne Speicher mentioned in her telegram was helping as much as it could, providing services such as financial planning programs and counseling for the children.

One of the most heartwarming visits we made during the war was to the Raytheon Missile Systems plant outside Boston, where they make the "SCUD-buster," the Patriot missile that was such a hero in the war. It saved thousands of lives by knocking Iraq's SCUD missiles out of the air.

For years this plant had been criticized for making weapons, and it was exciting to see what pride the workers had in their product and their work as they heard about their success night after night on TV.

George toured the plant, and then we went into a giant rally of about three thousand workers. It was jammed, and men and women literally hung from the rafters. It was so much more emotional than I expected, and I was reminded of World War II and Rosie the Riveter. Patriotism flooded the room, and I must confess that tears ran down my cheeks. They cheered for their country, for their own work—and for George.

After the visit we drove up to Maine to spend two nights in the three cozy rooms that are winterized in the house. We read, took long walks, and watched movies. That Sunday morning we went to our winter church that we love. When Pat Adams, our minister, called for prayers for people who are sick or in need, a well-dressed stranger jumped to his feet and asked us to pray for the thousands of innocent children who were being killed every day in Iraq. He really got warmed up, and then Pat thanked him for his words and asked him to sit down. On and on he went—babies being slaughtered by gas bombs, and so on. Suddenly the congregation rose to its feet and started singing "God Bless America" to drown him out. One amusing moment in this nightmare came when he said, "I can speak. I am a member of this church." Mary Philbrick, the matriarch of our church, said quick as a wink, "Oh, no you aren't," in a clear, loud voice that even he didn't dare to question. Eventually he did sit down and was quiet for a while, only to jump up again to get louder and uglier. In the interim the police chief had come in and sat next to him, and he and another policeman dragged him out at the request of the church deacons. (The Secret Service do not remove protesters unless they threaten the security of the President.) It was the most unpleasant happening, and I felt shaken and sick at heart that we had brought this on our friends. During the coffee hour, we apologized and they reassured us it was okay. In fact, I think we all felt even closer than before. The next day we read in the paper that the man was a frequent protester associated with the Berrigans.

On February 20 the Queen of Denmark, Queen Margrethe II, arrived with Prince Henrik for their long-planned visit. At age fifty-one, she was six feet tall and looked just like what a fairy-book queen should be. She appeared for the arrival ceremony in a stunning plum-colored coat and a marvelous sort of winged-looking hat. Had she flown off, I wouldn't have been surprised. I joined George; Jim Baker; Brent Scowcroft; our ambassador, Keith Brown; and all their counterparts and Her Majesty and the Prince for coffee and an interesting discussion. She is an artist, and Laurie Firestone and I later went by the National Women's Museum to see a Danish exhibit that included some of Her Majesty's work.

We had an interesting group of guests for that dinner. Staying with us was a baseball hero, Texas Ranger pitcher Nolan Ryan, and his beautiful wife, Ruth, and our good friends Maggie and Armando Codina, who are a great Cuban refugee success story.

I wrote:

> The State Dinner was one of our best. The food was absolutely delicious and Frederica Von Stade sang. She ended her program with "The Star-Spangled Banner" and it was so beautiful and moving. The Queen wore the most glorious diamonds—tiara, necklace, and brooch, all big with many large pearl drops. She wore a red velvet gown and looked very queenly. George said that she was a very good dinner partner.
>
> There were many guests, but the hit of the evening was Melanie Griffith. She came with her husband, Don Johnson, in a tiny dress that hardly covered her sensational body. Laurie had put Marvin at her side thinking that she would enjoy a young person and it might encourage Marvin to come again. He turned us down for almost all White House events. He really did not like to be in the media spotlight. All during dinner the butlers, who loved Marvin, slipped him notes saying things like, "Keep your eyes on your plate, your mother is watching" or "Eat your dinner and stop ogling the lady next to you."
>
> In any case, we had a nice visit with Melanie and Don upstairs before they left to go to their hotel. Several weeks later I received a letter from Melanie that said something like when she was a little girl, her mother told her if she had good manners and obeyed her, she might grow up and be invited to the White House. She said that her dream had come true. Then she said very nice things about the evening and thanked me for both of them.
>
> Then there was this P.S., which I loved: "I just wish my mother had told me what to wear when I went to the White House."

Melanie will probably never read this, but if she does, I want her to know she looked beautiful and adorable and certainly added to the evening.

* * *

The next night, George and I had planned two events in the residence for the same time. I was having a small reception for the Barbara Bush Foundation for Family Literacy Corporate Committee, a group made up of corporate CEOs and headed by Red Poling of Ford Motor Company and Martin Davis of Paramount. George was having a group coming for a light supper and then they were going to see the Ford's Theatre production of *The Black Eagles*. George generously suggested that we join forces, which made for an absolutely fascinating evening for me and my guests. We gave them all a drink and sat in a semicircle in the Yellow Oval Room. George's group included the Supreme Court Justice David Souter; Air Force Chief of Staff, General Merrill McPeak; and Dr. Benjamin Payton, President of Tuskegee University. George first thanked my group of CEOs for all the help they had given to the foundation and said that I had reported they were doing a superb job. We then talked about the economy and the Persian Gulf. George asked General McPeak to tell us about the surgical bombing and other aspects. I took a chance and said, "You know, General, my husband is under tremendous pressure from his four sons. They all say, 'Tell 'em you're going to bomb all bridges and hotels where you know they have strategic equipment and communications. Give them a set number of hours and then do it.'" I was fascinated, for Ben Payton spoke up and said that he agreed with our sons, then the others joined in, too. I really do think that's what most Americans were feeling.

As I kissed George good-bye, I told him that without my asking for anything he had raised $1 million for me that night. Wrong. Within the week two of those men pledged $1.5 million to the Barbara Bush Foundation for Family Literacy.

That same evening I flew to Arizona with Jimmy Symington, former Democratic congressman from Missouri and a former chief of protocol. Jimmy and his wife, Sylvia, are two of Washington's most attractive inhabitants. We were going to do a breakfast for his cousin, Fife Symington, who was running in a special election for governor. (He later won.)

While there I visited with the Arizona Air National Guard and their families and then had the usual rally. This visit was slightly different, however. I had very private visits with four families: one whose son/husband was a prisoner of war; one whose relative was missing in action; and two whose relatives were killed in action.

People always ask me how I handled these visits. I can't answer that, but I liked to be alone with the families and let them set the pace. They were always kind to me, and I never had an unpleasant experience. There was a lot of listening, a lot of tears and hugs. They all mentioned the strong help they were getting from their peers and support groups.

The first family was the family of Lt. Colonel Clifford Acree, the POW that we had seen on the tube, led in looking doped and beaten early in the air war. I visited with his wife, mother, father and aunt. I was so proud of the wife. She had organized a POW/MIA support group and seemed to be doing well. They all spoke well of George and it was a very moving visit. The darling mother was teary and I couldn't blame her. [He came home safely.]

The second meeting was with a Hispanic family of a KIA (killed in action). We had the whole family there, darling grandparents, an aunt who had a boy there herself whom she hadn't heard from in weeks, a sister, an uncle and a fiancée. The latter didn't fit the picture at all. She was very young and dressed to the teeth and very sensual looking. The others were all so warm, teary and darling and she seemed sulky and did not speak. I was shocked that the family seemed to shun her. Later Anna Perez told me that she had been paid a lot of money by a national magazine and was furious when the base would not let their reporters and cameras in the room while we were visiting. She had arrived separately from the family with two very Caucasian-looking people with cameras, saying they were "family." Anna said that it was very sticky, but they were kept out of the room. No wonder the family shunned her. We hugged, had tears, talked and promised to try to get in touch with the first cousin whom they had not heard from.

. . . Next was the wife of an MIA. She was so adorable and had such faith that although she had been told that the chances of his being alive were slight, she believed he was. I certainly hope so. [She was right; he came home!]

. . . The last visit was really sad, a Native American family, a very young widow and mother with her sister, brother-in-law and two young children. The baby was being taken care of by the sister, who seemed to love the precious child. I had trouble sorting it all out in my mind as the widow showed no affection toward the baby, the daughter of the dead

Marine. I don't know if it is the stoic Indian culture or if the wife was in shock, which certainly would be normal. It was so sad. I was so glad that she had that nice sister. We did offer to help her find affordable housing. My heart broke for all these families.

From Arizona we flew on to Campbell Air Force Base on the Tennessee and Kentucky border. We had been warned that this would be an "uptight" visit, for many of the 28,000 troops that had been deployed from this enormous base were on the front lines and, with a ground war on the horizon, they were frightened. I walked out to the largest, most enthusiastic rally ever. Lee Greenwood, that great patriotic country singer, was there and they loved him. So did I and so does George Bush!

February 23—The deadline came and went and (Saddam) did not withdraw. We are going to have an early dinner at Camp David and fly down to D.C. There George will announce that the ground war has started—8 p.m. our time and 4 a.m. their time. George had spent the day working at his office and talking to leaders around the world, Senate and House Leadership and all the former Presidents. It is a terrible, awful decision, but certainly had to be made. That madman has set over two hundred oil wells on fire in Kuwait and is continuing the killings. Dear God, let it be quick and let there be few deaths.

February 24—The ground war did start last night. George went immediately to the Oval Office. He made a short announcement on the ground war. Dick Cheney gave a short announcement at the Pentagon and then took some questions. . . . He has done such a good job. He seems so steady and no nonsense. Before we went to bed John Harper of St. John's Church was called. He had offered to help in any way that he could. He said that we could have an early morning communion service at church. So Patty Presock got on the phone and so did I and invited as many people as we could reach, making it clear that it was not a command performance. Many of the staff attended. I only saw Anna from my office. I was touched that both Doro and Marvin went with us at 7 a.m., which means that they got up at 5:30. It means a lot to have your children there. It was a lovely service. John gave the best sermon, I thought. It was sincere and sweet. We have been friends for a long time and that made the service even more special.

. . . At church Dick Cheney passed George a note telling him that "Norm says things are going well." There was a hard knot of drummers outside the church. When we saw them they were really odd looking and only about five people.

. . . George and Marvin gathered a crowd for lunch with horseshoes before: David and Ann Bates and their three children (David used to work for George and is like a son to us); Steve Quamme; Marvin, Margaret, Marshall and Abigail Meyer, Walker; Doro, Sam, Ellie, and Sam's friend Carlos, plus Doro's new friend, Bobby Koch (pronounced Cook). With Pop and me that made 18 for hamburgers, hot dogs, French fries, cherry pie and ice cream. I swam a mile while they were throwing shoes before lunch. I wonder what Bobby Koch thinks of this nutty family: a fat old mother swimming in the middle of the winter outdoors; and a father who plays horseshoes like it is the most important game ever while running an international war thousands of miles away that will affect the world for years to come.

By afternoon we got the word that we had lost twelve of our people. George was so sad. I didn't know how to console him.

February 26—We awakened this morning to a defiant speech by Saddam Hussein. He said that he has asked his troops to withdraw from Kuwait, but was by no means surrendering. He may not be, but his troops were surrendering right and left. George has stood firm and has resisted all pressure to accept the Russian or Iraqi plan. I am so proud of George. He has worked up a superb team and coalition.

February 28—Yesterday was a big day in the life of our country.

. . . George called and told me that he was going to give a talk to the nation at 9 p.m. I told him that I was out for dinner and would be speaking at the time to the National Foundation for Depressive Illness Foundation Benefit Dinner. He asked me if I couldn't speak before the dinner and get home in time for his speech, which is exactly what I did. I went over, gave my speech and got back and was sitting on a chair in the Oval Office when George announced that 100 hours after the ground war started (42 days after the air response to Saddam's invasion of Kuwait), he was calling for a ceasefire IF Saddam Hussein accepts unconditionally all 12 U.N. resolutions. It is so thrilling. All the pundits said that it would be a long war, that we would have thousands of dead, that it would cost billions of dollars more than it did, and on and on. We awakened this morning to hear Saddam declaring victory. It makes you want to go in and bomb the whey out of him. The reason we didn't go all the way into Baghdad was that we never wanted to devastate Iraq. We just wanted to get him out of Kuwait and cripple him militarily. We are assured that has been done.

I was a little surprised to hear the drums going the day after the war ended and must say I wondered why. I suspect that they are now protesting our having gone at all.

The next day I went to Baltimore to help cut the ribbon at the International Book Bank. The Governor and Mayor were there along with many dignitaries. Governor Donald Schaefer, a longtime dear friend in the literacy world, said such nice things about George. He said he was proud to be an American with a president like this, that he felt a "quiet pride" in our country. Anna Perez and I talked about it and decided that he was right. We felt a "quiet pride," not only because we had won the war, but in the way we won.

From there, I visited Fort Meade in Maryland. The trip was originally planned as a rally to cheer the troops on, but instead it was a celebration of the cease-fire and victory the night before. It was so touching with flags and such cheering. Unfortunately, the wives and children were thinking their husbands and dads would be home immediately, but I knew there would be a lot of peace-keeping and mopping up.

March 2—I wish I could freeze the newspaper columns in a time capsule. They are raving over George today. It won't last, but nobody thought that a war could be fought like this and won in this manner. I am so proud of him and his team that I could burst. Dick Cheney, the Secretary of Defense, is as competent as they come. He seems very laid back and reassuring. He does not have a Dr. Strangelove image that so many of our Secretaries of Defense get, whether they deserve it or not. Colin Powell, Chairman of the Joint Chiefs of Staff, has been superb. These two, along with Norm Schwarzkopf, Commander of the Allied Forces, have been strong, reassuring and have made *NO* mistakes that I can see. Jim Baker, Secretary of State, has done what he does best, which is diplomacy, the very best. And I can't leave out Brent Scowcroft and Bob Gates. They worked hard behind the scenes. They are two of the finest public servants. They are wise and good. George Bush has been well served.

I want to add here Dan Quayle, who was at George's side, loyal and supportive in every instance. I also don't want to forget to mention that we were really part of a worldwide team, just one of thirty countries in a coalition that stood and fought together.

That weekend George invited Al and Ann Simpson to join us at Camp David. Al was having a hard time in the press for a statement he had made about Peter Arnett of CNN being an Iraqi sympathizer. George wanted to show his support for Al, who, besides having an unbelievably good sense of humor, is a true, loving friend. We were joined by Fred and Martha Zeder and Jack and Bobbie Fitch, friends from Texas.

About that time I learned that *Millie's Book* was going into its eighth printing—400,000 copies—and was on *The New York Times* best-seller list for the twenty-third week. In fact, the book was climbing back from number 7 to number 5. Nobody could believe it, but I couldn't help but wonder, "Could it have anything to do with the fact that George is 91 percent in the polls?"

I continued my base visits, especially since most of them had been scheduled before the war ended. On March 6, I headed to Jacksonville, Florida, to visit the Mayport Naval Air Station. I wrote:

First I spoke to some members of the families of those deployed in the Gulf. I said a few words and then invited discussion. Of course the first question they had was when was their husband or wife, father or mother coming home? To that I could say soon. In regular service life they are at sea for 6 months and then home for 6 months . . . The only sour note was one male spouse who asked me when Congress was going to update the laws . . . when was a reservist who gives up a high-paying job going to get compensation for being called back into the service? They asked the wrong person that because I feel so strongly that if someone has been in the reserves for 9 years, getting their education or accepting pay for their training and then gripes about serving when called, they are wrong, dead wrong. Before I could answer the woman standing next to me said, "Do you mean you can't live on what we have been living on for years?"

Next to the USS *Forrestal* (aircraft carrier) where we made the most dramatic entrance coming up on the plane elevator to find 4,000 troops lined up on the flight deck. I was led to a mike, introduced and invited to speak. To hold that speech and pray that my dress would not blow up was no mean feat. After a few words of thanks on the windiest deck, I walked the lines and shook hands and smiled at those I could not touch. It was amazing. They had just been told that they were not going to be deployed and were so disappointed. Isn't that funny? They, too, wanted to be part of the action!

I had run into the same thing at an earlier visit at Quantico Marine Base near Washington. They were sad they weren't in the desert. Somehow I suspect their families felt differently.

    On March 7, Margaret Thatcher, now Lady Thatcher, visited us at the White House, and George bestowed on her the highest medal a foreigner can receive from the U.S. government, the Medal of Freedom. We had heard that Margaret was crushed about her recent defeat, but she seemed her old self. I wrote:

We sat in the Oval Office with John Sununu, Brent Scowcroft, the two she called "Tweedledee and Tweedledum"—Bob Gates and Larry Eagleburger, Sir Antony Acland and several of her people. She hasn't changed much. She is still on top of the world situation and still seems to do most of the talking. She does have a lovely voice, is a joy to hear and we were very glad to see her looking so well. Denis doesn't say much. I am crazy about him. What a rock he is for Margaret.

After a receiving line and reception, we all retired upstairs for a small dinner of 60 in the Yellow Oval Room. As Denis and I walked into the dinner, he asked me if he could ask a personal question. He said: "I have met Dan Quayle several times and I found him bright and very nice. Why doesn't the press like him?" I had to tell him that I did not know as Dan was all he said and much more. At that moment Katharine Graham (owner of *The Washington Post*) walked up to our table and I suggested rather facetiously that he ask her. I should have known that Denis would, and he did. He came back and reported that Kay had said that Dan was "superficial" and she didn't like him. She also told Denis that she didn't know him.

. . . George made a nice toast to Margaret, and Margaret answered— at some length. Denis said in a loud stage whisper, "Don't go on, Mum." Then George stood up and invited others who knew Margaret and loved her to please feel free to speak. He turned and said, "Bar, you start it off." I should be prepared but never am, but stood and toasted dear Denis and sat down. Denis stood and said, "As Anthony said to Cleopatra as he walked into her tent, 'I did not come to talk,'" thanked us and plunked down. George told me later that it reminded him of Henry the VIII saying to his 6th wife, "I won't keep you long."

March 10—We attended the annual Ford Theatre Gala. This year country music was featured and George was, to use a little country music lingo, in "hog heaven." Some of the entertainers were Randy Travis, Alabama, Clint Black, the Statler Brothers, Tammy Wynette, K. T. Oslin, Ricky Skaggs and Pendley and Wolz. The hosts were John Ritter and Teri Garr. Morgan Freeman did the tribute to Lincoln and ended with "Thank you, Mr. President," looking up at the box where Lincoln had sat the night he was shot. He then turned with the most loving expression, looked George right in the eye and said, "And thank *YOU*, Mr. President." It was a moment of great emotion.

Later that week George took a trip to Ottawa, Martinique, and Bermuda to meet with Brian Mulroney, François Mitterrand and Margaret Thatcher, in that order. I headed to Houston for several days of rest and exercise. Since the trip was strictly personal, I flew down and back commercially. I wrote:

People were so nice to me on the plane. They smiled and sent me notes, asked to have their pictures taken with me, etc. When they were asked to stay in their seats until the "unnamed VIP" unloaded, they clapped. It was *NOT* for me, but GB. Everyone I met or spoke to raved over George and told me just how good they felt about themselves and our country.

We ended our trip on a real high. Peggy (Swift) and I were sitting talking in the car when . . . a man in a yellow beat-up truck drew up beside me at a red light. He glanced at me, recognized me and his face broke into the biggest, most handsome smile. I smiled and he rolled down his window and said, "I didn't think you stopped at lights." I said that I did. He asked for an autograph. I handed him one that Peggy had in her bag that I had signed before, and as he drove off, he was shaking his head saying, "Nobody will believe this. God bless America." It was so sweet.

As you can see, this was almost a euphoric time for us. However, there was something bothering me deeply. In March, at our annual meeting to decide the theme of this year's graduation speech, I said that I wanted to talk about tolerance, doing unto others as you would have them do unto you. It seemed to be needed that year more than any other; the papers were filled with terrible stories about racial and religious intolerance. I felt so strongly that we could not let our troops come home from the Gulf War to any racial problems. All races and religions had worked side by side in the desert; I felt we must do the same at home.

I did talk about intolerance last year, but without the controversy that had surrounded my Wellesley speech the year before, my remarks did not get as much media coverage. And sad to say, as I write this in early 1994, our papers are still filled with stories of intolerance. It's a part of America I despise and pray so fervently we one day will overcome.

૭~ In the next few weeks, the cease-fire was signed, and slowly but surely our troops started coming home. On June 8 we had a huge celebration in Washington with an old-fashioned parade and supposedly the biggest fireworks display ever in Washington. But the beginning of the day is what touched me the most:

We went early in the morning to a wreath-laying service at Arlington Cemetery. It was a most glorious day. It was warm, but not too hot. As we drove to Arlington we could see people walking toward the parade route in shorts and comfortable shoes, often carrying picnics and folding chairs. They waved and cheered when they saw George. The service at Arlington was very moving. We first marched up that long stairway in front of the Tomb of the Unknown Soldier. George laid the wreath in a solemn ceremony. So far in this war there are no unknowns. Then on into the Amphitheater, where George went with Generals Powell, Schwarzkopf, and Streeter (commanding general of the local military district), Secretary Cheney, the Ambassadors of Kuwait and Saudi Arabia and some other military men to the stage. I was with several of the wives to the side. From where we were sitting we could see the faces of the families who lost loved ones in the war. They were dear sweet faces and many had smiles with tears. It was so tough to look at them. My heart ached for George as I know he feels these deaths as though they were his own children. The service was filled with beautiful music and prayers. George spoke as did the Ambassador of Kuwait. After the last song George came over, took me by the hand and led me down to the families. We hugged, had pictures taken and shook as many hands as possible. We would have stayed longer if they had let us, but all those people had to get to the parade. We did feel that they personally deserved our thanks.

As a footnote to Desert Storm, we went to Kuwait in March of 1993 as guests of the Kuwaiti government. It was an extraordinary trip, and I wish all those families who lost loved ones could have been with us. The gratitude toward the United States was overwhelming. People waved American and Kuwaiti flags for mile after mile everyplace we went, and the Arab women made that wonderful trilling sound as a welcome. They stood for hours just to catch a glimpse of George, whose face was everywhere on posters, flags, and billboards.

We saw such devastation and heard tales of horror and just plain meanness. We met with families whose sons and husbands were still hostages or MIAs in Iraq. We saw museums that were burned the last two days of the war. We heard of rapes and visited a hospital where the handicapped were thrown out on the streets and babies in incubators were put on the floor so the machines could either be broken or taken as loot. We visited the blackened oil fields where eventually over seven hundred wells had been set on fire as the Iraqis fled the country. Everyone we met had a death of a family member to report.

However, nature and the human spirit are amazing. We saw rebuilding going on everywhere, including the Bayan Palace, where we stayed. There were patches of green shooting through the thin layer of oil and I even saw some yellow wildflowers. I was told the oil on the ground actually was holding in what little moisture they have, thus the growth.

We went one morning to visit with the families of the POWs and MIAs and they gave George an antique door. As we approached we were so moved to see that they had inscribed on the door in gold the names of the American men and women killed freeing Kuwait. The inscription read:

> When a man gives you the key to his home, it means that you are the best and most valuable friend to him; and when

a man gives you the door of his home, it means that you are one of his family.

This beautiful old door symbolized to us more than anything their gratitude, and it will be forever on display at the George Bush Presidential Library Center in College Station, Texas, for all to see and honor those courageous Americans who died.

22

Of Cabbages and Queens

After the war ended, it was nice to settle back into a somewhat normal, although busy, routine. Springtime brought,
among other things, the commencement season, and George and I both
had a full schedule often taking us in opposite directions.

So I was very happy on May 4, a Saturday, to find myself on *Air
Force One* with George headed for the University of Michigan, where he
was to give the commencement address. Three congressional friends
from Michigan—Guy Vander Jagt, Carl Pursell, and Fred Upton—
also were on board, and they warned George he could expect some protests during his speech.

We were taken immediately to a huge stadium filled with seventy thousand people, and despite the dire predictions, George got a
great reception with the exception of a very small group with mega-
phones who yelled "Bulls—t" the whole time George spoke. At one
point, when he was talking about the importance of freedom of speech,
he stopped, looked over at them and said: "When I wrote that, I didn't
know you guys were going to be here!" He got a huge laugh and
applause. I do not know how he got through that speech, but he did—
and did it well—and said he hardly noticed the protesters. Everyone
was thrilled, including Governor John Engler, who had worried that
the protesters would ruin the day.

We flew back to Camp David, bringing with us Bob Teeter,
an old friend from past campaigns, and his wife, Betsy. Craig Fuller,

George's chief of staff from the vice presidential years, and his wife, Karen, also drove up from Washington to spend the night. We all separated to do our own thing: I went to ride my bike and swim laps; George to nap and go for a jog; and the Fullers and Teeters to ride bikes and take walks.

Halfway through my swim I was interrupted and told that George was in the dispensary. I was told not to worry, that he just had a little shortness of breath while jogging. I put on a robe and went to find him hooked up to a cardiac monitor and with an IV in his arm. He told me that he had felt exhausted while jogging and had to stop and walk several times. When he finished his run, the doctor suggested that he stop in the Eucalyptus Cabin (the very appropriate name for the medical cabin) to be examined. They discovered that his heart was out of sync. Simply stated, the upper chamber was pumping at a different rate than the lower chamber. It was fibrillating.

George, of course, was joking about the whole thing. When I walked in, he took one look at my face and said: "Remembering how sympathetic I was when you broke your leg, I know you'll be caring." That was a family joke, as I had kidded him about continuing to sled while I went off in the ambulance to be X-rayed.

Meanwhile, Dr. Mike Nash, the White House doctor on duty, and John Herrick, assistant to the press secretary, were attempting to get a protesting George to Bethesda Naval Hospital. I was so impressed with how everyone worked so efficiently and calmly. George suggested that I stay with our guests, but that was out of the question; they were our friends and would understand.

We got on the helicopter with the monitoring machine and the needle still feeding something into his vein. The latter was there just in case he went into cardiac arrest; they could shoot a stimulant into his system immediately. It was necessary, but hardly comforting to an amateur like me.

George, on the other hand, opened his briefcase and worked the twenty-minute trip to the hospital as though he felt fine. In fact, he was bemoaning the fact that he had complained in the first place. As I sat there, the most dreadful thoughts ran through my mind: Dear God, this wonderful man must not die. A little later, as he worked away, I thought: Don't you dare die. I'll never forgive you. Hardly courageous, but that's what I thought.

Before leaving Camp David, I asked the Secret Service to please let our children know that we were headed for the hospital but they should not worry. Their father was making jokes and we were going just as a precaution. The message was passed on right in front of me, but it must have gotten garbled in transit, because all of them heard it from friends or television. We hated that, but it was just one of those things.

While the doctors ran their tests, I sat quietly with George in the large presidential bedroom at Bethesda. Again, he was quite funny and very regretful that he had even mentioned feeling tired. He said that he'd rather be at Camp David. We both got more respectful, however, when the doctors told us that when the heart stops fibrillating and kicks back into sync, there is a danger of blood clots shooting through the body and causing a stroke. I noticed that George stopped talking about going back to Camp David.

I spent the night in the hospital, going home the next morning to change my clothes and bathe. When I went back for lunch with George, Doro had brought Ellie and Sam over to see their grandfather. He loved that.

At one time during the afternoon George got up to go into the bathroom, which was complicated since he was still attached to an IV. He came back and got into bed, and we were watching TV when we suddenly heard a voice say, "We caught a glimpse of the President at the window a minute ago." Immediately a picture of George appeared on the screen. You could tell it was taken from far away, but it was definitely George. Little did they know what they had just filmed. I peeked out another window and there on a hillside, a hundred yards away, was a little knot of press with their cameras aimed at George's bathroom. What a dreadful job. I don't often sympathize with the press, but a lot of their lives are spent just sitting and waiting.

After George was settled down for the night I went home. I did this partially to reassure the world and our own children that it was not serious. I was promised that the doctors would let me know if there was any change. Before I got to the White House they called to say that his heart was back to normal.

He came home Monday and went right to work, although he continued to be hooked up to the cardiac monitor. A few days later, George was diagnosed and treated for Graves' disease. What a peculiar illness—it attacked my eyes and George's heart. It is unusual for a husband and wife to both have this problem, but not unheard of. I received several letters telling me of other couples who shared our same disease. I also heard from people who weren't as lucky as we were. They were not diagnosed as quickly and really suffered. I have to give credit to the doctors at Bethesda and Walter Reed hospitals for jobs well done, and later, to the doctors at the Mayo Clinic.

Not surprisingly, the press began to speculate on George's health, and rumors ran wild—some, I suspect, started by political opponents. One day, the rumor that George had lupus swept across the United States and the stock market dropped forty points. I loved setting people straight: THE DOG had lupus; George was fine. George W. heard the rumor and called from Dallas to say we could end all the talk if his dad and I would just stop drinking out of Millie's bowl.

Then story after story appeared about the fact that George, Marvin, Millie, and I all had autoimmune diseases. There was much speculation about this, one sillier than the next. Some suggested that we received bad rays when we lived in China, and then the water supply at the Vice President's House came under great scrutiny. We probably will never know the answer. I remember once asking a doctor why a terrible illness had afflicted a darling child, and he said: "Barbara, our body is made up of millions of cells. All it takes is for just one to go bad. The miracle is that more of us aren't sick."

Actually, we're still searching for answers. In December 1993, George, Millie, and I gave blood to Dr. Jonathan Jaspan at Tulane University to be tested for a possible common virus that might be responsible for our autoimmune diseases. A virus conceivably might trigger one type of disease in George and myself (that is, Graves' disease) and another type in Millie (lupus). If such a virus is found and proved to be the cause, it will be an important breakthrough.

As much as I hated George's illness, some very sad things happened that spring that made it seem quite insignificant. Our very dear friend Bill Liedtke died of cancer. He was one of our first friends in Midland, and he and his family have been very much a part of our lives ever since. Then Senator John Heinz was killed in an airplane accident. It was a double tragedy, as a helicopter and plane crashed over a school yard and two little boys on the ground also were killed, along with five in the air. John was a wealthy man who well could have sat home and never lifted a finger in his life. He chose to serve his country. He was young, bright, and caring. The very next day, our dear friend John Tower was killed in a commuter flight with his daughter Marian. Then later that year Dean Burch died after a long and horrible fight against cancer. George had a special rapport with Dean and will miss him always. And Lee Atwater died in March. It was a very difficult period.

But of course many exciting things were happening, too, and that's what we chose to focus on. In April, as chairman for the 75th Anniversary Celebration of the National Park Service, I had the pure pleasure of seeing the Grand Canyon for the first time.

In early May we had the Second Annual Great American Workout at seven A.M. led by Arnold Schwarzenegger. Arnold gathered many great athletes for this event, and at his own expense visited all fifty states to urge governors, schools, and parents to help get our nation into shape. All statistics show that exercise not only prolongs life but improves its quality.

Also that spring we dedicated the ecumenical chapel at Camp David, with leaders of all religions taking part in the ceremony. Among those attending were Adele and Don Hall, who, along with many others, had helped raise the money to build it.

I was continuing to travel to promote literacy. One trip I particularly enjoyed was to the Martin County Literacy Council in Stuart, Florida. George's cousin Shelley Jansing was a volunteer in the day-care center connected to the literacy program and had urged me to come. About three hundred volunteers were tutoring nine hundred students, six hundred of whom were prisoners. I was very impressed with the program, and proud of Shelley for her commitment.

One night I came home very late from a trip to be met by a White House electrician. He asked me if I wanted to know where everyone was sleeping. I was exhausted and said, "No," then went to bed and lay awake wondering just who "everyone" was. George Bush hates an empty bed.

Back home I had a reception for the Washington Parent Group Fund to celebrate its tenth anniversary. I had been involved with it almost from the beginning. Founded by lawyers, businessmen, parents, and educators, it had grown from helping nine schools in 1981 to more than seventy schools in 1991 through 515 different programs. One of this program's strengths is that it insists on parental involvement. Family is the answer to so many of our problems, and the sooner we accept responsibility for our own children, our own neighborhoods, villages, and communities, the better off we will be as a country.

We had several foreign visitors that spring: President Lech Walesa and his wife, Danuta, from Poland; President Violeta Chamorro from Nicaragua; and President Turgut Ozal of Turkey and his wife, Semra.

However, the visit all of Washington was talking about was the Queen of England's state visit in May. As the date approached, excitement ran high. Finally the big day came, May 14. I wrote in my diary:

She arrived on the Concorde from London this morning and we had the arrival ceremony at 11 a.m. People were really excited and started gathering on the South Grounds 1 to 2 hours ahead of time. It was muggy! Several people fainted. Her Majesty looked lovely in a purple linen suit with a smart straw, purple, black and white hat. She is sweet and has a nice sense of humor. Thank heavens, as the podium step was not pulled out for her to step up on and she looked, according to the press, like a "talking hat." You literally could not see her face as she spoke; just the hat bobbing up and down.

We had a quiet lunch with HM Queen Elizabeth II, HRH the Duke of Edinburgh, the British ambassador and his wonderful wife, Antony and Jenny Acland, George and Laura and Will and Sarah Farish. Nan Ellis, George's sister, breezed in at the end of the lunch and joined the group. I jokingly told Her Majesty that I had put our Texas son as far away from her as possible at the table and had told him that he was not allowed to say a word to her or, for that matter, to our only daughter's beau, who was coming to the dinner that night. She asked him why that was. Was he the black sheep in the family? George W. allowed as how he guessed that was true. (Not true at all.) Then she said, "Well, I guess all families have one." George W., of course, asked her if their family had one and who it was. She laughed and asked me why I thought him so dangerous. I told her that he said what he felt and besides that, he threatened to wear cowboy boots in the evening to the State Dinner. I told her that they had Texas flags on them or GOD BLESS AMERICA. She asked him which pair he was going to wear that night and he said, "Neither. Tonight's pair will say GOD SAVE THE QUEEN."

And as for Doro's beau, she has four brothers who love her and tease her all the time. They constantly were threatening her that they would ask what her dates' intentions were, etc. The Queen laughed. Incidentally, when George W. came through the receiving line at the State Dinner, Her Majesty, with a smile, looked down and without a word, he pulled his pants' leg up to show her his boots with an American flag on them.

After lunch we retired to the Rose Garden, where the Queen presented George with the Winston Churchill Award. It was truly miserably, burning hot and George jokingly said that he had a 45-minute speech and in the interest of good sense and because he did not want to cook Her Majesty, he would just say thank you. Which he did. I only mention this as the next day I read that he had torn up a 45-minute speech. Of course he wasn't going to give a 45-minute thank you!

The Queen and George replaced a tree that her father had planted and that had fallen over in a big storm last fall. And then she went off to place a wreath on the Tomb of the Unknown Soldier. Joseph Reed, our unique Chief of Protocol, told me that the Queen saved the day when out of the blue the heavens opened up and the queen whipped a tiny umbrella out of her pocketbook. Otherwise, Joseph said, we would have had two faux pas in one day.

The State Dinner that night was lovely with tables covered with white peonies with dark centers and lavender and pink roses. . . . The British ladies all wore varying degrees of tiaras, the Queen's being the largest and right on down to an adorable one that Jenny Acland wore. I sat next to the Duke and General Norman Schwarzkopf. The latter is a warm funny man who happens to be great. He is so new to the political world that he needs a keeper. He is in demand, his upcoming schedule is awful, and he has yet to learn that you do not have to accept everything. This morning's paper had him apologizing for some politically incorrect thing he had said. The world of politics is a tough one.

The Prince is charming and I gave him Libbie Reilly as his other partner. Her husband, Bill, was president of the World Wildlife Fund and now heads the Environmental Protection Agency. Libbie is a great beauty, very bright and has the singing voice of an angel.

Jessye Norman sang for us after supper. One of the many joys of living in the White House is that great entertainers generously come to perform. Often you can sneak down in the afternoon and hear a dress rehearsal. Jessye Norman's voice in an empty East Room is magnificent and fills the room and the house.

The next morning I picked Her Majesty up at Blair House, and we rode out for a visit to the Metropolitan Police Boys and Girls Club. On the way people waved and cheered. I waved back very enthusiastically until I realized that, number 1, they were waving at her; and number 2, after watching her, I realized that ladies do not almost fall out of the car waving. They do "The Light Bulb," which she has made so famous. All the Brits had on their hats and gloves. I didn't own a hat, but I did wear my gloves.

The program we visited is another excellent one in which the police mentor children and keep them in school and off the streets. The children put on quite a show for us.

From there we went to visit the Marshall Heights Community Development Organization to meet with three first-time homeowners. This area had the most dreadful reputation for guns and drugs, and the good people of the neighborhood started their own patrol and took back their streets.

In the first house, a wonderful woman named Mrs. Alice Frazier got so carried away that she just put both her arms around Her Majesty and gave her the biggest hug—the hug that went around the world. It was so sweet and the Queen's smile was a joy. Mrs. Frazier had spent the whole morning cooking and of course we could not stop for one bite. But her house smelled wonderful.

Hundreds of schoolchildren, several bands, and lots of just plain people were crowding the streets. It was a rousing welcome for the Queen. Even though it was very hot, she plunged into handshaking, didn't flick an eyelash, or even glow (a ladylike term for "perspire"). She, poor soul, went on to several more events, including a garden party at the British Embassy for some 1,800 people.

That night the Queen and Duke joined us for a helicopter ride over to see the Baltimore Orioles play several innings of baseball. Her Majesty told us the garden party had turned into a large crush, but that she had a lady-in-waiting who puts her elbows up and charges into a crowd, making a path for the Queen. This same formidable lady also carries a parasol with a point on the tip. If the crowd gets too close, she pokes the ladies on the instep. They jump back, never knowing what happened to them. We all got the giggles, with Her Majesty leading in the laughter.

There was some reluctance on the part of the Secret Service and

Scotland Yard to have the Queen go out onto the playing field. However, George talked her into it, and they went out through the dugout. She received a tremendous ovation. We left after two long innings and I was glad that they could get home and to bed.

The next morning the papers all had pictures of the podium with only the talking hat showing. When the Queen addressed a Joint Session of Congress, she opened by saying, "I do hope you can see me from where you are sitting." She had them in the palm of her hand from that moment on. The speech was only twelve minutes long. The fascinating thing is that she can only speak words that the elected government has okayed or written.

That night we went to the beautiful return dinner at the British Embassy, and then the trip was over. Both Her Majesty and the Duke were warm and gracious, and we enjoyed the visit very much.

  Summer began with a great fun event for us. During a visit to California, Jerry and Jane Morgan Weintraub gave a party for us at their lovely house in Malibu, Blue Heaven, named for one of the songs that Jane made famous. They have been loyal friends of ours for years and stuck with George through thick and thin. It wasn't always easy, especially in 1992, when much of Hollywood backed Bill Clinton.

We had a receiving line in the house and then went into a tremendous clear plastic tent covered with "A Thousand Points of Light." I wrote:

> The guest list was a moviegoer's dream: For starters, Mr. and Mrs. Johnny Carson, Don and Barbara Rickles, Gloria and Jimmy Stewart, Danny DeVito and Rhea Perlman, Tom Hanks, Chevy Chase, Olivia Newton-John, Goldie Hawn, Sally Field, Raquel Welch, Sylvester Stallone, Dinah Shore, Angie Dickinson, Merv Griffin and Eva Gabor, Julie Andrews, Billy Crystal, a very pregnant Demi Moore and her husband and George's friend, Bruce Willis, Janet Jackson, Clint Eastwood, Richard Gere, his girl with the mole, Cindy Crawford, Bernadette Peters, Jon Bon Jovi, Warren Beatty, Steven Spielberg, Sidney Poitier, Arnold Schwarzenegger, another great friend of ours, and his wife, Maria Shriver (also very pregnant), and her parents, Eunice and Sarge Shriver, Lod and Carole Cook, our great friend and head of ARCO and many, many more.

George sat at the table with Goldie Hawn and Sally Field and found them both captivating and fun. I sat next to Warren Beatty, Sidney Poitier and later Richard Gere. They were all very nice. I remember telling Warren Beatty that I had loved *Reds* and he suggested that I might be one of the only people who had seen it. Not a success, I guess. It was a most glamorous night and to top it all off I danced with a very bright Sylvester Stallone and a very attractive John Travolta. That was great fun and I had my picture taken with them both. I was thrilled as I wanted to send the picture with John to Mildred Kerr. In 1978 she and I had taken her daughter-in-law Mimi and some other young friends to see *Grease* after they helped me address some political mail that I was sending out for George W. We loved *Grease* so much that the next afternoon we took in *Saturday Night Fever*. The latter film turned out to be filled with words that embarrassed us and especially embarrassed those young women with us. Unfortunately the same words are used today almost as common words, but not by us.

(The Weintraub party) was the most glamorous night ever and such fun. Jane has the most beautiful voice and she once again came out of retirement for us. Fortunately I now have a disc of her songs and so can hear her year-round.

On July 1 in Kennebunkport, George announced the appointment of Clarence Thomas to fill the vacancy left by Thurgood Marshall on the Supreme Court. Clarence arrived in Maine at lunchtime with John Sununu, White House Counsel Boyden Gray, Deputy Chief of Staff Andy Card, and Attorney General Dick Thornburgh for the announcement. They sneaked him past the press, stationed across the bay from the Point in a van with tinted windows. We had a quiet lunch and then walked down to a press conference where George made the announcement.

The press had gone mad speculating on who the nominee would be. I was told that Rita Beamish with the Associated Press had been on the phone to possible candidates and if they were at home, she knew they were not the one. Great ingenuity on her part. I should add we liked her a lot. I believe that George surprised them.

We were touched when Clarence choked up when talking about his family. He is the most extraordinary man. He talked about how he came from a very poor family in Pinpoint, Georgia. After his father abandoned the family, he was raised by his mother, grandmother, and grandfather. He never dreamed as a child he would even see the Supreme Court, much less be nominated to it. "Indeed, my most vivid childhood memory of the Supreme Court was the 'Impeach Earl Warren' signs which lined Highway 17 near Savannah," Clarence told the press. "I didn't quite understand who this Earl Warren fellow was, but I knew he was in some kind of trouble." He went on to tell us that he had attended an all-black Catholic school taught by white nuns and that his mother, grandparents, and nuns all were adamant that he make something of himself. It was very sweet.

~ The Fourth of July was spent parading, literally. Returning Desert Storm veterans were being honored across the country. We started in Marshfield, Missouri, a darling little town that has had a Fourth of July parade for 110 years. They march everything by: at least two sanitation trucks, loads of horses, with or without riders, trick dogs, Boy and Girl Scouts, trucks, fire engines, farm equipment, bands, and of course many, many Desert Storm troops. We were accompanied by Governor John Ashcroft and his lovely schoolteacher wife, Janet, and both of Missouri's senators, Jack Danforth and Kit Bond. John told us how thrilled he was by the Clarence Thomas appointment. They had worked for two years in the same tiny office for then Attorney General of Missouri Jack Danforth. John said and still says that no finer, more decent man exists than Clarence Thomas. And of course his former boss, Senator Danforth, was a huge fan. In light of what happened to Clarence later, this is interesting.

Our second parade was in Grand Rapids, Michigan, with Governor John Engler and his bride, Michelle. It was huge, but the same good feeling ran through both communities and it was heartwarming to see. That night we got home in time to see the fireworks from the Truman Balcony. We invited Marilyn and Dan Quayle and their family to come watch with us. Marilyn and I went upstairs and watched the show from the catwalk on the roof with many of the children. It was wonderful, even when it drizzled. Umbrellas were brought up and we looked like a group of Mary Poppinses. The South Lawn of the White House and the whole Mall were filled with families on blankets. It was a sight to behold.

July 8—Tough times . . . going to lift the sanctions on South Africa, Israel causing trouble and we have the MFN [Most Favored Nation] vote on China. Then you add to that the tough time the Senate is giving our wonderful friend Bob Gates, G's nominee as Director of the CIA, and Clarence Thomas, G's nominee for the Supreme Court. I asked Bob how his kids were doing with the awful attacks being made on him. He said that their friends were great, they all have rallied around the children, but that several of the teachers have said ugly things. How outrageous! Clarence is also being raked over the coals. They are saying he is "anti-Israel, pro-life, a white man in a black man's skin." The women's group NOW and the Black Caucus have come out against him and on and on.

On July 13 we left for the annual G-7 Economic Summit, this year to be held in London, but we stopped en route in Rambouillet, France, so George could meet with François Mitterrand. During a formal arrival ceremony in the courtyard of the chateau, George presented General François Roquejeoffre with the Legion of Merit medal for his leadership during Desert Storm.

While the leaders met, Danielle Mitterrand and their charming granddaughter Justine gave me a tour of the lovely summer home of the President of France, open to the public when they are not in residence. We took a walk through the grounds and toured the Shell House and the Queen's Dairy. They are both made to look like one thing and then turn out to be another. We walked up to a tiny cottage covered with a thatched roof, walked in, and found an exquisite room all decorated from head to toe with shells. They were beautiful. I have seen only one other like it and that was in a marvelous villa at Gasparilla Inn in Boca Grande, Florida. Another tiny room was painted in the fashion of Versailles. This incredible place was a playhouse built for Marie Antoinette. It took ten years to build and they said she rarely, if ever, visited it. The dairy was equally grand when we went inside.

When we arrived in England, we went almost immediately to Number 10 Downing Street for dinner with John and Norma Major:

. . . The security is unbelievable. But remembering the bomb that had gone off about four months ago in the tiny backyard of Number 10, I was pleased. George gave the Legion of Merit to General Peter de la Billière, who led the British Troops in Desert Storm. After the ceremony we went into dinner with Norma and John, just the four of us. They are the most attractive couple. He seems well in command of his role and she seems very less intimidated by the job than she did at Camp David, in fact very comfortable. They took us upstairs to their residence for after-dinner coffee. The only thing I remember is that they had a painting by Winston Churchill. He was a much better painter than I thought. The men talked at length about what must come out of this Summit for Gorbachev (he had been invited to come at the end) and the world.

Once again we stayed at Winfield House, this time with Ambassador Ray Seitz and his wife, Caroline. We heard good things about both of them from everyone. Ray is a career Foreign Service officer, and George appointed him for that reason and for many others, including ability. He felt that the State Department needed the appointment of one of their own—as opposed to a political appointee—to this illustrious post for morale purposes.

It struck me as funny that right in the heart of the city and on this elegant estate we were awakened early in the morning by the cock-a-doodle-do-ing of a rooster who lived nearby!

Norma Major had planned a lovely tour for the G-7 spouses, including a boat ride and lunch on the River Thames, and a visit to Kew Gardens, which was founded in 1759 and is now three hundred acres and exhibits thirty thousand different species. We walked in the gardens and the roses were absolutely at their glorious peak. That night we went to see *Carmen Jones* in the Old Vic Theatre while the heads of state met. The next day we visited a Spinal Injuries Center at Stoke Mandeville Hospital, followed by lunch at Chequers.

That evening Queen Elizabeth and Prince Philip were hosts for a state dinner at Buckingham Palace:

(It was) every little girl's dream and maybe the dream of some not so little girls. . . . We got dressed in black tie and drove to Buckingham Palace with Jimmy and Susan Baker and Nick and Kitty Brady. We were met by HRH Prince Philip and a Lady-in-Waiting. It amused us that François Mitterrand beat us to the party. I'm afraid that he had heard reports that he was always late to everything. Protocol-wise, we should have preceded him, but he came early this time. We were met in the Blue Room by HM the Queen. She looked lovely in a yellow silk gown. No tiara! There were

64 participants, all the regulars and the Prince and Princess of Wales, the latter looking so beautiful in a one-shoulder, many-colored chiffon dress. The young prince seemed so sad. I feel sorry for them as they should be the happiest people in the world. Three former Prime Ministers were there—Heath, Callaghan, and Margaret Thatcher. I sat next to HRH Prince Philip and Former PM Callaghan. Both more than pleasant and charming. The minute the Prince was served he started in, down goes the food and then his plate was whisked away. Hard on Callaghan as he was in what we called "starvation corner," last to be served, and HRH was sitting waiting for the next course. I said: "Don't put your fork down, Sir, or your plate will be taken." He laughed, put down his fork and away went his dinner! Hardly a bite eaten. After dinner our numbers swelled and we had coffee with the new arrivals. George was talking to a group of people when a woman turned to him and said: "Peter, how are you?" and went right on talking to him. He quickly realized that she thought she was talking to somebody else and said: "I'm George Bush, the President of the United States." Needless to say, she was humiliated. A rather humbling experience for my truly humble husband. How we teased him. He later sent her a picture of himself with Ranger and on it he wrote: "I enjoyed meeting you. I'm the one on the left." He hoped that she would think it was funny and that it would put her at ease. Obviously it did not, as he never heard back from her.

Her Majesty then said she had a surprise for us. We went outside on a balcony that overlooked the courtyard. No words can tell how exciting it was. We were led out in the exact middle of the courtyard and stood under an arch. The view in front of us was three great arches into which troops marched, the Air Force, Marine and Guard Bands, about 250 of them. At one time they were joined by about 24 bagpipers. The pièce de résistance was James Galway, the flutist. When he played "Danny Boy," it was, I believe, the sweetest sound I ever heard. They had a laser beam show that out-Disneyed Disney. At one time they flashed the names of the G-7 countries on the far walls and then flashed something symbolic of that country. In our case it was the Statue of Liberty. At the same time they played "God Bless America." It was most generous of Her Majesty. Then came the most amazing fireworks, shooting from the chimneys, rooftops and balconies. Remembering how singed everything gets at Walker's Point after fireworks, I wondered the next day just what Buckingham Palace looked like in the morning. In any case, Her Majesty gave us a storybook evening.

The next morning Princess Diana came by Winfield House with her sons, William and Harry. The two boys were absolutely like any others their age and were very excited to see *Marine One,* which was tethered on the lawn under guard. They asked all the right questions and had a twinkle in their eyes. We asked them if they wanted to see *Air Force One,* the giant Boeing 747, and they rapidly agreed that they did. So we sent them out to Heathrow Airport. I later heard that Danny Barr, the President's pilot, gave them a first-class tour of the whole plane, although I think they were a little disappointed he didn't give them a spin.

Meanwhile their mother and I went to Middlesex Hospital/Hospice to visit the AIDS ward. It was a very moving morning. We met many patients and talked a little about their concerns, one of which was visiting the United States, since our country was not issuing passports to anyone who tested HIV-positive. They didn't specifically ask me about changing the policy; my impression was they wanted to make sure I was aware of it.

I have visited hospice programs twice with Princess Diana and feel that I have learned from watching her. She is so warm and loving to the sick. Their faces light up as she takes time with each person, and she seems to know the right questions to ask.

Before we left London, George and Mikhail Gorbachev had a joint press conference. It was an accident waiting to happen. The press advance team changed their minds three times about the location of the conference, and the White House communications team had to work all night to set up the cables. As it turned out, the wires got mixed and the two leaders' statements and answers were broadcast into their own countries in the other person's language. Now it sounds funny; then, it was very embarrassing. Nevertheless, it was an exciting conference. It was announced that we would visit Russia at the end of July to sign another weapons reduction treaty.

From London we flew to Athens, where we were met by our old friends, Prime Minister Konstantinos Mitsotakis and his wife, Marika. The second morning of our visit, we took a walking tour of the Acropolis. I was so glad I had worn sneakers, for it was very hot and slippery. (Out of respect for our country, you'll be happy to know, I wore matching ones!)

Next stop was Crete, where we toured the Greek ship *Limnos* and the U.S. naval vessel the U.S.S. *Dewert*. The men on the two ships had one thing in common—they were young. Later George told me that he saw the ships tied up stern-to-stern and remembered that in his talk he referred to them as tied bow-to-bow. He corrected it in the speech and sent it back to the writers with a note that said, "The pointy end is the bow."

We went to the Prime Minister's house and were greeted by Marika Mitsotakis and the children. They lived in the most heavenly house high on a hill overlooking the harbor with a view of the mountains and room for the whole family, including four children and nine grandchildren. Although it was beautiful, the best part is being invited into one's home. That is the greatest honor that can be bestowed on a person. It does not matter if the home is large or tiny. I remarked to the Prime Minister's daughter that the house was lovely and she said: "Yes, the house is beautiful, but my mother is the house. It is not the same when she isn't here." A nice tribute to a very nice friend.

We finished our visit with a big evening reception in Athens given by our very able ambassador and wife, Michael and Estelle Sotirhos, and an early morning greeting to the American community at the U.S. Embassy. This was something we did—or at least tried to do—in every country we visited, to greet the American community, particularly those serving in our embassies, and let them know how much we appreciated their hard work and dedication to their country.

We flew on to Ankara, Turkey, where we renewed our friendship with President and Mrs. Ozal. We were represented there by one of the wisest and most senior of our diplomatic corps, Morton Abramowitz, and his wife, Sheppie, who were retiring after a long and distinguished career, and there was a medal ceremony upon our arrival honoring them.

I have to mention one of the banquets we attended while in Turkey. The table was set with very old gold ware that was not in great condition, but was very beautiful with filigree work. We discovered that it came from the Ottoman period. There was a gold plate in front of each of the 150 guests. I read in the paper that Semra Ozal had bought the plates for our visit. The writer in the paper suggested that they were so ugly (they weren't) that he wouldn't be surprised if she sent them back to France, where she bought them. When you think that Nancy Reagan took so much criticism for china that was given to the White House in her name. Imagine the stir if she had bought gold plates!

Semra and Turgut took us to the beautiful old city of Istanbul, where we toured the Blue Mosque, St. Sophia Cathedral, and Topkapi Palace. It was all too fast, but worth every minute. We saw many Ottoman treasures, an exhibit of whirling dervish dancers, and a small concert using ancient musical instruments. We had lunch during a boat trip on the Bosphorus, almost reaching the Black Sea. I wish we could have. I hadn't realized Turkey is literally in two continents. We had a nice lunch facing Asia, and then the boat turned and we were looking at Europe. This is a beautiful part of the world.

Turgut Ozal was a courageous leader who backed the United Nations Coalition against Saddam Hussein, his very threatening neighbor. He and George were on the phone to each other a lot, and George respected his judgment a great deal. We last saw him in Houston shortly after George left office. The four of us had a cozy lunch and a nice visit. When he died just a short time later, we and the United States lost a good friend.

A few days after we returned home, George signed the National Literacy Act of 1991. Needless to say, I was thrilled. Secretary of Education Lamar Alexander, Secretary of Labor Lynn Martin, and several congressmen and senators were there. Most had very legitimate reasons for attending, like Senator Paul Simon and Congressman Bill Goodling of Pennsylvania, who have been champions of literacy. As for some of the others, I wasn't sure what their role had been. I was amused to see that when George invited the members of Congress to stand behind him when he signed the bill, there was a lot of elbowing and they all got as close as they could.

I must say that I got more credit than I deserved. I had heard that George was going to give the pen to me, but before he could, Senator Simon spoke up and said: "That pen ought to go to Barbara." I have donated it to the George Bush Presidential Library Center. In the end, however, it's not pens and pictures that count; it's the National Literacy Act that *really* counts. It was the first piece of legislation—and to date, the only one—ever enacted specifically for literacy, with the goal of ensuring that every American adult acquires the basic literacy skills necessary to achieve the greatest possible satisfaction professionally and personally. But even more than that, the act seeks to strengthen our nation by giving us more productive workers and informed citizens.

That summer Joseph Reed announced his resignation as Chief of Protocol. He certainly is one of a kind. He cared for the Diplomatic Corps as though they were his babies. He entertained them at Blair House and made all our foreign guests feel most welcome. He treated the doorman the same way he treated the King of Spain, and that's pretty nice.

~ We were barely home when it was time to turn around and fly to Moscow for the treaty signing. We arrived very late on July 29 and went straight to Spaso House, the ambassador's residence. If ever I saw a house that needed a face-lift, this was it. It suddenly looked very shabby and run-down. We were greeted by Ambassador Jack Matlock and his wife, Rebecca, who also were getting ready to retire after years of service.

The next morning we were received in St. George's Hall at the Kremlin. It is large and impressive and very dramatic. Raisa and Mikhail greeted us and after the ceremony was over, Raisa and I went for a tour of the Kremlin:

Just before we went on our tour Raisa took me into a little room and changed her shoes. Much to my amazement she changed from very high suede shoes to very high leather heels. Remembering how her feet got blistered at Camp David in stilts, I thought that she would put on walking shoes. But no—beauty first. We walked to and into the Annunciation Cathedral, by the Cathedral of the Archangel, past the Czar's cannon and bell and into the Armory to see a small portion of the gold, jewels and diamonds. The diamond coronation crown and necklace of Catherine the Great put all the Ottoman Empire jewels to shame. They were so delicate and beautiful with their double-headed eagles.

Back to the Palace for tea. There were loads of tourists. Raisa still loves to plunge into crowds. It is fun.

In the afternoon we went to the Novodevichy Park, where we presented a *Make Way for Ducklings* sculpture to the children of Moscow from the children of the United States. It is an exact replica of the sculpture Raisa and I had visited in Boston Gardens. This was an idea that was thought up and executed by Susan Porter Rose. It took an unending amount of planning and fund-raising to do. The artist who sculpted the original statue, Nancy Schon, offered to duplicate it, and she and her husband were there for the unveiling, along with Robert McCloskey, who had written the book fifty years before. We also brought with us copies of the book in Russian. The setting was perfect, on the Moscow River across from the Novodevichy Monastery and right by a duck-feeding station. Susan literally did not leave a stone unturned: The cobblestones from Boston were surrounded by the black stones from Moscow. Everyone said that the workmen from both countries worked well together. It was a happy and lovely gift. I got the credit and did not deserve it; Susan did.

We met the Gorbachevs at the studio of Zurab Tsereteli, the artist who made the magnificent statue of St. George that is on the United Nations grounds in New York City. This is the most remarkable man, who paints a picture a day just to keep his hand in. Every inch of his studio was covered with paintings, many of them just finished, as George's personal aide, Bill Farish, can testify. Bill had backed up to let us by and had a nice flower on his jacket for the rest of the day. We were led into a back room where the artist unveiled two bronze models of Columbus. He invited us to pick one out, explaining with great enthusiasm that the actual statue would be larger than the Statue of Liberty and would go on the tip of Roosevelt Island, where it will be seen from the United Nations. I know George's heart sank. Who was going to pay for this? Then we were told that it was privately funded. I could see the relief on George's face. We loved that visit and the magnificent artist.

That night the Gorbachevs had a lovely dinner for us in the Kremlin:

We started in the Garden Room, then into the Hall of St. Vladimir for a receiving line—In they poured. Some we knew like Dwayne and Inez Andreas (he is head of the Archer Daniels Midland Co.). Mrs. Yeltsin came through, but no husband—until the very end of the line. We were about to break up the line when in he came, bigger than life. He is outrageous. He wanted a "photo op" with George and Mikhail with himself in the middle, but Mikhail would not turn around, but kept his back to the press pool. "Gorby" moved him on to me and Raisa. Raisa seemed very welcoming—for the press, I guess. Jack Matlock had told me that Yeltsin had criticized Gorbachev in the Parliament and had ended by saying that "besides all other complaints, he was sick of having four telephone calls a day from Raisa Maksimovna Gorbacheva." As everyone had gone into dinner, Boris Yeltsin offered me his arm and said, "As I am going to sit by you at dinner, please let me take you in." I started in with him and then thought better of it and went back to ask Raisa what I should do. She suggested that we all go in together and kept me from making a mistake. I sat between the President of Russia and the President of the Soviet Union. Both men were charming. I must confess that I thought that Boris was using me to needle Mikhail. Evidently they need each other right now, but it is clear that they don't like each other.

The dinner was held in the Palace of Facets—one of the oldest rooms in the Kremlin, built in 1472 by Ivan the Great. It served as a throne room and a reception hall by Ivan and his successors.

The next day we went to a dacha in the countryside where the men talked and Raisa took me for a boat ride on the Moscow River. I loved every minute in the tiny little speedboat. There was a driver and a security guard in the two front seats; Raisa and I were directly behind them; and her interpreter and Jim Sloan, the head of my Secret Service detail, were behind us. Raisa had a small parasol with her and, to her credit, she did offer it to me. I turned it down. It must have been a funny scene as the poor interpreter had to lean forward to hear Raisa and took a chance every time she turned her head that he might lose an eye. All along the way we saw families having a swim in the dirty river and sitting on bare dirt patches, which Raisa called beaches. I couldn't believe the bathing suits. The biggest men and women were in tiny little strings of suits. I got the giggles thinking of how shocked they'd be by my bathing suits with skirts.

Later that day George and President Gorbachev signed the START treaty, another step in ending the Cold War.

That night we had a reciprocal dinner at Spaso House. Almost everything was brought from the White House kitchen. For the first time we produced something really bad—a watercress soup that normally tastes wonderful. If we hadn't been the hosts, I almost would have enjoyed it, since the faces of people as they had their first bitter sip were so funny. The rest of the meal was delicious, but the evening was made because the wonderfully talented Isaac Stern offered to come and play the violin for us.

The next morning we left for Kiev, a city which touched me deeply. It is beautiful and old but with so many problems. I rode in the car with Mrs. Antonia Kravchuk, the wife of the Ukrainian leader and now the President, Leonid Kravchuk. She was the nicest young woman, a math teacher who had absolutely no interest in politics. The crowds along the way were tremendous, so we slowed the motorcade down to enable the people to see George, who was riding in the car ahead of us. We waved and talked all the way in:

Mrs. K. told me some of the awful consequences of Chernobyl that is only sixty miles away. It was and is dreadful in a real sense. They know the ground is contaminated for miles around. They no longer can go into the really lush green forests we passed on the way into town for berries and mushrooms. They don't plant vegetables and wheat anymore even though this Kiev is known as "the breadbasket" of the Soviet Union. Their other main source of income was from tourists, but who would want to come here now? They don't know what will happen to their children and babies. It is so much bigger than I thought.

We and many other countries have sent teams in, but it is all so new. The ghastly part is that it did not need to happen. (The Soviet scientists) were sloppy.

Our last stop before leaving Kiev was a very moving visit to the Babi Yar Holocaust Memorial:

The Germans occupied the Ukraine for two years. When they saw the war was ending, they lined the Jews up, marched them to the field, had them dig trenches, strip and fold their clothes, put their jewelry in another spot and line up by the trenches and they shot them. They killed 33,000 people at the end. I sat next to some of the survivors. One lady was twelve at the time. Her brother and sister were killed. One lady had a baby in her arms, she fell into the trench protecting her baby with her body. When it was all over she pushed her way out through the dead or dying and she and her baby lived. One lady near me had hidden a Jewish family for two years at great personal risk. It is inconceivable to us. What horror—what courage.

Soon after returning home I took off for Maine and the grandchildren. I loved how they loved seeing each other, their great-grandmother, and their cousins, the Stapletons. George and Noelle spent hours with Walker and Wendy Stapleton, the children of George's much younger cousins.

Like the summer before, however, this was not to be a real vacation. It all started on August 19:

George and I were going to play golf at the crack of dawn with (Boston Red Sox pitcher) Roger Clemens and his wife, Debbie. Roger was to bring a group of Red Sox players, and the wives and I were going to play after the men. BUT everything was against this game. First of all we were called in the middle of the night and told that there had been a coup in the Soviet Union and that Mikhail Gorbachev and Raisa were under house arrest in the Crimea, where they were on vacation. Our host for some of the trip we recently took, Vice President Yanayev, is now in charge. He is a hard-line Communist. We are seeing tanks in Moscow on the tube. My heart goes out to our friends the Gorbachevs. To his credit Boris Yeltsin is working hard to bring Gorbachev back. When John Major talked to Boris he said, "I only have a few minutes left." He was in his office at the Parliament building and was under siege. We knew it was tenuous at best, but this is such a shock. Rumors are running wild. We heard that Gorbachev was "undergoing treatment." That he has been "put on a ship in the Baltic," that he was "taken to a military base," etc. There are so many questions. Is Raisa with him? I hope so because they are so devoted. It is so frightening. Will the new group keep the recently signed agreements? And there are so many more questions.

Then Hurricane Bob came roaring up the coast and if the coup hadn't cancelled the game the weather would have. The Red Sox came by with tons of souvenirs for the grandchildren and nephews and nieces. The house was like a madhouse. George and Brent (Scowcroft) were on the phone between cups of coffee, the builders had run over to board up our house against the hurricane, and plans were being made for George and Brent to return to Washington. Everyone departed the Point and we who were left spent a quiet day putting away all the porch furniture, toys and the chil-

dren's tent. In the afternoon the Secret Service said that we must all evacuate. Before we could go we had to move George's mom and aunt to a safe
place and then Colu, little Jeb, Paula and I went up to Blueberry Hill, Jane
and Jerry Weintraub's beautiful old farmhouse, and settled in for a nap.
Noelle and George went to their cousins' house. The winds and rains were
fierce and the electricity went out on the farm. The eye of the hurricane
went by at 5 p.m. and high tide came at 8 p.m. and so we were lucky. We
went back home at 6 p.m. and the swell of the waves in the cove was absolutely magnificent. At 8 p.m. the cousins returned with the other children
and we all stood out on the deck and marveled at the sea. George checked in
every few hours and all was well with us. Not so great on the Soviet front.

George returned on the 20th.

We awakened to pouring rain. We are getting tired of being damp.
They say we have had more rain this August than any other August in history. I really think that 18 inches came down in two or three days.

G. spent the morning on the phone with Yeltsin. He sounds fairly
assured or at least not hopeless. Brent and George say that this is the most
important day. We will know whether the coup will be overturned. Two of
the eight who headed the coup are "ill" and have been removed.

. . . Our house is like a circus. Doro and Colu alleviated some of
the strain by taking the three little kids, Sam, Ellie, and Jebby, to the
movies . . . we ended up by being 11 at the table. In the middle of it
all Pop called me into the bedroom and told me that he was talking to
Mikhail Gorbachev. It was very exciting. The coup had failed and we were
thrilled. There were so many ramifications if the coup had succeeded and
the hard-liners had taken over—back to the days of the Cold War. What
would have happened to the Mideast talks? The weapons treaty that was
signed just a few weeks ago in Moscow? The giant steps that the Soviet
Union had taken towards democracy? . . . Both Gorbachev and Yeltsin
thanked George profusely for his statements and for not recognizing the
insurgents.

In September I received a letter from Raisa, responding to a letter I had written her. We had heard and read that she suffered greatly
during the coup. Among many things she said:

> Those three terrible days were a severe trial for us all.
> However, we are deeply convinced that such values as free-

dom, democracy and human dignity, in the name of which perestroika was initiated, have already become irreversible. It makes us happy and inspires optimism.

How relaxing was the rest of the summer? Here are a few excerpts from my diary:

Walter Cronkite and Betsy came by for dinner with an old friend, Bill Harback, and his wife, Barbara. They were cruising up the coast.
. . . Jimmy Dean, the sausage man, came into the river in his boat *The Big Bad John,* named after his big song hit.
. . . G. had a meeting at the house with (Bob) Teeter, (Dick) Darman, (Andy) Card, (John) Sununu . . . Jim Baker just back from talking to NATO Foreign Ministers. He had interrupted his vacation in Wyoming for the meeting.
. . . Arnold and Winnie Palmer came for a few days.
. . . Brian and Mila Mulroney arrived with their four children.
. . . G. had a briefing from Bob Strauss, Dick Cheney, John Sununu, a Russian expert, Bob Gates and Brent Scowcroft. [Bob Strauss had just become Ambassador to the Soviet Union when this all happened. Talk about timing! He did a great job.]
On the 28th Norma and John Major arrived with their children, Elizabeth and James. They are very relaxed guests and eager to sunbathe and walk. The men, of course, talked business.
. . . George had a great tennis match on Thursday afternoon with Jeb as his partner against Craig Stapleton and (Maine Senator) George Mitchell. We had a small group at the house (Nick and Kitty Brady, Speaker Tom Foley, Senate Majority Leader George Mitchell, our family and the Majors) for a drink and then down to the River Club for a Clambake with a larger group including the governors of Maine, Vermont, New Hampshire and Massachusetts. Frankie Hewitt of the Ford Theatre gathered the disbanded cast from *Forever Plaid* who had acted in the show in Washington and we went across the street to the Casino for that great musical. It was a perfect evening.

Before leaving Kennebunkport for the summer I decided, almost as an afterthought, to take the advice of Craig Stapleton, who, after Hurricane Bob, suggested that perhaps I should remove fifty years of scrapbooks and photo albums from the house. He had seen them in our bedroom the day after the storm and just thought maybe they would be safer somewhere else. So Peggy Swift and I boxed them up and shipped them to Washington to be put in storage. Considering what was to happen to our home in a few months, Craig saved those scrapbooks, which I definitely needed to help write this book.

We ended the summer by going home via Lewiston, Maine, where George, Lamar Alexander, and Maine Governor Jock McKernan kicked off America 2000 for the state. A week later I was doing the same thing in Maryland with Governor William Donald Schaefer, Undersecretary of Education David Kearns, and many others, including Lou Sullivan, Bill Reilly, and Jim Watkins from the cabinet. America 2000 was an innovative, bipartisan effort to improve education in our country, and I would attend several more state kickoffs in the coming months. I always loved the enthusiasm and dedication to our children that I found, whether I was at the huge Arsenal Technical High School in Indianapolis or in tiny, rural Winona, Mississippi.

At all the kickoffs I shared with the participants one of the more amazing statistics I had come across. Did you know that if a child never misses a day of school from first grade to twelfth grade, he or she would have spent only 9 percent of his or her life in the classroom? The other 91 percent is spent in the home or out in the community. We cannot expect teachers and the schools to solve all our children's problems.

September 13—This week we have been involved with three black men; three amazing black men. Clarence Thomas, whose mother could not care for him and whose grandparents took him in, sent him to parochial school, expected him to do well, and he did.

Then yesterday at a brown sack lunch at the Dept. of Education I heard Dr. James Comer from Yale University speak on the Comer Schools, a system he created that is being tested in the public schools and it seems to be doing very well. It has a lot to do with getting input from parents, having a strong principal, a strong social aid, great expectations along with a good academic course. Empowering parents seemed to make the big difference. His mother, a housemaid, went through the seventh grade; his father, a laborer, went through third grade. His mother made up her mind that she would marry a man who had the same values that she had. She knew that she would never go to college, but her children would get an education. She had five children who between them got THIRTEEN degrees. Amazing.

Then the third man we saw was Stan Scott, an old friend of ours from the Nixon days. Stan was born into a newspaper family in Atlanta, Georgia. He remembers his grandmother sitting in the back of the segregated trolley listening to him conjugate verbs. She felt that he had to learn to speak correctly to move to the front of the trolley. Stan was one of the first black writers for a white paper. He was nominated for a Pulitzer Prize because of his coverage of Malcolm X's assassination. He worked for Nixon, Ford, Philip Morris and then bought a Miller's Beer franchise which he has just sold for a lot of money. Stan has three children and a magnificent wife, Bettye. He also is riddled with cancer. We saw Stan at a dinner in Washington where the money will go to set up a scholarship in his name at the United Negro College Fund. Stan gave a talk filled with love and gratitude. What a man! [He died April 4, 1992.]

All three of these men had something in common—someone who cared for them, a family member who urged them on.

. . . I read Hume Cronyn's book *Terrible Liar: A Memoir.* I so admire both Hume and his truly talented wife, Jessica Tandy.

. . . I taped thirty-six introductions for the Disney Channel's "Salute to the American Teacher." It is such a worthwhile program. This series runs for nine months and it recognizes excellence in teaching.

September 18—Dee Jepsen (wife of former Senator from Iowa) came by one morning this week to brief me on The National Coalition against Pornography. They are keeping their focus on things that are illegal and those things where children are concerned, so all those disgusting magazines like *Hustler*, etc., are out of children's first strike zone. I am eager to help them as it does have something to do with a healthy child and we have already decided that a child must be healthy in order to learn. (America 2000's first of six goals.) The sexual exploitation of children must be stopped!

. . . I visited the Baptist Senior Adult Ministries Adult Day Care Center. This is on the edge of the University of Maryland and is a wonderful place where older people, retarded adults and people with Alzheimer's can go for the day, 5 days a week, thus giving the caretaker a little relief and not costing what a home or a hospital would cost. I took Millie with me thinking that they would like to see her. I think they did.

I did lots of other programs. Too many to mention.

. . . Joseph Reed gave a lunch for the King of Swaziland. The King came with one of his seven wives. He must marry one lady from each of his tribes. He is twenty-three years old. His wife asked Anna Perez just how old she was and how many children she had. Anna told her that she was forty and that she and Ted had three children. Her Majesty asked Anna what was the matter with her. Anna was nonplussed for once!

Also that fall I did a little work for Childhelp USA, a wonderful group of people who help abused children. Childhelp was founded by two dynamic women, Yvonne Fedderson and Sara O'Meara, who are absolute stars. They also have a star-studded group of Childhelp ambassadors, including Cheryl Ladd, Florence Henderson, Jane Seymour, Dionne Warwick, and Efrem Zimbalist, Jr. I attended the dedication of their new residential treatment facility near Culpeper, Virginia, which means they will have places for children to get help on both the East and West Coast.

⊷ At the end of September, George and I spent several days at Sea Island, Georgia. This was our first trip back since our honeymoon forty-six years earlier, although we had planned to return every year. There were people along the route into the Cloisters with signs saying HAPPY ANNIVERSARY, MR. PRESIDENT. It wasn't our anniversary, but it was sweet anyway.

Former Attorney General Griffin Bell arranged golf games for both of us. George played with Griffin, Bill Jones, and Jack Lumpkin. My game was and still is poor, but after a hiatus of thirty years, I had taken it up again and was loving it. I like to play in a twosome right after George's foursome for two reasons: He plays so quickly that he clears the way for me; and I love to see him having fun with his friends. Since he has left office we play a lot together. I can't give him any competition, but I am the only one who will play at 6 A.M. with ten minutes' notice!

Griffin arranged a foursome for me with Louise Suggs, one of the first great professional women golfers who started the women's golf tour. Now a teacher in Florida and Sea Island, she hits the straightest, longest ball with absolutely no effort. He also lined up two other ladies, Fran Green and Carolyn Carter. All three were so much better than I was, but they were a lot of fun and very nice. I think that they were surprised that anyone who played as badly as I did was eager to play the second day. But out they came. Louise took me over to the practice tee and gave me a mini lesson before the game.

We were there for two nights and got a great rest. I only hope we don't have to wait another forty-six years to return.

⁓ We had some fascinating visitors during the fall of 1991. King Juan Carlos and Queen Sophia of Spain came for an overnight at Camp David with their friends and ours, Bob and Georgette Mosbacher. Her Majesty and I visited the National Rehabilitation Hospital. It is such a wonderful place that I loved taking foreign visitors there—and besides that, our Doro was working there.

Another treat for me was that Maeve Binchy, an Irish writer and one of my favorites, came to the White House for lunch with her very nice husband, Gordon Snell. She has written *Light a Penny Candle, The Lilac Bus,* and many others. I invited several of my friends whom I thought would enjoy her: Flo Gibson, who reads books on tape for the blind and others; Nan Ellis, George's sister, who happened to be in Washington; and, of course, Andy Stewart. I also included Maeve Gallagher, the wife of the new Irish Ambassador. We laughed our way through the meal.

Also that fall, as part of the upcoming five hundredth anniversary of Columbus's discovering America, the "Circa 1492: Art in the Age of Exploration" exhibit came to the National Gallery. This extraordinary show was a cross section of the world's great art at the time of Columbus. There were many treasures that had never been seen outside their own country. The centerpiece for me was the Leonardo da Vinci *Portrait of a Lady with an Ermine* (Cecilia Gallerani). Now I have seen all three of his ladies, the *Mona Lisa* in Paris and the National Gallery's *Ginevra de' Benci.*

We lost another friend that fall. Nan Rehnquist, wife of Chief Justice Rehnquist, died after years of fighting cancer. It was so sad. Many people did not even know Nan was sick.

And we were agonizing through Clarence Thomas's confirmation hearings. Our whole country suffered, and it was awful to watch the disgraceful procedures on television:

October 11—Clarence Thomas and his wife (Virginia) came over to see George. They are in shock. They cannot believe what is happening. All the women's groups are up in arms and the hue and cry for Clarence's blood can be heard from every side. It is setting a picture that anyone can testify if he or she wants and cause doubts.

Sexual harassment is wrong. Let's hope some good will come of this. Women will now testify if, in truth, they are being harassed.

The question is: Is this woman telling the truth? It is Clarence's word against Anita Hill's. I do not mean to sit in judgment, but I will never believe that she, a Yale Law School graduate, a woman of the 80s, would put up with harassment for one moment, much less follow the harasser from job to job, call him when she came back to town and later invite him to speak to her students at Oral Roberts University. It just makes no sense at all. It also makes no sense to me that this was all publicly aired on television. We are talking about reputations here and a good man was smeared.

October 15—Clarence Thomas's nomination was passed by a 52 to 48 vote.

. . . It is becoming very obvious that the 1992 campaign has already started. George wanted a Civil Rights Bill, a Crime Bill, Tort Reform, a Capital Gains Tax reduction, the Line Item Veto, Health Care Reform and many more things that the country needs and wants. None of which will happen because the election is a year away. [He did get a Civil Rights Bill later that fall.] I mentioned to George that it had been a sad and ugly week and he said, "Every day is ugly in my life." I hated that. I think I got him when he was very tired.

October 28th—As the election year creeps up on us things get tense. It isn't just the Democrats that knock George, but the press is all over him. It is interesting how they can slant a story by using an ugly word, a qualifier. Like: "Last night a WEAKENED president"; or "The IRRITATED president said."

In late October I flew down to Atlanta at the invitation of Rosalynn Carter to speak at a luncheon for one of her causes, Project Interconnection, a wonderful program that houses mentally ill homeless. After the lunch we went out to visit the Carter Center. It is a glorious seventeen-acre compound that consists of a library, museum, and a center that serves as an umbrella for President Carter's various projects and is connected to Emory University.

We had a minute to visit with the former President, who was gracious and pleasant. I sometimes find Rosalynn to be a complicated person. She is very partisan and not comfortable with me. Earlier in George's administration, I had asked Rosalynn for lunch at the White House, which would have been her first opportunity to see their portraits on display. I told her that we had revived the White House Endowment Fund that had been started under their administration but died during the Reagan years. Her answer: "Good. Republicans have all the money." Huh? Since when have the Harrimans, Roosevelts, Rockefellers, and Kennedys all been Republicans?

I get the feeling that she is a nice lady who loves her husband very much and is not as happy and content as she should be. I could well be wrong and I certainly hope I am. Both President Carter and Rosalynn have made a large contribution since leaving the White House, working for the good of others, housing for the homeless, and so forth.

The next week I went to Dallas to visit George W., Laura, and the girls while George went to Spain for the beginning of the Middle East Peace Talks. One night, while having dinner at the home of Elvis and Joan Mason, we watched George and Mikhail Gorbachev open the talks.

It was so thrilling to watch what was going on in Spain. It was such an amazing group of people sitting at the same table—Israelis and Arabs—who harbored so many ancient animosities. Just the fact they had sat down together was a miracle.

The next day I visited the Scottish Rite Hospital, where they are doing marvelous things for children with learning disabilities, and then on to Brian's House, where Laura works with AIDS babies.

That afternoon I was working away on my computer when Peggy Swift and Jim Sloan came into my room looking very serious. As George was just returning from Spain, they scared me. They quickly reassured me that he was okay, but said that a terrible storm was raging in Kennebunkport and it looked like we had lost our house. There were thirty-foot waves at Kennebunk Beach. Thirty feet! The agents had to abandon Walker's Point, but our longtime agent and friend Tom Clark was watching from a safe house and reported seeing waves breaking over the three-story house. It was so hard to believe. We had to wait and see what the next high tide would do in the middle of the night, but they could see horrible damage already.

I called George. I needed to talk to the one other person who cared as much as I did—even more, if possible. George had gone into a meeting before the agents could brief him, so I was the one who broke the news to him. He said he would call me right back. When he did, he told me that everything I had heard was true, but that I must not worry. It would be all right. It was such a comfort to talk to him.

I called Laura and George W. Then Doro called me "just to check in" and I had to tell her.

That night I went to a dinner honoring Ralph Rogers. What a remarkable man he is. He founded Texas Industries, and then, in 1970, helped found PBS and later the Children's Television Workshop, which does "Sesame Street." At this time he was working hard on a preschool children's program, P.E.P. He has been a great contributor to many community programs. I love Ralph, but I don't know how I got through that evening.

After the event I flew to Houston, where I was to meet George and spend the weekend. Neil met me at the airport and, yes, I had to tell him. I hated being the one having to deliver all this bad news. What a Halloween! More trick than treat. It was a dreadful night.

Early in the morning George called and told me that the house was standing, but the damage was extensive. Unfortunately, we had several agonizing days of commitments in Texas, but George's thoughtful brother John went to Maine immediately and reported back. He said it was awful, that among other things, our first-floor bedroom was a wreck. I asked him about the bookshelves (where our scrapbooks and photo albums had been up until two months ago!) and he said, "What bookshelves, Bar?" At that point we decided we had to cancel the weekend in Texas and go to Maine.

We couldn't believe what we saw. The deck was totally ripped up, the stone walls were down in many spots, the Wave was ripped off its foundations, and the porch was gone. I had just redone the Wave, a little guest house, and I just could not bring myself to even look in the door. I should have, for after it had been moved, propped up on blocks, and moved back onto a new foundation, we discovered that only one glass had been broken. Lamps, books, and china had stayed put, and the little bedroom looked spic-and-span.

That was not true of the big house. The living room walls were gone, and with them, every stick of furniture. It looked like a ballroom. The whole downstairs was either broken or demolished or gone. Forty percent of the dock was gone. The dock, the stone walls, and the house had been there since 1902. Now all eleven acres were strewn with our books and belongings.

Betsy Heminway had dropped everything and driven to Kennebunkport to help. Our nephew Billy Bush and our cousin's child Jay Field came down with two other boys from Colby College and worked alongside us shoveling sand, rocks, broken glass, and china out of the downstairs rooms. Amazingly, the second and third floors had not been touched.

I ran the gamut of emotions. What did I feel about the house in Kennebunkport? Of course I had dark moments. It had meant so much to George and his whole family and, in all honesty, to me. But for some reason I also felt so fortunate, so loved, and so surrounded by family and friends. Then I would remember my little garden, our beautiful living and dining rooms that Mark Hampton had helped decorate, and I would feel like weeping again. Then I would think about the many people up and down the coast who lost everything and who didn't have George Bush and great kids and I would realize how lucky I was.

That Christmas our cousin Susue Robinson suggested to all our relatives that this might be a great year to give us something that plugged into the wall. Just think about what we take for granted: lamps, toasters, waffle irons, washing machines, dryers, irons, ovens, TVs, refrigerators, dishwashers, and on and on. George, of course, replaced big kitchen appliances. Susue offered to coordinate the gifts to be sure we didn't receive ten toasters. All this was unbeknownst to us. Our Christmas was a large surprise, and needless to say, we were very touched.

Our builders, the Philbricks, started work immediately and did a great job working under the worst conditions. George's mother once again gave us the tennis court as a present. (It had been a joint birthday present in 1980.) Then I traveled to High Point, North Carolina, to the furniture store of Edgar Broyhill, the son of the former senator and our friend Jim Broyhill, and I picked out materials and ordered couches, chairs, tables, and some odds and ends for the first floor. As much of our old furniture as possible was repaired by a superb refinisher in Maine, John Dickinson. By May we were in our finished and furnished house thanks to the hard work and generosity of many friends.

As I write this in January of 1994, I feel very lucky all over again. The people of Los Angeles are digging out from underneath a horrible earthquake and parts of the East and Midwest are suffering from one of the worst winters on record. Mother Nature can be so brutal and unforgiving sometimes, and I hope and pray that all those hurting now will find the same love and support we did.

In November we went to the opening of the Reagan Library, which is in a most glamorous setting on a hillside in the Simi Valley. Lady Bird Johnson, Dick and Pat Nixon, Jerry and Betty Ford, and Jimmy and Rosalynn Carter also came, and it was a nice reunion for us all. Now we have seen the libraries/museums of all the living former presidents and a few of the others.

All the presidents spoke briefly. Jimmy Carter was very amusing when he said that the Republicans were getting four times more speaking time than the Democrats. He also went on to say that he was the only person on the stage who had never met a Democrat president. (He has now, darn it.)

President Reagan gave a marvelous speech which brought back great memories of that lovely man. There was one sad thing. Pat Nixon did not look well at all. She was very frail-looking and through her smile you could see that she was in great pain and having a terrible time getting air into her lungs. She and Dick did not come to the lunch, but quietly slipped away. This gentle lady died in June of 1993. She was a wonderful person and First Lady, and my memories of her are all good.

Also in November we took a quick four-day trip to Italy and Holland. In Rome, while George attended NATO meetings, I of course got to have all the fun. First I visited the Capitoline Museum, then went to Valentino's thirtieth anniversary show of unbelievably beautiful dresses, many loaned by their owners, including Audrey Hepburn, Jackie Kennedy, and Brooke Astor. The money from the show, which also traveled to the United States, went to benefit AIDS. Next I went to Boys' Town, a home for boys from seventeen foreign countries, including political refugees. Many Americans support this community, including Pete and Joan Secchia, our ambassador and his wife, who had planned this marvelous trip for me. Monsignor John Patrick Carroll-Abbing, the founder, took me on the tour.

Something very funny did happen there, which shows how quickly—and innocently—you can get into trouble. They asked me to get up and say a few words to a school assembly, which was difficult since I didn't know Italian and few of the boys spoke English. At one point during my talk, I used sign language to say "I love you." As it turns out, a slight variation of that gesture has an obscene meaning in Italy! At least one Italian newspaper mentioned it the next day.

Before leaving Rome, we had a nice visit with the Pope and the American community. His Holiness, a true man of peace, was most generous with his time. We then flew on to the Netherlands, where we were happy to see Prime Minister Ruud Lubbers and his wife, Ria. We had dinner with Her Majesty Queen Beatrix at the Noordeinde Palace, and I sat next to the Prime Minister, who told me an interesting piece of trivia.

I was asking Ruud about the beautiful lady who was on the wall looking down at us. He said that she was a Russian princess with very extravagant tastes, a Romanov. After ten years of marriage she ran out of money and wrote her father, the Czar of Russia, to please send her some. He said that he would, but that she had some pictures that he would like in return. Thus the beginning of the incredible Hermitage Collection—which explains why they have so many Dutch and Flemish masters' paintings!

⁓ Shortly after we returned home President Carlos Menem came for a state visit from Argentina. He is a charming man and George told me he really was working hard at privatizing his country and making a democracy. He and George struck up a real friendship and over the years had fun playing tennis both in Argentina and the United States.

All that fall the press was swirling. It seems to me, looking at my diary, that both sides were making mistakes, and the press was waiting to pounce. Senator Bob Kerrey of Nebraska, and a Democratic presidential candidate, told a filthy, insensitive joke about lesbians to Bill Clinton and a live microphone picked it up. Then Dan Quayle's press secretary, Dave Beckwith (whom I like very much), made a tasteless remark about that and had to apologize. Mario Cuomo called Dan Quayle "Danny boy" in a most denigrating way, and yet when Dan called him Mario, the Governor said that it was an ethnic slur. John Sununu attacked Ann Devroy of *The Washington Post* and that caused great excitement. She had been attacking him for weeks in the paper and that was okay, but he got clobbered for retaliating. I guess along with never putting on a hat or a helmet for the cameras, one of the first lessons someone in public life must learn is: THE PRESS HAS THE LAST WORD.

The pressure was mounting on John, who had come under criticism for a variety of things, including misuse of government planes. On December 1 he turned in his letter of resignation. He had been such a great friend and it hurt, but he knew best. He has gone on to great things in the private sector, including appearances on CNN's "Crossfire," where he makes the conservative argument with humor and sanity.

The day George was having a press conference to announce John's replacement and his campaign team, I tuned in to TV to watch:

I sat watching CNN and suddenly realized that they were not going to leave the Willie Smith rape trial for George's press conference. I finally found him on C-SPAN. He announced Sam Skinner as his new Chief of Staff, Bob Mosbacher as campaign chairman, and Bob Teeter, Fred Malek, Mary Matalin, Rich Bond, Charlie Black and George W. as the team.

The Willie Smith trial is dominating the news . . . I'm not sure that this should be on television. It is such an intrusion on both the accused and the accuser.

On December 7 we flew to Hawaii for the fiftieth anniversary of the bombing of Pearl Harbor. What an emotional day that was:

We went by launch to the USS *Arizona* Memorial. Many of the fleet was in port and sailors were lined up saluting their Commander in Chief as he went by. I had expected to be moved, but never as much as I was. There were survivors there and families of those who to this day are below in the sunken ship. Within sight of where we were sitting we could see the hull of that enormous ship itself just below the surface of the water, and every few minutes a dot of oil from the ship popped up and a tiny shiny oil slick appeared for a moment. After all these years it was still leaking. Eleven hundred men were entombed right below us. Pearl Harbor must have been much as it was that morning fifty years ago, beautiful, sunny, calm and peaceful when those planes came over. An 89-year-old Congressional Medal winner introduced George. He was not only moving, but visibly moved. We kept silent at the infamous moment when the raid started—7:55 a.m., I believe, and then taps were played, a flyover, and George and I dropped leis into the hole where one looks down to see the hull. I know that this day brought back many memories for George. One man yelled out to George and said: "George, San Jac!" George turned around and looked at the man and said, "Frank, how are you?" Frank said, "You have a great memory," and George said, "I read your name tag, but I certainly remember you." I asked him in the car if he really remembered Frank and he did—forty-seven years later. Amazing. I thought that George looked younger than anyone else we saw there. At one time during the day we went over to the enormous *Missouri* and George did some tapings, which were then played during halftime of the Army-Navy game. Think how the world has changed in these fifty years. Then we did not have TV for civilians, and now George can be seen in a football stadium in Philadelphia when he is in Hawaii.

We returned home to a totally decorated White House. This was our prettiest Christmas of all, I believe. It was a needlepoint Christmas: The tree was covered with needlepoint ornaments, plus a town, a Noah's Ark with all the animals, and of course the crèche—all of needlepoint.

December 8—I have just returned from the press showing of Christmas at the White House. I think they all agreed that it looked spectacular. There are 26 trees on the State Floor. It took 40 volunteers approximately 1,600 hours to do the decorating. They started on December 2nd and finished on the 8th at 3 p.m. More than 100,000 people will tour the White House between now and December 29th. The State Dining Room has the 22nd Gingerbread House made by Hans Raffert with Hansel, Gretel, the witch and this year Millie. Hans was careful to explain that the reason Ranger wasn't there was because Millie was the "First Dog." It's in the eyes of the beholder, I guess, or maybe Ranger's forays into the kitchen were not always welcome. More than 500 people contributed to the needlepointing, 314 Saintly Stitchers from St. Martin's Church in Houston and another 290 people including White House staff, friends and relatives. (Even Skip Allen in the Usher's Office needlepointed a jack-in-the-box.) There are 1,370 pieces. (Florist) Nancy Clarke, who truly is an artist, made most of the patterns and organized the whole project. She estimates that 150,000 working hours were spent on this year's decorations.

What really made that Christmas special, however, was that all the hostages finally came home! Terry Anderson, Thomas Sutherland, Joseph Cicippio, Alann Steen, and Jesse Turner helped George light the National Christmas Tree on the Ellipse and then came to the White House for a reception. How good it was to see those fine men home and with their families.

All our children with the exception of Jebby and his troop came for Christmas. We missed them badly, but talked often.

On Christmas Day President Gorbachev resigned and the Soviet Union ceased to exist. It was not a shock—the country had been unraveling ever since the August coup as one republic after another declared its independence. And yet, it was a shock. Suddenly, the Cold War truly was over. The country that had been our enemy most of my life no longer existed. We were excited at the prospect of democracy coming to all these new republics—including Russia—but still nervous at the uncertainties ahead.

And we felt great sadness for the Gorbachevs. He was, after all, the one who introduced perestroika and glasnost, which eventually brought freedom to his country. He was instrumental in ending the arms race and the Cold War—and now he was out of power. I wondered about Raisa, whom I had grown to like very much, and whom I knew loved her country and husband deeply. A new wind was blowing . . .

Speaking of which: Exactly one week before Christmas, I flew to Concord, New Hampshire, on a cold, snowy day and officially filed the papers declaring George a candidate in the Republican New Hampshire primary. Pat Buchanan had just thrown his hat into the ring, challenging George from the ultraconservative right wing of the party.

It had begun.

23

"Back & Forth
and Ups & Downs"

O ur New Year began on the other side of the world—literally. We landed New Year's Eve in Sydney, Australia, the first leg of a trip to the Far East. We immediately cruised out to the Admiralty House Dock, where we walked into a reception and watched New Year's Eve fireworks with Prime Minister Paul Keating and his wife, Annita, and Governor General Bill Hayden and his wife, Dallas.

When this particular trip had been planned, Bob and Hazel Hawke were in office, and she had sent me a letter saying she was looking forward to our visit. Suddenly they were out and the Keatings were in. We did see the Hawkes, whom we liked very much. Like Margaret Thatcher, they were beaten by a challenger from their own party, which is not much fun. We knew that we had Pat Buchanan to look forward to when we got home, and we were reminded of the new breeze blowing. At that time, I didn't think that George and I would be caught in it.

We immediately liked the Keatings, too. Annita, a lovely, slender native of the Netherlands with long curly hair and a great smile, had met Paul when she was working for Alitalia, and he courted her all over the earth.

Accompanying us on the trip were Secretary of Commerce Bob

452

Mosbacher and a group of American businessmen, most of whom were connected to the auto industry. George had invited them to join us to promote American exports abroad since trade issues were a prime focus of the trip.

I should note here that soon after returning home, Bob Mosbacher left Commerce to go to the campaign. Barbara Franklin, an old friend and a very smart businesswoman, became the new Secretary, joining Lynn Martin and Carla Hills in the cabinet, the first time three women served at the same time.

We flew on to Canberra, the capital, a beautiful new city which we have watched grow over the years. When we got off the plane for the arrival ceremony, I noticed that George's military aide's back was covered with flies. Suddenly, I realized that I was, too. This is sheep country, and we came right during the fly season. We were teased about how quickly we learned the "Australian wave" because you just have to keep fanning your face to keep the flies away. We stayed with our Ambassador and his wife, Mel and Betty Sembler. They are a magnificent couple from Florida who started STRAIGHT, a very successful drug rehabilitation program. Betty had a fly "zapper" right in the kitchen.

There is so much that is lovely about Canberra that helps you forget those darn flies. The buildings are magnificent and the vistas lovely, and the people of Australia are warm, relaxed, and very much like Texans, the biggest compliment I can pay anyone.

One night we had dinner with the Governor General and Dallas Hayden. Their house and the view through the park in the back were glorious. We saw kangaroos jumping about, which I loved. I suspect that they are like our deer, who eat our gardens and generally are a pain.

Next stop was Singapore. Our Ambassador was the former Governor of Indiana, Bob Orr, and his wife, Josie, had done a stunning job of redoing the temporary residence, all in black and white.

That night, President and Mrs. Wee Kim Wee gave us a grand dinner. George, as usual, put a lot of pepper on his food, and the next morning he awakened feeling fine but with a black tongue. I went for Burt Lee, who took one look and in amazement said: "Holy Cow!!" I told Burt that that was hardly comforting from your doctor. They were not sure if it came from medicine that George was taking for his fire ant bites that he got while hunting in Beeville, Texas, just before the New Year, or from the pepper, or from all the octopus we had been eating. We told George not to stick his tongue out and all would be well.

We flew on to Korea, where our Ambassador, Don Gregg, and his wife, Meg, met us. When George was vice president, Don was his National Security Adviser. We were thrilled to have a chance to see them again and stay in their home.

A small group of us had a beautiful Korean dinner with President and Mrs. Roh Tae Woo, after meeting their children and two of their grandchildren. They were living in a new official residence, the Blue House, named for the blue titles on the roof. The old house was built by the Japanese when they occupied the Korean peninsula before and during World War II, and the Koreans hated it for that reason. I noted in my diary that in Australia, Singapore, and Korea I found real distrust of the Japanese—if not hatred. It always amazed me that you still can find the same feeling today in Europe about Germany.

The next night, at the state dinner, the Rohs (pronounced "Nohs") had an enormous cake wheeled in to celebrate our forty-seventh wedding anniversary. I sat next to the President on my right and the Chief Justice on my left. I asked the latter if he spoke English, and his exact answer to me was: "I cannot communicate with you." And he didn't. It could have been worse. I remember another Korean dinner that went on forever where neither partner spoke a word of English.

We left Korea the next morning for a marvelous day in Osaka and Kyoto, Japan, with our old friends former Prime Minister and Sachiyo Kaifu. They are such a nice, positive couple. Yuko Kojima, newly engaged to the Kaifus' son, was there and interpreted for me on the whole trip. We toured the Kyoto Imperial Palace and ate lunch in the famous Tsuruya Restaurant, sitting on pillows on the floor. It was exotic and very good.

We went on to Nara to visit a recently opened Toys "R" Us store, which was a real breakthrough for American trade.

Then on to Tokyo, where we stayed at the Akasaka Palace, the Japanese guest house. It was as I remembered it, the grandest, most ornate palace I have ever seen, copied from the gilded European Victorian era, I believe. The service was the same, the very best. The next morning we had the official arrival ceremony in the courtyard of our Palace.

. . . The Emperor and the Empress were the official greeters. She, Michiko, is a lovely, graceful, thin lady. She was a commoner, the first. We were told by PM Miyazawa that her mother-in-law made her life miserable. We loved her gentle ways. On this trip we discovered that she quietly goes to the U.S. Embassy to play duets with Bonny Armacost on the piano. The whole Imperial family is musical. The Crown Prince Naruhito is very attractive and not married. He must marry a girl who is willing to give up her job and live a secluded life. We keep hearing rumors that he is in love with our friends the Owadas' daughter, who is at their state department.*

. . . We climbed into a car and went to pay a courtesy call on Emperor Akihito at the Imperial Palace. We sat in the same room where we had talked with his father and where we had met with this Emperor and wife when he came to his father's funeral in 1989. The exchange of gifts was embarrassing. We gave them a quilt. Granted, it was pretty, but I did not feel very appropriate. [I think the State Department thought it was a very "American" gift to give.] They gave us a big painting, a lovely plate and a box. They will go to GB's museum.

Mrs. Miyazawa (wife of the Prime Minister) and I visited the American Trade Fair in the Mitsukoshi Department Store, their Bloomingdale's. We saw everything from cars to electrical appliances.

I think by now most of us know how that day ended:

At 3:20 I went and took tea with the Empress and her daughters-in-law and the young prince. We watched George and our Ambassador, Mike Armacost, play and be beaten in tennis by the Emperor and the Crown Prince. After tennis we went back to our rooms and George told me he didn't feel very well, but not too bad. He saw the doctor and then took a nap for several hours, after which we rushed to a dinner that the Prime Minister was having. We stood in a receiving line for quite a while and then George asked to be excused. I thought he had been called to the phone. Not true. He had been violently sick to his stomach.

This was a big dinner, mostly men, the two Cabinet members, Nick (Brady) and Bob (Mosbacher), the businessmen who were traveling with us, a lot of George's traveling squad and many Japanese businessmen and

* For once, rumors were right. He married Masako Owada in 1993.

officials. We were in a long thin room with a balcony at the far end where several cameras were set up. I do know that our hosts had been very strict about no aides hovering about. There was a head table and three long tables going the length of the room. Not another living human could have been seated and left room for waiters to serve.

It was a beautiful meal and all seemed to be going well, but George certainly did not look well. I noticed that Rich Miller, the head of George's Secret Service detail who was seated halfway down the room, never took his eyes off him. George was seated between the PM and his very nice wife. Suddenly he leaned over and told the Prime Minister and me that he wasn't feeling well and thought he better leave—the next thing you knew—he passed out, his eyes rolling back in his head while getting sick. The PM caught him and held him. I was so proud of our Secret Service and medical team. They were there in a second. It all happened so quickly. A large agent charged down the middle aisle and the PM said in a firm voice: "You stand there and guard your president." I believe that he meant for him to stand between George and the cameras. That big man did not move. We all learned later, one camera was left on and unattended and that's how the word of George's ailment was instantly seen around the world. I hated that because Doro saw it as she was getting dressed to go to work.

George came to immediately, realized where he was and said: "Maybe you better roll me under the table, let me sleep and you just go on with your dinner." They had pushed a stretcher down one side of the room and Rich Miller told George he was going to help him walk to it. George said absolutely not. He would walk out of that room by himself. He asked for his tie, which they had removed, and put it back on lying on the floor, which in itself is no mean feat, and walked out smiling and apologizing after asking me to give his toast. He looked awful, and, I guess, felt the same. How I wanted to go with him, but I felt I must stay or people would think he was really ill. You are not trying to fool the public or press, but you don't want to panic the world either unnecessarily. Once again I was really scared—was he really sick? That was one long dinner!

Prime Minister Miyazawa made a friend for life in me. He held George with such care before Rich Miller tried to stretch him out on the floor. I can remember Rich saying to Dr. Roberts, who was on duty that night, "I can't lift him," and the quiet voice of Kiichi Miyazawa saying, "You have my leg." No wonder he couldn't lift him. That's quite a load, a president and a prime minister at the same time.

I also remember Nick Brady saying "Give him air." I had nightmares about the fact that I hadn't moved to my precious husband's side. Several weeks later I was relieved to see a series of TV pictures that showed me wiping George's face and trying to help and then stepping back to let the medical team in. Once again, it reminds me that eyewitness accounts are not always true. I could have sworn that I had not touched George and that really worried me.

I do not know how to explain what happened later during the toast, but I do know that whatever I said must have worked. Sometimes somebody up there just leans down and the right thing happens. I remember making a joke about George being such a poor sport for losing his tennis game that afternoon. I later apologized to our ambassador for making a little fun of his tennis game and blaming him for the whole incident. His response: "That's what ambassadors are here for."

When we got home from our trip we had lots of mail about George's sickness, but the letter that I liked best said:

Dear Mrs. Bush,
   Tell Mr. President not to be embarrassed that he threw up on international TV. I once threw up on my dog.
                                        Love,
                                        Jennifer

The next morning I kept my regular schedule while George slept. By the afternoon he was feeling better and was able to hold his meetings and get back on schedule.

(I went to a) luncheon hosted by Bonny Armacost at the U.S. Residence. Bonny is a lovely person who does her country proud as does her fine husband. Hanae Mori, the great dress designer, was there, a concert pianist and other ladies who all star in their fields. One of the Japanese ladies gave us a second day of lectures on male dominance in Japan. This came up because many wives had not been invited the night before to the dinner. She elaborated on her life in Washington, saying that Japanese men did not include their wives even in the District of Columbia.

That night we went in black tie to a beautiful dinner that the

Emperor and Empress had for us. The Emperor and Empress were waiting for us at the door. They led us upstairs and introduced us to their family. There were about ten members there. The brother of the late Emperor, his son, etc. Then into dinner. Their Highnesses had shortened the evening by an hour, which was most kind. The most thoughtful thing of all was that Her Highness had a special dinner cooked for George that the four of us ate, bland and pureed food. It was delicious and just what he needed. I did see several of the wives that had not been invited the night before.

. . . I sat next to the Empress and the Crown Prince. He studies medieval transportation, especially as it relates to travel on the Thames River, I believe. He was a great dinner partner. Because they live such restricted lives, so to themselves, they must develop interests in order to survive. The Empress told me that their tiny lovely little princess daughter studies the kingfisher.

. . . We are reading that the trip was a failure. That is not true. It was a trade trip and many of the things we went for, we got. We are trying to get a level playing field for our manufacturers and workers. Many restrictions were lifted.

Unfortunately, George's illness, which was blown out of proportion, put a shadow on the trip. I was disappointed to learn that many people in the traveling party—including press—had come down with the same flu, but that was never reported, so rumors about George's health started again.

ᴄ◈〉 We came home to plunge into New Hampshire and the first primary, while still trying to carry on real-life duties. The experience was so different from previous years. First, Iowa was not a factor. Since one of their senators, Tom Harkin, was in the race on the Democratic side, and because on our side Pat Buchanan was concentrating on New Hampshire—partially because the economy was getting better in Iowa—there was just no race there.

On the other hand, the economy was bad in New Hampshire and the other New England states. During previous campaigns, I was told their kids were dropping out of high school as soon as the law would allow (age sixteen) because they could make $9 an hour in fast-food

Dancing with Sylvester Stallone at Jerry and Jane Weintraub's house. Look at that smirk! (Susan Biddle)

Floating down the Thames River in London with friends. From left: Hannelore Kohl of Germany; Mila Mulroney of Canada; Norma Major of Great Britain; and Sachiyo Kaifu of Japan. (Carol Powers)

Meeting the future King of England, Prince William, along with his mother, Princess Diana; Caroline Seitz, the wife of the American ambassador to England; and Prince William's little brother, Prince Harry. (Carol Powers)

Cruising the Moscow River with Raisa Gorbachev. (Carol Powers)

Relaxing with a friend. (Carol Powers)

George gets a phone call from Mikhail Gorbachev that the coup has ended and he and Raisa are safe, August 1991. (Susan Biddle)

George and his mother
in Kennebunkport.
(Family photo)

Strolling in Kennebunkport
with two of my favorite
friends, Mila Mulroney and
Millie. (Susan Biddle)

Sharing a thought
with my husband
during the Reagan
Library dedication,
November 1991.
(David Valdez)

Everybody at the White House
had to wear ID tags, including
Ranger. (Carol Powers)

Volunteering at the Goodwill
book sale in Washington, D.C.
(Carol Powers)

Topping the National Christmas Tree, one of twelve times I did the honors. Helping out are grandchildren Lauren and Pierce Bush and Joe Riley, chairman of the Pageant of Peace. (Carol Powers)

Grandson Walker Bush checks out the train under the White House Christmas tree, December 1991. (Joyce Naltchayan)

A Christmas tree covered with needlepoint ornaments. If you look hard, you can find the Raggedy Ann and Andy dolls I stitched. (David Valdez)

Bundling up with Naina Yeltsin at Camp David, February 1992. (Carol Powers)

Getting tips on how to use the computer from some young experts in
Winona, Mississippi. (Carol Powers)

Millie meets with some of the fourth graders touring the White House. (Carol Powers)

Heading to Kennebunkport with granddaughter Ellie LeBlond, Millie, and Ranger. (Carol Powers)

"Sure, I can take your picture with the President." (Carol Powers)

Doro is absolutely radiant; please don't look too carefully at what the
father of the bride is wearing. Neil and Sharon are at left, and behind them are
my brother Jim and his wife, Margie. (David Valdez)

Naina Yeltsin meets some young Americans outside Martha's Table in Washington, D.C., June 1992. (Carol Powers)

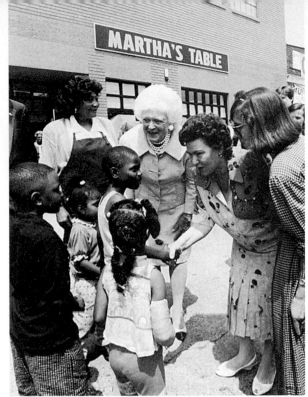

Sharing a laugh with Boris Yeltsin, June 1992. (David Valdez)

The family whoops it up on the first night of the Republican National Convention, August 1992. (Susan Biddle)

The clan gathers for the Republican National Convention in Houston, August 1992. Sitting on the floor are, from left, grandchildren Jenna, Marshall, Ashley, Lauren, Ellie, and Jebby. Second row, sitting down, from left: Laura, Barbara, Pierce, me and George, Sam, and Jeb and Columba. Back row, from left: Marvin holding Walker, Margaret, George W., Sharon, Neil, Doro, Bobby, George P., and Noelle. The only one missing is our thirteenth grandchild, Robert, who is still nearly a year away. (David Valdez)

George P. addresses the convention surrounded by his family. (Susan Biddle)

The last night at
the convention.
(Carol Powers)

Actor Gerald
McRaney keeps
me dry during a
campaign stop in
Florida.
(Carol Powers)

Making a new friend in
Louisville, Kentucky.
(Carol Powers)

Millie tries to explain to Larry King why George Bush should be reelected president. (David Valdez)

The Bush women campaign team, from left: Doro Koch, me, Noelle Bush, Nancy Ellis, and Margaret Bush. (Carol Powers)

Our son Marvin hams it up on the campaign trail, Halloween 1992. I never knew we looked so much alike. (Carol Powers)

Whistle-stopping toward the end of the campaign. Sam LeBlond and I
huddle to keep warm. (Carol Powers)

The White House staff bids us good-bye as we head to Houston for Election
Night. I'm about ready to hug James Selmon. (Carol Powers)

Telling Hillary Clinton how wonderful life in the White House is. (Carol Powers)

Oh, good. Santa Claus didn't forget me on our last Christmas in the White House.
(Carol Powers)

One last walk around the
White House grounds,
January 20, 1993.
(Susan Biddle)

Welcoming the Clintons
to the White House,
January 20, 1993.
(Carol Powers)

Three women with two things
in common: We've all been
married to the Vice President
of the United States and we all
showed up in purple.
(Susan Biddle)

Houston, we're home!
(David Valdez)

restaurants at the mall. Every window would have a Help Wanted sign.

This year, there were no jobs, malls were closing or had boarded-up stores, and kids were staying in school. Was that the silver lining in a very black cloud?

On February 17, the day before the primary, I ate an early lunch and took off for one last day of speaking and shaking hands in New Hampshire. It was sort of sad after twelve years.

While campaigning hard for George, I was watching the five Democrats flail away at each other. The one thing they had in common was George, and they were really bashing him, to say the least.

In a state that small it was hard not to cross paths. On that last night, I was at a Manchester TV station at the same time as Bill Clinton and Jerry Brown. We didn't see the former, but Jerry and I ran right into each other. He stuck out his hand and said, "Hi, I'm Jerry Brown." I said, "Hi, I'm Barbara Bush." We smiled, shook hands, and went our separate ways.

The final vote in New Hampshire was Bush 58; Buchanan 40. The original estimates were that the vote would be much closer, so we were pleased. It was interesting to me that George got much of his vote from women. The gender gap had narrowed, at least in this state. The exit polls also showed that the higher the education, the more people voted for George.

~~∽~~ Of course there was no time to rest and, in fact, George was already campaigning in the Super Tuesday states. Earlier in February he had gone to Orlando, Florida, to attend the National Grocers Convention:

He saw the newest state-of-the-art device for checking out. It is not on the market yet, but the press all had a week of fun acting like George was "out of touch" and had never seen a checkout scanner. They knew darn well that this was new and revolutionary. The author of the original story, Andrew Rosenthal of *The New York Times,* hadn't even been there, but just wrote (his story) from the press pool report.

Eventually some of the press did write about how the story was blown out of proportion, but not until after media all over the country had picked it up and the damage was done. Columnists used it right up until Election Day.

What's almost even more frustrating, however, is that nearly two years later, we're still hearing about this erroneous story. I was watching "60 Minutes" on January 16, 1994, when I heard Andy Rooney refer to the fact that George was "out of touch." His proof: George had never seen a grocery store scanner. Baloney! Once these stories get into the computer systems, they never die, even if they are not accurate.

I did wonder sometimes in the White House if it was worth awakening every day to the abuse that opponents and the press give the President. I knew that George was the best. I could not have survived without that knowledge. AND, I could not have survived without friends. Andy Stewart, of course, was the very best, but Betsy Heminway and Phyllis Draper were also so great about checking in and coming by when they were in town. And my 90th Club ladies were all supportive. I also knew that I could call Mildred Kerr, Betty Liedtke, Bobbie Fitch, or Marion Chambers in Houston.

∽ In February George asked Doro to head the U.S. delegation to the Winter Olympics. The rest of the delegation consisted of Don Johnson, Melanie Griffith, Nancy Ellis, and George's friend from Andover and Yale days, Osborne Day. Ossie had been in the ski patrol during World War II and had skied in the very place where the Olympics were to be held, Albertville, France.

For the last year or so Doro had been getting back into the mainstream of single life. It was not easy to date, however, when you were the daughter of the President. It was a job sorting out who liked her for herself and who liked her for being George Bush's daughter. She is so funny and kept us laughing about some of her experiences.

For example, she had learned not to accept a date for cocktails *and* dinner. Instead, she would say, "I can't have dinner, but I'd love to meet you for a drink. You see I have to get home to my *two children*." That immediately cut the list down. Then, if they stayed on board, she would meet them for the drink and if she liked them, she could say that if they still wanted to have dinner, she had gotten a babysitter after all. I can't remember that she ever got beyond the drink with many men. I do remember that one time she went to meet a man whom one of her cousins felt she must meet. They barely had sat down when he said: "Let me tell you what I don't like about your father . . ." Doro jumped up and explained that she had just come by to tell him that she couldn't meet him after all—a crisis at home!

But by February of 1992, Doro had met a man who seemed very nice and it was becoming apparent to her father and me that she was getting serious. While Doro was on her Olympics trip to France, Bobby Koch called and asked if he could come up to Camp David to talk to George. He told George that he wanted to ask Doro to marry him when she returned home. Bobby worked for Dick Gephardt, a Democratic congressman from St. Louis who as House Majority Leader often attacked George, sometimes pretty viciously. Bobby told George that it was time for him to change jobs and he would before the marriage, if she accepted. George would not have asked him to do that; Bobby offered.

I could hardly stand it when Doro got home from Europe. I so wanted to tell her, but I didn't. On the fifteenth of February she called in tears to tell us that she was engaged. Bobby had taken Sam, Ellie, and Doro out to dinner and proposed to all three of them. Doro said that Sam's reaction was: "Oh, yeah!" He gave Doro a lovely ring with three beautiful diamonds, one for each of them. We instantly adored Bobby. When your children are happy, everything seems better.

February 23—I had a nice quiet morning yesterday. I did my mail and rode the stationary bike for an hour and read Margaret Truman's *Murder on Capitol Hill.* That's fun. I recently had finished Maeve Binchy's *Circle of Friends* and hated to see it end.

. . . I went over to thank the volunteers who sort and answer my mail. They say that I am still getting over 100,000 letters a year. I only see a sample of my mail. They claim that I see the bad with the good. I do get letters from people who are hurting. Darn this economy. There is just no reason that it does not pick up, interest rates are down, inflation is down and there are signs that things are moving in the right direction.

. . . Walked over to see the most wonderful show at the Corcoran Gallery, a picture of the black world called "Songs of My People." It is very powerful and moving.

George and I traveled, separately and together, to campaign and do fund-raisers, from Florida to California, Texas to Colorado, back and forth and up and down.

One afternoon I flew to Peoria, Illinois, and spoke at the Annual Washington's Day Birthday Dinner with and at the request of the Minority Leader of the House, Bob Michel, and his wife, Corinne. What a rock Bob had been for his president. George always knew he could count on him. He will be missed by his country when he retires, as he is not running for reelection in 1994.

We visited the Reagans in their beautiful new house in California.

We had a Drug Summit in San Antonio attended by the presidents of Mexico, Colombia, Ecuador, Bolivia, Peru, and the Minister of Foreign Affairs from Venezuela.

In Houston I helped dedicate the Barbara Pierce Bush Elementary School. Now that was exciting—I had my own school. I couldn't help but wonder what my father would think. This past Christmas (1993), I went to hear their choir sing and they were very, very good—of course!

As we toured the country I met more hairdressers than I could believe. I never traveled with a hairdresser, either at home or abroad, but instead found someone locally. They all were nice, some better than others, but they all were willing to come at the crack of dawn to comb out my hair. Some looked so teased up or disheveled themselves that I would give them my head with fear and trembling.

One morning on the campaign trail I walked into Peggy Swift's room to have my hair done and there was a middle-aged man who had brought his wife with him, thank heavens. This poor man seemed nervous, but that was normal in little towns. Often people were nervous when they had to do the hair of the wife of the president. What wasn't normal was that the poor fella had not zipped up his trousers. As he did my hair I could see his wife notice the omission and begin to try to catch his eye. After he was finished, Peggy brought the photographer, Carol Powers, in to take my picture with the couple. I took pity on the man and asked them to wait one moment while I put on my pearls and lipstick. While I was gone the wife took care of the problem, but I bet they have had fun telling that story and I hope they had a laugh. We certainly did.

On a trip to England a young man came dressed from head to toe in black leather, had an earring in his left ear, long stringy hair, and what looked like a week-old beard. He was late because the Secret Service was reluctant to let him up to the room—and he wondered why. I sort of mentioned that he did not look like your run-of-the-mill hairdresser and asked him why in the world did he want to look like Arafat? He said that he looked like Don Johnson. I quickly told him that I knew Don—in fact, had just seen him—and he was clean-shaven. The next morning he came without the beard and told me that his "mum" was thrilled.

Another hairdresser told me that he had hung his picture with me in his salon and a fellow worker had torn it to shreds. I noted in my diary that I guessed we should put that man down as doubtful!

≈≫ I didn't write much about the Democrats in my diary in 1992. I will confess, however, that I wrote over and over again that Bill Clinton did not have a chance. The American people would never vote for him. I wrote him off from the start. I am such a bad politician that I thought that Senator Bob Kerrey would be the hardest to beat. He seemed to have so little baggage and he was a Congressional Medal winner for heroism in Vietnam. If it comes to politics and you want to know who is going to win, ask me. Then go the other way!

The week before Super Tuesday George won South Carolina with 67 percent of the vote to Pat Buchanan's 2 percent and David Duke's 7 percent. Then George swept the Super Tuesday states by hefty margins. I should also note that 166 of 167 Republican congressmen had endorsed George. It was obvious that his party was solidly behind him.

However, Pat Buchanan claimed victory during the evening by saying that he beat David Duke ten to one in Texas, three to one in Louisiana, and so forth. But the thing I loved best was he said that he might not be winning many votes, but that he had "won the hearts of the American people." Huh?

Anna Perez told me during the campaign that she felt Pat was a racist, that he was saying all the "code" words that tell her that. I think her exact words were "a mean-spirited racist." Certainly his speech at the Republican Convention later that year sent the message loud and clear. I worried about some of the racist things I was hearing. Whether they were specifically racial or not, the perception was there. Mildred

Mottahedeh, that brilliant businesslady who reproduces some of the most magnificent porcelains from around the world and who has been so generous to the White House, wrote me in a letter: "The USA is really a prize concoction of the world and that's what makes us so special." George and I both believe that, and to feel our country fragmenting off into more defined racial pockets was and is of great concern.

⁓ In March we took Sam LeBlond with us to Arkansas to meet another "Sam"—George gave "Mr. Sam" Walton the Medal of Freedom. Mr. Sam was the founder of Wal-Mart, which had grown from a little store in a small Arkansas town into a national retail giant. Mr. Sam, who died a short time later, gave George a Sam's Club card that day, and little did we know that we soon would become regular shoppers in Maine and Texas.

March 27—I cut the ribbon on the Smithsonian Exhibit of First Ladies. They are no longer showing just the gowns and furnishings of the time. This new exhibit will also show the lady herself, her political involvement, her writings, her interests, etc. I thought it was well done until I came across Mrs. Kennedy's and Nancy's. There, prominently displayed, were Kitty Kelley's books about both ladies. These were both ugly books written by someone who did not know either woman and both books were largely discredited. Somehow or other I thought the Smithsonian was better than that [and mentioned it at a later date to Roger Kennedy, the director of the National Museum of American History. He agreed and I hope they are gone].

We tried hard to keep up with noncampaign events. In late March, for example, we attended Joe and Pat Gibbs's Youth for Tomorrow Gala at the Kennedy Center. This is a great program for kids at risk which is run by Joe and Pat with the Washington Redskins taking an active, personal interest. America is filled with good and caring people.

In April I had a luncheon for the Morehouse School of Medicine and a few days later a reception for Tuskegee University. I went to a lunch given by my 90th Club ladies and attended the Congressional Club's annual luncheon for the First Lady on April Fool's Day.

As a joke, they had the room decorated like Christmas Day. But they also gave a donation to Christmas in April, a marvelous program that started in Midland, Texas, and has now spread across the country. I visited Covenant House in New York City with Nancy Dickerson Whitehead and met the wonderful, loving Sister Mary Rose. I spoke at a fund-raiser in New York City for Boston College, where Doro got her degree, and I visited various literacy programs.

I also would like to tuck in here a luncheon I went to for Elayne Bennett's Best Friends program. Elayne has done the most marvelous job gathering prominent black women to mentor young girls. The goal is to keep them in school and off the streets, to prevent teenage pregnancies, drug abuse, and so on. The program has spread to several junior and senior high schools.

But the most fun of all was planning Doro's wedding, which was coming up in June. Arnold Scaasi was designing a lovely soft peach chiffon gown with a lace top for our very happy, beautiful daughter.

❧ Like past campaigns, I was having trouble watching or reading the news, so I was reading a lot on the plane and at night. I read two books that I loved in April, *To Dance with the White Dog*, by Terry Kay, and John Grisham's third book, *The Pelican Brief*. I still liked his first book best, *A Time to Kill*.

At the end of April we invited John Grisham and his wife, Renee, to a state dinner for President and Mrs. von Weizsacker of Germany. I sat between the President and John. One of the perks of being the hostess is that you can invite and sit next to whom you want. During the dinner John asked me what I thought of the verdict. I asked him what verdict, and he said the beating in Los Angeles involving Rodney King. He told me the jury had found the police officers involved not guilty. NOT GUILTY? How could that be? We had seen the tapes, like everyone else. John and I discussed that we hoped the city would not riot. A few days later I wrote:

Los Angeles had two days of burning and looting. There were breakouts in Atlanta and San Francisco, but things are calming down. I know it can't be compared, but I thought of Lincoln. Imagine being President when your country is at war with itself? How awful. There are undercurrents that are ugly. Blacks turning on Koreans. Blacks pulling whites out of their cars and trucks and beating them. Over fifty people got killed. I kept thinking of all those families and what suffering they are going through. I thought of all those black mothers and how do they explain a "not guilty" verdict. I wondered how we would explain it to our own grandchildren when we don't understand it ourselves. [I know that I am being judgmental and I don't really approve of that, but this is what I put in my diary.] George was in touch at all times. At first the Governor and Mayor did not want federal aid in quelling the riots, but finally they asked for it and got it immediately. One of the saddest hours in our four years.

George went to California . . . The thing that really bothered him was what happened to the Koreans. Over 2,000 small businesses owned by the Koreans were burned. Could some in the black community be racists?

Here is a sampling of some of the other things we were up to that spring and of the thoughts going through my head:

May 3—I do not know whether George will survive this political year or not, but I do know that he is the only stable person running. He has the Congress, top labor leaders and the press against him. They smell blood. There is a life after politics. My only concerns are for the country and I'd hate for George to lose for his sake. Think how good it would be for our children. They could get on with their lives.

May 15—The Gorbachevs, who are on a whirlwind speaking tour of the country, came for dinner with us, the Bakers, Brent and George W. On this visit they brought their tiny pretty daughter, Irina. She was just as peppy and bright as she could be, this Ph.D. mother of two little girls. Raisa looked tired, but who wouldn't be on a trip like the one they are on—14 cities in 12 days . . . Mikhail was careful not to criticize Boris Yeltsin too much and then Raisa would speak up because she thought he was not being tough enough. That reminds me of me sometimes. I am often not as generous as George. It was a fascinating evening and good to see them again.

I gave the graduation speech at Marquette University and George at Notre Dame . . . heard on CBS that George had had a lukewarm reception at Notre Dame. It worried me. When he got home and I asked and then told him about the report—he was shocked. He said it was really very warm and enthusiastic. He later got a letter from the president of Notre Dame saying that he could not believe the "lukewarm" report. He said that they were very enthusiastic. I wish he'd told the world that.

May 18—Did Literacy Volunteers of NYC annual fund-raiser, I believe my favorite fund-raiser. This year the readers were Arthur Miller, William Styron, Gwendolyn Brooks, Anna Quindlen and Amy Tan. Each year it gets better and this year was another great evening. I love the readings and I must confess that I love not having to sit through a long dinner.

May 20—Had Mary Pohlmann and Debbie Stafford for lunch. (Two young friends that I had gotten to know and like so very much from Iowa.) I had not seen Andy Stewart for several days and asked her to join us. As she was playing tennis, she said that she might come in tennis clothes. I said that was fine, but she must be there by 12:30 as I had a full afternoon and I was sure that the others did also. She came running in on time, but in a state of disrepair, if there is such a word. No necklace, no earrings and two *LEFT* shoes, one a wedge heel and one plain. We all laughed until we cried. How I love Andy and how she brightened my life.

May 21—LSU Graduation speech . . . What a gentle part of the country. (Louisiana State University in Baton Rouge)
. . . Flew from Louisiana to Kennebunkport. The Nebletts from Houston spent the weekend with us. I was so excited to see George's face when he saw the house. He thought it was perfect. I am so happy.

June 5—The trips are good. The press is bad. Margaret brought the children by for a swim. I know our children are worried about us. Margaret, Marvin and Doro come by often just to be sure that we are all right. How we love our children! Andy came by. All is well.

Pop arrived Sunday night from California. He said he had a great trip. . . . I might as well write it now because it caused me great unhappiness. He had a great trip, but Evans and Novak wrote the most damaging article saying that our campaign was in such disarray that Pop didn't even meet with his State Vice Chairman, state Sen. Ken Maddie. In fact it said that the senator refused to meet his plane and that the senator was an authority on farming and that George met with farmers that the senator didn't even know. The fact is that the senator met the plane, spent the day with Pop, knew all the farmers and even came back and toured the plane with him. How can we fight that?

. . . On June 2nd I flew to San Antonio, Texas, to speak to the AARP Convention at 8:30 a.m. I was followed by Ed Bradley of "60 Minutes" fame. After my talk and as I was walking out of the convention hall I heard Ed Bradley saying, "Do you think if Kuwait's main product was bananas instead of oil this administration would have risked the lives of our young men and women?" I wanted to march back in and tell him, "You bet oil made a difference, but so did standing up against brutal aggressors." I also would have asked him if he knew what would have happened if 29 other U.N. member countries hadn't formed a coalition and stopped Saddam Hussein? He probably would have sent his army into Saudi Arabia. All the world would be dependent on Iraq for energy. We would have high inflation, long lines at the gas stations, high unemployment and on and on. I wanted to ask him if he remembered that one country invaded another, raped the women, killed, stole and burned. We are not to interfere in the internal affairs of a country, but when one of our member nations gets invaded, we are obligated to go to the rescue. As long as I stayed in the building I could hear Ed Bradley trashing the administration. I hated that.

. . . John and Norma Major came for the night at Camp David. The men talked and the ladies walked. Sometimes we all did both.

One of the happiest things that happened to us that spring was the birth of the ducks. This has happened before at the White House, but this year we made an effort to save them from these hideous black birds that had been seen swooping down and carrying the babies off. After the ducklings hatched, the mother pushed them out of the nest and then led them to the water in the fountain on the South Grounds. It was the cutest sight to see her waddling down the lawn with her ducklings following. After the first raid by the black birds, the White House carpenters made a little cage that fit into the fountain, then herded the mother and the babies into the cage to remain there until the babies were old enough to fend for themselves. The father, a beautifully colored male mallard duck, swam and hovered outside the cage, would then leave and come back for visits. We ended up by having two families in two cages. Mallards could teach humans a lesson about monogamy. Anyway, George and I walked the dogs down to the fountain several times a day to see those darling little ducklings.

  ∾ On June 11 we left on what promised to be one of our more difficult trips abroad, to attend the UN Conference on Environmental Development—known as the Earth Summit—in Rio de Janeiro. En route, we were going to stop for a visit in Panama. We fully expected protesters in both countries. I also knew the wives of the heads of state in both countries were in their twenties, so I worried about not having much in common with my hostesses.

 First stop, Panama:

The hot air blasted us as we stepped off the plane. Silk is not the material to wear in this part of the world. The humidity must have been at 98%! President Endara, a heavyset 55-year-old man, and his very exotic 25-year-old Chinese/black wife, Ana Mae, were awaiting our arrival, as were our Ambassador Deane Hinton and his wife, Patricia. He has been a great troubleshooter for his country.

 After coffee with Mrs. Endara and a large lunch, we went to a big rally at the Plaza Porras put on by the dynamic Mayor of Panama City, Mayin Correa. Sad-to-say an American soldier had been killed yesterday by terrorists and so the security had to be tight. The death breaks our hearts, but George says that we cannot let terrorists rule our lives . . . I sat in on the briefings so I know that 80% of the people like us. The drive to the rally was wonderful, streets lined with crowds waving American flags and cheering people. The plaza was jammed and enthusiasm ran high. We barely got there when a few students started throwing rocks and what we thought were firecrackers. It turned out that the Panamanian police panicked and what we thought were firecrackers was tear gas and it was ghastly. The poor people in the plaza with babies could not get out and the gas was so painful. We finally had to leave the platform. My eyes still feel burned. We were thrown into our cars and took off. It was heartbreaking for the crowds on the streets who were still waving, cheering, but some had tears flowing down their faces. It was so sad that the few can ruin it for the many. If you have never been around tear gas, it is just impossible to stand. It burns your eyes, throat and lungs. It is truly unbearable.

 We arrived at Rio at twelve midnight. The next morning a very nice military wife came to comb out my hair. She says that they cannot walk the streets with even a wedding ring on because of the crime. We heard that from everyone. Evidently for the Conference they cleared the streets of bands of young boys and the street people and trucked them out to the country. It is so sad. These are the children who leave home or are pushed out because their parents can't feed them. [These are the same children who are being gunned down in 1994 to get rid of them.]

. . . The view from our hotel window was sensational. Right out front were big rocks and a tremendous surf breaking. With the doors open the sound was lulling. On the side we looked over a tremendous pool and three tennis courts and if you looked slightly further you saw a hillside favela, which I believe means a slum. It was a slum. There is no running water and it reminded me of the ride into Caracas, Venezuela, from the airport, but the proximity to this luxurious hotel made the contrast even more noticeable. Further off in the distance we could see a glorious beach, but we were told that it is unsafe to swim as the water is so polluted. What a tragedy!

Libbie Reilly, Peggy Melton, the wife of our ambassador, and I took a thirty-minute drive to Ramoa de Mattos Duarte Orphanage, run by sisters. I loved it and wanted to take most of the children home with me. The drive was lovely. For some reason the hills surrounding the city reminded me of Kweilin in China. [I'm beginning to feel like Miss Marple in the Agatha Christie stories. Everything and everyone reminds me of something or somebody else. Old age, I guess.]

After a lunch we went into the Conference Hall to hear George speak. It was very interesting. Things were running a little behind schedule and I got to visit with Shirley MacLaine, Bianca Jagger and Seymour Topping (of *New York Times* fame) and his wife, Audrey. They were all very pleasant and all, I'm sure, against us. I saw Castro from a distance.

Castro got a lot of applause which made a lot of news. But why not? He was advocating enormous environmental changes for the Third World which the developed countries would pay for. As the Third World so outnumbers the developed countries, their cheers were deafening. At the same time Senator Gore was at the Conference advocating a policy that would have cost the U.S. taxpayers billions of dollars and many thousands of jobs. It, too, sounded great, but the consequences to our people would have been earthshaking.

We went by a rain forest close to town. It was beautiful, lush and so thick that I don't think we could have walked through it without a machete. It had been a plantation until 130 years ago, all cleared and planted. Then the owner had six slaves plant two hundred thousand trees which today is this amazing jungle. It is never too late. We must continue our tree-planting program in the United States that George initiated.

We had dinner that night with President and Mrs. Collor at the Palacio Laranjeiras. This is a really beautiful palace that the governor lives in. It was built by a private family about 80 years ago. They must have been very rich! I sat next to Fernando Collor, an extremely attractive young man whom George liked and we had such great hopes for. [He left office abruptly, accused of corruption. Sad.]

The Tuesday after we came home the Yeltsins arrived for a state visit. It was a historic occasion—the first state visit ever of a *Russian* president. It was the most beautiful day and the ceremony was magnificent.

We had the usual tea for the ladies and then Naina Yeltsin and I went to visit Martha's Table to make sandwiches, stir the soup, and play with the children. They had moved since my last visit and are in a much better, bigger place. They feed nine hundred people in five parks and in four locations; they tutor adult literacy students; and they have a place for children to come after school. How I love this place and the wonderful people who run it, Veronica Park and Olivia Ivy. They also have seventy volunteers a day and they could not exist without them.

Naina was great. She listened to everything and said exactly the right thing to the press. I already had grown to like her very much. She and Boris had come to Camp David in February for an informal visit. It was freezing but she never complained. She wore pants as requested and two very pretty sweaters. There is just something about her that is warm, cozy, and relaxed. Late in the morning Doro arrived with Ellie, Sam, and Bobby Koch. They came bouncing in, pink cheeks and all. When I introduced Ellie, she went right over and gave Mrs. Yeltsin a great big hug. Naina is that kind of woman; you want to hug her. During our talk she told us some of their troubles: Those in the old regime will not give up the power; the President has passed new laws, but they won't conform to them; the press does not print what happened. We all laughed, as we hear that all around the world. She went so far as to call them a third party. She told us that one of their problems was that the family was disintegrating. I remembered thinking that we have so many of the same problems.

Anyway, on with the state visit:

Ranger, Millie and I were down visiting the ducks when I looked up and saw George and Boris walking down to also see our ducklings and the tennis court. Boris prides himself on his tennis game, but George tells me that "the ranking committee" (an imaginary group known only to my husband, our sons and his brothers) says that he is not very good. George gave him a tennis ball machine. We looked at the ducks and the court for a while and then Boris went off to his luncheon and George came home for a little chicken salad à la Pierre. It was a joy to have George home for lunch—alone!

At the State Dinner for the Yeltsins Naina seemed dear, but nervous. She told me the next day that she had been running late, rushed in to turn on her bath and the shower poured down on her hair. What a good sport. She brushed it back in a hurry and came on as she was. She is the most unselfish woman. Rather than make us wait, she came with a damp head. I must say she looked lovely and no one noticed.

. . . The dinner itself was truly superb. I sat next to Boris and Bob Allen of AT&T. Two easy dinner partners. I put Robin Gerstner (whose husband now heads up IBM) on Boris's right. She is so pretty and such fun. During dinner Boris leaned over and said, through an interpreter, "Barbara, I don't know the protocol, but what should I do if a woman has her foot on my foot?" I looked over at Robin Gerstner and said, "Oh, dear, I don't know what to tell you." Just then Boris lifted his leg and up came mine! We both burst out laughing. I was, in truth, stepping on his foot. Heaven only knows if I had been grinding his foot into the ground! He then told me that in Russia that meant that the woman loved the man. I quickly told him that was not true in our country. We did laugh.

When the violins came in Boris asked me to dance. I told him that I *DID* know the protocol to that, "Protocol demands you dance with the woman on your right." He had been teasing me all night about protocol, saying that he was a "bad boy" and did not go by protocol. Well, he grabbed Robin Gerstner and they spun around to music in the State Dining Room. It made the party more fun! He has a great twinkle in his eye and really seems to like people.

When we left the State Dining Room and headed down the hall-way, Boris and I did take a spin in the hallway to the violin music. He is fun.

⮑ The next day I hosted a lunch at Mount Vernon for Naina with the gracious help of the Mount Vernon Ladies Association. We had a wonderful meal on the veranda with a sensational view of the Potomac River.

The men signed seven more treaties that afternoon—including an agreement that eventually would lead to another drastic cut in nuclear weapons—and then we went to a return dinner given by the Russians. I asked Boris to sign my menu, and he wrote: "Barbara, remember it was you who stepped on my foot and you know what it meant. I feel the same way. Boris."

George and I were home in bed early that night. The Yeltsins told us that they only need three and a half hours' sleep a night; George and I need six to seven hours. The Yeltsins came back for breakfast and we waved them off.

Only one thing marred this wonderful visit. Our good friend George Bell died and we had to miss the funeral. How I wanted to be with my friend Bertie, but it just could not be helped.

⮑ Immediately we went back to the campaign. George left that same day for California, and I went the next day to Dallas to give the keynote speech at the Texas Republican State Convention. That night I went to a private dinner and saw many old friends. Dallas was a problem for us, as some of our big backers and friends were neighbors of Margot and Ross Perot. I got the impression it was hard to live in Dallas and be for George Bush, especially since it appeared Ross held grudges.

. . . A *Washington Post* article this morning says that Ross has had investigators looking into our boys and Hugh Liedtke for years. It is sick. Ross also tells a story about visiting us in Maine back in the 60s and going out in the boat with George when the motor failed and George "almost cried." That is the craziest story I ever heard.

I barely remember the visit to Maine, but I know that George *never* came close to crying. All this from a man who offered George a big job when he left the CIA in 1976. Thank heavens he didn't take it. I confess to liking Margot and the children very much and will resist saying all I feel about Ross. Some of his quotes are truly off the wall, such as this "quote of the week": "When I go to a meeting and they open with a prayer, I put my wallet away and leave. I know all they want is my money." I'm reminded of what people used to say about a man in Houston: "If he didn't have all that money, he'd be the most disliked man in town." I wonder if that applies to Ross?

June 24—Poor Dan Quayle got into the worst thing. It could have happened to anyone . . . especially me (I am the world's worst speller). A teacher handed him a cue card with POTATOE written on it and then Dan asked a little kid to spell "potato." Dan tried to make the child put an "e" on the end as his misspelled card had it. The press and all the comedians had a field day with this. My heart ached for him. My heart should have ached for the teacher who made the mistake, but it was Dan who got the blame and for days this very important mishap wiped out other unimportant news like the signing of the weapons treaties with Yeltsin.

. . . During the past week I kicked off the Summer Quest Reading Program in a public library and another time I visited one of the Boys and Girls summer programs. Both do a great job and need all the support they can get.

On June 26 we had Bobby and Doro's rehearsal dinner at the White House. The Kochs wanted to give the party, but the children wanted privacy, which we could guarantee only at the White House. I should apologize right now to Marlin Fitzwater, George's press secretary, who gave Anna Perez, my press secretary, a very hard time about the wedding. He just could not understand why Anna was being so closemouthed about something as simple as a wedding. Anna was doing exactly what I asked: "No press about the wedding, please, not one word." That's what Bobby and Doro wanted and Anna kept her word.

The White House was abuzz with excitement, and so many people volunteered their time to make this a spectacular wedding. We had to limit the rehearsal party to seventy-four people and tried to be sure that Doro and Bobby had their friends. Of course all our children came and brothers and sisters and spouses. Bobby's family turned out en masse and were so nice. Bobby's parents, George and Helen Koch, are absolutely the best, the easiest, and most relaxed people. The dinner was in the State Dining Room and it looked wonderful. The whole White House did. There were lots of toasts, all loving, mostly funny, but the one I liked best was the rap song that Sam, Ellie, and Doro had worked on for days to sing to Bobby:

> *We're Doro, Sam, and Ellie,*
> *And we're making a toast,*
> *To Bobby Koch, who is the most,*
> *Extraordinary person we ever met,*
> *He'll make a great family man, you bet!*
> *Tomorrow is the big day we become a family,*
> *When Bobby Koch joins us three.*
> *We'll have a great life, that we know is true,*
> *But the message of this rap is: We love you!*

The wedding itself was to be held the next day at Camp David. Laurie Firestone really put on this wedding. She can make magic and knows the right way to do anything and everything. All the off-duty White House butlers volunteered to serve as a present to Doro, and although George paid for the flowers, Nancy Clarke, Wendy Elsasser, and Dianne Barbour from the florist shop decorated the chapel and the tables on their day off. White House chefs Pierre Chambrin, Franette McCulloch, and Roland Mesnier made a beautiful cake and cooked a lovely buffet supper, including an enormous fresh salmon that Ted and Cathy Stevens had sent us straight from Alaska. I wrote in my diary:

The guests arrived at 4 p.m. and were taken to Laurel to freshen up and have a cold drink or tea. At 4:30 the father of the bride showed up to change into his clothes and asked what people were wearing to the wedding. I told him his navy blue suit would be just fine. I couldn't believe it when he confessed that he hadn't brought a suit. He said that he thought it would be informal! He did come up with a blue blazer, a white shirt and some 20-year-old white summer pants with a thin blue stripe which the boys call his "New York Yankee" pants. Bobby Koch had given him a wedding tie and that added to his look. How I love that man. He thought it was informal! Wait until he gets his Scaasi bill!

The chapel looked so beautiful with peach roses, and there was music in the balcony. The groom walked in from the back of the altar followed by Sam and his three brothers, P.C., Danny and Monte Koch . . . All four boys had on blue suits and the ties Bobby had given them. Bobby was so dear to have Sam at his side. (This was Sam and Ellie's second wedding in two months. Their dad had gotten married in April and they were in that wedding, also.) Everybody was in place and then to great trumpets down the aisle came Ellie LeBlond in a floor-length lavender gown holding a miniature nosegay like her mother's. Her face was literally beaming. Behind them came my precious George with Doro on his arm looking incredibly beautiful. She looked exactly right. Chaplain Jonathan Frusti led the service. George W. read a passage as did a friend of Bobby's. The little church choir, made up of several service personnel and some of their wives, sang three lovely songs (our young chaplain leaves the altar to join the choir). Their voices are clear and sweet. Sam and Ellie wiggled a lot. It didn't seem to bother Doro or Bobby. Doro put a loving hand on Ellie every now and then. When Doro and Bobby knelt to be blessed there was a BUSH/QUAYLE sticker on Bobby's soles. His brothers put it there. Neither George nor I noticed. I suspect we were praying.

After the wedding we walked back to Aspen and took a lot of pictures; the bride and groom formed a receiving line. The parents mixed and mingled and had fun. Everything about the wedding was happy and we will forever be grateful for all who made it so perfect.

. . . All during the weekend George had been on the phone with other heads of state about the problems in Yugoslavia. I heard him talking to Major, Kohl, Miyazawa, Lubbers, Cavaco Silva (of Portugal) and Mulroney. Then we awakened the morning after the wedding to find that California had suffered another dreadful earthquake. All this on his mind and a wedding, too.

We flew back to the White House and I took Ellie to see the ducks. We still have seven. Then Ellie and I went up on the Truman Balcony to read books. I got so tired that I took her into my room and we both climbed on the bed. She read aloud to me and did a great job. I sat up and looked and SHE COULD READ! She had broken the code and could really read. Hurrah, another grandchild can read! Ellie is going into first grade this fall. She could read because she was read to by her mother and baby-sitters. Seeing a child read is such a miracle.

The next morning we were back on the campaign trail—George to New York City and Detroit and me to Nebraska and on and on and on.

We were back in time to have Luciano Pavarotti for lunch on Tuesday. It was such fun as he has an air of joyous energy that fills a room. We talked about Italian politics, a subject he seems to love.

That night we had our annual diplomatic picnic, and for the second year in a row, the heavens opened up and the rain crashed down. I guess I deserved that because after Doro's glorious weather I had said, "I don't care if we have hail or sleet from now on, if we can just get through the wedding." Luckily, the staff moved everything in quick as a wink.

On July 5 we left for the annual G-7 Economic Summit in Munich, Germany, stopping in Warsaw en route. We had a rousing welcome all the way from the airport to the Royal Palace. It was nice to see Lech and Danuta Walesa again. She is a great beauty and looks very young despite the fact they have eight children, ages six to twenty-two, and are grandparents. They say she is a very steadying influence on him.

On this trip we officially returned the remains of Ignace Paderewski to the Polish people. A great composer, concert pianist, and statesman, Paderewski had died in New York City in 1941, when his country was occupied by Germans. His dying wish was to be buried in his homeland—but not until it was free. So he was entombed in Arlington National Cemetery until we took him home in 1992. It was a very moving ceremony.

Afterward George spoke in Castle Square to a tremendous crowd. Lech Walesa told us only the Pope had drawn that many people.

That evening in Munich, while George went to a working dinner with François Mitterrand, I had a quiet dinner with Kitty Brady and Susan Baker. I then intended to crawl into bed but instead got all involved in Wimbledon. I was so excited because Andre Agassi won the men's singles. Hurrah!

Several years before, George had invited Andre to play tennis at the White House. Although his manners were great, his clothes and appearance were not. It was pouring rain, and I told him that he was darn lucky because I wouldn't let him play in those awful clothes on the White House court. He was very funny and promptly gave George one of those strange psychedelic-colored pants with those even stranger underpants hanging down. How we all laughed at the thought of George wearing them. It wasn't long after that he was in another Wimbledon when he *had* to wear all white. I sent him a telegram wishing him well and telling him I admired his costume and that now he could play on the White House court. When he returned he came by to see George at the Oval Office and brought me the shorts and shirt he had worn! Pretty cute. Another time Andre and Wendy, his girl of many years (he was twenty-one at the time, and he told me that he had known her since she was eight), came to spend a night at Camp David for a little tennis and golf. I was very touched when both of them showed up in church at 9 A.M. and he had a well-worn Bible in his hands. I wrote at the time:

Thank heavens he has shaved. He still has the dyed stringy, long blond hair and the earring. I cannot criticize another part of him, having been so bad about his clothes. He wore whites at Wimbledon and here at Camp David. He was telling us about the house he is building in Las Vegas—instead of a dining room he will have a pool table, instead of a formal living room he will have pinball machines and penny arcade games. He is just a little kid, but a nice little kid.

And now he had won Wimbledon. I was thrilled for him.

The first day in Munich the spouses all met at the Seehaus Restaurant, known for its good food, atmosphere, and beautiful English gardens. Hannelore Kohl was our hostess. While at the luncheon I got a note from Anna Perez:

Danielle Mitterrand's motorcade was bombed in Northern Iraq this a.m. Potential 4 deaths, 12 injured, children involved. Mrs. Mitterrand's safety has been confirmed. Info is sketchy. Will get more to you later. Anna.

One of the ladies said: "What in the world was she doing there?" I said I was sure that she was trying to help the Kurds. It was criminal what was happening to those poor children and people. Saddam Hussein just would not leave them alone.

We later learned that a car bomb had detonated as the motorcade drove by. Three security people and a ten-year-old girl had been killed.

After lunch we got into a bus so fancy it was impossible to see out the windows with ease. We headed for the Glyptothek Museum:

We hadn't gone one moment when we came to a bridge and, believe it or not, hit the bridge. Poor Hannelore, she had planned everything so carefully. The explanation was that the driver had pushed a button to raise the shock absorbers and thus raised the level of the bus! We were able to back out, but it meant missing many of the sights that were planned. So the tour was, "If you could see, you would have seen a pavilion . . ." It was funny, but not to our hostess. The truth was that by the time the charming man, Professor Everding, who was guiding us, told us about a building, we had long since passed it. From then on the afternoon was fine.

That night we saw a performance of "Carmen" which I enjoyed enormously . . . Roger Porter (of George's staff) thought the production was more sensual than any he had seen before. I must say that the TV and everything is more sex-oriented here than even in the USA. Rose Zamaria went for a walk across the park and came upon a man with absolutely no clothes on walking her way. (I would have loved seeing Rosie's face.) She also saw another man in a cut-off tee-shirt and nothing more riding a bike. That is evidently OK in Germany although it does not sound very comfortable to me!

The next morning we went by helicopter to Hohenschwangau and then by horse-drawn carriages up a hill to Neuschwanstein Castle. This was a fairy-tale castle built by Ludwig II. It was described to us as "a monument to Wagner." Poor old Ludwig II was engaged briefly, but broke the engagement. It was intimated to us that he was in love with Wagner (the composer), who did live with him. This castle was enormous. We walked up miles of spiral staircases. There was a glorious chapel, a music room and a grotto right in the castle. Every inch of the castle was carved, painted, gilded and on and on. . . . Poor Ludwig II got dethroned because of the money he was spending on this castle and shortly afterwards drowned— whether by his own hand or another's is unknown.

The next day President and Mrs. von Weizsacker hosted a luncheon, and I sat between him and Boris Yeltsin. The latter is so easy and funny. He constantly teased me, including reminding me of the foot incident at the state dinner.

We went on to Finland in the late afternoon—although it was hard to tell what time of day it was. At that time of year, sunset was around 11 P.M. and it came back up by 4 A.M. Very confusing. We stopped in Helsinki to attend the CSCE (Conference on Security and Cooperation in Europe).

While we were there Bill Clinton announced that Al Gore would be his running mate. Again, I showed just how politically astute I am:

> I can't understand him picking another southerner from a small state. Al has a good military record and a very nice family. He is a liberal and a demagogue. Neither he nor Clinton have ever been in the private sector. They are just professional politicians. They have made their living in politics. Amazing.

Tellervo Koivisto, the wife of the Finnish president, had planned a wonderful program for us which included a luncheon cruise and museum visits. I was very pleased to see that she carried the lovely Judith Lieber bag that I had given her. While at the White House I gave these exquisite little bags as gifts to the heads of state's wives. They are made in America, they are beautiful, everyone loves them, and I know and love Judith.

～ We went home to Maine for the weekend, and I noted in my diary that the planting on Walker's Point was coming back from the Halloween disaster:

> The bayberry and rosa rugosa are pushing up through the rocks and are looking pretty good. I am thrilled. I guess I should have trusted God a little more.
>
> George's mother seems so much better. At church on Sunday as part of the children's service, Jack Allin said: "Pussy Cat, Pussy Cat, where have you been? I've been to London to visit the queen. Pussy Cat, Pussy Cat, what did you do there?" And before a child could answer a loud clear voice said, "I frightened a little mouse under the chair." And it was our precious

mom. We almost cried, it was such a sweet moment. It is so amazing. Mom is just floating in and out so gently.

George left for California, and ended up fishing in Wyoming with Jim and Susan Baker during the Democratic Convention. I stayed in Maine with the grandchildren and Mom, resting up for the big push ahead.

24

The Campaign

This is a most painful chapter to write. The weeks leading up to Election Day almost seemed like a game we played as children where we'd take one step forward and two steps back.

July 17—There is a new poll out this morning that shows Bill Clinton 23 points ahead of George. Pretty frightening. Somehow or other it seems impossible for George to win, a Congress that bucks you on every turn, a tough press corps, 5 Democrats, 1 Republican and 1 Independent, all railing against him for months. AND THE ECONOMY! It just seems impossible to me, but we will do our best.

. . . I am hiding my head like an ostrich. It hurts too much to see George and the children so lied about. Only 3½ more months to go.

Yesterday morning as I was driving out to play golf I heard Ross Perot on the radio saying that he would no longer remain in the race. The fact that he chose this day for the announcement came as a surprise. This was the last day of the Democratic Convention and should have been Bill Clinton's day. Whether Ross did it on purpose or just did it we will never know. I'm tempted to think that he did it without thinking of Bill or anyone else. He seems to be extraordinarily self-oriented.

July 21—The political picture could not be any worse. Clinton came out of the convention 25 points ahead.

. . . George is being trashed by one and all.

. . . George spoke to the National League of Families (of American Prisoners and Missing in Southeast Asia) in Crystal City (Va.). He got booed. Darn that Ross Perot. He has really hurt these people by making them think that their loved ones are alive and that their government has not done everything they can to find them. The government is absolutely convinced after years of intelligence that they are still not holding our men. What purpose could it possibly serve to lie about this?

Lest you think I was obsessed with the election—and of course we actually were—I'd like to share some other diary entries from that time period.

I flew down to Washington on July 22nd for the Medal of Arts Luncheon where Marilyn Horne, for one, was honored. She is a great lady with a glorious voice.

Winnie Palmer and her daughter and three granddaughters and one grandson came for iced tea. We walked down to see the ducks. The baby ducks have grown so much that they could now be released. Nice Dale (Haney) had waited for me to come home, and he cut the cage while the Palmer group was standing there. Dale (one of the groundskeepers) is so dear to all the animals and takes Ranger for walks while he does his chores. (He invites Millie, but she is a mother's girl.)

I visited Martha's Table while I was home and read one of my favorite books, *Amazing Grace,* to thirty bright little kids. They all sat on the floor and listened and entered in while sitting next to or on a volunteer's lap. . . . One child spent the whole time softly rubbing or feeling a volunteer lady's hair. It was very sweet. These little ones are from the homeless shelters or the worst public housing projects. They were bright eyed and smart. These are the kids we are losing, and it must not happen.

I went to Boston for a RIF (Reading Is Fundamental) event and on to the Thyroid Foundation luncheon. As we stood in the receiving line and doctor after doctor came through the line, I wondered what in the world I was doing being their speaker? You may be sure that I did not speak about the medical side of Graves' disease! I went on to Maine to be with George W., Laura, the girls and their houseguests, Jimmy and Debbie Francis.

When George joined us in Maine for a short weekend, he told me that people around the country, Republicans included, were calling for him to dump Dan Quayle from the ticket. Even a former president called and advised giving Dan another job. The pressure was enormous.

I'd like to go on record right now as saying that Dan Quayle was a superb vice president. He is loyal and smart. There is no question that he had a perception problem, and it was politically chic to kick Dan around. It was darned unfair, and how he and Marilyn kept their cool, I will never know. When I think of the ridicule Dan got for talking about family values in 1992, and now hear our opponents talking about them in 1994 without ridicule, it hurts me for the Quayles. Dan was right, you know. So many of our problems stem from dysfunctional families. And our welfare system locks people into poverty and discourages two-parent households. We give incentives for all the wrong things: not working and having more children.

⁓ Once again, friends came to my rescue. Andy Stewart drove over from New Hampshire and we had two days of terrible golf and lots of laughs.

After taking political trips to Baltimore, New Jersey, Ohio, and Florida, I flew back to Maine to be with our gang and my dear friend Bertie Bell. She's another one of the group of close friends who made my life at the White House such a joy. She hung in and stayed in touch.

The Prime Minister of Israel, Yitzhak Rabin, and his wife, Leah, came to Maine on August 10 to spend a night. We had known each other over the years and it was nice to see them again. In fact, many years ago, Leah and I had played tennis in Washington with Jessica Catto, whose husband, Henry, was then Chief of Protocol.

The men worked all day while Leah and I went to have a delicious lunch at Jerry and Jane Weintraub's Blueberry Hill farmhouse, where they generously let us pick blueberries every summer. Leah wanted to go antiquing, but because there was a very radical Jewish group in town protesting the visit, Security didn't think it was safe. This group rented a boat and sat off the Point yelling ugly things about the Prime Minister over a loudspeaker. The men broke for dinner, but then worked all through the night.

The next morning an agreement was announced that we would give Israel $10 billion in loan guarantees, but they agreed to curtail building settlements in the occupied territories. This had been a source of tension between the United States and Israel for some time, so the agreement was an important announcement.

At the end of the news conference, CNN's Mary Tillotson asked George the most scandalous question about a story that had run in one of the New York City tabloid newspapers. There was not a word of truth in the story, which concerned an alleged affair that had been looked into for years. Yet, it dominated the news, burying the real story about the agreement with Israel. Marlin Fitzwater later told me that he asked Mary why she had done that, and she said that her boss ordered her to ask that question.

Jim Miklaszewski of NBC told me that the Clinton people had blasted him because he had said during a panel discussion that their campaign was calling around trying to get reporters to go with that ugly story. I asked him if, in truth, they had done this, and his answer was "Absolutely." That's definitely playing hardball.

About this time the campaign took a definite turn for the silly when *Family Circle* magazine decided to sponsor a chocolate chip cookie contest between me and Hillary Clinton. I can't speak for Hillary, but my office knew nothing about the contest until it came out in the magazine. And to make matters worse—it wasn't even my recipe! As it turns out, *Family Circle* had found the recipe in a 1986 *McCall's*, which got it from a chef who worked at the Vice President's House. *My* chocolate chip cookie recipe was one that Patsy Caulkins had given me years ago when we were housemates at Yale. Just to make sure all of you got the right one, here it is:

Mix: *1 cup butter*
      1 cup granulated sugar
      1 cup brown sugar

Add: *2 eggs and beat*

Sift and add: *2 cups flour*
      1 teaspoon soda
      1 teaspoon salt

Add:	*2 cups quick-cooking rolled oats*
	2 teaspoons vanilla
	1 12 oz. package chocolate chips

Bake:	*Drop by tablespoons onto ungreased cookie sheet and bake for 10 minutes at 350 degrees.*

This silly contest popped up all over the place during the conventions and the campaign and even prompted some serious columnists to write about it as "anti-feminist." Yikes. And then on top of everything else, *I lost.*

Actually, this story reminds me of a true scandal in my office, which I don't think ever has been revealed before: Let's call it "Recipegate."

My office got hundreds of letters requesting recipes for cookbooks, articles, and other publications, and we had a select few that we sent out. Then a woman wrote in inquiring if I was trying to kill George: Most of my recipes were loaded with fat and cholesterol. (Please keep in mind that back when I cooked for my family, we didn't worry about such things.)

A volunteer in my office, a wonderful woman named Alicia Lee, who also happens to be a great cook, took it upon herself to make my recipes "politically correct," substituting margarine for butter, egg whites for eggs, and so on. Finally she gave up and started sending out some of *her* favorite recipes.

I knew nothing about this until a woman told me one day how much she loved my bean recipe. Bean recipe! My bean recipe was to open a can. What on earth was she talking about? So there it is. There are cookbooks all over the country with "Barbara Bush's favorite recipes" that I've never seen before. I just hope they're good.

❧ Finally it was August 17, time to head to Houston and the Republican Convention at the Astrodome. The first stop was a huge rally where we saw all our children and grandchildren and many dear friends from across the country. We called on the Reagans, and then went to the Houstonian, our home away from home, to get ready for the big week ahead.

Unfortunately, before we even left the plane, the convention was off to a bad start.

There was a pro-life plank in the Republican party platform (which is decided by a platform committee and not the President) and some very specific judgmental words about homosexuals that did not reflect George's views at all, and that set a bad tone for our convention. I believe that a platform should set *broad* guidelines and that religious beliefs should not be in the political arena. Unfortunately, I made that view known in an interview just before we arrived, so the "Barbara Bush is pro-choice" rumor ran wild—exactly what I had tried to avoid for years.

Let me say again: I hate abortions, but just could not make that choice for someone else. And contrary to the platform plank, which was opposed to *all* abortions, George was against abortions with the exception of rape, incest, and where the life of the mother was threatened.

The very first night I went to the convention and heard Pat Buchanan and Ronald Reagan speak. I wrote in my diary:

(Buchanan) endorsed George strongly after cutting him to ribbons for month after month and was very extreme. It is hard for me to accept his kind of campaigning . . . I hate "gay bashing." I sat next to (his wife) Shelley, whom I remember from the Nixon White House and like. I noticed all through the campaign that his sister, Bay, walked next to him and that Shelley walked behind them all the time. That made me think of George's mom, who always noticed if the husband waited for the wife. She gave Ron Reagan high marks for being thoughtful to Nancy. She would have given Pat very bad marks. I remember one time we were with the Reagans at some ceremony or another. We were briefed and told that the Reagans would walk through the door followed by George and me. When the door opened and they started through, Ronald Reagan stopped, stepped aside and said, "After you, Barbara." He is innately polite.

Speaking of Ronald Reagan, he gave a very good speech, vintage Reagan, and had a great reception from the delegates.

 The next day I had the most unbelievable schedule: Along with our grandson George P., I dropped by a "Black America Salutes the First Family" breakfast; did a ton of press interviews; toured the American Spirit Pavilion, where they had every kind of convention and other souvenirs you can imagine, including *Millie's Book*; and attended a fund-raiser for a local candidate. But the most fun of all was a reception that evening at the Museum of Fine Arts. The Ashmuns, Kerrs, Fitches, Nebletts, and Liedtkes had gathered family and friends, which was our only real opportunity to see them since everyone was so busy.

I left the reception with such a wonderful warm feeling and went to the Convention Hall, where the first stop was the PBS booth and an interview with Judy Woodruff:

It was truly unbelievable—starting out with a hideous editorial from the *Houston Post* (against George) and fast moving into "politically incorrect" things said by speakers at the Convention, at least according to the press pack. It was so combative that I finally said, "Stop. Where were you at the Democratic Convention? Were you asking these questions? How come it is OK for them to allow only a pro-choice person to speak and you do not say a word or ask a question? Be fair. We have pro-choice speakers and pro-life speakers and we all have one thing in common—we're all pro-Bush. We showed our congressional people and they showed NONE. And you asked no questions! Be fair." She cut it short. I felt abused.*

You can't beat the press. They always have the last word, and the next morning I turned on the tube to see a panel discussing how badly *I HAD ABUSED JUDY WOODRUFF!* If George hadn't been running for President that might have been funny!

Secretary of Labor Lynn Martin, who is pro-choice, keynoted the convention that night and did a superb job. She is a bright, enthusiastic, energetic woman. As she spoke, I remembered sitting in a living room in Rockford, Illinois, twelve years earlier and listening to this young woman, a single parent of two girls. She was running for the congressional seat that John Anderson was vacating. Since that time, Lynn and I had campaigned together a lot, sharing long bus rides and

---

* I probably should explain this diary entry. The Democrats refused to let Pennsylvania Governor Robert Casey, who is pro-life, or any other pro-life Democrats, speak at their convention. Also, their senators and congressmen had little or no role in the convention since the Democratically controlled House was in the middle of the Post Office scandal.

marching in freezing parades, and here she was keynoting the convention and sitting in the President's cabinet.

Mary Fisher also spoke and was magnificent. She has tested HIV-positive and is dedicating her life to the research, prevention, and the cure of AIDS. Mary is the daughter of our friends, Max and Marjorie Fisher, and is a single mother of two young boys. She believes passionately in what she is doing. We have kept up our interest in her work and value our friendship with her immensely.

Jack Kemp and Phil Gramm also spoke Tuesday night and did well, I thought. It was interesting to hear them, knowing that both were probably thinking ahead—four years ahead, to be exact. But now they were 100 percent behind George.

The next day was as crazy as the first. I visited the Texas Children's Hospital, met George at the huge Republican Gala, rushed home to do more press interviews, practiced my speech, which was coming up that night, and then had dinner with all our family, seventy of us. I ate with my brothers and their wives, and George ate with his. Both our families have been so supportive during George's political career.

Unfortunately, George P. and I had to leave early to change clothes and head for the convention and our big night.

We were preceded on the program by six of the most amazing "Points of Light" recipients, and then Marilyn Quayle spoke. She is a great wife and mother and a very bright woman. Unfortunately, her speech did not convey her warmth or caring and she was very much criticized for it. The work Marilyn has done with breast cancer is far-reaching, and she got little or no credit for that. She started the "Race for the Cure" in Washington, and has raised millions of dollars for the fight against this dreadful disease that needlessly kills 46,000 American women every year.

Then it was my turn. In all honesty, I can't remember a word that I said, but the highlight of my talk came when I called the family out and ten children and twelve grandchildren appeared. I asked George P. to speak for the family:

Among other things, George read a letter that his grandfather had written him after his trip with AMERICARES to Armenia after that devastating earthquake several years ago.

George P. gave a loving endorsement of his grandfather, ending with a last minute addition of "VIVA BUSH," which resounded through our trips for the next few months. "P" wrote his own speech and delivered it so well. He stood straight and gave that beautiful smile that Dick Darman mentioned several years before. He made us so very proud [see Appendix D].

One thing that happened gave me the giggles. George came out after our little talk and was immediately rushed by the grandchildren—as primed by the handlers. Jenna and Barbara were very enthusiastic and at (age) 10 were like big puppy dogs. They charged their grandfather and for a moment I feared that he might buckle under their weight. Now that would have been a photo op!

The next morning we attended an early-morning prayer breakfast at the University of Houston with Jim Baker. George spent most of the day working on his speech for that night. I would not have been able to sleep if my speech had not been finished the day it was to be given!

At noon the Harris County Republican women hosted a Tribute to the First Lady. I was very touched. Representative Olympia Snowe, Senator Nancy Kassebaum, Ambassador Carla Hill, and cabinet secretaries Barbara Franklin and Lynn Martin all attended. Jane Morgan Weintraub sang, and not only looked sensational but sounded like an angel. Rich Bond, Janet Steiger, and Jeb Bush all spoke. Every one of them lied about me and I loved it! They had a film narrated by Charlton Heston that made me sound like a saint. I knew better, but loved it also!

That night I raced to the Convention Hall so I could hear Jerry Ford speak. He and Betty were so great to be there and he gave a marvelous speech. Jerry had campaigned hard for George, and they had been very generous with their words and time. He was followed by Senator Jack Danforth, Dan Quayle, and Bob Dole, who in his very commanding yet funny way, introduced George.

Of course I think George was great. But I wasn't the only one. He was interrupted so many times that his thirty-five-minute speech took almost an hour.

. . . The place went wild. We went up to sit behind the stage to listen to the end. There were all the little grands, full of it, and dying to get up on that stage. They had had a taste of applause the night before and liked it, I guess. I joined George and then all the family did. They had an overkill of a balloon drop. If any more had come down we would have been buried! All the kids loved it and they all looked adorable.

So a convention that had started out on rocky footing ended on a very high note for us. The polls showed that the gap between George and Bill Clinton had nearly closed, and we felt ready to go.

⌒ I spent the first three days traveling with George, which was fun, and despite terrible weather, we felt a rush of excitement and high hopes.

August 21—We flew to Gulfport, Mississippi, to the biggest hottest rally ever. It was there that George and I saw a sign that we loved: "George P. for President in 2024!" From there to a fund-raiser where we had some of the "sweatiest" pictures ever taken with supporters!

On to Branson, Missouri, where we went to a rally of 17,000 people in a theme park. There were Glen Campbell, Loretta Lynn and Moe Bandy, all great supporters, working up the crowd. One forgets that these poor people have stood there for three hours in some cases. It was truly a great start. We went that evening to Moe's theater for a wonderful show . . . He is giving the proceeds of the night to literacy and that is just great! So ended Day One of the official 1992 campaign.

August 22—Up early. Flew to Woodstock, Georgia, a town of 3,500, and there were greeted by 25,000. . . . It was the darndest thing you have ever seen—it poured rain and people stayed for hours. It was drizzling when we arrived and several times it poured again. I was under an umbrella. Paul Coverdell and Newt Gingrich were there. On to Birmingham, Alabama, where exactly the same thing happened. It rained and 17,000 people stayed. We were with Helen and Governor Guy Hunt and Ray Scott, a fishing pal of George's.

In every town we did a fund-raiser. The people who come are always so fresh and eager and we are always so tired and rushed. It hardly seems fair to them. They are so generous and deserve more than they get.

We went from Alabama to Dallas, where we had supper with George and Laura and then George spoke at a Baptist meeting. So ended Day 2 of the 1992 official campaign.

August 23—Day 3 of the campaign was spent at church and the State Fair in Illinois with (Governor) Jim Edgar and Brenda. I could not get over the numbers of people who met us at every stop . . . It was amazing. In Georgia and Alabama they stayed through the rain, and in Mississippi and Illinois through intense heat. I know that George is going to win.

August 24—71 more days.
. . . Other things are happening in the world. At this very moment Miami, Florida, is being hit by the big hurricane—big. Our children (Jeb and Colu) have been evacuated from their home. I can't wait to hear that they are all right.
. . . Woody Allen and Mia Farrow are having a disgusting public separation.
. . . "Fergie" is all over the news with pictures of her swimming topless with some young man other than her husband and her children standing by.
George flew to N.J., Connecticut and right to Florida. He declared the area a disaster. He says that it is the worst devastation that he has ever seen, 250,000 homeless. Horrible.
. . . I watched from Los Angeles and Hurricane Andrew is the worst in our history. It also ripped through Louisiana. I have just seen G. there on the TV.

Later I went with George when he toured both south Florida and Louisiana again. It was so hard to believe. This hurricane didn't cut a swath through an area, it absolutely demolished everything as far as the eye could see. The one bright spot was seeing the volunteers from the Red Cross and religious groups, victims of Hurricane Hugo, medical teams from all over the country, the National Guard, and other military units, all setting up day-care centers, medical clinics, soup kitchens, and centers for dispensing water and for helping people with their insurance. Not only did the hurricane victims lose their homes, schools, and hospitals, but in many cases their places of work and therefore their jobs.

The campaign went on and on. It seemed like endless meals one week—and none the next. I rediscovered that all pillows at hotels and motels feel like rocks and everyone wakes up with stiff necks. The windows don't open and the heat or air-conditioning is never adjustable, so you cooked or you froze. Sometimes you would get lucky. Doro and I once were put in honeymoon suites. Right next to my bed was a big bathtub for two, and from the bed you could see the toilet. What happened to the blushing bride? There is a generation gap.

We felt rushed all the time and very grateful to all the people who were working so hard.

Despite the long hours, it was exciting to meet so many interesting people and hear their stories. Many of our experiences were wonderful. One great example is when Gayle Wilson, wife of California Governor Pete Wilson, and I visited a Hispanic housing development in Los Angeles. The locals had taken charge of their own area and were crime free. As we were walking out of this truly humble housing project, a young girl came up and said, "Mrs. Bush, I go to Phillips Exeter Academy." She told me that another girl from the same complex also goes there. She said, "I want you to know that we don't only bring up gang members here." I was so touched and wondered how these two young women felt among so many children from considerably more comfortable backgrounds in that cold, cold New England climate. Exeter should be proud. I am sure that this girl will do well in life because she not only earned, but also was given, this opportunity.

In North Carolina a man gave me a check for $100,000 in response to George's plea for the American Red Cross and their Hurricane Andrew relief work. Later I heard that the Red Cross got 53,000 telephone calls pledging more than $4 million in response to George's message. In addition, the government of Kuwait gave $10 million.

Actor Gerald McRaney of "Major Dad" fame spent a day campaigning with me in Florida. The people loved him and he was a great campaigner.

In early September, George and I had lunch with the Roy Harris family in Asheville, North Carolina. Several months earlier, Mr. Harris had been in the audience during a Rose Garden interview George did with "CBS This Morning." After asking George a question, he thanked him for asking him to the White House and invited us to his house. Well, we took him up on it and went for lunch with the whole family, including his wife, Diantha, and their two daughters, Stacy and Lisa. Their community all had pitched in and they had a delicious spread.

The family was involved in their church, the Girl Scouts, the schools, and so on. It was another bright spot.

The very next day we went to Louisville, Kentucky, to attend a Triple A baseball game with Will and Sarah Farish and Dan Ulmer, one of the owners of the Louisville Redbirds, and his wife, Helen. Everyone who came brought a can of food for the hurricane victims. We got a huge standing ovation when we walked out onto the field for the singing of "The Star-Spangled Banner," and then George threw out the first ball and got another standing ovation from 20,000 people. We did not see one bad sign or hear one boo. We were thrilled and surprised when George got yet another ovation when we left.

While we were at the baseball game, Bill Clinton was at a car race in South Carolina, where he got booed badly. Almost all the press reported it except for our old friend David Broder of *The Washington Post*. His column said that George threw out a ball at a baseball game where his people expected him to be booed, and Bill Clinton went to a car race where there were 100,000 people. Period. Not one word that George was cheered or Bill was booed. I just could not understand that. Many years before we had established a friendship with Dave and Ann Broder with the full understanding that they were Democrats and politics would be put aside in our friendship. I respect Dave, but this article was so blatantly partisan and untrue. That was a dark spot.

On Labor Day we walked the four-and-a-half-mile Mackinac Bridge in Sault Ste. Marie, Michigan, an annual event that brings out about 100,000 people, with Governor John Engler and Michelle. Then it was on to Milwaukee, where we attended a Labor Day picnic with Wisconsin Governor Tommy Thompson and Sue Ann Thompson, and then back to Michigan for the Hamtramck Polish Festival Parade.

Despite the great events we were doing, I wrote in my diary about this time: "I am back to my bad feelings and feel discouraged about winning these days. The crowds are great, but the playing field is not level. It is hard to run against the world!!"

∾ George and I rarely traveled together, which I hated. He was great about calling and checking on me. Most of my campaign trips were built around big rallies, then smaller fund-raising lunches or dinners. Anna Perez and I worked on two talks: one to be given at the rallies, and since I am not a rah-rah speaker, these were not easy for me; and a second warm and cozy talk for the smaller groups. I much prefer the latter. George, meanwhile, was doing his job *and* speaking around the country.

Between speeches we managed to tuck in visits to literacy programs, which I loved. In Lexington, Kentucky, I helped dedicate the Carnegie Lexington Literacy Center, which Will Farish had supported. They have a wonderful, big-picture approach to literacy: in-house poets and writers, classes for new learners, writing classes, children's story hours, state-of-the-art computers.

We often visited shopping malls to shake the hands of shoppers, and I would stop in the bookstore to promote "Mrs. Bush's Storytime" and read to a group of children. Sometimes local campaign staffs would point out to my staff that children couldn't vote, so maybe I shouldn't take the time. Ridiculous.

In Louisville, Kentucky, Sharon Darling, who is a member of my foundation board and is director of the National Center for Family Literacy, took me to a great family literacy program, Parents and Children Together, where the mothers spend their mornings studying and the afternoons working with their children:

They are the poorest group of women, all have several children, some as many as four, no man in the household, most, if not all, dropped out of school early, black and white, and all felt alone and forgotten. There was an outpouring of gratitude for the program and the most amazing feeling of "sisterhood." We talked about what they hoped for their children. We talked about sex and the fact that there was something worth waiting for IF THEY GET THEIR EDUCATION. I was touched—one shy lady asked me to hug her and the whole visit turned into a hugging, crying time. Then we went into a class with the mothers and their children. Each one of my new friends wanted me to see her child or children. This is what I mean when I talk about family values.

In Barberton, Ohio, near Akron, I visited the Decker Family Development Center. The entire community supported it, including the hospital, local university, and service clubs, and they received funding from the federal, state, and local governments. I was so impressed with all the services the center offered the entire family—and under one roof—that I suggested that they apply for a grant from the Barbara Bush Foundation for Family Literacy. There was an awkward silence and then someone told me that they already had received one! Now that was embarrassing. We also visited another impressive foundation recipient in Denver, the Bishop Richard Allen Center.

⟜ On September 17 I logged in my diary that in one week I had visited eleven cities in seven states. My events had included the ceremonial receiving of the Olympic Flag in Atlanta for the 1996 games (which George also attended); eight fund-raisers; five school, library, or literacy events; two cultural centers; three rallies; and one fair. Yes, I was exhausted. Several times during September I noted in my diary that both George and I feel very good on the road and discouraged when we get back to Washington. The reception on the hustings was great, but bad press "inside the Beltway" got us down.

September 28—I am flabbergasted by this campaign. We are allowing the Clinton campaign and the press to walk all over us. George Bush has been a great president. Interest rates are at a 20-year low; inflation ¼th of the 1980 levels; the U.S. is the world's number 1 exporting nation; George negotiated a North American Free Trade Agreement (NAFTA) with Canada and Mexico which will open more markets for U.S. goods and create more jobs; overall drug use is down by 13%; more assistance in drug crop destruction; tougher law enforcement against drug dealers; net farm income at record levels and government supports have declined; a transportation bill that will pump millions of dollars in the economy, create hundreds of thousands of jobs and strengthen the infrastructure of our country; the first Clean Air Act in a decade; 1990 Child Care Bill; a revolutionary Americans with Disabilities Act; a Civil Rights Bill with no quotas; on George's watch the Cold War and the nuclear nightmare have ended and he won the release of the hostages in Lebanon; he helped bring about the end of the civil war in El Salvador; he restored a democratically elected president to Panama and the victory in the Persian Gulf made us all proud; he vetoed 33 bills that would have cost the American public billions of dollars. He did all this with the Congress bucking him on every positive program he sent to them. The Congress, Democratically controlled, on the other hand, has been found to be filled with corruption, check kiting, drug and sex scandals. It has all been swept under the rug, covered up. I do not understand it!

As you can see, I was frustrated. So we would just get back out there on the road and try harder.

One of the most fun, exhausting, and interesting things we did was take train trips across the Midwest and later in the South. The first one, in late September, began in Columbus, Ohio, and included five scheduled stops and one impromptu. We learned right away that after every rally stop, we had to get back on the train and wait twenty minutes while the press corps reboarded. There were around two hundred traveling with us, and they had quite a distance to go to get back to their cars. As the train pulled out of the station we would go back to the caboose and wave:

Then I thought I would work on my computer. Not at all. People lined the tracks at every intersection waving and cheering. We ended by standing on the back of the train and waving for hours. It was exhausting, but fun. If the crowd was big we were sad that we couldn't stop or slow down. There were some Clinton/Gore people out, not many, and they were friendly. There were two who mooned us. I thought that was quite funny and certainly different!! One man, who was on a pickup truck in the middle of a field with several children, dropped his pants and mooned us while his wife took pictures. Great example for the kids. The train tracks in Ohio and Michigan go by many attractive homes. Many families were having picnics and waving flags as we went by. There were "Where's Millie?" signs. Many people ran along the track or rode bikes alongside of the train until the road ran out. People stood on hilltops with flags as we went by. All along the 130 miles people put pennies on the track and the minute we went by children were collecting the flattened pennies as souvenirs of the Presidential train. The leaves are beginning to change and we love the beauty.

On a smaller scale, I took several bus trips with Nancy Ellis, Doro, Margaret, and Noelle. We each would give a short talk and then work the crowd. I spoke first, introducing Nan, who spoke as a sister and then introduced Margaret, who spoke as a teacher and daughter-in-law and then introduced Doro, who spoke as a daughter and then introduced Noelle, the cleanup hitter, who spoke as a granddaughter.

We had great crowds every place we went in Illinois, Wisconsin, Ohio, Pennsylvania, and New Jersey.

October 3—This morning I am absolutely convinced that George is going to lose. It is wrong, but all the press are printing such negative things. I will miss the White House life, but I can already feel a little splurge of excitement about going home to Neil and Sharon, friends, to play golf, and to setting up a home in Houston. I could die for my George, who has been a superb president and will go down in history as a great leader for the free world. The momentum is so strong against him.

October 8—Great news. The *Weekly Reader* Poll came out and George wins 55% of the vote. They have never been wrong since Ike's day. The only good poll I've seen. Gosh how I hate all this!!

October 11—23 MORE DAYS TO GO!
. . . This morning George said to me, "The hill may be too high to climb." I don't like to hear him say that, but I certainly have felt that he was going to lose. I have this terrible feeling that he is worrying about me. He needn't. Wherever he is, I will be happy. I will just hurt for him.

In October, there were three debates among George, Bill Clinton, and Ross Perot, who had jumped back into the race. They all run together in my mind. My memories are of lots of tension on all sides, lots of advice, and great relief when they were over. We always felt George did well. I also felt that it was a crime to let Ross Perot be there. He had not gone through the primary process, but had just bought his way in, and out, and back in. The morning after the first debate in St. Louis I wrote:

I can still hear (Perot's) voice: "Those people sit up there in Washington with their pointy little heads and don't do anything. Send me up and I'll set up my town meetings and by Christmas we'll have things going." Bill Clinton sat there smiling and loving all the cutting down Ross was doing of George.

The Richmond, Virginia, debate was the toughest for George. The audience was chosen by a polling firm but didn't seem to represent a cross section of our country. As far as we could tell, there were no businessmen or -women or any small businesses represented:

> It was a funny set-up. Carole Simpson, the moderator, asked George to answer first every time and then gave no rebuttal time. The questions were things like "Mr. President, do you care? Do you really care about people?" As George is not too great about tooting his own horn, he did not hit this one out of the ballpark and I think he knew it. Generally speaking we thought he won that one, also. But then we always thought he won.

Something very touching happened right before the Richmond debate. Earlier that day, while I was visiting a bowling alley, a Vietnam veteran gave me a poem and his medal and asked me to give it to George to carry at the debate that night. That touched George. He did carry it, and after the election sent it back to the owner. I know that he felt that he let this veteran and all others down when he lost the election.

The next morning after the debate George P. and I left to campaign together in Texas. On the way down he worked on his talk, and Anna Perez suggested that he add something personal as he had done at the convention. We didn't know what he had come up with until the first stop and we heard his talk:

> Last night at the debate someone asked my grandfather if he cared. He cares all right. Once when I was playing baseball someone yelled "Get the *spick* off the field." That really hurt, and I told my dad. He told his dad and my grandfather cried. He believes you judge people for themselves and not for their skin.

It almost killed me to hear that story and yet think of how many children of all heritages have had that same thing happen.

I went to the third debate, in East Lansing, Michigan, with Jeb and Marvin. The only thing I really remember is that Ross Perot accused the Republican party of investigating his children. That is not true. He also had accused us of trying to ruin his daughter's wedding by doctoring some pictures of her. That's just plain nutty. Margot and his children always have been friends, and for them to even suggest that was wrong, and I told Ross that after the debate. He didn't answer me.

He continued his accusations during a "60 Minutes" interview later in the month, then he said the next morning that he had no proof. NO PROOF! After spending part of the debate and twenty minutes on "60 Minutes" talking about nothing else!

There also was one vice presidential debate, and we thought that Dan Quayle was great. He was very relaxed and called Al Gore several times on untruths. It was a good debate and exchange between two good men. Politically, I do not agree with Al Gore, but I would agree that he is a fine, decent man. I am afraid that all Americans remember that debate because it became apparent that retired Admiral Jim Stockdale, Perot's running mate, was physically not in shape to run for public office. I had much respect for this man, and it was a shame that he was put in that position.

While all of this was going on, we also were celebrating a very important event in Washington: the two hundredth anniversary of the laying of the White House cornerstone. Curator Rex Scouten and his staff, who did such a superb job taking care of the White House and preserving its history, headed up the celebration, and we had a variety of interesting and educational events.

One of my favorites was the "Very Special Arts" art exhibit. Disabled students from across the country were told about the White House, and then asked to draw their impressions. The winners from all fifty states and the territories came to the White House and had their art on display. Some of the pictures were very good; some were very simple. But they all were special. Many had pictures of Millie, George, and me. My favorite was of a state dinner. In the middle was a little black girl surrounded by a king and queen and then George and me. The artist had made herself the guest of honor. It was so sweet. Another little girl explained to me that her painting was of a dance at the White House. George and I were there, along with Barbie and Ken, and several of her other heroes. I asked who the person was with her back to the front, and she said it was she. When I asked why she had not let us see her face, she answered, "I was looking at you."

On October 13, we buried a time capsule to be opened in one hundred years. George wrote a letter, and I put in *Millie's Book*.

Also that fall, Julie Cooke of my office was spearheading one of my favorite projects: inviting fourth grade students in District of Columbia public schools to the White House for special tours. We actually had begun this program in January of 1992, and before it ended, well over nine thousand students came through. Even though some of them lived just blocks away, they had never visited the People's House, and we were thrilled to give them this opportunity.

A lot of thought and volunteer hours went into this program. Before they arrived, for example, the classes were sent a packet to help them prepare for their visit, including a video. United Bus Owners of America and Gold Line Tours provided free transportation for the students, and Merrill Lynch donated books about the White House to each school's library.

We set aside Monday, the day the White House is closed to the public, for the tours. The students arrived through the "front door," the North Portico, and when they reached the Grand Foyer, the Marine Band played "Hail to the Chief." National Park Service guides then ushered the students through the State Floor. Each room was set up to illustrate a different White House function. In the East Room, for example, students participated in a mock bill signing. Boys and girls were chosen to play the parts of White House characters, such as the president, a congressman, a press person, and so forth. I remember that the Red Room had some hidden things the children were supposed to look for, and the State Dining Room had two tables set as they would look for a state dinner. The "President" and "Head of State" toasted each other.

We learned the hard way to give the students their chocolate chip cookies as they were leaving the White House to go out to the South Grounds. Millie, Ranger, and I sometimes caught up with them there. They took home with them a booklet of interesting facts and games.

Some lucky classes got to witness actual White House events. For example, one class witnessed a signing ceremony in the Rose Garden with President Bush, and several groups of students watched the helicopter land on the South Lawn.

Many of the kids wrote us letters after their visits. They talked about how great the guides, band, and cookies were. Comments on the music ranged from "wonderful" to "cool" to "the best I have ever heard." The cookies rated "quite good," "very, very, very, very good," to "MMM-MMM good." Many thanked *me* for baking them. One boy knew better. He said, "Never fire the cook."

Here are some of my other favorite lines:

"Thank you for inviting us to your humble home. Maybe Mr. Bush can come over and play Nintendo."

"You keep the grass a nice length."

"Do you pay rent?"

"You have a nice dog. She is as beautiful as you are."

October 22—Marvin Bush's birthday.

12 MORE DAYS TO GO.

Such a sad day. Our truly precious friend Betty Liedtke died. This breaks my heart for Hugh, for their children and all of us—her friends. Betty was the best kind of friend. I hurt for Mildred (Kerr), Bessie (Liedtke), Sidney (Hover)—and me. I can hear her saying, "Say, Bar . . ." and then something funny. After much discussion it was decided that Pop would go to the funeral. He wanted to be there for Hugh. I thought about Betty all day and smiled. When she came to the White House for a State Dinner she wore a large, maybe 3 inch by 4 inch, obviously plastic diamond on a ring around her neck. When I kidded her about it she said, "Oh, you like it? Why then I'll wear the bracelet that goes with it." And she did. I wondered all night what the people sitting with her thought!! She laughed at everything and yet was loving and caring all the time.

October 25—The polls look bad, but I just know that when the people get in that booth, they will vote for George. Look at the alternate choices.

I feel guilty. George is on the trail and will go until the end. I went out to see Sam play in a baseball game. I was so impressed with the feeling of good sportsmanship we saw. Both teams were going to have a picnic after the game. It was a great family feeling. I couldn't help but think that just a year ago Bobby Koch was not engaged—and now he is married, coaching a baseball team, father of two, having a baby and voting for a Republican for president. What a joy for our family.

. . . George got home last night around 10:20. He was dead. He signed 33 bills and did some mail. He tried to stay awake to the end of the (World Series) game. Toronto won in the 11th. That's good news as a Republican wins when the American League wins. He fell asleep before the end of the game. He feels good about the campaign.

. . . People are pulling back from George—(Terry) Considine in

Colorado and (Senator) D'Amato in NYC. It is so ugly. He understands it. I don't.

Just when I thought the pressure and long hours were unbearable, something would happen to break the tension and make me feel better. I'll never forget when I did the Larry King show. Larry and I talked a while, then we took calls. The first four callers were anti-Bush, and I said to Larry, sort of kidding, "Where are the Bush people?" The next two callers were pro-Bush. I should have asked sooner! Millie went along with me and lay quietly at my side the whole time. Larry asked me if she was always that good, and as the camera focused on a sleeping dog, I said, "Always." When we left the studio, Peggy Swift and Anna Perez were in hysterics, for Millie had thrown up the minute the camera turned away from her. How awful for whoever found that little gift!

Toward the end of the campaign Marvin traveled with me quite a bit, which was a lifesaver. He is such good company and kept us laughing. And for a guy who truly hates politics, he is a great campaigner and speaker. During one of my interviews I looked up and there was Marvin in a Barbara Bush rubber mask. It was such a thing of beauty.

We worked mall after mall and shook thousands of hands. People waited hours to see us. I found myself thinking again: I just know he is going to win.

Then Margaret told me that Marshall's teacher called to ask if she could help prepare Marshall for either contingency, win or lose.

The last week we literally crisscrossed the country and ran into family and friends everywhere we went. I did unending radio, TV, and print interviews.

October 30—5 MORE DAYS TO GO!!!
. . . In New Jersey a reporter told me that the CNN Poll said we were within a point of Clinton.

October 31—I met up with George in Wisconsin finally and he had a dreadful cold. Several of his group have had the worst flu. He has had both. I thought he had a fever, but he had to get up and do a live Larry King show for an hour and a half.
. . . He did a superb job in spite of the darndest allegations from the Walsh Committee, the independent prosecutor's second indictment

of Cap Weinberger, and some suggestions about George. There is nothing new, but it feels as though it has brought our momentum to a halt. The Congress has already spent 42 million dollars looking into the "Arms for Hostages" deal and found absolutely nothing wrong with George and yet new allegations are brought up the Friday before the election? Now come on!! George had the Congressional Report of 1987, which is open to the public—the whole testimony—nothing new. This was looked into by the Tower Commission, the Congress and the Walsh Committee.

This dreadful man finally handed in his report in January 1994 after spending a reported $100 million of taxpayers' money. He went out swinging at everything and everyone in sight, but with absolutely no proof of wrongdoing. There was none to find.

ℝ I spent the Monday before Election Day campaigning with Marvin in Iowa, North Dakota, and Colorado, then home to Houston and George. It was over.

I wrote that night that I did not believe we would win, but I'm not sure I believed it. George woke up on Election Day and said that he still thought he was going to win. I must say that I thought he would, too. All that gloom and doom in the diary was just a way to protect myself. I know this all sounds mixed up—and it was. I just could not believe that when people got in the booth they wouldn't look at the three men and vote for George.

We voted early, then I visited with Jack and Bobbie Fitch for a while. I exercised, napped, visited with the family. In late afternoon, George W. told us, based on the exit polls, it was over; we would lose. Election evening dear Bill Moss had a buffet supper for family and friends. It was not easy.

Later that night we went to the hotel for George to make a concession speech. It was short and generous. When we saw all our dear friends who had been loyal for years, it really hurt. Our boys had killed themselves for us. I was glad that all their states had gone for George. George W. and Jeb had devoted almost full time to their dad. Marvin also worked hard, but he is more like me and couldn't stand to watch the news. Neil, all the wives, Doro, and Bobby all had worked. Noelle and George P. had actively campaigned. It was hardest of all on Neil and Sharon, who had longed to campaign but had to keep a low profile because of the vicious and untrue attacks on Neil. Margaret and Doro could not stop weeping. It hurt.

The week before the election Doro told me that a little classmate had said to Ellie, "Your grandfather is going to lose." The teacher told Doro that five-year-old Ellie just stood there shaking, fists clenched, and then she took her paintbrush, raised her arm, and starting at the face, painted the girl red with one big swipe! The teacher said that Ellie looked so frustrated. I knew the feeling. How I wanted to get my hands on a paintbrush.

≈ Why did we lose? George Bush says it was because he didn't communicate as well as his predecessor or successor. I just don't believe that.

I think we lost because people really wanted a change. We had had twelve years of a Republican presidency. The Cold War was over, and now it was time to turn our attention toward the home front and the many problems that were and are facing our country. People were worried about jobs and the economy. There was an impression that George was more interested in foreign affairs and did not have a domestic program, which was not true. He had accomplished so much, and still had so much he wanted to do. But that was the impression.

For more than a year, George had been attacked by five Democrats, one Republican, and one Independent. I think people began to believe what they heard.

And the press. I honestly believe that most of them wanted Bill Clinton to win. He was one of them—baby boomers. Many of them had shared experiences with him, including the Vietnam War protest. David Broder told *The Los Angeles Times* after the election: "The feeling was that a second Bush term would be boring . . . for a lot of reporters of (Clinton's) generation, there was a sense of anticipation: 'Our folks are going to be in charge.'"

An excellent example of what Dave was talking about is Strobe Talbott. Strobe and Bill Clinton were college roommates at Oxford. They were friends. His wife traveled with Hillary during the campaign. That was okay, but Strobe also was an editor at *Time* magazine. Today he is the number two man at the State Department.

Another example was the "MacNeil/Lehrer Newshour," where Mark Shields represented the Democratic side and David Gergen the Republican side. I would listen in shock, waiting for Dave to speak up in George's defense. He hardly ever did. It turned out, of course, that David Gergen, who also was an editor at *U.S. News and World Report*, announced after the campaign that he voted for Bill Clinton and was not a Republican but an Independent. He also said that they had been friends for years, having met at the annual Renaissance Weekend held over New Year's. Today he is a senior adviser in President Clinton's White House.

And then there was Rick Kaplan, who produced ABC's "Prime Time Live" while helping advise the Clinton campaign, according to *Los Angeles Times* reporter Tom Rosenstiel's book *Strange Bedfellows.*

It all added up to some very lopsided reporting at times, which simply was not fair. I recently heard ABC's Brit Hume say on C-SPAN that the media greatly exaggerated the state of the economy during the election; he called it a "dark chapter in the recent history of the American media."

A study conducted by the University of California at Irvine found that campaign coverage of George in the three major news magazines from May 1991 to November 1992 was 17 percent favorable, 75 percent unfavorable. For Bill Clinton, coverage was 60 percent favorable, 34 percent unfavorable.

Yes, many reporters did do a fair job of covering the campaign— in fact, too many to mention. But I will be honest in telling you that the overall experience has left a bad taste in my mouth about the media, and makes me question what I read. I hate that. I respect and like many members of the press. I just wish I could respect more of what they do.

25

"One Last Time"

The trip home on Wednesday was sad. The three grandchildren who were with us, Marshall, Ellie, and Sam, watched movies on the plane. The Secret Service and the staff were sweet and didn't quite know how to act. George worked all the way back, writing notes, making phone calls, and generally cheering everyone up. It might have been easier if he had kicked somebody.

Our helicopter landed at the Pentagon and we drove to the White House, with Marvin and Margaret in the car with us. As we crossed Memorial Bridge, two military men who were jogging stopped and saluted when they saw the car. For the first and only time, I saw George's face crumble. He slammed his fist into his palm and said a few profane words. I knew that he felt he had let down the men and women in the military. We felt his anguish and were crushed.

By the time we arrived at the White House he had recovered. The Quayles met us at the bottom of the South Lawn and we walked up through a crowd of supporters and staff. They were very dear to welcome us home, but it wasn't easy to go through that. George, as usual, tried to be funny. When the cheering died down, he went to the microphone and said something like, "Haven't you guys heard? We lost."

Brent Scowcroft and Jim Baker came upstairs to have a drink in the West Hall Sitting Room and saved the day. They told us that Ross Perot had called them both because he wanted George to know that he had led "his people" in three cheers (hip, hip, hurrahs) for George on election night. He felt that George wouldn't have seen it because it happened at the time he was giving his concession speech. What an amazing, insensitive man!

Everything we did after the election had a "this is the last time we will ever do this" feeling. It also was an extraordinarily busy period. The mail was tremendous—we tried hard to answer it all—and our phone rang nonstop:

. . . Many Heads of State are calling in and George is assuring them that Bill Clinton will be great. I'm not so sure.

We have seen pictures of Saddam Hussein dancing in the streets of Baghdad and former Prime Minister Shamir (of Israel) is rejoicing and says that George deserves it. He blames his defeat on George.

. . . Goldwater says that it was the worst campaign that he had ever seen. He should certainly know. His campaign in 1964 was a lulu!

But Jimmy Carter takes the cake and I quote the Atlanta/Reuters Report: "Jimmy Carter said that he would not accept a 'permanent position,' such as a Cabinet job in Bill Clinton's administration. But Carter said that he would be willing to accept an 'ad hoc' advisory position in a Clinton administration, perhaps on foreign policy issues. Carter said he considers Clinton's victory more a rejection of President Bush than an endorsement of Clinton, who won with a minority of the popular vote"!! I'm sure that endeared Carter to Clinton! George wrote under that clipping in a note to Brent Scowcroft: "Brent, Jimmy Carter is one gracious fellow, managing to p.o. both Clinton and me in one sentence!"

. . . Nancy Reagan called to assure me that the Cindy Adams column saying that she was going to vote for Ross Perot was not true. (Hadn't seen it.)

The first weekend after the election we went to Camp David with family and friends. George's brother Johnny and his wife, Jody, came, and we watched movies and relaxed. Colin and Alma Powell came for one night with two of their children, a daughter-in-law, and one grandson. He and George talked of many things. One conversation that I remember was about homosexuals in the service and how difficult that would be for Colin. He was opposed, as was George. This is part of the generation gap that I think was one cause of our defeat.

It was interesting that Bill Clinton's first pronouncement was on this issue, when he said they should be allowed into the military. In fairness, I suspect that he was asked many things in a press conference and this one answer was highlighted. Should homosexuals be denied the right to serve their country? There are many pros and cons, but like Bill Clinton, I have never been in the service and so have little to base my judgment on.

Later, when it came time to deal with the issue, General Powell, a good soldier and a great man, obeyed his Commander in Chief.

George spent a lot of time on the phone that weekend thanking people for their help and comforting them. I hated how everyone was attacking and blaming the campaign and George for the loss.

Exactly one week after the election we attended the Senate Republican Dinner on the Hill honoring George and Dan Quayle. Senate Minority Leader Bob Dole, a great war hero and certainly a congressional hero of the Bush/Quayle years, was the host and had us very close to breaking down. No man ever served his president more loyally or with more grace under very difficult circumstances. With the Democrats controlling both houses of Congress, every piece of legislation was an uphill battle. We saw many of our friends who had started out with us in politics, and now it was time to start saying good-bye. It was an emotional evening.

The very next day we left for a long weekend on Gasparilla Island in Florida with Will and Sarah Farish and Sarah's great parents, Mary and Bayard Sharp. We golfed, fished, and most important, spent time surrounded by good friends. Millie and Ranger went, too, and we took glorious early-morning walks on the beaches and golf course.

I went directly from there to Houston and looked for the perfect house for two old retired people. I stayed with Bobbie and Jack Fitch and saw twenty-two houses in a day and a half. They were either too grand, too expensive, or not what we wanted. The long and the short of it was that we decided to build a "patio" house on our own property, a tiny lot that has great neighbors. This was the same lot everybody had been saying for years was too small to build on, so there was something sort of fun in doing just that.

On November 19 George flew up to Greenwich, Connecticut, with Doro to see his darling mother, who had slipped into semiconsciousness. They sat and held her hand for several hours and told her that they loved her, which she well knew. No mother has ever been more loved than Dorothy Walker Bush by her children—and her in-laws, I might add.

That afternoon Hillary Rodham Clinton came by the White House for her tour. She was very easy to be with and, I believe, we had a good visit. We talked about the office, the mail volume, and Chelsea. I suggested that she might bring a cousin or a best friend to spend the first year and go to school with Chelsea. It's a big lonely house for one little girl.

Then I went downstairs to join George on the State Floor while he received the credentials of the new ambassadors and I had tea with their wives and children. Upstairs, Hillary was going through the White House with Chief Usher Gary Walters and two or three people who were going to help her with decorating.

At the end of the credentials ceremony I was slipped a piece of paper saying that George's mother had gently passed away. I am so glad that he had been with her that day.

The next day I flew to Atlanta to campaign for Paul Coverdell, who was in a run-off race for the U.S. Senate. Paul had been our campaign chairman in Georgia in 1980, and he served George as director of the Peace Corps. He and his wife Nancy were good friends, so even though I had sworn off politics for life, I couldn't say no. Nor did I want to. He did us proud by winning that race and has been a fine addition to the U.S. Senate.

I headed straight for Camp David, where George had planned a big weekend, including a Vespers service with Amy Grant. He had invited five Republican governors and wives who had been such good friends and worked so hard for us: Bill and Susan Weld of Massachusetts; Tommy and Sue Ann Thompson of Wisconsin; Jock McKernan and Olympia Snowe of Maine; Carroll and Iris Campbell of South Carolina; and John and Janet Ashcroft of Missouri.

In addition we had the Sununus, plus Bruce Willis, Demi Moore, and their two children. Amy, her husband, mother, and baby made up the rest of the house party. Where they all slept, I do not know. Amy and her wonderful guitar-playing husband, Gary Chapman, performed with the Camp David choir. John Ashcroft, then the Governor of Missouri, got up and sang a great, rousing gospel song. George also invited an additional fifty or so people—all good friends and people who had worked hard—to come for the service. Frankly, I had dreaded the weekend. I was tired with a deep fatigue from defeat, death, and the uncertainty of getting out of the White House on time. As usual, George had done all the planning and all the work and the whole weekend turned out to be a joy.

That Sunday afternoon at the White House we had our last "National Literacy Honors" evening that ABC-TV has sponsored for several years, and later that week we announced at a White House luncheon the latest Barbara Bush Foundation for Family Literacy grant recipients. This was not the last such announcement, of course, since the foundation would go on, but it was our last time at the White House.

On Monday we had the happiest, most loving funeral for George's mother, surrounded by family and friends of this magnificent woman. It was a beautiful day as we laid her to rest by her beloved Pres and our little Robin.

All our children with the exception of Sharon, who had another commitment, came to the funeral. The boys were wonderful and kept us laughing and crying on the plane going up and coming back. John Bush gave me an envelope with George's name on it that had been found in Mom's safe. In it were a group of letters that George had written his mother and father over the years. Everything George is, is so much a part of his Ma and Pa.

Ten years before her death Mom had written her children a letter "to be opened at her death" describing in minute detail her very modest funeral plans. Her last instructions were: "Let us after the benediction rise and sing gaily, as we depart, that lovely hymn we sang at Pres' service, 'Hark, Hark My Soul.'"

November 23—The third quarter growth figures were announced today. When George announced that the growth would be 2.7%, the Clinton campaign said that George was doctoring the numbers and guess what? When the figures came out for the third quarter the numbers were 3.9%, better by far than George said. Every time George suggested that things were getting better he was accused by one and all of "being out of touch."

Having said that (and feeling better because I said it), we are both looking forward to getting on with the next phase of our lives. I *AM* panicked about getting out of here on time, but I will.

George, Brent, and I went to Kennebunkport for Thanksgiving. It was a quiet, reflective weekend, and although it was cold, we three plus Kenny Raynor, our dear friend and the golf pro at Cape Arundel Golf Course, ran around the course every day playing eighteen holes of golf. And I mean ran. I was so flattered to be included, but then just how many nuts do you know who would drop everything and run around a wet, cold golf course with five minutes' notice? As the club was closed, the dogs were allowed to come with us and ran miles.

We went to our little winter church on Sunday, and as George walked to the door, the whole congregation came to its feet clapping. I could hardly walk in and had trouble controlling my tears.

It wasn't long before we were in the thick of the Christmas season. On December 1, Marvin and Margaret's little Walker joined me and Joe Riley, chairman of the Pageant of Peace, to put the star on top of the National Christmas Tree. I should have gained a place in the Guinness Book of Records as this was my twelfth year to do this.

On Sunday we hosted our fourth and final Kennedy Center Honors reception and then attended the celebration. This was always an evening of great pleasure and performances. So many superb members of the entertainment world have been honored on this evening in the past. This year's honorees were Lionel Hampton, Paul Newman, Joanne Woodward, Ginger Rogers, Paul Taylor, and Mstislav Rostropovich. Lionel and Slava Rostropovich were very dear to us, so this was a happy "last time" for us. At the very end, Master of Ceremonies Walter Cronkite gave a lovely, kind tribute to George.

George had such fun that week planning a surprise for the White House staff. He invited Dana Carvey, the funny "Saturday Night Live" George Bush impersonator, to go to the Kennedy Center Honors and then spend the night with us. He then called a White House–wide staff meeting for 9 A.M. Monday, which set the East and West Wings to buzzing. What was going to happen? Was he going to resign early? You name it, they thought of it!

The staff all gathered in the East Room, and at the appointed hour, the Marine Band played "Hail to the Chief" and in marched that tiny Dana Carvey. The room broke up. What followed was an hour of Dana imitating George and George imitating Dana imitating George. It was very funny, and really helped break the tension that had permeated the place since the election.

Later that morning we officially opened the Christmas season with the traditional showing of the decorations to the White House Press Corps. The theme was "Gift Givers," and the geniuses in the flower shop had dressed about ninety sixteen-inch dolls in authentic costumes of gift-givers through the centuries, starting with the Magi.

As usual, I prayed that I wouldn't make any news when talking to the press. I only made a little when I told them that they have no sense of humor and I thought they made up some of their sources who "wish to remain anonymous." They of course argued with me. I do think one easy way to improve reporters' credibility would be if they all agreed not to use anonymous sources. Only people who are willing to stand behind what they say should be quoted.

I went to my last Toys for Tots party, and was so surprised when General Walt Boomer, the assistant commandant of the Marine Corps and the general who had shown us around the Saudi Arabian desert on Thanksgiving Day, met me at the door. He had such kind words about George, which I appreciated very much.

While all of this was going on George was still consumed with the duties of being President. He had announced the previous week that in cooperation with a United Nations resolution, he was sending American troops into Somalia for "Operation Restore Hope," to help end the starvation there. The food we had been sending to those desperate people had not been getting through, and hundreds of thousands of people were starving or being killed. Before he made his decision, George first consulted with Bill Clinton.

It was around this time that I decided I would write my memoirs. Our lawyer, Terri Lacy, came to Camp David to talk about the future, and I sort of panicked when I realized what was ahead. There is no government money for any expenses of a former First Lady—as there shouldn't be—and I wondered how I was going to manage to answer my mail and cope with public appearance requests. What to do? An answer sort of fell in my lap. I got several very generous offers for my book and also some speech requests, which would help me pay for a couple of helpers. But then I worried how to give speeches, write a book, travel with George, build a house, run a house, play golf, be a good friend and a mother, grandmother, and wife all in one lifetime? Terri assured me that it would all work out, and it has. My troubles were minute compared to the ones George faced: paying for a new house and keeping up Kennebunkport, answering huge stacks of mail, a demanding speaking schedule, and so on. They, too, have worked out, thanks to George's amazing energy and his staff.

December 11—MEDAL OF FREEDOM AWARDS. Johnny Carson, wife and sons stayed with us. They are so nice. I later heard that Johnny said that the Lincoln Bed (an overlong double) was the closest he had slept with anybody in years. I'm sure that other guests feel that way, but like Johnny, are so thrilled to sleep in the Lincoln Bedroom, they are willing to forgo the sleep.

. . . Blair House. This party was to be a surprise thank you for Brent and it was. It was also a surprise for George Bush. I think that Jon Howe got them both to agree to come to honor each other. Then Admiral Jonathan Howe, the quiet gentle No. 2 at the NSC, gave a great talk and we were very moved. He said that General Sherman said about Lincoln that which he would say about George: "Of all the men I ever met he seemed to me to possess more of the elements of greatness combined with goodness than any other." I loved that. Because, God knows, George Bush is all that and more.

On December 13 we attended for the last time "Christmas in Washington," the marvelous star-studded annual NBC event that benefits Children's Hospital. Spike and Betsy Heminway came from Greenwich, Connecticut; Ken and Linda Lay from Houston; and Reverend Pat Adams from Kennebunkport for the evening. We also invited for dinner George's respected friend Jack Welch, head of General Electric, and Bob Wright, CEO of NBC. It was so much fun to share that great house with friends, and we just wish now we had shared it with even more. (I can hear the White House staff laughing—George kept the house pretty full.)

John and Norma Major came to spend a night at Camp David, along with two of his top aides, Stephen Wall and Gus O'Donnell, and Brent Scowcroft and his daughter Karen. We are devoted to the Majors, and it was a warm farewell to two great friends.

We hosted the usual evening Christmas receptions, which took on an even more special meaning. We knew so many of the staff would scatter around the United States.

Then we took our whole little family to Camp David for one

last Christmas. Not so little, I guess. We had two grandchildren when George was elected vice president, and we had grown to twelve in 1992. It was a very, very happy time. These wonderful children look forward to being with their cousins, and this year they once again put on a play written by Jenna and Barbara. Six-year-old Pierce, Neil and Sharon's son, played Santa in a glued-on beard and a Santa cap. He has the dearest, smiling face, reddish hair, glasses, and the deepest voice that you ever have heard on a little boy. As in so many things in life, the planning was almost as much fun as the actual doing. Several days were spent in secret play rehearsals, costume and prop preparation. Then there was the well-known snowball fight where George got a black eye from a snowball that had a tiny piece of ice in it. The guilty party was so upset that George swore her to secrecy and he, in turn, never told on her. She didn't do it on purpose! Santa was good to us all.

George went hunting in Beeville, Texas, and I really started into some serious packing and sorting, although most of the work was done by the White House staff.

On January 1 George went to Somalia to visit the troops, and I joined him in Russia for the signing of the START II treaty, the broadest disarmament pact in history, according to the press. Among other things, it barred all Intercontinental Ballistic Missiles, the dreadful rockets that had scared the wits out of generations of kids all over the world.

We stayed at Spaso House and I am happy to report that repairs have started. It is still ugly, but they have started. Our guest room was the same, horrid brown curtains. It did look cleaner. I must say that brown sheets turn me off a little. Having said all these mean things, the water was piping hot, we had plenty of blankets, the beds were comfortable, I couldn't see the sheets (when my eyes were closed) and we slept like logs.

As Yogi Berra would say, "It was déjà vu all over again." We went to the Kremlin to the same building that the Gorbachevs had entertained us in. Naina and Boris met us at the door and we marched up that enormous red carpeted staircase past those very elite blond soldiers who stand with their noses up in the air, knees locked and their bodies leaning stiffly forward. They follow with their eyes the Head of State, looking down their noses all the time. Fascinating.

Same reception room, receiving line and on into that beautiful Facet room. This time I noticed what looked like delicate wrought iron chandeliers, but turned out to be solid silver that had blackened with time. I sat next to Boris and the mustached Vice President (Aleksandr Rutskoi), who I understand is giving Boris a very hard time.

. . . Sad to say they did not serve caviar as they did in the old days when you just shoveled it out on your plate. Boris talked mostly to George, which was all right as that was what we had come for. He did tap my foot just to remind me of our little game. He did tell George that he'd like to come to Kennebunkport. We said that we'd love to have him (and we would), but that it had to be a private visit.

Naina, Susan Baker, and I toured a little more of that beautiful Kremlin and then joined the men for the signing of the START II treaty. I know that George felt a personal satisfaction over that signing and it was a thing of pride for me.

On the way home we stopped in Paris for a few hours to say good-bye to François Mitterrand. The men talked and then had a press conference which both François and George handled with humor and warmth.

. . . On into cocktails. My, but the French do it well. Their canapés look and taste delicious, small, bite-sized, and they manage to avoid the plastic look that we have perfected. Dinner was even better, ending with the lightest, most delicious dessert.

. . . François was very funny and relaxed. He told several stories about his being a prisoner during WWII. He also told us a story about how Margaret Thatcher asked Ronald Reagan why she had not been invited to the 200th anniversary of the Revolutionary War Victory at Yorktown. I don't know if the story was true, but it is funny.

Good-byes are never easy, but when François said: "Good-bye, my dear friend," I was very moved.

That word "good-bye" hung over our heads for the next few weeks; it became a part of everything we did.

(On January 5th) George spoke at West Point. I was so glad that I had decided to go with him. By the time we got there it was a sunny bright day at that glorious spot on the Hudson River after a dreary start. We ate in the most tremendous dining room with the whole corps—

4,000 great-looking kids. We walked to General Graves's house for dessert and coffee and stood on the porch and watched the "Long Gray Line" march by to go to the auditorium where Pop spoke. The speech was well received. Brent went with us, as did Col. Larry Mohr, one of the White House doctors. When Brent went to the academy, the Corps was half its present size. It was such a happy, impressive day.

The next day was our anniversary, and after a full day of official events, we came upstairs for dinner with Marvin, Margaret, Doro and Bobby. All four grands came and ate in the kitchen. They are wild and enjoy each other. How I love them and how I am going to miss them!

. . . Then one of those magic moments happened. Marvin asked us to go to the first floor with him and there was the "President's Own," the Marine Band, all ready and they played and the household staff sang "Happy Anniversary to you." They had stayed all that time while we had dinner. It was so sweet, private and personal. The grands danced, and George and I were very touched. I wonder if our grandchildren will remember that they danced at the White House on their grandparents' 48th anniversary with the Marine Band playing for them? They passed champagne. It was very thoughtful, and I suspect Gary Walters thought of it. In fact I'm sure he did.

. . . Kitty Brady had the cabinet wives for a final time on the 12th of January at the Treasury Department. This group of ladies have really bonded. I shall miss them a lot.

Marvin and Margaret and their friend Lloyd Hatcher, and Bobby and Doro and all their children, came to Camp David the weekend of January 9 for the last time.

We had very teary good-byes with Doro and Margaret. Doro took her little family to Florida to stay at Betsy and Spike Heminway's. Marvin went to Hawaii with his family to get out of the first strike zone of the Inaugural festivities. I'm afraid that I took for granted those wonderful children and their grandchildren. The drop-in trade at the White House had been a joy. I would hear those little voices around the pool or on the South Grounds and go out to find Sam, Ellie, Marshall with her sidekick, Abigail Meyer, and our little Walky Talk, Walker. I mention Abigail for she adopted us as her "Ganny and Gampy" also and we love her. Marvin, who hates politics, was wonderful about popping by quietly to check on his Dad and be sure he was all right. We will really miss them. That's the bad news. The good news was that we were leaving Doro happily married to the world's nicest man with a great big loving family. And the very best news was that while we were moving away from those children we were moving closer to Neil, Sharon and their children and George, Laura and Barbara and Jenna.

Esther and Dick Moore came up on Saturday night with Andy. It is all so final.

. . . Meanwhile down in Houston, the Fitches, Paula, Barbara Patton, Jack Steel, Don and Ariel are working away trying to make some sense out of all those boxes. What to send to storage and what to unpack. Many phone calls back and forth. Were any two people luckier than George and I? We certainly have good and loyal friends. I am beginning to really look forward to the move.

. . . I had a tea for my staff. So many of them have been with me for twelve years. I get a very heavy feeling in my heart when I think of them, how great they have been and what fun we had all working together . . . I wonder if I still have a brain. We'll certainly find that out and very soon! [I wrote that because I had become so reliant on my staff.]

On January 13 George gave the Medal of Freedom to Ronald Reagan. It was a real reunion of the Reagan White House. We were eager to have a lunch, but they really wanted a large crowd and had to fly back to California that day, so 280 came for the ceremony and refreshments. That was probably just as well:

. . . Saddam Hussein was violating the U.N. sanctions and at 1:20 p.m. British, French and American bombers were going to retaliate and hit missile sites. How we hated to see this happen during our last week, but that, of course, was exactly why it happened. (Saddam thought he could get away with it during the transition.) We just could not let this go by. Needless to say, George consulted with Bill Clinton and got total approval. I later saw Henry Kissinger on the tube and he said that Bill Clinton should be very grateful to George Bush for doing this for him. I also saw people like Donahue who said that George was just trying to regain some of his glory! Baloney!!!

Although all the weeks after the election had been emotionally draining, the last was the worst. I don't know what touched us most, but sometimes the love and support came from very unexpected sources. Shortly before we left, George received a phone call from actor Chevy Chase, whom we knew only casually and who was in town for the inauguration. He told George that although he had not supported him, he felt that George had served his country with honor and he wanted to say "thank you." That really touched George; it was a phone call Chevy didn't have to make.

Certainly anything that had to do with the military hit the tear button as George loved those young men and women. So you can imagine how difficult it was when we went to Fort Myers in Virginia on January 14 for the "Armed Forces Salute to the President."

Doro went with us. When George reviewed the troops for the last time I was almost overwhelmed with emotion. The speeches by Dick Cheney and Colin Powell were absolutely the most warm and touching. I'm not even a member of the bawl team and the tears flooded. Colin's speech:

"Mr. President, there comes a time every so often in a soldier's life when he has to say good-bye to an especially honored, respected and revered leader.

"It is always a profound and emotional moment. Anyone who has ever worn a uniform understands the ties that bind a great sergeant-major, or a ship captain, or a squadron CO to the men and women he leads.

"A loyalty grows in the unit—the loyalty of family—and the heart and soul of each member of that family is touched when the time comes for the leader to depart.

"For the over two million of us who serve in the Armed Forces, such a time has come for us today.

"To be sure, you have been the leader of the *ENTIRE* nation, in all its glorious and trying complexity. You have met the diverse challenges of an historic age and been equal to all of them.

"And yet, sir, despite the breadth of your cares and accomplishments for all Americans, a generation of American soldiers, sailors, Marines, airmen and Coast Guard will always think of you and regard you affectionately above all as *their* leader, *their* president and *their* Commander in Chief.

"That's because you have been unstinting in your faith in us, your pride in us, your respect in what it is we do for the nation.

"You have lived by the code we set for ourselves as warriors: dedication to one's troops, moral integrity, judgment, tenacity, courage . . . and to put it in military terms: DUTY, HONOR, COUNTRY.

"You have sent us into harm's way when you had to, but never lightly, never hesitantly, never with our hands tied, never without giving us what we needed to do the job.

"Your deep concern for the lives and sacrifices of those who serve in America's Armed Forces and their families has been felt in every barracks, on every flight line, in every berthing space of every ship.

"We have fought under your leadership for true and noble causes . . .

". . . In the Cold War, where the enemy was a hostile way of life . . .

". . . In Panama and Iraq, where the enemy was brutal tyranny . . .

". . . In Bangladesh and South Florida, where the enemy was nature's violence . . .

". . . And in Somalia, where the enemy is chaos and unspeakable human misery.

"History will remember you as a stirring leader of this nation in war and in crisis.

"History will remember you well for your leadership in peace-time . . . for your steady efforts to build a strong and capable military . . .

". . . For your steadfast support of the men and women who stand guard day and night, in every far-flung corner of the world, even when the glare of the world's attention is focused elsewhere.

"In 1981 you helped President Reagan begin to correct what the long, neglectful 'hollow force' days of the 70s had done to the spirit and sinews of America's military.

"Under your leadership our weapons have been the best, our magazines full, our training the most demanding and sophisticated in the world. Our leaders from the very top on down understand the use of force and the priceless value of our young men and women.

"America's revitalized forces shall be among your most honored legacies, Mr. President. They shall be the pillar of America's trusted power that you bequeath to the world.

"They shall be one of the tokens of greatness that you leave in tomorrow's history books.

"We are here today to honor you as a leader whom we have served with great pride.

"But no matter how heartfelt I try to make my words here, no matter how stirring this ceremony, no matter how warm our hearts, the honor we can offer in this hall cannot match what's written on the faces of our troops all around the world . . . the faces that America and the world see on their TV screens . . . the faces of courage, professionalism, compassion and hope . . . the bright faces of America's future.

"In their faces is written the highest and truest testimony to your leadership. And for that, Mr. President, the entire nation owes you its most sincere and profound thanks."

This was followed by a ceremony with singing put on by the combined services, and then a representative from each branch came forward and remembered something very personal about George. It was almost more than I could stand. So tender.

That night George's cabinet had a going-away party and presented him with his cabinet chair, his third. George was in the cabinet as UN Ambassador, Vice President, and President of the United States. The chairs are now in his office in Houston and are very handsome. I believe that George would tell you that he was served very well by the distinguished men and women in his cabinet.

. . . Everything is sort of emotional and "last time." Yesterday we left the White House "for the last time" in a helicopter. In like manner we arrived at Camp David for "the last time."

Our last weekend at Camp David was very touching—and very hard. We had become so close to the service families who lived there, and we had many good memories with friends and family. For four years we jokingly had called it "Camp Marvin," since he had complained in jest one time that if President Eisenhower could name the camp for his grandson, why couldn't we change it in his honor.

As usual, we had a campful. Brian and Mila Mulroney and their children came from Canada to say good-bye. George planned one last Vespers service and asked George and Norma Strait and their son Bubba to come participate, and we also invited the Joint Chiefs of Staff and Supreme Court Justices and their spouses; and the heads of both transition teams: Vernon Jordan and Warren Christopher for the Clinton team, and Andy Card, who once again had come to our rescue and headed ours. When it came time for the service, the back of the chapel was filled with young Marine recruits.

We had to start the program without George and Brent Scow-croft, who were on the phone with François Mitterrand, John Major, and other world leaders about the situation in Iraq. George Strait had us laughing when he got all our guests to join in singing "All My Ex-es Live in Texas." Whoever thought that we'd see the members of the Supreme Court and Joint Chiefs singing that funny song. He sang my favorite, "A Father's Love," and ended the program with a song dedicated to George, "The Cowboy Rides Away." I'm sure that it will come as no surprise that we all cried.

The Mulroneys left the next morning after our last church service at the chapel. We said good-bye to Chaplain Jon Frusti, the choir, and all the little children. We had shared so much with them all, and I honestly feel that they are the true meaning of loving families and abiding faith.

George and Norma Strait were scheduled to leave early in the morning, but we found out that they were leaving just so Bubba and George could race home in time to see the football play-off games. George is a rabid Dallas Cowboy fan, as is George Bush, so we persuaded them to stay on for the games and watch on our big screen. Between games Bubba and his dad played Wally Ball. For a very big star—George pulled in a record 87,000 swooning fans at the Houston Astrodome last year—they are the most natural, unspoiled family. George reminded me of our boys.

There was yet another teary good-bye with the Camp David personnel in the helicopter hangar. It was a surprise ceremony with a short speech by the wonderful Commander of the Camp, Joe Camp. (Yes, that's his name.) When it came time for George Bush to speak, he couldn't. I am sure that the Straits wondered just what they had gotten themselves into—a tear-soaked weekend, that's for sure.

On Monday night we had Al and Ann Simpson, Lud Ashley, and Fred and Martha Zeder for dinner. They told awful jokes and everything seemed funnier.

We ate dinner our last night in the White House with Pres, George's older brother, Johnny and Jody Bush, Billy and Ruth Graham, and Bobby Koch. Then we went to bed "one last time" in that glorious house.

26

A New Beginning

There is life after politics! Hurrah!

George and I quickly settled into our little rented house on West Post Oak. We were taken back into the community as if we had never left, and the "welcome home" still continues a year later. Houstonians truly have been loving and kind.

At 7:30 A.M. on January 21, George went to his new office on Memorial Drive to settle in and sort out, among other things, how in the world he was going to answer all his mail. A skeleton crew headed by Rose Zamaria came down with us, and a small army of volunteers—many of whom had helped George with his first congressional campaign—appeared to deal with the seven hundred letters a day that poured in.

I was getting reacquainted with shopping, cooking, and driving after twelve years of living a grand life. George took me out to buy a car and I had lots of fun shopping for the color I liked. Thank heavens he went with me to see that I also got a good car—American made, I might add. As it turns out, driving is something you do not forg*

Now, cooking is a little different. I never loved cooking, jus*at*ing. Why is it when people see someone who is a tad overweigh*they* assume she loves to cook? I don't. I can turn out a meal for fifty*it you* would never go home afterward and say: "WOW! What a*B* I can light the fire and throw something on it. I can bak* cook vegetables. So while we didn't starve, we did h* n meals. George lost two pounds without even trying; I, of course, .idn't.

Just a few days after we moved home George W. and Laura and Neil and Sharon came for dinner. George W. was running the next day in a marathon and requested pasta for dinner. I made a tasteless dish of leftover turkey with a sauce to put over the pasta and served it up. The children kept straight faces, but George couldn't resist and said that he liked his pasta rare. It was just plain undercooked. The next day we watched George W. go racing by mile 19 of the 26.2-mile race and he finished in better than average time—in spite of my cooking.

Another afternoon Lauren, our nine-year-old granddaughter, came over after school. As she is a vegetarian, I decided to show off and use a new juicer we had been given. We cleaned a few carrots and jammed them into the machine along with some celery and a piece of tomato. All seemed well at first, but then suddenly food shot out of the juicer and reached as high as the ceiling and as low as the floor. Lauren couldn't control herself and got the giggles, and so did I.

Sharon came for Lauren just as George walked into the house to find me scraping carrots off of everything. He said not to worry, he had brought dinner home. He had made his first foray to Sam's Club and bought the world's biggest jar of spaghetti sauce and some spaghetti. While he watched the evening news, I continued to clean up my mess and start dinner. I turned around and in my haste knocked off the jar of sauce. Ugh, now I had sauce and glass mixed with the rest of the mess. That was the night George and I made an amazing discovery: You can call out for pizza!

We *were* having a lot of fun taking care of ourselves. We had all the modern equipment and our needs were not great. Paula, our housekeeper of thirty-four years, no longer was living with us, although she still was coming for a few hours every day to help out, and dog-sat when we were out of town.

We both longed to become truly private citizens, but that, I g s, is not to be. We live on a quiet, horseshoe-shaped street, and th urists are a menace. On the weekends there is a steady parade of ars veral amusing things have happened, however. There are two inger spaniels that live on our street. Sometimes they are tied t yard, and people will see them and jump out and have s taken with dogs they think are Millie and Ranger. That

makes me furious, as they are not as handsome as our dogs and because I don't want anyone to think that I would chain our dogs to a tree in the front yard!

Another morning I was walking the dogs in my jogging suit and stopped to talk to our neighbor and friend Jack Fitch. We saw a small bus appearing around the corner and I immediately went and stood behind Jack's brick wall. A woman got off the bus and said, "I hope I'm not imposing, but I have a busload of British tourists. Can they get off and take pictures and talk to you?" Jack told her that she *was* imposing and that she also was breaking the law. She took off fast!

To solve this problem, which was ruining our gentle little street, the neighborhood got together and petitioned for state legislation and a city ordinance that allow us to gate our street. The revised Texas statute says cities can "regulate and restrict access to streets, avenues, alleys and boulevards in the municipality on which the dwelling of a former president of the United States is located, including the installation and maintenance of fences, gates, or other structures." Since there are very few "former presidents," the law does not affect many people. Barbara Patton, a beautiful volunteer in George's office and a neighbor and friend, along with Cassandra Manley, the head of our street association, and Jack Fitch joined forces with the help of many others to get this done.

George and I also changed our house plans to include a six-foot-high brick wall around our tiny drive-in courtyard.

I know that people don't realize how miserable they make the life of people who have been in the public eye, including actors and athletes. Some are kind and courteous, but others can be just plain rude. I have tried hard to get back to real life and am driving and shopping on my own. I know it is out of affection, but to be asked for your autograph, grabbed and hugged, or have your picture taken when you are racing to buy your groceries, or, even worse, something personal in the drugstore, is a little much. Sometimes when someone sidles up to me in a store and says, "Aren't you Barbara Bush?" I answer, "No, she's much older than I am," or sometimes I'll say, "No, but I am mistaken for her all the time," and march on. Often in my wake I can hear a voice say, "See, I told you that wasn't her!" My own grocery store is so used to me that I can shop pretty much like other people.

George, on the other hand, is much nicer than I and would never do that. Eating out can be especially hard at times. He stops eating,

stands up, and is polite to everyone. He and I both love Sam's Club and are dangerous shoppers when we go there. We come out with stacks of paper napkins, office supplies, and huge jars and boxes of everything. However, it takes George hours to shop because he is mobbed.

On February 13 George and I flew to Miami for a much needed rest. He surprised me with something we always said we wanted to try, a cruise. We went on the *Regal Princess*, one of the "Love Boat" ships that advertises on TV. We were met by Captain Cesare Ditel, along with the TV captain, Gavin MacLeod, and the director of the ship company, who had come all the way from England. (The last two did not go on the cruise.) Something incredibly touching happened as we left the harbor: Earlier, George had visited a submarine that was in port, and as we passed by, the sailors were up on deck, saluting their former Commander in Chief.

Our ship had 1,600 guests and 900 staff. We fast learned that we could not walk out the door of our room without George's being swamped with requests for pictures and signatures. But the wonderful Italian captain invited us to use his deck up on the flying bridge during the day and to eat our dinner with him in his quarters. He was charming and we enjoyed that very much.

We worked out early in the gym. I rode the stationary bike and kept my head down reading a book; George jogged around an open deck with a large following. One morning George went into the sauna after his jog and came out stark naked toweling off. There stood a persistent photographer who asked George if he could take his picture! For the first time in his life George Bush said, "Absolutely NOT!"

We got off the ship in San Juan, Puerto Rico, where Governor Pedro Rosselló and his truly beautiful, vivacious wife, Marga, had a dinner for us in a tent under the stars at the Fortaleza. It was one of those magical nights with a cool breeze blowing from the harbor. They kindly let us bring the ship's captain with us. They gathered about seventy of our Puerto Rican friends, including several from the States.

We jumped ship in St. Martin, as planned, and flew to Miami to see Jeb and Colu and their three children. The next morning we went to Deering Bay, a marvelous development that Jeb's great friend and partner, Armando Codina, founded. George played golf with Jeb,

Arnie Palmer, who designed the course, and Joe DiMaggio, who loves golf. Both men are amazingly unspoiled after years of being loved by their fans. After a light lunch the Palmers dropped us off in Jacksonville. Arnold pilots his own Cessna jet, and we love how he makes announcements just like an airline pilot.

George and I had a cozy dinner with June and Dan Jenkins. Dan is a sportswriter who also has written several best-seller books. His latest, *Bubba*, is very funny—I would call it men's humor. Since reading it I sometimes refer to George as "Bubba." Bubba's dad would always come home, plunk down in front of the TV, and then mumble and talk back to the screen. I have occasionally found George Bush doing just that. I myself could be called "Mrs. Bubba" because I don't mumble at the screen, I yell gentle things like "IDIOT" or "FOOL," and feel better for it.

We had come to Jacksonville so I could attend my first meeting of the Board of Trustees of Mayo Foundation. Rochester, Minnesota, is the home base for the Mayo Clinic, but there are satellites in Scottsdale and Jacksonville, where this particular meeting was being held.

I was thrilled when they invited me to join such a prestigious board, but I quickly realized how much I had to learn. The other members represent the worlds of business, education, law, media, and, of course, patient care, healing, treatment, and research. Then there's me. I'm afraid that so far I only have brought a good name—my husband's. The Mayo Clinic certainly is one of the best health care facilities in the world. During this time of medical care reform, they not only are on the cutting edge of patient care, but also have kept costs 20 percent lower than the national average while constantly striving to make medical care better and accessible.

When the meeting was over, I caught up with George in Albany, Georgia, at Nilo Plantation, the home of Gene and Evie Williams. George went to high school with Gene and we have known and loved both of them since then. Their plantation is lovely, with enormous live oaks covered with Spanish moss, green fields, ponds and lakes, pine and magnolia trees. There is every kind of wildlife you can imagine: horses, mules, swans, peacocks, ducks, cranes, deer, and so on. George had a great time hunting quail.

* * *

꙳ This was sort of typical of our first year out of office. There were so many friends we wanted to see, so many things we wanted to do, but we seemed to race from place to place.

In March, for example, we went back to Florida for spring training with George W.'s Texas Rangers and the Houston Astros. We went to games, played golf in the pouring rain with an old Andover and Yale classmate of George's, Bill Howe, and his great wife, Joan, and visited with Mary and Bayard Sharp, Sarah Farish's parents. In May George went to the Kentucky Derby with Will Farish, now chairman of Churchill Downs, and fishing in the Bahamas with Nick and Kitty Brady.

And in April we took the thrilling trip to Kuwait, which I already have shared with you. One thing I did not mention, however, was the planned terrorist attack on George which was thwarted. Fortunately, we knew nothing about it until we returned home.

In between the traveling we were working on our house in Houston, which was going up just two doors down from our rented house, and we were redoing Mrs. Bush's bungalow in Kennebunkport, which we had inherited by default. It had to be overhauled from stem to stern without losing the essence of the house that the family grew up in. In all honesty, both houses were a joy to work on as everyone wanted to do a good job for George.

And both of us were trying to write books. George and Brent Scowcroft are working on a book about the seven dramatic changes in the world during the four years of the Bush administration. Since they both are speaking and doing so many other things, the book has been slow going for them.

George, for example, became chairman of the Eisenhower Exchange Fellowship, a group that tries to identify young people from abroad with leadership potential and brings them to the United States for six weeks. We went to Philadelphia to meet about thirty fellows who were finishing their tour and had been all across the country meeting with our leaders on every level in every field.

This is just one of the many causes that we are trying to support, including leukemia, the Crohn's and Colitis Foundation, and Boys and Girls Clubs. We both have become involved with M. D. Anderson Cancer Hospital in Houston, and George has gone on the Texas Medical Center Board. He also has become active in the Greater Houston Business Partnership, and I have accepted the job as Ambassador at Large for AmeriCares. We are encouraging volunteerism and want people to try to take back their own communities by being responsible, supportive, and interested. In short, we are trying to live up to George's Thousand Points of Light credo: "From now on any definition of a successful life must include service to others."

I will be honest and tell you we also have learned to say no. We are trying to keep a balance and stay focused on just a few causes.

For me, of course, my number-one cause is still literacy, with emphasis on the Barbara Bush Foundation for Family Literacy. With Benita Somerfield at the helm as executive director, we have many exciting plans for the future as we continue to raise money for literacy programs. We still strongly feel that focusing on the family is the best place to start to make this country more literate, and I still feel that being more literate will help us solve so many of the other problems facing our society.

∽ In the spring my older brother, Jim, who had been in bad health for many years, began to fail rapidly. His problems made Job's troubles seem light in comparison. Just everything was wrong with his body. I flew up to see him at the hospital, and although he was in considerable pain from cancer, he maintained a great sense of humor, optimism, and courage. That was a privilege to see. We talked intermittently, when he could. He told me how much Dave Peake's loyalty had meant (Dave was a childhood friend who now lives in Houston); what our brother, Scott's, great love and strength had meant to him; that our sister, Martha Rafferty, had been there for him through thick and thin; and above all just how much he loved and depended on Margie, his wife. He said that she was everything to him, and that is so true: My sister-in-law has been the greatest wife and mother.

Jim Pierce was unique, to say the least. I'll never forget when George was vice president and he showed up for a visit dressed in blue jeans and riding a motorcycle. I loved him. He died in a bed in his living room holding Margie's hand and looking out a window at a redbird in a magnolia tree.

I was very proud of what the editor of *Sports Afield* and Jim's boss, Lamar Underwood, wrote after his death: "Jim Pierce made hundreds of close friends and served the interests of sportsmanship everywhere.

His magazine leadership and influence transcended traditional editorial/ advertising lines to achieve reader reward. Jim was always on the front line in the battle for editorial integrity and useful, illuminating editorial coverage."

But as is so often the case when there is a death, there also is a new life: Robert Daniel Koch weighed in at ten pounds, six ounces on May 20. Doro and Bobby, along with Sam and Ellie, were thrilled.

We had another great sadness that spring: Our poor Ranger died of cancer. George, along with Don Rhodes, was devastated. I truly believe that George, who had not let us see him mourn the election or the loss of his mother, let his grief for all come out when his dog died. I really did not know how to help him, but it was very touching how Millie tried to take Ranger's place. Then George got a note from Fred Zeder that said, "Sorry. I've just heard Ranger's gone paws up." That brought a smile.

It was one night about this time that I absolutely couldn't sleep, and I got to thinking about what I have learned in life—sometimes the hard way—and the advice I'd like to give my precious children, if I could or would. I found myself at my computer composing a letter, which I never sent but would like to share with you now:

. . . Faith, Family and Friends.

Try—and oh boy, how hard it is—to find the good in people and not the bad. I remember many years ago that I wasted so much time worrying about my mother. I suffered so because she and I had a "chemical thing." I loved her very much, but was hurt by her. (I am sure that I hurt her a lot, too.) Grace Walker said to me once, "Think of all the lovely things about your mother . . . all the things you love and are proud of about her." There were so many that I couldn't count them all. I think that I expected her to be perfect. Nobody is perfect. Certainly not me. So LOOK FOR THE GOOD IN OTHERS. Forget the other.

Clara Barton, founder and president of the Red Cross, was once reminded of a wrong a friend had done to her years earlier. "Don't you remember?" the friend asked. "No," replied Clara firmly. "I distinctly remember forgetting that." Not bad advice. Take a lesson from your dad.

He says when I remind him that someone has been hateful, "Isn't it better to make a friend rather than an enemy?" He's right, too.

Don't talk about money . . . either having it or not having it. It is embarrassing for others and quite frankly vulgar.

DO NOT BUY SOMETHING THAT YOU CAN- NOT AFFORD. YOU DO NOT NEED IT.

If you really need something and can't afford it . . . for heaven's sake call home. That's what family are all about.

Do not try to live up to your neighbors. They won't look down on you if you don't have two television sets. They will look down on you if you buy things that you can- not afford and they will know it! They are only interested in their possessions, not yours.

Be sure that you pay people back. If you have din- ner at their house or they take you out, have them back, but remember you don't need the expensive thing. You can make the best spaghetti in the world. People love to come to your home. Plan ahead and it will be fun.

Value your friends. They are your most valuable asset.

Remember loyalty is a two-way street. It goes up and down. So be loyal to those people who are loyal to you. Your dad is the best example of two-way loyalty that I know.

Love your children. I don't have to tell any of you that. You are the best children any two people ever had. I know you will be as lucky. Your kids are great. Dad and I love them more than life itself. I think you know that about your dad. I do also.

Remember what Robert Fulghum says: "Don't worry that your children never listen to you; worry that they are always watching you."

For heaven's sake enjoy life. Don't cry over things that were or things that aren't. Enjoy what you have now to the fullest. In all honesty you really only have two choices; you can like what you do OR you can dislike it. I choose to like it and what fun I have had. The other choice is no fun and people do not want to be around a whiner. We can always

find people who are worse off and we don't have to look far!
Help them and forget self!

I would certainly say, above all, seek God. He will
come to you if you look. There is absolutely *NO* down side.
Please expose your children and set a good example for
them by going to church. We, your dad and I, have tried to
live as Christian a life as we can. We certainly have not been
perfect. Maybe you can! Keep trying.

In early May we headed for Kennebunkport and a glorious summer in Maine. We were barely there when Esther and Dick Moore and
Hugh and Anne Sidey spent the weekend. It was cold but fun. They
were the first of 177 different overnight houseguests, counting our
children and grandchildren. I would remind you that is 344 sheets and
344 pillowcases. I dread to think of the towels we washed!

One of the most fun groups we had come up were the six military
nurses at the White House who had taken such good care of George.
To explain this weekend I first have to give you a little background:
When they had treated George for shoulder spasms with hot packs
and deep heat therapy, they played music, and Art Wallace brought
a Roger Whittaker tape (he is a famous British balladeer) which they
all loved. As these things happen, they formed a Roger Whittaker Fan
Club. Kim Siniscalchi became the president and George became the
recording secretary of the club. The other four were Paula Trivette,
Mary Jackson, Debbie Beatty, and Ellen Tolton.

Just before we left office in January, George made the nurses
promise they would take leave and come to Maine for a weekend. He
then tracked down Roger Whittaker through his agent and called his
home outside London and talked to his wife, Natalie. I would have
loved to have seen her face when she picked up that telephone. (I bet
she checked on the authenticity of the call.) They accepted for the
weekend of June 12.

I raced around getting the Point ready for its first big weekend of
guests, and George had more fun planning the visit. He had big pins
and polo shirts made that we all were to wear that said "Nurses Weekend; Roger Whittaker Fan Club," with the dates and the club slogan:
"More Roger in our lives."

The Whittakers arrived and turned out to be fun-loving, ready-

A New Beginning 533

for-anything people. We raced them out to the golf course as Roger loves golf and got back to the house just in time to greet the nurses' minivan. They poured out of the bus all wearing T-shirts with blown-up pictures of Roger on one side and themselves on the other and "MORE ROGER IN OUR LIVES" underneath. They had left Washington at 5 A.M. and driven all day, and every time they stopped, people asked them about the club. When they got to our gate, the guard who checked them in looked at their shirts and said: "I never heard of this guy until today. He's up at the house now." So George's surprise was a surprise until the last minute! Thus began a weekend of golf, tennis, walking, biking, and lots of singing. It was a treat.

In July the George Bush Presidential Library Foundation Board of Trustees came to Kennebunkport for a meeting. The majority of the people, about one hundred strong, stayed at the Colony Hotel, a big beautiful old wooden hotel, but Will Farish and Walter and Lee Annenberg stayed with us and were our first guests in the refurbished bungalow. Lee and Walter were so great. The room they stayed in was about the size of the closet in their guest room when we stayed with them in the desert. To hear them talk you would have thought we'd put them up in Buckingham Palace. Peddie, the preparatory school that Walter attended and to which he had just made a large donation, sent a big banner which we put outside their bedroom door on the side of the house.

The trustees, along with officials from Texas A&M University, came from as far away as California and Puerto Rico. Former Governor Don Luis Ferré and his wife, Tiody, attended. (He turned ninety in February 1994 and George was thrilled to go to the party.) I believe that George was as moved by the numbers of people who have wanted to help with the library and who came to this meeting as by anything that ever happened to him. We tried to show them a good time. We brought all the guests to the Point for cocktails by trolley in the evening and then took them back to the Boat Club for a Maine dinner. Dick Cheney, Tip O'Neill, and Dick Jackman spoke, after which Jane Morgan Weintraub sang. Dick Cheney gave a very warm testimonial, and Tip was so dear and funny. Dick Jackman, a vice president at Sun Oil, has helped George out many times and is not only really funny, he also is motivational. He starts out rather seriously and then sneaks up on you and you realize that here is one funny man.

The next morning after breakfast we met at the Colony Hotel to discuss the library. The presentation by Texas A&M impressed everyone: They are the third largest university in the country, rank fifth in the number of Merit Scholars and eighth in research. Walter Annenberg announced that when he went back to college for his Ph.D., he thought he'd go there.

Several universities wanted George's library, but I believe the A&M spirit was the deciding factor. When it opens in 1997, the entire complex will include the library and museum, administrative offices, a teaching and research facility with classrooms, meeting rooms, and conference facilities. The George Bush School of Government and Public Service will offer a master of public administration degree, and George looks forward to teaching and working with the students.

The lunch crowd and drop-in trade were pretty heavy all summer, including President and Mrs. de Klerk of South Africa, who came for lunch. We feel that he is trying to set his country on the right road as peacefully and fairly as possible without ripping it further apart.

One day I wrote in my diary:

Very few people would believe our yesterday. We had the "Book Group"* for lunch; three Cardinals: O'Connor from New York, Law from Boston, Baum from St. Louis and now the Vatican, and Father Murphy from Boston. They are at Proutt's Neck for a few days' rest. They mentioned that they knew Jack Allin, former President Bishop of the Episcopal church and our summer minister at St. Ann's by the Sea. George got on the phone and invited Jack for lunch. At one time Wendy Stapleton came in with our grandchildren Marshall and Walker and some little boy who is staying at the Stapletons'. (Wendy was baby-sitting our grands while Margaret went to the airport to pick up Marvin.) Then Johnny Walker (GB's first cousin and a federal judge), his wife Katharine, their baby little Katy and Kimba Wood, the judge who was put up for Attorney General, then so unfairly caught up in "Nannygate," dropped by in the middle of the lunch. (She was an attractive young woman and seemed very nice.) Griffin Bell, Marlin Fitzwater, Wick Sollers and Boyden Gray appeared. Margaret

---

* These are the people helping George and Brent Scowcroft on their book: Condi Rice, provost at Stanford University; Ginny Lampley and her husband, Robb Mulberger; Arnie Kanter; and Flo Gantt.

came back with Marvin, Chrissy Evert, Andy Mill, little Alex and a nanny. A few minutes later Don and Adele Hall drove in. At four eight of us rushed out to the golf course and got in thirteen holes and had to quit on account of darkness and the fact that Paula was going to kill us. Suddenly instead of eight for dinner we had four Marvin Bushes, four Mills, three from the Griffin Bell group as Boyden left and two Halls. Paula told me it would all work out and it did. It was a case of the fishes and the loaves.

We were so busy and hectic that I can't believe what I did one day. For weeks I had looked forward to Phyllis Draper's coming for lunch with four Smith classmates. When the big day came I was just sitting down to lunch with George when they called from the gate to say that they were on their way up. I had totally forgotten. George suggested that I tell them I thought they would like to see the town and that we would have a cool glass of something and then I'd take them to Mabel's Lobster Claw, made famous by the press during our presidential years. I confessed, and they all were kind. We did have that cool drink and I did show them our favorite eating spot in Kennebunkport.

We did some great whale-watching that summer, a new sport for us, and we are kicking ourselves that we did not discover this sooner. Some of our guests I'm sure wish we never had, since they got seasick bumping around out in the ocean. About forty porpoises raced alongside our boat and dove and played when we were out looking for whales with little Jebby one day. They are hard to find, but well worth the search.

One day George let Sam and Jebby, both ten, take our tiny dinghy out on the sea. The little outboard motor quit and they could only move whichever way the wind blew them. Their mothers and I watched out the window with great fear as they bobbed up and down on the waves; George laughed at their plight. Finally, a lobsterman took pity and towed them in.

So George decided that the grandchildren needed a bigger boat, which they will have for the summer of 1994.

And, of course, we did not stay home all summer. In August, thanks to Trammell and Margaret Crow, who gave us their beautiful boat, *Michaela Rose*, we took a cruise in the Mediterranean. Noelle, now sixteen, went with us along with George's young cousins Craig and Debbie Stapleton and their sixteen-year-old daughter, Wendy.

Included in the adventure was a visit with King Hassan II of Morocco, where George played golf. We cruised to Gibraltar and up the Spanish coast and had a fabulous time. It was a dream trip.

⌒ On September 13 George was standing on the South Lawn of the White House when Prime Minister Rabin of Israel and Yasir Arafat of the Palestinian Liberation Organization signed a peace accord. I also had been invited, but just wasn't ready to go back yet. However, it was right and proper that George be there. The signing would never have taken place without George. Ronald Reagan also must get credit for rebuilding our defenses and keeping us strong. If George hadn't held firm against the pressures to make immense loan guarantees to Israel without an agreement from them that they would not build in the occupied territories, the Arabs would not have come to the table. If George had not formed and held together the coalition to free Kuwait, the Arab world would not have come to the table in Madrid. Many friends, domestic and foreign, called to congratulate George after the signing.

George met with Arafat and said he was charming. Amazing! Who ever thought that we would recognize a sworn terrorist?! Let's hope something comes of this famous handshake as many, many people have worked years to get peace in the Middle East.

George stayed on in Washington to help show support for NAFTA, joining former presidents Jerry Ford and Jimmy Carter and President Clinton in the NAFTA push. The Clintons invited him to spend the night, and George said he loved seeing the White House staff. He also said that the house looked lovely.

We watched the NAFTA debate with great interest and I found myself on the same side with Al Gore and voting for him all the way. He showed great control, reason, and ability. He also showed Ross Perot to be devious. Ross made many damaging statements that night, but the things he said about Mexico alone would make him unfit for public office. It was so insulting to our friends and neighbors to the south. I can't imagine how hurtful those words were to them. It hurt us. George was very happy when NAFTA passed, as he truly feels it will be good for the country. Incidentally, more Republicans than Democrats supported Bill Clinton on this vote.

I did go to Washington with George for Colin Powell's touching, dignified retirement ceremony. There is no finer man, American, or friend, and we also love his wife, Alma.

We moved into our dream house on October 18. Every person who worked on our house did a splendid job, and we are so grateful to them all. It is everything anyone would ever dream of or want at our age. We are surrounded by people we love; we have every modern appliance we could ever want; every room is really bright and pretty; Imelda Marcos would be jealous of our closets, if not my clothes; we are handicap accessible. We are so happy that every day we awaken and say to ourselves: "How could we be so lucky?"

The answer to that is that we might stay at home a little more. We both gave numerous speeches in the United States that fall, and George went to Brazil, taking along Jeb; Cannes, France, Genoa, Italy, and Switzerland, taking along Margaret; and Puerto Rico, taking Doro and her friend Jodie Dwight. In November he and I took a trip to the Far East with Carole and Lod Cook, going to China, Hong Kong, and Taiwan, then stopping in Sweden and England before coming home just before Thanksgiving.

We had a happy holiday with Neil and Sharon and children and my two nephews, Jim and Scott Pierce, and their darling young families. Then on Sunday we once again joined Lod and Carole Cook and flew back to London for a fascinating four days. (Everyone needs a Lod Cook in their lives. He is one of the most generous people.)

John and Norma Major hosted a wonderful lunch at Number 10 Downing Street, where we saw many old friends, and Ambassador Raymond and Caroline Seitz also gave a lunch at Winfield House. But the highlight was going to Buckingham Palace for lunch with Her Majesty Queen Elizabeth II and His Royal Highness Prince Philip.

They received us in their private quarters and the four of us sat to have a glass of sherry. At one time the door opened and six Welsh corgi puppies came in. They were all well behaved and dear, smiling little dogs. Then Her Majesty said something like, "Before we forget we must do what we are here to do," and handed George two leather boxes. One held an enormous heavy gold chain with a big burst on the end. This "Collar" with enamel on one side and gold on the other literally came well past George's waist. It was very impressive. The other box held another big burst on a large ribbon to be worn across the chest, I guess. So much for ceremony. The actual title of the award is Knight Grand Cross of the Most Honourable Order of the Bath. George is the eighth American to receive it, the other seven being Ronald Reagan and six World War II generals.

We went in to lunch and had a lovely time. Both the Queen and Prince Philip know a great deal about the United States and the world, so it was a stimulating visit. I remember that we talked about what George had observed on our trip around the world; our mutual friends, Will and Sarah Farish, with whom the Queen has stayed in Kentucky; and our sons' races for governor: George W. in Texas and Jeb in Florida.

When we got home from the luncheon George's aide, Michael Dannenhauer, asked me to witness a paper that George had to sign. It said that if for any reason George withdrew from the order or became deceased, the collar would be returned. So, as long as George lives, the stunning collar—valued at more than fifty thousand British pounds—will be on display in the George Bush Presidential Library Center.

David and Carina Frost had a lovely dinner at their absolute jewel of a house with many friends. I loved it when we were talking to, and I quote them, "two lesser Knights" at the dinner and they asked if we had signed the paper.

Several months later, German Chancellor Helmut Kohl presented George with the Grand Cross, special class of the Order of Merit, to recognize his world leadership, and while in Kuwait, the Amir had presented him with the Necklace of the Most Excellent Order of Mubarak, which had been given only four times in the history of the country. These, too, will be on display at the library—forever.

In the middle of December I took a completely different kind of trip: I went with a group from AmeriCares to Croatia, carrying food and medicines to the people of Sarajevo. We were a crew of volunteers along with Nancy Huang, my new aide, and Ben Orman, my new doctor, and Dr. Larry Mohr, who was with us at the White House. We didn't know what to expect and were disappointed to discover that we could not take the supplies ourselves to Sarajevo. It just was not safe. Bob Macauley was determined to go, but the airport was closed and, I believe, eleven people were killed that day. So we flew into Split, where the cargo was unloaded and trucked to Sarajevo the next day.

We visited the refugee camps, one drearier than the next. These people are feeling hopeless. They want to go home. They have no jobs and nothing to do. They worry about their families and friends. They live in barrack-type rooms with two other families in many cases. Several things impressed me. The number one request that the doctors have is medicine for depression, which I was told time after time was their biggest enemy. They also constantly fight dysentery, and hepatitis had broken out just before our visit in one of the camps. The women all knit, but they don't have much yarn, so they make a garment, tear it out, and make another. The last camp we went to was the worst: one hundred people sharing four toilets and sinks and no showers. The smell was pretty bad. We were gone four days in all, and in a way, it was the perfect way to start the holiday season.

A quiet Christmas was spent in our new home with Neil, Sharon, and their family. Our other children spent Christmas in their own homes. We talked to them all, missed them, but were so glad that they had each other and were well.

So now we have come full circle. Nineteen ninety-four is upon us. I remember years ago saying to George when we were first married: "I can't wait for you to retire." He looked surprised and said that he couldn't think of anything worse and that he hoped he never would.

Well, I'm glad he still feels that way. There are so many more things to do. This new life is a beginning and not an end. This year alone has two gubernatorial races ahead, which we are very excited about. We are proud that Jeb and George W. have chosen to serve their country in this way. They have paid their dues: They both have been successful in business—met payrolls, paid taxes, and supported their families; and they both have been community activists, both socially and politically. They will make outstanding governors.

We have so many plans for trips and events and friends in 1994 that it boggles the mind. But I know it will be fun. Certainly it has never been boring.

George Bush and I have been the two luckiest people in the world, and when all the dust is settled and all the crowds are gone, the things that matter are faith, family, and friends. We have been inordinately blessed, and we know that.

Appendix A

It's impossible in one book to recognize all the people who have made a difference in your life over the years, but certainly there are two groups of people without whom I never could have accomplished one thing: our Houston volunteers, who stuck with George and me through victories and defeats; and my White House staff.

The volunteers I especially would like to recognize are: Marjorie Arsht, Betty Baker, Mary Stuart Baker, Susan Baker, Melza Barr, Kay Bruce Baxter, Taylor Blanton, Sarah Bergner, Dot Burghard, Flo Bruenig Carroll, Betty Lou Carter, Janet Cartwright, Bill Cassin, Kristi Cassin, John Cater, Roland Chamberlin, Marion Chambers, Nancy Cook, Nancy Crouch, Linda Dyson, Ida Fahey, Daphne Murray Gawthrop, Sarah Gee, Bebe Gow, Peggy Green, Sara Green, Ada Grundy, Pat Halla, Margi Jenkins, Mary Louise Knowlton, Betty May, Dossett McCullough, Ed McCullough, Betty Kyle Moore, Betty Ann Murray, Becky Orr, Barbara Patton, Caroline Pierce, Mary Sage, Helene Speights, Bill Spence, Nancy Spence, Jack Steel, Margaret Voelkel, Kris Anne Vogelpohl, and Jane Wainright.

And the following were the members of my White House staff. Some of them were with me just a few months; some were with me for twelve years, beginning in 1981 in the Vice President's Office. They all helped make a difference: Susan Porter Rose, Julie Cooke,

Laurie Firestone, Sondra Haley, Susan Green, Celeste Dorsey, Anna Perez, Joan DeCain, Ann Brock, Cathy Fenton, Jean Becker, Peggy Swift, Sally Runion, Jane Moore, Jay Suchan, Kathy Steffy, Jeanie Figg, Anne Griffith, Diana Kellogg, Deborah Underhill, Diane Limo, Kim Brady Cutler, Catherine Coughlin, Casey Healey Killblane, Lea Uhre, Rosemary Gonzalez, Jean Wallace Leach, Aida Cipriani, Karen Connell, Ruth Mankin, Susan Hubbard, Deborah Scott, Courtney Dur, Don Mains, Elaine Speiser, Juanita Doggett, and Shirley Campolieto.

Appendix B

The mission of the Barbara Bush Foundation for Family Literacy is:

To establish literacy as a value in every family in America by helping every family in the nation understand that the home is the child's first school, that the parent is the child's first teacher, and that reading is the child's first subject.

To break the intergenerational cycle of illiteracy by supporting the development of family literacy programs where parents and children can learn to read together.

BOARD OF DIRECTORS

Dr. Joan Abrahamson, Chairman
President
Jefferson Institute

The Reverend Dr. Anderson Clark
President
READ America

Sharon Darling
President
National Center for Family Literacy

Dr. John E. Harr
Vice President, Office of Corporate Initiatives (Retired)
Capital Cities/ABC Inc.

Harold McGraw, Jr.
Chairman Emeritus
McGraw-Hill, Inc.

Sydney Olson
Director, Governmental Affairs
American Speech-Language-Hearing Association

Susan Porter Rose
Former Chief of Staff to Barbara Bush

Benita Somerfield
Executive Director
Barbara Bush Foundation for Family Literacy

Margot B. Woodwell
Vice President and General Manager
WQED

ORIGINAL CORPORATE COMMITTEE

Martin S. Davis, Co-chairman
former Chairman and Chief Executive Officer
Paramount Communications, Inc.

Harold Poling
Chairman and Chief Executive Officer (Retired)
Ford Motor Company

Joseph Antonini
Chairman, President, and Chief Executive Officer
K mart Corporation

Frank A. Bennack, Jr.
President and Chief Executive Officer
The Hearst Corporation

John J. Curley
Chairman, President, and Chief Executive Officer
Gannett Company, Inc.

Louis Gerstner, Jr.
Chairman and Chief Executive Officer
IBM

Thomas Murphy
Chairman of the Board (Retired)
Capital Cities/ABC, Inc.

Donald E. Newhouse
Samuel I. Newhouse Foundation, Inc.

Reece A. Overcash, Jr.
Chairman and Chief Executive Officer
Associates Corporation of North America

John J. Phelan, Jr.
Chairman and Chief Executive Officer (Retired)
The New York Stock Exchange, Inc.

Ralph Rossi
Vice Chairman
UST, Inc.

William A. Schreyer
Chairman and Chief Executive Officer
Merrill Lynch and Company

Appendix C

Text of Remarks of Mrs. Bush at
Wellesley College Commencement
Severance Green, Wellesley College,
Wellesley, Massachusetts,
June 1, 1990

Thank you, President Keohane, Mrs. Gorbachev, Trustees, Faculty, Parents, Julie Porter, Christine Bicknell, and the class of 1990. I am thrilled to be with you today, and very excited, as I know you must all be, that Mrs. Gorbachev could join us.

More than ten years ago when I was invited here to talk about our experiences in the People's Republic of China, I was struck by both the natural beauty of your campus . . . and the spirit of this place.

Wellesley, you see, is not just a place . . . but an idea . . . an experiment in excellence in which diversity is not just tolerated, but is embraced.

The essence of this spirit was captured in a moving speech about tolerance given last year by the Student Body President of one of your sister colleges. She related the story by Robert Fulghum about a young pastor who, finding himself in charge of some very energetic children, hit upon a game called "Giants, Wizards, and Dwarfs." "You have to decide now," the Pastor instructed the children, "which you are . . . a giant, a wizard, or a dwarf?" At that, a small girl tugging on his pant leg asked, "But where do the mermaids stand?"

The Pastor told her there are *no* mermaids. "Oh yes there are," she said. "I am a mermaid."

This little girl knew what she was. She was not about to give up on either her identity *or* the game. She intended to take her place wherever mermaids fit into the scheme of things. Where *do* mermaids stand . . . all those who are different, those who do not fit the boxes and the pigeonholes? "Answer that question," wrote Fulghum, "and you can build a school, a nation, or a whole world on it."

As that very wise young woman said, "Diversity . . . like anything worth having . . . requires *effort.*" Effort to learn about and respect difference, to be compassionate with one another, to cherish our own identity . . . and to accept unconditionally the same in all others.

You should all be very proud that this is the Wellesley spirit. Now I know your first choice for today was Alice Walker, known for *The Color Purple.* Instead you got me—known for . . . the color of my hair! Of course, Alice Walker's book has a special resonance here. At Wellesley, each class is known by a special color . . . and for four years the class of '90 has worn the color purple. Today you meet on Severance Green to say good-bye to all that . . . to begin a new and very personal journey . . . a search for your own true colors.

In the world that awaits you beyond the shores of Lake Waban, no one can say what your true colors will be. But this I know: You have a first-class education from a first-class school. And so you need not, probably cannot, live a "paint-by-numbers" life. Decisions are not irrevocable. Choices do come back. As you set off from Wellesley, I hope that many of you consider making three very special choices.

The first is to believe in something larger than yourself . . . to get involved in some of the big ideals of your time. I chose literacy because I honestly believe that if more people could read, write, and comprehend, we would be that much closer to solving so many of the problems plaguing our society.

Early on I made another choice which I hope you will make as well. Whether you are talking about education, career, or service, you are talking about life . . . and life must have joy. It's supposed to be fun!

One of the reasons I made the most important decision of my

life . . . to marry George Bush . . . is because he made me laugh. It's true, sometimes we've laughed through our tears . . . but that shared laughter has been one of our strongest bonds. Find the joy in life, because as Ferris Bueller said on his day off . . . "Life moves pretty fast. Ya don't stop and look around once in a while, ya gonna miss it!"

The third choice that must not be missed is to cherish your human connection: your relationships with friends and family. For several years, you've had impressed upon you the importance to your career of dedication and hard work. This is true, but as important as your obligations as a doctor, lawyer, or business leader will be, you are a human being first, and those human connections—with spouses, with children, with friends—are the most important investments you will ever make.

At the end of your life, you will never regret not having passed one more test, not winning one more verdict, or not closing one more deal. You will regret time not spent with a husband, a friend, a child, or a parent.

We are in a transitional period right now . . . fascinating and exhilarating times . . . learning to adjust to the changes and the choices we . . . men and women . . . are facing. I remember what a friend said, on hearing her husband lament to his buddies that he had to baby-sit. Quickly setting him straight . . . my friend told her husband that when it's your own kids . . . it's not called baby-sitting!

Maybe we should adjust faster, maybe slower. But whatever the era . . . whatever the times, one thing will never change: fathers and mothers, if you have children . . . they must come first. Your success as a family . . . our success as a society . . . depends *not* on what happens at the White House, but on what happens inside your house.

For over fifty years, it was said that the winner of Wellesley's Annual Hoop Race would be the first to get married. Now they say the winner will be the first to become the CEO. Both of these stereotypes show too little tolerance for those who want to know where the mermaids stand. So I offer you today a new legend: The winner of the hoop race will be the first to realize her dream . . . not society's dream . . . her own personal dream. And who knows? Somewhere out in this audience may even be someone who will one day follow in my footsteps, and preside over the White House as the President's spouse. I wish him well!

The controversy ends here. But our conversation is only beginning. And a worthwhile conversation it is. So as you leave Wellesley today, take with you deep thanks for the courtesy and honor you have shared with Mrs. Gorbachev and me. Thank you. God bless you. And may your future be worthy of your dreams.

A Transcription of Mrs. Raisa Gorbachev's Remarks
at Wellesley College Commencement,
Wellesley, Massachusetts,
June 1, 1990

Dear Friends, I am pleased to be with you at this momentous and exciting day when you are leaving your college and entering a new life. I congratulate you on this important occasion. I am grateful to Mrs. Barbara Bush and to the college administration for this chance of coming to Wellesley during our stay in America. I thank college officials, professors, and all of you for your kind words and warm feelings.

I distinctly remember a similar summer day in Moscow. The years of my studies at Moscow University were over. We were then full of plans and hopes just like you are today. Being young is a marvelous time, a time of actions and expectations, of being confident of one's abilities, and sure that everything is still ahead. I wish that all your dreams of the future come true. The President of the Soviet Union asked me to convey to you his warm regards. He also wishes you happy roads in your life.

We know that people in America show great interest in what is happening in the Soviet Union, the land of Perestroika. This word, nowadays, sounds the same in all languages of the world. We associate with Perestroika the future of our country whose millions of people speak over 120 languages. Perestroika was conceived and is being implemented for the sake of the people, their dignity and equality. This goal is to make human ideals and values a reality. This vast and difficult task is a tough challenge, but we are confident that Perestroika will succeed. The guarantee of that is the patriotism and talent of our people, their tenacity, their strength, and their desire to overcome obstacles on the way on the road they chose.

In renewing our country, we want to make it open to the world.

The Soviet people know the value of peaceful lives. We wish to have good relations with the Americans and other peoples. Of course all of us, [as] daughters and sons of our own countries and peoples, are different. The Soviet Union and the United States have different histories, traditions, and cultures. That, however, is not [a] reason for mutual estrangement and suspicion. People on both sides of the great ocean realize more and more clearly that our values bring us closer. Such values are love for one's own native country, love for one's relatives, children, the belief in what is good, and belief in solidarity to combat wars, violence, hunger, catastrophes, and other threats to mankind. These values are now more important than anything else. Hamlet's question, "To be or not to be," today confronts not only individuals or nations but the entire humanity.

So, what will our society be like? Not only the leaders of states, but the world community as a whole, share this responsibility. We women have our special mission. Always, even in the most cruel and most troubled times, women have had the mission of peacemaking, humanism, mercy, and kindness. And if people in the world today are more confident of a peaceful future, we have to give a great deal of credit for that to women who are active in advocating friendship, cooperation, and mutual understanding among nations.

You are entering a complex and multifaceted world. Your generation will soon assume the responsibility for everything that takes place on our planet. May good luck and happiness be with you. I wish you many good accomplishments. Thank you.

Appendix D

*Text of Remarks Given by George P. Bush
to the Republican National Convention,
Houston, Texas,
August 19, 1992*

Thanks, Ganny. I would like to talk about a member of the family that is not here tonight. You know him as the President, but I know him as the greatest man I have ever known. Despite the enormous pressures of his job, he always has time for his twelve grandkids.

In the presidential campaign, it's hard for people to get a sense of what makes a candidate tick. The family is what makes my grandfather tick.

I would like to read excerpts from a letter that he wrote to me after my dad and I came back from a relief mission in Armenia before he was inaugurated. I hope it gives you a better understanding of what my grandfather is all about.

He wrote:

Dear George P.,

A few days ago I met with the Deputy Mayor of Yerevan, in the Soviet Union. He was a stolid-looking guy and he came in with some people from Cambridge, Massachusetts, because Yerevan and Cambridge are sister cities.

He told me about how things were going back there in the U.S.S.R. He told me that the outpouring of generosity and caring from America had really meant a lot to the people there. And then he said this: "When your son wept, it was on every TV set in the Soviet Union and those tears said more than anything else about the decency of the American people."

My grandfather went on to say:

Men are not supposed to cry, says convention; but we do and we should and we should not worry when we do.

I cry when I'm happy and I cry when I'm sad, but when I saw you and your wonderful dad in that church in Armenia on Christmas Day I cried because I was both happy and sad. Don't ever forget what you saw there. Don't ever forget what you participated in. In less than two weeks I will be President of the United States. I know I will not forget what that little trip of yours meant to people all over the world.

You're a good man, Charlie Brown, and I miss you a lot.

Devotedly, Gampy.

This letter means a lot to me because it shows the heart of this man I love so much. I just wish people who see George Bush on TV or read about him in the newspapers could know him as I do. A man of enormous integrity and love for his family . . . and for all of America.

Thank you.

Index